PARLIAMENTARY HISTORY: TEXTS & STUDIES
18

THE BOOKSELLERS' BILL 1774

'The Devil Tavern in Fleet Street' by John Cleghorn, 1746 (image licensed from Alamy). The signatures for the London Booksellers' Petition were collected at a meeting held at the Devil's Tavern in 1774.

The Booksellers' Bill 1774

Legislating in the 18th Century: A View from Sir Henry Cavendish's Parliamentary Diary

by
Phillip Johnson

WILEY
for
THE PARLIAMENTARY HISTORY YEARBOOK TRUST

John Wiley & Sons

Registered Office
John Wiley & Sons Ltd, The Atrium, Southern Gate, Chichester, West Sussex, PO19 8SQ, UK

Editorial Offices
101 Station Landing, Medford, MA 02155, USA
9600 Garsington Road, Oxford, OX4 2DQ, UK
The Atrium, Southern Gate, Chichester, West Sussex, PO19 8SQ, UK

For details of our global editorial offices, for customer services, and for information about how to apply for permission to reuse the copyright material in this book please see our website at www.wiley.com/wiley-blackwell.

Library of Congress Cataloging-in-Publication Data

ISBN 9781394180776

The Booksellers' Bill 1774. Legislating in the 18th Century: A View from Sir Henry Cavendish's Parliamentary Diary / by Phillip Johnson

••

A catalogue record for this title is available from the British Library
Set in 10/12pt Bembo
by Aptara Inc., India
Printed and bound in Singapore
by C.O.S. Printers Pte Ltd
1 2022

Parliamentary History: Texts & Studies

CONTENTS

Acknowledgments ix

Abbreviations x

Note on Biographic and Bibliographic Information xi

Part I: The Story

Introduction 1
- 1. Lobbying for Change (or Staying the Same) 9
- 2. The Tools of Persuasion 21
- 3. Parliamentary Procedure and the Booksellers' Bill 43
- 4. Evidence and Argument: The History 73
- 5. Evidence and Argument: The Investment and Other Arguments 96
- 6. The Bill 119
- 7. Parliamentary Reporting 125
- 8. The Reporting of the Booksellers' Bill 140
- 9. The End ... 158

Part II: The Diaries 164
- Henry Cavendish's Diary 170
  - Report on Petition (24 Mar) 170
  - First Reading (21 Apr) 193
  - Second Reading (10 May) 194
  - Second Reading (13 May) 208
  - Committee (16 May) 223
  - Report adj (19 May) 252
  - Third Reading (27 May) 253
- Lord Folkestone's Diary 255

Part III: Newspaper Reports 259
- Petition Presented (28 Feb) 267
- Petition Committee (9 Mar) 271
- Bach & Abel Petition (15 Mar) 272
- Petition Committee (16 Mar) 273

Petition Committee (17 Mar) 275
Report on Petition (24 Mar) 280
First Reading (22 Apr) 303
Donaldson's Petition (26 Apr) 312
Second Reading adj (4 May) 313
Second Reading (10 May) 315
Second Reading (13 May) 330
Committee (16 May) 346
Report adj (19 May) 364
Report (20 May) 366
Third Reading (27 May) 367
First Reading (HL) (2 Jun) 371

Part IV: Petitions, Cases and Papers 378

Booksellers' Petition 378
Bach and Abel's Petition 379
Booksellers' Case 380
Case Observations 382
Remarks on the Booksellers' Petition 386
Farther Strictures 389
Petition Committee Report 393
Committee Evidence Observations 399
Goldsmith's Hints 405
Edinburgh Booksellers' Petition 407
London Stallholders' Petition 409
Glasgow Booksellers' Petition 412
Donaldson's Petition 413
Petition of Booksellers of York 417
Remarks on Donaldson's Petition 417
London Booksellers' Considerations 421
Glasgow Memorialists 424
General Observations/Hints 442
Further Remarks 463
Country Booksellers' Petitions 475
Burke's Notes on Copyright Bill 475
Copies of Five Letters 477
Printed Books 483
Expense of Printed Books 489
Booksellers' Bill 492
Donaldson's House of Lords Petition 496

Select Bibliography 501

Index 521

ACKNOWLEDGMENTS

The creation of a book, particularly a mixture of monographs and primary sources, is not a work which can be created by an author as an island, entire of itself. It requires pieces from many continents to give it form. The original material used to make this book comes from the British Library, Bodleian Libraries, University of Oxford, the National Library of Scotland, London Guildhall Library, Glasgow University Library, the Historical Society of Pennsylvania and the Beinecke Library at Yale. I would like to thank all the staff at these great libraries and in particular Robert Betteridge and Lee Arnold for their more substantial help. In addition, I would like to thank the librarians at the Institute of Historical Research for their assistance as well as Malcolm Langley at the Queen Mary Intellectual Property Archive and Lynn Goodhew at Cardiff University Library.

I extend my thanks to the earl of Radnor for his kind permission to reproduce the second earl's parliamentary diary and Felix Waldmann for some guidance on sources connected to David Hume. I must also thank Linda Clark, who has been a very helpful series editor, as well as Sarah Worrall, Ajay Patel and Chris Burton, who helped during the final publication process. As always, I am thankful to Jo, my wife, for supporting me throughout, and finally I must acknowledge John Donne for my opening sentence.

ABBREVIATIONS

app.	apprentice
BIHR	*Bulletin of the Institute of Historical Research*
BL	British Library, London
CJ	*Journals of the House of Commons*
Cobbett's Parl. Hist.	William Cobbett, *Parliamentary History of England from the Earliest Period to the Year 1803* (36 vols, 1806–20)
EHR	*English Historical Review*
ESTC	English Short Title Catalogue
HC 1754–1790	*The History of Parliament: The House of Commons 1754–1790*, ed. Sir Lewis Namier and John Brooke (3 vols, 1964)
HC Debate	Hansard, Official Reports of Parliamentary Debates (Commons)
HC Paper	Parliamentary Papers, House of Commons
HJ	*Historical Journal*
Judges of England	*The Judges of England, 1272–1990: A List of Judges of the Superior Courts*, comp. Sir John Sainty (Seldon Society, supp. ser. x, 1993)
LJ	*Journals of the House of Lords*
TNA	The National Archives, Kew
tr.	trading
Votes 1774	*Votes and Proceedings of the House of Commons, 1774*

NOTE ON BIOGRAPHIC AND BIBLIOGRAPHIC INFORMATION

The Booksellers' Bill involved the interests of four different professions: authors, booksellers, lawyers and politicians. The bibliographic details of most of the characters involved are well known and easily accessible. Accordingly, all that has been provided here is the key bibliographical dates and an asterisk (*) where there is an entry in the *Oxford Dictionary of National Biography*,[1] a dagger (†) where the person was a member of parliament between 1754 and 1790 and so was included by Sir Lewis Namier and John Brooke in *The House of Commons, 1754–1790*,[2] and a double dagger (††) where he is included in another of the publications in the *History of Parliament* series. The details relating to the dates of appointments of the English judiciary come from *The Judges of England, 1272–1990*, compiled by Sir John Sainty.[3]

There are many excellent sources of biographical information for booksellers in the late 18th century. The starting points would now be the *British Book Trade Index*, a database hosted by the Bodleian Library,[4] and the *Scottish Book Trade Index*, a database hosted by the National Library of Scotland.[5] These databases rely on extensive earlier work by numerous scholars, and it is often easier to refer to these earlier sources than to the databases. The work of Ian Maxted, and his Exeter Working Papers on the Book Trade,[6] provide most of the information used for the bibliographical details used here, in particular *The London Book Trades, 1775–1800*,[7] and the shorter *London Book Trades, 1735–1775*,[8] as well as his checklist of bankrupts[9] and apprentices.[10] The apprentices and masters of the Stationer's Company

[1] http://www.oxforddnb.com

[2] *The History of Parliament: The House of Commons 1754–1790*, ed. Sir Lewis Namier and John Brooke (3 vols, 1964).

[3] *The Judges of England, 1272–1990: A List of Judges of the Superior Courts*, comp. Sir John Sainty (Seldon Society, supp. ser. x, 1993).

[4] http://bbti.bodleian.ox.ac.uk/

[5] https://www.nls.uk/catalogues/Scottish-book-trade-index

[6] These have now been made available online: https://bookhistory.blogspot.com.

[7] Ian Maxted, *The London Book Trades, 1775–1800: A Preliminary Checklist of Members* (Exeter Working Papers in Book History, 1977).

[8] Ian Maxted, *The London Book Trades, 1735–1775: A Checklist of Members in Trade Directories and in Musgrave's Obituary* (Exeter Working Papers in Book History, iii, 1984).

[9] Ian Maxted, *The British Book Trades, 1731–1806: A Checklist of Bankrupts* (Exeter Working Papers in Book History, iv, 1985).

[10] Ian Maxted, *The British Book Trades, 1710–1777: An Index of Masters and Apprentices* (Exeter Working Papers in Book History, ii, 1983).

are provided by Donald McKenzie's *Stationers' Company Apprentices 1701–1800*.[11] Some booksellers became members of parliament or were otherwise prominent enough to be included in more general bibliographic sources and they have additionally been marked with an asterisk or dagger as appropriate.

The details available for a particular bookseller varies. The dates of birth and death have been included where they are available, and those booksellers whose apprenticeship (app.) was recorded have the date noted. In the 18th century, the average age a person began an apprenticeship was between 14 and 16 years old,[12] and so even when a date of birth is unavailable it is possible for the reader to make a reasonable estimate. The dates where the bookseller has been identified as trading (tr.) are also included, however the accuracy of these is patchy as they depend on the records of activity. The addresses recorded for the booksellers represent their trade addresses in 1774 or, if they ceased trading before that time, the last address where they were known to trade. Where a person, bookseller or otherwise, appears in none of these sources then the source of any biographical information is provided in the text.

The story of the Booksellers' Bill is a story of books, and editions of books. There are numerous references in debates and publications to a particular impression. Any impression individually mentioned has been identified and where there is a general discussion of publication the first edition is identified to provide a temporal context. Every book is identified by its citation number on the English Short Title Catalogue hosted by the British Library.[13] This catalogue builds on the work of Alfred Pollard and Gilbert Redgrave, *A Short-Title Catalogue of Books Printed in England, Scotland, & Ireland and of English Books Printed Abroad 1473–1640*,[14] and Donald Wing, *A Short-Title Catalogue of Books Printed in England, Scotland, Ireland, Wales, and British America and of English Books Printed in Other Countries 1641–1700*,[15] as well as the *Eighteenth Century Short Title Catalogue*,[16] and items catalogued by the American Antiquarian Society as part of the *North American Imprints Program*. Using the online catalogue and the ESTC citation provided in the text allows readers to find the libraries which hold all the extant copies of that particular impression.

There are many references to newspapers published in 1774 throughout the book and are mostly included in Part III. However, where an extract from a newspaper from 1774 is not included it will be marked with the symbol §.

All cross-references to material reproduced in Parts II, III and IV use the page numbers in the original manuscript or document. All inflation calculations have been undertaken using www.measuringworth.com and calculated to 2020.

[11] D.F. McKenzie, *Stationers' Company Apprentices, 1701–1800* (Oxford, 1978).

[12] Patrick Wallis, Cliff Webb and Chris Minns, 'Leaving Home and Entering Service. The Age of Apprenticeship in Early Modern London', *Continuity and Change*, xxv (2010), 377–404.

[13] http://estc.bl.uk/

[14] (3 vols, Bibliographical Society, 1976–91).

[15] (3 vols, Modern Language Association of America, 1972–98).

[16] For a discussion of this project, Henry Snyder, 'The Eighteenth Century Short Title Catalogue', *IFLA Journal*, xvi (1990), 79.

PART I: THE STORY

Introduction

The history of copyright and publishing in the 18th century is well trodden,[1] and an event in 1774 is one of the most explored of all.[2] The house of lords heard the infamous case of *Donaldson v Beckett*[3] in February that year when it was found that copyright in printed books was by then a purely statutory creation. The case had attracted great public interest at the time, as it was put by one newspaper, 'No private cause has so much engrossed the attention of the public, and none has been tried before the House of Lords, in the decision of which so many individuals were interested',[4] and there were even said to be celebrations by all the printers in Edinburgh.[5] It has also had a long-term significance, being seen as the end of the old protectionism which had been started hundreds of years earlier by the Stationers' Company.[6] The case is thought to be the end of the story, but immediately

[1] Those at the time have been said to have made copyright history a sub-discipline: 'Introduction' in *Privilege and Property: Essays on the History of Copyright*, ed. Ronan Deazley, Martin Kretschmer and Lionel Bently (Cambridge, 2010), 1–2.

[2] The most well known are the following: Mark Rose, *Authors and Owners: The Invention of Copyright* (Cambridge, MA, 1993); H.B. Abrams, 'The Historic Foundation of American Copyright Law: Exploding the Myth of Common Law Copyright', *Wayne Law Review*, xxix (1983), 1120; Trevor Ross, 'Copyright and the Invention of Tradition', *Eighteenth-Century Studies*, xxvi (1992), 1; J.F. Whicher, 'The Ghost of Donaldson v Becket', *Bulletin of the Copyright Society of the USA*, ix (1962), 102, 194; L.R. Patterson, *Copyright in Historical Perspective* (Nashville, TN, 1968); Ronan Deazley, *On the Origin of the Right to Copy: Charting the Movement of Copyright Law in Eighteenth-Century Britain (1695–1775)* (Oxford, 2004); John Feather, *A History of British Publishing* (2005); John Feather, *Publishing, Piracy and Politics: An Historical Study of Copyright in Britain* (1994); H.H. Ransom, *The First Copyright Statute: An Essay on An Act for the Encouragement of Learning, 1710* (Austin, TX, 1956); Brad Sherman and Lionel Bently, *The Making of Modern Intellectual Property Law* (Cambridge, 1999); R.J. Coombe, 'Challenging Paternity: Histories of Copyright', *Yale Journal of Law and the Humanities*, vi (1994), 406–7; A.F. Pollard, 'Some Notes on the History of Copyright in England, 1662–1774', *The Library*, iv (1922), 97; H. Tomás Gómez-Arostegui, 'Copyright at Common Law in 1774', *Connecticut Law Review*, xlvii (2014), 1; Ronan Deazley, 'The Myth of Copyright at Common Law', *Cambridge Law Journal*, lxii (2003), 106; Mark Rose, 'The Author as Proprietor: *Donaldson v Beckett* and the Genealogy of Modern Authorship', *Representation*, xxiii (1988), 51 (an amended version was published as 'The Author as Proprietor: *Donaldson and Beckett* and the Genealogy of Modern Authorship', in *Of Authors and Origins: Essays on Copyright Law*, ed. Brad Sherman and Alain Strowel (Oxford, 1994), 23); Augustine Birrell, 'The "Battle of the Booksellers" for Perpetual Copyright', in *Seven Lectures on the Law and History of Copyright in Books* (1899), ch. 4; Mark Perry, 'The Legacy of *The Seasons*: Confusion and Misdirection', in *Forgotten Intellectual Property Lore: Creativity, Entrepreneurship and Intellectual Property*, ed. Shubha Ghosh (Cheltenham, 2020), 206.

[3] *The Cases of the Appellants and Respondents in the Cause of Literary Property, before the House of Lords* (Bew, 1774) (ESTC: T90592); *The Pleadings of the Counsel before the House, in the Great Cause concerning Literary Property* (Wilkin, 1774) (ESTC: T90593).

[4] *Edinburgh Advertiser*, 25 Feb.–1 Mar., 132 (although the *Advertiser's* proprietor was the son of the victorious party in *Donaldson v Beckett* (1774) 2 Br PC 129 (1 ER 837–8)).

[5] *Caledonian Mercury*, 2 Mar.

[6] Feather, *A History of British Publishing*, 68; for the early period, see P.W.M. Blayney, *The Stationers' Company and the Printers of London, 1501–1557* (Cambridge, 2013).

afterwards the Booksellers, that is those responsible for publishing books,[7] petitioned the house of commons for a bill that would have delayed the full impact of *Donaldson v Beckett* for over two decades. The Bill passed the Commons but was resoundingly defeated in the Lords now sitting in its legislative capacity.

Why the Booksellers' Bill?

It is this Booksellers' Bill of 1774 which is central to the narrative. It is copyright paint upon a parliamentary canvas. The Bill is used to tell the story of parliament in 1774 by opening a window upon how the public interacted with parliament, how it then legislated and how its work was viewed. It might be asked why an obscure bill which passed only the house of commons should be the protagonist. In some ways its obscurity makes it a better hero. The Bill was not championed by the government, yet it was hard and bitterly fought. Neither was it a bill of high politics, such as those relating to North America[8] or to the royal family.[9] So while there were parliamentary fights they did not fit into any bigger political picture and had limited broader significance. The Bill presents a microcosm of parliamentary activity in the period in a way that would not be possible again for decades.

The Booksellers' Bill of 1774 was the end of something, rather than the beginning. The Booksellers had spent decades trying to protect their monopolies and interests in books, and 'old' books in particular.[10] As Feather puts it, '[t]he workings of the London book trade depended essentially on the continuity of ownership of copyrights in which the leading booksellers had invested so much capital'.[11] *Donaldson v Beckett* had put all this in jeopardy or even annihilated it. The Bill began at the end of February and was dead by early June; it was before parliament for about nine weeks. The history of copyright has been written from many perspectives,[12] and with lenses that encompass hundreds of years,[13] or at least decades,[14] so why would nine weeks at the end of the third quarter of the 18th century be important enough to warrant extensive study?

[7]At the outset, it is important to understand that a bookseller was not simply a trader in books. As the industry was structured in the 18th century, the booksellers were closer to the publisher and retailer combined: James Raven, *Publishing Business in Eighteenth-Century England* (Woodbridge, 2014), 50.

[8]The 'Intolerable' and 'Coercive' Acts were passed the same year: Boston Port Act (14 Geo. III, c. 19); Massachusetts Government Act (14 Geo. III, c. 45); Administration of Justice Act (14 Geo. III, c. 39); Quartering Act (14 Geo. III, c. 54).

[9]Such as the Royal Marriages Act 1772 (12 Geo. III, c. 11).

[10]Those no longer protected by the Copyright Act 1709 (8 Anne, c. 19).

[11]Feather, *A History of British Publishing*, 72.

[12]Kathy Bowrey, 'Who's Writing Copyright History?', *European Intellectual Property Review*, xviii (1996), 322; Bowrey, 'Who's Painting Copyright's History?', in *Dear Images: Art, Copyright and Culture*, ed. Daniel McClean and Karsten Schubert (2002), 257.

[13]Patterson, *Copyright in Historical Perspective*; Ransom, *The First Copyright Statute*; Feather, *A History of British Publishing*; Feather, *Publishing, Piracy and Politics* (and earlier articles such as 'The Book Trade in Politics: The Making of the Copyright Act 1710', *Publishing History*, viii (1980), 19; 'The Book Trade and the Law 1695–1799', *Publishing History*, xii (1982), 51).

[14]Deazley, *On the Origin of the Right to Copy*.

Booksellers[15] on both sides printed significant material in support or against the Bill,[16] a factor which facilitates an examination of how cases were presented, and how the public tried to seek support from members of parliament by what would later be called lobbying. The art of parliamentary persuasion was rarely confined to the printed word, but in contrast to so much 18th-century legislation it is possible to see the arguments presented clearly. Arguments from documents, whether parliamentary or legal texts, and law reports dealing with 'legal and aesthetic questions' which are often 'indistinguishable' provide a broad canvas for the Booksellers' Bill.[17] The booksellers' easy access to newspapers meant the message was more widely broadcast than in other cases, and so the voice is louder. While much activity of interest groups, such as the private conversations with MPs and meetings in coffee houses, is now lost, the booksellers' tendency to print and record means we have a much greater insight into their activities and it is possible to see how members of parliament might have been influenced by such printed records. The completeness of the records surrounding the Booksellers' Bill means a good picture can be painted of a 'standard' bill at the time.

The Booksellers' Bill faced the full brunt of parliamentary tactics. The procedures that were followed in the Commons at the time, earlier and later, developed from precedents, Speakers' rulings, and similar. For the most part, these are determined by parliamentary minutes recorded in the *House of Commons Journals*.[18] Henry Cavendish's shorthand record provides an opportunity to see procedure in action. While the Commons' processes in the 18th century have been studied before,[19] this has largely been a view from above – that is how procedure developed and evolved over time. This story is about a single bill (albeit one which pushed the boundaries of parliamentary practice) and so it is possible to look closely at ground level to see how procedure worked, and how MPs viewed its import.

There were many such bills in the period, but what sets the Booksellers' Bill apart from others is how much documentation survived.[20] The debates in the Commons were recorded by Cavendish,[21] using his own version of Gurney shorthand.[22] As a member of the House he was ever present and so was able to record almost every word spoken.[23] His shorthand notes were transcribed and from this we have a near complete record of the

[15]The trade in pamphlets and similar sheets was much closer to the book trade than is often acknowledged, so their sellers too might have had an interest: Raven, *Publishing Business in Eighteenth-Century England*, 35.

[16]That which remains is included in Part III, below.

[17]Rose, *Authors and Owners*, 6.

[18]The publication of the journals' index assisted Erskine May in the preparation of his seminal treatise on parliamentary practice: Martyn Atkins, 'Persuading the House: The Use of the Commons Journal as a Source of Precedent', and Paul Evans and Andrej Ninkovic, 'From Manual to Authority: The Life and Times of the Treatise', in *Essays on the History of Parliamentary Procedure: In Honour of Thomas Erskine May*, ed. Paul Evans (2017), 82, 84, 116.

[19]P.D.G. Thomas, *The House of Commons in the Eighteenth Century* (Oxford, 1971) (he also relies heavily on Cavendish).

[20]It has already been pointed out that the interest in the literary property debate might come in part from the substantial material still in existence: Lionel Bently, 'A Few Remarks on Copyright at Common Law in 1774', in *What is the Point of Copyright History? Reflections on Copyright at Common Law in 1774* (CREATe Working Paper, 2016/04), 29.

[21]He had yet to inherit the baronetcy, so he was only Henry at this point. For biographical details see Part II.

[22]Thomas Gurney, *Brachygraphy, or Swift Writing made Easy to the Meanest Capacity* (1750) (ESTC: T134667); the earliest surviving version is the 2nd edn.

[23]P.D.G. Thomas, 'Sources for the Debates of the House of Commons, 1768–1774', *BIHR*, special supp., iv (1959), vi. For a more detailed account of his reports see Part II.

debates on the Bill and its turbulent passage. The newspapers were full of the debates on the Bill, with many editions having a quarter or more of the space taken up with matters relating to it, and, by this period, almost all of the leading London and Edinburgh newspapers still exist in libraries.[24]

Policymaking is based on beliefs, but how legislators come to believe something is a more complex question. It is too simple to suggest that policymaking is based on evidence;[25] the question is really where that evidence comes from and the weight it is given. In the 18th century, parliament could, and often did, hear witness testimony and consider documents while deciding whether to enact a bill. Indeed, for private bills, hearing evidence was theoretically essential.[26] In contrast to debates, Cavendish did not record witness evidence,[27] either that heard in a committee room or on the floor of the House, but there are other less extensive records that provide a picture.[28] Nevertheless, from the debates it is possible to see the facts or beliefs that MPs had when making their argument – not only can these be weighed and considered but it is possible to go further and try to determine where these views originated.

The newspapers' interest in the Booksellers' Bill is shown by the extensive coverage and reporting of the debates, which was often comparable to that received for significant debates of state.[29] These reports were nascent at this time and so, using Cavendish's diary once more, it is possible to consider the nature, accuracy and content of parliamentary reports. Assuming the Bill is typical of debates more generally, it enables the historian to extrapolate the quality of reporting to other debates and bills both during and after 1774.[30] Therefore, the Booksellers' Bill might be insignificant in terms of high politics, and even an afterthought in the history of copyright, but it provides a useful tool to examine how parliament worked at a key time in its history. We therefore must introduce the protagonist.

A Bird's Eye View

The Booksellers' Bill was the last hurrah in attempts to protect old, classic, books. It was the stillborn child of a common law copyright in published books. Much had been written on the common law right – whether it ever existed, and what its origins were – and the parliament of 1774 had its own version of the history.[31] Even now it is far from a fixed

[24]As to the precise coverage see Part III: Introduction.

[25]For a recent perspective, Paul Cairney, *The Politics of Evidence-Based Policy Making* (New York, 2016), chs 1 and 2.

[26]However, to prove the preamble a contemporary source highlights that for unopposed bills 'very tender Proof serves to support the Preamble': *The Liverpool Tractate: An Eighteenth-Century Manual on the Procedure of the House of Commons*, ed. Catherine Strateman (New York, 1937), 47.

[27]Except where it affected debate: Cavendish {41, 47, 49}.

[28]The committee records were lost in the fire of 1834: Caroline Shenton, *The Day Parliament Burned Down* (Oxford, 2012).

[29]For instance, if one compares the records of debates in *Cobbett's Parl. Hist.*, xvii (largely taken from newspapers): the Booksellers' Bill occupied cols 1077–110 and 1400–2, whereas both the Boston Post Act 1774 (cols 1163–92) and the budget (cols 1330–50) occupied significantly fewer columns.

[30]Cavendish's diary ended in 1774 when he left parliament. He later kept reports of the Irish parliament.

[31]See, Chapter 4.

thing; there are developed histories of copyright – orthodox views, revisionist approaches and even returns to the orthodoxy.[32] This history will not be considered afresh here, but a short introduction is necessary to provide context.

The Booksellers' Bill was promoted by the London Booksellers. The group was responsible for publishing, rather than simply selling, books, and they had dominated the book trade since the turn of the century. Central to their way of doing business was the buying and selling of 'copies' – what were later called copyrights. During the 18th century there was little or no technological advance in printing technology,[33] with the first major development being the metal press which arrived around 1800.[34] So the business was all about ownership of copies. The Statute of Anne (the Copyright Act 1709)[35] had created a statutory copyright, but the London Booksellers also traded another right in copies even where there was no statutory copyright (later to be claimed as the common law copyright). These rights in copies were often divided into shares, with most London Booksellers holding a share in the more profitable books. In simple terms, the house of lords' decision in *Donaldson v Beckett* meant that there was no copyright in old books (those no longer protected under the Statute of Anne). It was this which the London Booksellers wanted to change with their bill so as to resurrect their 'old' copyright.

On the other side were the Scottish Booksellers, with a figurehead of Alexander Donaldson.[36] Donaldson had started printing books in Edinburgh in the 1750s, and in 1763[37] he opened a shop in London from which he sought to sell cheaper books to undercut the London Booksellers. At the time books could be made cheaper by reducing their size[38] or length. Donaldson took both options, abbreviating text and printing in smaller sizes to reduce the price. The more books unprotected by any copyright,[39] the more he could print and sell. In addition to Donaldson and the Scottish Booksellers, there was another group of opponents: the London Stallholders.[40] These were the people who sold books in London. The books they sold were usually cheaper, provided from Scotland or outside the capital

[32] Gómez-Arostegui, 'Copyright at Common Law', 1, 4, 6; H.B. Abrams, 'The Persistent Myth of Perpetual Common Law Copyright', in *What is the Point of Copyright History?* (CREATe Working Paper, 2016/04), 16.

[33] Raven, *Publishing Business in Eighteenth-Century England*, 33.

[34] With the invention of the 'Stanhope' press: James Moran, *Printing Presses, History and Development from the Fifteenth Century to Modern Times* (1973), ch. 3 (the precise date it was invented is unknown, and it was not patented).

[35] There is some confusion over the dating of the Statute of Anne. It received royal assent on 10 Apr. 1710 and so it is often dated as 1710. However, before the Parliament (Commencement) Act 1793 (33 Geo. III, c. 13), which commenced (and so dated) statutes when they received royal assent, an act commenced (and so should be dated) at the start of the parliamentary session in which it was passed (in this case the relevant session began on 15 Nov. 1709): *Partridge v Strange and Croker* (1553) 1 Plowd 77 (75 ER 123). Accordingly, it is properly an act of 1709, hence its short title, Copyright Act 1709, in the chronological list of statutes.

[36] Alexander Donaldson* (1727–94). For a simplified biography, see W. Forbes Gray, 'Alexander Donaldson and the Fight for Cheap Books', *Juridical Review*, xxxviii (1926), 180.

[37] Part IV, Donaldson's Petition {10}.

[38] The price of books was largely concerned with their size. The most expensive books were folio, which was two pages to each side of paper (four per sheet); the second most expensive was quarto (4to), eight per sheet, then sexto (6to), 12 per sheet, octavo (8vo), 16 per sheet, and duodecimo (12mo), 24 per sheet. In other words, six times as many books could be produced from the same paper in 12mo than folio, and the binding would also involve fewer materials.

[39] He also printed those protected under the Statute of Anne, or so it was claimed: see *Public Ledger*, 11 May.

[40] They called themselves London Booksellers as well, but this use of 'sellers' was more literal.

and the London Booksellers treated them disparagingly.[41] But unlike the 'Booksellers' the Stallholders held no copyright, so their interests lay in reducing the price of books and thereby selling more: opening the market as it were.[42]

The battleground between the London Booksellers and Donaldson was marked out by the Statute of Anne. There could be no dispute that a book which was first published after 10 April 1710 was entitled to copyright for two terms of 14 years[43] from the date of first publishing (that is 28 years in total).[44] The Statute also protected 'old books', that is any book published before 10 April 1710, for a total period of 21 years (so statutory copyright in all old books ended on 9 April 1731).[45] Long before Donaldson had inherited his starting capital,[46] and within a few years of the statutory copyright expiring, the London Booksellers tried to protect old books by petitioning parliament for a bill: in 1735[47] and again in 1737.[48] This was followed by a more limited public bill in 1738,[49] which prohibited the importation of printed books and, finally, a similar restricted bill was finally enacted in 1739.[50] Yet by the time the first public bill was before the Commons, the Booksellers had changed tack and started to see the courts as the place to protect their rights.[51]

The London Booksellers took to the courts both in England and Scotland, claiming that publishing 'their copies' was an infringement of what they eventually called common law copyright. This began with a handful of cases in England[52] and then in Scotland[53] in the 1730s before turning into the full-blown 'Battle of the Booksellers'[54] through the 1750s and on to the determination in *Millar v Taylor*. Over this period, there were many claims, and some injunctions, based on a common law copyright. The cases heard before the

[41] They were compared to Sussex smugglers by the *Lloyd's Evening Post*, 25–7 Apr., 399.

[42] One letter to the newspapers says none of the names of petitioners were known to be booksellers: *Public Advertiser*, 4 May§.

[43] Also see, Chapter 5: Reversion.

[44] Copyright Act 1709, s. 1.

[45] Copyright Act 1709, s. 1; it may have ended on 10 Apr. 1774 (*Millar v Taylor* (1769) 4 Burr 2303 at 2324 (98 ER 201 at 213), as it depends whether the first day is immediately after 10 Apr. or is 10 Apr. itself.

[46] R.B. Sher, *The Enlightenment and the Book: Scottish Authors and their Publishers in Eighteenth-Century Britain, Ireland and America* (Chicago, IL, 2006), 312–14.

[47] Booksellers' Bill 1735 (*CJ*, xxii, 431, 438, 451, 470, 475, 480, 482). The Bill failed when second reading was deferred in the Lords (*LJ*, xxiv, 543, 544, 548, 550); for a discussion of its passage: Deazley, *On the Origin of the Right to Copy*, 94–104.

[48] Booksellers' Bill 1737 (*CJ*, xxii, 741, 756, 761, 764, 769, 800, 803, 832–3, 836, 838; *LJ*, xxv, 73, 81, 91, 99, 106, 111, 142); for a discussion of its passage: Deazley, *On the Origin of the Right to Copy*, 104–8.

[49] Importation of Printed Books Bill 1738 (leave 19 Apr. 1738: *CJ*, xxiii, 157): for a discussion of its passage: Deazley, *On the Origin of the Right to Copy*, 108.

[50] Importation Act 1738 (12 Geo. II, c. 36). As to the year of the enactment see p. 5 n 35. Order 6 Apr. 1739 (*CJ*, xxiii, 320); for a discussion of its passage, Deazley, *On the Origin of the Right to Copy*, 109–10 (there was one minor alteration).

[51] Deazley puts it down to the decision in *Baller v Watson* (1737): *On the Origin of the Right to Copy*, 110–12; also see Feather, *Publishing, Piracy and Politics*, 92, and the speech of De Grey LCJ, *Donaldson v Beckett* (1774) *Cobbett's Parl. Hist.*, xvii, cols 991–2.

[52] For example, *Eyre v Walker* (1735), *Motte v Faulkner* (1735), *Walthoe v Walker* (1737), and *Tonson v Walker* (1739), 1 Black W 331.

[53] The first case was *Millar v Stalker (and Nineteen Others)* (1738): Warren McDougall, 'Copyright Litigation in the Court of Session, 1738–1749, and the Rise of the Scottish Book Trade', *Edinburgh Bibliographical Society Transactions*, v (1971–87), 3–5.

[54] So named after ch. 4 in Birrell, *Seven Lectures on the Law and History of Copyright in Books.*

court of chancery[55] involved some of the finest advocates of the day: William Murray (later Lord Mansfield),[56] William Blackstone,[57] and Alexander Wedderburn[58] for the London Booksellers; whereas Joseph Yates,[59] Edward Thurlow,[60] and John Dunning[61] acted for their Scottish opponents. Many of the same men were present when the Bill was before the Commons.

Yet it was only in 1769, in *Millar v Taylor*, that the court of king's bench, or indeed any law court, recognised the existence of a common law copyright in a published book,[62] namely Thomson's *The Seasons*.[63] The court in *Millar* had been led by Lord Mansfield (chief justice) with Sir Edward Willes and Sir Richard Aston making a majority, albeit there was a strong dissent[64] from Sir Joseph Yates.[65] The attempt to appeal *Millar*[66] did not proceed and the decision stood (and in 1770 the injunction was granted). Soon thereafter, Donaldson published Thomson's *The Seasons* himself,[67] and Thomas Beckett, a shareholder in the book, brought a claim in chancery where, as expected, Donaldson lost with Lord Apsley LC granting an injunction on 16 November 1772.[68] A few weeks later, on 10 December, Donaldson petitioned the house of lords.[69] The case was heard a little over a year later in February 1774.

[55] Likewise, the Scottish cases: Hector MacQueen, 'Literary Property in Scotland in the Eighteenth and Nineteenth Centuries', in *Research Handbook on the History of Copyright Law*, ed. Isabella Alexander and H. Tomás Gómez-Arostegui (Cheltenham, 2016), 129.

[56] Solicitor-general 1742–54, attorney-general 1754–6, lord chief justice 1756–88: advocate, *Tonson v Walker* (1752) 3 Swans 672 (36 ER 1017); judge, *Tonson v Collins* (1761) 1 Black W 301 (96 ER 169); *Tonson v Collins* (1762) 1 Black W 321 (96 ER 180); *Millar v Taylor* (1769) 4 Burr 2303 (98 ER 201). He actually discusses his extensive involvement in *Millar*: 4 Burr 2408 (98 ER 257).

[57] Vinerian professor of English law, Oxford, 1758–66, justice of king's bench 1770, justice of common pleas 1770–80: advocate, *Tonson v Collins* (1762) 1 Black W 321 (96 ER 180), *Millar v Taylor* (1769) 4 Burr 2303 (98 ER 201).

[58] Solicitor-general 1771–8, attorney-general 1778–80, chief justice of common pleas 1780–93, lord chancellor 1793–1801: advocate, *Tonson v Collins* (1762) 1 Black W 321 (96 ER 180), *Donaldson v Beckett* (1774) 2 Br PC 129 (1 ER 837).

[59] Justice king's bench 1762–70, justice common pleas 1770: advocate, *Tonson v Collins* (1762) 1 Black W 321 (96 ER 180); dissenting judge in *Millar v Taylor* (1769) 4 Burr 2303 (98 ER 201).

[60] Solicitor-general 1770–2, attorney-general 1772–8, lord chancellor 1778–93: advocate, *Tonson v Collins* (1762), *Millar v Taylor* (1769) 4 Burr 2303 (98 ER 201), *Donaldson v Beckett* (1774) 2 Br PC 129 (1 ER 837).

[61] Solicitor-general 1768–70: advocate, *Millar v Taylor* (1769) 4 Burr 2303 (98 ER 201), *Donaldson v Beckett* (1774) 2 Br PC 129 (1 ER 837).

[62] As Deazley says, considering Mansfield's early role in the dispute, the outcome was almost inevitable: *On the Origin of the Right to Copy*, 189.

[63] Lord Camden had foreshadowed his decision in *Donaldson v Beckett* (1774) 2 Br PC 129 (1 ER 837) in an earlier part of the proceedings of *Millar v Taylor* (1769) 4 Burr 2303 (98 ER 201): Gómez-Arostegui, 'Copyright at Common Law', 21.

[64] The first dissent during Lord Mansfield's tenure: *Millar v Taylor* (1769) 4 Burr 2303 at 2395 (98 ER 201 at 250).

[65] Who apparently generally fell out with Mansfield: Wilfrid Prest, *William Blackstone: Law and Letters in the Eighteenth Century* (Oxford, 2006), 260.

[66] By way of writ of error: see Chapter 4: The Battle of the Booksellers.

[67] He was obviously not bound by the injunction in *Millar* and probably chose the book to directly challenge the decision in that case: Rose, *Authors and Owners*, 113.

[68] Entry Book, Decrees and Orders, Book A, 1772: TNA, C 33/439, ff. 26–7.

[69] *LJ*, xxxiii, 476. As to petitioning the Lords at this time (which would have included judicial petitions), see M.W. McCahill, *The House of Lords in the Age of George III, 1760–1811* (Oxford, 2009), 258–60.

The house of lords in *Donaldson v Beckett* found against the London Booksellers and their common law copyright disappeared.[70] While the reasoning was unclear,[71] and has even been called a 'judicial black hole',[72] the outcome was not: copyright in published works existed only because of the Statute of Anne.[73] The London book trade was (potentially) thrown open to competition,[74] and the Booksellers proclaimed that they were staring at ruin.[75] Within days they were petitioning for a new bill: the Booksellers' Bill 1774. The numerous histories of copyright have only ever touched on the Bill. Like the earlier bills in the 1730s, it made its way through the Commons and while it was opposed the suggestion that the most effective opposition came from booksellers who did not own copyright,[76] that the arguments raised were difficult to sustain, that the Bill 'had no hope',[77] or that it 'falls on deaf ears',[78] misses the point or at least grossly simplifies it.[79] Similarly, the suggestion that there was a 'flood' of Scottish petitions against the Bill suggests the opposition was greater than it was, but it is fair to say it had an 'acrimonious' passage through the Commons.[80] Yet the Bill did pass the Commons at least and so it found the Booksellers' claims to be proved. The Bill fell because their lordships,[81] and Lord Camden in particular, strongly disliked it.[82] We turn back to the beginning and how interest groups, like the Booksellers, could exert pressure and seek legislative change.

[70]There are so many accounts of this decision it will not be explored further.

[71]There are a multitude of views on what was opined by the judges. A good summary is in Gómez-Arostegui, 'Copyright at Common Law', 23–4.

[72]Mark Rose, 'Donaldson and the Muse of History', in *What is the Point of Copyright History?* (CREATe Working Paper, 2016/04), 40.

[73]The broader question of whether there was ever a common law copyright was not authoritatively decided therefore: Lionel Bently, 'A Few Remarks on Copyright at Common Law in 1774', 24 (or, of course, it was decided in *Millar v Taylor*).

[74]But see discussion at Chapter 5: Monopolies.

[75]Feather, *Publishing, Piracy and Politics*, 93.

[76]Patterson, *Copyright in Historical Perspective*, 178.

[77]Feather, *Publishing, Piracy and Politics*, 93–4.

[78]Ronan Deazley, *Rethinking Copyright: History, Theory, Language* (Cheltenham, 2006), 21.

[79]Albeit Deazley mentions it in passing: *On the Origin of the Right to Copy*, 213–15; *Rethinking Copyright*, 21–3.

[80]Rose, *Authors and Owners*, 103.

[81]In a letter from the marquis of Rockingham to Edmund Burke on 1 June it appears that Lords Gower, Weymouth, Denbigh and Radnor were already against the Bill, and that most other peers were of that mind: *The Correspondence of Edmund Burke, Volume 2, July 1768– June 1774*, ed. Lucy Sutherland (Cambridge, 1960), 540–1.

[82]See Chapter 8.

Chapter 1
Lobbying for Change (or Staying the Same)

Introduction

The Booksellers petitioned for their bill almost immediately after the house of lords ruled against them in *Donaldson v Beckett*.[1] There was no mounting pressure to legislate, there were no pushes for reform,[2] rather the petition and bill came from nowhere. This chapter is concerned with the actions of the respective interest groups to promote or oppose the legislation – what would subsequently be called lobbying.[3] At this time, lobbying went in two directions – to government and to parliament.[4] Once a petition was lodged before parliament, as in the case of the Booksellers, the lobbying of government became otiose. The decision whether the petition, and subsequently the Bill, passed was in the hands of members of parliament both individually and collectively, the government only playing a role as a power within that sphere, with its support affecting any bill's chances of success.

The Structure and Nature of Interest Groups in the 18th Century

The interest groups that had engaged in lobbying, well into the 18th century, were institutions: trading companies, guilds and other formal associations of craftsmen,[5] or municipal corporations, such as town councils and the City of London.[6] These bodies had clearly defined memberships,[7] and while they remained rich and powerful such groups had very privileged access to government and parliament.[8] By comparison other interest groups were created and were in 'constant construction'.[9] With the development of *political* movements, such as those led by the radical John Wilkes (so called Wilkesite groups), a new approach was starting to take hold, with groups being open to everyone[10] wishing to pursue a similar aim

[1] *LJ*, xxxiv, 29–30 (21 Feb.). While not within the scope of this chapter, it appears that lobbying could also occur in relation to judicial decisions of the house of lords: Anita Rees, 'The Practice and Procedure of the House of Lords 1714–1784', University of Aberystwyth PhD, 1987, p. 158 (stating how vested interests could turn the tide of legal opinion).

[2] Ronan Deazley, *On the Origin of the Right to Copy* (Oxford, 2004), ch. 2.

[3] The term is an anachronism as it would not have been used at the time: F.G. James, 'The Irish Lobby in the Early Eighteenth Century', *EHR*, lxxxi (1966), 543; Vivienne Dietz, 'Before the Age of Capital: Manufacturing Interests and the British State, 1780–1800', University of Princeton PhD, 1991, p. 18.

[4] Dietz, 'Before the Age of Capital', 32 (it was 'bifurcated').

[5] E.g. White Paper Company.

[6] A.G. Olson, 'The Virginia Merchants of London: A Study in Eighteenth-Century Interest-Group Politics', *William and Mary Quarterly*, xl (1983), 365; Dietz, 'Before the Age of Capital', 33; John Brewer, *The Sinews of Power: War, Money and the English State 1688–1783* (Cambridge, MA, 1990), 231. These groups were also the most likely to petition parliament: Julian Hoppit, 'Petitions, Economic Legislation and Interest Groups in Britain, 1660–1800', *Parliamentary History*, xxxvii (2018), 59.

[7] The membership was exclusive or ascriptive: Graham Wootton, *Pressure Groups in Britain 1720–1970* (1975), 13.

[8] Brewer, *Sinews of Power*, 248.

[9] Dietz, 'Before the Age of Capital', 19.

[10] For example, public meetings: Wootton, *Pressure Groups in Britain*, 39.

or having similar political beliefs.[11] In most cases[12] this development had not touched the economic interest groups, such as booksellers, which remained formed of people coming together with a common cause to prevent or promote a policy or bill.[13]

The 18th-century parliament could be responsive to a wide range of political, social and industrial interests represented by traditional interest groups[14] because these were rarely opposed to ministerial positions. Some such groups have even been described as having a 'comfortable advisory relationship'[15] with minsters who would support their preparation of testimony and come to exchange information[16] about the industry concerned.[17] This sort of gentle influence was thought quite acceptable and proper, whereas the more overt agitation and opposition to government (exemplified by John Wilkes)[18] was thought to be less acceptable among the more conservative classes.[19]

The Booksellers

In many respects the London Booksellers would have started like the older fragmented[20] interest groups who often had no strict meeting place, subscription or fixed membership.[21] London society, and indeed commercial society, was strongly based around the coffee houses where deals could be done, gossip exchanged and groups with common interests formed.[22] *The Chapter* coffee house,[23] on Paternoster Row, had strong links with the book trade.[24] As early as 1715 an association of booksellers (set up to divide shares) had been based at

[11] Wootton, *Pressure Groups in Britain*, 13; Hannah Barker, *Newspapers, Politics and English Society 1695–1855* (1999), 155.

[12] Cf. the transformation of the American traders' lobby: A.G. Olson, '"The London Mercantile Lobby" and the Coming of the American Revolution', *Journal of American History*, lxix (1982), 29–35; Olson, 'The Virginia Merchants of London', 383–6.

[13] Dietz, 'Before the Age of Capital', 33.

[14] Lee Davison *et al.*, 'Introduction' to *Stilling the Grumbling Hive. The Response to Social and Economic Problems in England 1689–1750* (Stroud, 1992), xxix, xxxiv–xxxv (response to urban middle class and activity of economic and social interests).

[15] Olson, "The London Mercantile Lobby", 25.

[16] The information exchange became more reciprocal as the century progressed: Brewer, *Sinews of Power*, 227.

[17] Olson, 'The Virginia Merchants of London', 382. It was often better informed than that through official channels: Brewer, *Sinews of Power*, 232.

[18] P.D.G. Thomas, *John Wilkes: A Friend to Liberty* (Oxford, 1996), ch. 7; Olson, 'The Virginia Merchants of London', 384.

[19] Olson, "The London Mercantile Lobby", 25, 30.

[20] Olson, "The London Mercantile Lobby", 22.

[21] Dietz, 'Before the Age of Capital', 33.

[22] Indeed, printing houses were themselves often used to co-ordinate projects and lobbying: James Raven, *Publishing Business in Eighteenth-Century England* (Woodbridge, 2014), 114; but this is unlikely as between booksellers themselves, who would have been further up the social ladder.

[23] Bryant Lillywhite, *London Coffee Houses: A Reference Book of Coffee Houses of the Seventeenth, Eighteenth and Nineteenth Centuries* (1963), 151–5, no. 234.

[24] Markman Ellis, 'Coffee-House Libraries in Mid-Eighteenth Century London', *The Library*, x (2009), 3 (relevant to this discussion, Ellis also describes the book holdings of various coffee shops); as to the role of the coffee shop in society, see Ellis, *The Coffee House: A Cultural History* (2004); Brian Cowan, *The Social Life of Coffee: The Emergence of the British Coffeehouse* (New Haven, CT, 2005).

the site,[25] and by the 1770s booksellers, writers and others associated with the trade were customers.[26] While there is nothing specifically linking the Booksellers' Petition to the *Chapter*[27] and there were other coffee houses linked to the trade,[28] in 1774 it was a central meeting point and had strong links to old alliances,[29] so at least some of the booksellers promoting the Bill would have met there. What is known, however, is that the signing of the petition itself took place at another literary haunt: *The Devil Tavern*.[30] Handbills were given to booksellers for a meeting at the tavern where a speech was given on the Bill's importance to the trade, and then all present were asked to sign.[31]

At coffee houses and taverns, like the *Chapter* and the *Devil*, it was possible to politicise groups within the trade, essentially leading[32] a core of people co-ordinating and motivating others within an interest group towards a particular end. Yet by the 1770s lobbying even by traditional interest groups was changing in a number of respects. In the first half of the century their engagement had been led by the proponents of legislation or those scrutinising the legislation of others,[33] rather than agents or dedicated professionals.[34] Interest groups developing a more managed structure allowed them to grow in size and thereby engage the public.[35] Such engagement meant to the more conservatively minded (such as Samuel Johnson) that these wider groups were not representing a particular interest as each person might sign a petition for a different reason.[36] Thus, smaller close-knit groups, like the Booksellers were often as effective as larger less defined associations.

In other respects, the London Booksellers and their opponents were different from other interest groups. They had formed and identified leading players much earlier than the 1770s,[37] and in particular the 'honorary monopoly' had been set up in 1759[38] with a subscription and committee (comprising Jacob Tonson, Andrew Millar, Charles Hitch, John and James Rivington, John Ward and William Johnston).[39] The 1759 project had facilitated subgroups to litigate cases ultimately leading up to *Donaldson* in the Lords. In other words,

[25]Lillywhite, *London Coffee Houses*, 152.

[26]The 'Chapter Coffee House' was seen as having a large collection of books or even being a reading society: Lillywhite, *London Coffee Houses*, 153.

[27]The Letter by Colineus in the *Morning Chronicle*, 16 Mar., described how the subject was being discussed in coffee houses albeit by those against the London Booksellers.

[28]For instance, the 'Grecian Coffee' (Lillywhite, *London Coffee Houses*, 243–5) and the 'London Coffee House', where later copyrights were sold, 338–9.

[29]For a detailed history of the congers, Norma Hodgson and Cyprian Blagden, *The Notebook of Thomas Bennet and Henry Clements* (Oxford Bibliographic Society, new ser., vi, 1956), ch. 3.

[30]It was at 2, Fleet Street, and was famously home to Ben Jonson's 'Apollo Club'. In the 1770s, Thomas Longman and others ran a literary society for booksellers at the tavern: Henry Curwen, *A History of Booksellers, the Old and New* (1873), 86.

[31]Part IV, Remarks on the Booksellers' Petition.

[32]Olson, "The London Mercantile Lobby", 23; Olson, 'The Virginia Merchants of London', 367.

[33]Brewer, *Sinews of Power*, 232.

[34]Dietz, 'Before the Age of Capital', 19.

[35]Olson dates the London Merchants taking similar steps to 1763: "The London Mercantile Lobby", 29.

[36]Samuel Johnson, *The False Alarm* (Cadell, 1770) (ESTC: T88127), 42–3.

[37]Indeed, it was probably always like that. For a discussion of Elizabethan printers, see Feather, *Publishing, Piracy and Politics*, 20–1.

[38]See Chapter 4: The Honorary Monopoly.

[39]Letter 26 Apr. 1759: Part IV, The Five Letters.

the Booksellers were used to working and acting within a committee structure and with substantial sums of money.[40] Indeed, it appears that the spending to promote the Booksellers' Bill itself totalled £1,500, including over £1,000 raised by the Stationers' Company from a general subscription.[41] This brings us to the people they were trying to influence.

Party Politics?

The role of political parties or groupings in the 18th century house of commons[42] is not without controversy, particularly after the 'rage of the party' ended in 1714.[43] The traditional view was that there was a two-party system – Whig and Tory – which began after the Glorious Revolution and continued well into the 19th century.[44] A new orthodoxy, led by Sir Lewis Namier, developed which suggested 'the political life of the period could be fully described without ever using a party domination',[45] and in this absence power was used to satisfy local or personal needs, with any groupings being 'for' the government or in 'opposition' to it.[46] This premise has now been tempered substantially and for a time the tide turned in favour of the two-party view once more,[47] with Thomas more recently taking the stance that individual MPs and groups came together and broke apart as issues, or particular ministers or policies, changed.[48]

In this framework, there were ministers, and those strongly opposed to the government, but many MPs of the age are often described as 'independent country gentlemen'.[49] They

[40]This seems to have been mentioned in 1759. As to the need for subscriptions and agents, see Brewer, *Sinews of Power*, 237.

[41]Feather, *Publishing, Piracy and Politics*, 94; Court Book M, 5 Nov. 1775, p. 480: *The Records of the Stationers' Company 1554–1920* (1986), reel 50; *Literary Print Culture* (Adam Matthew, 2017): TSC/1/B/01/10 (£1,030 raised from trade already, of which £210 from the court, asking for £471 18*s*. 11*d*. to meet the shortfall).

[42]In the house of lords, as would be expected, it largely followed what might be termed 'the party of the Crown': M.W. McCahill, *The House of Lords in the Age of George III, 1760–1811* (Oxford, 2009), 128, followed by empirical data on 129–35.

[43]The 'rage of party' is usually tied to the triennial parliaments (under the Meeting of Parliament Act 1694 (6 & 7 Will. & Mar., c. 2) it ended with the Tory party breaking down due to its Jacobian support and the Septennial Act 1715 (1 Geo. I, St. 2, c. 38) was passed in 1716. The term itself was coined by J.H. Plumb as the title to ch. 5 in *The Growth of Political Stability in England, 1675–1725* (1969). Other notable works in this field include Geoffrey Holmes, *British Politics in the Age of Anne* (2nd edn, 1987); and *Britain in the First Age of Party, 1680–1750: Essays Presented to Geoffrey Holmes*, ed. Clyve Jones (1987).

[44]The high point of this orthodoxy was G.M. Trevelyan's Romanes Lecture of 1926: 'The Two-Party System in English Political History', in Trevelyan, *An Autobiography and Other Essays* (1949), 183. Some copyright scholars have taken this view as well and put great weight on the party system: Deazley, *On the Origin of the Right to Copy*, 11–12 (albeit this is a comment during the 'rage').

[45]Lewis Namier, *The Structure of Politics at the Accession of George III* (2nd edn, 1957), xi (he does note, on p. x, however, that 'party names and cant were current').

[46]Namier, *Structure of Politics*, 133–4.

[47]P.D.G. Thomas, 'Party Politics in Eighteenth-Century Britain: Some Myths and a Touch of Reality', *Journal of Eighteenth-Century Studies*, x (1987), 202. As to the criticisms of his arguments, see Jeremy Black, 'Eighteenth-Century English Politics: Recent Work and Current Problems', *Albion: A Quarterly Journal Concerned with British Studies*, xxv (1993), 420–1.

[48]Thomas, 'Party Politics in Eighteenth-Century Britain', 208.

[49]For a definition of such a member, *HC 1754–90*, i, 146; see more generally Lewis Namier, 'Country Gentlemen in Parliament 1750–1783', *History Today* (1954), 676.

could be expected to give 'general support' to the government of the day;[50] in other words, the government might expect certain members to vote to support most (but not all) of its measures.[51] This absence of firm party lines was central to practice and procedure before the house of commons.[52] Yet those who argue most strongly against the existence of parties in the latter part of the 18th century often take it further and argue there was an absence of political principle,[53] and that local and personal interests most strongly influenced how MPs acted. The debate over the role of the 'party' in 18th-century politics remains and while there were groups of MPs who opposed each other at different times it is probably better to see the matter on this basis rather than in terms of the 'monolithic' parties that would rise in the 19th century.[54]

Whether the party was a strong, or a weak, factor in voting, it is important to understand that any particular debate would attract only a few speakers; even where there were weighty political questions at stake fewer than 30 would usually speak.[55] More precisely, during the parliament of 1768–74 of the 692 members who could have spoken only 303 ever did so,[56] and of those 62 spoke only once, with 40 members speaking at least 100 times.[57] In the absence of reports and with many truly safe seats there was little need to speak and, in any event, most MPs usually lacked clear political vision.[58] Accordingly, debates in the Commons were led by a very small minority of members and in many respects the affiliations and beliefs of these men mattered most.

In the absence of official party labels, and with little debate recorded (other than by Cavendish), it is difficult to attribute whether a member was for or against the government; other than by considering how he voted on each division (that is vote in the House),[59] and

[50]S.M. Lee, 'Parliament, Parties and Elections (1760–1815)', in H.T. Dickinson, *A Companion to Eighteenth-Century Britain* (Oxford, 2000), 73; Thomas, *The House of Commons in the Eighteenth Century*, 240 (39 out of 101 country members spoke, and of those ten spoke only once).

[51]Lewis Namier, 'The Circular Letter: An Eighteenth-Century Whip to Members of Parliament', *EHR*, xliv (1929), 589.

[52]Thomas, *The House of Commons in the Eighteenth Century*, 6; it did not preclude MPs being whipped to vote for the government, however: Namier, 'The Circular Letter'.

[53]The so-called Rockingham Whigs, for instance, were concerned about 'secret influence', that is advice being taken from the wrong advisors and not the government: Lee, 'Parliament, Parties and Elections', 74.

[54]Thomas, 'Party Politics in Eighteenth-Century Britain', 208 (he also provides a historiography of the issue until that time).

[55]Thomas, *The House of Commons in the Eighteenth Century*, 202. The highest number of speakers appears to be over the printers' debate on 25 Mar. (see *CJ*, xxxiii, 283–5) where there were 65 different speakers. In Cavendish, there were 30 speakers recorded across the various stages of the Bookseller's Bill.

[56]It has been suggested that the presence of about 400 members was considered a 'full house' at this time and even when in London many members did not attend: P.D.G. Thomas, 'Division Lists, 1760–1774', in *The Parliamentary Lists of the Early Eighteenth Century: Their Complication and Use*, ed. Aubrey Newman (Leicester, 1973), 146; Thomas, *The House of Commons in the Eighteenth Century*, 229–30; Josef Redlich, *The Procedure of the House of Commons: A Study of its History and Present Form*, trans. A.E. Steinthal (3 vols, 1908), ii, 112. There were attempts to increase attendance, but this largely failed: Redlich, ii, 114.

[57]P.D.G. Thomas, 'Check List of MPs Speaking in the House of Commons, 1768 to 1774', *BIHR*, xxxv (1962), 221. Alexander Wedderburn and Edward Thurlow, the solicitor- and attorney-generals, were some of the most active speakers: Thomas, *The House of Commons in the Eighteenth Century*, 238. Over a longer period of 1747–96 it has been suggested about one fifth of members made a 'discernible contribution' to debate: L.D. Reid, 'Speaking in the Eighteenth Century House of Commons', *Speech Monographs*, xvi (1949), 135.

[58]Thomas, *The House of Commons in the Eighteenth Century*, 231 (unless a constituent was present during a debate, absent reporting, they would not know whether a member spoke or not).

[59]As to the procedure see Chapter 3.

the view of John Robinson of whether an MP was pro or anti-government at the time of the 1774 election.[60] At the time, division lists were not officially published and only very occasionally were they collected for publication in newspapers or privately.[61] In the parliament of 1768 to 1774 there were a total of 301 divisions[62] but only a few lists are known.[63] Nevertheless, the existing division[64] lists of the period have been recorded[65] and analysed.[66] In contrast, for votes in the Lords most of the existing division lists are minority lists,[67] that is they detail only those peers who voted with the minority (lost the vote) rather than who voted in favour. From party power we move to petitioning.

Petitioning

The 18th century still had very formalised lobbying[68] which revolved around the right[69] to present a petition.[70] It was a practice which was routine and ubiquitous and undertaken by all levels of society,[71] with an average of 1.4 petitions being presented per sitting day in the 1770s.[72] A petition would set out a grievance, or arguments for or against a bill,[73] and, as would be expected, the petitioners would vary depending on the issue.[74] In simple terms petitions provided the 'key' to parliament, unlocking access, provided a parliamentarian

[60] P.D.G. Thomas, 'John Robinson's "State" for the General Election of 1774', *Parliamentary History*, xxx (2011), 215.

[61] And usually when printed it was for opposition purposes: Thomas, 'Division Lists, 1760–1774', 46–7.

[62] Thomas, *The House of Commons in the Eighteenth Century*, 262 (this only includes divisions of the House and not of a division committee of the whole House or in select committees).

[63] Many are minority lists.

[64] Or almost all: Grayson Ditchfield, 'Numbered, Weighed and Divided: The Voting of the House of Commons During the Reign of George III', *Parliamentary History*, xv (1996), 231 n. 3, 233, for omissions during the 1770s; Clyve Jones, 'New Parliamentary Lists, 1660–1880', *Parliamentary History*, xxv (2006), 401 (identifying no further lists for the 1770s). It is likely that as more manuscript collections are explored more lists will be discovered.

[65] There are of course significant questions about their accuracy: Thomas, 'Division Lists, 1760–1774', 48–51; there are also questions whether the list records the division or is a canvasing list, that is a list predicting a vote.

[66] *Voting Records of the British House of Commons, 1761–1820*, ed. D.E. Ginter (6 vols, 1995). It does not, however, include some division lists of the period, including the partial division list in the *Public Advertiser* for 24 Mar., relating to the order to bring in the Booksellers' Bill.

[67] William Lowe, 'Politics in the House of Lords, 1760–1775', University of Emory PhD, 1975, appendix IV, supplementary notes.

[68] This formality is suggested to be one of the advantages of petitioning: Hoppit, 'Petitions, Economic Legislation and Interest Groups', 65.

[69] The contested nature of this right existed throughout the 18th century, including the time of the Booksellers' Bill: Mark Knights, '"The Lowest Degree of Freedom": The Right to Petition Parliament, 1640–1800', *Parliamentary History*, xxxvii (2018), 24.

[70] For a review of the subject matter of such petitions, Hoppit, 'Petitions, Economic Legislation and Interest Groups'.

[71] Knights, "The Lowest Degree of Freedom", 18; albeit it appears the *most* powerful were less likely to petition: Hoppit, 'Petitions, Economic Legislation and Interest Groups', 70.

[72] Philip Loft, 'Petitioning and Petitioners to the Westminster Parliament, 1660–1788', *Parliamentary History*, xxxviii (2019), 347 (this only includes what Loft calls large responsible petitions, so the number would have been a little higher).

[73] National lobbying had begun very early. For instance, the leather workers presented over 150 petitions from around the country against a proposed tax at the end of the 17th century: Brewer, *Sinews of Power*, 233.

[74] Loft, 'Petitioning and Petitioners', 350. In this respect the challenges to the London Booksellers' petition on the basis that many who signed it had not suffered any loss seems particularly relevant.

would present it.[75] Presentation could lead to committees being formed to examine the issue or to consider ordering in a bill, but it was also possible for petitions to be laid on the table and no more. This would usually, although not always, result in it not progressing further. This is why 'inside' contacts would have been a vital resource. In the 18th century it was still possible for parliamentary officials to work as agents (so called 'indoor' agents) for interest groups. For instance, engaging Edward Barwell (who was a clerk without doors)[76] in 1774 meant he could not only give notice to clients of petitions being lodged but possibly even provide a copy before it was presented,[77] enabling its opponent to get a head start on any counter-petition, or persuading members to vote against any proposal.

Informal Pressure

Campaigns and so petitions might need renewing again and again if they were ever to progress. For instance, the Booksellers in the 1730s petitioned and pushed for legislation repeatedly. But militant activism,[78] such as demonstrations and crowding outside parliament, was not well received and even led to parliamentary motions condemning the groups.[79] So what sort of activity was acceptable? It could take three forms. The first would be personal contacts with members of interest groups seeking opportunities to call on MPs, peers, ministers or even senior officials.[80] The second would be more formal steps, such as producing printed materials, 'lobbying documents' (sometimes called 'cases') for circulation among parliamentarians and others setting out the arguments being relied upon; these were sometimes published in newspapers. Eventually, such printed materials could support the witness testimony which might follow if the lobbying had some success. Third and finally, it was possible to use the newspapers or other media to seek support either by writing letters, printing cases, seeking editorial comment, writing tracts or even performing plays.

Personal Contacts

Whether a group had influence or contacts with leading politicians would substantially determine the success of many lobbying efforts; knowing the right person could bring the issue to the attention of the minister or parliament almost immediately.[81] In Scotland, the role of the Burghs could be significant, and through the annual convention, something

[75] Brewer, *Sinews of Power*, 233; which of course was also a drawback of this method of lobbying: Hoppit, 'Petitions, Economic Legislation and Interest Groups', 66.

[76] O.C. Williams, *The Clerical Organization of the House of Commons 1661–1850* (Oxford, 1954), 282. As to the role of 'clerks without doors', that is principal committee clerks, Williams, ch. 7.

[77] Sheila Lambert, *Bills and Acts: Legislative Procedure in Eighteenth-Century England* (Cambridge, 1971), 50.

[78] Indeed, even more moderate delegations were frowned upon: J.M. Norris, 'Samuel Garbett and the Early Development of Industrial Lobbying in Great Britain', *Economic History Review*, x (1958), 451.

[79] Brewer, *Sinews of Power*, 238; as occurred in 1733 after Walpole withdrew the excise bill and a large mob descended on the palace of Westminster: J.H. Plumb, *Sir Robert Walpole: The King's Ministers* (2 vols, 1960), ii, 270–1; *CJ*, xxii, 115, 12 Apr. 1733.

[80] Olson, 'The Virginia Merchants of London', 368.

[81] Norris, 'Samuel Garbett and the Early Development of Industrial Lobbying', 452; Brewer, *Sinews of Power*, 240.

close to national support could be signalled.[82] Meetings with MPs might be formal affairs or, more likely, gatherings over food and drink paid for by the interest groups.[83] This was a time when candidates for parliament would routinely spend vast sums of money securing election support through 'treating' – that is giving food, wine and banquets,[84] and so it is almost certain that these things worked the other way around. Conversely, it would be necessary to take account of political rivalries,[85] and so while the Booksellers had had very influential members recently on the payroll as counsel in *Donaldson* (the solicitor-general, Alexander Wedderburn, and John Dunning MP) as well as support from the more literary minded members (for instance, Edmund Burke) they also had credible adversaries.

Printed Material

What the Booksellers' Bill shows us so clearly is how parties, and non-parties, lobbied for and against a bill. The most formal type of lobbying was presenting a petition praying to be heard and, as discussed below, this applied to private and public bills.[86] At the other end of the spectrum, it appears that cards (the size of postcards) might be handed out to members with the key message being printed upon them amounting to little more than flyering.[87] In contrast to these throwaway cards, what is more commonly retained in archives and libraries are the 'cases' in favour or against the Bill. These and similar documents bearing names such as Remarks, or Observations, were not required under standing orders or convention.

In contrast to petitions, breviates and the Bill itself, these cases had no formal or substantive requirements and so the length, layout and content was entirely in the hands of the party producing them. With printing and wider circulation, it became possible for one party to respond to the other and so on creating a conversation in documentation.[88] These papers would have been handed out in the lobby of the house of commons by the promoters, or given to the doorman to hand out to members entering the chamber;[89] some

[82] Indeed, Edinburgh Booksellers petitioned the annual convention in 1774, and received its support, which led to a letter to all burghs to push for their MPs to oppose the Bill: *Caledonian Mercury*, 27 Apr§. (and the letter of 14 Apr. it published).

[83] Brewer, *Sinews of Power*, 239.

[84] William Morgan, 'An Eighteenth-Century Election in England', *Political Science Quarterly*, xxxvii (1922), 596–8; John Phillips, 'The Structure of Electoral Politics in Unreformed England', *Journal of British Studies*, xix (1979), 97 (treating a common practice); Zoe Dyndor, 'The Political Culture of Elections in Northampton, 1768–1868', University of Northampton PhD, 2010, pp. 182, 184–7 (treating rituals occurring daily during elections); Matthew McCormack, *The Independent Man: Citizenship and Gender Politics in Georgian England* (Manchester, 2005), 15 (an accepted practice).

[85] Norris, 'Samuel Garbett and the Early Development of Industrial Lobbying', 452.

[86] This distinction is discussed in Chapter 3: Public and Private.

[87] While there is no evidence it happened in relation to the Booksellers' Bill, there is the copy of such a card on Hornblower's Patent Bill 1792, which simply reads 'Mr Hornblower's Bill is merely for an Extension of the Term of his *Patent* … without the Intention of taking away any *Rights* of the Opposers of his Bill, or *Adding* to his Own': Birmingham Library, MS 3147/2/36/5. It appears that Donaldson circulated cards encouraging members to attend the second reading: *Middlesex Journal*, 7–10 May§.

[88] David Zaret, *Origins of Democratic Culture, Printing, Petitions, and the Public Sphere in Early-Modern England* (Princeton, NJ, 2000), 250–2.

[89] With a fee being paid: Brewer, *Sinews of Power*, 241. A tip of 5*s*. had been paid in 1711 to ensure all members had a copy of a paper; it would probably have been a little more by the 1770s.

MPs even made arrangements to have lobbying documents forwarded to them.[90] Cases had begun as short one page documents,[91] but as the 18th century progressed they became longer and longer as the cost of printing declined.[92] These cases were an effective and cheap method of lobbying[93] as they involved a few meals, the odd tip and the cost of printing: a couple of pounds at most.[94] In the case of the Booksellers' Bill, it would have been cheaper still as both sides would have access to printing at cost. It is hardly surprising, therefore, that an assortment of lobbying documents, and more than might usually have been expected, were produced for the Booksellers' Bill (for instance, the following year the Porcelain Patent Act 1775,[95] which was also heavily opposed, attracted at least seven lobbying documents).[96]

Newspapers

The circulation of newspapers had grown substantially over the second half of the 18th century. There were around 7.3 million newspapers printed (not sold) in 1750 and this had risen to 12.6 million by 1775.[97] By the end of the 1770s it was estimated that some of the leading papers[98] had daily or tri-weekly circulations of between 2,000 and 5,000,[99] with higher circulations when parliament was in session.[100] The method of printing at the time meant that using a skilled workforce a single printing press could produce about 250 copies an hour: that is about two four-page newspapers a minute.[101] So to meet this high level of demand multiple presses would have been needed,[102] causing minor discrepancies between editions.

[90] Brewer, *Sinews of Power*, 241.

[91] Bob Harris, 'Parliamentary Legislation, Lobbying and the Press in Eighteenth-Century Scotland', *Parliamentary History*, xxvi (2007), 76.

[92] Brewer, *Sinews of Power*, 241.

[93] In general, it appears that print played a lesser role in Scottish political culture than in England, albeit this was starting to change by the time the Booksellers presented their bill: Harris, 'Parliamentary Legislation, Lobbying and the Press', 77–8; however, the Scottish Booksellers, like their English cousins, clearly had significant reliance on print.

[94] Brewer, *Sinews of Power*, 241–2.

[95] 15 Geo. III, c. 52 (a private bill extending a patent).

[96] Phillip Johnson, *Parliament, Patents and Inventions* (2018), 228 (PRVA19) (more could have existed which have now been lost).

[97] Barker, *Newspapers, Politics and English Society*, 30 (this figure is based on treasury stamps so includes only the stamped press); this must also be considered in line with the demographics and the rapidly increasing population. This led to annual profits of between £1,500 and £2,000: Barker, 35, 95.

[98] Advertising revenue being so important to newspapers of this and later periods means a larger circulation could attract more and greater value advertising.

[99] Barker, *Newspapers, Politics and English Society*, 32; for instance, the *Public Advertiser* was selling about 3,000 issues per day: Ivon Asquith, 'Advertising and the Press in the late Eighteenth and Early Nineteenth Centuries: James Perry and the *Morning Chronicle* 1790–1821', *HJ*, xviii (1975), 723 (Appendix B2).

[100] John Brewer, *Party Ideology and Popular Politics at the Accession of George III* (Cambridge, 1976), 143 (sales peaked in February or March just before parliament started sitting).

[101] The standard format for the 18th century was made by printing on both sides of one sheet and then folding it into two. There were usually four columns and about 5,000 words per page by the 1770s.

[102] Barker, *Newspapers, Politics and English Society*, 37.

By the 1770s the London newspapers were routinely sent by Post Office employees[103] (and by this point, MPs)[104] around the country[105] using their franking privileges. This not only facilitated local papers[106] and inspired many newspaper titles (*Morning Post* and *Evening Mail* for instance) but it also provided the bulk of the income for six Post Office clerks of the road.[107] The circulation through the Post Office was growing so rapidly that by 1782 it despatched over three million London newspapers to the regions each year and 46,000 came back into the capital.[108] Nevertheless, the number of newspapers was still small compared with the population as a whole; for instance there were around three newspapers produced each *year* for every two adults in England.[109]

This did not reflect readership however. It was estimated that every newspaper would have been read numerous times, as they were often taken by coffee houses,[110] clubs and similar venues. The number of readers per copy probably increased over the century and one estimate in 1782[111] put it at ten readers per paper, while another later suggested around 30.[112] The readership might also have reached a reasonable cross-section of society, not being confined to the middle and upper classes but extending to the 'lower orders' as well.[113] For instance, many engravings of the period show working class people reading newspapers,[114] despite only a minority of the working class being literate.[115] But the reading aloud of

[103] Who had franking privileges, meaning the newspapers could be franked and sent without payment to the postal service, just payment to the relevant post office clerk. Over £1,800 was spent on franking and sending out newspapers in 1764: *CJ*, xxix, 1000 (28 Mar. 1764).

[104] From the 1760s, commercial or private individuals could start making use of the MPs' privilege and while the franking privilege had long existed it only became relevant from this point: Michael Harris, 'The Structure, Ownership and Control of the Press, 1620–1780', in *Newspaper History: From the Seventeenth Century to the Present Day*, ed. George Boyce, James Curran and Pauline Wingate (1978), 89.

[105] They were therefore vulnerable to the regional press: Harris, 'The Structure, Ownership and Control of the Press', 87.

[106] As to copying the news see Chapter 7: Copying and Part III; and more generally Will Slauter, *Who Owns the News? A History of Copyright* (Stanford, CA, 2019).

[107] Jeremy Greenwood, *Newspapers and the Post Office, 1635–1835* (Reigate, 1971), 34 (financially dependent on the income); Raven, *Publishing Business in Eighteenth-Century England*, 132; Dennis Griffiths, *Fleet Street: Five Hundred Years of the Press* (2006), 60.

[108] *Report from the Committee for the Reform and Improvement of the Post Office* (1807 HC Papers 1), ii, 95 (Appendix 26).

[109] Barker, *Newspapers, Politics and English Society*, 46.

[110] Anon, *The Case of the Coffee-Men of London and Westminster. Or, An Account of the Impositions and Abuses put upon Them and the Whole Town by the Present Set of News-Writers* (Smith, 1728) (ESTC: T128525), 15 (laments the fact coffee houses had to spend up to £20 p.a. on newspapers); Raven, *Publishing Business in Eighteenth-Century England*, 123 (suggesting up to four copies of leading newspapers a day/issue might be taken by each coffee house); Harris, 'The Structure, Ownership and Control of the Press', 91.

[111] Based on a letter from Dennis O'Bryen to Edmund Burke, March 1782: Sheffield City Archives, BK 1/1557, p. 4: 'There are 25 thousand papers published every day in London, allowing ten readers for each paper, I am sure these 250 thousand include by much the majority of the reading class of the community.'

[112] Arthur Aspinall, *Politics and the Press, 1780–1850* (1949), 24–5 (suggested for the year 1829).

[113] However, suggestions that over half the London population was regularly 'in touch' with the contents of newspapers is probably too high, as claimed by Adriano Bruntini, 'Advertising and the Industrial Revolution', *Economic Notes*, iv (1973), 109.

[114] This could of course have been an artist's idealised view.

[115] Barker, *Newspapers, Politics and English Society*, 51–3.

newspapers was common depending on where it took place,[116] with some papers being written in a rhetorical style to facilitate this practice.[117]

Newspapers could be used to influence public opinion,[118] and they could have a powerful effect; it was said in 1795 that people would obstinately believe what was in a newspaper even when notorious facts suggested it was a lie.[119] It was unusual for the newspapers to have editorial comment or leaders in the 1770s[120] but a newspaper clearly had a communicative role allowing electors[121] to know what the issues before parliament were and occasionally to garner support for a particular position.[122] The London papers, in particular, would also have been read by the more active MPs[123] and so reporting might have made new information available to the House. Newspapers therefore ran three sorts of political content: printing lobbying papers, publishing parliamentary debates, and letters from readers.

This readership and coverage meant that newspapers could play various roles in the promotion of, or opposition to, a bill whether public or private. For instance, petitions and lobbying papers relating to the Booksellers' Bill appeared in various newspapers.[124] This was common when local support was needed for a bill (or opposition to be overcome), but as parliament started to be seen as reflecting a more national public mood then it becomes less surprising that there were attempts to influence that mood through the press.[125] Yet it was something contemporary MPs had yet to come to terms with; many still thought that pamphlets or publications designed to encourage the public to put pressure on parliament were not acceptable.[126]

Conclusion

It is clear that parliament could be influenced by many different things, by direct lobbying undertaken by interest groups and individuals, petitioning government or the House,

[116]Jeremy Black, *The English Press in the Eighteenth Century* (1987), 302.

[117]Barker, *Newspapers, Politics and English Society*, 55.

[118]There was no agreement on who the 'public' was at this time – the electors, all the general population, the educated classes or something else: Barker, *Newspapers, Politics and English Society*, 23; yet the papers were not the 'fourth estate' they later became: Barker, 27.

[119]Vicesimus Knox, *The Spirit of Despotism* (1795) (ESTC: N21542), section 6, 'On the Venality of the Press under the Influence of the despotic Spirit, and its Effects in diffusing that Spirit', in the *Works of Vicesimus Knox* (7 vols, 1824), v, 176, showing it is an issue that long predates the dissemination of digital news.

[120]Although it did happen in some form. For instance, the 'call to arms' in the *Edinburgh Advertiser*, 18–22 Mar., 182, and the editor said in the *Morning Chronicle*, 19 Mar§, 'that property should rather accrue from prosperous pillage and plunder, than from any conscientious tenure derived from an equitable bargain and sale'.

[121]There were about 305,400 voters in 1774: Peter Jupp, *The Governing of Britain, 1688–1848: The Executive, Parliament and the People* (2006), 235.

[122]Brewer, *Sinews of Power*, 242.

[123]Christopher Reid, 'Whose Parliament? Political Oratory and Print Culture in the later Eighteenth Century', *Language and Literature*, ix (2000), 130.

[124]As to the printing of petitions in newspapers more generally, see J.E. Bradley, 'Parliament, Print Culture and Petitioning in Late Eighteenth-Century England', *Parliamentary History*, xxvi (2007), 99–101.

[125]Brewer, *Sinews of Power*, 243.

[126]A.G. Olson, 'Parliament, the London Lobbies, and Provincial Interests in England and America', *Historical Reflections*, vi (1979), 377.

the circulation of lobbying papers and stories in the newspapers. On the other hand, political factions might play a limited role in influencing voting behaviour in the Commons. These insights into how matters work more generally enables us to move on in the next chapter to explore how the Booksellers' Bill followed or departed from this norm.

Chapter 2
The Tools of Persuasion

Introduction

We have explored how influence might be exerted on political decision making. In this chapter we move from how it was done in the abstract to the sorts of documents which existed, and still exist, to evidence how parliament was swayed in relation to the Booksellers' Bill. This chapter begins by looking to 'cases' which formed the main lobbying papers but, unusually, in the case of the Booksellers' Bill another key method of influencing legislators was case reports, that is, decisions of the court. This chapter will examine both these forms of case before the house of commons as well as having newspapers called in aid to support or oppose a measure. Looking at the tools and agents forming the methods of persuasion, it will set out the role, if any, of party and the sides taken. As has now become clear, members of parliament were not short of information to use to support a position, even if that information was not necessarily accurate.

Cases

The printing and distribution of cases was a central part of lobbying. It is when, at this distance, the voice of the parties is clearest. It is their words, making their arguments to support or oppose a measure. The Booksellers' Bill is well served with 26 different documents surviving,[1] with the cases from both sides. Unfortunately, the limited history of the Bill has concentrated on just one or two of the documents.[2] Some of these papers were also published in the newspapers, not only providing a perspective on the interrelationship between the two but also an opportunity to see the variations that could be introduced – by both expansion and contraction – to the arguments raised. We explore these cases by looking at their style, their timing, and finally their authorship to better understand how lobbying took place.

Style of Cases

Cases could adopt many different styles. The *Case of the Booksellers* provides a slightly longer summary of the arguments in favour of the Bill than had been presented in the petition.[3] As would be expected, the counter-petitioners attempted to address the allegations in that *Case* by taking each allegation and providing an 'answer'.[4] A question, or issue is set out, then an answer is presented. These points were often later supported by counsel's submissions, but for the most part, lobbying documents were not used to foreshadow pleadings or counsel's oral submissions. Of course, there are instances where particular arguments or factual examples were made in both a lobbying document and by counsel (such as their

[1] Some in multiple versions: see Part IV.

[2] Most concentrate on the Petitions and Papers, which mainly provide those cases against the Bill. Likewise, Gwyn Walters, 'The Booksellers in 1759 and 1774: The Battle for Literary Property', *The Library*, 5th ser., xxix (1974), 287, makes use of the lobbying paper the *Glasgow Memorial*: Part IV, Glasgow Memorialists.

[3] Part IV, Booksellers' Petition; Booksellers' Case.

[4] Part IV, Case Observations (showing the long history of 'briefing notes').

reference to the conference between both Houses during the final stages of the passage of the Statute of Anne),[5] however it is unclear which came first, whether they had a common origin, or whether there was a causal link. Yet it is apparent that many of the arguments raised in the Cases, and Observations, were relied upon by members during the debate, giving them ideas and debating points and 'facts' to support a particular side of the argument. In simple terms, the lobbying documents worked.

Timing of Lobbying Documents

The publication of lobbying documents had no fixed cycle. The dates upon which petitions were presented is recorded in the *Votes* and the *Journal*,[6] but there is no record of the date upon which other lobbying documents were disseminated. Nevertheless, in some cases the publication date can be pinpointed accurately. It was reported that the *Case of the Booksellers*[7] was presented to the committee on 9 March 1774, and that on 15 March the other side distributed its *Observations on the Case*.[8]

The *Remarks on the Booksellers' Petition* was, to judge from its content, published while the petition was before the committee (so between 28 February and 18 March) or soon afterwards as a variant version was published in the *Edinburgh Advertiser* on 1 April.[9] The follow up document, the *Farther Strictures on the Booksellers' Petition* must have been published after the newspaper articles[10] to which it refers, and probably in time for the debate on the report of the petition committee held on 24 March. *Dr Goldsmith's Hints* must have been published after he died on 4 April as he is referred to as 'the late' and, probably, before the Bill was presented on 22 April, as it does not refer to the Bill itself.

The Booksellers had to present their bill to the House at its first reading.[11] The Bill would be printed and distributed to MPs. At this point, in theory at least, the debate moved on from the broad policy set out in the petition to a slightly narrower question, namely whether the Bill itself should pass. Even at first and second reading the Bill's policy was still only provisional; key elements had yet to be agreed (the 'blanks' filled in); for instance, the term of the exclusive right remained blank through both readings.[12] Donaldson presented his petition on 26 April,[13] four days after first reading, and it is likely that the *Remarks on his Petition*[14] was printed within a few days; and soon thereafter the response to those *Remarks*

[5] Case Observations {1}; Cavendish, Murphy {257}; *CJ*, xvi, 395–6 (5 Apr. 1710); it was also raised in *Donaldson v Beckett: Case of the Appellants and Respondents in the cause of Literary Property* (ESTC: T90592).

[6] See *Votes 1774*, pp. 245–6 and *CJ*, xxxiv, 513 (London Booksellers); *Votes 1774*, p. 346 and *CJ*, xxxiv, 562 (Bach and Abel); *Votes 1774*, pp. 523–5 and *CJ*, xxxiv, 665 (Edinburgh); *Votes 1774*, p. 532 and *CJ*, xxxiv, 668 (London Stallholders and Glasgow Booksellers); *Votes 1774*, pp. 554–5 and *CJ*, xxxiv, 679 (Donaldson); *Votes 1774*, p. 597 and *CJ*, xxxiv, 698 (York Booksellers); all petitions read: *Votes 1774*, p. 648; *Votes 1774*, pp. 684–5 and *CJ*, xxxiv, 757 (country booksellers).

[7] See Part IV, Booksellers' Case.

[8] *Caledonian Mercury*, 21 Mar.

[9] *Edinburgh Advertiser*, 29 Mar.–1 Apr., 201.

[10] These are the *Middlesex Journal*, 17–19 Mar.; *Gazetteer*, 19 Mar.; *Morning Chronicle*, 19 Mar.

[11] *CJ*, xv, 18 (12 Nov. 1705); the Bill as presented and as passed, is at Part IV, Booksellers' Bill: (the difference is marked).

[12] The 14-year term was added in bill committee.

[13] *CJ*, xxxiv, 679.

[14] Part IV, Remarks on Donaldson's Petition.

were published, probably all in time for second reading on 10 May. The *Observations on the Evidence*,[15] which appear to be based on the petition as reported, were also prepared for second reading. It is likely the other opponent printed the *Considerations in Behalf of the Booksellers of London and Westminster* around the same time.[16] Finally, the *Glasgow Memorial*[17] was dated 25 April, just after first reading, but before its author would have had an opportunity to see the Bill itself.[18]

The next paper,[19] that is, the *Hints and Grounds of Argument* (General Observations) was printed in the *Morning Chronicle* between 5 and 13 May (and was started again on 2 June).[20] The *Further Remarks* include the text of the Bill with blanks and Edmund Burke appears to have had a copy in his possession during committee.[21] It is probable, therefore, that it was printed just before committee on 16 May. The *Further Remarks* adopted an approach similar to a briefing document setting out remarks on each clause suggesting why it would be inappropriate to enact.[22] These comments, provision by provision, were followed by a general argument against the Bill. It can be seen that each party kept up the pressure by publishing and disseminating lobbying documents throughout the time the petition and then the Bill were before the House: each time one side published a document the other side did likewise. This exemplifies, very acutely, that pervasive and iterative lobbying was a dynamic and intense process.

There was also a booklet published by opponents of the Bill, which did not include most of the papers in favour of the booksellers: namely, the *Case of the Booksellers*, *Remarks on Donaldson's Petition*, *Considerations in behalf of the Booksellers* and the *General Observations*. It appears to have been published in time for second reading; it was followed by a proposal for the London Booksellers to do likewise with a booklet entitled *The Memoirs of Perpetual Literary Property*,[23] clearly a joke.

The Authors and the Failure to Sign

While the position of a particular lobbying document is clear, its author is less certain. A petition would be signed by the petitioners and the names of subscribers known;[24] cases on the other hand, as unofficial lobbying documents, may or may not be identified with an individual. The *Observations on the Case of the Booksellers* were published as a lobby document but carried no name; its author (Arthur Murphy, counsel to Donaldson) is known because his name was published in the *Caledonian Mercury*.[25] Similarly, the *Hints and Grounds* is signed

[15] Part IV, Committee Evidence Observations.

[16] Part IV, London Booksellers' Consideration.

[17] Part IV, Glasgow Memorialists.

[18] Glasgow Memorialists {22}.

[19] Donaldson's house of lords petition (signed by Donaldson on 31 May) (see Part IV) was of course later.

[20] A letter responding to these *Hints and Grounds* was published in the *Morning Chronicle*, 9 May.

[21] Cavendish, Burke {5}.

[22] Part IV, Further Remarks.

[23] *Morning Chronicle*, 7 May§.

[24] Albeit the original petitions are now lost (Maurice Bond, *Guide to the Records of Parliament* (1971), 241), the names would have been known at the time and this is clear from the debates: Cavendish, Dalrymple {229}.

[25] *Caledonian Mercury*, 21 Mar.

'TC', so it is probably by Thomas Caddell.[26] Yet there was no identification (even by initials) when a variant of the *Hints and Grounds* was printed as *General Observations*. Likewise, the arguments in the London Stallholders' Petition, the *Remarks on the Booksellers' Petition* and the *Farther Strictures on the Booksellers' Petition* suggest common authorship.[27] Yet the publication of the *Remarks* in the *Edinburgh Advertiser* also suggests a connection with Donaldson.

The 'Hints' upon the petition was published as those of 'the late Dr Goldsmith'. Oliver Goldsmith[28] died on 4 April 1774. Accordingly, this document must have been printed after that date and, if not falsely attributed, written before it. Goldsmith had been a poet, an eccentric and broke. He had attended the house of lords to hear the appeal of *Donaldson v Beckett* and so he clearly had some interest,[29] but he fell ill in the middle of March[30] and while it appears he was still writing immediately beforehand[31] by 25 March he was very sick. There is no other evidence of Goldsmith's view on the question of perpetual copyright,[32] but the examples put forward in his *Hints* are common to those raised by booksellers rather than what would be expected from an author; for instance, it is doubtful that authors would talk of auctions for buying and selling copyrights or mentioning decrees in king's bench. Indeed, Goldsmith was a strong friend of Edmund and William Burke and so it is more likely he would have written in support of the Bill (even though he was intermittently in dispute with his publisher in the last years of his life).[33] So, while the attribution might be genuine, it is also quite possible that the opponents took advantage of the death of a well known and popular author, and simply attributed words to him in support of their cause.[34]

The Goldsmith document may not be the only gilded lily. The Booksellers wrote to authors seeking support for their bill, and while some authors such as David Hume[35] did support them, it appears that they falsely claimed endorsement from Samuel Johnson. In *Hints and Grounds*, it was said that Johnson sought further support from his publisher to complete his *Dictionary*; an example used to promote the virtue of London Booksellers. Dr Johnson disputed this claim and wrote to Arthur Murphy to this effect, his letter being read out during committee stage on the Bill.[36] Indeed, before *Donaldson* was heard, Johnson

[26] There were only a handful of Booksellers with the initials 'TC'. Another possible candidate is Thomas Carnon, but he petitioned against the copyright in Almanacks Bill: *CJ*, xxxvii, 355–6 (29 Apr. 1779).

[27] The only surviving copies of the *Remarks* and *Farther Strictures*, held by Beinecke Library, Yale, belonged to William Fox (or carry his initials); and while he gave a witness statement (Part IV, Further Remarks), there is no reason to suppose he was also the author (although it is of course possible).

[28] Oliver Goldsmith* (?1728–1774).

[29] Along with Edmund Burke and David Garrick among others: *Edinburgh Advertiser*, 8–11 Feb., 91§.

[30] John Forster, *The Life and Times of Oliver Goldsmith* (1855), 457.

[31] Forster, *Life and Times of Oliver Goldsmith*, ch. 20 details his last days.

[32] There is an odd chapter (ch. 21) at the end of Forster, *Life and Times of Oliver Goldsmith*, which discussed the case of *Donaldson v Beckett* (1774) 2 Br PC 129 (1 ER 837).

[33] Forster, *Life and Times of Oliver Goldsmith*, 429 (albeit he sold his *Grecian History* for £250 the year before he died, 439).

[34] There are numerous forged letters which were at one stage attributed to him: Katherine Balderston, *The Collected Letters of Oliver Goldsmith* (Cambridge, 1928), Appendix II.

[35] He wrote a letter on the matter: Hume to William Strahan, 1 Mar., in *Letters of David Hume*, ed. J.Y.T. Greig (2 vols, Oxford, 1932), ii, 286–7 (no. 496); and appears to have handed a different letter to Strahan saying he did not think the harm would be very bad: ii, 288 (no. 497); Samuel Johnson to Strahan, 7 Mar.: *The Letters of Samuel Johnson*, ed. Bruce Redford (3 vols, Oxford, 1992–4), ii, 129–30.

[36] Cavendish, Johnstone {79}.

expressed his view against the perpetual right,[37] and when he was subsequently approached by the bookseller William Strahan he reiterated this view, asserting a term of 50 years was appropriate.[38]

Use of the Lobbying Documents

It is clear that cases were used and referred to during debates, and vice versa. In his opening speech, following his report from the petition committee, Paul Feilde[39] expressly refers to the 'Answer to the Bookseller's case'.[40] Edmund Burke, in bill committee, had been given a 'brief for debate',[41] which he says included objections to every clause of the Bill.[42] Similarly, Thurlow made reference to the subscription raised for the honorary monopoly taking a figure from Donaldson's petition,[43] and John Dunning brought forward an example which could have been based on a comment in the opponent's case,[44] namely the attempts to pursue an extension of copyright in the 1730s.[45] Finally, much reference was made regarding a series of letters setting up of the honorary monopoly,[46] which were printed[47] and seem to have been circulated to MPs. While these lobbying documents might have provided information to members of parliament, those closest to the Bill received briefings more directly.

Edward Thurlow (for Donaldson), Alexander Wedderburn and John Dunning (both for Beckett, that is the London Booksellers) had all been counsel in *Donaldson v Beckett*.[48] In their speeches they provided information directly to the House based on their preparation for, and presentation of, the case to the house of lords (and before). Indeed, in the debate on the report from the petition committee, these three men spoke for a little over 50% of the time.[49] In contrast Feilde provided details about the history of the 'common law'

[37] *Letters of Samuel Johnson*, ed. Redford, ii, 123–4, Johnson to James Boswell, 7 Feb. (albeit he admits without reading the case); also see James Boswell, *The Life of Samuel Johnson*, ed. David Womersley (2008), 406–7 for a copy of the letter. In *Letters of Samuel Johnson*, ii, 231 (20 July 1763) there is a view in favour of the Booksellers, and at 399 (8 May 1773) a view against. For a more general discussion of Johnson's view, E.A. Bloom, 'Johnson on Copyright', *Journal of English and Germanic Philology*, xlvii (1948), 165.

[38] *Letters of Samuel Johnson*, ed. Redford, ii, 129–31, Johnson to William Strahan, 7 Mar. For new books, this term would have been longer than that given under the Statute of Anne and the Booksellers' Bill, but old books would already have expired.

[39] Cavendish, Feilde {S281}.

[40] This was almost certainly a reference to *Case Observations*.

[41] This was probably Part IV, Further Remarks.

[42] Cavendish, Burke {69}.

[43] Cavendish, Thurlow {S7}; also see Merrill letter, in Part IV, The Five Letters; but he might have had it previously from his role as counsel.

[44] *Case Observations*.

[45] Cavendish, Dunning {S16–17}; he was also involved in *Donaldson v Beckett* as counsel.

[46] Cavendish, Thurlow {S7}.

[47] Some of these had been printed earlier by Alexander Donaldson, *Some Thoughts on the State of Literary Property* (Donaldson, 1764) (ESTC: N23843).

[48] The remaining counsel, Thurlow's junior, Sir John Dalrymple, was now the leading counsel for the Bill's opponents. Arthur Murphy had drawn up the case: *Letters of Samuel Johnson*, ed. Redford, ii, 123–4, Johnson to James Boswell, 7 Feb.

[49] Based on the number of words recorded by Cavendish for the petition debate.

right and outlined some of the key cases, including details of the reports in *Millar v Taylor*.[50] While the collusive nature of *Tonson v Collins* was mentioned in the *Observation on the Case of the Booksellers*, which he referred to in the same speech, Feilde had far more detail than it provided.[51] The source of this information must have been the petitioners or other supporters of the Bill. There was additionally information put forward by MPs, which appears to have been largely anecdotal, such as the comments about the notorious *Hawksworth*[52] and its extraordinary price,[53] and the statement of William Mason,[54] who might 'burn his papers'[55] following *Donaldson*. Thus, the cases and lobbying documents were merely part of a rich tapestry of sources before the house of commons; another being law reports.

Law Reports

Unusually, the Commons' debate of the Booksellers' Bill includes repeated references to court cases.[56] This is not entirely surprising as the Bill was predicated upon two earlier judgments. The first, *Millar v Taylor*, which supported the London Booksellers' position on the common law, and *Donaldson v Beckett*,[57] which necessitated the seeking of relief. To understand the nature of references to jurisprudence before the House, it is critical to understand how cases were cited before the courts in the second half of the 18th century.

Citing Law Reports in Court

In preceding centuries, it had been common for the courts and counsel to refer to 'our books' instead of actual cases when extolling the common law.[58] By the 18th century, references were made to reports in court, but usually this was little more than the case's name and the relevant legal principle.[59] Indeed, Wedderburn's own notes[60] provide very

[50] Cavendish, Feilde {S281–2}. While there was a partisan version of the report, *Speeches or Arguments of the Judges of the Courts of King's Bench in the Cause of Millar against Taylor* (Coke: Leith, 1771) (ESTC: T117122), it is clear that only Burrow's report was used before the House: *The Question Concerning Literary Property, Determined by the Court of King's Bench of 20th Apr. 1769, in the Cause between A.M. and R. Taylor. With the Separate Opinion of the Four Judges* (1773) (ESTC: T88999).

[51] Part IV, Case Observations.

[52] John Hawkesworth (?1715–1773), *An Account of the Voyages by the Order of His Present Majesty for Making Discoveries in the Southern Hemisphere* (Strahan and Cadell, 1773) (ESTC: N34379). See Thurlow {S10}. This led to some defence of the book in letters to the press, suggesting that it cost the public nothing to print and it was a person's choice whether to buy it or not: *Public Advertiser*, 4 May§; in any event, the book was copied: *Morning Chronicle*, 9 Apr§. (the relevant case was probably *Strahan v Newberry* (1773–5): H. Tomás Gómez-Arostegui, *Register of Copyright Infringement Suits and Actions from c. 1560 to 1800* (2009).

[53] Not included on the Book Lists, see Part IV, Printed Books.

[54] William Mason (1725–91).

[55] Cavendish, Onslow {S23}.

[56] Many MPs had acted for the parties.

[57] *Cobbett's Parl. Hist.*, xvii, col. 953.

[58] David Ibbetson, 'Legal Printing and Legal Doctrine', *Irish Jurist*, xxv (2000), 346.

[59] Absence judicial challenge.

[60] He has notes of two copyright cases: Wedderburn (Lincoln's Inn MS 384) which were as follows (abbreviations expanded):

Giles v Wilcocks (6 Mar. 1740), 283 [now reported (1740) 2 Atk 141 (26 ER 489)]
Abridgement not within Statute 8 Anne

little detail about the cases themselves. It was still the case during the 1770s that manuscript reports were seen to have the same or even more authority than the printed reports,[61] and there were many reports which were cited in manuscript long before they were printed.[62] So when MPs spoke of cases and reports they did not yet mean the printed version of a reasoned judgment.

Source of Law Reports

During the second half of the 18th century, the law reports were starting to move towards their more modern form: that is a report of a judgment intended for publication. While this was still in process, lawyers and judges were still happy to cite their own manuscript notes of cases before the courts. Notes may have been recorded by the lawyer based on his personal attendance at the hearing or copied from notes made by other lawyers past and present who were trusted by the advocate.[63] For instance, while preparing for *Tonson v Collins*[64] William Blackstone[65] wrote to the then solicitor-general, Charles Yorke, asking whether he had any manuscript cases[66] relating to a perpetual copyright.[67] This very process of manuscripts being passed around and copied allowed for additions and alterations to be made, thereby affecting what was thought to be reported.[68]

The Quality of Printed Law Reporting

The printing of law reports had begun in earnest towards the end of the 17th century,[69] but such reports before 1750 have been described as mostly of an 'inferior nature',[70] and

60 *(continued)* Upon the St. 8 Anne – to secure the property of books – to the Authors – not a monopoly – the words are confined to the same Book it would hinder persons from making of abridgement which is another Book, another work

Bridgeman v Dove (27 Nov. 1744), 422 [(1744) 3 Atk 201 (26 ER 917)]

Books won't pass as furniture, Lord Hardwicke

A Library of Books won't pass by Devise of furniture – Adjudged so in D's Beaufort's Case

61 David Ibbetson, 'Report and Record in Early-Modern Common Law', in *Case Law in the Making: The Techniques and Methods of Judicial Records and Law Reports: Volume 1: Essays*, ed. Alain Wijffels (Berlin, 1997), 65.

62 Sir John Baker, *An Introduction to English Legal History* (Oxford, 2019), 193 (referring to the reports of William Dalison, William Bendlowes, Sir Edmund Anderson and Sir Francis Moore).

63 David Ibbetson, 'Report and Record in Early-Modern Common Law', 65.

64 (1762) 1 Black W 321 (96 ER 180).

65 It appears Blackstone was not entirely reliable in his account of earlier cases: Deazley, *On the Origin of the Right to Copy*, 58–60. This may have been caused by him working from the manuscript notes of others, rather than going back to check the original records (which clearly happened, as evidenced by Thurlow's reference: Cavendish, Thurlow {S6–7}).

66 Having examined Yorke's Case Books (Lincoln's Inn MSS 347–50); albeit one volume was missing, there were no copyright cases.

67 *The Letters of Sir William Blackstone*, ed. W.R. Prest (Seldon Society, lxvi, 2006), 82–3, from Blackstone to Charles Yorke, 21 June 1761.

68 Van Vechten Veeder, 'The English Reports, 1537–1865', *Harvard Law Review*, xv (1901), 21.

69 Baker, *Introduction to English Legal History*, 193 (and these were often misattributed); it has been suggested that the monopolies actually hindered the printing of law reports: T.A. Baloch, 'Law Booksellers and Printers as Agents of Unchange', *Cambridge Law Journal*, lxvi (2007) 389; cf. Veeder, 'The English Reports', 4, suggesting this process made the reports more accurate.

70 Baker, *Introduction to English Legal History*, 194.

some as 'quite worthless',[71] being based on private notes rather than intended for publication.[72] Indeed, in *Donaldson v Beckett* a report was criticised as being merely 'in the book of a special pleader'. The variety of reports means that critically the printed reports were often so poor that judges required counsel to refer to manuscript sources instead of the published versions.[73] A variant of this occurred in *Millar v Taylor* itself where Arthur Murphy cited a manuscript letter in an attempt to contradict the printed report of *Midwinter v Kincaid*, albeit the court appears to have preferred the latter. Law reporting of a higher quality started to appear at the same time as *Millar v Taylor* itself, with Sir James Burrow's reports marking the beginning of a new 'epoch'.[74] Thus, his report of *Millar*, which was published in 1773,[75] represented the highest standard of law reporting at the time.[76] This aided the Booksellers before the house of commons, as the report was fully explained and reasoned in a way few other law reports were and, critically, the judges' conclusions in *Millar* could be understood by the country gentleman as well as the seasoned lawyer.

Use of Law Reports in the Booksellers' Bill Debates

It is evident some MPs had access to the printed report of *Millar*. Paul Feilde referred to Burrow's report (erroneously, as that of Sir James Bruce)[77] and it is likely the other speakers[78] who discussed the case had seen that report at some time. The other side did not have it so easy. Edward Thurlow, the attorney-general, referred to the Bill, Demurer and Answer[79] in *Horne v Baker*,[80] so it is reasonable to assume he had actually seen these documents (or his junior or clerk had seen them) and made notes or a copy of the same. In his submissions, Arthur Murphy also refers to something which appears to come

[71] Veeder, 'The English Reports', 3.

[72] Nevertheless, not all early reports should be written off. For instance, *Mitchel v Reynolds* (1711) 1 Peere Williams 181 (24 ER 347) was described by the supreme court as an 'immaculate report' which 'any study of the contribution made by law reporters to the development of our law would do well to include': *Tillman v Egon Zehnder Ltd* [2019] UKSC 32, [2020] AC 154 at [25].

[73] Baker, *Introduction to English Legal History*, 194.

[74] *Millar v Taylor* (1769) 4 Burr 2303 at 2321–3 (98 ER 201 at 211–12); J.W. Wallace, *The Reporters Arranged and Characterized … Fourth Edition Revised* (Boston, MA, 1882), 446–7; Veeder, 'The English Reports', 5.

[75] *The Question Concerning Literary Property, Determined by the Court of King's Bench of 20th Apr. 1769, in the cause between A.M and R. Taylor. With the Separate Opinion of the Four Judges* (1773) (ESTC: T88999). It was probably printed in time to be referred to in *Hinton v Donaldson* (1773) and while it is not mentioned in Boswell's Report it is likely to be what their Lordships referred to.

[76] It may even have been read by Lord Mansfield before publication: Wallace, *The Reporters Arranged and Characterized*, 30 (but see 451 as to its accuracy); it is also clear that he did not include the entirety of the judgments, as he notes Sir Joseph Yates spoke for three hours and he reports only the key points made: *Millar v Taylor* (1769) 4 Burr 2302 at 2354 (98 ER 201 at 229).

[77] Cavendish, Feilde {S281–2} and {91–3} (the error may have been that of Cavendish).

[78] Cavendish, Thurlow {S6–7}, Graves {S16–17}, Murphy {259–60} and {45–50}, Mansfield {35–6}, Johnston {78}, Fox {104–5}.

[79] There are two documents (1) a Bill of Complaint and (2) a Demurer and Answer: TNA, C 5/290/70.

[80] Albeit he called it the case in relation to the work of Samuel Butler: *Hudibras* (1663, 1664, 1678); there is a complex history to its publication: J.L. Thorson, 'The Publication of "Hudibras"', *Papers of Bibliographical Society of America*, lx (1966), 418.

from Lord Kames' report of *Midwinter v Hamilton*[81] and others just referred to the case simpliciter.[82]

There were other cases referred to by MPs. Most importantly, *Donaldson v Beckett*[83] of course, where the speeches had been published in various newspapers,[84] and Boswell had published his report of *Hinton v Donaldson*[85] in time for the hearing in *Donaldson* before the house of lords so it too was out when the Booksellers' Bill was before the House. But reference was made to numerous cases lacking any printed report at the time: *Tonson v Collins*,[86] *Tonson v Walker*,[87] *Motte v Faulkner*,[88] *Midwinter v Kincaid*,[89] *Millar v Donaldson*,[90] *Macklin v Richardson*.[91] So there was either reliance on the references in *Millar* or something else. Conversely there are lots of cases which were referred to in *Millar* which were not referred to before the Commons.[92]

These cases were not published until much later. *Tonson v Collins*[93] was eventually reported in Blackstone's *Reports*, which appeared after his death in 1780;[94] the reports of

[81] (1743) Kam Rem 154; *Lord Kames's Remarkable Decisions of the Court of Session from the year 1730 to the year 1752* (Edinburgh, 1766). It was also included in Morison's *Dictionary of Decisions* (1748), Mor 8295.

[82] Cavendish, George Johnstone {77}.

[83] Cavendish, Dalrymple {254–5}; Murphy {260}.

[84] These are listed in H. Tomás Gómez-Arostegui, 'Copyright at Common Law in 1774', *Connecticut Law Review*, xlvii (2014), 51–5. It was still a breach of privilege at this time to print the Lords' proceedings, but 1774 was the year when the Lords started to follow the Commons by turning a blind eye to such reports: see Chapter 7: The Printers' Case; and William Lowe, 'Peers and Printers: The Beginning of Sustained Press Coverage of the House of Lords in the 1770s', *Parliamentary History*, vii (1988), 241.

[85] *Decision of the Court of Session upon the Question of Literary Property* (1774) (ESTC: T8898); advertised in *Morning Chronicle*, 1 Feb§. Apparently, some of the judges were given the opportunity of perfecting their judgments before publication: Frank Brady, *James Boswell: The Later Years 1769–1795* (New York, 1984), 88.

[86] Cavendish, Feilde {S282}; Thurlow {S6}; Murphy {259–60}; cited in *Millar v Taylor* (1769) 4 Burr 2303 at 2354–5, 2400 (98 ER 201 at 228, 229, 253).

[87] Cavendish, Thurlow {S6}; Murphy {258–9}. It was also referred to in later cases: *Tonson v Collins* (1761) 1 Black W 301 at 310, 311 (96 ER 169 at 173); *Millar v Taylor* (1769) 4 Burr 2303 at 2325, 2353 (98 ER 201 at 213, 228).

[88] It had likewise been cited in *Tonson v Walker* (1752) 3 Swans 672 at 675 (36 ER 1017 at 1018); *Tonson v Collins* (1761) 1 Black W 301 at 305 (96 ER 169 at 171); *Tonson v Collins* (1762) 1 Black W 322 at 331 (96 ER 180 at 184); *Millar v Taylor* (1769) 4 Burr 2303 (98 ER 201).

[89] Cavendish, Mansfield {31}; cited (as *Millar v Kincaid*) in *Millar v Taylor* (1769) 4 Burr 2303 at 2319, 2379, 2388 (98 ER 201 at 210, 242, 247).

[90] Cavendish, Murphy {258}; *Millar and Osborne v Donaldson* (1765) 2 Eden 327 (28 ER 924). Although there was a record of a note of the case published in Lord Coalston, *Information for Alexander Donaldson and John Wood* (Edinburgh, 1773) (ESTC: T90591), 70.

[91] (1770) Amb 694 (27 ER 451).

[92] *Stationers' Company v Seymour* (1676) 3 Keb 792 (84 ER 1015); 1 Mod 256 (86 ER 865); *Ponder v Braydall/Braddill* (1679) 1 Lilly's Modern Entries 67; *Stationers' Company v Parker* (1685) Skin 233 (90 ER 107); *Stationers' Company v Partridge* (1712) 1 Mod 105 (88 ER 647); *Tonson v Clifton* (1722); *Webb v Rose* (1729); *Eyre v Walker* (1735); *Walthoe (Walker) v Walker* (1736); *Baller v Watson* (1737); *Austin v Cay* (1739); *Tonson v Walker* (1739); *Pope v Curll* (1741) 2 Atk 342 (26 ER 608); *Forster v Walker* (1742); *Manley v Owen* (1755); *Baskett v Cambridge University* (1758) 2 Burr 661 (97 ER 499); *Duke of Queensbury v Shebbeare* (1758); *Millar v Donaldson and Osborne v Donaldson* (1765); *Roper v Skinner* (1765): H. Tomás Gómez-Arostegui, *Register of Copyright Infringement Suits and Actions from c. 1560 to 1800* (2009).

[93] (1761) 1 Black W 301 and (1762) 1 Black W 329 (96 ER 180 and 184).

[94] Wallace, *The Reporters Arranged and Characterized*, 443–4.

Macklin v Richardson,[95] *Millar v Donaldson*,[96] *Tonson v Walker*[97] and *Midwinter v Kincaid*[98] were not published until 1790, 1818, 1827 and 1849 respectively. While *Motte v Faulkner*[99] was mentioned in *Millar v Taylor* it was referred to as little more than a case where an injunction was granted under the Statute of Anne. The closest that exists to a report of the *Motte* decision is a three-line summary in the report of *Tonson v Collins*[100] (and later *Millar v Taylor*). This three-line report does not appear to follow the order of the court particularly closely.[101] Finally, *Horne v Baker* (the *Hudibras* case) was cited by Thurlow[102] for which there is a limited (manuscript)[103] report concerning a question of discovery.[104] Accordingly, as in court, it appears cases were cited in parliament often without producing a printed report (or even a manuscript) and probably largely relying on the earlier citations in the published report in *Millar v Taylor*, which is somewhat circular.

Witnesses

Testimony from witnesses was still central to how evidence was received by parliament. In relation to the Booksellers' Petition and Bill there were ten witnesses heard: in the petition committee, William Johnston, John Wilkie and Augustine Greenland; at second reading, Thomas Merrill snr, John Merrill jnr, William Fox, John Murray, George Bulkley, Albany Wallis and William Smith,[105] and by the petitioners, Wilkie once more.[106] Thus, seven booksellers gave evidence, the clerk of the Stationer's Company, and two attorneys. Each of these witnesses, save maybe the attorneys, would have been coached and fed at coffee houses or other similar places.[107] Whether lawyers were involved in this process or it was merely the interest groups themselves is less clear.

[95](1770) Amb 694 (27 ER 451).

[96](1765) 2 Eden 327 (28 ER 924).

[97](1752) 3 Swans 672 (36 ER 1017).

[98](1751) 1 Paton 488; but it was in the Lords' Journal: *LJ*, xxvii, 489 (11 Feb. 1750/1).

[99](1735) TNA, C 11/2249/4 (pleadings).

[100](1762) 1 Black W 321 at 331 (96 ER 184); *Millar v Taylor* (1769) 4 Burr 2303 at 2325 (98 ER 201).

[101]Chancery: Entry Books of Decrees and Orders: Book B: TNA, C 33/366, 28 Nov. 1735.

[102]Cavendish, Thurlow {S5}.

[103]For related discussion, H. Tomás Gómez-Arostegui, 'The Untold Story of the First Copyright Suit Under the Statute of Anne in 1710', *Berkeley Technology Law Journal*, xxv (2010), 1247; *The State Trial of Doctor Henry Sacheverell*, ed. Brian Cowan (Parliamentary History Texts & Studies, vi, 2012). The only report of this case is in Lincoln's Inn, William Melmoth's Reports, MS 10, p. 1 (reproduced on p. 177, n. 117).

[104]Where one party has to disclose documents in his or her possession to the other party under order from chancery: Alan Goldstein, 'A Short History of Discovery', *Anglo-American Law Review*, x (1981), 257.

[105]John Bell, bookseller on the Strand, was also prepared as a witness, but not called: *Caledonian Mercury*, 16 May.

[106]William Johnston (Johnson) (d.1804), app. 1743–8, tr. 1745–73, 16 Ludgate Street; John Wilkie (d. 1785), app. 1743–50, tr, 1753–75, 71 St Paul's Churchyard, clerk of auctions; Augustine Greenland, attorney, Newman Street and Oxford Street: *Browne's General Law-List* (2nd edn, Whieldon and Co., 1777) (ESTC: T85768), 22; Thomas Merrill (d. 1781), tr. 1736, and John Merrill (d. 1801), Regents Walk, Cambridge; William Fox; John Murray (1745–93), The Ship, Fleet Street; George Bulkley, tr. 1774–1811, Bridge Street, Cheshire; Albany Wallis, attorney, Wallis and Parker, Norfolk Street, The Strand; William Smith, tr. 1760–82, Glasgow West Side, Salt Market.

[107]Brewer, *Sinews of Power*, 239.

One of the lobbying documents, that is the *Further Remarks and Papers on the Booksellers' Bill*, included various printed statements from William Cavell, Simon Vandenbergh, William Fox and John Wade.[108] This document was printed after second reading, but it is not clear if these were printed versions of sworn affidavits, more informal statements which were seeking to give additional information to the House, or whether they were be treated in a like manner to letters in support (testimonials).[109] Only one of those who gave a statement, William Fox, also gave live evidence. However, as they were produced after the evidence had been heard, they could not have been part of any formal procedure.[110] So the statements were simply a part of a lobbying document handed out to MPs.

Once before parliament, the evidence of witnesses was obtained in the same way as in court, examination-in-chief and then cross-examination. Thus, witness preparation would have been important (rules against coaching witnesses did not exist at the time),[111] but if this occurred it was not successful as the testimony in the case of the Booksellers' Bill taken during second reading was poorly received.[112] In any event, as is clear from the following chapters, information was routinely received from MPs which had little basis in the formal rules of evidence. Thus, beyond the need for formal proof of allegations, looking towards the expediency of the Bill, witnesses were not key but other forms of lobbying were.

Newspapers

It is extraordinary that throughout 1774 the literary property debate, first before the house of lords in *Donaldson v Beckett*, and later the Booksellers' Bill before the Commons, received so much attention in the press. While the newspapers clearly had an interest in the Bill, it was more than that: their readers, and the literate classes more generally seemed genuinely engaged. Newspapers were only four pages long, and many ran only three times a week. Yet they still carried columns of copy on the Bill. It attracted editorial comment,[113] essays and letters as well as formal petitions.[114] The daily *Morning Chronicle*, with its link to the book trade,[115] was particularly engaged as was the slightly less frequent *Caledonian Mercury*. So, for instance, in the *Morning Chronicle* a correspondent said that some just pirated on 'principle',[116] and another that literary property should be well protected,[117] and other

[108]Part IV, Further Remarks; William Cavell, tr. 1766–1804, 29 Middle Row, Holborn; Simon Vandenbergh (1728–1808), Bow Street, Westminster; William Fox, tr. 1773–82, 128 Holborn Hill; and John Wade, app. 1766, tr. until 1801, 20 Bride Lane, London.

[109]There was mention of affidavits in Cavendish {82–3}.

[110]It would have been possible for them to give testimony during bill committee, but it did not happen.

[111]It appears that some degree of coaching continued well into the 19th century: T.E. Crispe, *Reminiscences of a K.C.* (1909), 228–9; W.W. Boulton, *A Guide to Conduct and Etiquette at the Bar of England and Wales* (1953), 12.

[112]*Morning Chronicle*, 11 May.

[113]Where a 'correspondent' says something or it is published with little more besides a general statement.

[114]The reasons these were published in one case was explained in *Middlesex Journal*, 23–6 Apr.; Part IV, Booksellers' Petition.

[115]Ivon Asquith, 'Advertising and the Press in the late Eighteenth and Early Nineteenth Centuries: James Perry and the *Morning Chronicle* 1790–1821', *HJ*, xviii (1975), 709.

[116]*Morning Chronicle*, 9 May§.

[117]*Public Advertiser*, 5 Apr§.

papers just included general comments in favour[118] or against.[119] It even got to the stage where jokes about the dispute were printed.[120]

The positive coverage was not an attempt to seek public support for the Bill as the interests were very private; whereas the opponents – who claimed to be acting for cheaper books – might well have used the newspapers, particularly those in Scotland, to support the case. Nevertheless, there was a short paragraph dropped in numerous London papers[121] suggesting that *Donaldson v Beckett* would increase the price of books as booksellers would need to recoup their losses within the statutory term, and some weeks later another paragraph suggesting that the case would not reduce litigation,[122] and even that it might endanger new books.[123] Maybe it was felt that if enough concern was raised in the coffee houses it might reach MPs.

In most respects, therefore, the publication of material in the London papers was for the benefit of a more limited group of people, that is members of parliament. It is less likely this would be the case for those in Edinburgh and Glasgow, yet the *Caledonian Mercury*,[124] the *Edinburgh Advertiser* and the *Edinburgh Evening Courant* carried the Booksellers' Petition and those of Donaldson, the Edinburgh Booksellers and London Stallholders and some lobbying papers (the *Mercury* carried *Observations on the Case of the Booksellers* and the *Advertiser* the *Remarks on the Booksellers' Petition*).[125] These Scottish papers would have made it back to London, but only in small numbers and probably to a limited audience. The coverage must, therefore, have been to interest readers or sate the editor's passions on the subject. In London, the *Morning Post* and *Public Advertiser* carried petitions[126] related to the Bill,[127] and the *Morning Chronicle* also carried the *Hints and Grounds* which turned into the lobbying paper entitled *General Observations*.[128] This was referred to and rebutted (in relation to a comment as to Dr Johnson seeking subscriptions) on the floor of the House,[129] so whether the newspaper was read or it was the printed paper is unclear, but the existence of the document and the fact it was seen by members of the House is without doubt. Thus, it

[118] See for instance, *St James's Chronicle*, 14–17 May§.

[119] In particular, the *Edinburgh Advertiser*.

[120] Suggesting it was a battle between cobblers and shoemakers: *Morning Chronicle*, 28 Apr§.; or booksellers comparing dramatists to pastry chefs: *Craftsman's Weekly Journal*, 26 Mar§.; booksellers made the butt of other jokes: *Middlesex Journal*, 26–9 Mar§.

[121] *Middlesex Journal*, 17–19 Mar§.; *Gazetteer*, 19 Mar§.; *Morning Chronicle*, 19 Mar§.; it was mentioned in *Farther Strictures on the Booksellers' Petition* (see Part IV); it was raised again later: *Morning Chronicle*, 26 Apr§.

[122] *General Evening Post*, 26–8 Apr§.

[123] *St James's Chronicle*, 16–19 Apr§. (more precisely indicating a hope that this will not happen).

[124] These *Observations* were also published in a booklet along with certain of the petitions, the letters of Whiston and Wilkie, some of which also had the observations of 'Dr Goldsmith' attached: *Petitions and Papers relating to The Bill of Booksellers Now Before the House of Commons* (1774) (all reproduced in Part IV).

[125] *Edinburgh Advertiser*, 29 Mar.–1 Apr., 201; *Edinburgh Advertiser*, 22–6 Apr., 261; 29 Apr.–3 May, 273–4; *Caledonian Mercury*, 2, 9 May; the *Edinburgh Evening Courant*, 7 May, also carried Donaldson's Petition.

[126] As the *Votes* carried shortened versions of the petitions, this might have been one of the ways of getting a full copy into the hands of MPs.

[127] All versions are in Part IV, Booksellers' Petition.

[128] A second round of these arguments started for the second reading in the house of lords, but stopped after it was rejected at first reading. Only the first part was printed in the *Morning Chronicle*, 2 June: see Part IV, General Observations/Hints.

[129] Cavendish, Johnstone {78–9}.

appears, newspapers played an active role in disseminating some of the lobbying papers connected with the Bill; albeit it is not clear how the papers were chosen for inclusion.

Letters

People writing to the editor to express a view, or to challenge something previously published, had been established long before the 1770s. The number of letters published, and the issues raised, exemplifies what readers felt was important enough to write about and editors thought worthy of publishing when space was so short across four pages of four columns. So, the high number of letters printed on the Booksellers' Bill shows its interest both to some readers and editors. Indeed, on the day of second reading the *Morning Chronicle* even explained to readers that there had not been enough room to publish all the 'essays' (that is letters) received.[130] The sorts of letters varied and came from both sides, some papers took a side (or its readers had but one side), others clearly did not.[131]

The *Public Advertiser*[132] had a letter from an unnamed 'celebrated' author,[133] which was strongly in favour of the Bill. It claimed the trade was open to all and in the absence of the monopoly no 'man will venture to print a *splendid* or *good* Edition of any Book', and likewise no cheap books would be produced because of the Bill, so Donaldson himself would be undone by his victory.[134] Conversely, it appears that letters were shared with both the *Edinburgh Advertiser*[135] and *St James's Chronicle*[136] having had a letter from a 'great author' setting out an anecdote as to a John Dryden manuscript[137] not being worth much before the Statute as he would so quickly be copied.[138] Nevertheless, for some balance, the writer accepted that some works would need longer terms than those offered by the Statute of Anne, but in such cases acts of parliament could be obtained to extend the term when they warranted longer than the statute allowed.[139]

At the moment of greatest public interest, the day of second reading, the *Morning Chronicle*[140] carried a series of letters such as an attack on Donaldson (bolstered by a claim that

[130] *Morning Chronicle*, 10 May§.

[131] Almost all of the letters are cited at some point in this work, albeit only a few here.

[132] It was also published in the *London Evening Post*, 8–10 Mar§.; *London Chronicle*, 8–10 Mar., 233§; *General Evening Post*, 8–10 Mar§.; *Lloyd's Evening Post*, 11–14 Mar§., 241; *Gazetteer*, 9 Mar§.

[133] *Public Advertiser*, 9 Mar§. There was a reply to the letter, dealing with the work of John Hawkesworth* (?1715–73) in the *Lloyd's Evening Post*, 6–8 Apr., 332§.

[134] Indeed, nearly half a century before W.F. Lloyd wrote *Two Lectures on the Checks to Population* (Oxford, 1833), which was later used as the basis of Garrett Hardin, 'The Tragedy of the Commons', *Science*, clxii (1968), 1243: the letter of the 'celebrated author' says in the absence of copyright, 'The Field wherein he claimed an equal Right to graze his Cattle with supposed Proprietor is laid open to be trampled on, and rendered useless by all the Cattle in the Neighbourhood.'

[135] *Edinburgh Advertiser*, 31 May–3 June, 346§.

[136] *St James's Chronicle*, 24–6 May§.

[137] It is not apparent if this is just a reference to a very famous author: John Dryden (1631–1700), poet laureate from 1668 until his death.

[138] Strangely, a letter was carried summarising Dryden's assignments after the Bill had been rejected: *Morning Chronicle*, 11 June§.

[139] As to patent term extension, which might be considered similar, see Phillip Johnson, *Privatised Law Reform: A History of Patent Law through Private Legislation* (2017), ch. 8.

[140] *Morning Chronicle*, 10 May§.

before his time the Edinburgh and London Booksellers got along well) in a response from 'A Counter-Petitioner'[141] to an earlier letter from Literatus,[142] who defended the reputations of the Booksellers. There was even a satirical petition from the 'London Trunkmakers'[143] praising how *Donaldson v Beckett* helped supply wastepaper. The range and interests of letter writers was significant. Doctor Kendrick wrote a letter on the editing of Shakespeare, lamenting that the Booksellers' influence was sufficient 'to support ... an exclusive Right, unwarranted by law' which had made a part of his life 'useless'.[144] Others simply supplied material they thought would support one side or the other,[145] or like 'Colineus' wrote in to do little more than summarise the talk in the coffee shops.[146] There was also, of course, much left over in the public minds from *Donaldson v Beckett* itself.

As newspapers were usually only four pages long and letters could take up over half a column (and some of the lobbying papers and essays took up many pages) the subject of the Booksellers' Bill would have formed a significant part of the paper and could well have influenced readers, including those in powerful places. The Junius letters[147] had made correspondence a point of conversation only a few years earlier, so those writing letters on the Booksellers' Bill could expect them to be read, discussed and to influence MPs and peers.

Plays, Literature and Culture

The Bookseller's Bill even inspired the farce *The Author*[148] to be performed again for the benefit of Jane Pope[149] on Drury Lane, with John Moody as Vamp the Bookseller and Charles Bannister[150] as Cadwallader (who mimicked Samuel Foote very well apparently). The play had originally been written and performed in 1757, but it appears to have been modified for its 1774 run as Vamp laments the lack of his books being 'tangible' and how without 'tangible property' his trade was hardly worth carrying on.[151] Debating societies

[141] It would have been William Cavell, Richard Dymott (tr. 1757–89), of Somerset House, or Henry Serjeant (tr. c.1775), Temple Bar, based on the reference in the letter to being improperly sued over the 'Beggar's Opera': *Strahan v Cavell & Others* (1774): H. Tomás Gómez-Arostegui, *Register of Copyright Infringement Suits and Actions from c. 1560 to 1800* (2009).

[142] Which had been published in the *Morning Chronicle*, 9 May§.

[143] *Morning Chronicle*, 10 May§.

[144] *Morning Chronicle*, 11 May§.

[145] A correspondent reproduced advertisements for Joannes Sleidanus, *A Famous Cronicle of Oure Time, called Sledanes Commentaries, concerning the Raigne of the Emperor Charles the First* (1555 and 1561) (ESTC: S115934, S115937) asking not to be copied: *London Chronicle*, 26–9 Mar., 301§.

[146] *Morning Chronicle*, 16 Mar§.

[147] The use of a pseudonym might have been linked to the fervour that arose with the Junius Letters (letters published under the name Junius in the *Public Advertiser* between 1769 and 1772 criticising George III and his ministers). The potential authorship was a hot topic long after they ceased, and the excitement their authorship attracted led many others to write under a pseudonym. It is now believed they were authored by Philip Francis (1740–1818), then a clerk in the war office. The Letters were all published numerous times as a collection.

[148] Samuel Foote, *The Author* (1757). It was included in *The British Drama Comprehending the Best Plays in the English Language: Operas and Farces* (1804), 199.

[149] Jane Pope* (1744–1818), an English actress.

[150] John Moody* (?1727–1812); Charles Bannister* (1741–1804).

[151] *Middlesex Journal*, 19–22 Mar§.; with shorter reviews in *General Evening Post*, 19–22 Mar§.; *London Chronicle*, 19–22 Mar§.

considered questions such as 'Whether Lord Camden's Speech[152] on Literary Property was the Speech of an *Advocate* or a *Judge?*'.[153]

There were also those, like Catharine Macaulay and William Enfield, who published tracts in support of the Bill.[154] Macaulay had become an overnight sensation[155] in 1763 with the publication of the first volume in her *The History of England from the Accession of James I to the Accession of the Brunswick Line*,[156] so it had an impact when over a decade later she published her *A Modest Plea for the Property of Copyright*,[157] and made 'pleas of equity – of moral fitness – and public convenience'[158] on behalf of the Booksellers.[159] While a historian, *A Modest Plea* was directly addressing the suggestion by Lord Camden[160] that great authors did not write for money, and so she addressed the fate of particular authors and whether they needed copyright to survive or not,[161] as well as the argument that authors and inventors could be equated. It shows a successful attempt by the booksellers, along with authors, to promote the value of the Bill. Not only by this time was Macaulay a celebrated historian, but she was also a celebrated author, and the sister of John Sawbridge MP, who seconded the Booksellers' Petition Report, and was strongly in favour of the Booksellers. It is not clear whether the brother was supporting the sister's stance or vice versa, however there is little doubt that many in the Commons would have had access to her pamphlet and her historical narrative would have painted them a picture.[162]

William Enfield wrote his *Observations on Literary Property* while the Bill was before parliament referring to its 'wisdom and equity' but calling for improvement to the current temporary protection. He was seeking to build on the arguments of Macaulay by suggesting that the right should exist by labour and occupancy and that the term of protection should be longer because of it. Its link to the Bill comes from the conclusion where he

[152]In *Donaldson v Beckett* (1774) *Cobbett's Parl. Hist.*, xvii, col. 992.

[153]*Lloyd's Evening Post*, 30 Mar.–1 Apr., 311§.

[154]There were also tracts in support of the respondents in *Donaldson v Beckett* (1774) *Cobbett's Parl. Hist.*, xvii, col. 953, still circulating, for instance, Francis Hargrave, *An Argument in Defence of Literary Property* (2nd edn, 1774) (ESTC: T014300); as well as some related papers dealing with literary property: William Kenrick, *An Address to Artists and Manufacturers of Great Britain: Respecting an Application to Parliament for the Futher Encouragement of New Discoveries and Inventions in the Useful Arts; to which is added an Appendix Containing Strictures on some singular Consequences Attending the Late Decision on Literary Property* (Domville, 1774) (ESTC: T20406; N30789). Hargrave was possibly a junior counsel in the case, but it is not entirely clear whether he had lost the brief for the hearing (cf. Rose, *Authors and Owners*, 124).

[155]Bridget Hill, *The Republican Virago: The Life and Times of Catharine Macaulay, Historian* (Oxford, 1992), 16.

[156](John Norse, 1763) (ESTC: T106230).

[157](Cruttwell, 1774) (ESTC: T57030); the foreword was dated 9 Mar. and it was published on 16 Mar. (advertisement indicating its publication that day in *Morning Chronicle*§, and advertisement in *Public Advertiser*, 15 Mar§. that it is to be published 'tomorrow' – as sometimes an advertisement ran for a few days saying published 'today'). A significant extract was published in the *London Chronicle*, 15–17 Mar., 257§, and in the *Lloyd's Evening Post*, 30 Mar.–1 Apr., 311§.

[158]Macaulay, *A Modest Plea for the Property of Copyright*, 9.

[159]And in her own interest as was clear in the day from an anecdote in the *London Chronicle*, 24–6 Mar., 290§.

[160]It is possible, but unlikely, that the tract was just written as an outraged response to Lord Camden.

[161]Subsequently there was a poem published mocking the 'Mrs' Freeman [Anna Maria de Burgh Coppinger], *Modest Plea:* Doctor Dissected (Stella). *Modest Exceptions, from the Court of Parnassus to Mrs Macauly's Modest Plea* (Ben, 1774) (ESTC: T129596).

[162]Part IV, General Observations/Hints {MC13}, which set out a simplified history; it was a history criticised in a letter by a counter-petitioner: *Morning Chronicle*, 10 May§.

refers to 'the favourable attention' being paid to the subject by parliament and hoping for a perpetual copyright.[163] The pamphlet appears to have been written in May while the Bill was before the Commons,[164] and must have been an attempt to get the house of lords to support the Bill and, somewhat ambitiously, to change the term of years granted by the Commons to a perpetual right. Yet in the week it was published[165] the Bill was killed in the Lords and it came to nothing. This did not prevent reviews of the works being published in the *Monthly Review*,[166] with a somewhat mixed review of Macaulay's arguments and glowing reviews for Enfield.[167]

Party Politics

In the previous chapter, the role of party in the 18th century was explored and at this point we will consider whether the Booksellers' Bill was a party matter. The stance of MPs on the Bill is identified in the table below and this is correlated with whether they generally supported the government of Lord North over the decade, making it possible to ascertain whether the Bill was largely supported or opposed by the government and whether there were any 'party' lines.[168] For this purpose, the table below lists all the speakers recorded by Cavendish or included in the one known division list on the Bill,[169] and divides them into groups whether for or against the Bill by using that list and the content of their speeches. Sometimes the side might be evident from their comments, but at other times it arises from a desire to delay the Bill or make its passage more difficult.[170]

While there were nine divisions[171] held on the Booksellers' Petition and bill, only a partial division list for one vote is known to have survived;[172] accordingly, an MP could speak one way and vote another, meaning his comments during debate do not show conclusively how he would have voted. This assessment of government support has been made in three ways. First, John Robinson, secretary to the treasury, compiled a list for the general election of 1774, assessing which MPs were 'pro' the government, hopeful or doubtful supporters, or in opposition.[173] It is generally said that his predictions were not always that accurate, but

[163] William Enfield, *Observations on Literary Property* (Johnson, 1774) (ESTC: T41748) 8, 52.

[164] The preface is dated 26 May.

[165] It appears to have been published on 30 May. An advertisement in the *Gazetteer*, 28 May§, suggests publication on the following Monday. However, advertisements in two issues of the *Morning Chronicle*, 1 and 2 June§, suggest it was published that day. It is more likely that the prepublication advertising is correct.

[166] It also carried much on *Donaldson v Beckett*.

[167] *Monthly Review or Literary Journal*, li (1774), 272–3, 357.

[168] The number of division lists is small and so the conclusions drawn must be tentative. However, there have been attempts based on far fewer lists to allocate parties more firmly, for instance, Dan Bogart, 'Political Party Representation and Electoral Politics in England and Wales, 1690–1747', *Social Science History*, xl (2016), 271 (where just two lists for an entire parliament have been used to give a Whig or Tory affiliation).

[169] *Public Advertiser*, 25 Mar.

[170] It may of course be that there were those who wanted to ensure certain parliamentary procedures were followed or changed irrespective of the legislation in question, but this possibility cannot be explored further.

[171] Petition report (*CJ*, xxxiv, 590; 24 Mar.) – 2 divisions; second reading (*CJ*, xxxiv, 752; 13 May) – 5 divisions; committee (*CJ*, xxxiv, 757; 16 May) – 1 division; and third reading (*CJ*, xxxiv, 788; 27 May) – 1 division.

[172] And it may be that they were never made in the first place as members were simply counted at this point.

[173] P.D.G. Thomas, 'John Robinson's "State" for the General Election of 1774', *Parliamentary History*, xxx (2011), 215.

his indication is recorded under the name in question. Secondly, the division on Grenville's Election Act,[174] where Lord North has marked some MPs as friends of the government[175] with an 'O' (and those with places who voted against the motion were marked with an 'X'). Thirdly, an assessment has been conducted to see whether a member largely voted with or against the government in the course of that decade. This is based on the 29 known divisions,[176] other than that on the Bookseller's Bill itself. As the government was led by Lord North throughout the decade there was only one administration to oppose. Finally, there is an extract from the *History of Parliament*[177] setting out any suggestion of affiliation.

For the Booksellers' Bill	
William Baker	15 Votes (1770–9): G: 1; N: 1; O: 13
[Con]	('attached himself to the Rockinghams, and voted constantly against the Grafton and North administration, though throughout his career he always put great emphasis on his independence')
Issac Barré	19 Votes (1770–9): G: 0; N: 1; O: 18
[Con]	('For more than twenty years he was Shelburne's closest friend, and chief spokesman in the House of Commons.')
Frederick Bull	8 Votes (1774–9): G: 0; N: 0; O: 8
[Con]	('He steadily opposed the North Administration')
Edmund Burke	11 Votes (1770–9): G: 1; N: 0; O: 10
[Con]	('the story of his political career is bound up with that of the Rockingham group')
William Burke	9 Votes (1770–4): G: 1; N: 0; O: 8
[Con]	(he said he was 'willing to be called a follower, the humblest and meanest of that set [Rockingham]')
John Carnac	6 Votes (1770–4): G: 0; N: 0; O: 6
[Pro and 'O']	('voted with the Opposition, following Clive, whom he also supported at East India House')

[174]The vote was for the Parliamentary Elections Act 1774 (14 Geo. III, c. 15), which made the Parliamentary Elections Act 1770 (10 Geo. III, c. 16) permanent; for the vote see *CJ*, xxxiv, 505.

[175]There are two versions of this list, the one used here is that from *The Correspondence of King George the Third, from 1760 to December 1783*, ed. Sir John Fortescue (6 vols, 1967), iii, 71 (no. 1403).

[176]Twenty-four of the lists come from those complied by Donald Ginter: *Voting Records of the British House of Commons*, 1761–1820, ed. D.E. Ginter (6 vols, 1995). A further four lists relating to the Dissenters Bills have been added from Grayson Ditchfield, 'The Subscription Issue in British Parliamentary Politics 1772–9', *Parliamentary History*, vii (1988), 70–2 (these only mention William Jollifee in one non-governmental vote (N)); there was an minority list for a vote challenging the commission of two lords of trade in the *Middlesex Journal*, 15–18 Feb. 1772 (including John Sawbridge, Lord Folkestone, Richard Oliver and William Baker): identified in Grayson Ditchfield, 'Numbered, Weighed and Divided: The Voting of the House of Commons During the Reign of George III', *Parliamentary History*, xv (1996), 231 n. 3).

[177]HC *1754–90*: Ambler (ii, 18), Baker (ii, 42), Barré (ii, 50), Bull (ii, 130), E. Burke (ii, 147), W. Burke (ii, 156), Carnac (ii, 194), Cavendish (ii, 202), Crosby (ii, 278), Cholmley (ii, 213), Cooper (ii, 251), Cornwall (ii, 255), Dempster (ii, 315), Dunning (ii, 368), Feilde (ii, 416), C. Fox (ii, 457), S. Fox (ii, 466), Fuller (ii, 477), Graves (ii, 534), Harley (ii, 587), Harris (ii, 590), Johnstone (ii, 684), Jollifee (ii, 689), Mackworth (iii, 91), Martin (iii, 117), Montagu (iii, 154), Oliver (iii, 224), Col. Onslow (iii, 227), Mr Onslow (iii, 230), Pleydell Bouverie (iii, 303), Popham (iii, 308), Pulteney (iii, 341), Savile (iii, 406), Sawbridge (iii, 410), Seymour Conway (iii, 424), Sutton (iii, 512–13), Van (iii, 572), Wedderburn (iii, 618–20), Sir Charles Whitworth (iii, 634), Richard Whitworth (iii, 634–5).

Henry Cavendish [Con]	9 Votes (1770–4): G: 1; N: 1; O: 7 ('regularly voted with the Opposition, and spoke against Administration on every political issue during his first years in the House … on American affairs, supported the Administration's punitive measures')
Grey Cooper [Pro]	21 Votes (1770–9): G: 13; N: 1; O: 7 (secretary to the treasury; ['treasury; As…'] As a junior minister, Cooper spoke frequently in the House, mainly on financial matters, sometimes on matters of procedure, and also to introduce and to forward Government business in general: but he did not take any part in the great political debates')
Brass Crosby [Con]	8 Votes (1770–4); G: 0; N: 0; O: 8 ('closely associated with Wilkes … and consistently opposed Administration both in the House and in City politics')
John Dunning [Con]	17 Votes (1770–9): G: 0; N: 1; O: 16 (counsel for Beckett; 'he adhered strictly to Shelburne')
Paul Feilde [Con]	8 Votes (1773–9): G: 0; N: 0; O: 8 ('attached to no party')
Rose Fuller[178] [Pro]	6 Votes (1771–4): G: 4; N: 0; O: 2 ('Generally he supported Administration, but took a different line on America')
Samuel Martin[179] [Pro]	4 Votes (1771–4): G: 4; N: 0; O: 0 ('In the Parliament of 1768–74, Martin played a very small part; spoke rarely; and voted regularly with Government')
Fredrick Montagu [Con]	17 Votes (1770–9): G: 1; N: 0; O: 16 ('he belonged to the inner circle of the [Rockingham] party, was consulted on all important occasions, and was a frequent speaker in the Commons')
Richard Oliver [Pro crossed out]	17 Votes (1771–9): G: 0; N: 1; O: 16 ('associated with Wilkes … [later] helped to found the Constitutional Society in opposition to Wilkes … refused to sign Radical declaration')
Col. George Onslow [Pro]	9 Votes (1771–9): G: 8; N: 1; O: 0 ('remained with the court and supported [Lord] North to the end')
Mr George Onslow [Pro]	8 Votes (1770–4): G: 7; N: 1; O: 0 ('His zeal and bustle for the rights of the Commons, and his absolute reliability as a Government supporter … made him a laughing stock with the Opposition')
John Sawbridge [Con]	19 Votes (1770–9): G: 0; N: 1; O: 18 ('his attacks on the ministry were often couched in violent language')
Charles Van [Pro; 'O']	2 Votes (1773–4): G: 0; N: 0; O: 2 ('In general Van was a supporter of North's Administration …')

[178]While Rose Fuller voted in favour on 24 Mar., during the debate he suggested the arguments of George Dempster were very strong: Cavendish, Fuller {S31}.

[179]The *Public Advertiser* refers to 'Mr Martin'. It is possible it was referring to the less active Joseph Martin (who voted 'constantly with Opposition, but had no strong ties with either Rockingham or Chatham').

Alexander Wedderburn [Pro]	8 Votes (1770–9): G: 3; N: 1; O: 4 (solicitor-general; counsel for Beckett)
Sir Charles Whitworth [Pro]	2 Votes (1771–4); G: 2; N: 0; O: 0 ('a regular and obedient follower of Government')
Richard Whitworth [Pro;[180] 'X']	13 Votes (1770–9): G: 2; N: 1; O: 10 ('At first he voted with the Opposition ... From 1774 to 1780 Whitworth was a regular Government supporter')
Against Booksellers	
Charles Ambler [Pro; 'O']	7 Votes (1776–8): G: 5; N: 1; O: 1 ('Ambler voted with the court throughout this Parliament')
Lord Beauchamp (Francis Seymour Conway) [Pro]	17 Votes (1771–9): G: 8; N: 0; O: 9 ('During the American war Beauchamp was a regular supporter of North's Administration')
Nathaniel Cholmley [Con]	8 Votes (1770–4): G: 0; N: 1; O: 7 ('Cholmley voted with the Opposition')
Charles Cornwall [Pro; 'O']	13 Votes (1776–8): G: 2; N: 0; O: 11 (he 'soon became known as one of the most prominent speakers on the Opposition side')
George Dempster [Con]	14 Votes (1770–9): G: 1; N: 1; O: 12 ('Under North's Administration Dempster maintained his reputation for candour in opposition')
Lord Folkestone (Jacob Pleydell Bouverie) [Con]	8 Votes (1772–5): G: 0; N: 0; O: 8 ('at the end of the session he was clearly in Opposition, yet he never identified himself with any party')
Charles Fox [Con, but Pro in constituency list]	14 Votes (1771–9): G: 6; N: 0; O: 8 (dismissed from government February 1774 and 'by the end of the next session of Parliament he was on the way to becoming the acknowledged leader of the Opposition in the House of Commons')
Stephen Fox [Deceased]	7 Votes (1771–4): G: 4; N: 0; O: 3 ('He supported Administration 1768–72' and 'in politics he followed the same line as his brother [Charles James Fox]')
William Graves [Con]	8 Votes (1770–9): G: 2; N: 0; O: 6 ('remained in opposition till the end of the Parliament')
Hon Thomas Harley [Pro]	5 Votes (1773–9): G: 5; O: 0; O: 0 ('Harley consistently supported North's Administration, and became the leader of the court party in the City')
James Harris, Snr [Pro]	5 Votes (1772–9): G: 4; N: 1; O: 0 ('steadily supported North')
George Johnstone [Con; 'X']	9 Votes (1770–9): G: 0; N: 0; O: 9 (he took 'an independent line in Parliament')

[180] His name is not included in Thomas, 'John Robinson's "State" for the General Election of 1774' (but his constituency is marked as 'pro'); however, the 'original' (BL, MS Facsimile 340(4), ff. 43–51) has 'Whitworth' twice in the Pro column, and so his omission from Thomas must be an error.

William Jollifee [Pro]	7 Votes (1771–9): G: 5; N: 2; O: 0 ('by the advice of my father I ... continued my support Lord North')
Herbert Mackworth [Pro]	9 Votes (1770–9): G: 1; N: 1; O: 7 ('in Parliament he was thoroughly independent, and spoke very frequently on a wide variety of subjects')
Alexander Popham [Hopeful]	12 Votes (1770–9): G: 0; N: 0; O: 12 ('voted with the Opposition ... at the general election [in 1774] he ...[was] opposed by ... Administration candidates')
William Pulteney [Con]	10 Votes (1770–9): G: 1; N: 0; O: 9 ('Pulteney was completely independent')
Sir George Savile [Con]	18 Votes (1776–7): G: 0; N: 1; O: 17 ('He was a Whig who never wished for office and never belonged to a party')
Richard Sutton [Con; 'O']	5 Votes (1770–9): G: 1; N: 0; O: 4 ('voted repeatedly with the Opposition ... [later] Sutton was a convinced adherent of the Government's American policy, and this made him ... into their steady supporter')
Edward Thurlow [Pro]	1 Vote (1771–4): G: 1; N: 0; O: 0 (attorney-general; counsel for Donaldson)

G: A vote for the government; N: A vote where the government did not take a side; O: A vote for the opposition.

It appears that most of the speakers, both for and against the Bill, were generally in opposition to the government. Party therefore had little influence on an MP's stance on the Booksellers' Bill in the Commons.[181] In contrast, in the house of lords there was a full division list printed for the single vote (21:11 against)[182] held on the Booksellers' Bill.[183] This can be used to examine whether their lordships generally voted for or against Lord North's government[184] from February 1770 to the end of 1775.[185]

[181] Also see F.P. Lock, *Edmund Burke, 1730–1784* (2 vols, Oxford, 1998), I, 362 (the Bill was 'not a party issue').

[182] J.C. Sainty and David Dewar, *Divisions in the House of Lords: An Analytical List 1685–1857* (1976); *Minutes of Proceedings of House of Lords* (*Manuscript Minutes*), Parliamentary Archives, HL/PO/JO/5/1/121, 2 June.

[183] *Edinburgh Advertiser*, 3–7 June, 357; this appears to have been copied by John Debrett, *The History, Debates and Proceedings of Both Houses of Parliament* (7 vols, 1792), vii, 4, but stated to be the vote on *Donaldson v Beckett*. However, that was an aural vote as no vote on the appeal was recorded in the *Minutes of Proceedings of the House of Lords* (*Manuscript Minutes*): HL/PO/JO/5/1/121, and so not recorded by Sainty and Dewar, *Divisions in the House of Lords*. It was also specifically said it was agreed 'without a division' in the *Annual Register for the Year 1774* (1775), 95. The 'Donaldson' vote being identified as that for the Booksellers has been long accepted by parliamentary historians as that for the Bill: Lowe, 'Politics in the House of Lords', 853 n. 55; Grayson Ditchfield, David Hayton and Clyve Jones, *British Parliamentary Lists, 1660–1800* (1995); and more recently stated by Gómez-Arostegui, 'Copyright at Common Law', 23, n. 108.

[184] Lowe, 'Politics in the House of Lords' did not include the Booksellers' Bill on the list.

[185] This list is built on the assessments in Lowe, 'Politics in the House of Lords', 966–74, Appendix IV. He does not include every division now known and his work ceases in 1775, which means there is a slightly different time scale than for the Commons (where most of the divisions are in the latter part of the 1770s). For a list of known divisions, Ditchfield, Hayton and Jones, *British Parliamentary Lists*, 67–72; and there are a few additional lists subsequently discovered: Clyve Jones, 'New Parliamentary Lists, 1660–1800', *Parliamentary History*, xxvi (2006), 401.

For the Booksellers' Bill

1st duke of Northumberland (Hugh Percy)	O: 5; p: 1
3rd duke of Portland (William Cavendish-Bentinck)	O: 11 (2P); unknown: 1
2nd marquis of Rockingham (Charles Watson-Wentworth)	O: 12 (1P)
5th earl of Carlisle (Frederick Howard)	G: 1; p: 11
4th Earl Fitzwilliam (William Fitzwilliam)	O: 12 (1P)
2nd Viscount Dudley (John Ward)	G: 1; p: 7
4th Viscount Torrington (George Byng)	O: 1 (1P); p: 1
2nd Lord Bruce of Tottenham (Thomas Brudenell-Bruce)	G: 1; p: 12
2nd Lord Lyttelton (Thomas Lyttelton)	O: 4; p: 2
Archbishop of Canterbury (Frederick Cornwallis)	G: 1; p: 12
Bishop of Chester (William Markham)	G: 1; p: 5

Against the Bill

3rd duke of Ancaster[186] (Peregrine Bertie)	G: 1; p: 11
6th duke of Bolton (Henry Powlett)	O: 4; p: 6
6th earl of Denbigh (Basil Feilding)	G: 1; p: 11
2nd earl of Gower (Granville Leveson-Gower)	G: 1; p: 12
4th earl of Sandwich (John Montagu)	G:1 (1P); p: 9
1st Earl Spencer (John Spencer)	O: 4; abs: 1; p: 2
1st earl of Radnor (William Bouverie)	O: 6; p: 3
4th earl of Jersey (George Busy Villiers)	G: 2; p: 9
2nd earl of Northington (Robert Henley)	G: 1; O: 1; p: 3
4th earl of Oxford (Edward Harley)	G: 1; p: 8

[186]The division lists (which are included in Part III) include the duke of Roxburghe, although he was not a representative peer – M.W. McCahill, *The House of Lords in the Age of George III, 1760–1811* (Oxford, 2009), Appendix 5 – and he was not marked as in attendance on 2 June. The only duke who was in attendance and not otherwise accounted for was the duke of Ancaster. The mistake probably came from the fact that Roxburghe's appeal was heard the next day: *LJ*, xxxiv, 233.

8th earl of Abercorn (James Hamilton)	G: 1; p: 12
4th earl of Loudon (John Campbell)	G: 1; p: 10
3rd earl of Roseberry (Neil Primrose)	p: 9
6th Viscount Say and Sele (Richard Fiennes)	G: 1 (1P); O: 1; p: 7
3rd Viscount Weymouth (Thomas Thynne)	G: 1; p: 7
2nd Viscount Falmouth (Hugh Boscawen)	G: 1; p: 11
1st Lord Camden (Charles Pratt)	O: 9; p: 1
1st Lord Ravensworth (Henry Liddell)	O: 3; unclear: 1; p: 3
7th Viscount Montague (Anthony Browne)	G: 1; p: 8
Bishop of St Asaph (Jonathan Shipley)	O: 3 (1P; 1 uncertain); p: 6
Bishop of Litchfield and Coventry (Brownlow North)	G: 1; p: 7

G: a vote for the government; O: a vote for the opposition; p: present but no indication of the vote; 1P: one vote by proxy; 2P: two votes by proxy

In the Lords, records for most of the surviving division lists are minority lists,[187] that is, providing details of only those peers who voted with the minority (lost the vote). Those voting in the majority, usually with the government, would not be listed. However, it is reasonable to assume in most (but not all) cases that a peer who was present ('p') but did not vote with the opposition voted with the government. In any event, while there were some key government opponents in the Lords who supported the Booksellers' Bill there were numerous opponents voting against, and some government men were in favour. This confirms its status as outside the realms of high politics and fits a pattern identified from an earlier period where it was said in the case of purely private legislation there was probably little 'party' influence.[188]

Concluding Remarks

The house of commons did not consider the Booksellers' Bill in a vacuum, it took place as part of maelstrom of debate in the press and the public. There remains so much material that it is possible to see the canvas upon which the MPs and later peers were working. It was a picture painted by the Bill opponents and promoters and the wider public. The arguments will be explored in chapters 4 to 6, but first the discussion turns to the procedure.

[187]Lowe, 'Politics of the House of Lords', Appendix IV, supplementary notes.

[188]Robert Tennyson, 'Private Legislation: Function and Procedure in the Eighteenth Century', University of Berkeley PhD, 2009, p. 57 (this comment appears more directed to the first half of the century).

Chapter 3
Parliamentary Procedure and the Booksellers' Bill

Introduction

The passage of legislation follows traditions and rules, and these rules can have a profound effect on what the houses of parliament do. Rules of parliamentary procedure had begun as an oral tradition, but by the 18th century, procedure was largely based around precedents set out in the journals, which had been carefully prepared since the 16th century as a way to ensure there was procedural continuity. The 18th century was a period in history when the fewest changes to parliamentary procedure took place,[1] and by the beginning of the 1770s the procedure had long been very stable,[2] with only a few standing orders governing practice.[3] Precedent books, were starting to be published, most notably in 1781 that of John Hatsell,[4] who collected together rulings and other matters recorded in the *Votes and Proceedings* and the *Journals*.[5] Indeed, when Erskine May wrote his first *Treatise upon the Law Privileges, Proceedings and Usage of Parliament*[6] it was derived in part from his experience indexing the journals.[7]

Precedent and practice, therefore, originated with what was recorded in the official minutes of the house of commons. In respect of only a few rulings do any records of debates survive. Yet due to Henry Cavendish a vivid picture can be drawn of how procedure was implemented and used tactically by MPs. The Booksellers' Bill, and the surviving reports demonstrate the sorts of procedural tricks undertaken by proponents and opponents of legislation. There were so many opportunities during the passage of legislation for its opponents to resist that the rules have been called 'the procedure of an opposition'.[8] These opportunities were rarely taken and undue use of procedure was uncommon, which is probably why procedure changed so little.[9] This means the practice and procedure surrounding the Booksellers' Bill tells us much about the day-to-day approach to contentious bills and, more importantly, a bill where some of these procedural devices *were* employed. While the failure of the Booksellers' Bill meant that it did not make it to the statute book, only about a quarter of legislative initiatives[10] ever succeeded and in contrast to many others, the Bill

[1]Josef Redlich, *The Procedure of the House of Commons: A Study of its History and Present Form*, trans. A.E. Steinthal (3 vols, 1908), i, 43, 44, 54.

[2]Redlich, *Procedure of the House of Commons*, i, 26 ('highly developed form of its procedure').

[3]Sometimes called the 'pre-standing order' period: This is the title of ch. 3 in O.C. Williams, *The Historical Development of Private Bill Procedure and the Standing Orders in the House of Commons* (2 vols, 1948–9), i.

[4]John Hatsell, *Precedents of Proceedings in the House of Commons* (Dodsley, 1781) (ESTC: T114572).

[5]As to the history of the *Votes and Proceedings*, see Maurice Bond, *Guide to the Records of Parliament* (1971), 213–14; for the decision to routinely publish the votes, Lois Schwoerer, 'Press and Parliament in the Revolution of 1689', *HJ*, xx (1977), 545.

[6]Thomas Erskine May, *A Treatise upon the Law Privileges, Proceedings and Usage of Parliament* (1844).

[7]Martyn Atkins, 'Persuading the House: The Use of the Commons Journal as a Source of Precedent', 82, 84, and Paul Evans and Andrej Ninkovic, 'From Manual to Authority: The Life and Times of the Treatise', 116, both in *Essays on the History of Parliamentary Procedure: In Honour of Thomas Erskine May*, ed. Paul Evans (2017).

[8]Redlich, *Procedure of the House of Commons*, i, 57.

[9]P.D.G. Thomas, *The House of Commons in the Eighteenth Century* (Oxford, 1971), 11.

[10]*Failed Legislation: Extracted from the Commons and Lords Journal, 1660–1800*, ed. Julian Hoppit (1997). In the 1774 session there were 80 failed legislative measures (pp. 426–33) and 118 public Acts and 114 private Acts

made it all the way through the Commons so it can tell us much; but first it is important to turn to the nature of the Bill.

Public or Private

The petition from the Booksellers seeking a bill was lodged only a few days after the vote of the house of lords which decided *Donaldson v Beckett*.[11] This was the beginning of the Bill, but it was initially uncertain what form it might be: that is whether the Bill would be public or private.[12] The distinction between the two is largely that a private bill (or act) affects a particular and identifiable person or persons, whereas a public law affects the public at large.[13] There is no difference in the parliament's powers when enacting private legislation. It could relate to anything and could repeal or modify the common law or other (public) enactments.[14] The right of a person to petition the House for a change in the law was, by the late 18th century, very well established.[15] And while a petition was necessary to start any private bill,[16] it could also be used as a general plea for law reform, that is for a public bill.[17] Indeed, the prayer[18] of the London Booksellers petition does not refer to any named individual as being harmed, rather it asks for the House 'to take their singularly hard case into consideration, and to grant them such relief' as the House thought fit.[19] And in due course the Bill referred to 'every author'.[20] Both were hallmarks of public legislation.

The classification of whether a bill should follow the public or private procedure, certainly at the time of the Booksellers' Bill, turned not on the nature of the Bill as such but on the extraction of fees,[21] with the distinction between the public and private bill procedure being finally codified only a little over 20 years earlier with the introduction of the table

10 *(continued)* (a 25.6% failure rate). The average failure rate over the period 1760–1800 was 59.7% (p. 4). All Acts before 1797 were classified as private or public – but it was not a particularly useful classification (p. 6).

11 *LJ*, xxxiv, 32 (22 Feb.); the petition was presented on 28 Feb.

12 John Feather, *Publishing, Piracy and Politics: An Historical Study of Copyright in Britain* (1994), 64 suggests the Statute of Anne was not really a public bill, as it was started by petition: also see *Tonson v Walker* (1752) 3 Swans 672 at 673 (36 ER 1017 at 1018).

13 *Erskine May's Treatise on The Law, Privileges, Proceedings and Usage of Parliament*, ed. Sir David Natzler and Mark Hutton (25th edn, 2019), para. 42.2.

14 Numerous editions of Erskine May have said this basic proposition has been 'questioned', but it remains law: *Erskine May's Treatise on The Law, Privileges, Proceedings and Usage of Parliament*, ed. Natzler and Hutton, para. 42.9; something the Glasgow Memorialists seem to have skated over: Part IV, Glasgow Memorialists {19}.

15 Fredrick Clifford, *A History of Private Bill Legislation* (2 vols, 1968), i, 271–2 (originally published in 1885). He refers to a lords' election of receivers of petitions in 1278.

16 This had been required since 1685: *CJ*, ix, 719 (26 May 1685); a similar order was passed by the Lords on 7 Dec. 1699: *LJ*, xvi, 482.

17 As to the lack of distinction, Josef Redlich, *The Procedure of the House of Commons: A Study of its History and Present Form*, trans. A.E. Steinthal (3 vols, 1908), i, 13.

18 That is, the request to the House at the end of the petition.

19 Part IV, Booksellers' Petition {4}.

20 Part IV, Booksellers' Bill cl. 1.

21 *The Liverpool Tractate: An Eighteenth-Century Manual on the Procedure of the House of Commons*, ed. Catherine Strateman (New York, 1937). *The Liverpool Tractate* does not refer to private bills as such, but bills upon which fees must be paid and so go through the private bill procedure: Sheila Lambert, *Bills and Acts: Legislative Procedure in Eighteenth-Century England* (Cambridge, 1971), 85.

of fees in 1751 which provided that 'every bill for the particular interest of any person or persons, whether the same be brought in upon petition, or motion, or report from a Committee, or brought from the Lords, hath been and ought to be, deemed a private bill, within the meaning of the table of fees'.[22] Thus, while the classification of bills became more firmly set it did not necessarily follow that all members saw each as entirely separate. For instance, during the protracted debate on whether adequate notice had been given for the sitting of the committee on the Booksellers' Bill, Sir George Savile mooted (then dismissed) the suggestion that the mere committal of the Bill to the whole House could change the nature of it from private to public.[23] The decisive difference was that private bills involved the House in a mixed judicial and legislative function, as it was put by Erskine May over half a century later:[24]

> This union of the judicial and legislative functions is not confined to the forms of procedure, but is an important principle in the inquiries and decisions of Parliament upon the merits of private bills. As a court, it inquires and adjudicates upon the interests of private parties; as a legislature, it is watchful over the public interests of the public.

This distinction was actually highlighted during the passage of the Booksellers' Bill when George Dempster said that the Bill was private, because it was necessary to enable a party to call evidence to rebut an allegation made by a member of the House or another person.[25] In any event, long before 1774 it had been a requirement that all private bills should be started by petition,[26] and it is to this which the discussion now turns.

The Petition

For a private bill the petition was key to the whole proceedings. It was one of only a handful of things that *must* be provided for a bill to progress.[27] Yet the petition for the London Booksellers was brief and very general. The allegation it contained extended to little more than reciting the Statute of Anne; the belief in a common law copyright based on *Miller v Taylor*; and how the petitioners would suffer through their erroneous belief unless granted relief.[28] It is hardly surprising, therefore, that the petition was described by Edward Thurlow as 'dark and ambiguous',[29] but it was a difficult line to draw between generality and precision, as explained in a near contemporary source on procedure, the so called *Liverpool Tractate*:[30]

[22] *CJ*, xxvi, 277 (4 June 1751).

[23] Cavendish, Savile {83}.

[24] Erskine May, *A Treatise upon the Law, Privileges, Proceedings and Usage of Parliament* (1844), 385.

[25] Cavendish, Dempster {82} (this was in the context of the notice required for bill committee making this course of action difficult).

[26] *CJ*, ix, 719 (26 May 1685); a similar order was passed by the Lords: *LJ*, xvi, 482 (7 Dec. 1699).

[27] As to the papers and cases, see Chapter 1.

[28] See Chapter 4.

[29] Cavendish, Thurlow {S1}.

[30] *The Liverpool Tractate* was only ever a manuscript, so dating is uncertain, but Strateman dates it to about 1762: *The Liverpool Tractate*, p. xxii.

> it may not be absurd to remark that all Petitions ought to be drawn as short and in Terms as general as can possibly be conceived … for by descending to Particulars you frequently embarrass your Proceedings not only in Committee but in the future progress of the Bill … and to remedy these Faults … you are often obliged to have recourse to supplementary Petitions.[31]

If one contrasts it with other similar contemporary petitions on related subject matter, such as those private bills seeking to extend the term of individual patents, the Booksellers' Petition was short but not atypical. There were four patent extension[32] petitions in the following two parliamentary sessions (1774–5 and 1775–6),[33] some of which had a controversial passage through parliament,[34] and while two petitions[35] were much longer, two were shorter than the Booksellers' Petition. Nevertheless, the patent petitions were largely in a similar form: the grant of a patent, the inadequacy of the remuneration so far, and so asking for an extension.[36] So while in terms of lines in the journal[37] the Booksellers' Petition was of comparable length, the subject matter was much broader: it covered *every* book and not just a single patent.

The petition's lack of detail at presentation was probably because the London Booksellers had yet to work out the relief they sought. The petition was lodged only six days after the Booksellers lost their case in *Donaldson v Beckett*.[38] It had to be lodged so quickly to meet the deadline for petitions for private bills being presented in the current parliamentary session (28 February 1774).[39] In other words, the booksellers *had* to issue their petition within days. Indeed, if the London Booksellers really did believe they had a perpetual right (which remained disputed throughout the passage of the Bill) they would probably have been reasonably confident that the house of lords would have supported them in *Donaldson*.[40] So while some basic contingency planning might have taken place, it is unlikely to have got further than an intention to petition the Commons. Furthermore, the Booksellers were probably not united in what they wanted, or thought they could achieve, before the House. Some may have still held out hope for a perpetual right, others a further time for an exclusive

[31] *The Liverpool Tractate*, 28.

[32] Richard Champion's petition (*CJ*, xxxv, 138; 22 Feb. 1775); James Watt's petition (*CJ*, xxxv, 142; 23 Feb. 1775); John Liardet's petition (*CJ*, xxxv, 546; 12 Feb. 1776); Walter Taylor's petition (*CJ*, xxxv, 559; 15 Feb. 1776).

[33] There had not been any in the 1774 session or indeed since Meinzie's Patent Act 1740 (24 Geo. II, c. 28); albeit there were further petitions in the 1750s; Phillip Johnson, *Privatised Law Reform: A History of Patent Law through Private Legislation* (2017), 124–6.

[34] Phillip Johnson, 'The Myth of Mr Burke and Mr Watt: for Want of a Champion!', *Queen Mary Journal of Intellectual Property*, vi (2016), 370.

[35] Or at least the summary included in the journal.

[36] Walter Taylor also had a petition to lodge a petition: *CJ*, xxxv, 559 (15 Feb. 1776).

[37] The following sets out the number of lines each petition takes up in the *Commons Journal*: Booksellers' petition, 36; Champion's petition, 22; James Watt's petition, 46; John Liardet's petition, 49; Walter Taylor's petition, 11.

[38] And seven days after they discovered the judges were mainly against them, as they gave their opinion on 21 Feb.: *LJ*, xxxiv, 29–30. It was noted that a petition was to be lodged even more quickly: *Middlesex Journal*, 24–6 Feb.

[39] This date had been ordered on 14 Jan. (*CJ*, xxxiv, 395) (it was possible to ask the House to dispense with this order so as to allow late petitions, but there would need to be some grounds for making this request).

[40] As to belief see Chapter 5: Ignorance, Counsel and How to Know.

right to publish, and maybe a third group wanted compensation from the public purse.[41] By ensuring the petition was vague it was possible for the Booksellers to lodge it without excluding any particular relief – keeping all options open as it were: exactly what *The Liverpool Tractate* suggests.

Presenting the Petition

A private bill would only pass where the petitioners proved their petition, and ultimately, the preamble to the Bill.[42] In simple terms, it was for the petitioners to establish that the enactment of the Bill was expedient (the traditional test for all parliamentary legislation).[43] First, however, there was a very formal procedure to present a petition: the relevant standing order said 'That every member, presenting any Bill or Petition to this House, do go, from his Place, down to the Bar of the House, and bring the same up from thence to the Table'.[44] In fact, it was even more formal than this suggests. A member would stand, his name would be called by the Speaker, the member would say 'a petition' and then summarise its contents to the House. This was followed by three formal questions: that the petition now be brought up; once it had physically been brought to the table of the House, the next question was whether it should be read; and then the third question was whether it should be referred to a committee and on what basis.[45] Each of these questions needed proposing and seconding,[46] and any one of them could be negatived. These questions, like any other, could only be debated after being put; it was not possible to attack the motion in advance.[47]

The consideration of the London Booksellers' Petition upon presentation is not well documented and so it is unclear how much more would have happened other than these formal steps.[48] All that is known is that it was presented by Thomas Harley[49] and seconded by John Sawbridge,[50] after which it was referred to a committee.[51] Many petitions would have been laid on the table[52] and not proceeded with further, or possibly read, without any reference to a committee: in both cases effectively killing them.[53] In other words, reference to a committee was *not* a formality. On the other hand, there was no requirement for

[41] Which as we know was proposed by Folkestone: see Chapter 3: Scope. This would also have required the assent of the crown under an earlier standing order: *CJ*, xv, 18 (12 Dec. 1705).

[42] Once enacted, the preamble helps explain the policy of the Bill. In relation to the Statute of Anne, see *Millar v Taylor* (1769), 4 Burr 2303 at 2332, 2366–7 (98 ER 201 at 217, 235).

[43] Clifford, *History of Private Bill Legislation*, ii, 865.

[44] *CJ*, x, 740 (10 Dec. 1692).

[45] *The Liverpool Tractate*, 21.

[46] Only then was something in the 'possession of the house' as it were: Thomas, *The House of Commons in the Eighteenth Century*, 173.

[47] Thomas, *The House of Commons in the Eighteenth Century*, 17.

[48] *CJ*, xxxiv, 513 (28 Feb.).

[49] Alderman Hon. Thomas Harley†* (1730–1804), MP for London.

[50] Alderman Hon. John Sawbridge†* (1732–95), MP for Hythe. As to seconding, see for instance, *Public Advertiser*, 4 Mar.

[51] *CJ*, xxxiv, 513 (28 Feb.).

[52] As the petition from Innkeepers presented immediately beforehand was just left on the table: *CJ*, xxxiv, 513.

[53] Although it was possible for a bill to be ordered immediately upon reading the petition: *The Liverpool Tractate*, 29.

debate before it was referred, and it may be that little more was said about the petition than that recorded in the newspapers. There is no record in the Cavendish diary at all,[54] suggesting there was no substantive debate at this stage but considering the resistance the Bill faced throughout its passage it cannot be ruled out that such debate was simply not recorded.

The Committee on the London Booksellers' Petition

Formation of the Committee

Once a petition had been referred to a committee, any member of the House interested in being on that committee would stand up and be counted in.[55] There was no set number to constitute a committee,[56] but we know that 14 people attended the second day of committee on the Booksellers' petition.[57] Quorum, unless otherwise ordered,[58] was the entire committee.[59] Once formed, its powers would be agreed by the House; critically, a select committee only had the power given to it by the order constituting it. Therefore, the committee on the Booksellers' petition could only hear witnesses or evidence because the order gave it 'Power to send for Persons, Papers, and Record'. As soon as the Booksellers' petition was referred to a committee there followed a motion by William Graves proposing an (unusual) order that a list be laid before the House of the entries in the Register Book of the Stationers for the books claimed.[60] It is presumed that such a list was sought to substantiate, and particularise, the allegations in the petition.[61] Nevertheless, the order was discharged a few days later due to it be too onerous and time consuming for the committee.[62] Even so, throughout its passage the opposition to the Bill kept emphasising no loss was identified for any particular book. The London Booksellers did, however, produce something entitled 'List of Books',[63] which was provided to show how long it takes for the full stock of books to be sold after printing.

[54]Matthew Brickdale's diary does not include anything on the Bill at all: P.D.G. Thomas, 'Sources for the Debates of the House of Commons, 1768–1774', *BIHR*, special supp., iv (1959), viii.

[55]It appears that at an earlier time a person could not be on a committee if he had spoken against the petition or bill already: Redlich, *Procedure of the House of Commons*, ii, 205; Sir Simonds D'Ewes, *The Journal of all the Parliaments During the Reign of Elizabeth* (Shannon, 1682), 634 (*CJ*, 11 Nov. 1601); *The Liverpool Tractate*, 45.

[56]Quorum was usually eight: *CJ*, i, 169 (12 Apr. 1604); *The Liverpool Tractate*, 40–1. As to the earlier period, it was not so fixed: Redlich, *Procedure of the House of Commons*, ii, 206.

[57]*Public Advertiser*, 17 Mar.

[58]There was usually a formal meeting of the committee to set a date for the committee proper to meet. The time for this would be that ordered when the petition was referred to committee (*CJ*, xxxiv, 513: 'meet Tomorrow, at Nine of the Clock, in the Speaker's Chamber'). This required the presence of five members: *The Liverpool Tractate*, 22.

[59]Erskine May, *A Treatise upon the Law, Privileges, Proceedings and Usage of Parliament*, 232–3.

[60]*CJ*, xxxiv, 513 (28 Feb.); as to who sought the order see *London Chronicle*, 26 Feb. to 1 Mar.

[61]The *Remarks on the Booksellers' Petition* (Part IV, below) suggested a more detailed list particularising how much each work was bought for and how much money it had made to calculate the loss.

[62]*CJ*, xxxiv, 525 (2 Mar.); *Gazetteer*, 3 Mar.

[63]See Part IV, Printed Books. There are two versions: a shorter version entitled 'Books' (ESTC: T16363) and a longer one entitled 'List of Books' (ESTC: T8900).

It was possible for the opponents of the petition to lodge a counter-petition at this early stage,[64] but only the year before counter-petitioners had been prevented from having their petition considered or counsel appearing before petition committees[65] and so there was little point in doing so. An early method of delaying or even killing a petition was to adjourn the committee repeatedly, and there is some evidence that this tactic was used. Edward Thurlow admits he suggested 'a definite line be drawn' for the examination of witnesses which broke up the committee, leading to an adjournment of a week.[66] As Thurlow was a vociferous opponent, delay was almost certainly his intention. Nevertheless, when the committee met again a little over a week later[67] it proceeded without further delay, demonstrating a determined opponent could be met by those coming in the other direction.

Purpose of the Committee

The object of a petition committee was to establish that the proposer had made a *prima facie* case that the Bill would be expedient.[68] Members therefore questioned witnesses on what was in the petition; George Onslow chastised the attorney-general for asking questions of the witness 'out of their petition' regarding the book trade in general.[69] Assuming this was typical, it demonstrates a very strict approach to handling cases before the committee. This strict view could either have arisen because the committee was a delegate of the House and its power extended no further than the order to examine 'the Matters of Fact contained in the said Petition',[70] or because, as a private bill,[71] the proceedings were *judicial* and so some sort of pleading rules applied as they would before the courts. In the courts, the rule was simple: the fact finder is to take no matters into consideration, except for the matters in issue from the pleadings.[72] Thus, it appears that parliament used petitions in the same way as contemporary courts used pleadings.

Witnesses before the Petition Committee

The Booksellers' petition committee met three times. The first time, as described, was abortive; the subsequent meetings involved a very lengthy examination of witnesses, which

[64] Although a petition was lodged by music publishers it was not against the Booksellers' petition: *CJ*, xxxiv, 562 (15 Mar.); see Part IV, Bach and Abel's Petition.

[65] *CJ*, xxxiv, 300 (5 May 1773); even before this it was thought to be too early for the policy of the Bill to have been properly formed: *The Liverpool Tractate*, 42–3.

[66] Cavendish, Thurlow {S1}; *Public Advertiser*, 10 Mar.

[67] It met again on 16 and 18 Mar.

[68] This was still the case 50 years later: T.M. Sherwood, *A Treatise upon the Proceedings to be Adopted by Members in Conducting Private Bills* (1828), 7. Had any standing orders been relevant it would have checked for compliance with those as well, but other than starting by petition there were none relevant to the Bill in the 1770s.

[69] Cavendish, Onslow {S20}.

[70] *The Liverpool Tractate*, 44 ('the Power is contained in the Order which constitutes them and without which they are nothing at all').

[71] As mentioned above this was not clear at the time.

[72] While somewhat later, the best exposition of the rules of pleadings in contemporary courts was Henry Stephens, *A Treatise on the Principles of Pleadings in Civil Actions* (1824), and in the relevant respect, pp. 106–7.

would *not* be on oath.[73] In relation to private bills, the witnesses presented were usually more than happy to attend and testify. So while it was possible to order a person to attend as a witness[74] it was rarely necessary.[75] These committee meetings appeared to have run for around four hours from noon to 4 p.m.; we can be more confident of the end time than its start because the House usually began public business around 4 p.m.[76] and so any select committees would have been expected to have concluded their work by that point.[77] Indeed, it was usual for an order to be made each session whereby once the serjeant-at-arms' gives notice to the committee that the House was sitting ('going into prayers') anything occurring thereafter was null and void.[78] Indeed, on 17 March 1774 it appears that the committee was brought to an abrupt end due to the want of members in the House and the need for a quorum (that is, it was probably a little after 4 p.m.).[79]

While the division of the hearing between evidence and debate in a petition committee might have varied between bills, it is difficult to know much of what occurred at this remove of time. All the minutes of Commons' committees were lost in the fire of 1834,[80] and while the reports of the committee are set out extensively in the journal[81] these detail only the final factual findings of the committee and not the evidence heard (or a record of the debate). In the case of the Booksellers' petition, unusually, there was some limited reporting in the newspapers, but this was more succinct than even the restricted parliamentary reporting of the proceedings from the floor of the House.[82]

In this case, it appears that most of the time was taken up with examining the main witness (William Johnston)[83] who gave evidence for nearly three hours on 16 March and appears to have done so again on the next day. The length of time taken for his evidence on the second day is not clear, but from the newspaper reports it appears he was asked about 'prosecutions' for 'piracy'.[84] The report of his evidence extends to around four columns in the *Commons Journal*. The evidence on injunctions, or 'prosecutions' as it were, are in the second half of the third column of the report. If the report was compiled sequentially, based on the questioning (and it is not clear this is the case), this would suggest that a significant

[73] As to this see Chapter 3: Witnesses; it would be on oath before the house of lords however.

[74] Erskine May, *A Treatise upon the Law, Privileges, Proceedings and Usage of Parliament*, 239.

[75] A failure to attend could lead to the witness being arrested by the serjeant-at-arms and held in custody: Erskine May, *A Treatise upon the Law, Privileges, Proceedings and Usage of Parliament*, 239.

[76] Thomas, *The House of Commons in the Eighteenth Century*, 159–60; sitting at 4 p.m. had become a firm rule by the 19th century: Redlich, *Procedure of the House of Commons*, ii, 77; Hatsell, *Precedents of Proceedings in the House of Commons*, 114.

[77] Erskine May, *A Treatise upon the Law, Privileges, Proceedings and Usage of Parliament*, 237.

[78] Sessional order for 1774: *CJ*, xxxiv, 394 (14 Jan.); as to it being routine see Erskine May, *A Treatise upon the Law, Privileges, Proceedings and Usage of Parliament*, 237; this required attendance with the mace; where the serjeant attended without the mace a polite request might be made to invite members to attend the House: P.D.G. Thomas, 'The Parliamentary Diary of John Clementson, 1770–1802', *Camden Miscellany, XXV* (Camden Society, 4th ser., xiii, 1974), 148.

[79] *Public Ledger*, 18 Mar.

[80] Maurice Bond, *Guide to the Records of Parliament* (1971), 219; by 1834 practice had changed in many respects so records after that date are not particularly helpful.

[81] For the Booksellers' Bill: *CJ*, xxxiv, 588–90 (24 Mar.); reproduced in Part IV.

[82] See Part III, Petition Committee, Days 1–3.

[83] William Johnston or Johnson (d.1804), app. 1743–8, tr. 1745–73, 16 Ludgate Street.

[84] *Public Ledger*, 18 Mar.

part of the sitting of 18 March was also taken up with Johnston's evidence. His evidence was followed by that of John Wilkie,[85] as well as some formal exhibiting of materials.

The petition[86] of Bach[87] and Abel[88] was also before the committee and their attorney, Augustine Greenland,[89] gave evidence regarding musical copyright, but this does not seem to have been considered in great detail.[90] In other words, the petition committee was dominated by witness testimony (not debate), and in the Booksellers' cases that of one witness. So, the meeting does not appear to have been the appropriate place for detailed policy discussions – albeit there was *some* such discussion, as on 16 March the newspapers report there was a debate on the appropriate term for the Booksellers' proposed right (Richard Whitworth suggesting ten years and Peter Burrell that it be reduced to seven).[91]

The Report

The chair of the petition committee would draw up its report (a summary of the facts proven) and this would be approved by a vote of the committee. As the chair was also the proposer of the Bill it potentially risked the evidence being considered in an unduly favourable light. For instance, during the petition committee there was evidence given that the valuation of certain copyrights had been reached by someone less than impartial.[92] But all that was recorded was the valuation and not the method. However, the report was of the facts that had been *proved* and so any conflicts of evidence had to be resolved and valuations may have been one of these. It is not entirely clear the extent to which MPs (and particularly those who were on the committee) were subsequently free to depart from those findings of fact. It appears from the debates on the petition, and later, that MPs took the findings with some latitude and felt free to add their own facts or even to contradict those findings. Yet in principle it seems strange that committee members could determine their own view of the evidence and the rest of the House only had as a guide that which was reported. But this appears to have been what happened at least in relation to the Booksellers' petition.

Report on the Petition

When the petition committee wished to report its findings back to the House, its chair, Paul Feilde, would stand and say 'Mr Speaker. The Committee to whom the Petition [of the Booksellers] was referred have pursuant to the order of the House examined the Matter of the said Petition and have directed me to report the same as it appears to them to the House'. The question was then put whether the report should be read, and assuming this

[85] John Wilkie (d. 1785), app. 1743–50, tr. 1753–75, 71 St Paul's Churchyard; clerk of auctions.

[86] Part IV, Bach and Abel's Petition.

[87] Johann Christian Bach* (1735–82).

[88] Karl (Carl) Fredrich Abel* (1723–87).

[89] Augustine Greenland, attorney, Newman Street and Oxford Street in London: *Browne's General Law-List* (2nd edn, Whieldon and Co., 1777) (ESTC: T85768), 22.

[90] For a discussion, John Small, 'The Development of Musical Copyright', in *The Music Trade in Georgian England*, ed. Michael Kassler (Farnham, 2011), 249–54. It was suggested at one point that there was more sympathy for musical copyright than literary: *Morning Chronicle*, 27 Apr§.

[91] *Middlesex Journal*, 15–17 Mar.

[92] Part IV, Petition Committee Report; Committee Evidence Observations.

was agreed, a clerk read it out to the House.[93] Unlike those of bill committees, the report was recorded in the *Commons Journal*.[94] After the report was read, its findings could be debated by the House. The purpose of the debate was to determine whether a bill should be ordered or not. As the report on the petition would usually end with a vote (or more commonly, a general acclamation) this was the first difficulty any legislative proposal faced.[95] Thus the debate was crucial in determining progress. Some committee reports were bound along with the near daily publication of the *Votes*,[96] but the report on the Booksellers' petition was included only in summary[97] and was not printed in 'full' until the *Journal* was published.[98] This means that MPs would be either relying on notes they made during the actual testimony or those made during the reading of the report. Indeed, reliance on memory alone is likely in many instances as the factual details often appear to be imperfectly recalled or based on other sources.

Edward Thurlow, one of the main opponents to the petition, referred to George Scott purchasing Edmund Gibson's translation of *Camden's Britannia*[99] for £500,[100] but the report suggests this was purchased for £800.[101] He refers to a witness (and this could only have been William Johnston) purchasing copyrights for £1,200 in the previous June and selling it to a branch of his family.[102] The report refers to purchases of between £8,000 and £9,000 and the transfer being to his son.[103] Thurlow also refers to the finding in the report that the subscription raised by the Booksellers was £3,140, but nowhere is this recorded in the report.[104] The information may have originated from letters sent to John Merill jnr[105] from John Whiston,[106] which Thurlow might have become aware of whilst counsel in *Donaldson v Beckett*, or it may be that he had already seen Donaldson's draft petition.[107]

While evidence could be, and indeed was heard later during the progress of the Bill, the evidence in committee clearly remained important. It also appears that the evidence in the petition committee was relied upon later,[108] something which was said to be improper by the opponents.[109] When the petition was reported, the supporters of the Bill relied

[93] *The Liverpool Tractate*, 23.

[94] *CJ*, xxxiv, 588–90.

[95] Thomas, *The House of Commons in the Eighteenth Century*, 261; unless the petition was just laid on the table.

[96] Bond, *Guide to the Records of Parliament*, 213.

[97] *Votes 1774*, p. 401.

[98] By this point it was usual for the *Commons Journal* to be published at some point during the following parliamentary session: Bond, *Guide to the Records of Parliament*, 211.

[99] The relevant edition is William Camden, *Britannia*, trans. Edmund Gibson (3rd edn, Ware, 1753) (ESTC: T145183).

[100] Cavendish, Thurlow {S8}; the sale price is not mentioned but Scott was his son-in-law and so it was not at arm's length: Sir Henry Ellis, *Original Letters of Eminent Literary Men of the Sixteenth, Seventeenth and Eighteenth Century* (Camden Society, xxiii, 1843), 106.

[101] Petition report (*CJ*, xxxiv, 588). In the report it is also spelt 'Cambden'.

[102] Cavendish, Thurlow {S12}.

[103] Petition report (*CJ*, xxxiv, 590).

[104] Cavendish, Thurlow {S7} (it may be that Thurlow was misheard and he said £3,150).

[105] Part IV, The Five Letters.

[106] Although the scheme was orchestrated by Andrew Millar: Feather, *Publishing, Piracy and Politics*, 83.

[107] Donaldson's petition was lodged much later so this is unlikely.

[108] Submissions of James Mansfield KC, which relied on petition committee evidence: Cavendish {22–38}.

[109] Part IV, Donaldson's Lords Petition {3}.

on Johnston as showing his losses were 'common with the whole trade',[110] and George Onslow went as far to say a single witness was all that was needed even if 100 witnesses could have been produced.[111] The impartiality of witnesses was a real concern: Johnston was put forward as an unbiased witness because he *no longer* held any copyright, despite the fact he had owned some in the past.[112]

Leave for a Bill

In contrast to the house of lords,[113] a bill could (and can) only be presented to the house of commons where leave has been given, so the outcome of the petition committee debate is for an MP supporting the Bill to propose a motion and eventually the question was put: 'Is it your pleasure that leave be given to bring in a Bill for the relief of Booksellers?'.[114] This was not a mere formality and it could lead to a division as it did for the Booksellers' petition.[115] It was possible to amend the motion for leave, as Lord Folkestone tried to do,[116] but once leave had been given the scope was set.[117]

Divisions

The order for the Bill to be brought in led to the first and second[118] of the nine divisions on the Bill, that is a counted vote on a question. The usual practice at this time was for a voice vote (where members shouted out 'aye' and 'noe' at the relevant point) after which the Speaker would give his opinion as to whether the ayes or noes had it (won the vote).[119] Only if this conclusion was challenged by a member was a division called, so a division was very unusual at this time.[120] Indeed, multiple votes, as occurred in relation to the Booksellers' Bill, were even more uncommon as it was more usual to ascertain the sentiment of the House on a bill by a single vote at one point during its progress.[121]

[110] Cavendish, Dunning {S15}.

[111] Cavendish, Dunning {S21}.

[112] Cavendish, Johnstone {42–3}, where George Johnstone discusses the competence of another witness.

[113] Where any peer could present a bill and lay it on the table and then present a motion for it to be read: Erskine May, *A Treatise upon the Law, Privileges, Proceedings and Usage of Parliament*, 271.

[114] *The Liverpool Tractate*, 23. For Booksellers' Bill motion, see *CJ*, xxxiv, 590. It appears that at this time the order to bring in the Bill was still a written document: *The Liverpool Tractate*, 5.

[115] Erskine May, *A Treatise upon the Law, Privileges, Proceedings and Usage of Parliament*, 271–2 suggests that debate should be avoided at this stage.

[116] See Chapter 3: Scope; also note the need for the crown's permission to give money: *CJ*, xv, 211 (11 Dec. 1706).

[117] There was usually a second question, asking whether it was the House's pleasure that a particular MP prepare and bring in the Bill: *The Liverpool Tractate*, 23.

[118] *CJ*, xxxiv, 590 (24 Mar.).

[119] Redlich, *Procedure of the House of Commons*, ii, 260. This practice was ancient: Henry Scobel (d. 1660), *Memorials of the Method and Manner of Proceedings in Parliament in Passing Bills* (1670) (ESTC: R203067), 24.

[120] There were only 205 votes for over 2,000 bills before the Commons during 1768–80: Thomas, *The House of Commons in the Eighteenth Century*, 262.

[121] Thomas, *The House of Commons in the Eighteenth Century*, 261. Even the serjeant-at-arms commented how for private bills' votes (other than the third reading) he did not need his hand on the lock: Thomas, 'Parliamentary Diary of John Clementson', 149.

When a division was called there could be additional complications, as voting one way might require a member to leave the chamber.[122] In the old house of commons there was probably only enough seating for 300 to 350 in the chamber despite[123] a membership of 558.[124] While the House would rarely have been close to capacity an MP had to leave the chamber to be counted in a division, meaning he might forfeit his seat[125] when the debate resumed.[126] The matter was complicated further by the lack of consistency over whether the 'ayes' or the 'noes' left the chamber to be counted, and the fact that when sitting in committee neither side left.[127] It depended on the nature of the motion and there was little rhyme or reason to which had to leave.[128] In any event, the division was in favour of the Bill being introduced, and so the supporters of the Bill (Paul Feilde, John Sawbridge, Alexander Wedderburn, John Dunning, Edmund Burke, James Harris and Thomas Harley) were ordered to bring it in.[129]

First Reading

Once a bill had been ordered it could be presented to the House. In the case of the Booksellers' Bill this was done by Paul Feilde.[130] It was usual that the presentation of a bill was followed by its first reading. In the house of commons, the vote on the first reading of a bill had, in most cases, become a formality,[131] yet it still remained important as it was the first time the House learnt of the Bill's contents and purpose.[132] Already by the time William Hakewill wrote his *Modus Tenedi Parliamentum or The Manner of Holding Parliaments in England*[133] in the 17th century it was the case that a first reading was seldom challenged,[134] and later in the same century in *Lex Parliamentaria*[135] it was said that it 'was not usual for a

[122] Apparently, the confusion during divisions even allowed a 'stranger' to vote in a division on 27 Feb. 1771: *CJ*, xxxiii, 212.

[123] As to the number who usually attended see p. 13 n. 56

[124] Thomas, *The House of Commons in the Eighteenth Century*, 127 (he also sets out some earlier more optimistic estimates).

[125] Hatsell, *Precedents of Proceedings in the House of Commons*, 56–8, deals with attempts of members to reserve seats with gloves, hats and so forth.

[126] Thomas, *The House of Commons in the Eighteenth Century*, 129; Redlich, *Procedure of the House of Commons*, ii, 261.

[127] As to how it was done in practice, and the exact way the door was held and locked for a committee vote, see Thomas, 'Parliamentary Diary of John Clementson', 147, 149.

[128] Hatsell, *Precedents of Proceedings in the House of Commons*, 122–34; Redlich, *Procedure of the House of Commons*, ii, 261.

[129] *CJ*, xxxiv, 590 (24 Mar.).

[130] *CJ*, xxxiv, 669 (22 Apr.).

[131] In the period 1768–80 there were four debates on first reading where two passed and two failed: Thomas, *The House of Commons in the Eighteenth Century*, 262.

[132] Redlich, *Procedure of the House of Commons*, iii, 109.

[133] (Benson, 1659) (ESTC: R210040). It had been written in manuscript much earlier as there was an unauthorised extract published in 1641: entry for Hakewell in *History of Parliament. The House of Commons, 1604–1629*, ed. Andrew Thrush and John Ferris (6 vols, Cambridge, 2010), iv, 501.

[134] Hakewill, *Modus Tenendi Parliamentum*, 139.

[135] George Petyt (Phillips), *Lex Parliamentaria: A Treatise on the Law and Customs of the Parliaments of England* (Goodwin, 1690) (ESTC: R4908).

Bill to be put to the Question upon the first reading'.[136] So while a first reading could in theory be refused, that was incredibly rare even where members were very dissatisfied.[137] Notwithstanding its usually formal nature, the first reading still required numerous steps to be taken by the proposing member as it was later explained by George Bramwell:[138]

> The member, intending to present the bill, seats himself at the bar of the House, with the written copy and two prints of the bill, the order of leave, and brief of the bill in his hand; and upon being called to by the Speaker, he answers 'a bill', upon which the Speaker without putting the question, desires him 'to bring it up'. The member then carries up the bill (making three obeisances to the chair) and delivers it to the clerk at the table.

A private bill had to be printed and left at the door of the House[139] for first reading,[140] and at the same time a breviate for the Bill, that is a summary of the Bill's effect, was made available.[141] It was once the case that the Bill was read out in full by a clerk[142] at the first, and subsequent, 'reading',[143] after which the Speaker would summarise the Bill's effect with help from the breviate. The practice of reciting the Bill at each 'reading' fell into abeyance and by Blackstone's time (and so that of the Booksellers' Bill) the substance of the Bill, and not the entire content was read:[144] in other words the breviate was read.

The reading of the breviate did not always serve its purpose, as is clear from George Dempster's comments on the first reading when he said the noise in the House meant he did not know the contents of the Booksellers' Bill.[145] It is well known that there were poor acoustics in the old house of commons,[146] and so even reading the whole bill might not have led to better understanding. Nevertheless, a summary of the Bill was recorded in the newspapers,[147] this being probably based on the breviate, though more likely coming from the reporters' examination of the paper copy rather than through listening to its

[136] Also see Anon, *Observations, Rules and Order Collected out of Divers Journals of the House of Commons* (1717), 60; the Speaker tried to forbid speaking at first reading on 21 Jan. 1580 (OS): *CJ*, i, 118.

[137] This was still possible, and for a long time after: Erskine May, *A Treatise upon the Law, Privileges, Proceedings and Usage of Parliament*, 276; an example over 50 years later: *CJ*, lxxxviii, 614 (20 July 1833), when the Labour Rates Bill was voted down at first reading.

[138] George Bramwell, *The Manner of Proceedings on Bills in the House of Commons* (1823), 58. This stems from the rule implemented on 11 Dec. 1692 (*CJ*, x, 740).

[139] *The Liverpool Tractate*, 24; it also says doing so for a public bill would be a breach of privilege.

[140] *CJ*, xv, 18 (12 Nov. 1705).

[141] Harper's Memorandum, in Lambert, *Bills and Acts*, 88.

[142] William Hakewill, *The Manner How Statutes are Enacted in Parliament by Passing of Bills* (John Belson, 1641) (ESTC: R11690), 10–11.

[143] There are instances of more than three readings before the Elizabethan period: Sir John Neale, *The Elizabethan House of Commons* (1949), 356–7.

[144] William Blackstone, *Commentaries on the Laws of England* (1765), gen. ed. Wilfrid Prest (Oxford, 2016), i, 176; (Prest Version, 119).

[145] Cavendish, Dempster {S235}.

[146] Catriona Cooper, 'The Sound of Debate in Georgian England: Auralising the House of Commons', *Parliamentary History*, xxxviii (2019), 60.

[147] For instance, *Morning Chronicle*, 23 Apr.; *Public Ledger*, 23 Apr.

formal reading. Indeed, the *Caledonian Mercury* printed the entirety of the Bill, including the blanks,[148] whereas most newspapers produced only a summary.[149]

At first reading of the Booksellers' Bill, after formal presentation by Paul Feilde,[150] George Dempster jumped up to criticise the Bill as being of a 'most uncommon nature'.[151] So despite the rule there should be no debate at first reading clearly it did occur; but even with Dempster's obviously strong objections to the Bill, which were manifested before and after first reading, he still accepted that it was improper to oppose the question whether the Bill should be read a first time.[152] Indeed, the *Caledonian Mercury* spoke to a lack of support of the Bill while not formally challenging it, so it progressed to a second reading being ordered.[153] The date for second reading was set a couple of weeks later and subsequently adjourned another week.[154]

Scope

In the 18th century the title of a bill set its scope. Thus, all provisions should fall within the title and, in the case of the Booksellers' Bill, no amendment could be made to the Bill[155] if it did not relate to the 'Relief of Booksellers and others, by vesting the Copies of Printed Books in the Purchasers of such Copies from Authors, or their Assigns, for a limited Time'. The idea of granting a property right seems to have been determined by the time the petition report was heard before the House,[156] but was at large during the petition stage right up until the Bill was ordered.[157] So when Lord Folkestone proposed amending the title of the Bill upon petition report[158] it would, as Rose Fuller MP indicated, have given much more freedom in committee.[159] Folkestone's proposal was for the value of the books to be determined and then money could be paid to the bookseller for each book sold (so a compulsory licence of sorts or some form of equitable remuneration) until the appropriate purchase money had been repaid.[160] It even appears that he tried to suggest some figures

[148] Blanks were commonly used where it was uncertain what would be agreed by the House (in the case of the Booksellers, for instance, the term of the exclusive right), and the practice probably developed because it was thought better to leave blanks than deface the Bill itself: *The Liverpool Tractate*, 14 (also noting that it could lead to uncertain policy).

[149] *London Magazine*, 1774, pp. 622–3; *Morning Chronicle*, 23 Apr.; *Public Advertiser*, 23 Apr.

[150] *CJ*, xxxiv, 669 (22 Apr.).

[151] Cavendish, Dempster {S235}.

[152] Cavendish says Dempster says 'second reading' (not first reading), as did some newspapers. However, Dempster clearly meant first reading.

[153] *CJ*, xxxiv, 669 (22 Apr.).

[154] Originally for 4 May but then adjourned, *CJ*, xxxiv, 702 (4 May).

[155] While it is much later, see Erskine May, *A Treatise upon the Law, Privileges, Proceedings and Usage of Parliament*, 280–1, 283 (an 1844 precedent is cited for allowing a clause to be added on report outside the title, so it seems to have been changing at this time).

[156] Cavendish, Feilde {S283}; but see Cavendish, Dunning {S12–13}.

[157] Cavendish, Dunning {S13–14}.

[158] Cavendish, Folkestone {S30}; Folkestone's Diary, 24 Mar.; *CJ*, xxxv, 590.

[159] Cavendish, Fuller {S31}.

[160] Folkestone's Diary, 24 Mar.; Cavendish, Folkestone {S30}. It is possible this idea was spurred by the call to particularise the loss from every book in the *Remarks on the Booksellers' Petition* (Part IV).

as to the appropriate level of payment.[161] When his motion was defeated it meant that the committee was compelled to only grant a 'limited Time' and not some other sort of relief. Once that order had been given the title could not be amended at any point throughout the rest of the Bill's passage.[162] It worked both ways. The opponents argued that the clause in the Bill which allowed rights to those who had 'otherwise acquired'[163] the copyright[164] went beyond the rights to *purchasers* of the copyright, so it was said to be out with the Bill.[165]

Petitions Against

Whether a bill was public or private, any person could petition the house of commons (or when in the Lords, that House) whether in favour of the Bill or merely suggesting a new provision in, or amendment to, it; conversely, a petition could be against the whole of the Bill or just against a particular clause.[166] By way of example, in the 19th century the Copyright Bill 1842 attracted four petitions,[167] although similar bills much later in the century attracted many more: the failed Patents for Inventions Bill 1875 provoked 50 petitions,[168] whereas in 1844 the repeal of the corn laws attracted around 3,850.[169] As to the proper time to lodge a petition, in the last quarter of the 18th century the rules were quite loose,[170] as explained in *The Liverpool Tractate*:

> I have heard scruples made as to the proper time of presenting Petitions against the Bill without doubt there can be no impropriety in Petitioning against a Bill in any Stage of it. It would be absurd to think the contrary. Counsel have been heard against a Bill on the third Reading but it seems the candid way if you are apprized of it and are absolutely against the Bill to Petition and be heard upon the Question for the Second Reading ...[171]

The Booksellers' Bill being somewhere between private and public,[172] it attracted numerous petitions in favour and against. The Booksellers' petition asking for relief (although not

[161] Cavendish, Folkestone {S30} (but no figures are mentioned in his diary).

[162] *The Liverpool Tractate*, 18; Cavendish, Sutton {118}.

[163] Clause 1. Labelled as Clause 3 by *Further Remarks* (see Part IV).

[164] *Further Remarks* {3; '3rd Clause'); {1; 'Title of Bill'}.

[165] Nothing changed due to this statement.

[166] *The Liverpool Tractate*, 34.

[167] Authors, Booksellers and Publishers &c, 16 Mar. 1842, *Select Committee on Public Petitions Report*, 271 (Petitions numbers 6252–5; App 303, p. 146).

[168] For details, Phillip Johnson, *Parliament, Patents and Inventions* (2018), 660–5 (the relevant entries are PET316–20, 322–55, 357–63, 365, 366, 368–73).

[169] This is based on a count of the number in the index to the *Select Committee on Public Petitions Report* (1844), calculated by working out the number of petitions in a column and counting columns; as occasionally some petitions took up two lines it is not precise.

[170] The year earlier, a new standing order precluded the consideration of petitions against (or hearing from counsel against) during petition committee: *CJ*, xxxiv, 300 (5 May 1773).

[171] *The Liverpool Tractate*, 35, also refers to counsel at third reading on the Staverton Inclosure Bill on 6 May 1751 (*CJ*, xxvi, 217).

[172] But not hybrid in the modern sense: *Erskine May's Treatise on The Law, Privileges, Proceedings and Usage of Parliament*, ed. Natzler and Hutton, para. 30.57.

expressly a bill) was read on 28 February.[173] A little over two weeks later, while the petition committee was still hearing evidence, a petition in favour (or at least seeking clarification) was filed on 15 March.[174] The first petition against the Bill (sometimes called a counter-petition) was presented in advance of first reading on 21 April,[175] and two further petitions followed the next day.[176] The main opponent of the Bill, that is Alexander Donaldson, presented his petition on 26 April,[177] with one more petition being presented on 4 May.[178]

Petitioners could request their counsel be heard at second reading, an opportunity Alexander Donaldson and the Booksellers of Glasgow and London took.[179] Donaldson instructed the same counsel[180] as he had for his case before the house of lords in *Donaldson v Beckett*, and the Glasgow Memorialists did not instruct anyone else. On 16 May,[181] during bill committee, five further counter-petitions against the Bill were presented.[182] The records of these are limited, but in addition to general complaints against the Bill they might have included complaints regarding standing orders. Ironically, maybe, there was a rule prohibiting the presentation of petitions after ten o'clock in the morning,[183] and it appears that Charles Fox may have raised this rule in the debate on 16 May as the petitions on that day were presented in the late afternoon. Ultimately, however, the petitions were read.[184]

Second Reading

The second reading of the Bill was (and is) the time when the expediency of the policy underlying the Bill was debated.[185] In the usual course of things, this meant that each member wanting to speak had to catch the Speaker's eye and then enter the debate either for or against the motion.[186] However, as the Booksellers' Bill was conducted under the private bill procedure, the second reading was largely taken up by the submissions of counsel.[187] The first day of second reading was entirely taken up by the submissions of counsel (Sir

[173] *CJ*, xxxiv, 513.

[174] *CJ*, xxxiv, 562 (Bach and Abel's petition).

[175] *CJ*, xxxiv, 665 (Edinburgh Booksellers' petition).

[176] *CJ*, xxxiv, 668 – (1) London Stallholders; and (2) Glasgow Booksellers.

[177] *CJ*, xxxiv, 679.

[178] *CJ*, xxxiv, 698.

[179] *CJ*, xxxiv, 669.

[180] Albeit the junior (Sir John Dalrymple) was now the leader. The leader in the house of lords, Edward Thurlow, being attorney-general and an MP could not appear before the House as counsel: *CJ*, viii, 646 (6 Nov. 1666).

[181] *CJ*, xxxiv, 757 (16 May). In contrast to the earlier petition these have very limited coverage in the journal.

[182] Two of which were by Sir George Savile: Cavendish {86}.

[183] *CJ*, xii, 83 (4 Feb. 1697/8); although this is often misquoted as the rule for notice of select committees.

[184] Cavendish, Fox {71}.

[185] Erskine May, *A Treatise upon the Law, Privileges, Proceedings and Usage of Parliament*, 408; Thomas, *The House of Commons in the Eighteenth Century*, 261–2.

[186] Sometimes MPs did not get the opportunity to speak even if they had prepared a speech: Thomas, *The House of Commons in the Eighteenth Century*, 192; in theory, where two stood up to speak the person against the Bill should speak first: *CJ*, i, 231 (4 June 1604).

[187] It was possible to have counsel called on public bills if they had a particular interest: Erskine May, *A Treatise upon the Law, Privileges, Proceedings and Usage of Parliament*, 278–9.

John Dalrymple and his junior Arthur Murphy) against the Bill and the witnesses they relied upon to establish their case,[188] the second day was consumed by the submissions of counsel for the Bill (James Mansfield KC and John Hett), after which there was a short reply from Murphy. Conventionally, following the submissions of counsel, the House debated the expediency of the Bill.[189] However, due to the late hour (after 1 a.m.),[190] and a motion to adjourn second reading failing, the Bill was committed with little or no debate on its merits.[191]

What is particularly interesting about the submissions of counsel is the approach and tone. As explored in Chapters 4 and 5 there was little reliance on evidence in the legal sense. Sir John Dalrymple, for instance, opened his submissions with an attack on the character, or at least the activities, of the London newspapers.[192] He narrowly avoided being ruled out of order.[193] Thereafter, making various allegations about book prices without any reference to any evidence (such as the list of book stocks with prices),[194] he rather presented his own experience[195] of the printing of *Harlein Voyages*.[196] Not only does this demonstrate different standards for advocates as to giving evidence during submissions but it shows reliance on pure supposition as to the cost of a book before it would be published. Indeed, subsequently Murphy likewise provided a price for the transcript of Macklin's *Love-A-La Mode* based on a then unreported case.[197]

In simple terms, the style of advocacy was closer to the sort of debate and speeches made by members of the House than it was to the sort of submissions that one would have expected before a court of law. A party petitioning for or against a bill had the right to call witnesses to give (unsworn) evidence before the House. By the 19th century, these witnesses would be heard only in committee, but in 1774 it was still common for them to be heard at the Bar of the House.[198] As would be expected, the purpose of these witnesses

[188] *Morning Chronicle*, 12 May. The party against the Bill had the right to begin: *The Liverpool Tractate*, 79; also see *CJ*, i, 369 (5 May 1607) which held that whomever was against the Bill should be heard first.

[189] *The Liverpool Tractate*, 79.

[190] Newspapers vary as to the time the House rose: *Edinburgh Advertiser*, 17–20 May, 317 (debate lasted until 12 p.m. then voted); *Middlesex Journal*, 12–14 May (past 1 a.m.); *St James's Chronicle*, 12–14 May (1.45 a.m.); *Public Advertiser*, 16 May 1774 (past 2 a.m.); *Lloyd's Evening Post*, 13–16 May, 463 (past 2 a.m.) and Cavendish suggests it was 2 a.m. (Cavendish, {57}).

[191] It had been acknowledged that the debate would run late: see *Morning Chronicle*, 10 May.

[192] Cavendish, Dalrymple {229–32}.

[193] *Public Ledger*, 18 Mar.

[194] Part IV, Printed Books.

[195] Cavendish, Dalrymple {234}.

[196] *A Collection of Voyages and Travels Consisting of Authentic Writers in Our Own Tongue, which Have Not Before Been Collected in English, or Have Only Been Abridged in Other Collections … Compiled from the Curious and Valuable Library of the Late Earl of Oxford. Th. Osborn* (Osborne, 1745) (ESTC: T97843).

[197] *Macklin v Richardson* (1770) Amb 694 (27 ER 451). These reports were said to be notoriously inaccurate: J.W. Wallace, *The Reporters Arranged and Characterized … Fourth Edition Revised* (Boston, MA, 1882), 33. As to reference, see Cavendish {257}. In any event this would have been hearsay evidence, which was probably not the concern to the courts that it later became: J.H. Langbein, 'Historical Foundations of the Law of Evidence: A View from the Ryder Sources', *Columbia Law Review*, xcvi (1996), 1187–9; cf. J.H. Wigmore, 'The History of the Hearsay Rule', *Harvard Law Review*, xvii (1904), 437, taking the view it had reached a developed form by this stage.

[198] A related (and unusually still existing) example of notes made of the evidence being given at the bar of the House related to the Hornblowers' Patent Bill: Birmingham Library, MS 3147/2/35/28.

was to provide evidence that the Bill should (or should not) get a second reading and be able to progress further.

Witnesses

In the case of the Booksellers' Bill, witnesses were called,[199] and the questioning of Mr Wilke is even set out in the *Morning Chronicle*.[200] Most questions asked of the witnesses would come from counsel for the parties (if instructed). However, MPs could also ask questions either directly or through the chair, depending on the circumstances.[201] As Cavendish took no shorthand transcript of the evidence heard in relation to the Booksellers' Bill it is unclear whether the questions were asked by counsel, MPs or the Speaker.[202] The evidence given, both before the petition committee and the House, was not on oath.[203] The anomaly of giving unsworn evidence continued for decades thereafter and in 1844 Erskine May exclaimed, 'By the laws of England, the power of administering oaths has been considered essential to the discovery of truth; it has been entrusted to small debt courts, and to every justice of the peace; but is not enjoyed by the House of Commons, the grand inquest of the nation.'[204] The house of commons admitted that it did not have power to administer oaths (in contrast to the Lords). Initially, this restriction was overcome by either calling for the assistance of one of their members who was a justice of the peace, or summoning a judge to administer the oath, or actually holding their inquiries at the Bar of the house of lords. But from the 18th century, the House started treating giving false evidence as a breach of privilege,[205] and so a witness giving false evidence, or refusing to give evidence, could be committed to prison.[206]

The Testimony

The best reports (from the newspapers, as Cavendish did not transcribe their evidence) suggests the witnesses for the opponents exhibited certain letters from 1759,[207] showing an attempt by the London Booksellers to set up what would now be called a cartel to pursue any non-member publishing books. However, this cartel or 'conspiracy' (as others called it) was not mentioned at all by Dalrymple. While it was relied upon greatly later on, it is

[199] As to the precise practice of calling a witness to the bar, see Thomas, 'Parliamentary Diary of John Clementson', 150.

[200] *Morning Chronicle*, 16 May.

[201] Hatsell, *Precedents of Proceedings in the House of Commons*, 95–6; but see Thomas, 'Parliamentary Diary of John Clementson', 159 (only the Speaker could ask questions).

[202] The closest in Cavendish is Fox's question: Cavendish, Fox {47}. The evidence of John Wilkes was adduced by questioning from counsel: *Morning Chronicle*, 16 May.

[203] This was commented upon, see Committee Evidence Observations {12}, which makes this point.

[204] Erskine May, *A Treatise upon the Law, Privileges, Proceedings and Usage of Parliament*, 244; for precedents, John Hatsell, *Precedents of Proceedings in the House of Commons* (4 vols, 1818), ii, 151–62 (it was not in the 1st edn); the rule changes, allowing evidence on oath, with the enactment of the Parliamentary Witnesses Act 1858 (21 & 22 Vic., c. 78).

[205] Hatsell, *Precedents of Proceedings in the House of Commons* (1781), 92–4.

[206] Erskine May, *A Treatise upon the Law, Privileges, Proceedings and Usage of Parliament*, 246.

[207] It is presumed these are the letters transcribed in Part IV, The Five Letters.

strange that the speech of leading counsel did not open the concepts and allegations. In any event, the account in the *Morning Chronicle* suggests that the witnesses were evasive and unhelpful to the party calling them and largely complained about exclusion from the book sales. It all went very poorly as there was 'almost of scene of laughter during the whole of the evidence'.[208]

After the live testimony, Murphy continued his submissions without any real regard to the evidence heard. Indeed, he returned to the same sort of arguments put forward by his leader, such as turning a few words in the *Commons Journal* regarding the conference between the Lords and commons during the passage of the Statute of Anne into a central point,[209] and providing a summary of some of the leading cases with little of the background behind them. (Unfortunately, some of his submissions were not recorded by Cavendish.)[210] Murphy largely concentrated on the advantages of cheaper books and he made the submission that by not passing the Bill 'learning is put within reach of everybody'.[211]

James Mansfield during his submissions addressed many of the criticisms of the opponents, and specifically looked at the allegations regarding newspapers. He challenged the value of the opponents' witness testimony suggesting that they did not prove what was alleged (indeed, it amounted to a wholescale challenge of the Merills' evidence). In other words, his submissions were more conventional: addressing the evidence against his client and presenting an alternative reading of it. For instance, the 'combination' he says provided books to those whom it pursued for selling non-London books.[212] So he was addressing head-on the allegation of the conspiracy and he set his clients' position clean against it. Like his opposing counsel he relied on letters to support his case. The first of these went without comment, but then a subsequent letter faced an objection. The objection, as was conventional, was heard without the parties present. Unlike the subsequent arguments over admissibility, the Speaker allowed the letter to be read, making some opaque reference to legal evidence. Strangely, and revealingly, Mansfield expressly said that he would not go into 'legal arguments' as 'this is not the place for it'.[213] This is an express acknowledgment of the political nature of counsel's submissions at the bar. While the law is relevant, it is only tangentially, as the relevant background to the belief, so the argument for a bill is one of policy; a need for a new law as it were.

Witness Competence

After presenting a somewhat different historical view of what had occurred, John Wilkie[214] was called by Mansfield to give evidence. His competence as a witness was immediately challenged.[215] The debate that followed gives a real insight into the thinking of 18th-century parliamentarians. George Johnstone moved that Wilkie was not a competent

[208] *Morning Chronicle,* 11 May.

[209] Cavendish, Murphy {257}.

[210] See comment in brackets '(he dwelt …)' at Cavendish, Murphy {257}.

[211] Cavendish, Murphy {263}.

[212] Cavendish, Mansfield {24–5}.

[213] Cavendish, Mansfield {34}.

[214] John Wilkie (d. 1785), clerk of auctions, 71 St Paul's Churchyard.

[215] The competency of witnesses was also raised in Donaldson's Lords Petition {3}.

witness and that his evidence be struck out of the report (at this stage, according to Cavendish, he had given only a few hundred words of evidence). He argued that Wilkie was a proxy for the petitioners and that petitioners should not be allowed to give evidence in their own case (even if not strictly a party). Edmund Burke said it was a 'universal practice of the House' to hear witnesses 'whether their own story of their own suffering' or otherwise.[216] Burke, and others, appeared to draw a distinction between 'legal' evidence and 'information'. The former, it was said, required strict formalities but the latter did not. In supporting the admission of the evidence, Burke made a straightforward point, namely what happens if a petitioner is the only witness? If this rule were followed then there would be no remedy.

There were clear rules that petitioners were not competent witnesses in their own cause.[217] But as to whether a person who benefits from a bill, but does not actually have his name on the petition, is a competent witness was uncertain. It appears, however, in the case of the Booksellers' Bill, the witness was found to be competent after a division.[218] Parliamentary lawyers often turned to the courts for guidance as to how to deal with evidence, but even there ambiguity reigned over whether such a witness was competent. Lord Mansfield suggested slightly over a decade later that 'The old cases, upon the competency of witnesses, have gone upon very subtle ground. But of late years the Courts have endeavoured, as far as possible, consistent with those authorities, to let the objection go to the credit, rather than to the competency, of a witness'.[219] This might imply that a person with an interest was thought to be competent before the courts, but their testimony might not be given much weight.[220] Likewise before the House.

Wilkie was called in to answer a further question, and after withdrawing again he was asked a frivolous one by Charles Fox,[221] probably drawing out his unhappiness at the competence decision (he could not have answered it either if he was not competent) or, possibly, to bring the evidence to an end.[222] This short debate shows how members might imagine, or apply, a rule which had no precedent, or try to extend a well-known rule to try to block a bill. And conversely the members promoting the Bill would appear to be willing to circumvent rules if they seemed to be against them. In any event, after Fox[223] asked his question whether infringers should be guilty of a felony (that is, put to death) for copyright

[216] Cavendish, Burke {43}.

[217] *The Liverpool Tractate*, 77; Clifford, *History of Private Bill Legislation*, ii, 870 (indicating the rule was abolished in 1844, about the same time as it was permitted in the court).

[218] *CJ*, xxxiv, 752.

[219] *Walton v Shelley* (1786) 1 Term Reports 300 (99 ER 1106); *King v Bray* (1736) Cases Temp Hardwicke 358 at 360 (95 ER 232), Lord Hardwicke LC; *Bent v Baker* (1789) 3 Term Reports 27 (100 ER 437).

[220] However, in later years the rule became more firmly against the competency of interested witnesses at law with more relaxed rules in chancery. The Evidence Act 1843 (6 & 7 Vic., c. 85), s. 1 being enacted to permit an interested person to give evidence. It took even longer before a party could give evidence: Evidence Act 1851 (14 & 15 Vic., c. 99), s. 2.

[221] Cavendish, Fox {47–8}.

[222] *St James's Chronicle*, 14–17 May.

[223] It appears that Fox often repeated or modified his speeches (or added outrageous comments like this) on the basis that members came and went from the House very frequently: N.W. Wraxall, *Historical Memoirs of My Own Time* (1815), ii, 497.

infringement,[224] Wilkie's evidence seems to have stopped and Murphy moved on to give a reply on behalf of the opponents. The reply once more seemed to rely on presentational flourish and anecdotes rather than any evidence. Critically, it appears that on second reading this (quite properly) led to submissions confined to the central policy of the Bill and not its clauses; only in passing were any individual provisions mentioned.[225] This meant the arguments were very simple and confined to the question of whether the London Booksellers deserved, or did not deserve, the Bill. As already explained, it was expected there would be a full debate on the policy of the Bill, but this simply did not happen due to the late hour.[226] To permit such a debate, there were two unsuccessful motions to adjourn the second reading;[227] after the motions failed the Bill was committed to the whole house.

Judicial Notice

The courts had strict rules regarding the proof of enactments. A public act, such as the Statute of Anne, could be judicially noticed, but a private act could not.[228] Thus, in *Millar v Taylor* it was suggested that the decrees of the star chamber and the proclamations could not be judicially noticed as the law of the land.[229] In strict terms they would have to be proved. As this never happened, Sir Joseph Yates in his dissent suggested they were not more than historical anecdotes.[230] While extensive reference was made to the said same decrees and proclamations before parliament, no admissibility issue was raised. While any type of Act of Parliament was sufficient proof[231] within the House it is not clear how much further this extended. Thus, it may be the history presented to the House could not be taken as evidence of what the law was but merely an anecdote of it. As the case turned on a belief, these distinctions probably mattered little.

Committee

While at this point it was still common to commit[232] public bills to the whole House ('below stairs'),[233] it was more usual for private bills to be committed to a select

[224]Cavendish, Fox {47}. This joke was picked up in the press and so it must have had an impact: *St James's Chronicle*, 14–17 May; and one bookseller took the idea of putting to death far too literally and failed to see it as a joke: *Morning Chronicle*, 17 May§.

[225]Murphy refers to clause 1 in his reply: Cavendish, Murphy {50}.

[226]See Chapter 3: Second Reading above.

[227]*CJ*, xxxiv, 752 (13 May); Cavendish {55}.

[228]Sir Geoffrey Gilbert, *The Law of Evidence* (4th edn, 1777) (ESTC: N10446), 12; the rule regarding private Acts was reported later in *Greswolde v Kemp* (1842) Car & M 63 (174 ER 668).

[229]This was not raised before the House, but see Yates J dissent in *Millar v Taylor* (1769) 4 Burr 2303 at 2371–2 (98 ER 201 at 238).

[230]*Millar v Taylor* (1769), 4 Burr 2303 at 2373 (98 ER 201 at 239). He also pointed out that the by-laws are private and so only bind the parties to them.

[231]By implication, Hatsell, *Precedents of Proceedings in the House of Commons*, 105–7.

[232]It was necessary, when committing, to name a member to take the Bill: *CJ*, I, 650 (29 Nov. 1621); *Standing Orders and Resolutions of the House of Commons* (Steward, 1747) (ESTC T114967), 30.

[233]It was still normal in the late 19th century: Redlich, *Procedure of the House of Commons*, i, 196.

committee ('committee above stairs').[234] The purpose of a bill being committed was for it to be considered in detail and where the Bill was opposed the procedure was explained in *The Liverpool Tractate*:

> when your committee meets, the first thing to be done is to read the Preamble and then proceed to examine evidence to prove it: if the Point is litigated, this Examination may probably be very tedious, especially if the parties have money enough to throw away in feeing counsel.[235]

In theory, the committee was meant to go through each allegation in the preamble and decide whether it was proved or not. For instance, the Booksellers alleged in their preamble that:

> ... it hath been a prevailing Opinion with Booksellers and others, that Authors and their Assigns had by the Common Law, independently of the said Act of Queen Anne, the sole Right of printing and reprinting Copies of their Works.[236]

The Bill committee had to determine whether the evidence supported this fact – in other words did Booksellers and others believe there was a common law right? As the Bill was reported positively the committee must have accepted there was sufficient evidence to support this statement. After the preamble, the committee would go through each clause and determine whether it should stand as part of the Bill.[237] The role of the committee was to recommend[238] amendments to the Bill and report on the allegations (that is, the preamble).[239] Its powers did not extend to rejecting the principle of the Bill as such,[240] although it could omit all the operative clauses – which is much the same thing.[241]

Timing of the Committee

While the Speaker was still in the chair (that is before the House formed itself into committee, which was symbolised by the Speaker leaving the chair),[242] the first objection to the

[234]Thomas, *The House of Commons in the Eighteenth Century*, 264. It was also possible to have a select committee appointed, where 'all who come to have voices' – in other words anyone who came was a member: Redlich, *Procedure of the House of Commons*, ii, 209.

[235] *The Liverpool Tractate*, 47; the practice of bills being revised in committee was long established by this time: Redlich, *Procedure of the House of Commons*, ii, 203.

[236]Second Recital; Part IV, Booksellers' Bill.

[237] *The Liverpool Tractate*, 47, 48.

[238]It did not change the Bill as such, this happened on report: John Hooker, *Sessions of Parliament in the Reign of Elizabeth*, in Lord Mountmorres, *The History of the Principal Transactions of the Irish Parliament from the Year 1634 to 1666* (Caddell, 1792) (ESTC: T70500), i, 146–8; Redlich, *Procedure of the House of Commons*, ii, 204.

[239] *The Liverpool Tractate*, 47.

[240]A later ruling demonstrates this: Charles Manners-Sutton (Speaker), *Mirror of Parliament*, ii, 7 Apr. 1829, p. 1142 (in relation to Crossley's petition (Gas Lights Bill 1829).

[241]See discussion of Nicholas Facio's petition, where this appears to have happened, in E.J. Wood, *Curiosities of Clocks and Watches: From the Earliest Times* (1866), 307–8.

[242]This meant that a motion for the Speaker not to leave the chair was essentially the same as a motion against forming committee.

Bill was raised. Colonel George Onslow[243] complained that a standing order had not been complied with. The order required 'That the Chairman of the Committee for any private Bill do not sit thereupon, without a Week's public Notice thereof set up on the Lobby'.[244] The Booksellers' Bill had been committed on Friday 13 May and the committee was sitting on Monday 16 May, the next sitting day.[245] Indeed, the debate raises an interesting issue about the use of standing orders. The order was referred to by Charles Fox as that made on '4 February 1697',[246] but the debate was about an order not made on that date but two years later. *The Liverpool Tractate* makes the same mistake,[247] which suggests that either Fox used the text as a reference or, more likely, the mistake had become common and MPs simply remembered the order by reference to a particular incorrect date (and so reference was not made back to the journal itself).

It was quite possible for standing orders to be dispensed with in suitable cases,[248] which caused a protracted and complicated argument about the rules of procedure. The opening salvos of this battle show how such debates could proceed, with the opponents of the Bill pushing for as many divisions as possible.[249] The timing of such divisions could be important, as was the wording of the question,[250] as it might affect the support received. Once a division was lost it could not be put again.[251] A short narrative provides a picture of what happened. Fox, a vigorous opponent, suggested that as the rule had been dispensed with there should be a full debate on whether the rule should be set aside generally – before a fuller House (that is, on another day). This led to a distinction being identified. The standing order, Edmund Burke suggested, applied to select committees, it did not apply when it was committed to the whole House. Accordingly, no new precedent was being set. He then cleverly elided the suggestion that the 'spirit of the order' applied to proceedings before the whole House, saying that it was a 'discretionary rule' and not a standing order.[252] The idea of a 'discretionary rule' is, of course, contradictory, as Thurlow subsequently pointed out.[253] It would be better called a parliamentary convention. Burke's argument proceeded on the practical basis that the purpose of the standing order was to

[243] There were two George Onslows, who were cousins: Colonel George Onslow†* (1731–92), MP for Guildford, and George Onslow†* (1731–1814), MP for Surrey. The title of colonel was used to tell them apart.

[244] Originally, *CJ*, xiii, 6 (24 Nov. 1699); by 1774, *CJ*, xx, 161 (5 Mar. 1722/3); see discussion of the setting of the sittings of bill committees in *The Liverpool Tractate*, 25.

[245] The House sometimes sat on a Saturday at this time but did not do so on this particular weekend.

[246] Cavendish, Fox {71}.

[247] *The Liverpool Tractate*, 26; it appears that the attorney-general made the same mistake on second reading: *Morning Chronicle*, 16 May.

[248] By the 1820s the routine dispensing with standing orders was being criticised: Williams, *Historical Development of Private Bill Procedure*, i, 49.

[249] This was not entirely proper. George Onslow made this point during the newspaper reporters' debate in 1771 where there were 23 divisions: *CJ*, xxxiii, 249–51 (12 Mar. 1771); Thomas, *The House of Commons in the Eighteenth Century*, 260.

[250] For instance, postponing something might win support, whereas rejecting it might not: Thomas, *The House of Commons in the Eighteenth Century*, 175.

[251] Thomas, *The House of Commons in the Eighteenth Century*, 171, 175; Hatsell, *Precedents of Proceedings in the House of Commons*, 83–91. This remains the rule: Speaker Bercow's statement on Brexit: HC Debates, 18 Mar. 2019, dcvi, col. 775.

[252] Cavendish, Burke {60–1}.

[253] Cavendish, Thurlow {62–3}.

ensure that notice was given of the committee sitting and that due notice had been given as evidenced by 'a whole wagon load of petitions from Glasgow'.[254] Thurlow, on the other hand, argued for the standing order to apply to committees of the whole House, as well as to select committees. He, rightly, pointed out that there is little difference in principle between a private bill committee 'above the stairs' and where it was the whole House.[255] He also brought in a further complaint that the debate at second reading had not taken place because it was after midnight when counsel submissions finished and the debate would usually have started.[256] As mentioned above, in committee only the clauses and not the principle could be debated and Thurlow wanted to attack the principle.[257] Essentially, he was arguing (rightly) that the Bill had been highjacked into the committee.

Edmund Burke had been given a 'brief for debate'. It is not clear which one he held, but as discussed in chapter 2, many were circulating. He mentions there were objections to every clause of the Bill.[258] This document, he argued, showed there had been notice enough. If the opposers could put together a speaking note opposing the clauses then they must have had due notice. Later, Richard Whitworth argued that publication of the *Votes* would be sufficient notice,[259] but it was pointed out that the *Votes* might not yet have been printed from the preceding sitting day.[260] Charles Fox returned to the fray,[261] saying the notice was within the letter (and not just the spirit) of the order, thereby trying to make the committal out of order. The procedural maneuvering continued, with Fox proposing that there were numerous issues which required a division of the House (a vote). Did committing the Bill on the next sitting, by that very fact, mean that standing orders were dispensed with? Division was required, he said, and once that is resolved another division was needed as to whether to go into committee at all.[262] In response to these proposed questions, William Burke, on the other side, claimed such a motion would not be permitted as it was after 4 o'clock.[263] Thurlow, to keep the ball rolling, suggested another motion to allow a motion to be made after 4 o'clock (why a motion for a motion was allowed after that time, but the motion itself was not, is unclear, but Hatsell seems to suggest it was).[264] It appears that even those involved thought what was going on was extreme: John Sawbridge commented that 'the manoeuvering today exceeded all manoeuver that ever were practised',[265] before he

[254] Cavendish, Burke {61}.

[255] Cavendish, Thurlow {64}.

[256] Cavendish, Thurlow {65–6}.

[257] In other words, challenge the preamble.

[258] Cavendish, Burke {69}; this makes it likely that it is *Further Remarks and Papers on the Booksellers' Bill* (see Part IV).

[259] Cavendish, Whitworth {85}.

[260] Cavendish, Chomley {86}.

[261] It was not possible for a member to speak to the same question again (although interventions did not end the main speaker's contribution). Nevertheless, speaking twice was a common problem, and the Speaker did try to take steps to restrict it: Thomas, *The House of Commons in the Eighteenth Century*, 195–7.

[262] Cavendish, Fox {73}.

[263] Hatsell, *Precedents of Proceedings in the House of Commons*, 120; it was also not possible to make new business part of the order of the day without notice. Accordingly, notice of any motion was usually given much earlier than 4 p.m. on the day itself: Thomas, *The House of Commons in the Eighteenth Century*, 97.

[264] Cavendish, Thurlow {73–4}.

[265] Cavendish, Sawbridge {74–5}.

went on to call for another vote on a different question. After a short detour through some of the merits of the Bill, those gathered returned to a vexed question as to whether this was a private or public bill, albeit the discussion was somewhat confused. It was significant, because if it was a public bill it clearly did not fall within the scope of the standing order requiring notice. But little came of that and it was pointed out that if the Bill were to pass in this session it would need to be passed quickly.[266]

The debate that followed was on the substantive merits of the Bill and was largely concerned with a reiteration of the same arguments as before. Paul Feilde, the proposer of the Bill, summarised the case for the Bill and Charles Fox that against. A brief attempt was made by Sir Richard Sutton to change the nature of the Bill from being the grant of a further term to some (unspecified) different form of relief. It will be remembered that Lord Folkestone had unsuccessfully proposed a different form of relief during the report on the petition.[267] As the Speaker indicated to Folkestone, the Bill introduced must be that pursuant to the leave which had been granted for a 'Bill for Relief of Booksellers, and others, by vesting the Copies of printed Books in the Purchasers of such Copies from Authors or their Assigns, for a Time therein to be limited'.[268] Any bill, therefore, had to grant a term of years of some sort.[269] The debate continued on the general merits of the Bill until eventually, after a division, the Speaker left the chair and the House went into committee.

Committee of the Whole House

Once the House entered the committee, the record of the debate by Cavendish is very short, but the newspaper reports give some further insight and suggest that it lasted many hours. It is clear that some amendments were made and the blanks filled up. This is evident from comparing the Bill as presented, which was reproduced in the *The Caledonian Mercury*, and the Ingrossment. However, Cavendish records only a proposal by Paul Feilde that the term should be 14 years, filling the blank in clause 1 (albeit James Harris suggested a term of seven years, which did not seem to be considered by the House).[270] The second change was a proposal for copies of the books to be delivered to the British Museum. While the Bill as introduced had included a legal deposit requirement, the addition of reference to the British Museum and the number of copies was agreed and added in committee.[271] It appears that Harris also proposed that the Bill should not extend to books first published before the commencement of the 18th century (and not to extend to ancient authors) which was opposed by the solicitor-general and led to a division. The proposed clause was not accepted. There were other blanks filled up, such as the date the Act would come into force (4 June), which did not appear to be mentioned by Cavendish although some newspapers reported this date being set.[272] (This report might have simply been looking

[266] Cavendish, Burke {54} and Whitworth {86}.

[267] The vote to remove the relevant words was unsuccessful: *CJ*, xxxiv, 590.

[268] *CJ*, xxxiv, 590 (24 Mar.).

[269] See discussion of scope at Chapter 3: Scope.

[270] Cavendish, Harris {135}.

[271] The text of the amendment is underlined in the Bill. See Part IV, Booksellers' Bill.

[272] *Public Ledger*, 17 Mar.; *London Magazine*, xliii, 627.

at the Bill, rather than listening to the debate.) The other amendments, such as setting the level of the fine for not entering the book in the register,[273] were also considered. The Bill was set to be reported the next day.

Report

The chairman of the Bill committee, whether of the whole House or select, is the person who had to report the findings back to the House.[274] This required him to report whether the allegations of the Bill had been examined,[275] and so when the report was made the chairman would be called to the Bar and would report that the 'Committee to whom the Bill had been Committed have made several amendments to the Bill which they have directed me to report to the House'.[276] The chairman would then read a token number of the amendments before they were presented to the clerk[277] on a sheet of paper (and not on the Bill itself).[278] Once the House was in possession of the amendments it could agree them or make further amendments as it saw fit.[279] It was the adoption of the committee's report that amended the Bill and not the committee itself. Unlike, with regard to the petition committee, evidence was not reported back to the House, only the amendments were.[280] Thus the report, along with any additional amendments, needed to be agreed to by a vote, after which the (former) chairman of the Bill committee proposed that the Bill with the amendments be ingrossed and a question was put to that effect.[281]

Quorum

On report, a proviso was presented 'that nothing herein contained shall prevent the booksellers of that part of Great Britain called Scotland, from printing and vending in Scotland all such books as they could have legally printed and vended before 1 of March 1774'.[282] While this proviso was being debated the quorum was called. The rule on quorum originated from a standing order of 1640,[283] which stated 'that Mr Speaker is not to go to his Chair till there be at least Forty in the House' and the Speaker could make up the

[273] Cavendish records a comment of William Pulteney that a failure to register the book should have led to forfeiting the rights: Cavendish, Pulteney {136}.

[274] *The Liverpool Tractate*, 13.

[275] *CJ*, xii, 625 (31 Mar. 1699).

[276] *CJ*, xxxiv, 775 (19 May); *The Liverpool Tractate*, 14 (unless no amendments were made when different words would have been used).

[277] On a separate sheet of paper. It was once the case that the amendments were each then read twice and agreed (Hakewell, *The Manner How Statutes are Enacted*, 148–9), but this had fallen out of practice by the late 18th century: *The Liverpool Tractate*, 14.

[278] *The Liverpool Tractate*, 11, 12 (this also appears to be a different practice from an earlier time); Hakewell, *The Manner How Statutes are Enacted*, 148.

[279] *The Liverpool Tractate*, 15–16. These further amendments were to the face of the Bill (or it is assumed the amendment sheet) and made by the Speaker personally.

[280] *The Liverpool Tractate*, 48; *CJ*, i, 378 (4 June 1607).

[281] *The Liverpool Tractate*, 16.

[282] *Morning Chronicle*, 20 May.

[283] *CJ*, ii, 63 (5 Jan. 1640/1).

40 members if need be.[284] This was not the first time quorum became an issue.[285] The decision to commit the Booksellers' Bill on 13 May only had sufficient members because the Speaker was included in their number.[286] Indeed, the quorum still remains,[287] although it is now the case that the quorum must be present on a division. There is no requirement for 40 to be in attendance within the chamber. The original rule appears to have been stricter and 40 members had to be present for a debate to take place. In uncontentious matters it was probably not raised where fewer than 40 members were present, but it would still be possible to kill a debate immediately by showing there was no quorum. This is exactly what happened on report of the Booksellers' Bill. While the debate was proceeding, George Dempster called for the Speaker to leave the chair,[288] as there were insufficient members present.[289] In such cases, the Speaker could send for members as they may have been elsewhere in the House, but this did not seem to happen.

Quorum could therefore be used to stall the progress of the Bill. If the opponents did not attend the chamber and those in favour were too few the House would adjourn and the matter would not progress. While this tactic could be used, it is probable it was not used very often, with the Booksellers' Bill being a notable exception.[290] What is more surprising is it appeared that Fox was actually trying to persuade fellow members (one being Lord Beauchamp) not to attend the House to make the quorum.[291] This led to a complaint being made to the House, but as the restraint was by persuasion, not force, the point was not pursued and the House adjourned to the following day. The next day, the report was accepted without further amendment and the Bill ordered to be ingrossed, it appears without any opposition.[292] The process of ingrossing a bill could take time and so while the date of a third reading was often proposed at report, it was usually done so dependent upon the condition that the Bill had by then been ingrossed.[293] This is precisely what happened in the case of the Booksellers' Bill.[294] The process of ingrossment, which became extinct in 1849,[295] was conducted by clerks in the Ingrossing

[284] Hatsell, *Precedents of Proceedings in the House of Commons*, 113; Redlich, *Procedure of the House of Commons*, ii, 75–6.

[285] The attorney-general had apparently tried the same tactic at the end of the second reading debate: *St James's Chronicle*, 12–14 May.

[286] *CJ*, xxxiv, 752: 35 in favour with an additional four members acting as tellers: total 39. The 40 is only made by counting the Speaker. Apparently, the tellers were not actually against the Bill, as the vote was none against, and this was commented upon as well: Cavendish {53}; Thomas, *The House of Commons in the Eighteenth Century*, 249.

[287] Now standing order no. 40.

[288] In this context, this would be asking for an adjournment (rather than going into committee); Hatsell, *Precedents of Proceedings in the House of Commons*, 75 (adjourn) and 136 (go into committee).

[289] Cavendish, Dempster {141–2}. The number who were actually present is uncertain – varying newspapers suggested different numbers: *Middlesex Journal*, 19–21 May (37 members present); *St James's Chronicle*, 19–21 May (25 members present).

[290] It must have been a rare example as it was the one used by Thomas, *The House of Commons in the Eighteenth Century*, 167.

[291] Cavendish, Fox {142–3}.

[292] *Gazetteer*, 21 May; *CJ*, xxxiv, 778 (20 May).

[293] *The Liverpool Tractate*, 16.

[294] *CJ*, xxxiv, 779 (20 May).

[295] *CJ*, civ, 52 (12 Feb. 1849), 625 (31 July 1849) (applies to private and local bills); *Resolutions Relating to the Ingrossing and Inrolling of Bills* (1849 HC Papers 20), xlv, 19; *LJ*, lxxxi, 18 (8 Feb. 1849).

Office.[296] A perfect copy of the Bill with all the amendments was presented to the ingrossing clerk,[297] who then wrote it out in a thick black and even handwriting on parchment.[298] This was a laborious process requiring great accuracy,[299] but still mistakes could be made, as they were in the Booksellers' Bill.[300] The Bill was only ingrossed once, in the first House; any subsequent amendments made to it in either House[301] would be by interlineation,[302] or by 'tacting' a 'rider'[303] to the Bill.[304] The cost of ingrossing was significant in 1774, amounting to 12*s.* 6*d.* per press,[305] and although the Booksellers' Bill was reasonably short, being on only nine presses, it would nevertheless have cost £5 12*s.* 6*d.*[306]

After it has been given royal assent, the ingrossed bill is the Act of Parliament.[307] It was vital to make sure it was correctly copied onto the parchment and so a standing order was passed that no ingrossed bill be brought to the table to be read a third time except by the chairman of the committee to whom that bill had been committed, after he had examined the same.[308] It appears the chairman had delegated the responsibility of checking the Bill was accurate to parliamentary clerks long before the Booksellers' Bill was before the House,[309] and in due course they would delegate it further.[310] Thus, the chairman of the committee (Richard Whitworth MP) would have collected the Bill from the ingrossment office and deposited it on the table for third reading.

Third Reading and the Bill Passing

Once it had been ingrossed and the breviate altered by the clerk,[311] third reading would be proposed by the chairman of the Bill committee,[312] the Speaker would read the breviate and the question would be put whether the Bill should be read a third time. It was possible for amendments to be made at third reading, and also for a bill to be rejected in its

[296]The office of ingrossing clerk had already become a sinecure by 1774: O.C. Williams, *The Clerical Organization of the House of Commons, 1661–1850* (Oxford, 1954), 229; indeed, later it seems to have been sent out of the House entirely to stationers: *Report from the Select Committee on the Present Method of Ingrossing Bills* (1823 HC Papers 552), iv, 69 at p. 24.

[297]Petition of James Goodiff (clerk): *CJ*, lxiv, 77–8 (22 Feb. 1809).

[298]As to the advantages of this hand, Clifford, *History of Private Bill Legislation*, 320–1.

[299]Williams, *Clerical Organization of the House of Commons*, 227.

[300]The Ingrossment (Parliamentary Archives, HL/PO/JO/10/2/53) has the word 'by' missed out.

[301]That is, on third reading or at any stage in the second House.

[302]Crossing out and writing between the lines.

[303]A 'rider' was always a distinct clause, whereas an 'amendment' was changing an existing clause: *Report from the Select Committee on the Present Method of Ingrossing Bills*, 31.

[304]An additional piece of parchment, usually a new clause or proviso, which was sewn to the main parchment: Clifford, *History of Private Bill Legislation*, 318.

[305]A sheet of parchment 27 inches by 12 inches of about 40 lines and 25 words to a line, and so about 1,000 words per parchment: Clifford, *History of Private Bill Legislation*, 319.

[306]Booksellers' Bill 1774, Parliamentary Archives, HL/PO/JO/10/2/53.

[307]Copies were sent to the chancery, but the official copy was that held in parliament.

[308]*CJ*, x, 406 (6 May 1690).

[309]Williams, *Clerical Organization of the House of Commons*, 227–8.

[310]*CJ*, lxiv, 77–8.

[311]*The Liverpool Tractate*, 16.

[312]*CJ*, x, 406 (6 May 1690).

entirety,[313] but amendments were avoided as they needed to be made to the Ingrossment itself.[314] However, in most cases the challenges to the Bill had already been heard, and so it was often little more than a last-ditch attempt to get a bill rejected.[315] In the case of the Booksellers' Bill, there were four short speeches criticising it and nothing said in favour. It appears even those present were resigned to it passing, although a division was called, and the Bill passed the House.[316]

House of Lords

The Bill was received in the house of lords on 31 May,[317] and the following week it faced its first reading.[318] In contrast to the Commons the quorum for the Lords was merely three,[319] and attendance was much lower, with an average of 35 peers[320] for every sitting day in 1774.[321] First reading of the Booksellers' Bill attracted only 28 peers.[322] This low attendance was a consequence of a mixture of lack of interest, infirmity and distance,[323] and, more crucially, the Lords in contrast to the Commons allowed voting by proxy.[324] As in the Commons, 25 or so peers dominated the proceedings and lawyers were particularly prominent.[325] The debates in the Lords were also generally thought to be of a higher quality than in the Commons,[326] and there were fewer formal votes,[327] with only 14 divisions in the Lords during 1774,[328] and business usually being conducted by voice votes alone.

[313]As to the process for recording amendments, *The Liverpool Tractate*, 17.

[314]Erskine May, *A Treatise upon the Law, Privileges, Proceedings and Usage of Parliament*, 285, 433. Technically, amendments were made *after* third reading.

[315]This still happened, but only infrequently: the following were identified for 1768–80 in *Failed Legislation*, ed. Hoppit (the six digit coding is that used by Hoppitt): Preventing Gashing of Skins (110.045; 25 Apr. 1769), Preservation of Game (111.046; 14 May 1770), East India Military Police (112.009; 23 Apr. 1771), Africa Company (113.045; 20 May 1772), Occasional Voters (114.039; 26 May 1773), Philips Lighthouse (116.015; 16 May 1775), Butchers Company (117.016; 26 Mar. 76), Workington Harbour (118.018; 28 Apr. 1777).

[316]*CJ*, xxxiv, 788 (27 May).

[317]*LJ*, xxxiv, 222 (31 May).

[318]It was clear even before this that the Bill's prospects were bleak: letter from the marquis of Rockingham to Edmund Burke on 1 June: *The Correspondence of Edmund Burke, Volume 2, 1768–1774*, ed. Lucy Sutherland (Cambridge, 1960), 540–1.

[319]Erskine May, *A Treatise upon the Law, Privileges, Proceedings and Usage of Parliament*, 151; Anita Rees, 'The Practice and Procedure of the House of Lords 1714–84', University of Aberystwyth PhD, 1987, p. 43 (quorum set by ancient convention).

[320]A 'full house' was about 100: Clyve Jones, 'Seating Problems in the House of Lords in the early Eighteenth Century: The Evidence of the Manuscript Minutes', *BIHR*, li (1978), 135.

[321]M.W. McCahill, *The House of Lords in the Age of George III (1760–1811)* (Oxford, 2009), 99.

[322]*LJ*, xxxiv, 226–7 (those attending is included at the start of every sitting day at this point).

[323]McCahill, *The House of Lords in the Age of George III*, 96, 103 ('the hunt periodically took priority over the appeals of party leaders').

[324]McCahill, *The House of Lords in the Age of George III*, 107–14.

[325]McCahill, *The House of Lords in the Age of George III*, 114–15 (this was in reference to a slightly later session).

[326]Contemporaries often gave laudatory accounts of Lords' debates: for instance, Sir William Anson, *Autobiography and Political Correspondence of Augustus Henry, 3rd Duke of Grafton* (1898), 361–2; *The Last Journals of Horace Walpole: During the Reign of George III*, ed. A.F. Steuart (2 vols, 1910), ii, 431–2, 462–3; ii, 481–2.

[327]Divisions also routinely had low attendance: a quarter of divisions had fewer than 30 peers voting: McCahill, *The House of Lords in the Age of George III*, 100.

[328]McCahill, *The House of Lords in the Age of George III*, 99.

By this time, it was rare for first readings to be challenged in the house of lords – like in the Commons – it was usually little more than a formality.[329] So the Bill was read for a first time.[330] However, it was immediately moved that its second reading be heard in two months' time – a way to effectively kill the Bill[331] as the adjourned date would be after the end of the current parliamentary session.[332] It appears that the debate on the matter was extensive and, unusually, it was reported in the newspapers in some detail.[333] It ended with the Bill being put off for two months following a division (21 not content and 11 content). This was a positive decision to kill the Bill.[334] In contrast to the Commons, the votes in a division were not recorded in the printed *Lords' Journal* until later, but they were recorded in the manuscript journal.[335] In the 1770s about 33% of bills started in the Commons failed in the Lords and so the failure of the Booksellers' Bill was not atypical.[336]

Conclusion

In the context of court proceedings, Sir John Baker explained how 'there is a world of practice and discretion which is understood by experienced practitioners but is not to be found in books',[337] and this equally applies to parliamentary practice. The Booksellers' Bill is a rare example of the broad range of parliamentary proceedings being brought to bear on a bill, and to see how rules were used and abused by those seeking to promote and hinder its progress. Parliament was a place of politics and procedure is only part of it. The evidence and arguments supporting the case for a bill played a far bigger role and it is this we start to look at in the next chapter.

[329] However, the Lords often did not follow its own rules very closely: McCahill, *The House of Lords in the Age of George III*, 120–1.

[330] *LJ*, xxxiv, 232.

[331] Erskine May, *A Treatise upon the Law, Privileges, Proceedings and Usage of Parliament*, 277–8.

[332] The session ended on 22 June. Private bills started to be carried over to the next session around the mid 19th century (it appears the first time was in 1859: *CJ*, cxiv, 114). Despite numerous attempts over the years, only since 1997 has it been possible to have a motion to carry a public bill over to the next session: *Erskine May's Treatise on The Law, Privileges, Proceedings and Usage of Parliament*, ed. Natzler and Hutton, para. 30.31 to 30.35.

[333] There is some mention of petitions being presented: *Edinburgh Advertiser*, 3–7 June, 356. The Lords' Journal does not record this, but we know that Donaldson had prepared a petition for the Lords.

[334] Here Ronan Deazley, *Rethinking Copyright: History, Theory, Language* (Cheltenham, 2006), 22, is wrong to call the Bill 'stalled': it was dead. Bills could be stalled, but a defer motion like this was a way to kill the Bill; it seems to be more clearly and accurately expressed in Deazley, *On the Origin of the Right to Copy*, 215.

[335] Manuscript Journal: Parliamentary Archives, HL/PO/JO/5/1/121, 2 June.

[336] McCahill, *The House of Lords in the Age of George III*, 293 (whereas 88.2% of bills started and failed in the Lords).

[337] J.H. Baker, 'Why the History of Law has not been Finished', *Cambridge Law Journal*, lix (2000), 78.

Chapter 4
Evidence and Argument: The History

Introduction

The Booksellers' Bill failed; the arguments its promoters made while sufficient to force the Bill through the house of commons did not even get a chance to be raised before the Lords. The purpose of this chapter and the next is to explore the arguments made, both for and against the Bill, and to evaluate the parties' evidence and assertions. The case had numerous facets, such as the belief in the common law right, the large investments lost as a result of *Donaldson v Beckett*, and the interests of authors, as well as some less substantial points.[1] This chapter considers the history, and the next chapter considers the other arguments. The Bill came at a time when copyright history was elevated to an 'academic sub-discipline',[2] and there is an inevitable disconnect when looking at it now, but the arguments and the evidence have been marshalled here to try to present a picture of the balance between rhetoric, evidence, supposition, extrapolation and simple hyperbole which was needed to get a bill through the House, or to try and stop its passage. As historians have the advantage of knowing what happened next[3] (that the book trade did not die but actually continued to thrive), we can test the merits of the arguments in a slightly more objective sense than could, or would, have been done at the time.

Counsel and politicians needed petitions to set the scope of the claim, yet the judicial nature of private bills,[4] with the attendant need for evidence or proof, can be seen firsthand as largely ineffective and often ignored.[5] The proceedings were based on the petitions, papers, 'cases', and witnesses before the house of commons and other less formal material.[6] For instance, in the petition committee the Booksellers relied upon the testimony of a single witness[7] to explain the whole trade;[8] it was even suggested that one witness was enough as 100 could have been called.[9] Later at second reading evidence was received from more witnesses,[10] but even then most of the evidence came from documents rather than live

[1] Part IV, Booksellers' Petition.

[2] 'Introduction', in *Privilege and Property: Essays on the History of Copyright*, ed. Ronan Deazley, Martin Kretschmer and Lionel Bently (Cambridge, 2010), 2.

[3] A nice point made by James Smyth, 'Lewis Namier, Herbert Butterfield and Edmund Burke', *Journal for Eighteenth-Century Studies*, xxxv (2012), 384 (that historians have an advantage over those living at the time as they can see the consequences of events), albeit it also brings in our assumptions of what things should be: S.F.C. Milsom, *A Natural History of the Common Law* (New York, 2003), xvi.

[4] Yet Mansfield said 'I meant not to go into the legal arguments this is not the place for it.': Cavendish, Mansfield {34}.

[5] But see the criticisms in Part IV, Donaldson's House of Lords Petition {3}.

[6] See Chapters 1 and 2.

[7] It appears that this was unexpected; in advance there was an expectation of 'several' booksellers giving evidence: *Public Advertiser*, 16 Mar§.

[8] A point seized upon by the opponents: Part IV, Committee Evidence Observations {12}, albeit there was some formal proof from others as well.

[9] Cavendish, Onslow {S21}.

[10] *Morning Chronicle*, 11, 16 May.

testimony. In a time when practice in the courts was largely oral it turns out the approach in parliament was very different.

Belief in Common Law Copyright: A History

There has been extensive consideration by scholars of whether there *was* a common law copyright before *Donaldson v Beckett*, or, put another way, whether *Millar v Taylor* was correctly decided. The Booksellers' Bill 1774 was not premised on whether such a common law right existed, but whether the Booksellers *believed* that such a right existed (whether or not it did in fact).[11] The belief question is different from the existence question.[12] What is central here is not the history of a common law right (or otherwise) but the *narrative* of that history put forward by the parties during the passage of the Booksellers' Bill. At some point these things will be the same – where the argument and history coalesce – but at other times it is the presentation of history: the historiography as it were. The history is something that can be divided into three stages, beginning with the prehistory, that is before the Statute of Anne; the Statute itself and its expiry for old books in the 1730s; and, finally, the 'Battle of the Booksellers' which then followed. It is a history with certain highlights which need particular examination, such as the 'honorary right' sought to be created in 1749, but largely it is a reimagined history – an invention of tradition.[13]

The Prehistory

The booksellers and their supporters relied on a relatively straightforward history of English practice.[14] In a nutshell, it was that there was a common law right[15] vested in authors in perpetuity before the Statute of Anne and which nothing in that act changed.[16] Yet little was presented supporting this right. Sir John Dalrymple, in his submissions on second reading, provided the most detailed history.[17] His purpose, as counsel against the Bill, was

[11] As John Feather, *Publishing, Piracy and Politics: An Historical Study of Copyright in Britain* (1994), 68, puts it 'the book trade behaved as if the law meant what they wanted it to mean, and ignored those parts they found inconvenient'.

[12] Some suggested it was 'wilful ignorance' and not belief: Cavendish, James Fox {161}.

[13] Trevor Ross, 'Copyright and the Invention of Tradition', *Eighteenth-Century Studies*, xxvi (1992), 1, following Eric Hobsbawm and Terrance Ranger, *The Invention of Tradition* (Cambridge, 1992); Ronan Deazley, *Rethinking Copyright: History, Theory, Language* (Cheltenham, 2006), ch. 2, explores how *Donaldson v Beckett* was received and believed over the next 75 years.

[14] The Scottish practice was different and was not really touched upon before the house of commons. For a history: A.J. Mann, 'Scottish Copyright before the Statute of 1710', *Juridical Review* (2000), 11; W.J. Couper 'Copyright in Scotland before 1709', *Records of the Glasgow Bibliographical Society*, ix (1931), 42; A.J. Mann, 'The Anatomy of Copyright Law in Scotland before 1710', in *Research Handbook on the History of Copyright Law*, ed. Isabella Alexander and H. Tomás Gómez-Arostegui (Cheltenham, 2016).

[15] John Hett argued that there were three properties that existed. The first the 'original right', the second the right to withhold printing (what might now be called the divulgation right or what became the common law copyright), and third the right to print: Cavendish, Hett {38}.

[16] Part IV, Booksellers' Case {1}.

[17] In contrast Cavendish, Mansfield {34–6} mentions it only in passing; other brief mentions by Cavendish, Feilde {S281, S282 and 95}; Thurlow {S5}; Folkestone {87}, and in Folkestone's Diary, 16 May.

to demonstrate that nothing in the history supported a common law right in literary property;[18] and that any protection the booksellers enjoyed had come from the prerogative and statute. Before turning to this history, a little context may assist.

William Caxton printed the first book in English in 1474 or 1475 and returned to England to print more a couple of years later.[19] The earliest printers were all foreign and it was not until the 1520s that Englishmen started to dominate the local trade.[20] During this time the king began granting privileges,[21] and it is here the history before the Commons begins with these privileges and, more particularly, the granting of printing patents[22] by Henry VII and Henry VIII.[23] The first king's printer, William Facques, was appointed in 1504.[24] These patents were usually for a particular type of book such as law books, books for private prayer, and almanacs.[25] The consolidation and management of these patents by the Stationers' Company[26] gave it great power,[27] enabling it to create tradable 'stocks'[28] in the patented

[18]Cavendish, Dalrymple {246–51}.

[19]Feather, *A History of British Publishing*, 15. It is put as 1471 in *Tonson v Collins* (1761) 1 Black W 301 at 303 (96 ER 169 at 170) although not expressly mentioned in the Commons.

[20]Feather, *A History of British Publishing*, 17; the Importation Act 1483 (1 Ric. III, c. 12) which restricted foreign merchants, did not extend to books.

[21]It appears that some privileges did not go through the full procedure for granting a patent. While these 'placards' were not conventional patents under the great seal they appear to have been recognised as privileges. For a discussion of 'placards' (which appears to be Blayney's term), P.W.M. Blayney, *The Stationers' Company and the Printers of London, 1501–1557* (2 vols, Cambridge, 2013), ii, Appendix D. It should be noted that shortcuts in granting patents (and so fees to officials) had sought to be remedied by the Clerks of the Signet Privy Seal Act 1535 (27 Hen. VIII, c. 11). As to issues before that, A.L. Brown, 'The Authorization of Letters under the Great Seal', *BIHR*, xxxvii (1964), 125.

[22]The value, and so success, of patents depended on the nature of publication. For instance, the Bills of Mortality once a valuable patent ceased to be once newspapers could use them to make news: Will Slauter, *Who Owns the News? A History of Copyright* (Stanford, CA, 2019), 32.

[23]For a general history of the printing patents, L.R. Patterson, *Copyright in Historical Perspective* (Nashville, TN, 1968), ch. 5. For the most complete list, A.F. Pollard and G.R. Redgrave, *A Short-Title Catalogue of Books Printed in England, Scotland and Ireland, 1475–1640* (London Bibliographical Society, iii, 1991), 195, 197–205, Appendices A–E.

[24]There does not appear to be a patent for the early king's printer: Blayney, *The Stationers' Company and the Printers of London*, i, 110–20; and in *Tonson v Collins* (1761) 1 Black W 301 at 304 (96 ER 169 at 170) the first is said to be Richard Grafton, 22 Apr. 1547: *Calendar of Patent Rolls*, 1547–8 (1924), 187. The early king's stationer had a very different role. The large number of patents granted by the Stuarts slightly undermined the copyright system run by the Stationers: Feather, *A History of British Publishing*, 42.

[25]Law Books (Richard Tottell, 12 Jan. 1559, *Calendar of Patent Rolls*, 1558–60 (1939), 62); Private Prayer (Richard Grafton and Edward Whitchurch, 22 Apr. 1547, *Calendar of Patent Rolls*, 1547–8, p. 100; a copy in Appendix 1 of Patterson, *Copyright in Historical Perspective*); Almanacs (Richard Watkins and James Robertson, 3 Dec. 1588: *Calendar of Patent Rolls, 31 Elizabeth I*, ed. S.R. Neal (List and Index Society, ccc, 2003), 75, no. 441). The almanac patent was successfully challenged in *Stationers' Company v Carnan* (1775) 2 Black 1004 (96 ER 590); as to the law patent, Feather, *Publishing, Piracy and Politics*, 12.

[26]Conversely, in Scotland it had no relevance: *Hinton v Donaldson* (1773), Lord Kennett at 1 *Boswell's Report.*

[27]This was probably an unintended consequence: Feather, *A History of British Publishing*, 35.

[28]The most valuable was the 'English' stock: Feather, *A History of British Publishing*, 36; Cyprian Blagden, 'The English Stock of the Stationers' Company: An Account of its Origins', *The Library*, 5th ser., x (1955), 163 and 'The English Stock of the Stationers' Company in the time of the Stuarts', *The Library*, xii (1957), 167. It basically worked by every bookseller paying a fee any time he wished to print a book within the English stock and was enforced by the Company (Feather, 39); also see Feather, 48–9. Other stocks included the Latin stock, Bible stock and Irish stock and the Ballard Partners: William Jackson, 'Introduction', in *Records of the Court of the Stationers' Company, 1602–1640* (Bibliographic Society, 1957), xi–xiv; Patterson, *Copyright in Historical Perspective*, 138.

books (which it later combined with its own licences to print).[29] The granting of these patents,[30] the monopoly rights given to the Stationers under its charter, and the licences it granted[31] meant that 'no other company … ever attained the same degree of monopoly that which the State thought it expedient to confer on the Stationers'.[32] This combination of patents and licences created two parallel systems of press regulation. While 'shares' were mentioned before the Commons,[33] the English stock, and the role of the Stationers' in it was not.[34] The complex and ambiguous relationships were simplified and sanitised.

The Commons heard[35] how the position of the Company[36] had been cemented[37] by decrees of the star chamber[38] and proclamations of the privy council.[39] Each of these instruments, Dalrymple said, demonstrated that the protection for printers required the royal prerogative,[40] and so there had been no common law right,[41] something even the proposers seemed to accept at times.[42] Dalrymple's history[43] progressed through the

[29]Patterson, *Copyright in Historical Perspective*, 113, suggests the importance of patents had been overtaken by the stationers' copyright (that is licences) by the end of the 16th century; the fact these were merely by-laws and could only bind members was not really picked up in the Commons, but see *Tonson v Collins* (1762) 1 Black W 322 at 335 (96 ER 180 at 186), submission of Yates.

[30]Which by the Elizabethan era covered only a minority of books: Feather, *Publishing, Piracy and Politics*, 14. There were also some printing grants (or rewards) given by parliament: for that to Bolton and Cheyanll: *CJ*, iv, 489 (25 Mar. 1646).

[31]Feather suggests that this created a unique right to print by the mid 16th century: *Publishing, Piracy and Politics*, 17; Rose points out that it was a system of regulation and not property: *Authors and Owners*, 15.

[32]George Unwin, *The Gilds and Companies of London* (1908), 261, albeit the difference was really only one of degree: Patterson, *Copyright in Historical Perspective*, 30–1. This position arose because the crown was interested in censorship, rather than giving the stationers greater control of the market: Rose, *Authors and Owners*, 12.

[33]Cavendish, Graves {S17}.

[34]The income generated from the English stock crashed following the loss of the almanac monopoly in *Stationers' Company v Carnan* (1775) 2 Black 1004 (96 ER 590): Feather, *Publishing, Piracy and Politics*, 95.

[35]As the court had before: *Tonson v Collins* (1761) 1 Black W 301 at 304–5 (96 ER 169 at 170–1), submissions of Wedderburn; *Tonson v Collins* (1762) 1 Black W 321 at 326–7 (96 ER 180 at 182). Submission of Blackstone, and the comment by Lord Mansfield: *Tonson v Collins* (1762) 1 Black W 322 at 329 (96 ER 180 at 183); *Millar v Taylor* (1769), 4 Burr 2303 at 2311–15, 2346–7 (98 ER 201 at 206–7, 225); *Donaldson v Beckett* (1774).

[36]Who actively sought the decrees: Patterson, *Copyright in Historical Perspective*, 120.

[37]Albeit these were largely for the purpose of censorship: Patterson, *Copyright in Historical Perspective*, ch. 6.

[38]In *Donaldson v Beckett* (1774) the appellants submitted that the star chamber was a criminal court so could not confer civil rights. While a good argument, this was not picked up before the Commons; the star chamber was just a judicial division of the privy council and so these are similar in nature (as to constitution, Sir William Holdsworth, *A History of English Law* (1938), i. 496–7).

[39]Star Chamber Decrees 1566, 1586, 1637: Edward Arber, *A Transcript of the Registers of the Company of Stationers of London, 1557–1640* (5 vols, 1875–94), i, 322; ii, 807; iv, 528. The incredible language of Yates J in *Millar v Taylor* (1769), 4 Burr 2303 at 2373 (98 ER 201 at 239) – 'despotic' prince (Henry VIII) and his 'bigoted' daughter (Mary) were not used before the House. As to the earlier system, Patterson, *Copyright in Historical Perspective*, 23.

[40]This view is still reflected: Feather, *Publishing, Piracy and Politics*, 11; and it appears to be the contemporary view: Ian Gadd, 'The Stationers' Company in England Before 1710', in *Research Handbook on the History of Copyright Law*, ed. Isabella Alexander and H. Tomás Gómez-Arostegui (Cheltenham, 2016), 83–4; Blayney, *The Stationers' Company and the Printers of London*, 170–2.

[41]This argument had been run by Thurlow before: *Tonson v Collins* (1761) 1 Black W 301 at 308–9 (96 ER 169 at 172).

[42]Cavendish, Feilde {S281 and 95}.

[43]He does not go into the fact that these were largely enacted to censor the press (that is, stopping things being printed rather than facilitating who prints them). As to censorship, Patterson, *Copyright in Historical Perspective*, ch. 6.

ordinances of the Commonwealth[44] to the various Licensing Acts,[45] which were enacted following the Restoration,[46] and to the final act lapsing in 1694.[47] While it was not explained during the passage of the Bookseller's Bill, the Licensing Act had been far from a dead letter. There had been as many as 19 prosecutions for unlicensed printing during the final six years before it lapsed.[48] Under this statute, the Bill's opponents admitted,[49] something property-like had been traded; nevertheless it was asserted upon the Act lapsing that the 'property vanished' and the 'copyright ceased'.[50] There was no discussion, however, of the nature of what might be called 'stationer's copyright',[51] that is, the licences to print granted by the Stationers' Company[52] which were registered with the clerk of the company.[53]

In the decade following the lapse, there were repeated attempts to resurrect some form of printing regulation,[54] with the Stationers and Booksellers petitioning

[44]A time when the Booksellers struggled as the regulation was not in their favour, albeit the system they had created largely survived the civil war: Feather, *A History of British Publishing*, 45.

[45]Ordinances 1647 (an Ordinance against Unlicensed or Scandalous Pamphlets, and the Better Regulating of Printing), 1649 (an Act against Unlicensed and Scandalous Books and Pamphlets, and for Better Regulating of Printing): *Acts and Ordinances of the Interregnum, 1642–1660*, ed. C.H. Firth and R.S. Rait (3 vols, 1911), i, 184, 1021; ii, 245. The Licensing of the Press Act 1662 (13 & 14 Chas. II. c. 33) adopted the 1637 decree with some variations, including a role for a licensor.

[46]Largely for political censorship and not religious reasons: James Walker, 'The Censorship of the Press During the Reign of Charles II', *History*, xxxv (1950), 219.

[47]Administration of Intestates' Estates Act 1685 (1 Jas. II, c. 17), s. 15. This act revived numerous earlier acts and it lapsed at the end of the next parliamentary session seven years after 20 June 1685 (so it ended 14 Mar. 1693).

[48]This is based on the thesis of P.A. Hamburger, 'The Development of the Law of Seditious Libel and the Control of the Press', *Stanford Law Review*, xxxvii (1985), 690, 714–17, that the trials at the Old Bailey purporting to be 'seditious libel' were in fact for unlicensed printing. Accordingly, at least some of the following 13 were convicted for this offence: John Pendergrass (3 July 1689), Francis West (9 Oct. 1689), John Lowthorp (3 Sept. 1690), John Evers (27 May 1691), Thomas Ross (8 July and 9 Sept. 1691), John Redman (9 Sept. 1691), Thomas Wyllan (7 Dec. 1692), Frances Salesbury (26 Apr. 1693), Bridget Laytus (31 May 1693), John Ludlum (13 July 1693), Hugh Hambleton (13 July 1693), Francis West (12 Oct. 1693), John Dyer (6 Dec. 1693), and J–D (3 Apr. 1695). There were also acquittals: Leonard Po-Jenner and Attbut Remmington (31 May 1693), Alexander Milbourne (31 May 1693), Paul Gervisset (13 July 1693), John Skidmore (21 Feb. 1694), and John Hall (18 Apr. 1684). All details are taken from the *Proceedings of the Old Bailey, 1674–1913* (available at: https://www.oldbaileyonline.org). Lois Schwoerer, 'Liberty of the Press and Public Opinion 1660–95', in *Liberty Secured? Britain Before and After 1688*, ed. J.R. Jones (Stanford, CA, 1992), 229, suggests there were 17 trials under the Acts, but it is not clear how this figure was reached. There were also two similar records for 'seditious libel' after the Acts lapsed – David Edwards (8 July 1696) and Thomas Moore (24 May 1699) – which means that the figure for unlicensed printing prosecutions in the earlier period must remain speculative.

[49]By the London Stallholders.

[50]Part IV, *Farther Strictures*; London Stallholders' Petition {4–5}.

[51]Patterson, *Copyright in Historical Perspective*, ch. 4; it was more complicated than this, however, as at one point there was a printer's right for the craftsman who actually printed the work and the right in the copy for the booksellers: Patterson, 49–51.

[52]Patterson, *Copyright in Historical Perspective*, 55.

[53]Order of 27 Sept. 1622: Court Book C, f. 74: *The Records of the Stationers' Company 1554–1920* (1986), reel 56; *Literary Print Culture* (Adam Matthew, 2017), TSC/1/B/01/01, f. 74. This was required by law for the first time by the decree of 1637, article 33; indeed, for many types of work the entry on the register was the only way to prove ownership: Feather, *Publishing, Piracy and Politics*, 26–7 (but it did not *confer* ownership).

[54]Deazley, *On the Origin of the Right to Copy*, ch. 1; this is mentioned in *Millar v Taylor* (1769), 4 Burr 2303 at 2317 (98 ER 201 at 209).

parliament.[55] Over 70 years later,[56] the parties could only explain this activity by relying on the *Journal*, which records little more than the prayer and a few additional details.[57] The relevance of these petitions, as with so much, depended on one's point of view. The promoters suggested that petitioning parliament evidenced how forcible the reasons must have been as the expense was so great;[58] whereas the opponents said it proved the absence of any common law right,[59] or as it was put by Dalrymple 'they came to Parliament knowing they had none'.[60] The opponents took it further, saying that from that time to the spate of court cases decades later, the London Booksellers never claimed a common law right.[61] While two other parliamentarians explored the pre-Statute of Anne history they added little to this superficial summary.[62] One was Dalrymple's leader before the house of lords in *Donaldson*, Edward Thurlow the attorney-general, and the other was the Bill's sponsor Paul Feilde.[63] Thurlow said that any common law rights were 'pure phantoms' at this time, as the monopoly was reliant upon the regulations and ordinances of the parliament which were transcribed into the Stationers' own by-laws.[64] It was upon the statute itself where the narrated history turned.

The Statute of Anne – Pre-Existing Right

At one level the argument of the opponents was straightforward: the Statute of Anne states for old books 'the sole Right and Liberty of Printing such Book and Books for the Term of One and twenty Years, to Commence from the said Tenth Day of April, and no longer'.[65] The final two words, they emphasised, showed there was a maximum term.[66] Conversely, while the origins of any common law right were barely considered by the parties or the House, the issue of whether the Statute of Anne preserved a right was hotly contested.[67] It had been an act for the Booksellers despite its grand

[55] Cavendish, Dunning {S15}; Dalrymple {249}; Part IV, Case Observations {2}; *Farther Strictures*; London Stallholders' Petition {5}; Donaldson's Lords Petition {3}; Feather, *Publishing, Piracy and Politics*, 50–63; Rose, *Authors and Owners*, 34–41.

[56] There is a detailed discussion of these bills in Deazley, *On the Origin of the Right to Copy*, 7–29; for a list of the Bills see Cavendish {248}.

[57] In the histories recorded before the court this period was often brushed over: *Tonson v Collins* (1761) 1 Black W 301 and 305 (96 ER 169 at 171), submissions of Wedderburn.

[58] Part IV, General Observations/Hints {MC13}; also see John Brewer, *The Sinews of Power: War, Money and the English State 1688–1783* (Cambridge, MA, 1990), 256–7.

[59] London Stallholders' Petition {5}.

[60] Cavendish, Dalrymple {248}.

[61] London Stallholders' Petition {5}.

[62] Lord Folkestone did mention them in passing: Cavendish, Folkestone {87–8}; Folkestone's Diary, 16 May.

[63] Cavendish, Feilde {95–6}.

[64] Cavendish, Thurlow {S5}; also see Part IV, Glasgow Memorialists {13}.

[65] Copyright Act 1709, s. 1.

[66] See further, *Farther Strictures*.

[67] In Part IV, Further Remarks {1; Preamble, Remark}; it was queried why the preamble to the Bill referred to the original 21-year term in the Statute of Anne if the common law right was separate.

title[68] of encouraging learning,[69] and so it is not surprising they argued that section 9[70] preserved a common law right:[71]

> Provided, That nothing in this Act contained shall extend, or be construed to extend, either to Prejudice or Confirm any Right that the said Universities, or any of them, or any Person or Persons have, or claim to have, to the Printing or Reprinting any Book or Copy already Printed, or hereafter to be Printed.

Thus, it applied to *any* person with rights,[72] and so, the London Booksellers argued, the Statute of Anne[73] had expressly saved pre-existing rights.[74] The opponents, on the other hand, asserted no rights could have survived beyond the Statute of Anne,[75] or alternatively it did not matter whether there was a common law right in 1710 or not, rather what was relevant was whether the right was believed to exist later when any 'lost' purchases were made.[76]

Stepping back from the arguments of the parties for a moment. If there had been a common law right it might be asked: why was the Statute of Anne enacted?[77] The answer is straightforward: the Act provides *statutory* remedies and *statutory* offences.[78] Under the Statute, a person who unlawfully printed books would have to forfeit the book to the proprietor and also pay 1*d*. for every individual sheet found in the printer's possession.[79] This means the proprietor of copyright could, if he wished, resell a forfeited book despite

[68]That the title changed from 'securing' to 'vesting' during the passage of the Bill might suggest against a pre-existing right. This was argued by Murphy in *Millar v Taylor* (1769) 4 Burr 2303 at 2332, 2334 (98 ER 201 at 217, 218) but not before the House (it was dismissed by the court); it was, however, accepted by the court of session in *Hinton v Donaldson* (1773) *Boswell's Report* 36, Lord President.

[69]Feather, *A History of British Publishing*, 67; Feather, *Publishing, Piracy and Politics*, 63 (continued business practices which had developed over the previous 150 years); Patterson, *Copyright in Historical Perspective*, 143 (he pointed out the 'author' is mentioned only once in the whole statute in s. 11 – other than in the title – and calls it a statute for 'trade regulation' at 150); Rose, *Authors and Owners*, 4 (it was a legislative extension of long-standing regulatory practice); and it was also noted at the time: *Hinton v Donaldson* (1773) *Boswell's Report* 35, Lord President; also see *Millar v Taylor* (1769) 4 Burr 2303 at 2350 (98 ER 201 at 227).

[70]Indeed, Patterson, *Copyright in Historical Perspective*, ch. 4, argues that the 'stationers' copyright' was protecting the same thing as the Statute of Anne: 43 (or was it a codification? See Patterson, 146).

[71]It was suggested in *Millar v Taylor* (1769) 4 Burr 2303 at 2352 (98 ER 201 at 227), Aston J that this was not needed to maintain the common law right.

[72]While the side note for section 9 now refers only to the rights of the universities, these were editorially added and are not on the Ingrossment itself (that is, the actual Act of Parliament).

[73]The Statute of Monopolies also excluded printing from its remit (s. 10) but this never seemed to get the same weight.

[74]Booksellers' Case {1}; this followed the argument of Ashton J in *Millar v Taylor* (1769), 4 Burr 2303 at 2351 (98 ER 201 at 227); he rejected the suggestion it was to preserve printing patents; cf. Patterson, *Copyright in Historical Perspective*, 149, who points to the Licensing of the Press Act 1662 (13 & 14 Chas. II, c. 33), s. 18 to suggest it must be referring to such patents.

[75]Further Remarks {1–2; Remark}.

[76]Cavendish, Dunning {S13}.

[77]A question still asked: Abrams, 'The Persistent Myth of Perpetual Common Law Copyright', 13.

[78]A point made by Lord Mansfield in *Tonson v Collins* (1762) 1 Black W 321 at 330 (96 ER 180 at 184).

[79]Copyright Act 1709, s. 1.

paying nothing to produce it.[80] For instance, a book with 240 pages[81] would lead to £1 damages per book,[82] and so 300 copies of the book would result in an award of £300,[83] this being shared between the crown and the informer (usually the proprietor).[84] An infringing printer might therefore be liable to pay a moderate penalty as well as forfeiting the infringing books themselves.[85]

Notwithstanding what appears to be a reasonable sanction, in his evidence before the petition committee, William Johnston stated that the statutory remedies were not worth seeking compared to those granted in chancery.[86] The most common remedy sought was an injunction or disgorgements of profits.[87] The former might also be obtained as a matter of course where the defendant did not respond in a timely matter, and would last until there was a 'full and perfect' answer.[88] So it might only take a few days from discovering the infringement to getting a remedy. Even where an answer was filed by the defendant it was still possible to seek an injunction on the merits, which would usually be granted.[89] If an injunction could be obtained quickly there would be little need to seek a disgorgement of profits (or damages) as the activity would not have been carried out long enough to generate a worthwhile claim.[90] The effectiveness of chancery remedies meant, in turn, that there was no incentive to record the publication of books in the Stationers' Company register.[91] The counter-petitioners, on the other hand, said it was clear to the House in 1710 that the Statute of Anne was creating a new right.[92] They pointed to the conference between the Lords and Commons[93] which took place on 5 April 1710 and, in particular, what was recorded in the *Journals*.[94] The conference arose because the house of lords disagreed with

[80]This was mentioned by Cavendish, Murphy {259}.

[81]It was not clear how sheets were measured. Was it that in a book each page (not side of the page) counted as one, or was it each printed sheet? The assumption here is that it was each page.

[82]There being 240 pence in the pound.

[83]This would be about £311 18*s*. in 1774 (and £40,120 now).

[84]This became the origin of statutory damages in the US Copyright Act 1790 (1 Stat 124), s. 2; and now 17 US Code §504(c).

[85]The deterrent effect of statutory damages is evident from the jurisprudence in the United States and with the issues that have arisen with conversion damages.

[86]Part IV, Petition Committee Report, {590, c. i, ii}.

[87]See generally, H. Tomás Gómez-Arostegui, 'Equitable Infringement Remedies before 1800', in *Research Handbook on the History of Copyright Law*, ed. Isabella Alexander and H. Tomás Gómez-Arostegui (Cheltenham, 2016), 195. A disgorgement was probably first ordered in *Gay v Walker* (1729): TNA, C 12/1817/67; Dealzey, *On the Origin of the Right to Copy*, 62–9.

[88]H. Tomás Gómez-Arostegui, 'What History Teaches us About Copyright Injunctions and the Inadequate-Remedy-at-Law Requirement', *Southern California Law Review*, lxxxi (2008), 1228–9; Gómez-Arostegui, 'Equitable Infringement Remedies', 197–207.

[89]Gómez-Arostegui, 'What History Teaches us', 1236–7; Deazley, *On the Origin of the Right to Copy*, 61–2.

[90]Gómez-Arostegui, 'Equitable Infringement Remedies', 225; albeit if the injunction was after the print run then the books would exist and statutory damages would have been available.

[91]As required by Copyright Act 1709, s 2.

[92]Case Observations {1}.

[93]As to such conferences, Josef Redlich, *The Procedure of the House of Commons: A Study of its History and Present Form*, trans. A.E. Steinthal (3 vols, 1908), i, 35.

[94]The only entry which could possibly be sufficient is on 5 Apr. 1710: *CJ*, xvi, 395.

what became section 4, which aimed to restrict the excessive price of books.[95] The Lords put forward two objections but only one was relied upon in 1774:

> Because Authors, and Booksellers having the sole Property of Copies of printed Books vested in them by this Bill, the Commons think it reasonable that some Provision should be made, that they do not set an extravagant Price on useful Books.

The Opponents argued the word 'vested' indicates that the right could not have existed beforehand.[96] It is not clear what was the basis of this claim. The term vested had been used in earlier and even in contemporary statutes to refer to the vesting of property after its transfer and assignment, and only existent property can be transferred.[97] This claim was not explored in depth. Conversely a more straightforward argument why was put by Thurlow: the Statute of Anne was founded on 'the petitioners expressly stating to the House ... [that] every man had thought proper, at his own pleasure, to print the works of every other man ... whatever'.[98] As before, the view from the London Booksellers was the right still existed, so their narrative jumped over the next couple of decades as time under the Statute of Anne ran.

Samuel Buckley's Act

The history restarts with Samuel Buckley. Both George Johnstone and Lord Beauchamp each referred to the term he was granted for *Thuanus*,[99] and indicated that parliament might be willing to help in similar *individual* cases.[100] While Beachamp suggested the term was for his 'extraordinary merit', it appears it was actually a grant for more mundane reasons. *Thuanus* was a Latin text and Buckley[101] believed that as such it fell outside the Statute of Anne, so he successfully petitioned parliament for a term of years[102] leading to the Printing

[95] This was to address the ineffective nature of the Printers and Binders Act 1533 (25 Hen. VIII, c. 15), s. 4 which had attempted to restrict excessive prices of books; Deazley, *On the Origin of the Right to Copy*, 27 n. 110, ignored this act when he suggested the origin of the clause was *The Case of the Free Workmen-Printers, Relating to the Bill of Preventing the Licentiouness of the Press*, Lincoln's Inn, MS 102, f. 307 (which merely mentions the high prices of books).

[96] Case Observations {1}; Cavendish, Murphy {257}; the same argument had been put in *Millar v Taylor* (1769) 4 Burr 2303 at 2332 (98 ER 201 at 217) and *Donaldson v Beckett* (1774); *Cobbett's Parl. Hist.*, xvii, col. 960 (it was rejected by Willes J both times).

[97] A particularly famous example is the Attainer of the Regicides Act 1660 (12 Chas. II, c. 30), s. 1; and one contemporary with the Statute of Anne is the Fortifications Act 1708 (7 Anne, c. 26), s. 2; also see comment in *Hinton v Donaldson* (1773) *Boswell's Report* (p. 12, Lord Monboddo and p. 30, Lord Coalston).

[98] Cavendish, Thurlow {S5}.

[99] Deazley, *On the Origin of the Right to Copy*, 87–8, 108, gives great weight to Buckley's Act. As to private Acts inspiring broader legislative developments, Fredrick Clifford, *A History of Private Bill Legislation* (2 vols, 1968), i, 266*–266**; Phillip Johnson, *Privatised Law Reform: A History of Patent Law Through Private Legislation, 1620–1907* (2017), 2–3.

[100] Cavendish, Johnstone {80}, Beauchamp {123–4}; a similar point made by Dunning: Cavendish, Dunning {S14}.

[101] Samuel Buckley, *Reasons humbly offered to the Lords Spiritual and Tempers in Parliament assembled, for granting to S Buckley such privilege for Thuanus in Latin as is already granted to every British Subject who is possessed of the Copy of any Book* (1733) (ESTC: T46461), 4.

[102] *CJ*, xxii, 242 (18 Feb. 1733 (OS)).

of Thuanus' Histories Act 1733,[103] which gave him a 14-year term.[104] Yet, as Thurlow said, there is a clear difference between an individual suffering harm and the whole trade doing so.[105] Indeed, in *Donaldson v Beckett*, Buckley's Act was used to suggest that because he was given 14 years then the time under the Statute of Anne must also have been so limited,[106] emphasising once more how the Commons debates were sitting on the back of the historical arguments made before the courts.

The 1730s

The Statute of Anne originally provided a term of 14 years (which could be renewed to 28 years) for new books and 21 years for books which had already been printed (old books).[107] The computation of the term for old books began on 10 April 1710 and expired on 9 April 1731.[108] In 1710, the Booksellers had simply not thought sufficiently about the temporal limitations under the Statute of Anne,[109] and so when the time expired they sought further relief.[110] Accordingly, in 1774 much was made of booksellers' petitions in the 1730s seeking further protection.[111] The first petition was presented in 1734, which led to the failed Booksellers' Bill of 1735,[112] and the second was presented in 1736,[113] with the subsequent bill failing in 1737.[114] In both cases, the Bills passed the house of commons yet were rejected in the Lords.[115] Albeit by the 1770s the reasons suggested for failure differed: William Joliffe, for instance, said that the plea of the booksellers was refused because the monopoly had already gone on too long;[116] whereas others said it failed for reasons other

[103] 7 Geo. II, c. 24.

[104] The Statute of Anne did not apply to Latin and other foreign language works printed outside the United Kingdom (Copyright Act 1709, s. 7: 'Provided, That nothing in this Act contained do extend, or shall be construed to extend, to Prohibit the Importation, Vending, or Selling of any Books in Greek, Latin, or any other Foreign Language Printed beyond the Seas; Anything in this Act contained to the contrary notwithstanding.'), so the Act could have been construed to preclude protection only for a Latin work printed outside Britain, and not those published domestically.

[105] Cavendish, Thurlow {S2–3}.

[106] *Donaldson v Beckett* (1774).

[107] Copyright Act 1709, s. 1. The reason for granting a monopoly in old books is difficult to understand but it was clearly a compromise settled upon by booksellers: Patterson, *Copyright in Historical Perspective*, 148.

[108] Or maybe the day later: *Millar v Taylor* (1769), 4 Burr 2303 at 2324 (98 ER 201 at 213).

[109] Feather, *A History of British Publishing*, 55.

[110] And in 1735, one of the provisions simply extended the protection for old books by a further 21 years: Act for the Better Encouragement of Learning: Parliamentary Archives, HL/PO/JO/10/2/38, cl. 1.

[111] It is suggested on more than one occasion (Cavendish, Dalrymple {249}; *Farther Strictures*; London Stallholders' Petition) that there were petitions in 1734, 1735 and 1736. It is not clear what the 1735 petition refers to unless there was double counting for 3 Mar. 1734 (O/C) which was 3 Mar. 1735 (N/C).

[112] Deazley, *On the Origin of the Right to Copy*, 94–103 (for more details, 95 n. 39); Rose, *Authors and Owners*, 58–61. The Bill promoted by the engravers passed: Engraving Copyright Act 1734 (8 Geo. II, c. 13).

[113] Cavendish, Dalrymple {249}; *CJ*, xxii, 800 (15 Mar. 1736).

[114] Part IV, London Stallholders' Petition; Folkestone seems to think that it was the 14 years for new books which was expiring: Folkestone's Diary, 16 May; Cavendish {97}; Booksellers' Bill 1737: Parliamentary Archives, HL/PO/JO/10/2/38); Bill Against Importing Books 1738: HL/PO/JO/10/2/39.

[115] The 1735 bill's second reading never progressed: *LJ*, xxiv, 550 (12 May), and the 1737 bill was rejected by a long deferral of committee: *LJ*, xxv, 111 (10 May).

[116] Cavendish, Joliffee {130}.

than the merit of the Bill,[117] such as the duty on paper.[118] So those in favour said the two bills of the 1730s should have been passed back then and so the Bill should pass now.[119] In fact, there were further public bills in 1738[120] and 1739,[121] the last of which was enacted as the Importation Act 1738.[122] This prevented the importation of books from abroad,[123] but these two public bills were not mentioned in 1774. It is unclear why.

The 1737 bill provided further ammunition to the opponents of the 1774 bill, who pointed to a proposed clause:[124]

> And forasmuch as the true Worth of Books and Writings is, in many Cases, not found out till a considerable Time after the Publication thereof, and Authors, who are in Necessity, may often be tempted absolutely to sell and alienate the Right, which they will hereby have to the original Copies of the Books which they have composed, before the Value thereof is known, and may thereby put it out of their own Power to alter and correct their Compositions, upon mature Judgement and Reflection; Therefore, be it enacted by the Authority aforesaid, That from and after the said Twenty fourth Day of June, One thousand seven hundred and thirty seven, no Author shall have the power to sell, alienate, assign or transfer, except by his last Will and Testament, the Right vested in him to the original Copy of any Book, Pamphlet, or Writing, to any Person or Persons whatsoever, for any longer Time than Ten Years.

This would have limited the period for which an author could alienate their copyright. The opponents postulated that such a clause was in the true interests of an author,[125] and additionally it was said (erroneously) that the 1737 bill only asked for a further seven years.[126] Not only do these provisions suggest against a common law right, but, as the opponents pointed out, the earlier bill would have granted a shorter term of protection than the 21 years[127] being requested in 1774.[128] But beyond pure policy what did lodging these petitions and the earlier bills demonstrate? If there was a common law right, it was said, why did the Booksellers desperately petition parliament for new relief?[129] Lord Folkestone emphasised that only when seeking a statutory solution failed did the Booksellers say 'what

[117]Cavendish, Dunning {S15}.

[118]Cavendish, Murphy {257–8}; the Bill allowed the universities to reclaim duty on foreign paper.

[119]Cavendish, Dunning {S16}.

[120]This was based on a petition: *CJ*, xxiii, 158 (24 Apr. 1738).

[121]Bill Order: *CJ*, xxiii, 320 (6 Apr. 1739).

[122](12 Geo. II, c. 36).

[123]Importation Act 1738, s. 1.

[124]Booksellers' Bill 1737: Parliamentary Archives, HL/PO/JO/10/2/38. A print version is available as An Act for the Encouragement of Learning (Draft), London (1737), *Primary Sources on Copyright (1450–1900)*, ed. Lionel Bently and Martin Kretschmer (www.copyrighthistory.org), cl. 13.

[125]Cavendish, Murphy {51}.

[126]For new works it asked for the author's life plus 11 years, or at least 21 years from death if the author died within ten years of publication: Booksellers' Bill 1737: HL/PO/JO/10/2/38, cl. 1. It is not clear where seven years came from.

[127]Cavendish, Dalrymple {249}.

[128]Ultimately, the Bill passed the Commons with it being 14 years.

[129]A point made in *Donaldson v Beckett* (1774) *Cobbett's Parl. Hist.*, xvii, col. 991, Gould J.

you will not give us, we have at common law already'.[130] It may of course have been the other way around: success in court meant parliament was no longer the only or best recourse.[131] The Booksellers sidestepped this difficulty and highlighted that petitioning and pursuing private bills was so expensive[132] that a very serious harm must have been contemplated.[133] In reality the 1730s provided a mixed picture and one which was not helped by the court cases that followed during the 'Battle of the Booksellers'.

The Battle of the Booksellers

Scholars have now identified numerous attempts to bring common law infringement cases during the 1750s,[134] and before,[135] but in the house of commons in 1774 only a few were mentioned. Those against the Bill emphasised the position in Scotland where the court of sessions had held in *Midwinter v Hamilton*[136] that no remedies were available beyond those set out in the Statute of Anne. On appeal to the house of lords, there had been an attempt to rely on the common law right,[137] but the opportunity to determine it on that basis was declined.[138] Indeed, *Midwinter* led the English Booksellers to avoid litigation north of the border and concentrate on actions before English courts.[139] What is more surprising is nobody in the Commons expressly referred to *Hinton v Donaldson*,[140] which had held there was no common law copyright in Scotland; the absence of the right was simply stated. Whether Scotland was treated differently will be explored below, but as far as the parliamentarians were concerned the situation in England dominated the debate. Edward Thurlow referred to *Horne v Baker*,[141] the first (largely unreported) case decided

[130] Folkestone's Diary, 16 May.

[131] Deazley, *On the Origin of the Right to Copy*, pp. xxv, 111–12, suggests that victory in *Baller v Watson* (1737) might have led the Booksellers to tactically change direction.

[132] For an introduction to the expense, Johnson, *Privatised Law Reform*, 27–9; Sheila Lambert, *Bills and Acts: Legislative Procedure in Eighteenth-Century England* (Cambridge, 1971), 37–8; Brewer, *Sinews of Power*, 236.

[133] General Observations/Hints {MC13}.

[134] H. Tomás Gómez-Arostegui, *Register of Copyright Infringement Suits and Actions from c. 1560 to 1800* (2009); Deazley, *On the Origin of the Right to Copy*, 122–32.

[135] Deazley, *On the Origin of the Right to Copy*, ch. 3, goes back much earlier (see in particular 59–61).

[136] (1748) Kames 158; *Millar v Kincaid* (1751) 1 Pat App 488.

[137] Deazley, *On the Origin of the Right to Copy*, 130; Hector MacQueen, 'The War of the Booksellers: Natural Law, Equity, and Literary Property in Eighteenth-Century Scotland', *Journal of Legal History*, xxxv (2014), 231; MacQueen, 'Literary Property in Scotland in the Eighteenth and Nineteenth Centuries', in *Research Handbook on the History of Copyright Law*, ed. Isabella Alexander and H. Tomás Gómez-Arostegui (Cheltenham, 2016), 119; Rose, *Authors and Owners*, 67. It was suggested there was evidence of a belief in 1748: Cavendish, Feilde {S280}, Thurlow {S4}.

[138] Part IV, The Five Letters {20}.

[139] Warren McDougall, 'Copyright Litigation in the Court of Session, 1738–1749, and the Rise of the Scottish Book Trade', *Edinburgh Bibliographical Society Transactions*, v (1971–87), 9.

[140] (1773) Mor 8307; 5 Br Supp 508; 5 Pat 505; James Boswell, *The Decisions of the Court of Session upon the Question of Literary Property in the Cause of John Hinton of London, Bookseller, against Alexander Donaldson and John Wood, Booksellers in Edinburgh and James Meurose, Bookseller in Kilmarnock* (Edinburgh, 1774); Hector MacQueen, 'Intellectual Property and the Common Law in Scotland', in *The Common Law of Intellectual Property: Essays in Honour of Professor David Vaver*, ed. Catherine Ng, Lionel Bently and Giuseppina D'Agostino (2010), 35–8.; MacQueen, 'The War of the Booksellers', 243–57.

[141] (1710).

under the Statute of Anne, pointing out that in that case no reference was made to the common law right.[142] It was not until over 40 years later in *Tonson v Walker*[143] that the existence of a common law right was first argued in a reported case,[144] and even that was not printed at the time. It is not surprising that Arthur Murphy, the junior counsel against the Bill,[145] cited only a few cases: those being *Motte v Faulkner,*[146] *Tonson v Walker* and *Macklin v Richardson*.[147]

In the absence of any jurisprudence, the opponents submitted that nobody could have believed there was a common law right which existed before *Millar v Taylor,*[148] and it seems that the Booksellers' own witness, William Johnston, had never heard of such a right before actions started being brought before the courts.[149] He further admitted in evidence[150] that *Millar* was the first time the common law courts had properly considered the issue,[151] as previously suits had been brought before the courts of chancery. This jurisdiction was elected, he said, because it was easier to commence a suit than pursue an action at law,[152] and injunctions could usually be obtained quickly. As already mentioned, few involved in the Booksellers' Bill referred to named (and so reported) cases; rather there were allusions to 'several injunctions' being granted.[153] While the House did briefly consider the precedential value of these injunctions,[154] probably spurred by Lord Mansfield's comment in *Millar*, in the end little was made of it.[155]

The first case identified in the Commons in which a common law right was claimed was *Tonson v Collins*,[156] but it was said to be collusively brought.[157] Even though the case was discontinued, it set the shape of the literary property debate,[158] right up to the Booksellers'

[142]Cavendish, Thurlow {S5–6}.

[143](1752) 3 Swans 672 (36 ER 1017); Cavendish, Thurlow {S6}.

[144]Swanston usually identified the source of the manuscript but did not do so for *Tonson v Walker.* It is unclear therefore whether Swanston's report is the same one used by the parties.

[145]Cavendish, Murphy {258–9}.

[146]TNA, C 11/2249/4.

[147](1770) Amb 694 (27 ER 451).

[148]London Stallholders' Petition {5}; Committee Evidence Observations {15}.

[149]Committee Evidence Observations {13}.

[150]He said he personally had brought two law suits: Petition Committee Report {589, c. i–ii}.

[151]That is the court of king's bench, common pleas or the exchequer.

[152]Petition Committee Report {589, c. i–ii}.

[153]Booksellers' Case {1}.

[154]Cavendish, Feilde {282}, Thurlow {S3}; *Millar v Taylor* (1769) 4 Burr 2303 (98 ER 201) where Lord Mansfield seems to give them more value.

[155]*Millar v Taylor* (1769) 4 Burr 2303 (98 ER 201); he says that the injunctions granted in those cases were 'equal to any final decree'.

[156](1762) 1 Black W 321 (96 ER 180); Cavendish, Murphy {258}.

[157]Case Observations {2}; Cavendish, Feilde {281–2}; but Thurlow who was asked to advise denied it was: Cavendish, Thurlow {S6}. It was probably agreed that there would be no appeal if Tonson lost: Rose, *Authors and Owners*, 75; or that the plaintiff would pay the defendant's expenses: Augustine Birrell, 'The "Battle of the Booksellers" for Perpetual Copyright', in *Seven Lectures on the Law and History of Copyright in Books* (1899), 110.

[158]Rose, *Authors and Owners*, 78.

Bill. Those for the Booksellers' Bill argued that had this case been finally determined, a majority of the judges would have found in favour of a common law right,[159] but the opponents suggested there was no such certainty,[160] some going further and alleging that *Millar v Taylor* itself became collusive,[161] Taylor being 'practised upon' to discontinue his pursuit of a writ of error to avoid a successful appeal.[162]

There are two very different procedures at work here, with very different tribunals. In *Tonson* it was a reference to the 12 judges, a procedure whereby a trial judge referred a difficult question of law for the opinion of all 12 common law judges.[163] In *Millar* it was for a writ of error heard by the exchequer chamber comprising at least six judges from the justices of common pleas and the barons of the exchequer.[164] The opponents suggested that six of the judges in the exchequer chamber would have been in favour of reversal of *Millar* and two in favour of the common law right never existing.[165] This was of course pure speculation. There were eight judges who could have sat on the appeal,[166] but it is not clear which six would do so.[167] The statements before the House were no more than guesses and, considering the vote in *Donaldson*, the London Booksellers were very optimistic.

The Honorary Monopoly

After the lapse of protection under the Statute of Anne,[168] the London Booksellers continued to buy and sell copyrights in old books and describe books printed by outsiders as

[159] Cavendish, Feilde {S281–2} (based on comments of Lord Mansfield in *Miller v Taylor* (1769) Burr 2408 at 2354 and (98 ER 228 and 257); in this case, before it was dismissed, Mansfield had unusually ordered that it should be heard by the 12 judges. This was probably an attempt to tie the entire judiciary into the finding.

[160] Committee Evidence Observations {2}; Cavendish, Thurlow {S6}.

[161] Case Observations {2}.

[162] Case Observations {2}; Glasgow Memorialists {17}. By this point it had long been the case that the exchequer chamber could hear a writ of error from the kings bench: Error From Queen's Bench Act 1584 (27 Eliz. c. 8) (other appeals from the kings bench still had to go to the house of lords); Holdsworth, *A History of English Law*, i, 244–6.

[163] James Oldham, 'Informal Law-making in England by the Twelve Judges in the Late Eighteenth and Early Nineteenth Century', *Law and History Review*, xxxix (2011), 181.

[164] Queen's Bench Act 1584 (the barons also had to be serjeants and the panel could not include the judges who heard the case below).

[165] Case Observations {2}; Committee Evidence Observations {16–17} (reference is made to Sir John Eardley Wilmot, who was a pusine judge of the kings bench at the time of *Tonson v Collins* (1762) 1 Black W 322 (96 ER 180), but by the time of the Booksellers' Bill was chief justice of common pleas).

[166] Common pleas in 1762 (*Tonson v Collins* 1 Black W 321 (96 ER 180)): Charles Pratt (Lord Camden) CJ; Edward Clive, Henry Bathurst and William Noel (who was replaced by Henry Gould); in 1770 (*Millar v Taylor*): Sir John Wilmot CJ, Joseph Yates (replaced by William Blackstone) and Henry Bathurst and Henry Gould remained; exchequer in both 1762 and 1770: Thomas Parker CB, Sidney Smythe, Richard Adams, George Perrott (who replaced Henry Gould); the king's bench in 1762 comprised Lord Mansfield LCJ, Thomas Denison, Michael Foster and John Wilmot: *Judges of England*, 13, 37, 51, 81, 98, 129–30.

[167] Joseph Yates could not sit on the appeal of *Millar v Taylor* as he had taken part in the original decision, so it would have been seven judges. Yates had moved to common pleas probably because he was distressed that he affected the unanimity of the king's bench: Holdsworth, *A History of English Law*, xii, 482–3.

[168] Graham Pollard, 'The English Market for Printed Books: The Sanders Lectures 1959', *Publishing History*, iv (1978), 27–9.

'piratical'.[169] They supported the exclusivity by forming 'congers'[170] and started to take aggressive action to protect their 'rights' in the late 1740s. The London Stallholders (and others) stated to the house of commons that it all began in 1746 or 1747 when John Osborne, a bookseller of substance,[171] fell out with the other booksellers and began printing copies of books which he did not 'own'. The Booksellers objected, eventually paying him off to quit the business.[172] This incident was not only admitted by the Booksellers but revelled in: they claimed it was quite proper.[173] The nature of the action taken against so-called infringers depended on the person who was being pursued. The poor were deprived of their property without compensation, but those who stood up to them such as Osborne were paid off to leave the trade.[174] These measures suggest (at least at this point) that the Booksellers were uncertain they had a legal right:[175] why pay someone to stop printing if you could spend less doing it through the courts?[176]

The Osborne case appears to have been an isolated incident, however soon afterwards the Booksellers took a more substantial step to protect their monopoly in books[177] by forming what would later be considered a cartel, but which at the time the members called an 'Honorary Property'[178] or 'honorary right'.[179] The exact nature of this right is unclear although it appears that old books were sold alongside books protected by the Statute, and for similar prices.[180] The scheme was formalised on 25 April 1759,[181] and its working was explained in a series of letters,[182] which were eventually presented to parliament.[183] The scheme was intended to prevent the sale of Scottish and Irish books where an edition of

[169] *Farther Strictures*; London Stallholders' Petition {5}; even where printing was lawful, for instance in North America: a point also raised by Slauter, *Who Owns the News?*, 9.

[170] As to the origin of the term, G.D. McEwen, "What is a Conger?": John Dunton and Scottish Booksellers', *Studies in Scottish Literature*, i (1963), 133; Stephen Parks, *John Dunton and the English Book Trade* (1976), 206–10; for a detailed history, Norma Hodgson and Cyprian Blagden, *The Notebook of Thomas Bennet and Henry Clements* (Oxford Bibliographic Society, new ser., vi, 1956), ch. 3.

[171] Goldsmith mistakenly calls him Thomas Osborne: the relevant bookseller was John Osborne of Paternoster Row: Walters, 'The Booksellers in 1759 and 1774', p. 309.

[172] *Farther Strictures*; London Stallholders' Petition {5}; Goldsmith's Hints {18; 2do}; Case Observations {1}; Cavendish, Murphy {258}; in *Farther Strictures* the payment is suggested to be £200.

[173] Cavendish, Mansfield {24–5}.

[174] It is alleged that they pursued under a penal statute, probably the Importation Act 1738 (12 Geo. II, c. 36).

[175] London Stallholders' Petition {5}.

[176] The cost of seeking an injunction would have been less than £100 (for two examples, Gómez-Arostegui 'Equitable Infringement Remedies', 228–34).

[177] They never denied it: Part IV, Remarks on Donaldson's Petition {2}.

[178] Part IV, Donaldson's Petition {11}.

[179] Petition Committee Report {588, c. ii}.

[180] Petition Committee Report {588}; it did not apply to classics.

[181] Letter 26 Apr. 1759: Part IV, The Five Letters; also evidence of Cavendish, Wilkie (witness) {41}. It is suggested that this honorary right was set up before the London Booksellers began issuing writs for common law copyright (Further Remarks {7}), but it is not clear how a suit in chancery would be acceptable without some form of right and there were cases in the 1730s, see Chapter 4: The 1730s.

[182] The same letters were suggested by the Bill's opponents to demonstrate there was no such right existing: Cavendish, Thurlow {S7}.

[183] Part IV, The Five Letters. Three of the five letters had been printed a decade earlier by Donaldson, in *Some Thoughts on the State of Literary Property* (1764) (ESTC: T049411).

the book had already been printed in England.[184] Or as Donaldson put it, 'suppression throughout England of all books whatever printed in Scotland'.[185] The basic idea was to bring proceedings in chancery against any person in England selling these books with agents being sent out to find 'pirates'.[186] While John Dunning argued there was nothing wrong in such a combination,[187] others called it a 'conspiracy' suggesting criminality,[188] or said it was 'impossible' to countenance.[189] One group of opponents even saying that endorsing it would encourage others.[190] In any event, it appears the scheme quickly raised a subscription of £3,150,[191] with only one fifth being initially called.[192] Once created, Donaldson said, it led to 'alarm' spreading throughout the country.[193]

In one of the advocacy papers *for* the Bill, it was accepted that this arrangement did not have any legal foundation but was based on the necessity of supporting the investments made by booksellers.[194] This, the opponent submitted, indicated that the scheme leant against a common law right existing.[195] Earlier, Thurlow had said the combination's lack of legal basis suggested it was not worth the money paid for the copyright, and so, he said, there could not have been any belief in a common law right.[196] Indeed, the Booksellers' counsel, James Mansfield, went as far as to admit the honorary copyright was not protected in law, but by members of the trade agreeing on their honour not to print the book until the first bookseller had had time to recoup his investment.[197] The combination was needed, he claimed, as one bookseller pursing a suit alone would have been destined to fail.[198] The combination was set up (in part at least) to pursue suits before the courts, suggesting they must have believed there was some legal basis for protecting old books.[199] On the other hand, the absence of claims in Ireland, where the common law was the same, it was argued, indicated an absence of belief.[200]

[184]The Five Letters, 23 Apr. and 26 Apr. 1759; Cavendish, Thurlow {S7}; in relation to classics see Chapter 6: Savings and Exclusions.

[185]Donaldson's Petition {9–10}.

[186]The Five Letters, 23 Apr. 1759; Cavendish, Thurlow {S7}.

[187]Cavendish, Dunning {S14}.

[188]Cavendish, Onslow {S20–1}; also see his comments in petition committee, *Public Ledger*, 18 Mar.

[189]Cavendish, Dempster {134}.

[190]*Farther Strictures*.

[191]The Five Letters, 23 Apr. 1759.

[192]The Five Letters, 26 Apr. 1759. This means only £630 was collected: cf. Deazley, *On the Origin of the Right to Copy*, 171.

[193]Donaldson's Petition {10}.

[194]General Observations/Hints {MC13}; Further Remarks {6}.

[195]Further Remarks {1–2; *Second Preamble*}; London Stallholders' Petition {5}.

[196]Cavendish, Thurlow {S7}.

[197]Cavendish, Mansfield {33}; indeed, it might have shown the Booksellers' impotence against the threat: Feather, *A History of British Publishing*, 65.

[198]Cavendish, Mansfield {25}.

[199]Feather suggests it was based on the Importation Act 1738: *A History of British Publishing*, 65; but this would have caught the Irish editions and not those from Scotland.

[200]Glasgow Memorialists {13–14} (mention is also made of Scotland).

The concerted actions of the London Booksellers led to Alexander Donaldson opening a bookshop in St Paul's Churchyard in 1763 to sell his own editions.[201] Soon afterwards he started a lobbying campaign against literary property.[202] He faced suits in chancery and the court of sessions under both the Statute and the common law right.[203] The fact, that Donaldson had defended[204] 11 suits brought by 'over 100' booksellers resulting in 13 injunctions,[205] was used by the Bill's proposers to suggest he knew all along of the common law right. But he claims he won every single suit,[206] while others said he lost some and won others.[207] In any event, the London Booksellers submitted that, had he wanted, Donaldson could have had a decision at law and petitioned the house of lords much sooner.[208] This final remark is quite extraordinary in that it seems to blame Donaldson for allowing the Booksellers to dare to dream and to continue trading in what was found out to be a fictitious property.

Origin of Belief

Edward Thurlow argued that no law book had ever set out the existence of a common law copyright,[209] and so it followed that any belief in it was writ on water. Contrary to his suggestion, the question was expressly addressed in Blackstone's *Commentaries*,[210] first published in 1766:[211]

> Neither with us in England hath there been any[212] direct determination upon the right of authors at the common law. But much may be gathered from the frequent injunctions

[201] Donaldson's Petition {10}. Yet it appears that not all of these suits were for the perpetual right (Cavendish, Onlsow {115}); while the Booksellers' shops were largely around St Paul's the retail trade was often further west: Feather, *A History of British Publishing*, 81.

[202] James Boswell, *The Life of Samuel Johnson*, ed. David Womersley (2008), 231 (20 July 1763); Patterson, *Copyright in Historical Perspective*, 167.

[203] Donaldson's Petition {10}.

[204] Donaldson like his adversaries raised a subscription to help fund his legal fees: Remarks on Donaldson's Petition {2}.

[205] Donaldson's Petition. These were: (1) *Millar v Donaldson* (1763), (2) *Osborne & Others v Donaldson* (1763) 2 Eden 328 (28 ER 924), (3) *Nourse v Donaldson* (1763), (4) *Doddesley v Donaldson* (1769), (5) *Dodsley v Donaldson* (1770), (6) *Becket, Abraham, Rivington & Others v Donaldson* (1771), (7) *Rivington & Others v Donaldson* (1771), (8) *Becket, Caslon & Others v Donaldson* (1771), (9) *Becket, Abraham and Cadell v Donaldson* (1771), (10) *Whiston & Others v Donaldson* (1771), (11) *Stationers v Donaldson* (1772), (12) *Donaldson v Donaldson* (1773), *Donaldson v Beckett* (1772–4): see Gómez-Arostegui, *Register of Copyright Infringement Suits and Actions*.

[206] Cavendish, Johnstone {131–2}.

[207] Cavendish, Onslow {131–2} and {115}; Feilde {132}.

[208] Cavendish, Mansfield {29}.

[209] Cavendish, Thurlow {S4–5}; but note the comments on Scots law specifically against it: Henry Home, Lord Kames (1696–1782), *Principles of Equity* (Kincaid, 1760) (ESTC: T70419), 185; (2nd edn, Millar, 1767) (ESTC: T67126), 265–6.

[210] William Blackstone, *An Analysis of the Laws of England* (6th edn, Oxford, 1771), ch. 26, p. 72 includes 'literary property' as something obtained by occupancy. It was not mentioned in previous editions (5th edn, Oxford, 1762).

[211] William Blackstone, *Commentaries on the Laws of England*, gen. ed. Wilfrid Prest (Oxford, 2016), bk. II, ch. 26, pp. 406–7; Prest Version, 275–6 (footnotes omitted).

[212] Blackstone, *Commentaries on the Laws of England*; in the 4th edn (1770) he said 'final determination' and footnoted *Millar v Taylor*; this was changed following Donaldson (in the 4th edn, but not the 5th and 6th, it mentioned the writ of error; these are all set out in the Prest Version).

> of the court of chancery, prohibiting the invasion of this property: especially where either the injunction have been perpetual, or have related to unpublished manuscripts, or to such antient books, as were not with the statute of queen Anne. Much may also be collected from the several legislative recognitions of copyrights; and from those adjudged cases at common law, wherein the crown hath been considered as invested with certain prerogative copyrights, for, if the crown is capable of an exclusive right in any one book, the subject seems also capable of having the same right in another.

The *Commentaries* was known to the parties and the parliamentarians; indeed, its publication was discussed during the passage of the Bill,[213] with Onslow even suggesting it was the source of the common law.[214] While the book was discussed, it is also apparent that Blackstone was potentially biased,[215] or at least he had been the London Booksellers' counsel in some of the court cases, and so the opponents (such as Thurlow) might simply have dismissed his opinion.[216]

Millar v Taylor

There were clear evidential problems for the London Booksellers. The Glasgow Booksellers (in contrast to others) specifically set out the lawyers who had opined against it: Sir Dudley Ryder, when attorney-general,[217] Alexander Hume Campbell,[218] and William Grant,[219] when lord advocate.[220] There was no list of those who had opined in favour of the right, although some MPs had been counsel in the matter so may have had such a view. The existence of the right, and the argument before the court in *Millar v Taylor*, have been explored extensively by commentators; however, the debate before the house of commons was much more straightforward than any more recent exploration. Before 1769,[221] as Lord Folkestone put it, there was not 'the authority of a single Lawyer, or the decision of any one Court to continuance it'.[222] Yet once Lord Mansfield acknowledged the right in *Millar* it was easy for the London Booksellers to embrace his 'ingenious and learned argument' and doing so 'without attempting to fathom the depth of the metaphysical subtleties, they had no difficulty in perceiving the force, the beauty and the truth of the argument'.[223]

[213] Cavendish, Burke {54}, Johnstone {78}, Feilde {97–8, 118}.

[214] Cavendish, Onslow {S22–3} (but he was not referring to copyright specifically).

[215] A similar allegation was made against Thurlow and Mansfield: Folkestone's Diary, 16 May.

[216] Deazley, *On the Origin of the Right to Copy*, 150, also seems to treat his *Commentaries* as similar to a pamphlet written by those connected with the various cases before the courts.

[217] Later chief justice of the king's bench (appointed 2 May 1754).

[218] As noted by the Memorialists, later lord clerk register (the second most senior judge in the court of sessions); George Brunton and David Haig, *An Historical Account of the Senators of the College of Justice in MDXXXII* (Edinburgh, 1832), xxviii.

[219] As noted by the Memorialists, appointed to the court of sessions, as Lord Prestongrange, 4 Nov. 1754; they also noted that his view was different in private (against the right) than in public.

[220] Glasgow Memorialists {5}.

[221] Cavendish, Folkestone {88}; Folkestone's Diary, 16 May.

[222] Folkestone's Diary, 16 Mar.; Cavendish, Folkestone {88}; save Blackstone's *Commentaries* as discussed above.

[223] General Observations/Hints {MC13}.

Millar was the first common law case recognising the right: it was decisive. The advocates of the Bill argued it 'confirmed'[224] the existence of a common law right and its opponents conceded (at best) that reliance on a common law right would have arisen from that date.[225] William Johnston merely said *Millar* removed any doubt he might have had regarding the common law right.[226] And this seems to have been accepted by some opponents: Lord Folkestone, before his position became more entrenched against the London Booksellers, said they 'clearly are entitled to relief' after that judgment, albeit he was less clear about what that relief should be.[227] Yet the counter-petitioners would not even accept this view. The London Stallholders, while admitting that the London Booksellers did buy and sell books during the period 1769–74, claimed this was despite knowledge that the right was contested: so it would have been more appropriate to see them as speculators and not investors.[228]

Donaldson v Beckett

While the London Booksellers argued that anything done by Donaldson after *Millar* in 1769 was undertaken at his own peril,[229] his fellow counter-petitioners claimed they never had any doubt he would ultimately succeed. So they carried on printing regardless. Conversely, and unsurprisingly, the Bill's promoters said they believed that when the question was put to their Lordships they would prevail,[230] with John Dunning, previously counsel for Beckett, saying as much in the House.[231] The action against Alexander Donaldson was brought by Thomas Beckett in 1771 over Thomson's *The Seasons*.[232] He argued that the work was in the public domain.[233] But the lord chancellor, Lord Apsley, nevertheless granted a perpetual injunction and ordered an account of profits.[234] This was on 16 November 1772; the petition to appeal to the house of lords was lodged on 10 December,[235] followed a week later by the respondent's petition.[236] Indeed, the Booksellers later said they would not have brought the question before the house of lords for a rapid determination had they thought they might lose.[237] As the respondents had few delaying tactics available it is difficult to understand the point being made.

[224] Cavendish, Wedderburn {S18}.

[225] Cavendish, Fox {105}; this date could be pushed forwards somewhat as a writ of error (which could be based on any error in the court records) was filed: *Millar v Taylor* (1769) 4 Burr 2303 at 2408 (98 ER 201 at 257).

[226] Petition Committee Report {589 c. ii}.

[227] Folkestone's Diary, 24 Mar.

[228] Part IV: *Remarks on the Booksellers' Petition*; *Farther Strictures*; London Stallholders' Petition {5}.

[229] Remarks on Donaldson's Petition {2}.

[230] General Observations/Hints {MC13}.

[231] Cavendish, Dunning {S14}.

[232] It is not clear which version of James Thomson, *The Seasons*, it would be: Donaldson (1768) (ESTC: T141531) is the most likely. The work was also the subject of *Millar v Taylor* (1769) 4 Burr 2303 (98 ER 201).

[233] *Beckett v Donaldson* (1771): TNA, C 12/61/24, mm. 1–2.

[234] Chancery: Entry Books of Decrees and Orders: Book A: TNA, C 33/439, ff. 26–7.

[235] *LJ*, xxxiii, 476; Parliamentary Archives, HL/PO/JO/10/3/263/50.

[236] *LJ*, xxxiii, 483 (17 Dec. 1772); HL/PO/JO/10/3/263/50.

[237] General Observations/Hints {MC13}.

The proceedings before the Lords have been dealt with extensively elsewhere, and little can be added by repeating matters here. It is sufficient to indicate that they resulted in 11 of the judges[238] giving their opinion on five questions. How they voted remains controversial,[239] and even the weight that should be given to their opinions is not accepted.[240] But what is clear is that the Lords reversed the decree, awarded Donaldson costs,[241] and held there was no common law copyright in 1774. This was what the Booksellers sought to remedy by their bill. While *Donaldson v Beckett* was claimed as a victory for the public by the Bill's opponents,[242] some took a very different view. The author William Mason[243] proclaimed that he intended to burn his papers after hearing of the decision.[244] Yet the supporters of the Booksellers' Bill[245] argued adamantly that they were not attempting to *overturn* the house of lords' decision,[246] but asking for an allowance for a mistake.[247] It appears that some parliamentarians saw this as a fight between the two houses of parliament, which might have raised constitutional ramifications. To avoid this, James Mansfield drew a distinction between the Lords acting in its judicial capacity in *Donaldson*; whereas for the Bill, parliament was acting in its legislative capacity. In other words, the House was being asked not to declare what the law is, but what it should be.[248] Similarly, John Hett, his junior, submitted that there was no intention to set one House against another.[249] Despite this argument being sufficient to get the Bill passed in the house of commons, once the matter reached the Lords it appears a different view was taken. Lord Camden put it simply: the Bill was proposing to turn the lawful into the unlawful and make the illegal legal.[250]

[238] All but Lord Mansfield.

[239] Deazley, *On the Origin of the Right to Copy*, ch. 8; H. Tomás Gómez-Arostegui, 'Copyright at Common Law in 1774', *Connecticut Law Review*, xlvii (2014), 1; H.B. Abrams, 'The Historic Foundation of American Copyright Law: Exploding the Myth of Common Law Copyright', *Wayne Law Review*, xxix (1983), 1120.

[240] There are those who suggest the statements of the Lords (not the judges) was the law of the case: Deazley, *On the Origin of the Right to Copy*, 217; Abrams, 'The Historic Foundation of American Copyright Law', 1169; cf. Gómez-Arostegui, 'Copyright at Common Law', 37–8.

[241] 22 Feb. 1774; *LJ*, xxxiv, 32–3; it was said that the booksellers eventually 'pushed the matter too far' in pursuing litigation: Committee Evidence Observations {15}.

[242] Cavendish, Beauchamp {124}.

[243] William Mason* (1719–91).

[244] Cavendish, Onslow {S23}.

[245] Cavendish, Feilde {S279–80, 289–90}.

[246] While there generally was a rule that proceedings in the house of lords could not be referred to, but only the journal (Thomas, *The House of Commons in the Eighteenth Century*, 216–17; James Harris's Parliamentary Diary, Hampshire Archives, 9M73/G715, 9 May 1765, p. 29; Cavendish Diary, 23 Nov. 1768; motion to hear John Wilkes' petition, Issac Barré, BL, Egerton MS 215, f. 204, 12 Feb. 1770; committee on the state of the nation, Richard Rigby, BL, Egerton MS 220, f. 68; *Sir Henry Cavendish's Debates of the House of Commons, During the Thirteenth Parliament of Great Britain, Commonly called the Unreported Parliament*, ed. John Wright (2 vols, 1841), i, 448), this clearly did not apply in the case of the Booksellers, as almost everything turned on what had happened there.

[247] Part IV, London Booksellers' Considerations {1}; Cavendish, Onslow {S22, 116}; in the Lords this was mentioned: Lord Lyttleton, *Public Advertiser*, 3 June.

[248] Cavendish, Mansfield {23}.

[249] Cavendish, Hett {38}.

[250] *Middlesex Journal*, 2–4 June; *General Evening Post*, 2–4 June.

The Role of Lord Mansfield

Before moving away from the decision of the Lords, it is important to consider the role of William Murray, Lord Mansfield. He admitted in *Millar v Taylor* that he had long been involved in the question of literary property including by his appearances as counsel in earlier cases.[251] Yet he failed to give his opinion on the question of literary property in *Donaldson*.[252] His long shadow goes much further than merely this absence. Some opponents highlighted that Mansfield, whilst at the bar, had been counsel for the *petitioners*,[253] and, as Lord Folkestone put it, his earlier advocacy for the booksellers lingered in his judicial views of common law copyright.[254] This view of Mansfield siding with booksellers has continued to the twentieth and now the twenty-first century. For instance, it is said that booksellers started bringing claims following his elevation to the bench,[255] and the judges (save for Baron Smythe)[256] who supported the common law copyright had all been judges of the king's bench under Mansfield. So as Folkestone claimed, the decision in *Millar* was his creation and he brought his brethren with him.[257]

It was not known in advance of *Donaldson v Beckett* that Mansfield would not be giving his opinion and it was even suggested midway through the proceedings that he would speak as a peer and not as law lord.[258] Ultimately, he did not appear at all (and neither did he appear when the Booksellers' Bill went to the Lords). This act of standing aside was thought of very poorly and led some to suggest that the law lords should be *compelled* to give their view.[259] On the other hand, there was a standing order which appeared to preclude a judge from hearing the appeal of a case they had heard below;[260] and some have claimed Mansfield recused himself because he would be defending his judgment in *Millar v Taylor*.[261] This is not a good reason. Not only did other judges in *Millar* appear unrestricted by the rule, as Sir Richard Aston and Sir Edward Willes both gave their opinions in *Donaldson*, but also Lord Apsley, the lord chancellor,[262] whose order was actually being appealed, gave his opinion overturning his own injunction.[263] Another, possibly stronger reason, is that Mansfield had

[251]And he was friends with some of the leading literary men, such as Alexander Pope: Rose, *Authors and Owners*, 59.

[252]The fact he failed to speak on the Booksellers' Bill at first reading in the Lords was also noted: *Middlesex Journal*, 11–14 June.

[253]In *Midwinter v Kincaid* (1751) 1 Pat App 488 and *Tonson v Walker* (1752) 3 Swans 672 (36 ER 1017); Deazley, *On the Origin of the Right to Copy*, 225 seems to suggest his rhetoric was unsupported by historical fact. The outcome might be true but one has to be careful not to extend this to suggest fabrication.

[254]Citing Horace, *Epistles*, bk 1, ch. 2, verses 69–70; Folkestone's Diary, 16 May; and of course, Joseph Yates was judge in *Millar v Taylor* 4 Burr 2303 (98 ER 201) but counsel in *Tonson v Collins* (1762) 1 Black W 321 (96 ER 180), and a similar accusation appears to have been made in *Donaldson v Beckett* (1774) *Cobbett's Parl. Hist.*, xvii, col. 968.

[255]Rose, *Authors and Owners*, 74; Deazley, *On the Origin of the Right to Copy*, 138.

[256]Judge of the exchequer appointed 23 June 1750, chief baron, 29 Oct. 1772: *Judges of England*, 98, 129.

[257]Cavendish, Folkestone {88}.

[258]*Public Advertiser*, 16 and 22 Feb.

[259]Cavendish, Onslow {S235}.

[260]9 Feb. 1641; *LJ*, iv, 156.

[261]*Millar v Taylor* (1769) 4 Burr 2303 at 2417 (98 ER 201 at 262).

[262]*Donaldson v Beckett* (1774) *Cobbett's Parl. Hist.*, xvii, cols 979–84, 1001–2.

[263]TNA, C 33/439, ff. 26–7.

previously had a public dispute with Lord Camden over jury trial,[264] and it may have been that he simply could not face another public fight,[265] particularly if he thought he would lose.

Hangs in the Balance

The London Booksellers urged the House to find their mistake was 'excusable' as a 'majority'[266] in the house of lords gave their opinion that the common law right existed before the Statute of Anne, and 'many' of those judges opined that the Statute did not take it away.[267] So belief mattered. And as Edmund Burke put it: why cannot a person rely on a view held by the 'majority of the judges of the king's bench and half the judges of the Lords'[268] who were induced 'to imagine that the common law was a larger and better thing than the common law could be'.[269] Alexander Wedderburn, at one point counsel for the London Booksellers, proclaimed that it had been as 'clear as the sun' that the property existed at common law.[270] And, as Onslow said, if the judges erred in their understanding of the law 'may not booksellers have erred?'[271] Much was also made of the lord chancellor voting to reverse his own decree,[272] but he himself suggested this occurred because he was bound by *Millar v Taylor* and not because of his own belief in the law.[273] The opponents simply referred to the number of judges who would have reversed the decree against Donaldson,[274] and the injustice to Donaldson himself: he wins in court and then has the decision overturned by Act of Parliament.[275] Yet contrary to the view in the Commons, Lord Camden[276] said the men in the profession were universally against the decree,[277] the law lords had particular powers of persuasion,[278] and so before the upper house this was enough to knock out the 'belief' in one swoop.

The Interval

The disputes over the history of copyright and the supposed existence of the common law right had little to do with how the question was resolved in *Donaldson v*

[264] Wendell Bird, *Press and Speech Under Assault* (Oxford, 2015), 59–63; the contest between them was sufficiently well known to attract comment in the *Morning Chronicle*, 3 Mar§.

[265] As suggested by Rose, *Authors and Owners*, 101.

[266] Whether this is accurate, or wishful thinking, by the Booksellers is open to dispute: cf. Gómez-Arostegu, 'Copyright at Common Law', 46; Deazley, *On the Origin of the Right to Copy*, 199–210; Cavendish, Feilde {91}.

[267] Booksellers' Case {2}.

[268] Cavendish, Burke {S27}.

[269] Cavendish, Burke {S28}.

[270] Cavendish, Wedderburn {S18}.

[271] Cavendish, Onslow {S22}.

[272] Cavendish, Feilde {93–4}.

[273] *Middlesex Journal*, 2–4 June; *Edinburgh Advertiser*, 4–7 June, 356–7.

[274] Case Observations {2}. They even prayed in aid the supposed vote of Sir Joseph Yates who died on 7 June 1770.

[275] Cavendish, Dalrymple {254}.

[276] He was Lord Mansfield's 'lifelong political opponent': Holdsworth, *A History of English Law*, xii, 306.

[277] *Middlesex Journal*, 2–4 June; *Edinburgh Advertiser*, 4–7 June, 356–7.

[278] McCahill, *The House of Lords in the Age of George III*, 114–15.

Beckett.[279] So the preamble was proven,[280] and so, in theory at least, the House accepted that the Booksellers believed that there was a common law right. This did not go so far as to vindicate the history that had been presented – a history which was truncated, and flavoured to the taste of the person speaking, yet was unduly complicated and convoluted by many other factors. That said it was not a new practice: Deazley suggests that advocates starting with William Murray himself ensured:

> that the history of copyright came to be dictated, not so much by historical fact, accuracy or veracity, but by those stories that could deliver the greatest rhetorical impact … for every story that could be spun out in favour of the perpetual right, for every thesis the booksellers could advance, there existed an equally plausible antithesis.[281]

It is not that Mansfield deliberately mislead the court, or fabricated history, but the gloss given upon facts meant that it was possible to present the history in many different ways. An uncertain and varied history which was slowly sculpted until it finally reached the house of commons in 1774. In reality what would determine the petition was whether or not the London Booksellers really lost fortunes or just the expectation of a fortune. It is to the value of their investment to which the discussion turns in the next chapter.

[279] Deazley, *On the Origin of the Right to Copy*, 166.

[280] See the special verdict of the jury in *Millar v Taylor* (1769) 4 Burr 2303 at 2306–9 (98 ER 201 at 203–5).

[281] Deazley, *On the Origin of the Right to Copy*, 136.

Chapter 5
Evidence and Argument: The Investment and Other Arguments

Introduction

The decision in *Donaldson v Beckett* was warmly received in Scotland with rejoicing in Edinburgh and bonfires being lit.[1] In England, it was quite the reverse; almost immediately there was the talk of 'property' being destroyed and lost investment. The following day the basis of the London Booksellers' arguments before the house of commons was foreshadowed by the *Morning Chronicle*:[2]

> … near 200,000l worth of what was honestly purchased at public sale, and which was yesterday thought property is now reduced to nothing. The Booksellers of London and Westminster, many of whom sold estates and houses to purchase Copy-right, are in a manner ruined, and those who after many years industry thought they had acquired a competency to provide for their families now find themselves without a shilling to devise to their successors.

In addition to the central debate about this 'lost' investment, the parties raised a host of other arguments: a blunderbuss as it were. The Booksellers following a general move towards interest groups relying on the broader effects of changes in the population such as employment, taxation, commodity prices and so forth, rather than simply the effect the law would have on themselves.[3] Accordingly, these policy arguments will be explored in this chapter after the central debates about the investments and fortunes lost.

Lost Investment

The advocates for the Bill argued that the Booksellers had made a great investment in copyrights,[4] some saying it was around £100,000,[5] others £200,000,[6] which had been lost. So that they had been 'great sufferers' by reason of *Donaldson*.[7] Individuals claimed to have spent 'many thousand pounds'[8] on copyright amounting to the 'greatest part' of their fortunes.[9] This 'loss' of investment was central to the case, both in terms of the call for

[1] *Caledonian Mercury*, 2 Mar§.; I.S. Ross, *Lord Kames and the Scotland of His Day* (Oxford, 1972), 143.

[2] *Morning Chronicle*, 23 Feb§.

[3] John Brewer, *The Sinews of Power: War, Money and the English State 1688–1783* (Cambridge, MA, 1990), 246–7.

[4] Cavendish Feilde {S280}.

[5] Cavendish, Mansfield {22}.

[6] Cavendish, Onslow {S21} (he also suggested the value in 1710 was £40,000).

[7] Cavendish, Sawbridge {S283}.

[8] Part IV, Booksellers' Case, {2}.

[9] It was suggested that the copyright in some mundane books was the most valuable; thus the copyright for Dyche's *Spelling Book* (probably Thomas Dyche, *A Guide to the English Tongue* (1st edn, 1707) (ESTC: N66051), sold for more than the combined value of the works of Isaac Newton, John Locke, Archbishop John Tillotson, Robert Boyle or Francis Bacon: Part IV, Further Remarks {6–7}.

compassion and as a proof of belief.[10] As Edmund Burke put it, 'no persons who commit a great part of their property, and trust by our laws, should be a loser by it',[11] yet those on the other side asked why a group of men who invented a property to trade between themselves and who had already made huge fortunes from it should be compensated when the courts said that the property was not real.[12]

That some booksellers 'lost' by *Donaldson* was conceded, but how many was not.[13] The nature of the bookselling business was also more complicated than at first appears. Most booksellers did not just sell books, but were also jobbing printers, that is, work came from printing blank forms, tickets, advertisements and so forth.[14] Indeed, the accounts of William Strahan, the master of the Stationers Company,[15] one of the richest booksellers of the day and a leading player in the Booksellers' Bill, show major contracts for jobbing work in addition to sales of books.[16] Fortunes, therefore, did not depend on books alone. The basic starting points accepted by both sides was that *some* petitioners were losers. 'Oliver Goldsmith' in his *Hints*[17] stated that about two thirds of the booksellers in London[18] had signed the petition for the Bill,[19] yet no more than eight or nine had actually owned any copyright,[20] Dalrymple and Donaldson were more circumspect suggesting it was about 20,[21] and even one of the London Booksellers' witnesses – John Wilkie, the clerk of the auctions – admitted there were eight or nine petitioners who did not own copyright at all.[22] It appears that a large number of signatures were obtained by leading booksellers holding a meeting and telling all who attended that putting their name on it was good for the trade.[23] What is significant about all of this is that some individual petitioners were complaining of a loss which their own side accepted had not actually been suffered,[24] so begging the question why a monopoly should be given to those without specific loss?[25]

[10]The making of such bold claims without clear substantiation was risky, as the Sugar Island lobby found out the same year when the government proved coffee consumption had gone up contrary to the lobby's claim: Brewer, *Sinews of Power*, 244.

[11]Cavendish, Burke {S26}.

[12]Part IV, Remarks on the Booksellers' Petition. The law has on other occasions recognised rights of action based on investment: *Douglas v Hello* [2007] UKHL 21, [2008] 1 AC 1, para. 124; *Irvine v Talksport* [2002] EWHC 367 (Ch), [2002] 1 WLR 2355, para. 39.

[13]Further Remarks {6}. There was also a counterclaim that the Stallholders' petitioners were not actually shopkeepers selling books.

[14]James Raven, *Publishing Business in Eighteenth-Century England* (Woodbridge, 2014), 7–8.

[15]He held the office during 1774.

[16]Raven, *Publishing Business in Eighteenth-Century England*, 85.

[17]As to the claim of authorship see Chapter 1: The Authors and Failure to Sign.

[18]It was signed by 87 persons: Cavendish, Dalrymple {251}; Part IV: Booksellers' Petition.

[19]Another group were counter-petitioners.

[20]Part IV, Goldsmith's Hints {19; 4to}; London Stallholders' Petition {4}.

[21]Cavendish, Dalrymple {229}; Part IV, Donaldson's Lords Petition {2}.

[22]Further Remarks {6}.

[23]*Remarks on the Booksellers' Petition.*

[24]Further Remarks {6}.

[25]Cavendish, Graves {S17–18}.

Even where an individual claimed loss, it was difficult to prove.[26] This uncertainty allowed much to be made of the wealth of a few key men. It was said that Jacob Tonson and Andrew Millar left at least £300,000 between them when they died,[27] (which would be almost £39 million now). It was also advocated that a handful of such 'opulent' booksellers could impede new books being published: any book of quality would be purchased by a few rich monopolists.[28] Yet the surviving booksellers said they were not rich men.[29] The evidence, however, proved little.

William Johnston's Evidence

William Johnston[30] was the star, and essentially only, witness on the issue of loss, and he described how he had started his business by buying copyright for around £1,500,[31] and as his business grew he bought more totalling another £10,000.[32] It appears that these investments had diminished to a value of £9,000 by June 1773 when he assigned all his copyright.[33] While the London Booksellers claimed this showed a substantial loss, the other side said all this proved was that a purchase was made and not that he lost money.[34] The opponents went further, highlighting that while Johnston claimed an interest in a large part of the books in the trade, he only identified a loss in respect of two of those editions.[35] In any event, Johnston's evidence was that following *Donaldson v Beckett* his copyrights would have been worth no more than £500 and this value would continue to fall.[36] Confusingly, he said he could have sold his copyright for 'a very considerable' loss a month *before* the house of lords' decision, suggesting a belief that *Donaldson* would be lost[37] contrary to what was suggested elsewhere.[38] Before coming to the value itself, it was never explained in evidence how, after the Lords' decision, common law copyright would retain any value at all. If there was no restriction on printing works outside the statute, it is unlikely anyone would pay for the privilege of doing so.[39] However, it may have been that the figure of £500

[26] Further Remarks {2; Remark}. Newspapers still carried bald statements of particular instances of loss however: *St James's Chronicle*, 28–30 Apr§.

[27] Part IV, Case Observations {3}. Their wills are TNA, PROB 11/928/110, 940/163, but they do not include the total value of their estates. Adam Budd, *Circulating Enlightenment: The Career and Correspondence of Andrew Millar, 1725–68* (Oxford, 2020), Appendix 1, includes an annotated version of Millar's will.

[28] Part IV, London Stallholders' Petition {6}; *Farther Strictures*.

[29] London Booksellers' Considerations {1}.

[30] William Johnston or Johnson (d. 1804), app. 1743–8, tr. 1745–73, 16 Ludgate Street.

[31] Part IV, Petition Committee Report (note this is half of the £3,000 opening capital), {588 c. i}.

[32] Petition Committee Report {588 c. i}; Cavendish, Feilde {S280}.

[33] Petition Committee Report {590 c. i}; Dunning seems to misremember the evidence: Cavendish, Dunning {S12}; Petition Committee Report {590 c. i}. Whether this fall in value was due to the price of individual copyrights falling or the commingling of statutory and 'common law' copyrights is unclear, as statutory copyright would clearly lose its value slightly each year as the number of years remaining reduced.

[34] Cavendish, Jolliffe {128}.

[35] Part IV, Committee Evidence Observations {15–16}.

[36] Petition Committee Report {590 c. i}. These figures are inconsistent with Cavendish, Dunning {S12}, who refers to property if sold at a shilling would not be worth a quarter of that.

[37] Petition Committee Report {590 c. i}.

[38] See Part IV, Booksellers' Petition.

[39] Although see Chapter 4: The Honorary Monopoly.

represents those copyrights still covered by the Statute of Anne, and as time passed their value would diminish leading to further loss. Finally, the sale at £9,000 was not at arm's length but between father and son.[40] There may have been all sorts of reasons why this transaction might have been completed at under or over value. The value of the copyrights itself was set by two other booksellers (Thomas Longman and Thomas Caddell),[41] but this is only half the story.[42] What actually happened was that Johnston valued the copyrights and then asked the other two booksellers to confirm his valuation without any independent calculation.[43] Not only does this highlight that the Booksellers' evidence of loss was not easy to quantify,[44] but it also shows that the author of the petition report took a very favourable reading of the evidence: he did not record the method of valuation.[45] This demonstrates an inherent flaw with the Bill's promoter drafting the report of the evidence heard before the petition committee. Finally, Johnston tried to bolster his claim by saying that had he believed there was any risk to any common law copyright he could (and would) have sold this interest some years ago for its full value,[46] and he would not have sold it to his son. Yet as the opponents pointed out when his parental assignment occured he should have known an appeal was pending and this presented a risk to the investment.[47]

Public Auctions

The investments were all linked to auctions and to the 'conger',[48] which, at the heart of the auctions, appears to have originated when the Licensing Acts expired. Its operation exemplified the trade throughout the 18th century with the intent of an inner circle of dominant booksellers dictating the practice of the whole trade.[49] The conger was not a partnership, rather it involved booksellers buying each other's books and agreeing to sell them at a set price: a cartel as it were.[50] It evolved into groups of booksellers getting together to finance a book throughout the publishing process, rather than just arranging to buy completed books from each other.[51] This developed further into a 'right' in copies, which were broken down

[40] Petition Committee Report {590 c. i}.

[41] Thomas Longman (1730–97), app. 1745–52, tr. 1754–96, Ship and Black Swan, 39 Paternoster Row; Thomas Caddell (1742–1802), app. 1758–65, tr. 1766–93, 141 Strand (he took over Andrew Millar's business on his death).

[42] Here it is assumed that the statement in the observations is correct.

[43] Committee Evidence Observations {16}.

[44] Cavendish, Thurlow {S8} as to difficulty of evidence.

[45] It was traditional for the MP promoting the Bill to write the report. While the report may be said to be entirely accurate, it might be asserted that he was practising equivocation; conversely, Cavendish, Dalrymple {254}, suggests what sold for £120,000 was worth £20.

[46] Petition Committee Report {590 c. i}.

[47] Committee Evidence Observations {16}.

[48] For a detailed history of the congers, Norma Hodgson and Cyprian Blagden, *The Notebook of Thomas Bennet and Henry Clements* (Oxford Bibliographic Society, new ser., vi, 1956), ch. 3.

[49] John Feather, *A History of British Publishing* (2005), 53; it had long been the situation in the Stationers' Company before that time: Gadd, 'The Stationer's Company', 93.

[50] For a discussion of this wholesale conger, Hodgson and Blagden, *The Notebook of Thomas Bennet and Henry Clements*, 67–85.

[51] Feather, *A History of British Publishing*, 53.

into shares,[52] and traded between members.[53] Shares were sold at auction, but subject to a condition that any subsequent resale must be under similar conditions.[54] This restriction existed because certain books had a very long life, much greater than a single impression, and if 'outsiders' got hold of the right to copy then the conger itself could have been taken over.[55] It is critical to remember the conger acted in a market with few long-term contracts and without any consistent or clear demand for anything but the most famous books.[56] So while they were called 'public auctions' they were conducted to ensure certain booksellers continued to control share ownership and with it the whole trade.[57]

Nevertheless, the promoters of the Bill put the value of the copyrights so high *because* they were bought at these auctions,[58] implying that sale at a public auction provided a fair reflection of the market price.[59] This assertion could easily be seen as a scam by the opponents; the sales were for the maintenance of copyrights and any incremental increase in value benefited all shareholders.[60] These 'Booksellers' Public Auctions' eventually took place in the *Queen's Arms* in St Paul's Churchyard and the *Globe Tavern* in Fleet Street, with an entry fee of £5.[61] William Johnston's evidence was that the sales were open to everybody,[62] but the opponents denied this saying sales were restricted and those without invitation cards were turned away,[63] as were any who did not comply with the rules prohibiting the sale of Scottish or Irish editions.[64] It was even claimed that all 50 booksellers who signed the London Stallholders' counter-petition had been turned away at some time.[65] Indeed, the witnesses called by the opponents at second reading appear to have been more concerned about their exclusion from these sales than the overall merits of the Bill.[66] Notwithstanding

[52]Where there was not a sole owner of the copyright, but shares (some queried what a share was as such: Cavendish, Graves {S16}) had been sold, then when a book was reprinted the publisher paid money to the person with the largest share who made up an account and divided the monies according to the size of the share: Petition Committee Report {589 c. i}.

[53]These shares could be in books within or outside the protection of the Statute of Anne; this is not mentioned in Hodgson and Blagden, *The Notebook of Thomas Bennet and Henry Clements*, 85–100, but it is widely described, see Patterson, *Copyright in Historical Perspective*, 152; W. Forbes Gray, 'Alexander Donaldson and the Fight for Cheap Books', *Juridical Review*, xxxviii (1926), 193.

[54]John Feather, *Publishing, Piracy and Politics: An Historical Study of Copyright in Britain* (1994), 66.

[55]Feather, *A History of British Publishing*, 54.

[56]Raven, *Publishing Business in Eighteenth-Century England*, 61.

[57]They are often called 'closed' sales in the literature: Raven, *Publishing Business in Eighteenth-Century England*, 40.

[58]Cavendish, Mansfield {33–4}.

[59]The exclusion of some booksellers would also deflate rather than inflate the price.

[60]Feather, *A History of British Publishing*, 54.

[61]Now £642; Part IV, Further Remarks, declaration of Simon Vandenbergh.

[62]Petition Committee Report {589 c. ii}.

[63]Case Observations, Answer {2}.

[64]Committee Evidence Observations {12–13}.

[65]Strangely, it appears that some booksellers were permitted to go to sales at one venue but not the other: Further Remarks {5} (it was alleged more copyrights sold at the *Queen's Arms* than the *Globe Tavern*): Further Remarks, Simon Vandenbergh; William Fox also explains that when he did not agree to a particular combination he was thrown out (Further Remarks, William Fox). Donaldson himself apparently had a secret proxy attending the *Globe* on his behalf: James Raven, *The Business of Books: Booksellers and the English Book Trade, 1450–1850* (New Haven, CT, 2007), 229.

[66]*Morning Chronicle*, 11 May.

the general assertion of being 'public', the London Booksellers accepted that some persons were excluded – for example, the sales were on credit and so men (and women) of lesser means could not attend.[67] Strangely, nobody mentioned that Donaldson himself was excluded from the sale of Thomson's *The Seasons*, a factor which had been central to his case before the house of lords.[68]

In any event, John Wilkie, the auctions clerk, gave evidence that £49,981 5*s*.[69] had been spent at auctions between 1755 and 1774,[70] with additional money being paid by private contract. This figure was admitted to be flawed because it included resales.[71] The following example explains why this is a problem: A sells the copyright to B for £5 at the auction and B subsequently sells it to C at the next auction for £6. The total sales at the auction will be £11, but the only person facing a loss (of £6) is C. There were other problems with the Booksellers' calculated loss. The 'exclusivity' in some books was traded at auction over 20 years before *Donaldson* and any purchaser would also have recouped some of the capital invested by 1774.[72] Donaldson himself suggested that booksellers often made a return of eight, ten or even 20 times their original purchase money.[73] While his basic point has some merit, the actual multiple is of course pure speculation. Nevertheless, rhetorically it supported the position taken by the opponents, namely that the London Booksellers were motivated by avarice and little else.[74]

Johnston's evidence demonstrated, albeit opaquely, that the sales included works still protected under the Statute. These works would still be protected for some time after *Donaldson* (particularly in light of the assignment of the renewal)[75] and while statutory exclusivity remained, some value could be recouped by the copyright owner. The opponents also alleged that the auctions were used to artificially inflate prices. For instance, it was claimed that when Jacob Tonson died his stock was sold secretly for £10,000 and subsequently resold at 'public' auctions for £23,000, enabling the secret purchasers to make a significant profit.[76] In other words, the London Booksellers would quite happily stab each other in the back.

Ownership and Assignment

The basic position of the Bill's proposers was that they would not have bought and sold 'copyright' at great expense if they did not believe it was protected under the common

[67] Part IV, General Observations/Hints {MC13}; but the opponents suggested men with credit were turned away: Committee Evidence Observations {12–13}; Further Remarks {5}; Cavendish, Mansfield, {25–6}.

[68] A.S. Collins, *Authorship in the Days of Johnson* (1928), 18.

[69] About £6.3 million now; in the Lords this was reported as about £60,000: Lord Lyletton: *Public Advertiser*, 3 June.

[70] Petitions Committee Report {590 c. ii}.

[71] Further Remarks {2}; Cavendish, Jolliffe {128}.

[72] Further Remarks {2}.

[73] Part IV, Donaldson's Petition {11}; albeit he ignored the cost of manufacture of the books.

[74] A term used by the Booksellers: Remarks on Donaldson's Petition {10}.

[75] Copyright Act 1709, s. 11; as to the assignment of the renewal see below.

[76] Cavendish, Murphy {262}; Further Remarks {2}; Goldsmith's Hints {18; 3*tio*}.

law.[77] But the assignments the Booksellers presented to parliament,[78] were to establish that the copyright sales had very low values;[79] they also did not specify whether they were for the 'Statute' or 'Common Law' right.[80] William Graves MP, who was against the Bill, admitted there had been assignments, but put their value 'in shillings',[81] and a prevailing and understandable theme was that if the Booksellers could not prove large sums were being paid for assignments[82] there was no loss and so no justification to pass the Bill.[83] In fact, the payment to authors had improved over the 18th century and by 1774 many were able to live by their pen,[84] albeit payment varied greatly between genre,[85] and, more obviously, fame. A well-known author could attract much higher fees for an assignment than someone who was more obscure, even after *Donaldson*, so, for instance, Frances Burney[86] received a 'low' 20 guineas[87] for her first book (*Evelina*),[88] £250[89] for her second (*Cecilia*)[90] and a very impressive £1,000[91] for her third (*Camilla*).[92] In short, booksellers were good at judging an author's worth in terms of expected sales;[93] and so assignments *could* be for a lot of money: as George Johnstone said, the payments to William Blackstone and others were a good bargain under the Statute of Anne.[94] However, those in favour of the Bill such as Alexander Wedderburn, were much more casual about the failure to establish very much, saying it was 'notorious' copyright that had been bought and

[77] Petition Committee Report {558 c. ii–589 c. i}; Cavendish, Feilde {97}; a point raised by the Glasgow Memorialists, which was not addressed by anyone, was how a property right could only be recognised in England and not elsewhere, because property rights were universal: Part IV, Glasgow Memorialists {5–6}.

[78] Later, there were details of assignments set out in the newspaper: *Morning Chronicle*, 31 May§.

[79] The assignment from Sir Richard Steele for *Tatler* was exhibited before the petition committee (*CJ*, xxxiv, 588, c. ii) and much made of Milton's assignment a century earlier: Kerry MacLenna, 'John Milton's Contract for "Paradise Lost": A Commercial Reading', *Milton Quarterly*, xliv (2010), 221.

[80] Petition Committee Report {589 c. i}; following a comment by Sir John Dalrymple, Cavendish, {255–6}, there was a letter in the *Morning Chronicle* demanding his assignment of copyright was disclosed to the Commons and the public: *Morning Chronicle*, 13 May§ ('Honesty').

[81] Cavendish, Graves {S17}.

[82] However, a correspondent did claim that one author had returned £1,000 and another had taken £200 rather than £500 since the decision in *Donaldson*: *St James's Chronicle*, 28–30 Apr§.

[83] Cavendish, Graves {S17}.

[84] Feather, *Publishing, Piracy and Politics*, 7, 80.

[85] David Fielding and Shef Rogers, 'Copyright Payments in Eighteenth-Century Britain, 1701–1800', *The Library*, 7th ser., xviii (2017), 16; as to the proportion of each type of publication, John Feather, 'British Publishing in the Eighteenth Century: A Preliminary Subject Analysis', *The Library*, 6th ser., viii (1986), 32 (drama being the most lucrative and philosophy, history and law being poor payers).

[86] Fielding and Rogers, 'Copyright Payments in Eighteenth-Century Britain', 16.

[87] The labour earnings now would be £34,950.

[88] *Evelina* (Lowndes, 1778) (ESTC: T145413).

[89] The labour earnings now would be £391,200.

[90] *Cecilia* (Payne, 1782) (ESTC: T102228).

[91] The labour earnings now would be £1.3 million.

[92] *Camilla* (Payne, 1796) (ESTC: T144705).

[93] But not necessarily in terms of each book they wrote: Fielding and Rogers, 'Copyright Payments in Eighteenth-Century Britain', 17.

[94] Cavendish, Johnstone {78}.

sold,[95] and if a *single* copy was worth less than it was before *Donaldson* no more proof of harm was needed.[96]

In relation to old works[97] there was little or no evidence put forward as to why a particular bookseller 'owned' the honorary or other rights in the book. Johnston in his evidence said little more than he was not aware that the assignments had ever been questioned before.[98] Indeed, he claimed ownership of a share of *Cambden's Britannia*, and in particular Gibson's translation, but he admitted to never having seen any assignment.[99] He went further, accepting that he often bought books without considering the title,[100] and that it was not usual to keep or request proof of the original assignment.[101] Instead, it was said that long possession[102] created a presumption of ownership, albeit the terminology was not entirely consistent.[103] It is quite extraordinary, particularly in a time of great legal formalism,[104] that it was thought a right could exist without any proof of it other than a *claim*[105] of long possession.[106]

Reversion

The opponents also relied on the argument that the reversion of copyright,[107] that is the second 14-year term of copyright which reverts to the author after the expiry of the first 14-year term,[108] vested in authors and not an author's assigns. In other words, it precluded the transfer of the reversion at the same time as the original grant. Had parliament meant to permit the author to sell the original grant and the reversion at the same time it would have, instead, merely extended the term. Indeed, they made the point that only by the time of the reversion could the author's reputation be secured and the value of the work be

[95] For this assertion, Cavendish, Wedderburn {S18}. It was reported that assignments had been made for £105 in 1738 and £505 in 1769 for Thomson's *The Seasons*: *Donaldson v Beckett* (1774) 2 Br PC 129 (1 ER 837).

[96] Cavendish, Wedderburn {S18}.

[97] The Bill applied to books whether published before or after the date of Donaldson and those published after the date cannot have created any loss (Further Remarks {1; Title}, {3; 2d Clause}. If published means printed this is flawed: if Bookseller A had paid for the copyright then either A had to continue to print it or its value had to be maintained for a term to make it a tradeable commodity.

[98] Petition Committee Report {589 c. i}.

[99] Petition Committee Report {588, c. ii}; Committee Evidence Observations {13}.

[100] Petition Committee Report {588, c. ii}.

[101] Committee Evidence Observations {13}.

[102] Brad Sherman and Lionel Bently, *The Making of Modern Intellectual Property Law* (Cambridge, 1999), 21–4.

[103] Petition Committee Report {589 c. ii}; a special case was made of those authors who wanted to remain anonymous: Petition Committee Report {589 c. ii}; Committee Evidence Observations {14–15}.

[104] See generally, F.W. Maitland, *The Forms of Action at Common Law* (Cambridge, 1936).

[105] Albeit by this stage the fiction of 'lost modern grant' (where long-used easements are pretended to have been granted in a long-lost document) was well established and might be seen as similar: Alan Dowling, 'The Doctrine of Lost Modern Grant', *Irish Jurist*, xxxviii (2003), 233–8. For a discussion of fictions more generally, S.F.C. Milsom, *A Natural History of the Common Law* (New York, 2003), ch. 2.

[106] Petition Committee Report {589 c. i}; Committee Evidence Observations {14–15}; Further Remarks {3; 2d Clause}; Cavendish, Feilde {94–5}.

[107] For a discussion of its purpose, Lionel Bently and Jane Ginsburg, '"The Sole Right … Shall Return to the Authors": Anglo-American Authors' Reversion Rights from the Statute of Anne to Contemporary U.S. Copyright', *Berkeley Technology Law Journal*, xxv (2010), 1482–91.

[108] Copyright Act 1709, s. 11.

known.[109] The evidence before the Committee, on the other hand, was that the witness (Johnston) had never seen an assignment where it expressly covered the reversion,[110] as all assignments were made forever (that is, in perpetuity).[111] The claim for the reversion was further undermined by the allegation that little (or no) additional remuneration was paid to the author for the additional 14 years.[112] Yet it turns out that the courts subsequently[113] held that the assignment of the original grant could include the reversion.[114] The assignment of future rights was just a form of trade-off.

Trade-off

To 'allow' booksellers to recover their investments in copyrights would, the opponents said, be taking away from the public:[115] as Charles Fox put it, compassion in giving relief to A is at the expense of B.[116] On one side, Edmund Burke said it was balancing larger gains by one group against smaller losses faced by another,[117] and on the other side Dalrymple said it was giving the advantage to 20 men over the rest of the population.[118] The latter view was picked up in the Lords when Lord Denbigh railed that the Bill violated the rights of individuals and so was totally unacceptable.[119] Clearly the Bill would have got wider support had the trade-off been avoidable.[120] A charge which the promoters faced, but was never pushed by the House, was that if an extension was given there could be no guarantee that they would not come back in 21 years asking for a further monopoly.[121] In other words, this 'repayment' of the investment would not finally resolve the matter.

Cost of Production

One of the key arguments put forward by and on behalf of the Booksellers related to the way books were manufactured. They argued that it was very risky to produce books, and indeed it probably was: Andrew Millar apparently used to say a book that did not sell quickly was a

[109] Petition Committee Report {589 c. i}.

[110] He suggested that authors got more for 28 years than 14 (Petition Committee Report {589 c. i}) but this might be seen as inconsistent with a perpetual right (although not with two tiers of protection); as to practice, Bently and Ginsburg, 'The Sole Right Shall Return to the Authors', 1494–1514.

[111] Petition Committee Report {589 c. i}.

[112] Committee Evidence Observations {17}.

[113] In *Millar & Dodsley v Taylor* (1765) it was accepted that reversions could be assigned, but the case was unreported and so may not have been known to counsel or others involved in proceedings: Bently and Ginsburg, 'The Sole Right Shall Return to the Authors', 1518–22.

[114] *Carnan v Bowles* (1786) 2 Brown's Chancery Cases 81 (29 ER 46); *Rennet v Thompson* (unreported, but cited in *Carnan; Rundell v Murray* (1821) 1 Jacob 315 (37 ER 870).

[115] Cavendish, Thurlow {S4}, Graves{S17–18}, Savile {S31}, Johnstone {76}; Goldsmith's Hints {19; 6to}.

[116] Cavendish, Fox {108–10}, Lord Beauchamp {165}, Graves {S18}.

[117] Cavendish, Burke {S24}.

[118] Cavendish, Dalrymple {244–5}.

[119] *Middlesex Journal*, 2–4 June.

[120] Cavendish, Saville {S31}.

[121] Goldsmith's Hints {18; 1mo}; Further Remarks {8–9}.

'blank' in the lottery of bookselling.[122] The problem was that publishing required very long lines of credit and the attendant strong reputation. Accordingly successful, well-tried books (which were often out of copyright) were particularly important, as the risks were lower.[123] The profits from other books might not accrue until the second or even later edition.[124] This cost structure arose because each book required printing plates to be typeset and then each individual sheet of the book to be printed.[125] Printing every additional sheet cost little compared to the original typesetting.[126] So printing on demand would have meant each book would cost many hundreds of pounds.[127] A bookseller therefore needed to produce an 'impression' – that is hundreds or even thousands of copies (the average was about 750 per impression)[128] – which might take 20 years or more to sell off.[129] Only when a sufficient number of these books had been sold would the production cost be recouped and the book turn a profit. In the absence of a monopoly, it was claimed no printer would publish a book[130] because another printer could come along and undersell the original bookseller (albeit they too faced the same high production costs – something the London Booksellers seem to have ignored). In the circumstances, the London Booksellers stated that in the absence of the Bill, books which were currently out of print would not be reprinted and might never be printed again,[131] aptly showing how their business model did not induce innovation and created little incentive to reduce production costs.[132]

The opponents, however, pointed out that even if the Bill did not pass, the London Booksellers had an incumbent position and so would face no competition in relation to many of the books they held.[133] This was supported by the practice of reusing type to reduce costs,[134] and copper plates for printing illustrations (unlike moveable type) were expensive to engrave and could be only used for one illustration.[135] Production methods thereby perpetuated the monopoly even without copyright.[136] Of course, the London Booksellers

[122]Glasgow Memorialists {8, 18} (although they were against the Bill there is no reason to think the alleged quote is not representative).

[123]Raven, *Publishing Business in Eighteenth-Century England*, 44, 49.

[124]Evidence before the petition committee on the Booksellers' Bill of 1734 (Robert Aynsworth), *CJ*, xxii, 411, 412 (12 Mar. 1734/5).

[125]Cavendish, Wedderburn {S19}.

[126]There would also be the high costs associated with having a wide variation of types: see Raven, *Publishing Business in Eighteenth-Century England*, 55, as to the expectations of holding different types.

[127]General Observations/Hints {MC13}; London Booksellers' Considerations {2}.

[128]Fielding and Rogers, 'Copyright Payments in Eighteenth-Century Britain', 17; the earliest printers would have had much shorter runs, maybe 50 per impression: Feather, *A History of British Publishing*, 14.

[129]Cavendish, Feilde {99}; Part IV, Printed Books; albeit the other side said that the cost of any copyright would usually be recouped by one impression or at the most two: *Remarks on the Booksellers' Petition*.

[130]Cavendish, Feilde {99}.

[131]Petition Committee Report, {590 c. i} (although this might have been only elegant editions).

[132]Raven, *Publishing Business in Eighteenth-Century England*, 47.

[133]Goldsmith's Hints {19; 8vo}.

[134]Raven, *Publishing Business in Eighteenth-Century England*, 48.

[135]It appears, however, that illustrations were shared and bought and sold between printers and could be used many years apart, albeit this had declined by the 18th century: Tessa Watt, *Cheap Print and Popular Piety* (Cambridge, 1991), 140–50 (and in particular 148–9); Slauter, *Who Owns the News?*, 26.

[136]Further Remarks {2; Preamble}.

countered that books were more expensive to produce than engravings and so they should get longer protection than engravers under their Act.[137]

Corrections, Translations and Protection of Ideas

The London Booksellers appear to have already accepted that copyright did not extend to ideas,[138] so, for instance, the way *Johnson's Dictionary* was arranged could not be protected.[139] Accordingly, any book which contained a new idea might be 'transposed, abridged, translated, anything but copied and published as the work of the author'.[140] As many of the works that were being claimed by London Booksellers were 'old' there were assertions of ownership based on corrections or translations[141] made by persons other than the author, such as those editing Shakespeare[142] or Malachy Postlethwayte's[143] translation of Jacque and Philémon-Louis Savary's *Universal Dictionary of Trade and Commerce*.[144] Indeed, it was said that few books with living authors (and indeed those of many deceased authors) were not revised or improved before being published again.[145]

A bookseller who bought an edition had to pay for every revision or correction and so, it was said, there should be some way to recoup this cost.[146] The London Booksellers published a list of books setting out the cost of producing books, and their supporters likewise emphasised the cost of editing works, such as Shakespeare.[147] Nevertheless, the assignment by Thomson of his *The Seasons*, the book central to both *Millar v Taylor* and *Donaldson v Beckett*, included the transfer of any benefit from corrections and amendments made later. However, the law's approach to translations was still not entirely clear by 1774. Much earlier, in *Burnet v Chetwood*,[148] Macclesfield LC had been sympathetic to the idea that a translation was a 'different' book, but the case was not decided on this basis. Indeed, the protection of revised and translated editions suggested against a need for common law copyright: if each new edition got statutory copyright this would cover any extra expenditure, a point

[137] Engraving Copyright Act 1734 (8 Geo. II, c. 13), s. 1 (14 years); Engraving Copyright Act 1766 (7 Geo. III, c. 38), s. 7 (increased to 28 years); London Booksellers' Considerations {3}.

[138] This is less clear, see dissent in *Miller v Taylor* (1769) 4 Burr 2303 at 2357–8, 2365 (98 ER 201 at 230–1, 234).

[139] General Observations/Hints {MC7}; Glasgow Memorialists {7–8}.

[140] General Observations/Hints {MC13}.

[141] The Booksellers also lauded the additional payments that they made to authors to complete works: General Observations/Hints {MC7; GO4}, {MC7; GO5}, (Postlethwayte).

[142] General Observations/Hints {GO3}; Printed Books. As to the 'improvers' of Shakespeare, A.F. Pollard, *Shakespeare's Fight with the Pirates* (Cambridge, 1920), ch. 4.

[143] First edition (Knapton, 1751) (ESTC: N35479).

[144] General Observations/Hints {MC7; GO6}. In *Hinton v Donaldson* (1773) *Boswell's Report* 7, Lord Hailes questions the ownership of Postlethwayte's compilation.

[145] London Booksellers' Considerations {3}; for instance, see the list of editors for Shakespeare: Printed Books {A3}.

[146] London Booksellers' Considerations {3}.

[147] Cavendish, Feilde {101}; Printed Books.

[148] (1721) 2 Mer 441 (35 ER 1008). For an introduction, David Saunders, 'Copyright, Obscenity and Literary History', *Journal of English Literary History*, lvii (1990), 437–8.

an opponent actually took to suggest the Booksellers' Bill was unnecessary,[149] although it was not picked up in the House.

Monopolies

Alexander Wedderburn suggested that an uncontrolled trade in books would not be in the interests of booksellers in general or the public,[150] whereas Dalrymple, the opponent's counsel, called for the promotion of free trade because any monopoly would increase the price of books, hurt the manufactories, hurt public revenue, hurt authors, and damage foreign trade.[151] Indeed, Donaldson, it was claimed, would have accepted a share in the monopoly if it had been offered, but his former counsel said he would not support his client in acknowledging a monopoly just to give him a share in it.[152] Edmund Burke tried to draw a distinction between acceptable and odious monopolies. He said no monopoly could be in things which by their nature are public, such as the right to sell or import a product, whereas when a person creates something 'original' it should give him the right to secure the profit.[153] In his Note on the Copyright Bill, Burke postulated that a monopoly could be justified either to encourage men to employ themselves in useful inventions or to take risks in useful undertakings,[154] but as Charles Fox pointed out this only works prospectively, as there has been no encouragement unless the incentive exists before the work.[155] In this respect contrasts were drawn between the term given to engravers under the Engraving Copyright Act 1766,[156] being prospective, and that claimed by the Booksellers, being retrospective.[157] He went further and came to a conclusion fit for a digital age, 'that all copies are as good as the original'.[158] Yet the opponents emphasised the importance of a limited monopoly.[159] The Booksellers' Bill was just trying to create monopolies for far too long.

The London Booksellers fervently disagreed: the risk they faced meant that the term of 14 years under the Statute of Anne was simply inadequate and doubling it, they said, would be barely sufficient (turning a blind eye to the fact this double term already existed).[160]

[149] Glasgow Memorialists {16}.

[150] Cavendish, Wedderburn {S19}.

[151] Cavendish, Dalrymple {232–3}; despite arguing based on a monopoly in *Tonson v Collins* (1761) 1 Black W 306–7 (96 ER 171) Thurlow took a different approach before the House: the closest he came to mentioning it is Cavendish, Thurlow {S9–10); Glasgow Memorialists {15}.

[152] Cavendish, Thurlow {S9–S10}; but see Chapter 9.

[153] Cavendish, Burke {S28}; Part IV, Burke's Notes on Copyright Bill {460–1}.

[154] Burke's Notes on Copyright Bill.

[155] Cavendish, Fox {108}; more recently these arguments have been part of the debates on the extension of copyright term: *Aldred v Ashcroft*, 537 US 186 (2003) (and the brief of George Alkerlof *et al.*); *Gowers Review of Intellectual Property* (HM Treasury, 2006), para. 4.39–4.44.

[156] (7 Geo. III, c. 38).

[157] Case Observations {3}.

[158] See Chapter 5: Quality Editions.

[159] Cavendish, Thurlow {S3}; this linked back to the Statute of Monopolies. It was Coke's view that a patent could be granted for a reasonable period, but this was capped (for inventions) at 14 years: Sir Edward Coke, *The Third Part of the Institutes of the Laws of England* (1648), 184. As printing patents were outside the Statute of Monopolies the grant had to be reasonable, but there was no cap.

[160] General Observations/Hints {MC7; GO5}.

Claims were made that in any one year the losses from book production would usually exceed the income,[161] citing an age old truth that it is difficult to know the value of a book until it has been to market and the public have given their view.[162] So, they proclaimed, a bookseller who has a book which is well received by the public 'considers himself as a successful adventurer in a very hazardous battery, of at least a thousand blank to a prize'.[163] In light of this, Burke urged that where a monopoly was granted to encourage taking a risk the monopoly must give full compensation for the value of the risk.[164] He went further, claiming that for books, and books alone, a perpetual monopoly would be reasonable,[165] because only that author (and no other) could have written that particular book. It is unclear whether it was pragmatism, and knowledge that perpetuity for booksellers would not pass, or the later rationale, that it would take a term of years to recover the investment, that led Burke to support the approach in the Booksellers' Bill, rather than perpetuity. Indeed, Colonel George Onslow said the change from permanence to a term of years was simply a concession.[166]

There were many who tried to draw a parallel between the protection of inventions,[167] under the grant of a patent, with the protection of books,[168] pointing out that monopolies for inventions are accepted 'every day'.[169] This comparison was resisted by the Booksellers,[170] as it potentially restricted their claim to a 14-year term.[171] The protection of inventions was in ideas,[172] whereas the protection of books was in the expression. Thus, they claimed, workshop improvements by an ingenious workman are rewarded by better prices and more constant employment and not by a monopoly. Intriguingly, the Booksellers argued that calico printers should be able to use each other's designs freely otherwise the business came to a standstill,[173] a short market lead time of a few days being enough to give the calico drawer the necessary protection.[174] Others pointed to great inventions that had

[161] General Observations/Hints {MC10}; albeit this would mean that most booksellers would go bust very quickly.

[162] General Observations/Hints {MC10}.

[163] General Observations/Hints {MC19}.

[164] Burke's Notes on Copyright Bill; it has a very 'slow sale': Booksellers' Case {2}.

[165] Burke's Notes on Copyright Bill; there is a commonly stated view that Burke was contrary to patents and similar monopolies, but this has been debunked elsewhere: Phillip Johnson, 'The Myth of Mr Burke and Mr Watt: for Want of a Champion!', *Queen Mary Journal of Intellectual Property*, vi (2016), 370.

[166] Cavendish, Onslow {115}.

[167] Including in *Donaldson v Beckett* (1774) *Cobbett's Parl. Hist.*, xvii, col. 974, Eyre B (case of appellants and respondents, 34); also see submissions of Yates in *Tonson v Collins* (1762) 1 Black 339 (96 ER 187).

[168] Cavendish, Feilde {122}; Burke's Notes on Copyright Bill {460–1}; London Booksellers' Considerations {2}; see for instance, Cavendish, Jolliffe {129}.

[169] Cavendish, Feilde {99}. The number of patents granted each year was small; it was not until 1783 that more than 50 patents were granted in a single year: Table A1 in Richard Sullivan, 'England's "Age of Invention": The Acceleration of Patents and Patentable Invention During the Industrial Revolution', *Explorations in Economic History*, xxvi (1989), 424.

[170] It had been previously resisted on the grounds that a patent suggested a privilege whereas copyright was a property right.

[171] Statute of Monopolies (21 Jas. I, c. 3), s. 6.

[172] But even this is not really true: *Regeneron Pharmaceuticals Inc v Kymab Ltd* [2020] UKSC 27, [2020] RPC 22, para. 58 (patents do not protect 'pure' ideas).

[173] General Observations/Hints {MC13}.

[174] General Observations/Hints {MC13}; however, a little over a decade later, parliament thought they needed three months: Designing and Printing of Linens etc. Act 1787 (27 Geo. III, c. 38); extended by Designing and

been given parliamentary prizes,[175] which were then in vogue,[176] and while Lord Folkestone touted payment, the London Booksellers simply said it would not work,[177] as books, unlike mechanical devices, had to be produced in bulk.[178] The fights over monopolies, and the effect on the market, came to nothing, but it is connected to another issued raised, namely the price of books.

Price of Books

One of the most straightforward arguments against the Bill was that it would tend to inflate the price of books or at least maintain the high price that already existed,[179] and without monopolies, it was said, books could be produced at 'moderate' price.[180] The London Booksellers countered[181] that the price of some books had not changed for half a century,[182] and some prices had even fallen before Alexander Donaldson entered the market.[183] Furthermore, the profit in books came from the volume of books sold[184] and so, for instance, the price of Shakespeare's works had fallen *only* because the volume purchased had increased.[185] Similarly, they claimed when costs had previously risen (for binding) the booksellers had absorbed it rather than passing it on to the customers.[186] Clearly booksellers paying large sums to authors increased the price of books,[187] and so Donaldson, it was claimed, could sell books more cheaply because he paid nothing for copyright.[188] Referring to the widely lampooned *Hawkesworth's Voyages*[189] it was said that the loss arising from bad books was

174 *(continued)* Printing of Linens etc. Act 1789 (29 Geo. III, c. 19) and the Act made perpetual by Linens etc. Act 1794 (34 Geo. III, c. 23); Sherman and Bently, *The Making of Modern Intellectual Property Law*, ch. 3.

175 General Observations/Hints {MC13}.

176 Robert Burrell and Catherine Kelly, 'Parliamentary Rewards and the Evolution of the Patent System', *Cambridge Law Journal*, lxxiv (2015), 423; Burrell and Kelly, 'Public Rewards and Innovation Policy: Lessons from the Eighteenth and Nineteenth Centuries', *Modern Law Review*, lxxvii (2014), 858; Phillip Johnson, *Privatised Law Reform: A History of Patent Law through Private Legislation, 1620–1907* (2017), ch. 9.

177 General Observations/Hints {MC13}.

178 London Booksellers' Considerations {1–2}.

179 Case Observations {3}; Cavendish, Dalrymple {235}; but see David Fielding and Shef Rogers, 'Monopoly Power in the Eighteenth-Century Book Trade', *European Review of Economic History*, xxi (2017), 393.

180 Donaldson's Petition {10}.

181 There was a comment in various newspapers that the price would rise due to *Donaldson*: *Middlesex Journal*, 17–19 Mar§.; *Gazetteer*, 19 Mar§.; *Morning Chronicle*, 19 Mar§.

182 General Observations/Hints {MC10}.

183 Remarks on Donaldson's Petition {2}; London Booksellers' Considerations {2} (they also said the quality was better).

184 General Observations/Hints {GO2}; London Booksellers' Considerations {2}.

185 General Observations/Hints {MC6; GO3}.

186 General Observations/Hints {MC10}.

187 General Observations/Hints {MC9} (and citing the widely lamented John Hawkesworth (?1715–1773), *An Account of the Voyages undertaken by the Order of His Present Majesty for Making Discoveries in the Southern Hemisphere* (Strahan and Cadell, 1773) (ESTC: N34379)).

188 Cavendish, Mansfield {30}.

189 Hawkesworth had been a high literary figure of his age, but his *Voyages* were lamented for having such a high price for such a short book: J.L. Abbott, 'John Hawkesworth: Friend of Samuel Johnson and Editor of Captain Cook's Voyages and of the Gentleman's Magazine', *Eighteenth-Century Studies*, iii (1970), 341–3. In the Commons the lampooning continued, saying if *it* sold for three guineas better books would sell for hundreds:

carried by the bookseller and not the public (and such losses would give a lesson encouraging booksellers to be more cautious).[190] Conversely, it was indicated that while the London Stallholders might not print books themselves, they still benefited from selling cheaper books.[191] Counsel for the opponents claimed the price would be higher simply because of the exclusive right granted but, both sides agreed, that as the number of books remaining of an impression fell the price would rise.[192]

There were even arguments about supply and demand. On one side it was argued that the small reductions in price would not affect consumption, on the other that when the price of commodities[193] increased sales would be reduced.[194] The price sensitivity was such that it was suggested that two impressions produced by different booksellers at the same time would 'ruin' a bookseller.[195] The relationship of price to quality was also raised: cheap books led to poor and inaccurate editions and this harmed both authors and the public.[196]

Quality Editions

Those against the Bill called for protection from their 'oppressors',[197] whereas the London Booksellers portrayed themselves as the 'good' booksellers and others (the Scots) as 'cheap' or 'bad' booksellers,[198] whose stock was sold at market stalls.[199] The Scottish printers might reduce the price, they said, but they would leave the public to guess at the 'havoc they will make, in correctness and perspicuity',[200] as a purchaser will only know the quality after the book has been bought.[201] On the same theme, William Graves MP proudly proclaimed that no gentleman would allow a poor quality edition into his library.[202] The London Booksellers gave numerous examples of what they suggested were editions of poor quality,[203] claiming Donaldson had published only a few *old* books and on 'bad paper' which were 'unpardonably incorrect' and 'scandalous[ly] mutilated' which (most claimed) were not even

189 *(continued)* Cavendish, Thurlow, {S10}; it also appears to have been mentioned in *Donaldson v Beckett* (1774) *Cobbett's Parl. Hist.*, xvii, cols 968, 970.

190 General Observations/Hints {MC9}; Cavendish, Thurlow {S10}.

191 Further Remarks {7}.

192 Cavendish, Dalrymple {233–4}; General Observations/Hints {MC13}.

193 They were referring to 'discretionary' purchases: Further Remarks {7}.

194 Cavendish, Dalrymple {235}; a similar sort of argument was made some time later regarding patents by James Maitland (Lord Lauderdale), *An Inquiry into the Nature and Origin of Public Wealth* (Edinburgh, 1804), 168–71.

195 General Observations/Hints {MC13}.

196 General Observations/Hints {MC5; GO1}.

197 Committee Evidence Observations {15}; and when the Bill reached the Lords, it appears that their Lordships saw them as oppressors and little more: Lord Camden, *Middlesex Journal*, 2–4 June.

198 A complaint was that the term bookseller was used as an 'invidious epithet', being indiscriminately applied: General Observations/Hints {MC5; GO2}.

199 General Observations/Hints {MC5; GO2}.

200 General Observations/Hints, {MC10}.

201 Cavendish, Wedderburn {S19}.

202 Cavendish, Graves {S18}.

203 There was some suggestion that false dating would occur on poor editions (see saving provision): Further Remarks {8}.

cheaper than the London editions.[204] An example was *Stockhouse's Bible* which had been published in two folio editions for three guineas,[205] whereas Donaldson printed it in six octavo volumes for six crowns[206] in basic prints with small letters making it difficult to read. Such abridgements (and the removal of notes) affected the quality of the edition, but the real complaint was that Donaldson did not tell the world what he had done.[207]

The opponents argued that with competition the quality of printing and books would improve and prices reduce,[208] so granting a longer exclusive right would actually *reduce* quality.[209] To cover all bases, they went further by asking what was wrong with cheaper coarse editions – coarse woollens and linen were accepted as necessary,[210] so why should the poor not have books too?[211] So battle was joined between those saying that if the market was open there would be a race to produce the cheapest and coarsest editions,[212] and those saying increased competition would improve quality. As time told us, little changed in terms of quality or access to books.

Loss of Employment

The Scottish booksellers were obviously concerned about the effect of the Bill on their business. Donaldson himself apparently started in business in 1750 soon after the court of session[213] 'held' there was no common law copyright,[214] and he sold new books, such as those by Lord Bankton, Lord Kames and David Hume;[215] but he also sold old books.[216] While he was fighting to continue his trade he also said it would give the country printing trade a share of the market in school books and other necessary

[204]Remarks on Donaldson's Petition {1}. This appears to be based on a like for like basis taking into account book sizes.

[205]£3 3*s*.

[206]£1 10*s*.

[207]Cavendish, Mansfield {28–9}.

[208]See for instance, Glasgow Memorialists {10 and 14}.

[209]Further Remarks {8}; reference was made to the high reputation of Paris printers; Cavendish, Dalrymple, {239–40}.

[210]Cavendish, Dalrymple, {239} (he also criticised the French approach and praised the Dutch); Cavendish, Murphy {263}.

[211]It is referred to as a comment of Lord Kames: Cavendish, Murphy {263}, which is probably based on a paragraph in *Midwinter v Hamilton* (1748) Kam Rem 160; Mor 8295.

[212]Cavendish, Mansfield {S30–1}; for a more modern economic view, G.A. Akerlof, 'The Market for "Lemons": Quality Uncertainty and the Market Mechanism', *Quarterly Journal of Economics*, lxxxiv (1970), 488.

[213]*Midwinter v Hamilton*, a court of sessions case which was appealed in *Millar v Kincaid* (1751) 1 Pat App 488; Deazley, *On the Origin of the Right to Copy*, 115–32.

[214]Donaldson's Petition {10}; Hector MacQueen, 'The War of the Booksellers: Natural Law, Equity, and Literary Property in Eighteenth-Century Scotland', *Journal of Legal History*, xxxv (2014), 231; Warren McDougall, 'Copyright Litigation in the Court of Session, 1738–1749, and the Rise of the Scottish Book Trade', *Edinburgh Bibliographical Society Transactions*, v (1971–87), 2.

[215]According to the English Short Title Catalogue he published the following volumes by those authors before his move to London: Andrew Bankton, *An Institute of the Laws of Scotland in Civil Rights* (1751–3) (ESTC: T90335–6); Lord Kames, *Essays on the Principles of Morality and Natural Religion* (1751) (ESTC: T70373); David Hume, *Political Discourses* (1752–4) (ESTC: T83618, T4007, T174609); *Essays and Treaties in Other Subjects* (1753–60) (ESTC: T217867, N70236, N8416, T167242, T199633, T33487, T33490).

[216]Donaldson's Petition {9}.

publications.[217] The flippant suggestion from the Bill's proposers, even said to be evidence, that shoemakers, weavers and others were now becoming publishers[218] each with literary agents going around hawking poor imitations of books.[219] In fact, this only mirrored the practices of the major booksellers who had long had a network of agents and retailers to sell their books.[220] So (even if true) the 'pirates' were merely copying the way the trade worked.[221]

Both sides claimed that the outcome of the Bill would change all this. The opponents pleaded that 'hundreds' of Scots in paper mills and many more working as booksellers, bookbinders and printers would lose their jobs.[222] In response, the London Booksellers simply said if you do not grant relief thousands will lose work; in other words our loss would be bigger than yours.[223] So, in turn, Dalrymple claimed at second reading that across the whole country 100,000 tradesmen would suffer from the Bill.[224] This question of loss directly led to an argument on the Bill's effect on the public revenue.

The Revenue

The Booksellers claimed, almost in passing, that the revenue would benefit more from the success of the London Booksellers than it would from that of the Scottish booksellers.[225] Counsel submitting boldly that as employment is higher without a monopoly so must be the taxes collected; and conversely the grant of a monopoly would reduce the return to the revenue. In terms of actual figures, the treasury gave no indication as to the revenue collected from booksellers.[226] So broad assumptions were made, such as that Thomson's *The Seasons*, which was successful, would bring significant receipts to the revenue.[227] The argument was entirely speculative and so it is not surprising it did not detain the House for long.

North American Trade

Exports to North America made up only a small part of the domestic business.[228] The London Booksellers' had a key role in supplying books to America,[229] but so did others,

[217] Goldsmith's Hints {19; 9no}.

[218] Cavendish, Mansfield {31–2}.

[219] Cavendish, Mansfield {32}.

[220] Raven, *Publishing Business in Eighteenth-Century England*, 39.

[221] Lord Auchinleck in *Hinton v Donaldson* (1773) *Boswell's Report* 4 says '*pirates* (a cruel name)', possibly demonstrating the term's inappropriateness.

[222] Part IV, Edinburgh Booksellers' Petition {7}; Cavendish, Dalrymple {235–6}.

[223] Remarks on Donaldson's Petition {3}; London Booksellers' Considerations {3–4}.

[224] Cavendish, Dalrymple {236}; in *Donaldson v Beckett* (1774) *Cobbett's Parl. Hist.*, xvii, col. 963, he had estimated that there were 30,000 involved in the book trade in London. It is not clear why the figures changed so substantially.

[225] Remarks on Donaldson's Petition {3}.

[226] Cavendish, Dalrymple {236}; the petitioners asked for the figures.

[227] Cavendish, Dalrymple {240}.

[228] James Raven, 'The Importation of Books in the Eighteenth Century', in *The Colonial Book in the Atlantic World*, ed. Hugh Amory and D.D. Hall (Chapel Hill, NC, 2010), 184, calculates that by the 1770s it was about 120,000 items or about 4% of British output.

[229] Raven, 'The Importation of Books in the Eighteenth Century', 185.

with ships leaving Scottish ports, in particular Glasgow, containing books.[230] The international trade was beset by issues, particularly due to the need for long lines of credit.[231] The challenges allowed the reprinters of books to gain market share by giving longer and more generous credit to American bookshops.[232] While it was rapidly changing during the third quarter of the century, many leading American booksellers still sold only imported books,[233] with local printing largely covering the bottom end of the market.[234] Even in larger towns, such as Philadelphia, there had been slightly over a dozen printers who had come and gone over the previous decades;[235] and in Boston, probably the most established town for the book trade, by 1771 there were only seven importing booksellers and ten printer-booksellers along with a handful of bookbinders and jobbing printers.[236] Thus, the book culture in America was closer to that in large provincial cities in England than its capital.[237] Nevertheless, by the time of the Bookseller's Bill the cheaper[238] reprint market was slowly starting to become localised,[239] but the Scottish and Irish booksellers were still fighting to protect their share of the market.

Accordingly, when the Scottish booksellers' counsel[240] argued that many merchants had warehouses in North America and they would send ships back to Scotland, or regional England, to buy more stock – including books – it was true; but it probably would have been a small part of their business. The fragile nature of the market led to a follow-on argument that to satisfy these book orders, if a monopoly existed, merchants had three options: to keep a large stock in Scottish warehouses; not send the books; or to send to London for the books. Each of which was said to be unacceptable: keeping the books in stock would undermine any profit, and if stock was requested from London the ship would have sailed before the order was met.[241] Accordingly, it was argued, that if the trade was not free in Britain it would go to North America where no restrictions existed.[242] In simple terms, passing the Bill would push trade to North America. In the end, of course, this happened as a consequence of the revolutionary war.

[230] Calhoun Winton, 'The Southern Book Trade in the Eighteenth Century', in *The Colonial Book in the Atlantic World*, 231, 239 (two ships from Glasgow to Maryland a year; one shipment of books being a mere 76 volumes).

[231] Raven, 'The Importation of Books in the Eighteenth Century', 191, and 193 for some specific examples of credit given.

[232] Raven, 'The Importation of Books in the Eighteenth Century', 194 (James Rivington gives 16% discount and a year's credit). Rivington largely relied on the Scots and Irish reprint trade: J.N. Green, 'The Middle Colonies, 1720–90', in *The Colonial Book in the Atlantic World*, 281–2.

[233] Winton, 'The Southern Book Trade', 236.

[234] Green, 'The Middle Colonies', 272, 279; Glasgow: Winton, 'The Southern Book Trade', 239.

[235] Green, 'The Middle Colonies', 272.

[236] Hugh Amory, 'The New England Book Trade, 1713–90', in *The Colonial Book in the Atlantic World*, 332.

[237] Green, 'The Middle Colonies', 277; Amory, 'The New England Book Trade', 316.

[238] Green, 'The Middle Colonies', 284–5. As to the price differential, a London copy of Blackstone's *Commentaries* sold in Philadelphia for $26, whereas a local imprint cost just $8.

[239] In 1775 there were still only 1,000 American imprints of any sort: Green, 'The Middle Colonies', 294.

[240] Similar arguments had already been presented in a lobbying document: Glasgow Memorialists {21}.

[241] Cavendish, Dalrymple {243}; it was also said that the terms of credit offered by London booksellers precluded stock being held.

[242] Cavendish, Dalrymple {244}.

Interests of Authors

It was disputed whether the interest of authors was protected by the Booksellers' Bill. Indeed, the link between the author and the text were far from axiomatic.[243] The London Booksellers said only those seeking copyright would procure the works of good authors,[244] and all such authors were in favour of the Bill.[245] The existence of copyright, it was claimed, enabled booksellers to patronise authors once kings and great men had ceased doing so.[246] Some going further and claiming all the principal works published since early in the reign of George II were made possible only by booksellers' patronage.[247] In other words, without copyright, authors could not reap any advantage from their bargains.[248] In support they sought testimonials,[249] cited laudatory statements of authors for their booksellers, such as those of Samuel Johnson,[250] and pleaded tales of authors' woes due to poor receipts:[251] Thomas Otway[252] died in poverty, Ben Jonson was constantly petitioning for relief,[253] and Milton's plight was the source of extensive discussion.[254] Indeed, the London Booksellers went further, saying that even when there was patronage it was for poets rather than works of history and prose.[255]

This attempt to canvas opinion was looked at unfavourably by the opponents,[256] who suggested that in fact the authors were quite against the Bill.[257] Going on to say it did not favour authors at all,[258] rather it was the London Booksellers alone who would be protected.[259] Indeed, the demand for old books would reduce demand for current authors

[243]Mark Rose, 'The Author as Proprietor: *Donaldson v Beckett* and the Genealogy of Modern Authorship', *Representation*, xxiii (1988), 73.

[244]General Observations/Hints {MC5; GO1}.

[245]Remarks on Donaldson's Petition {3}; cf. Cavendish, Onslow {114}, who said the Scots would welcome the Bill.

[246]General Observations/Hints {MC6; GO2, GO4}.

[247]General Observations/Hints {MC6; GO4}; in fact, booksellers' patronage had begun much earlier: Feather, *A History of British Publishing*, 28.

[248]General Observations/Hints, {GO2}.

[249]The Booksellers also cited testimonials of their fellow printers such as Jacob Tonson, by then deceased: General Observations/Hints {GO6–7; MC9}; and some opponents were careful not to criticise the dead, see Glasgow Memorialists {2–4} where much is made of Andrew Millar's achievements.

[250]General Observations/Hints {MC7; GO5–6}.

[251]General Observations/Hints {MC7; GO5–6}.

[252]Theophilus Cibber, *Lives of the Poets of Great Britain and Ireland* (5 vols, 1753), ii, 333–4 (suggesting he was begging on the street when he died).

[253]Frances Teague, 'Ben Jonson's Poverty', *Biography*, ii (1979), 260, 263, while mentioning the petitioning suggests that Jonson had more than enough money for his needs towards the end of his life.

[254]Cavendish, Murphy {262}; MacLenna, 'John Milton's Contract for "Paradise Lost"' (suggesting he was commercially astute).

[255]General Observations/Hints {MC7; GO4}.

[256]Petition Committee Report {589 c. i}.

[257]Goldsmith's Hints {19; 10mo}.

[258]Cavendish, Dalrymple {240–1}; the protection granted to authors who have yet to assign probably being taken to be illusionary.

[259]Cavendish, Beauchamp {125}, Jollifee {127–8}.

and so payments to them.[260] There was little evidence heard either way on the benefits to authors,[261] but much was made of the fact that no author gave testimony.[262] Indeed it was said that if authors wanted the right then let them rather than the Booksellers petition parliament for it.[263] Nevertheless, Edmund Burke eulogised that he had hoped literary property could be the 'exclusive perfect property right' of the author,[264] and even Thurlow and Murphy accepted that a privilege for authors was merited as they brought books to the world.[265]

Fame

While the argument was made that authors wrote, or at least should write, for fame and not money,[266] the Booksellers' supporters dismissed this almost contemptuously because it would mean authors must love fame more than eating or existing.[267] Shakespeare,[268] it was said, did not appear to love fame but needed pecuniary reward from his plays being performed.[269] Thus, it was claimed that without the passage of the Booksellers' Bill the 'lamp of science will be in danger of extinction'.[270] As copyright was for the 'encouragement of learning', Feilde said, it should be granted.[271] Indeed to ram the argument home, a return was made to quality editions, James Mansfield saying that low quality editions might lead to the wrong name being affixed and, critically, the name of a famous author being substituted for another – so even those who write for fame would suffer.[272]

Errant Newspapers and Other Plays to the Emotions

Counsel against the Bill, Sir John Dalrymple, argued that the Bill should be rejected, not only because of its lack of merit, but also because its proposers[273] were the owners of

[260] *Farther Strictures on the Booksellers' Petition* (where it also pointed out it caused a lack of transparency which would mean authors would not know the value of their work); Cavendish, Dalrymple {241–2}.

[261] Cavendish, Mansfield {27}.

[262] Cavendish, Murphy {52}.

[263] Case Observations {3}.

[264] Cavendish, Burke {S26}.

[265] Cavendish, Thurlow {46}, Murphy {51}.

[266] Cavendish, Onslow {111–12}; authors who write for money, Dalrymple submitted, write for the mob: Cavendish, Dalrymple {237–8}.

[267] General Observations/Hints {MC6; GO3}.

[268] As to the extent of the publication of his work during his lifetime, Pollard, *Shakespeare's Fight with the Pirates*, chs 2, 3.

[269] General Observations/Hints {MC6; GO3}; this of course would also lead to fame.

[270] General Observations/Hints {MC9; GO7}.

[271] Cavendish, Feilde {101}.

[272] Cavendish, Mansfield {32}.

[273] It was true that booksellers had significant shares in many of the newspapers, but how many of them were petitioners is less clear: Michael Harris, 'The Structure, Ownership and Control of the Press, 1620–1780', in *Newspaper History: From the Seventeenth Century to the Present Day*, ed. George Boyce, James Curran and Pauline Wingate (1978), 92–4; a letter to the *Morning Chronicle*, 13 May§ ('Florida Turf'), argued the shareholders had no editorial involvement.

scandalous newspapers who had insulted the king and members of the House.[274] This argument dominated many of the reports into his speech. Dalrymple suggested that it was only since the Bill had entered parliament that the insults had stopped, and they would restart once the Bill had left again.[275] A theme was picked up by his junior, who continued to allege that Henry Woodfall, the editor of the *Public Advertiser*, who had recently been jailed,[276] was connected with the promoters of the Bill.[277] Indeed, James Mansfield did not stand up for the newspapers, rather distancing his clients from their publication.[278] Others questioned whether the libelling of ministers or others should be a ground to refuse the relief.[279] These emotive arguments were not the only ones put forward, as attempts were made to turn it into a Scottish question; in other words, the English should be grateful for what the Scots gave them,[280] or conversely the Scots deserved no credit, because they had rebelled.[281]

Ignorance, Counsel and How to Know

The promoters had to address the fact that under the common law[282] ignorance[283] of the law is and was no excuse.[284] The most sophisticated argument was that where there was settled law or practice then deference should be given as this was more than a mere error of law.[285] To exemplify[286] this difficulty many MPs,[287] and indeed one of the counsel,[288] made a very imperfect analogy using the title to an estate.[289] The argument, simply expressed, is that John Doe holds the title of an estate, the judges differ as to whether John Doe is entitled

[274] General Observations/Hints {MC13}; Cavendish, Dalrymple {230–2}.

[275] Cavendish, Dalrymple {232}; he jokingly suggested a six-year term so that each election year the parliamentarians could have a year off from the abuse. It was also said that the 'liberty of the press' was something that should be protected: Cavendish, Dalrymple {230}.

[276] It was based on his publication of *Public Advertiser*, 15 Feb§.; *CJ*, xxxiv, 456 (14 Feb.); *CJ*, xxxiv, 526–7 (2 Mar.).

[277] Cavendish, Murphy {260–1}.

[278] Cavendish, Mansfield {24}.

[279] Cavendish, Onslow {110–11}.

[280] Cavendish, Dalrymple {238–9}; cf Mansfield {23}.

[281] Cavendish, Onslow {113–14}; the most likely one he was referring to was the return of 'Bonnie' Prince Charlie in 1745.

[282] Indeed, at this time the biblical rule would also be well known: Leviticus 5:17.

[283] At one point Murphy refers to it being a misconstruction of the law (Cavendish, Murphy {49}) but there seems little in the distinction.

[284] The rule was well known in relation to a criminal offence (*ignorantia legis non excusat*), while the matter was less clear in civil law: Sir William Holdsworth, *A History of English Law, Vol. 13* (1938), 513.

[285] Cavendish, Feilde {93–4}.

[286] Attempts to make literary property equivalent to land already having a long history. It is explored at length as a central theme of Rose, *Authors and Owners*; see also, Sherman and Bently, *The Making of Modern Intellectual Property Law*, 20–4, 26, in the context of using 'occupancy'.

[287] Folkestone's Diary, 16 May.

[288] Cavendish, Murphy {257}.

[289] There was a long history of this analogy in the literary property debate: Arthur Murphy, *The Gray's-Inn Journal* (Dublin, 1756), i, 20–5, no. 4 (11 Nov. 1752) (ESTC: T112211); Rose, *Authors and Owners*, 7. It also appears to have been used by some judges in *Donaldson v Beckett* (1774) *Cobbett's Parl. Hist.*, xvii, col. 979, per Willes J.

to do so, but ultimately John Doe is ejected. In such a case, parliament would not restore his estate. Indeed, the Glasgow Memorialists even found a specific example of an estate where the House of Lords had upheld a landowner's title to an estate in one appeal, but 20 years later ejected him following another;[290] albeit the real example was not taken up by any MP in the House.

A subsidiary point was that MPs suggested the Booksellers should have taken counsel's opinion on whether *Millar v Taylor* was correctly decided.[291] The solicitor-general retorted by asking whether they were meant to go into the coffee houses, ask students and note takers whether *Millar* was correct?[292] And Burke asked why a bookseller should rely on his own opinion over that of a judge.[293] The other side, returning to the estate example said that even if John Doe took counsel's opinion, once the court had ejected him parliament would not give him his property back.[294] The booksellers made much of the fact William Blackstone had sold the rights in his *Commentaries* perpetually[295] to Mr Strahan,[296] and later it was pointed out that Sir John Dalrymple had sold the perpetual rights in his *Memoirs of Great Britain and Ireland*[297] while he was counsel[298] for Donaldson, arguing against the existence of a right.[299] If these great men did not know, how could the Booksellers?

A risk, identified by George Dempster, was that if the Booksellers' Bill passed then parliament would face other bills seeking to reverse judicial decrees.[300] Sir John Dalrymple even took the argument so far as to say that parliament should not overturn a court decree and vice versa.[301] The basis of this suggestion is unclear, as even his own junior put it, over time 'laws change'.[302]

Weighing the Evidence

Sherman and Bently suggest that the house of lords in *Donaldson v Beckett* moved the arguments from ontological reasoning that there is 'literary property' to a more consequentialist

[290] Glasgow Memorialists {18–19}, based on *Antonius, son of Count Leslie v James Leslie* (1742) 1 Paton 324 (*LJ*, xxvi, 108, 29 Apr. 1742); and *Charles Cajetan, Count Leslie v Peter Leslie Grant* (1763) 2 Paton 68 (*LJ*, xxx, 326, 2 Feb.).

[291] Cavendish, Graves {S17}; no opinion was taken, Petition Committee Report, *CJ*, xxxiv, 590.

[292] Cavendish, Wedderburn {S19}.

[293] Cavendish, Burke {S27}.

[294] Folkestone's Diary, 16 May; Cavendish, Dalrymple {250–1} used other examples, such as the Ship Money Case and the Catholic fines being waived by James II; cf. Cavendish, Fielde {92–3}.

[295] Remarks on Donaldson's Petition {2}; Cavendish, Feilde {97}.

[296] Further Remarks {7}.

[297] *Memoirs of Great Britain and Ireland, from the Dissolution of the Last Parliament of Charles II until the Sea-battle off La Hogue* (Strahan and Cadell, 1771) (ESTC: T145644).

[298] General Observations/Hints {MC10}; Cavendish, Fielde {98}.

[299] He answers the comment in his speech, see Cavendish, {255–6}.

[300] In the 17th century there was a practice of reversing chancery decrees by seeking Acts of parliament: Elizabeth Read Foster, *The House of Lords 1603–1609: Structure, Procedure, and the Nature of its Business* (Chapel Hill, NC, 1983), 105.

[301] Cavendish, Dalrymple {252}; Deazley, *On the Origin of the Right to Copy*, 162, describes the various cases on common law copyright as considering the extent to which the common law could 'supersede' statute.

[302] Cavendish, Murphy {261}; a similar comment had been made by Paul Fielde already: Cavendish, Fielde {S235}.

approach,[303] so looking at why copyright should be granted rather than the intrinsic worth of authorship. The Booksellers' Bill precisely demonstrates this transformation with its discussion of the effect on the marketplace, the quality of books and trade, along with more traditional arguments mounted of a conflict between property owners and users.[304] But these larger narratives should not cloud the fact that evidence seems to have played a secondary role in the belief and positions taken by MPs. Those in favour of the Bill simply described their side's case as 'very true',[305] or merely discounted evidence presented by the other side;[306] others simply taking the view that even if there were evidence it did not justify the cases being made[307] or that their side's case was simply 'common sense'.[308] Maybe it was just *quod gratis asseritur, gratis negatur*.[309]

303 Sherman and Bently, *The Making of Modern Intellectual Property Law*, 39.

304 Remarks on Donaldson's Petition {3}.

305 Cavendish, Onslow {S21}.

306 Cavendish, Dempster {24}, Johnstone {79}.

307 Cavendish, Dalrymple {245–6}, Graves {S16}.

308 Cavendish, Thurlow {S9}.

309 'What is asserted gratuitously may be denied gratuitously'. Or, as it was put by Christopher Hitchens, 'What can be asserted without evidence can also be dismissed without evidence.': *God is Not Great: How Religion Poisons Everything* (2007), 150.

Chapter 6
The Bill

Introduction

The Bill itself was neither very long nor complicated even after it had passed the house of commons.[1] There were three preambles which set out the protection granted under the Statute of Anne,[2] the belief the Booksellers had in a common law copyright and the investments it caused them to make,[3] and the hardship caused by the decision in *Donaldson v Beckett*.[4] The Bill passed, so the Commons found the allegations to be true.[5] The key provision of the Bill was that a 14-year copyright would be granted in old books.[6] It also set the sanction, namely forfeiting 'pirated' books and damages of £10 per copy (half to the crown),[7] required booksellers to register the books before 29 September 1774 to enjoy the right[8] (with publication in the *Gazette* as an alternative).[9] There was to be a legal deposit requirement for the university libraries, Advocates Library and the British Museum.[10] Next, there were savings enabling existing legally printed works to be sold off,[11] and preserving the rights of the universities[12] before ending with procedural provisions.[13]

Exclusive Right

The wording of the first clause of the Booksellers' Bill began in a very similar fashion to the Statute of Anne,[14] setting out the exclusive right. The right was to be given to authors who had printed and published a book,[15] but not yet transferred the copyright; the only key difference was the earlier enactment referred to the transfer of the copy (and not the copyright). This purports to create a link between authors and the right granted, but in reality few authors would have retained the copyright if the book had already been published.[16] The Booksellers' Bill went on to make it clear that anyone who had acquired

[1] Ingrossment: Parliamentary Archives, HL/PO/JO/10/2/53.

[2] Recital (1).

[3] Recital (2).

[4] Recital (3).

[5] Likewise, a jury had found similar things proven in *Millar v Taylor* (1769) 4 Burr 2408 at 2354 (98 ER 228, 257); Ronan Deazley, *On the Origin of the Right to Copy* (Oxford, 2004), 174–5.

[6] Clause 1 (unpublished books, when first published would be protected by the Statute of Anne).

[7] Clause 1.

[8] Clause 2: there was a 2*s*. fee to register, although inspection was to be free.

[9] Clause 3; and £20 for the clerk.

[10] Clause 4.

[11] Clause 5.

[12] Clause 7; but it does not apply to 'any person': cf. Chapter 4: The Statute of Anne – Pre-Existing Right.

[13] Clauses 6 and 8; clause 9 deemed it a public act.

[14] Copyright Act 1709 (8 Anne, c. 19).

[15] The Statute of Anne referred only to printed (but not published). It is not clear what distinction was intended by the addition of the words 'and published'.

[16] A handful of authors would have paid for publication, but these are unlikely to have been economically viable books: Part IV, Further Remarks {33; 1st Clause}.

the copyright from the author had an exclusive right. In contrast to the Statute of Anne, it referred to the 'executors' and 'administrators' as well as assignees, leading Edmund Burke to say 'the Act of Queen Anne … made no provisions'[17] in cases where the author dies – something the Booksellers' Bill clearly did. Other than a few minor consequential changes the 1774 Bill lifted the wording from the provision protecting existing books from the Statute of Anne.[18] The main change was statutory damages being based on the number of books being printed rather than by the sheet.[19] So while complaints were made about the sanctions,[20] because they reflected the existing statutory regime such objections got short shrift. There had been some speculation during the passage of the Bill[21] as to the term that would be given.[22] But when the blanks were finally being filled up, a 14-year term was granted.[23] A shorter term of seven years had been suggested,[24] but Burke argued this was not enough as it was a replacement for perpetuity.[25]

Ex Post Facto Law

A repeated criticism of the Bill was that it created an *ex post facto* law – that is it changed the law in relation to things passed.[26] In strict legal terms this is not true as there was saving for books already printed.[27] But the Bill clearly would have given a right in relation to a work already created and, in that sense, it related to things already done.[28] The Booksellers' counter argument was that the Bill had become necessary only after *Donaldson* and it had been impossible to apply for the Bill any earlier,[29] and, as Burke argued, a person should not have to wait to suffer the injury before coming to parliament to avoid it.[30]

[17] Cavendish, Burke {135}.

[18] Omitting the 14-year term for books 'already composed' or 'hereafter … composed' and not printed and published.

[19] Compare Booksellers' Bill, cl. 1 and Copyright Act 1709, s. 1; this move had been foreshadowed in the Booksellers' Bill 1737, cl. 2: An Act for the Encouragement of Learning (Draft) (1737), *Primary Sources on Copyright (1450–1900)*, ed. Lionel Bently and Martin Kretschmer, www.copyrighthistory.org.

[20] Further Remarks {3–4; 3d to 5th Clause}.

[21] Burke also argued that the Booksellers' Bill would reduce copyright to 14 years. It is not clear why he came to this view. The exclusive right sought might have impliedly repealed the equivalent provision in the Statute of Anne (the now spent 21-year term for printed books), but there is no reason to suppose it would also repeal the 14-year term for new books. It is supposed the knock-on effect would be that there would be no 'said' term of 14 years to revert under Copyright Act 1709, s. 11.

[22] The *Middlesex Journal*, 24–6 Mar§. said 21 years; and 'an enemy' said the booksellers should ask for ten: *Morning Chronicle*, 8 Apr§. and *St James's Chronicle*, 5–7 Apr§. One of the opponents had proposed that the length of the exclusive right varied by the length of the book: Part IV, Glasgow Memorialists {11–12}.

[23] Cavendish, Fielde {135}.

[24] Cavendish, Mackworth {135}; also, the ambiguous statement of James Harris {135}.

[25] Cavendish, Burke {135}.

[26] Cavendish, Beauchamp {126}.

[27] Clause 5.

[28] Extending the term for existing works has been common ever since: Copyright Act 1842 (5 & 6 Vic., c. 45); Copyright Act 1911 (1 & 2 Geo. V, c. 46); Duration of Copyright and Rights in Performances Regulations 1995 (SI 1995/3297).

[29] Part IV, London Booksellers' Considerations; indeed, as mentioned in ch. 3, they applied within six days.

[30] Cavendish, Burke {S24–5}.

The London Booksellers also turned to precedent: Jane Hogarth had been given an individualised *ex post facto* law[31] in the Engraving Copyright Act 1766,[32] granting her an additional 22 years exclusivity for the engravings of her husband William Hogarth.[33] However, it was said that she had not been given a prospective right to compensate for 'loss', rather it was based on William Hogarth's extraordinary (and exceptional) talent,[34] or possibly because she was suffering hardship at the time.[35] It was probably thought to be tactically unwise to refer back to the Statute of Anne giving an almost identical right to that sought over 60 years later. Both were *ex post facto* laws or neither were.

Registration

The Booksellers' Bill copied the registration system from the Statute of Anne with only one material difference: it had a cut-off date of 29 September 1774, rather than as in the Statute of Anne, the date of publication.[36] The requirement to register a work with the Stationers' Company was very old,[37] but it lacked any incentive as the advantages of doing so did not necessarily outweigh the cost.[38] This flaw was perpetuated in the Statute of Anne[39] because registration was not a requirement to obtain equitable remedies such as an injunction or account of profits (only the remedies set out in the Act).[40] There is no reason to suppose the wording proposed by the Booksellers was intended to have a different effect – accordingly, the statutory sanctions sought in the Bill would probably not be sought before the court had the Bill been enacted; rather booksellers would have sought injunctions and disgorgement of profits. The deposit requirement was in real terms nugatory, like it was under the Statute of Anne. The Bill also proposed an alternative to registration which followed the Statute of Anne. However, the earlier provision had been enacted because of a concern that outsiders (non-members of the Stationers Company) would not be able to register works,[41] and so a mechanism was created whereby protection could be obtained under the Statute of Anne

[31] London Booksellers' Considerations {3}.

[32] Section 3; Cavendish, Feilde {121–3}.

[33] William Hogarth* (1697–1764). Nobody referred to the provision in the Engraving Copyright Act 1734, s. 5 which granted rights to John Pine to print engravings of tapestries depicting the Spanish Armada in 1588.

[34] He was probably the most famous English painter and engraver of the period. Cavendish, Lord Beauchamp {123–4}.

[35] Part IV, Remarks on Donaldson's Petition {3}.

[36] Compare Copyright Act 1709, s. 2 and Booksellers' Bill, cl. 2.

[37] Star Chamber Decree 1637, article xxxiii (see Edward Arber, *A Transcript of the Registers of the Company of Stationers of London, 1557–1640* (5 vols, 1875–94), iv, 528); and Licensing of the Press Act 1662 (13 & 14 Chas. II, c. 33), s. 17.

[38] Ian Gadd, 'The Stationers' Company in England Before 1710', in *Research Handbook on the History of Copyright Law*, ed. Isabella Alexander and H. Tomás Gómez-Arostegui (Cheltenham, 2016), 88–9; C.S. Clegg, *Press Censorship in Elizabethan England* (Cambridge, 1997), 17–19.

[39] It does not appear that the Scots had difficulties with registering in London: Hector MacQueen, 'Literary Property in Scotland in the Eighteenth and Nineteenth Centuries', in *Research Handbook on the History of Copyright Law*, ed. Alexander and Gómez-Arostegui, 123.

[40] Lord Mansfield in *Tonson v Collins* (1762) 1 Black W 321 at 330 (96 ER 184 at 184); Gómez-Arostegui, 'Equitable Infringement Remedies', 222–4.

[41] Deazley, *On the Origin of the Right to Copy*, 47–8 (which also discusses the poor drafting of the provision).

by advertising the book in the *Gazette*.[42] This mechanism was unsatisfactory, yet it would have been perpetuated by the Booksellers' Bill.

Deposit

The idea of booksellers being required to deposit a certain number of copies in important national libraries long predated the Booksellers' Bill or even the Statute of Anne. It probably began in 1610–11 with an agreement between Oxford University and the Stationers' Company whereby one book of every edition would be deposited at the Bodleian Library.[43] This requirement was included in the decree of the star chamber in 1637,[44] and then extended to the King's Library and Cambridge University by the Licensing of the Press Act 1665.[45] It was maintained and extended in the Statute of Anne,[46] and the presentation version of the Booksellers' Bill[47] mirrored the requirement. However, since 1710 a library had been started at the British Museum,[48] and so deposit at that institution was added in bill committee.[49] A proposal that the monopoly should be dependent on the delivery of books to the British Museum was specially rejected,[50] thereby keeping the approach consistent with the Statute of Anne.[51]

Saving and Exclusions

The Booksellers' Bill had many of the same savings, albeit slightly modified, as found in the Statute of Anne, but first it is important to consider those which were new. The Bill included a saving whereby copies of books which were printed before the passing of the Act (had that happened)[52] could be sold.[53] This was criticised on the grounds it would be open to fraud and vexatious litigation,[54] but it was an attempt to balance the public interest and that of the London Booksellers. Its remit was very narrow as it only applied to copies of books already printed, and books in production.

[42] Copyright Act 1709, s. 3; Further Remarks {4; 4th to 6th Clause}.

[43] Copy of Indentures for Sending Books to Bodleian Library, 28 Jan. 1611 (*The Records of the Stationers' Company 1554–1920* (1986), reel 99, no. 12; *Literary Print Culture* (Adam Matthew, 2017): TSC/1/E/5); Patterson, *Copyright in Historical Perspective*, 138.

[44] Clause 17.

[45] (17 Chas. II, c. 4), s. 2.

[46] Copyright Act 1709, s. 5 (to include the libraries of the four universities in Scotland, the Sion Library in London and the Advocates Library in Edinburgh).

[47] The Booksellers' Bill 1737, cl. 13 had proposed extending the requirement to every new edition, but this did not get carried through to 1774.

[48] It was founded under the British Museum Act 1753 (26 Geo. II, c. 22).

[49] Amendments marked up on bill at Part IV, Booksellers' Bill.

[50] Cavendish, Wedderburn {136}.

[51] Lord Mansfield in *Tonson v Collins* (1762) 1 Black W 321 at 330 (96 ER 184).

[52] This would not have protected anyone in relation to claims under the Statute of Anne if that term were still running.

[53] Booksellers' Bill, cl. 5.

[54] Further Remarks {4; 9th Clause}; Donaldson's Lords Petition {3} (as it would have to be proved when a book was published).

The Statute of Anne provided that it did not extend to Greek, Latin or other foreign language books printed overseas.[55] Throughout the debates in 1774 the Booksellers seemed to accept that rights should not vest in 'classics'. It was queried by William Graves why no such right was claimed and whether any money had been paid for the right to print such books.[56] The answer is not clear,[57] as it was suggested in the *Remarks on the Booksellers' Petition* that classics were bought and sold.[58] Indeed, if there had been common law right independent of the Statute of Anne, why would a restriction in that act matter? Nevertheless, the restriction on classics in the legislation still bit home.[59] It would be absurd to suggest Horace had assigned his rights to the predecessors of the London Booksellers,[60] but likewise there was no basis to say that Shakespeare ever sold the right to some of his plays.[61] Yet the Booksellers claimed the latter by occupancy,[62] so why not Caesar or Aristotle? There was no logic to their position but it enabled the Booksellers to say a particular part of the market ('the whole of learning') was open to all booksellers.[63] Stranger still was that the Booksellers' Bill as it passed the Commons did not actually exclude books in Greek or Latin, and so for all their grand statements it appears such books would (so far as they had a copyright owner) be covered by the Bill.

The Scottish booksellers had long faced a difficulty with copyright and had challenged it on patriotic grounds since the 1730s.[64] It was clear in 1774 before *Donaldson v Becket* that the common law of Scotland did not protect literary property and so George Johnstone asked why the Scottish booksellers, who relied on *Midwinter v Hamilton*,[65] should be punished.[66] Sir John Dalrymple, counsel for the opponent, likewise proclaimed the Bill could not be correcting any mistaken belief in that country.[67] Conversely, George Onslow said point-blank that a new right extending to Scotland would be to its benefit.[68] The Scottish booksellers also pointed out that Scottish authors usually printed in London and not

[55] Section 7; it was changed during the passage of the Statute of Anne to extend it from classics: Deazley, *On the Origin of the Right to Copy*, 40 n. 39. It appears the Glasgow opponents thought a short period for a new foreign book might be acceptable: Glasgow Memorialists {12}.

[56] Cavendish, Graves {S16}.

[57] The point is made by Goldsmith's Hints {19; 7mo} with no real elucidation.

[58] Part IV, Remarks on the Booksellers' Petition; this was repeated in the variant version in the *Edinburgh Advertiser*, 29 Mar.–1 Apr.

[59] Part IV, Petition Committee Report {588 c. ii}; Cavendish, Feilde {100–1}.

[60] Goldsmith's Hints {4; 8vo}.

[61] While some were sold, others were not: A.F. Pollard, *Shakespeare's Fight with the Pirates* (Cambridge, 1920); J.M. Gaba, 'Copyrighting Shakespeare: Jacob Tonson, Eighteenth Century English Copyright, and the Birth of Shakespeare Scholarship', *Journal of Intellectual Property*, xix (2011), 21; Giles Dawson, 'The Copyright of Shakespeare's Dramatic Works', in *Studies in Honor of A.H.R. Fairchild*, ed. C.T. Prouty (Columbia, 1946), 9.

[62] Occupancy was one of the main arguments put forward by William Enfield, *Observations on Literary Property* (1774), 18 *et seq.*; it was one of the ways that literary property could be equated with real property: Rose, *Authors and Owners*, 90. But it presented problems in that ideas could not be occupied in the same way: for a discussion, Brad Sherman and Lionel Bently, *The Making of Modern Intellectual Property Law* (Cambridge, 1999), 21.

[63] Cavendish, Fielde, {100–1}.

[64] John Feather, *Publishing, Piracy and Politics: An Historical Study of Copyright in Britain* (1994), 81; Mark Rose, *Authors and Owners: The Invention of Copyright* (Cambridge, MA, 1993), 68.

[65] (1748) Kames 158; *Millar v Kincaid* (1751) 1 Pat App 488.

[66] Cavendish, Johnstone {77}.

[67] Cavendish, Dalrymple {253–4}.

[68] Cavendish, Onslow {112–14}.

Scotland[69] and, it was claimed by the proposers, this was because there was no reward available to their own authors in their own country.[70] In the end, while a clause was proposed which would not extend the right to Scotland[71] there was no quorum to vote on it and so it did not make it into the Bill.

The Bill did, however, retain a saving for the universities,[72] albeit narrower than that in the Statute of Anne.[73] The material difference being that the newer version did not include the saving of right for 'any person', only for Oxford and Cambridge and the four Scottish universities.[74] The clarification fits with the arguments made earlier that 'any person' was in the Statute of Anne to preserve the common law right. If that right was now conceded there was no longer any need to protect anyone but the universities.

Concluding Thoughts

The Bill itself, without much regard to any evidence, tried to strike a balance between the two interests. Even those who put forward an extended monopoly still claimed the Bill balanced the public interest, and the loss arising from a misconception of law.[75] Yet as Lord Folkestone explained:

> … this is the case the Booksellers got all they could in the years and when their great advantage of that monopoly was over, they repeatedly petitioned Parliament for further advantages.[76]

This conclusion was surely right. The Bill created a monopoly for a handful of men and the countervailing provisions were toothless in comparison. So how did the press report and address this balance? Did newspaper proprietors and editors take a clear side or was the report balanced and fair? It is to this that we now turn.

[69] Part IV, Edinburgh Booksellers' Petition; London Booksellers' Considerations {4}.

[70] Part IV, General Observations/Hints {MC10}; Cavendish, Feilde {100}. This enabled the London Booksellers to claim they gave every encouragement to Scottish authors and the Scottish publishers were complaining about rewards to other Scots: General Observations/Hints {MC9; GO7}.

[71] The clause is included in the *Morning Chronicle*, 20 May; an indication of the debate is in Cavendish, {142}.

[72] Cl. 7.

[73] Copyright Act 1709, s. 7.

[74] The wording identifying the universities was also more precise in the Booksellers' Bill.

[75] General Observations/Hints {MC5}.

[76] Folkestone's Diary, 16 May.

Chapter 7
Parliamentary Reporting

Introduction

The parliament of 1768–74 is sometimes called 'The Unreported Parliament',[1] but it was far from it. The shorthand notes of Sir Henry Cavendish[2] make it one of the best recorded pre-Victorian parliaments, and by its end it was also the first to have routine and continuous reporting of proceedings in newspapers, something that would continue for over 200 years.[3] As will be discussed below, reports had existed before in various forms. But 1774 saw the majority of the London press starting to print reports the next day and, significantly, it was the only year where the Cavendish diaries overlap with this form of reporting.[4] While Cavendish is far from perfect, his diary is thought to be the best attempt at contemporaneous reporting for decades,[5] and in some ways it begins the history of parliamentary oratory.[6] So using it enables us to see how much was captured, or missed, by newspaper reporters. But to begin it is important to understand the problems and difficulties parliamentary reporters faced.

Prehistory

The house of commons had started restricting 'strangers'[7] from entering the chamber sometime before the Elizabethan era,[8] and anyone infringing the rule would have been removed and often imprisoned. A series of standing orders reinforcing these rules were to be passed,[9] and continued to exist long after the period being considered here. These orders resulted from the opposition between the crown and parliament in the 16th and 17th centuries,[10] with parliament attempting to maintain the complete secrecy of its proceedings so as to protect free debate and its members from the wrath of an unhappy monarch.

[1]Coined by John Wright's report of the parliament: *Sir Henry Cavendish's Debates of the House of Commons, During the Thirteenth Parliament of Great Britain, Commonly called the Unreported Parliament*, ed. John Wright (2 vols, 1841). Others, however, have suggested it was called this due to the attempts to strictly enforce the prohibitions against reporting: Michael MacDonagh, *The Reporters' Gallery* (1913), 168.

[2]See Part II.

[3]As the ending of newspaper reporting of parliamentary proceedings: Andrew Sparrow, *Obscure Scribblers: A History of Parliamentary Journalism* (2003), ch. 7.

[4]Also see the Preface to *Cobbett's Parliamentary History*, xiii.

[5]P.D.G. Thomas, 'Sources for the Debates of the House of Commons, 1768–1774', *BIHR*, special supp., iv (1959), vii.

[6]Christopher Reid, 'Whose Parliament? Political Oratory and Print Culture in the Later Eighteenth Century', *Language and Literature*, ix (2000), 127.

[7]Meaning anyone other than an MP or official.

[8]John Hooker, 'Sessions of Parliament in the Reign of Elizabeth', in Lord Mountmorres, *The History of the Principal Transactions of the Irish Parliament from 1634 to 1666* (Cadell, 1792) (ESTC: T70500); Sir Simonds D'Ewes, *The Journal of all the Parliaments During the Reign of Elizabeth* (Shannon, 1682) (ESTC: R473637), 334 (28 Nov. 1584), 394 (5 Nov. 1586), 512 (27 Mar. 1593).

[9]Josef Redlich, *The Procedure of the House of Commons: A Study of its History and Present Form*, trans. A.E. Steinthal (3 vols, 1908), ii, 34–5.

[10]Redlich, *Procedure of the House of Commons*, ii, 36.

To buttress the rule barring strangers from the chamber there were standing orders restricting the publication of proceedings.[11] These originated in 1641 following Lord Digby publishing one of his parliamentary speeches.[12] The original standing order read 'that no person whatsoever, do presume at his Peril, to print any Votes or Proceedings of this House, without the special Leave and Order of the House',[13] and it was reiterated numerous times with similar orders being made subsequently. As Thomas puts it, during the 18th century:

> Parliament's moral authority derived from its representative nature, [yet] the great majority of MPs were unwilling to acknowledge direct personal responsibility to the electorate, whether their own constituents or the wider political nation.[14]

Such restrictions remained in force until late in the 19th century,[15] despite parliamentary reporting being long established by this time.[16] Some of the earliest parliamentary reports were by Abel Boyer[17] in *The Political State of Great Britain* which ran from 1711 until 1737,[18] and later *The Gentleman's Magazine*[19] started printing reports in 1731[20] (largely copied and unattributed from the *The Political State* and later the *London Magazine*).[21] These early reports were printed during the recess, when parliament was not sitting, in the belief that the standing orders did not apply.[22] It also allowed time for more sources to be consulted to check the accuracy of reports.[23] Nevertheless, when a complaint was raised by the house of

[11] There were some reports which seem to have been tacitly accepted: for example, *Debates of the House of Commons*, ed. Anchitell Grey (10 vols, 1769); Redlich, *Procedure of the House of Commons*, ii, 37. Manuscript records of debates circulated even when print was banned: Jason Peacey, 'The Print Culture of Parliament, 1600–1800', *Parliamentary History*, xxvi (2007), 7–8; these continued until at least the mid-century; Markman Ellis, 'Philip Yorke and Thomas Birch: Scribal News in the Mid 18th Century', *Parliamentary History*, xli (2022), 202. As to the records of debates in the early days of printing, John Ferris, 'Before Hansard: Records of Debates in the Seventeenth Century House of Commons', *Archives*, xx (1992), 198.

[12] *CJ*, ii, 208–9 (13 July 1641). A year earlier, on 25 Apr. 1640 (*CJ*, ii, 12), steps had been taken to restrict the clerk, John Rushworth, from taking notes beyond orders and reports made: Redlich, *Procedure of the House of Commons*, ii, 36; for a more detailed account, Jason Peacey, '"Rushworth Shall Not Take Any Notes Here": Journals, Debates and the Public, 1640–60', *Parliamentary History*, xxxiii (2014).

[13] *CJ*, viii, 74 (25 June 1660).

[14] P.D.G. Thomas, *John Wilkes: A Friend to Liberty* (Oxford, 1996), 125.

[15] As to the attempts to revoke the standing orders: Sparrow, *Obscure Scribblers*, 48–52.

[16] Indeed, there was long a rule that it was improper to refer to what a member had said on a previous occasion due to the imperfections of memory: P.D.G. Thomas, *The House of Commons in the Eighteenth Century* (Oxford, 1971), 214–15 (later there would be complaints of the opposite); as to the history of the press, B.B. Hoover, *Samuel Johnson's Parliamentary Reporting* (Berkeley, CA, 1953), ch. 1.

[17] For his methods, Hoover, *Samuel Johnson's Parliamentary Reporting*; Mary Ransome, 'The Reliability of Contemporary Reporting of the Debates of the House of Commons, 1722–1741', *BIHR*, xix (1942), 69; Nikki Hessell, *Literary Authors, Parliamentary Reporters: Johnson, Coleridge, Hazlitt, Dickens* (Cambridge, 2012), 18–19.

[18] When access to the galleries became more restricted: Paul Mantoux, 'French Reports of British Parliamentary Debates in the Eighteenth Century', *American Historical Review*, xii (1907), 256.

[19] By Johnson's time it was the more accurate publication: Hessell, *Literary Authors, Parliamentary Reporters*, 34.

[20] P.D.G. Thomas, 'The Beginning of Parliamentary Reporting in Newspapers 1768–1774', *EHR*, lxxiv (1959), 623.

[21] MacDonagh, *The Reporters' Gallery*, 122; Ransome, 'The Reliability of Contemporary Reporting of the Debates', 76.

[22] Hoover, *Samuel Johnson's Parliamentary Reporting*, 9.

[23] Hessell, *Literary Authors, Parliamentary Reporters*, 36.

commons, the publications would cease or at least become more restricted.[24] For instance, mythical names were substituted for real ones, such as Lilliputia for the House itself,[25] and partial or anagrammatical names were used for speakers such as Sir R___t W__le for Sir Robert Walpole, and for anagrams keys were produced to assist the reader.[26]

Style of Early Reports

The reports were compiled by reporters attending debates and then retiring to a tavern to compare notes,[27] or from speakers providing their speeches privately. Where the reporter attended the Houses, any notes compiled would usually only set out the subjects of discussion, the names and order of the speakers, the side they took and some of the key points made,[28] meaning the majority of the report was largely an invention. One of the most famous reporters of this period was Dr Samuel Johnson,[29] who, some years after the event, described his process: he would be told a few details of the debate and the main arguments raised, after which he would write it up.[30] He even claimed he went to the gallery of the Commons but once,[31] which has led to a view that the eloquence perceived of the orators was largely imagined in his head and had little to do with reality. In fact, he had notes and comments for most of his work and this anecdote should not be taken literally.[32] His approach to remote working was not unusual,[33] and his 'creative' reports were simply a more elegant version of how everyone else worked.[34]

The reporting of proceedings with obscured or fictious names continued until the coverage of Lord Lovat's[35] trial for treason in 1747 when the *Gentleman's Magazine* and the *London Magazine* were both reprimanded. The former stopped parliamentary reporting entirely and the latter's reports became a very general summary. Such summaries continued until interest waned so much following Sir Robert Walpole's fall[36] that they stopped entirely in 1757. Soon reporting started once more, but the printers were soon found in contempt and in

[24] *CJ*, xxiii, 148 (13 Apr. 1738).

[25] Names began to be footnoted from 1743 so it became a little pointless: *London Magazine* (July 1743), 313.

[26] That for the *Gentleman's Magazine* was published as a mock advertisement for *Anagrammata Rediviva*: *Gentleman's Magazine* (supplement, 1738), viii, 700–2; and later *Gentleman's Magazine*, xii (supplement, 1742), 699.

[27] Sir John Hawkins, *The Life of Dr Samuel Johnson* (Buckland, 1787) (ESTC: T113903), 95.

[28] MacDonagh, *The Reporters' Gallery*, 122, 140.

[29] His role as a reporter is widely documented: MacDonagh, *The Reporter's Gallery*, ch. 16; Hessell, *Literary Authors, Parliamentary Reporters*, ch. 2; Hoover, *Samuel Johnson's Parliamentary Reporting*.

[30] Arthur Murphy, *An Essay on the Life and Genius of Samuel Johnson* (1792), 43–6. For instance, Johnson once reported a celebrated speech on the Press Ganging Bill (27 Jan. 1741) by William Pitt the Elder replying to a speech by Horace Walpole in support of his brother Sir Robert Walpole. It was said to be entirely invented by Johnson: William Coxe, *Memoirs of Horatio, Lord Walpole* (1802), 323. Johnson's version of the exchange is in the *Gentleman's Magazine*, xi, 569–70, Sept. 1741.

[31] Murphy, *Life and Genius of Samuel Johnson*, 44–5.

[32] William Coxe, *Memoirs of the Life and Administration of Sir Robert Walpole* (Cadell, 1798) (ESTC: T133960), i, pp. xxi–xxii. As to the views on Samuel Johnson's approach, Hessell, *Literary Authors, Parliamentary Reporters*, 4.

[33] Hessell, *Literary Authors, Parliamentary Reporters*, 19.

[34] MacDonagh, *The Reporters' Gallery*, chs 16, 17; also see Ransome, 'The Reliability of Contemporary Reporting of the Debates', 72.

[35] *Proceedings against Lord Lovat* (1746) 18 State Trials 529.

[36] He resigned in 1742.

1760 printed reports dried up once again. As the number of newspapers increased during the 1760s so did the competition that engendered, and eventually William Woodfall's *Morning Chronicle* and Edward Beckford's *Middlesex Journal* started including parliamentary reports. These began as brief summaries of reported speeches,[37] but the increased interest in political material led to John Almon publishing further accounts of the proceedings in parliament in his new *London Museum*.[38] This in turn led the *London Magazine* and the *Gentleman's Magazine* to restart publishing parliamentary debates. It appeared at first that the resumed activity would only attract intermittent parliamentary attention.[39]

The Printers' Case

When the new parliamentary session began in 1770[40] a larger number of daily and tri-weekly papers moved from occasional reporting in outline to fuller reports.[41] During the early part of the session, the newspapers would report a handful of debates at length, but the majority in summary.[42] The flashpoint, what came to be called the 'Printer's Case',[43] began on 5 February 1771 when Colonel George Onslow ('little cocking George') stood up in the Commons, complained about reporting and then required a standing order to be read out:[44]

> That it is an Indignity to, and a Breach of the Privilege of, this House for any Person to presume to give, in written or printed Newspapers, any Account or Minutes of the Debates or other Proceedings of this House, or any Committee thereof. That upon Discovery of the Authors, Printers, or Publishers, of any such written or printed Newspapers, this House will proceed against the Offenders, with the utmost Severity.

Reports followed in the *Middlesex Journal* and so Onslow moved that its printers (and also those of the *Gazetteer*) should be brought to the Bar of the house of commons. As the printers did not surrender, rewards were offered,[45] and by March the complaints had become more general and were not just directed against six editors.[46] A few days later

[37] Thomas, 'The Beginning of Parliamentary Reporting in Newspapers', 623, 624, 626.

[38] Patrick Bullard, 'Parliamentary Rhetoric, Enlightenment and the Politics of Secrecy: The Printer's Crisis of March 1771', *History of European Ideas*, xxxi (2005), 314.

[39] Robert Rea, *The English Press in Politics, 1760–1774* (Lincoln, NE, 1963), ch. 9.

[40] It began on 9 Jan. 1770.

[41] Thomas, 'The Beginning of Parliamentary Reporting in Newspapers', 626; he later suggested it was over a dozen: Thomas, *John Wilkes: A Friend to Liberty*, 127.

[42] Thomas, 'The Beginning of Parliamentary Reporting in Newspapers', 627–8.

[43] McDonagh, *The Reporter's Gallery*, chs 21–30. For a detailed discussion, Thomas, *John Wilkes: A Friend to Liberty*, ch. 8, which is a development of P.D.G. Thomas, 'John Wilkes and the Freedom of the Press (1771)', *BIHR*, xxxiii (1960), 86; R.R. Rea, *The English Press in Politics*, ch. 12.

[44] *CJ*, xxxiii, 142 (5 Feb. 1771); the standing order was made on 26 Feb. 1728/9 (*CJ*, xxi, 238). It appears that George III was unhappy about reports being published and this might have spurred on those opposing the printers: Thomas, *John Wilkes: A Friend to Liberty*, 129.

[45] The king offered a £50 reward for their arrest by a proclamation issued in the *London Gazette*, 9 Mar. 1771 (issue no. 11,125); also see Bullard, 'Parliamentary Rhetoric, Enlightenment and the Politics of Secrecy', 315; Thomas, *John Wilkes: A Friend to Liberty*, 129–30.

[46] William Woodfall, *The Morning Chronicle*; Thomas Evans, *The London Packet*; Henry Baldwin, *The St James's Chronicle*; John Miller, *The London Evening Post*; Samuel Bladon, *General Evening Post* and Thomas Wright, *Whitehall Evening Post*: *CJ*, xxxiii, 249 (12 Mar. 1771).

the Commons considered the appropriateness of debates being published; the issue was so controversial that there were 23 divisions (7.6% of all the divisions during the whole of the 1768–74 parliament)[47] causing the House to sit until 5 o'clock the following morning.[48] In their outrage, the Commons walked into a (not very secret) coup largely masterminded by the radical John Wilkes.[49] In contrast to earlier times the publishers were refusing to attend the Commons, rather hiding or remaining in their shops in the City of London.[50] The incident became more serious when the deputy serjeant-at-arms was arrested by a constable of the City for trying to 'illegally'[51] arrest the printers in their shops.[52] Incredibly, and probably collusively,[53] the two printers were brought before a City of London magistrate, who 'happened' to be John Wilkes.[54] He ordered their immediate release as they were detained under no law.

Thus, the question moved from whether the debates could be published to the power of the Commons to drag recalcitrant printers before the House. An alderman of the City appeared before the House in late March. He was followed a few days later by the lord mayor.[55] Both were imprisoned in the Tower until May,[56] although their incarceration was softened by gifts and expressions of support from around the country.[57] During the crisis the response of the press varied. Some more cautious publishers, such as the *Lloyd's Evening Post* and the *London Chronicle,* stopped parliamentary reporting immediately upon George Onslow's complaint in early February;[58] the publishers of a further two papers (*St James's Chronicle* and the *General Evening Post*) briefly stopped when they appeared before the House in March,[59] although the *General Evening Post* was back to reporting proceedings

[47] Thomas, *The House of Commons in the Eighteenth Century*, 262; the total number of divisions was 301.

[48] Thomas, *John Wilkes: A Friend to Liberty*, 139. As to the votes, *CJ*, xxxiii, 249–51 (12 Mar. 1771); there was a further 12 votes a few days later: *CJ*, xxxiii, 285–9 (14 Mar.).

[49] Thomas, *John Wilkes: A Friend to Liberty*, 124, 129. The interest in reporting had also arisen in part from the contested and controversial Middlesex election.

[50] Wilkes and his group were able to dominate the City of London for many years, due in part to their willingness to defy convention: Thomas, *John Wilkes: A Friend to Liberty*, 115.

[51] As the warrant was not backed by a City of London magistrate: Thomas, *John Wilkes: A Friend to Liberty*, 132. A transcript of the warrant is in Isaac Hitchcock, *A Supplement to English Liberty*, MS Notes: London Metropolitan Archives, CLC/253/MS03332/002, ff. 33–5.

[52] Bullard, 'Parliamentary Rhetoric, Enlightenment and the Politics of Secrecy', 316.

[53] But see Alexander Andrews, *The History of British Journalism* (2 vols, 1859), i, 202; Hitchcock, *A Supplement to English Liberty*, ff. 41–2, where it appears the person who arrested the printers was fined and imprisoned which suggests against collusion. However, he lived 'like a prince' during his imprisonment suggests the opposite: Thomas, *John Wilkes: A Friend to Liberty*, 138. If this is right, it is a hard punishment for someone doing as ordered. The solicitor-general, Alexander Wedderburn, described it as 'a plain and manifest collusion': Motion on Allowing Lord Mayor to be heard by counsel, 20 Mar. 1771: BL, Egerton MS 226, f. 355. It is included, with slightly different wording, in *Sir Henry Cavendish's Debates of the House of Commons*, ed. Wright, ii, 437.

[54] MacDonagh, *The Reporters' Gallery*, 223–4.

[55] Accordingly, MPs who wished for support in the City of London were compelled to give their full support to the printers: Thomas, *John Wilkes: A Friend to Liberty*, 133.

[56] Bullard, 'Parliamentary Rhetoric, Enlightenment and the Politics of Secrecy', 317. They sought their release earlier, but De Grey LCJ and Lord Mansfield LCJ both refused their writ of *habeas corpus* on 5 Apr. and before the exchequer on 30 Apr., before they were finally released on parliament proroguing: Hitchcock, *A Supplement to English Liberty*, ff. 40–1 (5 Apr.), 93 (30 Apr.), 103–4 (8 May).

[57] Thomas, *John Wilkes: A Friend to Liberty*, 137; Hitchcock, *A Supplement to English Liberty*, ff. 55–92, 93–101.

[58] Thomas, 'The Beginning of Parliamentary Reporting in Newspapers', 629; *CJ*, xxxiii, 142 (5 Feb. 1771).

[59] *CJ*, xxxiii, 258–60 (14 Mar. 1771); Thomas, 'The Beginning of Parliamentary Reporting in Newspapers', 629.

within a week. The defiant printers of the *London Evening Post*, the *Middlesex Journal* and the *Gazetteer* all published debates throughout, and even those who had stopped resumed after the Easter recess.[60] The episode had been a humiliation for the government[61] (as Wilkes had intended) and a bold move against the secrecy that marked the conduct of government.[62]

It was clear that if the house of commons tried to assert its privilege in this way in the future it would face the same difficulties and might cause another crisis.[63] As Thomas puts it 'the House, therefore contented itself with the token vindication of its authority',[64] and looking back it is clear that after the crisis the House completely abandoned any attempt to stop publishing parliamentary debates.[65] As MacDonaugh suggests, the House did not yield to the newspaper publishers because members believed there should be reporting of their proceedings, but because to stop it they would have to have implemented the most draconian laws.[66] However, the publishers were not yet sure they would not be sanctioned and so they began reporting again only hesitantly. In the two sessions following the crisis of 1771, the main reporter of debates, John Almon, still only reported on a Tuesday in the *London Evening Post* what had happened in the previous week, so he was only able to cover the major debates in brief. Similarly short reports appeared in the *Gazetteer*,[67] both newspapers being widely copied by other publications. While coverage continued to grow over the following sessions, the key year, as highlighted at the beginning, was 1774. It was a year when the interest in parliamentary news peaked, as Josiah Tucker put it 'this country is as much News mad, and News-ridden now, as ever it was Popery-mad, and Priest-ridden, in the Days of our Forefathers'.[68] It was when more of the London newspapers began to publish parliamentary reports of their own composition, albeit still routinely copying each other. By 1774 newspaper readers had started to expect reports of parliamentary debates and a failure to include them affected sales.[69]

The Problems of Reporting

The session of 1774 (when the Booksellers' Bill was before the house of commons) was the first where the London papers tried to report parliamentary proceedings routinely, but it was

[60]Thomas, 'The Beginning of Parliamentary Reporting in Newspapers', 630.

[61]Thomas, *John Wilkes: A Friend to Liberty*, 138.

[62]Bullard, 'Parliamentary Rhetoric, Enlightenment and the Politics of Secrecy', 317; MacDonagh, *The Reporters' Gallery*, ch. 26.

[63]It was not until 1774 that the peers agreed to open their doors: M.W. McCahill, *The House of Lords in the Age of George III (1760–1811)* (Oxford, 2009), 254; William Lowe, 'Peers and Printers: The Beginnings of Sustained Press Coverage of the House of Lords in the 1770s', *Parliamentary History*, vii (1988), 241.

[64]Thomas, 'The Beginning of Parliamentary Reporting in Newspapers', 630; Thomas, *John Wilkes: A Friend to Liberty*, 139.

[65]Arthur Aspinall, 'The Reporting and Publishing of the House of Commons Debates 1771–1834', in *Essays Presented to Lewis Namier*, ed. Richard Areas and A.J.P. Taylor (1956), 227–8; Thomas, *John Wilkes: A Friend to Liberty*, 139.

[66]McDonagh, *The Reporters' Gallery*, 260.

[67]Thomas, 'The Beginning of Parliamentary Reporting in Newspapers', 631.

[68]Josiah Tucker, *Four Tracts on Political and Commercial Subjects* (Raikes, 1774) (ESTC T85923), 82.

[69]Thomas, 'The Beginning of Parliamentary Reporting in Newspapers', 631–2.

also when reporters were still finding their feet.[70] Before examining how this manifested itself in the reports of the Booksellers' Bill itself, it is important to understand the conditions under which the reporters worked.

The difficulties faced by early parliamentarian reporters were so great it is incredible that anything was reported at all. There was no press gallery, indeed the press had no separate accommodation until the house of commons was rebuilt after the fire of 1834. The press had to compete with everyone else (and each other) to get a seat in the gallery.[71] However, it was not yet a public gallery, as a person needed a written introduction from a member of parliament to enter the gallery, or at least a willingness to pay a small bribe to the door-keeper (it appears that the reporters simply paid one larger bribe of a guinea each session).[72] And once inside, there was only one gallery, which was divided into sections, one of which comprised 200 seats 'below the bar' where the public (and press) could sit.[73] Once they began to be acknowledged, the reporters were even restricted to its back row, further limiting access.[74] They did not get any special access until 1803,[75] when they were allowed in first before the general public (but still after any members' guests, who could still fill the gallery on occasion).

The main chamber would usually start sitting at 4 p.m.,[76] but the public gallery would be open from noon so reporters might have to turn up before that time to get access. For the debates with the greatest public interest this would have involved turning up to queue very early in the morning.[77] It also appears that getting into the public gallery was not an orderly affair: William Woodfall describes how the public eager to hear the debates 'suddenly overpowered the doorkeepers and, pressing onwards through the front of the House, filled the gallery in a second'.[78] It was said later that the pressure in the passageway leading to the gallery could be so great at times there was a risk of legs or arms being broken.[79] Even if the reporters did get a seat, the debates could run for many hours; the second reading of the Booksellers' Bill did not adjourn until around 1 a.m., so its reporters may have been in their seats for at least 13 hours (and there were times when a reporter's shift could last a full 24 hours).[80]

[70] Later there was also the issue of government subsidies for newspapers which could have affected coverage: Aspinall, *Politics and the Press*, ch. 3; but as the sums involved were small it might not have been enough to affect [70 (continued)] coverage: Hannah Barker, *Newspapers, Politics and English Society 1695–1855* (1999), 81 (albeit some 'bribes' might have been paid to influence coverage: 83).

[71] Earlier in the century 'strangers' had not just been confined to the gallery; such a restriction began in George III's reign: Thomas, *The House of Commons in the Eighteenth Century*, 140.

[72] Thomas, *The House of Commons in the Eighteenth Century*, 148.

[73] Aspinall, 'The Reporting and Publishing of the House of Commons Debates', 232; O.C. Williams, *The Topography of the Old House of Commons* (1953), unpublished monograph held in the Parliamentary Archives: HL ARC/VAR/319.

[74] Aspinall, 'The Reporting and Publishing of the House of Commons Debates', 233.

[75] Sparrow, *Obscure Scribblers*, 30–1.

[76] Redlich, *Procedure of the House of Commons*, ii, 77.

[77] A little later, in 1800, Coleridge reported arriving at 7 a.m. to get into a debate: James Gillman, *The Life of Samuel Taylor Coleridge Vol. I* (1838), 207 (he later fell asleep due to the early start).

[78] *Morning Chronicle*, 12 Feb. 1780.

[79] *The Times*, 24 May 1803; *Morning Herald*, 18 Feb. 1783; Aspinall, 'The Reporting and Publishing of the House of Commons Debates', 235.

[80] McDonagh, *The Reporters' Gallery*, 307.

The house of commons was not a quiet place,[81] and any reporter might struggle to hear what was said either because of the poor acoustics or simply the background noise. Henry Cavendish made excuses for his reports saying:

> … the disorder that, now and then, used to prevail in the House; where sometimes Members from an Eagerness to hear others, or themselves, made so much noise as to drown the voice of the person speaking.

He continued:

> sometimes premature applause for a former part of a sentence prevented the House from hearing the latter; and sometimes those favourite words "hear, hear," so frequently echoed thro' the House, forbad all hearing.[82]

This meant there was a fairly constant hum of noise from private conversations, movements and general chatting.[83] Using a digital reconstruction of the old house of commons the acoustics have been analysed enabling it to be demonstrated that it was not a good venue for public speaking. It was also found that some seats had better acoustics than others, but not necessarily those seats which visually or politically were at a premium.[84] In other words, some backbenchers would hear better than leading politicians. It even appears that some positions in the gallery enabled reporters to hear better than many MPs, but in others much worse.[85] The poor acoustics meant reporters in some parts of the gallery would not have heard the debate very clearly at all.

While the house of commons tacitly allowed the reporting of its proceedings by 1774, it would still routinely clear the gallery of everyone (including reporters).[86] It was possible for a single member to notice a stranger in the House and the whole gallery would be cleared,[87] and it was also cleared for a division.[88] Once cleared any reporting of proceedings is precluded.[89] So very controversial debates, such as those relating to the loss of America,

[81] Williams, *Topography of the Old House of Commons*. Some reproductions of paintings and plans are discussed in Clare Wilkinson, 'Politics and Topography in the Old House of Commons, 1783–1834', *Parliamentary History*, xxi (2002), 141.

[82] Cavendish, draft Preface, BL, Egerton MS 263, f. 2. 'Hear ! Hear !' was not always support, of course, it might signify irony or sarcasm as well.

[83] Thomas, *The House of Commons in the Eighteenth Century*, 222.

[84] Including the Speakers' chair.

[85] Catriona Cooper, 'The Sound of Debate in Georgian England: Auralising the House of Commons', *Parliamentary History*, xxxviii (2019), 73. The best clarity was in the middle of the gallery at the rear of the chamber, and the worst was in the gallery on the left-hand side of the chair.

[86] Hatsell, *Precedents of Proceedings in the House of Commons*, 128–9. It appears that the opposition were usually in favour of admitting the press, probably to build support, whereas the government was less concerned: MacDonagh, *The Reporters' Gallery*, 270.

[87] This only ended with a modified rule in 1875: *CJ*, cxxx, 244 (31 May 1875); it had happened a few times in the decades before that point: 18 May 1849, 8 June 1849, 24 May 1870: Redlich, *Procedure of the House of Commons*, ii, 35.

[88] This ended in 1853: *Hansard*, 3rd ser., cxxix, cols 1112–3 (1 Aug. 1853); Aspinall, 'The Reporting and Publishing of the House of Commons Debates', 231; there were nine divisions on the Booksellers' Bill: see Part IV.

[89] Which is what makes Cavendish's reports so helpful in that he would not have had to leave.

could lead to the gallery being cleared and consequentially no record of proceedings in the newspapers.[90] While the Booksellers' Bill was interesting enough to get reported it was thankfully not controversial enough to lead to the gallery being cleared.

In the 1770s it was not permitted for reporters to take any notes,[91] and so any reports of proceedings in 1774 were either from secret notes made under the watchful eye of the House officials or made from memory.[92] Indeed, the requirement to rely on memory led to William Woodfall's moniker 'Memory Woodfall' for his seeming ability to remember vast amounts of what took place in the debate.[93] Apparently, he would sit in the gallery leaning forward with both hands clasped on a stick, and his eyes closed, so he could hear as much as possible; his only refreshment a hard-boiled egg.[94] In truth, memory was only part of it. Reporters' attendance at the House was supplemented by conversations in the lobby with members, gossip in coffee houses,[95] and, almost certainly, MPs providing copies of speeches to journalists.[96] Even later, when notes could be taken, it does not appear that any of the reporters could write in shorthand,[97] meaning that, at best, what was remembered was the gist or spirit of the speech and not its content.[98] As Thomas put it after comparing newspaper reports with those of Cavendish:

> Despite the fame of Woodfall's memory, the reports are not characterised by the retention of the actual phrases used by the speakers. At best only the general patterns of the speeches are the same: the wording is entirely different.[99]

Indeed, even Woodfall himself said his reporting was usually 'a mere skeleton of the arguments urged upon the occasion' and readers should not understand him to be reporting 'the exact phraseology used by the speakers'.[100] Speaking more generally of parliamentary reporters who did not rely on shorthand let alone notes McDonagh suggests:[101]

[90] MacDonagh, *The Reporters' Gallery*, 269–70.

[91] It appears that notes were allowed at an earlier time, so reporting may have been less accurate in the 1770s than in the 1730s: Ransome, 'The Reliability of Contemporary Reporting of the Debates', 76.

[92] Thomas, 'The Beginning of Parliamentary Reporting in Newspapers', 634. It is probable the ban on taking notes ended around 1783, but there is no clear evidence of when or why this happened: Aspinall, 'The Reporting and Publishing of the House of Commons Debates', 230–1.

[93] MacDonagh, *The Reporters' Gallery*, ch. 31.

[94] MacDonagh, *The Reporters' Gallery*, 268–9.

[95] John Almon, *Memoirs of a Late Eminent Bookseller* (1790) (ESTC: T6644), 119.

[96] Aspinall, 'The Reporting and Publishing of the House of Commons Debates', 237–8, 241–2; MacDonagh, *The Reporters' Gallery*, 192–2; Almon, *Memoirs*, 119; Barker, *Newspapers, Politics and English Society*, 90–1. Even vocal critics of the press might supply speeches, and Lord Perceval apparently did so: Robert Harris, *A Patriot Press: National Politics and the London Press in the 1740s* (Oxford, 1993), 19–22.

[97] In contrast to Cavendish, it appears the first reporter to use shorthand was John Collier, a reporter for *The Times*: MacDonagh, *The Reporters' Gallery*, 337, and, more generally, ch. 39.

[98] Even by 1820 shorthand writers were few and it was some time before it was thought appropriate to consider what was said rather than the spirit of what was said: Sparrow, *Obscure Scribblers*, 41–2.

[99] Thomas, 'The Beginning of Parliamentary Reporting in Newspapers', 635–6.

[100] *Morning Chronicle*, 26 Mar. (a reference to the report on the Booksellers' Petition); he makes a similar, but fuller, comment in his report of the Dublin parliament: William Woodfall, *An Impartial Sketch of the Debate in the House of Commons of Ireland, on a Motion for Leave to Bring in a Bill for Effectuating the Intercourse and Commerce between Great Britain and Ireland, on Permanent and Equitable Principles* (Dublin, 1785) (ESTC: N16791), ii.

[101] MacDonagh, *The Reporters' Gallery*, 340.

> It is to be feared that under the regime of the longhand reporters – who took beauty of expression and grace of form for their first object, and truth and accuracy for their second only – these speeches, of great personal as well as of political interest, have come down to us without any assurance whatsoever … that they rightly represent what was said, and still less that they preserve the distinctive individual diction of the orators.

Even where MPs provided their speeches to reporters, it would not have been precise. Reading out 'set' speeches or even the use of notes was frowned upon.[102] Nevertheless, it is likely that the speeches of Arthur Murphy, James Mansfield, Sir John Dalrymple and George Onslow, were first published in the *Morning Chronicle* and the *Middlesex Journal*,[103] and were provided by them or at least authorised by them.[104]

This means many records of speeches would have been fictions.[105] They could have been fictions propagated by the speakers themselves – getting published what they would *have liked to have said*. Or they could have been provided by those seeking fame or simply trying to mislead.[106] It has even been suggested that in the days of longhand reporting – which lasted well into the 19th century – the chief aim of the reporter was to reflect the 'qualities of his own mind much more than the mind of the speaker'.[107] Thus, the reports were a mixture of memory, hearsay, fraud and self-publicity. Yet, in relation to the Booksellers' Bill, there was an additional angle, namely self-interest. The proprietors of the newspapers had an interest in the outcome of the Bill and this too may have affected what was published.

Copying

News stories were often copied from elsewhere[108] and few editors hid it.[109] The copying might have been attributed, where the source was indicated, or straightforward lifting of material from rivals.[110] It may have been that the copying, for news at least, originated by reason of the cross-ownership of shares in other publications, but it was far more widespread than this allows. Copying of news made economic sense as the cost of reporting was a small part of production,[111] and so another paper using a story lost little 'value' invested in the paper. Indeed, the newspapers often saw news reports as a shared resource,[112] and by

[102] Thomas, *The House of Commons in the Eighteenth Century*, 203–4.

[103] *Morning Chronicle*, 12 and 16 May; *General Evening Post*, 14–17 May; *Middlesex Journal*, 14–17 May.

[104] Edmund Burke is known to have provided editors with corrected copies of his speeches as well, but not on this occasion: *The Writings and Speeches of Edmund Burke, Vol. III*, ed. W.M. Elofson, J.A. Woods and W.B. Todd (Oxford, 1996), 7–8.

[105] Thomas, 'The Beginning of Parliamentary Reporting in Newspapers', 634.

[106] 'Fake news' as it were.

[107] MacDonagh, *The Reporters' Gallery*, 339.

[108] This had long occurred in relation to the news; the *Grub-Street Journal* would run quotes to show the contradictions and others would join sources together for a complete account: Will Slauter, *Who Owns the News? A History of Copyright* (Stanford, CA, 2019), 2.

[109] Slauter, *Who Owns the News?*, 76.

[110] There seems to have been different standards for different types of material: Slauter, *Who Owns the News?*, 70–1.

[111] Slauter, *Who Owns the News?*, 68, 78.

[112] It enabled the news to spread more widely as well, as Richard Russel noted in the 1730s: Slauter, *Who Owns the News?*, 86.

the time parliamentary reporting became common copying was a part of the newspaper trade,[113] and copying from the better regarded reporters, such as Woodfall, was particularly common. There may have even been the sharing of type between certain papers.[114]

Nevertheless, publishers valued parliamentary reporting highly enough to obtain their own reports. This enabled them to represent the political persuasion of their readers or more precisely the editors and proprietors of the paper.[115] Yet copying was still rife (as demonstrated by the reports reproduced in Part III which have been edited so as to demonstrate this phenomenon), and there was an additional complexity: a report in *General Evening Post* may be copied from, say, the *Morning Chronicle*; a third newspaper, say the *Edinburgh Evening Courant*, may have copied from *General Evening Post*, but really it is an indirect copy of the *Morning Chronicle*. Thus, the permutations and modifications (made for space or style reasons) are often replicated down across titles. Further complexity arises as, occasionally, newspapers would print two versions of the same parliamentary proceedings from different sources.[116] While these versions were not contradictory, they were often very different in tone. Even when the number of reporters increased there would still be ways of trying to assist a defective memory, such as copying from earlier editions, and (probably) collusion between reporters as to what was said.[117]

Such copying clearly happened later in the history of reporting (even when shorthand notes were taken) as by the mid 19th century, the reporters would get together after a debate and one would read his notes to the others who in turn would complete the gaps or correct the transcript of the reader.[118] Thus, a collective or collaborative line might be taken as to what was said which may or may not have actually reflected the speech's content.[119] Critically, therefore, the more sources saying something – even different in style – does not necessarily make it accurate. Inaccuracies can arise from copying literally or non-literally and transposition errors can pass through many publications.

Limits of Space

The newspapers of the 1770s were usually four sheets. A full sheet would extend to about 5,000–6,000 words. In a typical day of reporting in the sixth series of Hansard about 70,000–80,000 words are recorded.[120] Assuming the total number of words spoken in the later 18th century was the same then even if there were verbatim reports less than 10% of material could be published. In these early days, reports of debates would occasionally stretch to a full page (and some for the Booksellers' Bill are this long), but they were often much shorter.

[113]Slauter, *Who Owns the News?*, 78.

[114]See Chapter 5: Cost of Production.

[115]Slauter, *Who Owns the News?*, 79.

[116]There are two versions in the *Caledonian Mercury*, 16 May (second reading) and *Edinburgh Evening Courant*, 23 Mar. (last day of petition committee).

[117]A slightly different issue is double typesetting where the same newspaper was printed on two different presses at the same time (due to demand). The copy had to be typeset twice and the versions might be fractionally different.

[118]MacDonagh, *The Reporters' Gallery*, 28.

[119]Sparrow, *Obscure Scribblers*, 46.

[120]As to what is reported and actually said see below: Chapter 7: Improving for Readership.

While parliamentary reporting was one of the central features of newspapers (along with advertisements), it was down to particular reporters or editors[121] whom to report and how much to report about each speaker. Thus, if a speaker was difficult to hear or had annoyed the reporters[122] they might get little or no coverage however elegant their speech, and those who gave poor speeches would not be worth inflicting on readers[123] (when other news could fill the space). Even the most famous of the 'orators' in parliament in 1774 were not necessarily comprehensible to listeners. Edmund Burke, one of the most famous members and a leading supporter of the Booksellers' Bill, was known to speak quickly but also with great complexity. His views were also often unpopular to his immediate audience and so there were sometimes attempts to stop him speaking or at least to get him to stop.[124] The significance of this, however, is not that speeches stopped but rather that if members of the House were unable to follow (or found the speech predictable or boring) then reporters faced the same problem and if speeches cannot be followed for any reason then reporting them was simply impossible.

This raises the question: why speak at all?[125] Tens or maybe a couple of hundred people would be present to hear an MP speak so why did orators bother to spend time preparing speeches which would be unlikely to affect any vote? A brilliant, but forlorn, speech being recorded for posterity or for one's electors is understandable,[126] but a great speech which would persuade nobody and possibly alienate those standing around the speaker are harder to comprehend. When Boswell asked Edmund Burke why he put so much effort into his speeches when he knew not one vote would be gained by them, he replied:[127]

> … I shall say, in general, that it is very well worth while for a man to take pains to speak well in parliament. A man, who has vanity, speaks to display his talents; and if a man speaks well, he gradually establishes a certain reputation and consequence in the general opinion, which sooner or later will have its political reward. Besides, though not one vote is gained, a good speech has its effect. Though an act which has been ably opposed passes into a law, yet in its progress it is modelled, it is softened in such a manner, that we see plainly the minster has been told, that the members attached to him are so sensible of its injustice or absurdity from what they have heard that it must be altered.

So it appears that striking passages, or great arguments, would be carried by the silent majority of members to the coffee houses and elsewhere thereby to the population more

[121] Who in the 1770s was often the same person.

[122] Famously, the comments of William Windham were ignored after he questioned the integrity of parliamentary reporters: Sparrow, *Obscure Scribblers*, 34–5; MacDonagh, *The Reporters' Gallery*, ch. 36. He did however publish his speeches: *Speeches in Parliament of the Right Honourable William Windham* (3 vols, 1812).

[123] MacDonagh, *The Reporters' Gallery*, 174–5 (referring to Burke's style and the failure of his speeches to make any impression at the time).

[124] Thomas, *The House of Commons in the Eighteenth Century*, 225.

[125] For a more detailed discussion of what it was like to speak, L.D. Reid, 'Speaking in the Eighteenth Century House of Commons', *Speech Monographs*, xvi (1949), 135.

[126] However, few ever read the speeches for recreation and many MPs, and even prime ministers, were contemptuous of reading parliamentary reports or *Hansard*: MacDonagh, *The Reporters' Gallery*, 435–7.

[127] James Boswell, *The Life of Samuel Johnson*, ed. David Womersley (2008), 650 (3 Apr. 1778); whereas Harris, 'What was Parliamentary Reporting?', 267, assumes there was an 'argument that divided the House'.

widely,[128] and so even if the House is not persuaded the respectable opinion elsewhere might be. While it might not yet have come to pass by 1774 it would soon be the case that leading parliamentarians would know that a significant speech would be 'recorded, reconstructed and textualized' during disseminations.[129] In addition, Burke and others spoke with the deliberate intention of publishing their speeches (and not merely in the newspapers) and it was necessary for a speech to be delivered – however long or difficult to listen to – before it could be published;[130] as Burke himself said 'It is very unlucky that the reputation of a speaker in the House of Commons depends far less of what he says there, than on the account of it in the newspapers.'[131]

Improving for Readership

In the context of parliamentary reporting the gold standard is that adopted by the official reports: *Hansard*. In 1907 such reports were originally written in shorthand and followed the recommendation of the *Select Committee on Parliamentary Debates*[132] requiring reports:

> which, though not strictly verbatim, is substantially the verbatim report, with repetitions and redundancies omitted and with obvious mistakes corrected, but which on the other hand leaves out nothing that adds to the meaning of the speech or illustrates the argument.

However, this is not all it seems. There have been studies of how much of what is actually said is recorded in *Hansard*. Sandra Mollin, taking four hours of debate on 13 June 2006, found that 18% of the words actually spoken in the House were not recorded in *Hansard*.[133] She presents numerous examples of how inelegant speech and repetitive phrases are tidied up.[134] Indeed, literalness in transliterating shorthand for the purposes of parliamentary reporting would not be welcomed by many politicians. It was even frowned upon by a 19th-century reporter, John Campbell, who later became lord chancellor, who mused that he 'knew nothing, and did not desire to know anything, of shorthand' as shorthand writers are 'wholly incompetent to report a good speech, because they attend to words without entering into the thoughts of the speaker'.[135] As McDonagh put it:[136]

[128]MacDonagh, *The Reporters' Gallery*, 178.

[129]Reid, 'Whose Parliament? Political Oratory and Print Culture in the later Eighteenth Century', 126, 128.

[130]See generally, Ian Harris, 'Publishing Parliamentary Oratory: The Case of Edmund Burke', *Parliamentary History*, xxvi (2007), 112.

[131]Letter from Edmund Burke to French Laurence, 16 Mar. 1797: *The Correspondence of Edmund Burke*, ed. T.W. Copeland (10 vols, Cambridge, 1958–78), ix, 284.

[132]*Select Committee on Parliamentary Debates* (1907 HC Papers 239), vol. vii, p. iii (in fact based on a definition from the earlier *Report from the Select Committee on Parliamentary Debates* (1893–4 HC Papers 213), xiii, 275, p. iii).

[133]Sandra Mollin, 'The Hansard Hazard: Gauging the Accuracy of British Parliamentary Transcripts', *Corpora*, ii (2008), 192. A similar exercise was conducted by Stef Slembrouck, 'The Parliamentary Hansard "Verbatim" Report: The Written Construction of Spoken Discourse', *Language and Literature*, i (1992), 101.

[134]See in particular, Mollin, 'The Hansard Hazard', 193, 194, 204; Slembrouck, 'The Parliamentary Hansard "Verbatim" Report', 105–7.

[135]*Life of Lord Campbell*, ed. Mary Hardcastle (2 vols, 1881), i, 105–6.

[136]MacDonagh, *The Reporters' Gallery*, 32–4.

> In first-person reports by even the leading parliamentarians it is sometimes necessary to smooth out intricacies, to suppress a trite or aimless phrase, to omit purposeless repetition, to make the halting sentence march in due line with its companions and to emphasise the main point by careful adjustment and proportion …

He continued:

> It would, indeed, be very cruel to report the Debates with absolute literalness. There is a great deal of matter that is rambling and irrelevant. Hazy ideas and slovenliness of expression are only too common.

Furthermore, many speakers in the house of commons were not great orators and many speeches were probably quite boring, repetitive and difficult to follow, and as was explained by Arthur Balfour in an after-dinner speech to the parliamentary reporters in 1908:[137]

> Most of us who have to make speeches … suspect that the speaker owes more to the report than, perhaps, we are always prepared to admit. I do not go to the length of saying that all the good things are put into a speech which the speaker never uttered, though that has been done … we all of us owe to the kind attention of the reporter the excision of many superfluities, not always, perhaps regard as superfluities by the orator, the correction of many gross errors of grammar, and an improvement in our oratory which we may be reluctant to admit, but which is nevertheless there. [I would like to thank you] for the work which you have done to improve our oratory, to spread our opinion, and to make clear the opinions … which we conceive, at any rate, that we hold.

Then, as in 1774, the papers would also write for their audiences.[138] The differences are that earlier papers had less to work with and fewer constraints. Many newspapers had particular audiences, while picking speakers or emphasising (or even embellishing) for a particular political audience would be expected.[139] In addition, there were some further influences arising from the trades a particular paper was directed towards. For instance, the *Morning Chronicle* was particularly strong with the book trade,[140] and so it is likely that Woodfall's reports would be tempered for that readership. The reporters were also attempting to record the speakers' ideas, rather than their words, recording the arguments presented by both sides, and setting out 'the sense of the debate'. Thus, reporters tried to pick out the most important arguments, whereas speakers simply reiterated arguments which had already been presented or at least would be confined to new arguments raised. There was no particular preference for reporting ministers over backbenchers,[141] but the most able speakers were more likely

[137] 'Mr Balfour and the Press', *The Times*, 11 Apr. 1908, p. 10.

[138] For a later instance, based on references to class, see Dror Wahrman, 'Virtual Representation: Parliamentary Reporting and Languages of Class in the 1790s', *Past and Present*, cxxxvi (1992), 83.

[139] E.g. Slauter, *Who Owns the News?*, 79.

[140] Asquith, 'Advertising and the Press in the late Eighteenth and Early Nineteenth Centuries', 709.

[141] Ian Harris, 'What Was Parliamentary Reporting? A Study of Aims and Results in London Daily Newspapers, 1780–1796', *Parliamentary History*, xxxix (2020), 261, 263, 265, 267, 270, 274. By the end of the 19th century, it had become the case that two-thirds of backbencher speeches were recorded in the third person and all of a minister's speech in the first person: MacDonagh, *The Reporters' Gallery*, 442.

to be reported, as usually it was they who would raise the new or important arguments.[142] Thus, reporters' views of the important issues in a debate set the tone in the country and, in turn, what we now see at this distant remove.

The Problems Summated

The problems faced by the reporters in the late 18th century were nicely summed up by James Stephen:

> No man was allowed to take a note for the purpose. To use a pen or pencil in the Gallery was deemed a high contempt … We were obliged therefore to depend on memory alone and had no assistance in the work … We … were obliged to sit in the Gallery from the sitting of the House till its adjournment, and afterwards, however late, to begin and finish our work before we retired to rest.[143]

Thus, the newspaper reports of this age cannot be taken as an accurate record of what was said. Such a luxury (if it ever existed before radio and television broadcasting)[144] did not appear until over 100 years later, but the reports of 1774 provide an interesting insight into the political discourse over a bill, and one which their publishers understood well.

[142] Harris, 'What Was Parliamentary Reporting?', 264, 271; this meant that when an MP unexpectedly said something significant it might have been missed.

[143] *The Memoirs of James Stephen*, ed. Merle Bevington (1954), 291; Thomas, 'The Beginning of Parliamentary Reporting in Newspapers', 633. As to the job requirements, see the advertisement in the *Star*, 21 Sept. 1796.

[144] Debate approving report to approve permanent broadcasting: *Hansard*, cdxvi, cols 1636–79 (3 Aug. 1976); also see *Sound Broadcasting First Report* (1975–6 HC Papers 494), xv, 935; *Second Report* (1975–6 HC Papers 723), xv, 979.

Chapter 8
The Reporting of the Booksellers' Bill

There have been very few attempts to consider the accuracy of parliamentary reporting as it became a routine matter in the 1770s. The earlier reports have had more evaluations. Those before 1738 have been said to be generally accurate, in that it was possible to discover the substance of what was said and the nature of the argument. After 1738 it is probable that the speeches of individual speakers are more reliable than the general reports, albeit at times they are misleading or entirely made up,[1] but no general statement can be made about the accuracy of the reports. Inaccuracies arose because some reports would have a deficient list of speakers, the order of speakers might be confused and the subjects spoken about be inaccurately recorded.[2] From this earlier period, we come on to the 1770s, for whose reports there has been a global assessment by Peter Thomas:

> The value of newspaper reports is therefore limited to names and general arguments. Points made by speakers were usually marshalled in the wrong order, and sometimes even ascribed to other members: never has the exact wording been captured ... The parliamentary columns of the newspapers ... are best regarded as the creation of imaginative artists, who often worked with scanty materials.[3]

Yet this general statement, without any examples used, explores the accuracy of the reports in a very different way to how it has been done for the earlier period. This chapter will therefore compare the manuscript of Cavendish's account and the petition report with the various reports of the Booksellers' debate. It will be assumed that the Cavendish manuscript is accurate,[4] which even Thomas accepts is not always the case,[5] but it does allow a consideration of how the debates were reported in the newspapers, what the reports represent and how they should be viewed. For instance, the editorial strategy of a newspaper might affect the selection of speaker and the style and dramatic mood of the report.[6] This chapter therefore examines each stage of the Bill.

[1] William Coxe, *Memoirs of the Life and Administration of Sir Robert Walpole* (1798), i, p. xxi; Mary Ransome, 'The Reliability of Contemporary Reporting of the Debates of the House of Commons, 1722–1741', *BIHR*, xix (1942), 78 (albeit it is unwise to attribute an argument to a particular speaker: 79).

[2] At least in relation to Samuel Johnson's accounts: B.B. Hoover, *Samuel Johnson's Parliamentary Reporting* (Berkeley, CA, 1953), 128–9; Michael MacDonagh, *The Reporters' Gallery* (1913), 146–7, where a comparison is undertaken between Johnson's report and the record of Archbishop Seeker. Hoover also compares records between published reports, which are less reliable due to the possibility of direct or indirect copying (also see Nikki Hessell, *Literary Authors, Parliamentary Reporters: Johnson, Coleridge, Hazlitt, Dickens* (Cambridge 2012), 47).

[3] P.D.G. Thomas, 'The Beginning of Parliamentary Reporting in Newspapers 1768–1774', *EHR*, lxxiv (1959), 636.

[4] In the context of the ideas and viewpoints, rather than precise words: Hessell, *Literary Authors, Parliamentary Reporters*, p. xviii.

[5] P.D.G. Thomas, 'Sources for the Debates of the House of Commons, 1768–1774', *BIHR*, special supp., iv (1959), vi–vii. Similar comments could apply to these reports as to the parliamentary diaries of the 17th century: C.R. Kyle, 'Introduction' to *Parliament, Politics and Elections 1604–1648* (Camden Society, 5th ser., xvii, 2001), 4–7.

[6] Hessell, *Literary Authors, Parliamentary Reporters*, 53.

The Early Stages: Lodging the Petition and it being Read

Most of the daily and tri-weekly papers simply mentioned the petition from the Booksellers, some with a very limited explanation of its purpose. A few days later the text of the petition was published in numerous papers, using a text taken from the *Votes*. What is more surprising about the Booksellers' Bill is the reporting of the proceedings of the petition committee. These would not have taken place on the floor of the House, but in a committee room.[7] Dedicating space in a newspaper to the proceedings in a committee (other than of the full House) was uncommon and remained so long after parliamentary reporting become routine. In these early days, a newspaper only had one reporter. Accordingly, reports were usually of business on the floor of the house of commons (unless the house of lords had a particularly controversial debate);[8] and a person could only be in one place at one time. Committees usually adjourned once debate started in the chamber,[9] which appears to have happened with the Booksellers' Bill,[10] therefore enabling a reporter to make his way from one part of the building to another. This meant that a reporter attending the committee still ran the risk of not getting a seat in the chamber. It would only have happened, therefore, where there was a particular interest in what was going on in committee either for the readers or, it is supposed, the publisher or reporter himself. The committee examining the Booksellers' petition committee might satisfy all three.

The reporting of the Booksellers' petition committee was a little confusing but it appears to have sat on three days. The reports of the first day of committee, 8 March 1774, and the second day, 16 March, are so brief that little can be taken from them other than that William Johnston gave evidence for some time and that he had invested significant sums of money in copyright. In fact, a large part of the report is made up by detailing who attended rather than what happened. Whether this is because attendance was of particular interest to readers, that there was little else to report, or that not much else was remembered is unclear. Indeed, there is little more than two facts recorded about the committee: first, that £12,000 had been spent on copyrights (which were now worth £9,000) and secondly, that Johnston's copyrights had now been left to his son.[11]

If these truncated newspaper reports are contrasted with the official report of the committee (which would, it is presumed, have been based on contemporary minute taking) significant discrepancies can be seen. For instance, there are different figures and a higher degree of complexity, with it being found that at one stage '£10,000 or more' was spent on copyright, at another £12,000.[12] Indeed, the paucity of details in the reports are such it would hardly be worth a reporter attending to retrieve them. Thus, it may well have been that one piece of lobby gossip was reported as fact and that this was picked up by most of

[7] O.C. Williams, *The Topography of the Old House of Commons* (1953), unpublished monograph held in the Parliamentary Archives, HL ARC/VAR/319.

[8] There were still difficulties reporting the Lords, which only began to be relaxed in 1774: William Lowe, 'Peers and Printers: The Beginnings of Sustained Press Coverage of the House of Lords in the 1770s', *Parliamentary History*, vii (1988), 241.

[9] *Public Ledger*, 18 Mar.

[10] The differing reports on the numbers when quorum was not reached: compare *Middlesex Journal*, 19–21 May 1774 and *St James's Chronicle*, 19–21 May.

[11] *Public Advertiser*, 17 Mar.

[12] *CJ*, xxxiv, 588 (c. ii).

the press. The *Middlesex Journal*[13] is shorter and even more speculative as it relates to the term sought for the new right. The single significant sentence it reports could easily have been obtained from a brief word with Richard Whitworth, the chair of the committee, or with Peter Burrell who proposed it. Indeed, it is difficult to imagine that it could have come from any other source.

The final day of committee, 17 March, was reported much more fully in numerous newspapers. As before, some of the reports seem to have been based on little more than gossip. The *Morning Chronicle*[14] merely listed members and reported the formal proceedings (that the preamble was proven, for instance). The *Edinburgh Advertiser*[15] shows outright partisan reporting. After commenting on the Booksellers' basic case, the paper actively calls for petitions against the Bill to be lodged. Its report is therefore not a record of the debate, but a call to arms. The majority of the newspaper coverage must, however, have been based on attendance at the committee meeting, probably by a single reporter due to the similarity in content. Interestingly, the coverage includes things which did not get a mention in the official report, such as an anecdote from George Onslow regarding the magistrate at Guildford (which he repeats later)[16] and details regarding the book (*Humphrey Clinker*)[17] which was central to one of the examples of infringement. The admission of documentary evidence was also reported along with some discussion as to what would be included in the committee report to the House.[18] Even with the increased coverage of the last day, the reports remain short, with a paucity of detail; nevertheless, they appear to be based on more than mere gossip.

Report on the Petition

The debate on the report of the petition committee was extensively covered in the press. In fact, it probably received the greatest coverage of any parliamentary stage. Cavendish's report extends to a little over 14,500 words and the longest newspaper report, that which probably originated from William Woodfall in the *Morning Chronicle*,[19] was a little under 5,000 words. Woodfall himself indicated that his record of this stage of the Bill was not to be read 'as an exact account of the debate on the subject but as a mere skeleton of the argument urged on occasion' as he was 'conscious of the impossibility of an auditor's carrying away the arrangements of the arguments, or the exact phraseology, used by the speaker'.[20] As the coverage was significant, it provides an excellent opportunity to consider the quality of parliamentary reporting. Woodfall managed to record all the speakers and in the correct order, the last speaker was omitted (a short comment from Herbert Mackworth and a point about the order of business from Lord North), further the two contributions

[13] *Middlesex Journal*, 15–17 Mar.

[14] *Morning Chronicle*, 18 Mar.

[15] *Edinburgh Advertiser*, 18–22 Mar., 182.

[16] *Morning Chronicle*, 26 Mar. (where it is said to be repeated).

[17] Tobias Smollett, *The Expedition of Humphry Clinker* (W. Johnstone, 1771) (ESTC: T55323).

[18] *Public Ledger*, 18 Mar.

[19] *Morning Chronicle*, 25/26 Mar.

[20] *Morning Chronicle*, 26 Mar.

of George Dempster were combined. The second most extensive of the reports was in the *Lloyd's Evening Post*: it too managed to get the speakers in the right order.

According to Cavendish the first speaker, Paul Feilde, referred to the evidence, *Miller v Taylor* and some general discussions of the merits.[21] The longest report, that of Woodfall, is little more than a summary of his key arguments with few details (other accounts record him summarising the petition report).[22] However, Woodfall includes a purported quote suggesting that the petitioners were 'Mea obstinate in error, and wilfully deaf to conviction'.[23] Turning to Cavendish, the relevant extract is that the petitioners are 'an obstinate persevering against the means of conviction'.[24] While there are common words between these two phrases, the original seems to be more moderate in tone: 'wilfully deaf' in contrast to 'persevering against'. The attorney-general, who was against the Bill, spoke at great length according to Cavendish. His speech demonstrates how shorter reports are sometimes more precise. For instance, the *Lloyd's Evening Post* mentions only three points: first, that the Booksellers are monopolists who combined together to raise a fund of over £3,000 for filing bills in chancery; secondly, they had purchased copies from Homer to *Hawkesworth* (noting, that this was 'trash');[25] thirdly, that the booksellers should have taken counsel's view on the issue. While the *Lloyd's Evening Post* report is short it is a reasonable summary of some (although not all) of the points made by Thurlow. In contrast, Woodfall has an extensive report of Thurlow's speech which is much more detailed and entertaining and imbues his speech with great passion. He includes some inflammatory language to emphasise what was said, such as to 'throw an odium' upon the petitioner. While he also records the monopoly allegation, he adds flavour calling it a 'dark, unintelligible, stupid prayer' (the *St James's Chronicle* has a very similar phrase). This reflects Thurlow's suggestion that the petition was 'dark and ambiguous'[26] but it goes much further: ambiguous becomes unintelligible. By recording the speech as a diatribe it is implicitly undermining the balance and merits of the argument actually made. Woodfall adopted this approach repeatedly. Cavendish records Thurlow explaining the purpose and limits of monopoly; he puts forward two cases where, in his view, a monopoly can be justified and says that neither of the cases apply to the booksellers.[27] These two cases are captured by the *St James's Chronicle*,[28] but Woodfall turns this into the booksellers' procuring 'an odious monopoly, prejudicial to the public interest, and of infinite mischief to many individuals'. While there are clearly gaps in Cavendish's account, and possibly issues of shorthand transcription, this does not reflect the tenor of the speech as recorded contemporaneously. In other respects, Woodfall reflects the key points made, albeit in much abbreviated language although (possibly inadvertently) leaving out important matters. Thurlow argues that the booksellers were not deceived, and Woodfall records this, but according to Cavendish he also states that he has a letter proving they

[21] Cavendish, Feilde {S279–83}.

[22] *St James's Chronicle*, 24–6 Mar.; *Public Advertiser*, 25 Mar.

[23] *Morning Chronicle*, 25 Mar.

[24] Cavendish, Feilde {S281}; this seems to originate from Case Observations {1} (see Part IV).

[25] This exact word was recorded by Cavendish, Thurlow {S10}.

[26] Cavendish, Thurlow {S1}.

[27] Cavendish, Thurlow {S2–3}.

[28] *St James's Chronicle*, 23–5 Mar., 287.

knew better,[29] of which Woodfall makes no mention. Clearly, there is a difference between a document demonstrating knowledge and supposition of knowledge based on circumstantial facts. In other instances, Woodfall has reimaged what was said. He claims Thurlow said that since the decision of the king's bench (*Miller v Taylor*) the price of books had risen most shamefully and if the Bill was adopted how much more they would increase; whereas it appears that what he was actually saying was that adopting the Bill would increase the price and there was not a suggestion of an increase after *Miller*.[30] While Woodfall's account is largely accurate of the sentiment expressed by Thurlow – that the Bill would increase prices – it adds additional facts which present a slightly different picture.

Likewise, the report in the *St James's Chronicle* invents whole phrases, some more poetic than the prosaic original, such as 'I suspect there is more Art than Folly in this Application, and more Imprudence than either … Their Imprudence has, indeed, been only exceeded by their Insolence.'[31] These phrases might indicate the sentiment but they are expressed in the first person and so it appears they are attempts to represent what was actually said. Whereas, according to Cavendish, none of the significant words – art, folly, imprudence or insolence – were uttered by Thurlow.[32] In contrast, Woodfall merely sets out the basic points made by the attorney-general, namely his opinion that the evidence is inadequate. The potential bias in reporting becomes evident when the attorney-general's speech is contrasted with that of John Dunning.

Dunning's speech is called 'masterly' and answering 'all his objections'.[33] In fact, in some of the shorter reports little else is said of his contribution.[34] The opening passage of his speech related to him having been involved in the question since the beginning and lamenting that he had been on the wrong side of the matter when it was before the house of lords,[35] and he then went on to suggest that Thurlow should forget his client. Woodfall's summary of Johnston's evidence is in a fashion similar to that recorded by Cavendish, likewise Dunning's rebuttal of Thurlow's[36] argument that relief would be given to one then it should be given to many.[37] However, this point was made early in Dunning's speech, according to Cavendish, yet Woodfall presents it as a crescendo. Once more the choice of language, not reflected in Cavendish, demonstrates the limitations of Woodfall's report. He reports Dunning saying 'Their petition was decent, their whole conduct strictly modest and respectful.'[38] Cavendish records nothing of the kind: rather than referring to the petitioners' conduct he records that they were seeking modest terms.[39] While it is quite possible that the common reference to 'modesty' is incidental, it is likely to be a word that remains in the memory, and if this were the case then Woodfall changes a claim that the

[29] Cavendish, Thurlow {S7}; that is the letter of 1759: Part IV, The Five Letters.

[30] Cavendish, Cavendish {S10}.

[31] *St James's Chronicle*, 23–5 Mar., 287.

[32] The closest was a reference to 'imprudent', see Cavendish, Thurlow {S7}.

[33] *Lloyd's Evening Post*, 23–5 Mar.

[34] *Middlesex Journal*, 24–6 Mar.

[35] He had been counsel for Donaldson.

[36] Cavendish, Thurlow {S9}.

[37] Cavendish, Dunning {S14}.

[38] *Morning Chronicle*, 25/26 Mar.

[39] Cavendish, Dunning {S15}.

Bill was modest (i.e. the law asked for does not go too far) to one that the petitioners had acted modestly and respectfully. The latter point might make the petitioners sound more reasonable, but does little for the merits of the case. In contrast to Woodfall, the *St James's Chronicle* once more reported the gist of what was said but little more. Indeed, it appears that it mixed up many of the ideas. It credits Dunning with saying the error was excusable as the judges were divided in opinion,[40] whereas Cavendish credits Onslow with this comment.[41] Similarly, the *St James's Chronicle* reports the sentiments of Lord Hardwicke being relied upon by Dunning, whereas Cavendish records only Thurlow mentioning the former lord chancellor. He records nothing in Dunning's speech where such a comment might fit.[42]

These speeches were followed by shorter speeches, such as those by William Graves, another opponent of the Bill. The speech recorded by Cavendish[43] and Woodfall[44] is of a similar length. Yet the content is somewhat different. As appears to be the usual case, the famous reporter introduces grand descriptions of the petitioners ('opulent men of the trade') and while it is right Graves criticised Scottish editions and suggested they should not be admitted into anyone's study,[45] Woodfall turns this into editions which are 'so badly printed, so very incorrect, so scandalously defective'[46] that they should not be so admitted. The *Lloyd's Evening Post* reported the statement more modestly, with the editions being described as 'generally incorrect'.[47] This is more likely to be closer to the original speech.

The reporting of the solicitor-general, Alexander Wedderburn,[48] is where divergences become even more apparent. The newspapers reported only short summaries of his speech but each seems to have included points he did not make. The *Morning Chronicle* reported that he said that a man after being evicted from his estate following the judgment of the court should be entitled to a parliamentary remedy.[49] However, this example does not seem to have been made by the solicitor-general. Indeed, it does not seem to have been used by anyone during the petition debate; but ironically parliamentarians might have read it and used it later.[50] The *London Magazine*[51] reported Wedderburn as saying that William Johnston was a legitimate witness (and not a party to the petition). Yet he made no such comment. Instead, the closest comment appears to have come from John Dunning, another supporter of the Bill.[52] Indeed, even when the solicitor-general did make a point which was properly reported in the newspapers, such as taking the opinion of Lord Mansfield and

[40] *St James's Chronicle*, 23–5 Mar.

[41] Cavendish, Onslow {S22}.

[42] Cavendish, Thurlow {S6}; cf. Dunning {S11–16}.

[43] Cavendish, Graves {S16–18}.

[44] *Morning Chronicle*, 25/26 Mar.

[45] Cavendish, Graves {S18}.

[46] *Morning Chronicle*, 25/26 Mar.

[47] *Lloyd's Evening Post*, 23–5 Mar.

[48] Cavendish, Wedderburn {S18–20}.

[49] *Morning Chronicle*, 25/26 Mar.

[50] For instance, it was referred to in committee by Lord Folkestone: Folkestone's Diary; Cavendish, {88}.

[51] *London Magazine*, 620–2.

[52] Cavendish, Dunning {S15}.

the kings bench over that of counsel, when it is compared to Cavendish's note[53] it shows how much Woodfall was willing to add and reimage the tone of the piece.[54]

Woodfall	Cavendish
They were of the most extraordinary nature he ever had heard. In the first place it was entirely a new doctrine, that the opinions of the bar were more to be relied on than the solemn decisions of the bench; and even allowing for the sake of argument that they were so, how were the Booksellers to procure the sentiments of all the counsel? Were they to make themselves masters of their opinions, by formally laying a brief before every barrister? Or were they to run from coffee-house to coffee-house, leave no accommodation house to an inn of court unvisited, and in conversation learn the opinion of all who were, or meant to be lawyers, from the youngest students to the oldest practitioners? The idea was in the highest degree repugnant to reason and possibility.	Did they not know that the judgment of the Supreme Court of King's Bench was contradicted at the bar? Were they to attend all the coffee houses ask all the students and note takers or come before the House? Whether the determination of the King's Bench should be a point of law but they are mistaken they are culpable. A gross neglect which makes them unworthy of attention of Parliament.

The shorter reports put the solicitor-general's case very simply, the *Gazetteer* simply saying he answered very 'fully and satisfactorily' many of the objections made, whereas others did not even mention that he spoke.[55] While this provides little indication of the content, it does once more show that many of the newspapers were, unsurprisingly, on the side of the London Booksellers.

While Colonel George Onslow spoke at some length in favour of the Bill,[56] much of what was reported related to the propriety (or otherwise) of the questions put to William Johnston and whether they lay within or without the petition. While the long account of Onslow's speech in the *Morning Chronicle*[57] has flourish and eloquence, there was no reporting of his comments on the suffering of authors,[58] which must have been the crescendo to his speech. Indeed, it appears that his more exuberant metaphors and anecdotes were remembered better by the reporters than his argument. The reports all tended to have some version of his 'flaming swords' comments, but as this was based on the well-known biblical passage[59] it is probable that the reporters remembered 'flaming swords' and made the rest up. Indeed, the differing accounts in the *St James's Chronicle* and *Morning Chronicle*[60] show a different tack and neither quite fits the more straightforward version recorded by Cavendish.

[53] Cavendish, Wedderburn {S19}.

[54] *Morning Chronicle*, 25/26 Mar.

[55] *Gazetteer*, 25 Mar.

[56] Cavendish, Onslow {S20–3}.

[57] *Morning Chronicle*, 25/26 Mar.

[58] Cavendish, Onslow {S23}.

[59] Genesis 3.24.

[60] *Morning Chronicle*, 25/26 Mar.; *St James's Chronicle*, 23–5 Mar., 287.

Onslow repeated his anecdote about the horse rustler in Guildford, with much fuller versions also recorded in the newspapers.[61] This might be because it was a well-known story or that earlier newspaper reports of the petition committee were relied upon.[62]

The confines of space also meant that many of the speeches that followed were abbreviated substantially. Edmund Burke spoke for longer than Onslow, but warranted much less space and few of his words or even the key points he made were reported. Woodfall has him stating that the case was 'now clear of that dogmatic clothing'; the contemporaneous report is more prosaic simply regretting the member 'resists a case of compassion'. A point recorded by Cavendish but not included in any newspaper report related to Burke's rebuttal of the concerns expressed elsewhere that non-lawyers should not be heard in the debate.[63] Burke's key point was a critique of monopolies, but importantly he highlighted why the Booksellers' case was different from odious monopolies. Most of the newspaper reports simply stated that he spoke that monopolies were usually problematic, but this case was an exception.[64] Woodfall's report simply records that monopolies were 'useful and necessary'. These two propositions are very different and it is clear that the short newspaper reports, although conveying nothing of the argument, are much more accurate. Looking back with access to Burke's notes,[65] it is clear what position he was taking, but more pertinently, Cavendish records that Burke argued for a distinction between monopolies for individual products, such as corn, flax or paper, and a thing which 'is an original production of any person'.[66]

First Reading

The first reading of a bill was already a largely procedural step by 1774, yet debate still occurred and it was possible for petitions to be presented as they were in relation to the Booksellers' Bill. Much of the reporting of first reading was a summary of the Bill being presented,[67] which might have been a recollection of the breviate for the Bill, but it is more likely that the reporters consulted the original and paraphrased (particularly as there were complaints that it had been difficult to hear at the time).[68] However, there were reports of the speeches of George Onslow and George Dempster, albeit the record in Cavendish of what they said is short.[69] Onslow argued the Bill was not overturning *Donaldson v Beckett* and criticised Lord Mansfield for not giving his opinion.[70] Yet many reports made the speech more emphatic than it was and some even added additional arguments. The *St James's Chronicle* had Onslow not only explaining in more detail why the Bill was not overturning *Donaldson* (the Booksellers' being 'fully satisfied of the Wisdom and Justice of

[61] Cavendish, Onslow {S20–1}.

[62] Report of committee in *Public Ledger*, 18 Mar.

[63] Cavendish, Burke {S24–9}.

[64] *St James's Chronicle*, 23–5 Mar., 287; *Gazetteer*, 25 Mar.; *Morning Chronicle*, 25/26 Mar.

[65] Part IV, Burke's Notes on Copyright Bill.

[66] Cavendish, Burke {S28}.

[67] Indeed, *The Caledonian* printed the entire bill on 2 May: Part IV: Booksellers' Bill.

[68] Cavendish, Dempster {235}.

[69] Cavendish, Onslow {S234–5}.

[70] Cavendish, Onslow {S235}.

that Decision') but also putting the basis of the Booksellers' case, namely the hardship they suffered.[71] According to Cavendish (and the *Morning Chronicle*) he said much less, and there was no reiteration of the basic case. These might sound like small things – clarification and explanation to the reader maybe. Yet it emphasises that in a time where reporting was in its infancy and reports were very short with only a few details added what was said could be fundamentally misrepresented by the addition of a sentence.

There is also what appears to be a later editorial correction to the speech of Dempster. He said he thought it 'improper' to oppose the *second* reading. This was recorded by Cavendish as his actual words.[72] But it is unlikely he meant this and what he actually meant was that it was improper to oppose the *first* reading. The former statement was incorrect – it was quite proper to oppose second reading – but opposing the first reading was not usual. This was corrected in Cobbett's *Parliamentary History*,[73] and so even when one moves away from the reporters who attended the meeting inaccuracies could be added later by editors. More fundamentally, Dempster's speech appears to have been almost completely rewritten (save the side he took) by the *St James's Chronicle*[74] and *The Edinburgh Advertiser*[75] which copied the *St James's Chronicle* almost exactly but then went on to add an entirely new passage where Dempster addressed the rights of Donaldson. It is difficult to see how this could not have been an editorial invention whereas Dempster's speech was only lightly embellished by other reporters. A debate that was so short as the first reading and which took place on an otherwise busy day allows the limitations of these reports to show through.

Second Reading

The second reading of the Booksellers' Bill would usually have been the point at which the policy of the Bill was debated and the Bill's expediency determined. It should have had two halves as it were. The first would have been the submissions of counsel and the evidence from their witnesses, and the second half dedicated to the debate by members. While second reading took place on two different dates[76] it was still the case that most of the time was taken up with counsel's submissions and evidence. These submissions were, however, reported extensively with notes of certain speeches being published a few days after the event, suggesting that a copy had been given to the reporter by counsel or his clerk or attorney.[77]

The opponents of the Bill spoke first, and Sir John Dalrymple led Arthur Murphy. In contrast to other stages of the Bill, it appears that there were numerous reporters, or at least providers of reports.[78] Yet many were very short indeed. Some reports of

[71] *St James's Chronicle*, 21–3 Apr.

[72] Cavendish, Dempster {S235}.

[73] *Cobbett's Parl. Hist.*, xvii, col. 1090.

[74] Compare Cavendish {S235} and *St James's Chronicle*, 21–3 Apr.

[75] *Edinburgh Advertiser*, 26–9 Apr., 266–7.

[76] 10 and 13 May.

[77] James Mansfield and Arthur Murphy seem to have supplied a summary to the *Morning Chronicle*, 12 and 16 May and likewise Sir John Dalrymple to the *Middlesex Journal*, 12–14 May.

[78] It may be that Murphy provided a report to some Scottish papers, such as the *Caledonian Mercury*, considering they published other material received from him: see *Caledonian Mercury*, 16 May (Second Account).

Dalrymple's submissions appeared to suggest much more clear bias than would be the case when members of the House spoke. The London papers were against him, the Scottish largely in his favour. The more tempered London papers opened with how he tried to 'inflame the minds of the House',[79] but many described his speech as 'long, dull and laboured'[80] or 'very tedious and laboured Harangue'.[81] Whereas many of the newspapers just criticised his approach calling it 'foreign matter' and noting how he 'most illiberally' abused the petitioners.[82] It may well have been that emotive language was used because he began his assault by claiming the proposers of the Bills were connected with the newspapers. Cavendish records how he said these newspapers had called parliament a 'knot of pickpockets' and the king a tyrant.[83] This appeared to make many newspapers ignore most, if not all, of what was said, simply reporting it as a philippic[84] or 'illiberal invectives against the licentiousness of the press'. Indeed, in some cases this was followed in one report by a curt dismissal of his whole argument as a 'jumble of absurdities' which even 'the enemies of the Bill could not allow'.[85] The *Caledonian Mercury* described the speech somewhat differently: it was 'an excellent speech'[86] with each of his heads of argument reduced to 'proper subdivisions' which he illustrated in a 'spirited and masterly manner', where he mingled 'wit with argument, and ridicule with serious fact'.[87] The most partisan of the Scottish papers, the *Edinburgh Advertiser*, simply asserted that Dalrymple had showed 'that the present application was contrary to all law and usage',[88] using many of the same plaudits of the *Mercury*. Yet neither publication really attempted to set out the arguments in substance. Those newspapers which carried a detailed account of the report seem to originate with Woodfall's *Morning Chronicle* and the slightly less detailed account in the *Middlesex Journal*.[89] Woodfall's account turns the strong words recorded by Cavendish from stern rebukes into vitriolic hyperbole, making his arguments look quite ridiculous when he rebukes the 'old for not being young, the young for not being old, the poor for not being rich, and the rich for not being poor'.[90] The *Middlesex Journal* adds to his speech by inventing references to meetings at Richmond and Hampstead to divide murdered reputations. One picked up by many newspapers was his comment that at different times the ills of England had been ascribed to another from Scotland, to France, to Holland, to Hanover and Scotland once more.[91]

[79] *Morning Chronicle*, 12 May.

[80] *Public Ledger*, 10 May; when it was copied by the *Lloyd's Evening Post*, 9–11 May, 447 and *London Magazine*, xliii, 623 (it just said 'long').

[81] *St James's Chronicle*, 10–12 May.

[82] *Morning Chronicle*, 11/12 May.

[83] Cavendish, Dalrymple {229}.

[84] *Gazetteer*, 11 May.

[85] *Public Ledger*, 10 May.

[86] *Caledonian Mercury*, 16 May (but note the *Caledonian Mercury* had an earlier report which was closer to that in London).

[87] *Caledonian Mercury*, 16 May (Second Account).

[88] *Edinburgh Advertiser*, 13–17 and 17–20 May, 309, 314.

[89] *Middlesex Journal*, 12–14 May.

[90] *Morning Chronicle*, 11/12 May.

[91] Cavendish, Dalrymple {254–5}; *Morning Chronicle*, 11/12 May.

In Cavendish, once more, it is recorded how Dalrymple said there had been a 'cessation of arms' of late which would end if the Bill passed.[92] This sentiment was expressed in a matter-of-fact fashion by the reporters.[93] It is not surprising that the reporting of these comments was unfavourable; the reporters were largely the owners, or at least editors, of the newspapers he was complaining about and so they had a real incentive to undermine him to protect themselves. Nevertheless, they *did* report these comments: they could have simply omitted them and concentrated on different aspects of the speech. Was this to show their outrage, because the comments opened Dalrymple submissions, or simply it was the most newsworthy? While it is true that Dalrymple did little more than play to sentiment at times (and probably misjudged his audience in the House) he did present some substantive arguments. For instance, while he lauded the quality of Scottish books[94] this was not recorded by the *Morning Chronicle* but was by the *Middlesex Journal*.[95] Looking at ten of the substantive points he made (in no particular order) there were only two which were not reported at all.

First, he argued that the Bill was a choice between free trade and monopolies, before setting out the evils of the latter.[96] The *Morning Chronicle* highlighted how he stated 'the bad tendencies' of monopolies,[97] and so reduced a substantial argument to a single line. Secondly, he argued that the Bill would increase the price of books.[98] While this might be seen as part of his overall argument against monopolies it was not mentioned by the *Chronicle* but was by the *Middlesex Journal*. Thirdly, he argued that if more books were produced, increased employment would result, as more workers would be needed to increase production. Again, this was mentioned by the *Journal* but not the *Chronicle*.[99] Fourthly, he argued that the Bill created an *ex post facto* law.[100] This was picked up by the *Morning Chronicle* but not the *Middlesex Journal*.[101] Fifthly, he argued that the Bill was for the benefit of a handful of booksellers and not the more general trade.[102] This was not recorded. Sixthly, he argued that the Bill was not for the benefit of authors and might actually be to their detriment, on the basis that if old books could remain very profitable then new books would not be sought, so authors would not be remunerated. Again, this was not mentioned. Seventhly, he referred to the North American trade and how lists of books were sent from America to the docks at Glasgow and there would be difficulties, by reason of credit and logistics, satisfying this order if books had to be sent from London, which in turn would lead to printing being removed to the colony.[103] This argument was reported.[104] Eighthly, he argued that the

[92] Cavendish, Dalrymple {231}.

[93] *Morning Chronicle*, 11/12 May.

[94] Cavendish, Dalrymple {237–9}.

[95] *Morning Chronicle*, 11/12 May; *Middlesex Journal*, 12–14 May.

[96] Cavendish, Dalrymple {233–5}.

[97] *Morning Chronicle*, 11/12 May.

[98] Cavendish, Dalrymple {233–5}.

[99] Cavendish, Dalrymple {235–6}; *Middlesex Journal*, 12–14 May.

[100] Cavendish, Dalrymple {252–3}.

[101] *Morning Chronicle*, 11/12 May.

[102] Cavendish, Dalrymple {244–5}.

[103] Cavendish, Dalrymple {242–3}.

[104] *Morning Chronicle*, 11/12 May; *Middlesex Journal*, 12–14 May.

Booksellers knew there could be no common law right setting out an historical summary, the number of failed petitions and similar other matters.[105] While this was picked up by the reporters it was summarised in a sentence or two. Ninthly, he argued that the revenue would benefit from more books being sold.[106] This too was picked up by the *Journal*,[107] but not the *Chronicle*. Tenthly, he defended the sale of his own book,[108] and the copyright in it.[109] This was reported in much more detail. Thus, by reading a plurality of newspaper reports it is possible to obtain a reasonable indication of what arguments had been made.

Cavendish did not record the evidence given on second reading. He simply noted that witnesses were examined. It is known from the newspapers who those witnesses were: namely, John Merill senior, John Merill junior, John Murray, William Fox, George Bulkney and Albany Wallis.[110] The content of their evidence received a short summary in most papers; indeed, in some cases more space was devoted to this than to Dalrymple's submissions.[111] As the evidence was not recorded by Cavendish[112] no comparison is possible with the newspaper reports.

The witnesses' evidence was followed by statements from Arthur Murphy, the junior counsel for the opponents. It was suggested that he spoke for about an hour and a half,[113] and his arguments, in contrast to his leader's, were described as 'shrewd'.[114] Yet only the *Morning Chronicle* and the *Edinburgh Advertiser* gave a more detailed account of his submissions and did so with much more accuracy. Murphy put forward only a few arguments, compared to his leader, yet many more seem to have been picked up by the two papers that reported his speech. His submissions were originally summarised in the *Morning Chronicle* on the day following second reading,[115] but the next day[116] a longer more detailed account was provided despite not (as was often the case) being foreshadowed in the earlier edition. While the second version is clearly not a transcript of the speech, and it differs in numerous respects from the first, its timing suggests that it was supplied by an interested party, most likely Murphy himself.

Cavendish seems to have struggled more with the submissions of Murphy than those of Dalrymple. This may be due to Murphy's speaking speed or the acoustics,[117] and so it is unlikely that the reporters would have done significantly better without a summary being provided. Indeed, there is a difference between the first version in the *Morning Chronicle*, which as usual exaggerated a simple statement such as 'ignorance of the law does not

[105] Cavendish, Dalrymple {245–53}.

[106] Cavendish, Dalrymple {236}.

[107] *Middlesex Journal*, 12–14 May.

[108] Sir John Dalrymple, *Memoirs of Great Britain and Ireland: From the Dissolution of the Last Parliament of Charles II, until the Sea-battle off La Hogue* (Stachan and Caddell, 1771) (ESTC: T145644).

[109] Cavendish, Dalrymple {255–6}.

[110] *Morning Chronicle*, 11/12 May.

[111] *Gazetteer*, 11 May; *Public Ledger*, 10 May; with other long accounts in *St James's Chronicle*, 10–12 May.

[112] Probably because minutes were taken by the clerk.

[113] *Morning Chronicle*, 11/12 May; or finished at 10 o'clock: *St James's Chronicle*, 10–12 May (the time estimate might be quite inaccurate).

[114] *Public Ledger*, 10 May.

[115] *Morning Chronicle*, 11 May.

[116] *Morning Chronicle*, 12 May.

[117] Or even the late hour.

excuse'[118] into one laced with hyperbole – 'no maxim more general; no maxim so notoriously inviolable, as that the ignorance of the law could not be urged or received as a palliative or an excuse'[119] – and the later version which is much more matter of fact. The provision of a note to Woodfall would also seem to demonstrate that the *Morning Chronicle* was already being seen as the account of record (and the *Advertiser* was of course owned by his client's son).

When the second reading resumed a few days later there seemed to be much less interest in the submissions of James Mansfield, the counsel in favour of the Bill. He did however receive a much better reception from the press. The *Public Advertiser* described him speaking for two hours 'in the most able manner' and answering everything the opponents had to say against the Bill.[120] It is quite possible that Mansfield or his clerk provided a note of his speech to the *General Evening Post*, where the report has a different style from most of the coverage. In terms of length, the *General Evening Post* has a word count of about half of that of Cavendish. Yet, like Woodfall, while many of the key points are present, there are notable differences. First, the order of the material is different. For instance, Cavendish records Mansfield's rebutting of the newspaper proprietorship before discussing the evidence of Merill junior and senior, whereas Almon does the reverse. Secondly, the level of detail is different, with much more recorded in the newspaper report than by Cavendish. For instance, the newspaper has a significant section on the Scottish trade,[121] whereas Cavendish records only a passing comment.[122] Similarly, a much fuller discussion is included in the newspaper[123] of the state of Scotland when discussing the letter[124] of William Creech,[125] a Scottish printer in favour of the Bill. While the general tenor of the reports remains the same,[126] critically, examples are used in the newspaper which did not appear to be recorded by Cavendish (notably, the discussion of Young's *Works*);[127] and as might be more expected examples caught by Cavendish are not included in the newspaper (the references to Milton and Pope's Homer for instance).[128] These small additions also appear elsewhere. Both Cavendish and the *General Evening Post* refer to the abridgment of Homer. Cavendish simply records that Donaldson 'greatly abridged those notes',[129] whereas the *General Evening Post* refers to 23,861 lines being omitted. These details may have been missed by Cavendish, but may also have been added improvements to the original speech by the reporter (or counsel, if that was the source). Indeed, the precise number of lines omitted is strange. The printed papers refer to 23,000 lines omitted.[130] If it were merely recorded as live debate

118 Cavendish, Murphy {49}.

119 *Morning Chronicle*, 11/12 May.

120 *Public Advertiser*, 16 May.

121 *General Evening Post*, 14–17 May.

122 Cavendish, Mansfield {27–8}.

123 *General Evening Post*, 14–17 May.

124 The newspapers, however, do not mention the challenge to its admissibility: Cavendish, Mansfield {31–2}.

125 William Creech (1745–1815) was the leading publisher in Edinburgh at the time.

126 Cavendish, Mansfield {32}.

127 Edward Young (1683–1765).

128 Cavendish, Mansfield {32}.

129 Cavendish, Mansfield {29}.

130 Part IV, London Booksellers' Considerations.

it would be incredible if that figure was remembered and other more important details were not. This suggests the precision is either an invention of the reporter or it comes from counsel (who may well while preparing the case have had a clerk or attorney count each one). A final example of the difference is the newspapers almost entirely omit Mansfield's summary of the 'history' of the right and his comparison with other countries.[131]

John Hett, Mansfield's junior, made only short submissions, which largely related to different types of property.[132] Unsurprisingly, the newspapers gave very little space to his speech, just saying he went 'though all the arguments'.[133] While Cavendish recorded some of the evidence of John Wilkie,[134] the proposers' main witness, most of his record covers the complaints of MPs. The debate over whether his evidence was admissible was covered by the *General Evening Post*, including Charles Fox's somewhat flippant question of whether copyright infringement should be a felony.[135] There were also summaries of the comments of the leading speakers, such as Edmund Burke. But the reply by Arthur Murphy after Wilkie's evidence was not reported at all.[136]

Committee

The debate recorded by Cavendish before and after the House went to committee on 16 May[137] represents the largest part of the record. Much of the debate was procedural as to whether or not there was a standing order prohibiting the committee being held so soon after second reading. The issue was raised by George Onslow before Paul Fielde addressed it, and he was then followed up by Charles Fox.[138] However, every single newspaper report ignored the contribution of Onslow and moved straight to the objection by Fox,[139] suggesting that Feilde was introducing his bill in the usual way before Fox jumped up to object. The reports then usually go on to combine two speeches of Fox, his first with his longer point made after a significant contribution by Edmund Burke and Edward Thurlow. While this might be seen as making the debates more readable and easier to follow, it can significantly change the nature of what was said. In Fox's case it was further compounded by adding general comments against the Bill which were not discussed in the procedural debates but later in the debate when he went on to discuss the substance of the Bill.[140] The standing order required a week's notice posted in the lobby, whereas the newspapers record eight days.[141] While it could have been misread out in the Commons it is more likely that it was a numerical misremembering by the reporter.

[131] Cavendish, Mansfield {34–6}.

[132] Cavendish, Mansfield {38}.

[133] *Public Advertiser*, 16 May.

[134] Cavendish, Hett {41, 47, 49}.

[135] *General Evening Post*, 14–17 May; Cavendish, Fox {47–9}. It was an attempt to stymie the debate.

[136] Cavendish, Murphy {49–53}.

[137] Cavendish {58 to 137}; around 40% of the total of his reports on the Bill.

[138] Cavendish, Fox {58–60}.

[139] *Morning Chronicle*, 18 May.

[140] Cavendish, {104–10}.

[141] It originated on 24 Nov. 1699 (*CJ*, xiii, 6); the versions in effect in 1774 were those reiterated on 5 Mar. 1772/3 (*CJ*, xx, 161).

According to Cavendish, Burke made much of a distinction between what he called a discretionary rule and a standing order, and this idea was picked up by the newspapers.[142] While the newspapers got the gist of what was said – that discretionary rules could be set aside with more ease than a standing order – the language used in the newspapers was quite different.[143] The longer newspaper reports also picked up his point that the opponents had been able to get from Scotland in time.[144] Most reports, however, glossed over much of what he said, simply reporting his speech as being 'exceedingly pleasant' and 'yet severe'.[145] The speeches of the other members on the standing order issue were similarly truncated. However, considering the relative technicality of the debate it would not have been that interesting to readers, so largely omitting it is not surprising. As in other cases, it appears that some of the content of George Johnstone's speech may have come from more than merely the reporter's memory, as it included a number of precise figures which appear to match those recorded by Cavendish.[146] Where one or two comments were made by members, such as by Herbert Mackworth[147] and Richard Whitworth,[148] they were often picked up by the newspapers.[149]

The reports of Lord Folkestone can be considered against two sources: Cavendish and Folkestone's own diary.[150] His speech involved a short discussion of the history of printing privileges and he concluded there was nothing supporting a common law right, a particular comment on Lord Mansfield and his role in the matter, and finally, a statement that the law was an *ex post facto*. The longer newspaper reports mentioned his history,[151] and one mentions his comment on Lord Mansfield, but his key point – the merits of the measure – was touched upon only once and imprecisely as 'necessary parliamentary considerations'.[152] Likewise, the reports of Paul Fielde each captured only one aspect of his speech, one providing a very brief summary of the history[153] and another, longer, emphasising that assignments were expressed as perpetual[154] when made by William Blackstone, the great lawyer and judge, and also by Sir John Dalrymple and, in addition, there was reference to payments made for corrections.[155] Cavendish, on the other hand, records Feilde making a number of other significant points in both his speeches,[156] many of which summarised the points made in earlier stages of the Bill. None were mentioned by the reporters. They may simply have been omitted to avoid reporting the same news twice.

[142] Cavendish, Burke {61–2, 69}; *Morning Chronicle*, 18 May.

[143] Cavendish, Burke {63} ('wagon load of petitions from Glasgow').

[144] Cavendish, Burke {61}; cf. *Morning Chronicle*, 18 May.

[145] *Public Ledger*, 17 May.

[146] Compare Cavendish, Johnstone {78–9} and *Morning Chronicle*, 18 May.

[147] Cavendish, Mackworth {85}.

[148] Cavendish, Whitworth {84–5}.

[149] *Morning Chronicle*, 18 May.

[150] Cavendish, Folkestone {87–9}; Folkestone's Diary, 16 May. As to a comparison between the two sources, the entry in Folkestone's diary is about 30 per cent longer than Cavendish's record of his speech.

[151] *Morning Chronicle*, 18 May; *Middlesex Journal*, 14–17 May.

[152] *Morning Chronicle*, 18 May.

[153] *Middlesex Journal*, 14–17 May.

[154] Compare Cavendish, Feilde {97, 118–19} and *Morning Chronicle*, 18 May.

[155] *Morning Chronicle*, 18 May.

[156] Cavendish, Feilde {89–103}.

The substantive speech of Charles Fox starkly shows some of the issues with the veracity of newspaper reports. Cavendish records that he said he had *two* parts to his argument:[157] the right to compensation and whether compensation can be given to them when it is an injustice to others.[158] The *Morning Chronicle* says he had three, with an additional limb based on the amount of relief justified.[159] The paper's reports of the first limb, that is the right to compensation, largely invents a narrative which touches on the same general theme as Cavendish records[160] – that there is no common law right – but little else. Likewise the *Chronicle* reports Fox arguing that they were seeking the extension of 'an odious and injurious monopoly',[161] whereas the *General Evening Post* reports that he was more in favour of extending the right under the Statute of Anne for authors rather than retrospectively for booksellers.[162] Cavendish reports[163] something more similar to the latter although, as usual, there was a much more exaggerated version in the newspapers (such as the invented, dramatic, statement: 'I am sure there is not a man in the House who wishes better to the cause of literature than myself').[164]

The speech of George Onslow was separately printed in the *Middlesex Journal*.[165] It is unclear who provided it. One might imagine that Onslow or an associate of his supplied it, although he had a chequered history with the newspapers. Cavendish records Onslow making a very long and detailed speech, but the *Middlesex Journal* includes only three comments, each a fair summary of points made by him. It is likely that the person who supplied the speech wanted to emphasise the best bits (or the editors cut out the less interesting passages) and this is the basis for what was published. Indeed, the three comments are what might be described as the entertainment or, dare one say, humorous part of his speech. The other newspaper reports of Onslow's speech picked these up with his talk of the Scots rebellion,[166] and the 'spunk' of clergymen.[167] Yet, even then, there was additional invention, with one reporter suggesting Onslow addressed the suggested link between the petitioners and the newspapers:[168] he did no such thing.

There are essentially two versions of Lord Beauchamp's contribution recorded by the reporters. One version included a general discussion of monopolies[169] and, as was usual for Woodfall, it was substantially embellished; in other versions much was made of the provision enacted for Mrs Hogarth in the Engraving Copyright Act 1766.[170] As before, many of the points Beauchamp made in his speech were entirely missed by the reporters,

[157] Cavendish, Fox {104}.

[158] Cavendish, Fox {105–7} (compensation) and {108–9} (injunctions).

[159] *Morning Chronicle*, 18 May.

[160] Cavendish, Fox {105–7}.

[161] *Morning Chronicle*, 18 May.

[162] *Middlesex Journal*, 14–17 May.

[163] Cavendish, Fox {110–17}.

[164] *Middlesex Journal*, 14–17 May.

[165] *Middlesex Journal*, 14–17 May.

[166] *Morning Chronicle*, 18 May; *Middlesex Journal*, 14–17 May.

[167] *Morning Chronicle*, 18 May; *Middlesex Journal*, 14–17 May.

[168] *Morning Chronicle*, 18 May.

[169] *Morning Chronicle*, 18 May.

[170] (7 Geo. III, c. 38); *Middlesex Journal*, 14–17 May; *Public Ledger*, 17 May.

and the emphasis was quite different to the tenor of the speech recorded by Cavendish. While the reporters did briefly report other matters there was not enough reported or recorded to make a comparison. Finally, once the Speaker left the chair and the committee sat, the reports of the proceedings[171] are as detailed as Cavendish managed with his tiring hand. Much could have been constructed from looking at the Bill with the blanks filled in so it may be that little was actually said during committee itself.

Aborted Report

On 19 May 1774, the Bill was reported from the committee. Cavendish only makes a short note of the hearing.[172] He simply records how John Stewart[173] presented a clause which was rejected. The *Morning Chronicle* actually sets out the text of the clause, which was to exempt Scotland from the Bill on the grounds that the common law had been different.[174] Like Cavendish, most of the newspaper reports concentrated on the House breaking up due to the lack of a quorum. When the Bill was reported (before a quorate House) no record was made in Cavendish and only the *Edinburgh Advertiser* carried anything more than a note,[175] suggesting it finally went through the stage on the nod.

Third Reading

In Cavendish, the speech of Charles Fox on third reading is recorded in full (but that of his brother is not) as are the speeches of George Dempster and Lord Beauchamp.[176] The newspapers, while noting the other speakers, did not report anything they said. In relation to Charles Fox, as seems to be the usual case, the newspapers added emphasis. Cavendish describes the Bill as a 'robbery' whereas the longest report described it as 'barefaced a robbery as ever was committed',[177] and the newspaper reports' dramatic opening to his speech that 'he could not let so infamous, so pernicious, so flagrant a Bill, pass through any stage without opposing it' is not recorded by Cavendish at all, even in a moderated form. In addition to these substantive additions there were also significant omissions. Cavendish records Fox lamenting Stewart's failed clause to exclude Scotland from the Bill, a comment not recorded by any of the newspaper reporters. Conversely, the two main versions of the newspaper reports spend a significant number of words reiterating the basic challenge to the case of the proposers. No such comments are recorded by Cavendish and comments about 'bad generalship' recorded by the *London Chronicle*[178] may be seen as pure invention.

[171] *Public Ledger*, 17 May.

[172] Cavendish {141–3}.

[173] John Stewart† (c. 1723–1781), MP for Arundel. There were two other potential Stewarts but he is the most likely.

[174] *Morning Chronicle*, 20 May.

[175] *CJ*, xxxiv, 778 (20 May); *Edinburgh Advertiser*, 20–4 May, 325.

[176] Cavendish {159–66}.

[177] *Edinburgh Advertiser*, 31 May–3 June.

[178] *London Chronicle*, 26–8 May, 512.

House of Lords

The Booksellers' Bill failed at first reading in the house of lords.[179] Obviously Cavendish was not present so the only records that exist are those in the newspapers. While the issues raised about the accuracy of reporting almost certainly apply with equal weight to the reports of the Lords' proceedings, it is almost as significant that the debate was reported at all. As mentioned at the beginning of this chapter, at this time, there would have been only one reporter for any newspaper and it was usual to report the debates in the house of commons rather than the Lords, particularly as there was still nervousness about reporting the Lords' debates.

What does this tell us?

The newspaper reports of the Booksellers' Bill, like that of *Donaldson v Beckett* itself, are woefully incomplete. In the same vein, it is not possible to know precisely what was or was not said. It is reckless to assume that reporters were accurate, even the legendary William Woodfall, either in their reports of the Bill or *Donaldson v Beckett*.[180] But with the contemporaneous reports of Henry Cavendish we have additional insight which brings to the fore both the strengths and weaknesses of the parliamentary reports in 1774. The truths missed, the truths invented, and the truths lost. Yet when the only remaining sources of debates are newspaper reports, they become the truth even if they were not the speakers' truth. If taken in that light parliamentary reports from this period are useful – but as historical records they stray slightly too often from fact to fiction. In one respect, when parliamentary reporters wrote about the creative genius of authors they were surely writing about themselves.

[179] Technically, it was read a first time and then the second reading was put off: *LJ*, xxxiv, 232 (1 June).

[180] Gómez-Arostegui, 'Copyright at Common Law', 21, 27, 33; Mark Rose, 'Donaldson and the Muse of History', in *What is the Point of Copyright History?*, 39.

Chapter 9
The End …

An ending of one story is always the beginning of the next, but like so many tales there is a need to know what happened next to the protagonists be they people, processes or paper. The literary property debates in 1774 were not something of isolated interest, but were documented heavily in the newspapers even at a time of potential crisis in North America. The abstruse and abstract nature of the literary property debate led to jokes being made in the context of complex legal matters more generally.[1] The day following the Booksellers' Bill being rejected saw claims that it was a loss for authors,[2] but, as correspondents observed, the rejection was like taking sugar with medicine.[3]

The London Booksellers

The Booksellers' Bill 1774 went down in flames, with commentators the next day suggesting such a bill should never have been brought. The defeat in the house of lords after a division meant that bringing it back the following year would have been an expensive waste of time. The London Booksellers did not give up and walk away. They tried as hard as they could to try to retain some form of protection from their common law 'copyrights' even if in a more limited way. In April 1775, the government introduced a bill[4] to grant perpetual copyright to the universities.[5] Unlike the Booksellers' Bill it passed quickly and without a single division.[6] In contrast to the newspapers' extensive reporting of the Booksellers' Bill, the Universities' Bill received, at most, mention in a single sentence,[7] save one small blip – involving the London Booksellers once more. There were some amendments made during

[1] The nature of a different claim was such that it was said it would baffle even the subtlety and cleverness of the literary property lawyers: *St James's Chronicle*, 16–18 June.

[2] *St James's Chronicle*, 2–4 June.

[3] *Morning Chronicle*, 4 June.

[4] It was proposed by the prime minister, Lord North, albeit he was also chancellor of the university of Oxford.

[5] It became the Copyright Act 1775 (15 Geo. III, c. 53). Ironically, the Glasgow Memorialists had suggested that the universities would be against restrictions on the freedom of printing: Part IV, Glasgow Memorialists {19}.

[6] Bill Ordered: *CJ*, xxxv, 299 (12 Apr. 1775); 1st reading: *CJ*, xxxv, 325 (28 Apr.); 2nd reading/committed: *CJ*, xxxv, 340 (2 May); report/ingross.: *CJ*, xxxv, 370 (11 May); 3rd reading: *CJ*, xxxv, 373 (15 May); 1st reading: *LJ*, xxxiv, 451 (15 May); 2nd reading/committed: *LJ*, xxxiv, 458 (17 May); committee/report: *LJ*, xxxiv, 462 (18 May); 3rd reading: *LJ*, xxxiv, 463; *CJ*, xxxv, 385 (19 May); royal assent: *CJ*, xxxv, 387; *LJ*, xxxiv, 465 (22 May).

[7] Commons Bill Ordered: *General Evening Post*, 11–13 Apr. 1775; *London Chronicle*, 11–13 Apr. 1775; *London Evening Post*, 11–13 Apr. 1775; *Lloyd's Evening Post*, 12–14 Apr. 1775; *Edinburgh Advertiser*, 5–9 May 1775, p. 293.
Committee: *Edinburgh Advertiser*, 12–16 May 1775, p. 309.
Report: *Morning Chronicle*, 12 May 1775.
Commons 3rd reading: *St James's Chronicle*, 13–16 May 1775; *London Evening Post*, 13–16 May 1775.
Lords 1st reading: *Morning Chronicle*, 16 May 1775; *Lloyd's Evening Post*, 17–19 May 1775.
Lords 2nd reading: *Morning Post*, 17 May 1775; *Daily Advertiser*, 17 May 1775; *General Evening Post*, 16–18 May 1775; *London Evening Post*, 16–18 May 1775; *Middlesex Journal*, 16–18 May 1775.
Lords 3rd reading: *London Chronicle*, 18–20 May 1775; *London Evening Post*, 18–20 May 1775; *Middlesex Journal*, 18–20 May 1775; *Morning Chronicle*, 20 May 1775; *Edinburgh Advertiser*, 16–19 May 1775, p. 316.
Royal assent: *Daily Advertiser*, 22 May 1775; *Lloyd's Evening Post*, 22–4 May 1775; *Edinburgh Advertiser*, 23–6 May 1775, p. 333.
Even the local Oxford paper only mentions royal assent: *Oxford Journal*, 27 May 1775.

bill committee to extend it to Eton, Westminster and Winchester Schools[8] and the four Scottish universities, but the only hiccup was that 'the friends' of the London Booksellers had tried to make certain amendments so that the universities could delegate their perpetual right to them. Even this received minimal reporting[9] in the London papers.[10] The *Edinburgh Advertiser*, still defending its victory[11] in *Donaldson v Beckett* and in respect of the Booksellers' Bill, reported[12] the adoption of a clause[13] to prevent such delegation. There was a 'heated debate' on the clause but no division was needed and it was accepted.[14]

The contrast between these two bills was stark. One led to massive lobbying efforts with pages of arguments, the other did not;[15] one had the full panoply of procedural tricks, the other more or less glided through parliament; one was reported extensively in the newspapers, the other just about got a mention. At one level this emphasises why the Booksellers' Bill, a failed legislative effort, is worth study in its own right. Far more happened with the Booksellers' Bill and it received substantially more consideration by the House than its successful cousin. It also demonstrated that despite the protestations made in 1774, the adoption of a perpetual copyright in the *right* hands was seen as fit and proper.[16]

One of the London Booksellers' responses to the failure of their bill[17] was to return to old habits. A scheme was discussed whereby the owners of copyright[18] formed a partnership, or company of sorts with collective management of certain 'unprotected' copies[19] with a sanction:

> That any person whatever, who shall hereafter print, or promote the printing and vending of any Copies, the objects of the protection of this Association, which are claimed, and have heretofore been considered as the property of any of the Trade, without their knowledge and consent, shall from thenceforth never be acknowledged as a partner in

[8]A direction was given to the committee to this effect: *CJ*, xxxv, 351 (5 May 1775).

[9]Henry Cavendish had lost his seat, so his reports ceased at the same time.

[10]Some comment about clauses being added was mentioned in *London Evening Post*, 11–13 May 1775; *Middlesex Journal*, 11–13 May 1775; *Gazetteer and New Daily Advertiser*, 12 May 1775.

[11]More accurately, his father's victory, as Alexander Donaldson had sold the paper to his son before any of these victories.

[12]*Edinburgh Advertiser*, 12–16 May 1775, p. 309; *Lloyd's Evening Post*, 22–4 May 1775 (taken from *Edinburgh Evening Courant*, 17 May 1775). The debate was also covered in a bit more depth in the *Public Advertiser*, 13 May 1775. There was actually concern expressed early on in a letter that it was a back-door Booksellers' Bill: *Edinburgh Advertiser*, 14–18 Apr. 1775, p. 245.

[13]Proposed by George Johnstone†* (1730–87), John Johnstone† (1734–95) and Edward Thurlow†* (1731–1806).

[14]Copyright Act 1775. s 1.

[15]As a government bill, lobbying was less common, as most government legislation was enacted.

[16]Indeed, the perpetual right was only brought to an end by Copyright, Designs and Patents Act 1988 (1988, c. 48), schedule 1, para. 13 (it expires 50 years after commencement); Deazley, *On the Origin of the Right to Copy*, 215–16.

[17]There is no proof of a link, but it is a likely response: Gwyn Walters, 'The Booksellers In 1759 and 1774: The Battle for Literary Property', *The Library*, 5th ser., xxix (1974), 309.

[18]Proposed Plan of the United Company of Booksellers for the Preservation of the Trade, and the Security of Literary Property, article ix (from the Strahan Papers held by the BL), reprinted in Appendix 15 of Norma Hodgson and Cyprian Blagden, *The Notebook of Thomas Bennet and Henry Clements* (Oxford Bibliographical Society, new ser., vi, 1956).

[19]Proposed Plan of the United Company of Booksellers, article ix.

> unprotected Copies. – It being the express Intention of this Association to preserve inviolate to every man the Shares he formerly possessed in such Copies.[20]

The scheme was never adopted and, as discussed in chapter 5, the structure of the market allowed booksellers to retain monopolistic prices for the rest of the 18th century.[21] The basic aim of booksellers was to have copyright protection for longer, and as time has gone by this has been achieved. The term was extended in 1814[22] to the author's lifetime or 28 years, whichever was longer, in 1842 to life plus seven years or 48 years if longer, in 1911 to life plus 50 years,[23] and eventually in 1995 to life plus 70 years.[24] These enactments[25] have pushed up the term of copyright albeit it has never *quite* become perpetual.[26] Even under the generous term regime in place in the 21st century, Shakespeare's plays[27] and Milton's *Paradise Lost*[28] would still be 'unprotected copies' in 1774, but the great cases of *Millar v Taylor* and *Donaldson v Beckett* would have been quite different, as the book at the centre of it all, Thomson's *The Seasons*, would have still been protected under statutory copyright.[29]

The Market in Books

The decision in *Donaldon v Beckett* and by implication the failure to delay its implementation with the Booksellers' Bill has long been said to have led to cheap books. It has been proclaimed as the beginning of 'modern' literature,[30] with the bookselling trade being 'transformed'[31] by the decision due to its being a critical 'turning-point'[32] or even the 'most decisive event' in the history of reading since printing was introduced.[33] So, it is said, following this decision cheap books began to 'flood' the market,[34] which led to the price

[20] Proposed Plan of the United Company of Booksellers, article xxi.

[21] Indeed, it appears to have lasted for a few years after *Donaldson v Beckett*: James Boswell, *The Life of Samuel Johnson* (Oxford, 2008), 724 (29 Dec. 1778).

[22] Copyright Act 1814 (54 Geo. III, c. 156), s. 4.

[23] Copyright Act 1911 (1 & 2 Geo. V, c. 46), s. 4.

[24] Duration of Copyright and Rights in Performances Regulations 1995 (SI 1995/3297) implementing Directive 93/98 harmonising the term of protection of copyright and certain related rights (since codified as Directive 2006/16).

[25] Albeit, the later changes brought about to comply with international law (Berne Convention for the Protection of Literary and Artistic Works, article 7) and European Community (EU) law.

[26] The perpetual copyright for the universities comes to an end in 2039. In any event, only a handful of books published each year have commercial value after copyright expires.

[27] Copyright would have expired at the end of 1686; albeit this ignores the protection still granted for newly discovered works, publication rights or manuscripts.

[28] Copyright would have expired at the start of 1735.

[29] James Thomson died on 27 Aug. 1748; copyright would have lasted to the end of 1818.

[30] Trevor Ross, 'The Emergence of Literature: Making and Reading the English Canon in the Eighteenth Century', *English Literary History*, lxiii (1996), 410.

[31] James Raven, 'The Book Trades', in *Books and Their Readers in Eighteenth-Century England: New Essays*, ed. Isabel Rivers (Leicester, 2001), 16 (albeit cautioning against 'too great an obsession with the 1774 contest'); B.M. Benedict, 'Readers, Writers, Reviewers and the Professionalization of Literature', in *The Cambridge Companion to English Literature, 1740–1830*, ed. Thomas Keymer and John Mee (Cambridge, 2004), 16.

[32] John Feather, *A History of British Publishing* (2005), 68; Feather, *Publishing, Piracy, and Politics: An Historical Study of Copyright in Britain* (1994), 94.

[33] William St Clair, *The Reading Nation in the Romantic Period* (Cambridge, 2004), 109.

[34] Mark Rose, 'The Author as Proprietor: *Donaldson v Beckett* and the Genealogy of Modern Authorship', *Representations*, xxiii (1988), 69.

of works falling 'sharply'[35] with 'multiple cheap editions of canonical works'[36] thereby creating a 'native literary tradition'.[37] Yet like so many other myths regarding *Donaldson* that the judgment caused a reduction in the price of books is probably untrue. The reprint market had been developed for some time,[38] the price of books changed little between 1750 and 1790,[39] and at least if the secondary market (that is resales) is indicative of prices in the primary market as Elliot has said:

> Whatever the Lords decided on that windy February day in 1774, it had little or no effect on what the average person paid – and would continue to pay – for his or her literary reading in the London and provincial bookshops.[40]

Likewise, David Fielding and Shef Rogers, after undertaking some substantial statistical and economic work based on prices and payments, concluded that there is:[41]

> no evidence copyright reform had any substantial effect on book prices, and evidence that it led only to a temporary increase in payments to authors … [o]ther economic factors led to a gradual reduction in booksellers' mark-ups, but there is no evidence that the legal reform made the market more competitive.

This was because before *Donaldson* the market in books was largely vertically integrated and had substantial market density, with existing distribution channels and agreements in place, and control of advertising channels and other commercial networks.[42] Both decisions came at a time when publishing had been forced to become more entrepreneurial in a changing commercial world.[43] This made a radical change following the Lords' decision unlikely. It may even have been the case that after the dust settled, the Scottish and the English booksellers joined forces and formed a British, rather than English, cartel.[44] So it appears that Donaldson and his countrymen took the share offered which his counsel would not countenance.[45] The price of books did not fall, but it did lead to a range of new forms

[35] Mary Poovey, *Genres of the Credit Economy: Mediating Value in Eighteenth- and Nineteenth-Century Britain* (Chicago, IL, 2008), 158, 160.

[36] Trevor Ross, 'Copyright and the Invention of Tradition', *Eighteenth-Century Studies*, xxvi (1992), 14.

[37] Benedict, 'Readers, Writers, Reviewers', 16.

[38] James Raven, 'Booksellers in Court: Approaches to Legal History of Copyright in England Before 1842', *Law Library Journal*, civ (2012), 129.

[39] J.E. Elliott, 'The Cost of Reading in Eighteenth-Century Britain: Auction Sale Catalogues and the Cheap Literature Hypothesis', *English Literary History*, lxxvii (2010), 355.

[40] Elliott, 'The Cost of Reading', 368.

[41] David Fielding and Shef Rogers, 'Monopoly Power in the Eighteenth-Century British Book Trade', *European Review of Economic History*, xxi (2017), 394. Other commentators have suggested investigating price-setting is largely impossible at this distance in time ('beyond our gaze'): James Raven, *Publishing Business in Eighteenth-Century England* (Woodbridge, 2014), 51.

[42] Elliott, 'The Cost of Reading', 375.

[43] John Feather, 'The Significance of Copyright History for Publishing History and Historians', in *Privilege and Property: Essays on the History of Copyright*, ed. Ronan Deazley, Martin Kretschmer and Lionel Bently (Cambridge, 2010), 366–7.

[44] Fielding and Rogers, 'Monopoly Power', 394–5.

[45] See Cavendish, Thurlow {S10}.

of publishing.[46] The law had been formed upon an assumption of how the business of bookselling could be transacted, but it was only one assumption and, while those in the trade did not necessarily know it, little would change as the monopolies crashed.

The Parliamentary Reporters

The reports of William Woodfall, John Almon and the other parliamentary reporters working on the Booksellers' Bill in 1774 were still in many respects similar to Samuel Johnson and the near fictional reports he and his colleagues wrote earlier in the century. The reports in 1774 covered very few of the debates in the House and when they did get reported, even by the legendary 'Memory' Woodfall, they were inaccurate and unreliable, missing out key facts, adding new arguments, changing arguments entirely, and generally trying to create an entertaining read or, perhaps, an idealised version of what had been said. These nascent reports were by men learning the skills and the right approach to what was essentially a new form of journalism. The fetters were removed slowly over time, note-taking was allowed,[47] so it would become rarer for entire arguments to be invented or completely moulded; and much later the adoption of shorthand facilitated a near complete account to be made. However nearly 100 years passed[48] before the quality of reports really changed and, of course, with the official reports the modern form of reporting began half a century later still.[49] Yet only with the broadcast of parliamentary proceedings,[50] and their digital retention, have truly accurate records been available.[51] So while there are extensive newspaper reports of the Booksellers' Bill, the record is not a mirror to the past, but a blurred lens letting though hints of what was said and aspects of what was not. It was a beginning after all.

Procedure

The parliamentary procedure of 1774 was little changed from 100 years earlier, but it was a turning point once more. Indeed, in his history of private bill procedure[52] Cyprian Williams

[46]Elliott, 'The Cost of Reading', 355–6. In the year after Donaldson, the almanac patent was found to be unlawful, even though it had been in existence for nearly 200 years: *Stationers' Company v Carnan* (1775) 2 Black 1004 (96 ER 590); Cyprian Blagden, 'Thomas Carnan and the Almanack Monopoly', *Studies in Bibliography*, xiv (1961), 23. The Booksellers considered a bill to remedy this decision and retain a perpetual right (An Act to vest the Sole Right of Printing Almanacks in that Part of Great Britain called England in the Two Universities of Oxford and Cambridge and the Company of Stationers of the City of London Respectively). A manuscript draft of the Bill was produced, but it was never taken further: *The Records of the Stationers' Company 1554–1920* (1986), reel 99, box D, item 10; box E, item 9; *Literary Print Culture* (Adam Matthew, 2017): TSC/1/E/EnglishStock/E/10/10.

[47]Arthur Aspinall, 'The Reporting and Publishing of the House of Commons Debates 1771–1834', in *Essays Presented to Lewis Namier*, ed. Richard Areas and A.J.P. Taylor (1956), 230.

[48]*Hansard* started having its own reporters to get a more complete report in 1870.

[49]The reports of the floor of the House began in 1909, but standing committees (now public bill committees) were only reported from 1920.

[50]*Sound Broadcasting Joint Select Committee* (*First Report* (1975–6 HC Papers 494), xv, 935; *Second Special Report* (1975–6 HC Papers 723), xv, 979); HC Debates, 3 Aug. 1976, cdxvi, cols 1636–79.

[51]Nikki Hessell, *Literary Authors, Parliamentary Reporters: Johnson, Coleridge, Hazlitt, Dickens* (Cambridge, 2012), xviii, somewhat cynically suggests even these might not be accurate as they can be digitally manipulated. While true there is no suggestion that this has happened at least in relation to the official broadcasts.

[52]O.C. Williams, *The Historical Development of the Private Bill Procedure and the Standing Orders of the House of Commons* (2 vols, 1948–9).

saw 1774 as the beginning of a new era: the move from the pre-standing orders' period towards the beginning of a code.[53] A milestone in this change was the appointment of a committee sitting alongside the Booksellers' Bill[54] to consider the proper rules and regulations to be observed for private bills.[55] Appointing such committees became a regular event during the remaining years of the 18th century[56] and from a handful of standing orders being in place in 1774 there were 39 by 1810,[57] and an 'impressive code'[58] of 149 orders over eighteen chapters by 1830.[59] The session where the Booksellers' Bill passed the Commons was the end of an era, albeit the new epoch grew only slowly. The changes in standing orders reflect the development of the great economic movements which came to dominate the 19th century – canals, railways and companies – all of which depended on more streamlined parliamentary procedure. While little changed quickly, momentum took over and a private bill in 1830 would have been quite different to that of the Booksellers'. The great counsel of the day had argued for their clients' cases at the Bar of the House, but this practice slowly petered out and by the end of the 1820s it happened no more.[60] The great debates on the merits of bills disappeared soon after,[61] and the petition committee eventually became merely about considering compliance with the (increasingly complex) standing orders, before being replaced entirely by examiners[62] who were officials of the House. Indeed, through the 19th century a private bill getting any parliamentary time on the floor of the House became increasingly rare. The great debate on the Booksellers' Bill simply would not have happened in the same way 50 years later, albeit the fear of monopoly had not diminished.[63]

The extensive records for the Booksellers' Bill have enabled us to look at the end of an age, or more accurately the beginning of a new era in book publishing, parliamentary reporting and parliamentary procedure. A failed bill rarely brings so much.

[53]This is evident from his chapter titles: ch. 3 'The Pre-Standing-Order Period'; ch. 4 'The First Advance Towards a Code: 1774–1835'.

[54]It was not the first such committee, but the previous one had been appointed nearly 25 years earlier in *CJ*, xxvi, 88 (5 Mar. 1750/1).

[55] *CJ*, xxxiv, 577 (21 Mar.); it reported on 30 Mar. (*CJ*, xxxiv, 608–9) recommending seven new orders and these with others were adopted on 15 and 25 Apr. (*CJ*, xxxiv, 649, 676).

[56]Over the next 25 years nine committees were appointed to review and develop standing orders: *CJ*, xxxviii, 407 (31 Oct. 1775); *CJ*, xxxviii, 224 (22 Feb. 1781); *CJ*, xliv, 530 (10 July 1789); *CJ*, xlvii, 674 (2 Apr. 1792); *CJ*, xlviii, 747 (7 May 1793); *CJ*, xlix, 422 (4 Apr. 1794); *CJ*, li, 425 (22 Feb. 1796); *CJ*, liv, 558 (27 May 1799); *CJ*, liv, 613 (10 June 1799).

[57] *CJ*, lvi, 658 (30 June 1801).

[58]Williams, *Historical Development of Private Bill Procedure*, i, 41.

[59] *Standing Orders of the House of Commons* (1830 HC Papers 692), xxx. 113.

[60]Williams, *Historical Development of Private Bill Procedure*, 56–7.

[61]'Private Business of House of Commons', *Law Magazine or Quarterly Review of Jurisprudence*, cxxix (1843), 132.

[62]This occurred in 1846.

[63]Debate on the Birmingham Plate and Crown Glass Company Bill: John Hodgson Hinde MP, *Mirror of Parliament*, iii, 28 June 1837, p. 2024.

PART II: THE DIARIES

Introduction

Biography of Sir Henry Cavendish

Sir Henry Cavendish was born in 1732[1] and educated at Eton and then Trinity College Dublin.[2] He entered the Irish house of commons in 1766,[3] and came over the Irish Sea in 1768 when he was given the seat of Lostwithiel in Cornwall by Lord Edgecumber, who was loosely described as his 'cousin'. In the Commons, he was part of the marquess of Rockingham's faction, and sat on the opposition side of the chamber,[4] and save in respect of America and the occasional Irish issue, he remained on the opposition lists,[5] which ultimately led him to lose his seat when his sponsor became a supporter of the administration. Cavendish then returned to Irish politics, re-entering the Irish parliament in 1776, whereupon his allegiance swung for and against the administrations in London and Dublin.[6] Cavendish was said to be mediocre but while 'steady to his interest, his politics were elastic' so that he 'changed his politics with different governments'.[7] While this comment might represent his conduct in the 1780s, from 1790 onwards he was a staunch government supporter and remained so until his political career ended with the Irish Parliament ceasing to be.[8]

Cavendish was a frequent speaker who was conspicuous and verbose;[9] he spoke at least 165 times,[10] almost always on the opposition,[11] but was not held in high esteem, being

[1] His father was said to have ruined Ireland as he was a teller of the exchequer and died owing the exchequer £67,000 – a debt which passed to his son: P.D.G. Thomas, 'Sir Henry Cavendish (1732–1804), Parliamentarian in Two Countries', *Parliamentary History*, xxxvi (2017), 190. He had a distant, illegitimate, connection to the duke of Devonshire: Thomas, 186.

[2] P.D.G. Thomas, 'The Debates of the House of Commons 1768–1774', University of London PhD, 1958, p. 1.

[3] For Lismore, Co. Waterford.

[4] Thomas 'Sir Henry Cavendish', 187–8; Thomas, 'Debates of the House of Commons', 2.

[5] Thomas 'Sir Henry Cavendish', 187–9. He remained on John Robinson's list of opposition members for the 1774 election: P.D.G. Thomas, 'John Robinson's "State" for the General Election of 1774', *Parliamentary History*, xxx (2011), 228.

[6] Thomas, 'Sir Henry Cavendish', 189–92.

[7] Sir Jonah Barrington, *Historic Memoirs of Ireland* (1833), i, 134–5.

[8] Thomas 'Sir Henry Cavendish', 197.

[9] Thomas, 'Sir Henry Cavendish', 185.

[10] He recorded 139 of them; in Thomas, 'Debates of the House of Commons', 6, it is suggested he made 168 speeches.

[11] Thomas, 'Sir Henry Cavendish', 187; as to the usual low number of speakers see Part I: Chapter 1: Party Politics.

seen as a bore or a joke.[12] Horace Walpole described him as 'a very absurd man'[13] and 'hot-headed and odd'.[14] In his time in the Irish house it was said on a government list of 1784 that he 'was a good shorthand writer but a tiresome speaker'.[15] Cavendish became incredibly unpopular, at one point so much so that he was hissed whenever he spoke.[16] He had a particular interest in parliamentary procedure,[17] having a particular regard for parliamentary dignity and constitutional propriety, and often intervened on the topic.[18] Despite all his flaws, Lord Clonmell conceded that through 'mere assiduity' he made himself the first sailor, skater, billiard player, fiddler, shorthand writer and master of several other accomplishments,[19] and grudgingly even Barrington described him as having 'good manners, good sense and some good qualities in private life'.[20]

Cavendish's Diary

Cavendish's account is 'uniquely'[21] significant because he was the only MP who wrote a regular series of reports of the British parliament of 1768–74,[22] making it far from being the 'Unreported Parliament' it was later called. His British diary covers more than 15,700 written pages,[23] extending to an estimated three million words,[24] and the majority of it has been in the British Museum (now the British Library) since 1835. The diary extends over 50 manuscript books and it is remarkably complete for its time, with only a few short periods omitted.[25] The length of each volume ranges from 200 to 500 pages.[26] It was Cavendish's aim to record every word spoken by every speaker – a true verbatim transcript – and he largely succeeded.[27] However, his record was mostly confined to public business and so private business was not usually included:[28] the Booksellers' Bill being a notable exception. There were only about 50 speeches that he failed to record (and a few days when he was

[12] A.P.W. Malcomson and D.J. Jackson, 'Sir Henry Cavendish and the Proceedings of the Irish House of Commons, 1776–1800', *Parliamentary History*, xx (2001), 131–2.

[13] *The Last Journals of Horace Walpole: During the Reign of George III*, ed. A.F. Steuart (2 vols, 1910), i, 201.

[14] Horace Walpole, *Memoirs of the Reign of King George the Third*, ed. Sir Denis Le Marchant (1845), iii, 213–4.

[15] G.O. Sayles, 'Contemporary Sketches of the Members of the Irish Parliament in 1782', *Proceedings of the Royal Irish Academy*, lvi (1953), 268.

[16] *Sketches of Irish Political Characters of the Present Day* [by H. MacDougall] (1799), 209.

[17] *HC 1754–1790*, ii, 202.

[18] Thomas, 'Sir Henry Cavendish', 185, 188; 'Debates of the House of Commons', 3.

[19] Malcomson and Jackson, 'Sir Henry Cavendish and the Proceedings of the Irish House of Commons', 145.

[20] Barrington, *Historic Memoirs of Ireland*, i, 135.

[21] Malcomson and Jackson, 'Sir Henry Cavendish and the Proceedings of the Irish House of Commons', 129.

[22] He also recorded debates during his time in the Irish house of commons: Malcomson and Jackson, 'Sir Henry Cavendish and the Proceedings of the Irish House of Commons', 129.

[23] For the most detailed account of the whole diary, Thomas, 'Debates of the House of Commons', 12–22.

[24] Thomas 'Sir Henry Cavendish', 186.

[25] A missing volume was found in 1954 and added to the rest. It did not relate to the Booksellers' Bill: P.D.G. Thomas, 'Sources for the Debates of the House of Commons, 1768–1774', *BIHR*, special supp. iv (1959), pp. v, vi.

[26] Thomas, 'Debates of the House of Commons', 12; one volume of 1,800 pages is really three volumes.

[27] Thomas, 'Sources for the Debates', p. vi.

[28] Thomas, 'Debates of the House of Commons', 16.

absent).[29] Like the reporters in the gallery he had to contend with the noise in the chamber, 'a few members, whose rapid delivery outran [his] ability to keep up with them',[30] and of course with tiredness.[31] From the sixth volume (long before the Booksellers' Bill) he started to leave out information that could be found elsewhere, such as the wording of motions, votes and precedents. He also did not identify speakers fully and so where members had the same surname there could be confusion. Yet Peter Thomas's conclusion on the diary is apt: 'despite the difficulties and hazards involved in the use of the Cavendish diary, it is the most detailed and accurate source available for the study of parliamentary debates before the nineteenth century.'[32]

While the diary was originally prepared for publication, Cavendish claimed he delayed until the speakers were no longer alive (for reasons of 'delicacy'),[33] albeit the reality was probably related more to him losing his enthusiasm for the project as time passed and Irish affairs became more important to him.[34] Yet his work has been largely neglected by historians,[35] and this has long been acknowledged. In 1887, Lord Rosebery while addressing the International Shorthand Congress, said the failure to publish Cavendish's reports was a 'great disgrace to us a Nation'.[36] There was an attempt to publish the diary by John Wright,[37] who in 1839 published the part of it dealing with the Quebec debates of May and June 1774. He had originally intended to publish the entire diary, but ultimately stopped midway through the second volume, taking the work as far as 27 March 1771. Wright did not publish the diary chronologically, but thematically, in the same way the *Parliamentary History* had been printed. He expanded abbreviations, inserted the motions and votes and so forth. He guessed the identity of the speaker where there were two possibilities and omitted entire paragraphs when these were unintelligible. Most troubling for historians, for other gaps he filled in blanks by guesswork, without indicating what was in the original text and what was his own invention. He also modified spelling and phrases and altered the style and grammar. This doctoring, as Thomas says, casts doubt on the precise words used and greatly reduces their value as an historical record.[38]

In the 1980s, Thomas published those parts of the Cavendish diary dealing with North America in his co-edited collection *Proceedings and Debates of the British Parliament Respecting North America, 1754–1783*.[39] However, the debates on the Booksellers' Bill, along with much of the debates between 1771 and 1774 have never been published. Cavendish's diary is far from perfect, however. He used a form of shorthand which had been recently

[29] Thomas, 'Sources for the Debates', p. vi.

[30] BL, Egerton MS 263, f. 1.

[31] Thomas, 'Debates of the House of Commons', 18; *The Grenville Papers: Correspondence of Richard Grenville and the Rt Hon George Grenville*, ed. W.J. Smith (4 vols, 1852–3), iv, 482–3.

[32] Thomas, 'Sources for the Debates', p. vii.

[33] BL, Egerton MS 263*, f. 2* (this was his son's explanation); also see his 'Instructions to the Printer': BL, Egerton MS 223, f. 1. He also wrote a Preface: BL, Egerton MS 263, f. 1.

[34] Thomas, 'Debates of the House of Commons', 14.

[35] Thomas refers to the fact that despite including 238 speeches by Charles James Fox none of his biographers refer to it: Thomas, 'Sir Henry Cavendish', 186.

[36] *The Times*, 27 Sept. 1887, p. 7.

[37] He edited volumes xiii–xxxvi of William Cobbett's *Parliamentary History of England* (1806–20).

[38] Thomas, 'Sources for the Debates', p. vii (the summary of failures is of those identified by Thomas).

[39] ed. R.C. Simmons and P.D.G. Thomas (6 vols, New York, 1982–6).

invented by Thomas Gurney,[40] and he often abbreviated words further than Gurney suggests in his text. Gurney shorthand is context dependent and so what was intended is not always clear. For instance, 'Cd nt h the lst alvity f the la had no'[41] has been transcribed as 'could not have the least validity if the law had no',[42] and as the reader of the shorthand becomes more in tune with the writer, common abbreviations become easier to follow: 'la' being short for 'law' and 'gr' being short for 'great' and so forth. However, this context dependency means that when the work was transcribed into longhand there possibly were ambiguities.

Most of Cavendish's diary was transcribed by a clerk named Clarendon.[43] His writing is perfectly legible, although he often used abbreviations, such as 'M' for member, 'C' for Committee,[44] 'h' for have and 'f' for from. Yet where he found words impossible to decipher, he left spaces for Cavendish to complete the longhand.[45] These spaces might represent a single word or two or a whole passage, making it difficult to know whether a blank or a new paragraph is intended. Cavendish, while he still intended to publish, went back and filled many of the gaps and sometimes these corrections involved entire sections being altered or rewritten. He went from adding new words to changing the meaning of phrases. It appears this was done to reflect accurately the shorthand notes rather than make what was actually said comprehensible.[46] In this, as explained below, he diverged from the modern *Hansard* reporter. In any event, Cavendish only corrected 12 of the 50 volumes and in relation to the Booksellers' Bill the second reading and committee stage were not fortunate enough to be in those 12. Three further volumes[47] were transcribed by Cavendish himself, one of them including the third reading of the Booksellers' Bill. As Cavendish's original shorthand notes have been lost it is not possible to complete the work.[48] Finally, for reasons unknown, Clarendon did not transcribe around 400 pages into longhand, but simply copied out the shorthand once more. The longhand went into shorthand and back to longhand in the middle of passages, and it is unclear why this happened. These shorthand notes were transliterated in the 1950s by Timothy Joyce[49] for the preparation of Namier and Brooke's volumes of the *History of Parliament*.[50] Joyce did not add punctuation and included only some, not all, of the spaces in the original text. Also, due to the nature of Joyce's work being typewritten with a ragged right margin, new 'apparent gaps' appeared. The report on the

[40] Thomas Gurney, *Brachygraphy, or Swift Writing made Easy to the Meanest Capacity* (1750) (ESTC: T134667); the earliest surviving version is the second edition.

[41] 'h' was also an abbreviation for have and 'f' for if.

[42] BL, Egerton MS 255, f. 29.

[43] Thomas, 'Sources for the Debates', p. v.

[44] Thomas, 'Debates of the House of Commons', 14.

[45] The shorthand notes were returned to Cavendish, but have since been lost: Thomas, 'Sources for the Debates', p. v.

[46] *Proceedings and Debates of the British Parliament Respecting North America*, ed. Simmons and Thomas, iii, p. vii.

[47] Some of which duplicated what was included elsewhere: Thomas, 'Debates of the House of Commons', 13.

[48] Thomas, 'Sources for the Debates', p. v.

[49] The shorthand transcriber is not named on the MS (BL, Add. MS 64869), but is identified in *Proceedings and Debates of the British Parliament Respecting North America*, ed. Simmons and Thomas, in the 'Introduction' to vol. iv, and in Thomas, 'Debates of the House of Commons', 27.

[50] *HC 1754–1790*, i, 523.

Booksellers' petition committee was one of the debates which Joyce transcribed from the shorthand.[51]

Cavendish v Hansard

Cavendish's style was to give statements of opinion in a blunt and direct form and record the essence of the argument.[52] He was a shorthand writer not a parliamentary reporter and as described in chapter 7 even now *Hansard* edits and rephrases passages to make them more understandable, thereby improving on what was said as a permanent record. So, in some ways, Cavendish's diary is not an early *Hansard*, but is closer to a record of what was actually said on the floor of the House – incoherent rambling and great eloquence alike. Maybe this is something which is more valuable.

Note on Transcription

The editorial approach has been to acknowledge that Cavendish's diary is a report of the often imperfect and imprecise spoken word. Where words were deleted or inserted in the original report these changes have been incorporated without any indication. Where there is a space for missing text in the original then an editorial suggestion[53] has been made in square brackets.[54] No other editorial changes have been made. Passages in the original which are so fragmented or for other reasons are incomprehensible have been retained in a footnote.

The Booksellers' debate comes in three parts, and there are some differences in handling between them. The first part covers the debates on the petition report and the first reading of the Bill, which both exist only in shorthand. Neither the original shorthand, nor Joyce's transliteration, included any punctuation. Accordingly, any punctuation in the text has been editorially added. To produce the report of these two stages, the transliteration by Joyce was digitally overlaid onto the original shorthand. This enabled a comparison to see if any words were missing and to identify the spaces in the shorthand. Certain words in the transliteration have been corrected from the shorthand, or alternative suggestions have been put forward. In cases where Joyce suggested a different word this is noted, but the text includes what is believed to be a better translation. The page numbers are provided from both the shorthand as, for example, **{S1}**, and the transliteration as, for example, **{T24}**; in the case of the latter the pencilled page numbers in the original are used in preference to the typewritten numbers, which have been crossed out on the manuscript.

The reports of the second reading, on both days, the Bill committee and its report were transcribed from the shorthand by Clarendon. Abbreviations[55] have been expanded with

[51]As discussed below, Joyce's work was checked by the author against the original shorthand and some alternative suggestions made.

[52]Michael MacDonagh, *The Reporters' Gallery* (1913), 171.

[53]Accordingly, a reader can see the brackets as blanks to replicate the original manuscript.

[54]In contrast to *Proceedings and Debates of the British Parliament Respecting North America* where the text is omitted. In footnotes '…' has been used for gaps where no sense can be discerned.

[55]The bulls eye symbol (ʘ) is used in the longhand as an abbreviation for 'of the'. In the transcription, this symbol has been replaced with 'of the' in italics.

the expanded letters being given in italics,[56] and as before, the gaps[57] in the text have been filled by editorial suggestions based on context or derived from other sources, all such editorial suggestions being in square brackets. Further, Clarendon did not start sentences with capital letters.[58] This practice has been retained, as has other capitalisation and contemporary spelling. He also had a practice of sometimes using a past tense apostrophe (for example, decid'd) or simply omitting the letter 'e' (for example, askd), but he was inconsistent and sometimes spelt the word out in full. The transcription simply copies whatever he did. The report of third reading was transcribed by Cavendish himself, but otherwise the same conventions have been applied.

The following sets out the location of debates in the original volumes:

Petition Debate	No record
Petition Report	
24 March 1774	Shorthand: BL, Egerton MS 254, ff. 279–84; MS 255, pp. 1–31 Transliteration: BL, Add. MS 64869, ff. 24–43
First Reading	
22 April 1774	Shorthand: Egerton MS 255, ff. 234–5 Transliteration: Add. MS 64869, f. 149
Second Reading	
10 May 1774	Egerton MS 257, ff. 228–63
13 May 1774	Egerton MS 259, ff. 21–57
Committee	
16 May 1774	Egerton MS 259, ff. 51–137
Report (aborted)	
19 May 1774	Egerton MS 259, ff. 141–3
Third Reading	
27 May 1774	Egerton MS 260, ff. 159–66

Diary of Lord Folkestone

Jacob Bouverie, born on 4 March 1750, attended Harrow and then University College, Oxford. He took the title Viscount Folkestone in 1765 upon his father becoming the earl of Radnor, and then added the name Pleydell in 1768 upon succeeding to his maternal grandfather's estate. The Bouverie family had held an interest in one of the seats in Salisbury since 1741. In 1768 Folkestone's uncle, Edward Bouverie,[59] was elected and he duly resigned his seat in 1771 once Folkestone came of age. Accordingly, on 15 June 1771, Folkestone was elected in the family's Salisbury seat, which he held until his father's death on

[56] Most commonly, h for have, w for with, w^t for without, bec for because, throu for through, G for Gentleman, c for country, M for Member, HG for Honourable Gentleman.

[57] A difficulty is that some gaps represent new sentences or paragraphs, some represent missing words, and some both. Where it is a new sentence or paragraph this has not been marked.

[58] This was probably as punctuation was added as the text was transcribed.

[59] Hon. Edward Bouverie† (1738–1810).

28 January 1776 when he took his place in the house of lords. Whether in the Commons or later in the Lords, as the second earl of Radnor, he had a host of idiosyncratic political interests. He sponsored estate, road and enclosure bills but also matters like poor relief and vagrancy, sewerage commissioners, the management of county gaols and the regulation of playhouses.[60] Like Cavendish, he kept a parliamentary diary, but his aim was much more modest in that he wanted to record his own parliamentary activity. His diary covers over 50 years in Parliament (from 1772 in the Commons to his death in 1828 as a member of the Lords), but extends to only three small volumes which are now held in the Wiltshire History Centre.[61] It is clear from his diary that Folkestone was particularly exercised by the Booksellers' Bill. In the 1774 session he spoke 13 times,[62] five of which speeches related to the Bill.[63]

It is not clear whether he read out a speech from his diary,[64] used it as notes to make a speech or wrote down a record of what he thought he had said (or had wanted to say) afterwards. It is apparent that some things recorded by Cavendish are not mentioned in Folkestone's diary but the correlation between the two sources is very high.[65] For instance, Folkestone proposed an amendment to the motion during the debate on the report on the petition committee. The amendment suggested a scheme for remunerating booksellers for their lost investment. Cavendish, in contrast to Folkestone, included proposed compensation figures. Omissions by Cavendish might be understandable for the reasons outlined above, but additional material must be because Folkestone said more than was recorded in his diary. In any event, his diary is a useful resource, setting out what a prominent opponent was unhappy about. In relation to other debates, Folkestone seems to have provided his speech to the newspaper reporters,[66] but not in the case of the Booksellers' Bill. His diary was written in longhand, and save for a few words is entirely legible, so the transcription included here is straightforward. There are no page numbers in the diary, and so every new page is marked with {NP}.

HENRY CAVENDISH'S DIARY

{S279; T25}
Thursday March 24
Booksellers Bill
Report *of the Committee* upon the Booksellers petition &c

Mr. Field[67] As this report has now been read and as I shall trouble the House with a motion. It will be **{S280}** in the first place before I trouble the House with a motion that I shall acquaint the House with the ground and with the nature of the relief. I shall

[60] M.W. McCahill, *The House of Lords in the Age of George III, 1760–1811* (Oxford, 2009), 116, 123–4.

[61] Catalogued as 1946/4/2F/1/3: Parliamentary diaries and speeches of 2nd Earl Radnor.

[62] *HC 1754–90*, iii, 303.

[63] In *HC 1754–90*, iii, 303, while all five speeches are included in his diary, there are only two included in Cavendish.

[64] As to whether this was thought proper see Part I: Chapter 7: The Problems of Reporting.

[65] Thomas, 'Debates of the House of Commons', 40.

[66] *Cobbett's Parl. Hist.* xvii, 410–19; Royal Marriages Bill.

[67] Paul Feilde† (1711–83), MP for Hertford.

pray for this petition. I hope I stand. That the petition have ground, the petition that they have evidence that the petition includes a [prayer] and in a long course of dealing, have **{T26}** conceived themselves[68] entitled to what has been called literary property. To that kind of property, which before the late judgment of the House of Lords. Which I am so far from even [thinking] to impeach their right,[69] depart from the principle of [law that is] perfectly consonant to every idea I always have had upon that subject. I do not mean to found myself upon any principle that should encounter the principle of that judgment but their judgment.

The idea of copyright which appears upon your report. The booksellers in common have laid out great sums of money in the purchase of that this is now become a shadow. Their property is sunk in nothing before this decision. Sir, the gentleman who has been before your Committee has showed that so long ago as the year 1748, at that time it was the current course of that trade to purchase these kind of copies; to consider these kind of copies as a perpetual right; and to invest money in them proportional to that idea. Sir, he[70] says upon first entering in trade he purchased to the amount of £3000 half of which he thought [included copy right and][71] after including [additional monies] he laid out £10,000 more, chiefly in this kind of right, and within these 22 months he has made over all copies upon valuable consideration to his son; and by this judgment the whole of it is sunk to a quarter of its value. Sir, it is upon this cause, I presume to move the House for a Bill to relieve this distress. It is the distress of a man thinking now worth this and now worth nothing. Sir, when I appeal to the compassion of this House it is that I appeal to their I appeal to their[72] on ground of merit in a precedent;[73] upon the ground of right that is at an end of compassion of the House. [This is a] case not of an individual suffering extraordinary prejudice[74] but it is for a body of men united in a useful and valuable trade of great importance to learning and [of importance to the] people. A body of men in this business [who made a] trade mistake, supported by great authority, in that mistake and by this judgment brought in a great distress. The sort of case **{S281}** will warrant my application.

Sir, it is said I have in my hand a paper[75] that seems to impeach the ground I stand on before [you, saying] error to combat or an obstinate persevering against the means of conviction. In the general turn of it [everywhere there is] obstinacy in error, even where conviction was to be had, and a desire to monopolise when no right existed (see the papers in answer to the booksellers' case). It is the plea not of merit, but of compassion. Not of obstinacy. Not where means can be had of conviction, but where no means of conviction can be had and where they err cum patribus.[76] Sir, I am far from wishing to [challenge the

[68]Joyce has 'myself', but the shorthand symbol is the same for both words.

[69]Joyce does not have anything for 'right'.

[70]William Johnston (*d.* 1804), app. 1743–8, tr. 1745–73; bookseller, 16 Ludgate Street.

[71]Part IV, Petition Committee Report, *CJ*, xxxiv, 588, c. ii.

[72]Joyce does not have 'to their'. In the shorthand it reads 'I appeal to their/there' followed by a repeat symbol followed by 'there/their on'.

[73]Joyce has 'privilege', but Gurney suggested using a single lower case 'p' for 'precedent'. It appears, however, that Cavendish did use it for 'privilege' elsewhere.

[74]Joyce has 'projects'; the shorthand is 'pr'.

[75]Part IV, Case Observations {3}.

[76]Trans. 'are with error'.

correctness of] the resolution of the House of Lords. I think they were highly warranted of the ground of their resolution in reciprocating the sort of ground as evidence, a court of law right upon which a contrary opinion has been supported. I perfectly unite in the idea that the common law was not to be looked for in the court of Star Chamber, of the King's Letters Patent, or in the injunctions of the Court of Chancery, or in the other ground.

But when I apply to the case of these Booksellers in their trade, as acting in the common course of their trade, I then think the question turns exceedingly different. Error in much[77] what the court of King's Bench determined: the common law right in property and could the Booksellers say that was an error? Could the Booksellers say previous to this when the case and motion[78] was argued? It is said in Sir James Bruce's[79] Reports in the last case of Millar & Taylor[80] he then said that the case of [Tonson & Collins][81] it has been argued twice by the greatest counsel at the bar. It was not intended to have been referred if not referred to all the judges of that chamber to take their opinion upon that important point. But, Sir, in the reports of Sir James Bruce in the case of Millar & Taylor in that report he does declare Lord Mansfield declares that the intention of the reference to the twelve judges[82] was not from any doubt of judgment of that court had; that they were **{S282}** united in opinion. I ask pardon for the mistake. To have the united opinion of the judges of the common law right – though not proceeding to the determination of that case was because they found it was not any real, but a fictitious or collusive action. Judges of Westminster Hall did not sit to try a fictitious, but a real one therefore, they did not proceed any further in that case. This is all an assurance to me of the error they were in.

Sir, the only ground taken notice of was the injunction **{T27}** that, Sir, was not authority of law it was very hard it should not be an authority to the booksellers, especially when that weight was given to the injunction. Not now allowed to the injunction.[83] Because in that very report of Sir James Bruce it is asserted by Lord Mansfield and the[84] two learned judges, they did assert that the injunction before the resolution is a decided opinion upon the merit of the case.[85] I do understand that the doctrine is denied, I always wonder at it. I have myself experienced a case where the injunction [was upon] the ground upon that ground when the case is doubtful the court will not grant injunction. The only idea I ever entertained. I understand the idea now stands that the reason of injunction by a final resolution, that the thing may not be done by [any earlier stage]. When once it is done there is an end of the resolution could they say that that would rise? Could the King's Bench say [what it did] with regard to other patents, and Star Chamber decrees they are now decrees, but do

[77]Joyce then has 'of'. There is nothing in the shorthand.

[78]'…'.

[79]This seems to be an error: it should be Sir James Burrows* (1701–82).

[80]*Millar v Taylor* (1769) 4 Burr 2303 (98 ER 201).

[81](1761) 1 Black W 301; (1762) 1 Black W 321; as to being the case see *Millar v Taylor* (1769) 4 Burr 2303 (98 ER 201).

[82]While not clear from the text, this is a reference to *Tonson v Collins* (1761) 1 Black W 301 and 321 (96 ER 169 and 180): see *Millar v Taylor* (1769) 4 Burr 2303 at 2327 (98 ER 201 at 214).

[83]'…'.

[84]Joyce has 'of'; both are represented by a dot.

[85]See *Millar v Taylor* (1769) 4 Burr 2303 at 2399–2400 (98 ER 201 at 253) where Lord Mansfield seems to give them more value.

they not decree the current opinion: some go up as far as 1550.[86] Certainly it remains a general proceeding, Booksellers include the trade concern trade can feel what the general proceedings lead them to. They know the practice, they do not know the history.[87] It created the effect of their opinion confident before such authority, that any man might have ventured ever [forward]. On this authority, I say on such **{S283}** authority. I hope it will not be thought it was in this [respect an] error etc. I ask pardon for having gone so far. I say I hope it stand there is a ground of involuntary error, an error in a prudent man, an error that any man might be liable to and such as will go, I hope, to the relief. Say something to the mode. Definitive and distinctive in every mode. Open to every gentleman's observation [on it without] restriction, my general idea is to give some time in the discussion of the House to those who have been purchasers of this copyright under the idea of a property which should not stick, I hope to God never will stick. To make amends for the great prizes they have given. To impress to dispose of large copies in hand less by the continued gate they want for them the whole world will come in. Totally destroyed with regard to the whole circumstance. I shall propose to follow the model of the Act of Queen Anne for the encouragement of learning that gave [to] books already printed the term of 21 years to printers[88] and in case another had not published [14 years].[89] Exceedingly proper and necessary should concur in the idea of printers and booksellers who have in pursuit the real right and under that idea, that they may not be sufferers in the copies they have published. I am afraid I have troubled the House too much. The House will give me leave to make a motion that leave be given to bring in a Bill for the relief of booksellers and others by vesting the copies of printed books in the purchaser of such copies [from authors] and their assigns for the time therein to be limited.

Mr. Sawbridge[90] Immediately upon the determination of the House of Lords, I did myself imagine that the booksellers who had been purchasing the copyright must be great sufferers by that decision. It was therefore with cheerfulness that[91] I second the motion for bringing up the petition, [and subsequently] referred the evidence that did appear before that Committee. More confident my **{S284}** in the[92] [great injury] that these booksellers would sustain if the legislature did not give some relief. The Honourable Gentleman that gone so fully into the question. Unnecessary for me to say anything at present. Satisfactory [to] second this motion.[93]

{S1; T28} Attorney General.[94] [I] at once took the opportunity of going into the Committee to learn, if I possibly could, upon what foundation in principle there would

[86] In fact, the earliest relevant decree was a little later, in 1566: Edward Arber, *A Transcript of the Registers of the Company of Stationers of London, 1557–1640* (5 vols, 1875–94), i, 322.

[87] '...'.

[88] Copyright Act 1709, s. 1.

[89] Assuming he knew the effect of the Copyright Act 1709, s. 2.

[90] John Sawbridge†* (1732–95), MP for Hythe.

[91] Not in Joyce, but in the shorthand.

[92] Joyce has 'any' rather than 'in the'.

[93] Ends with 'This debate continued in the next volume'. The start of volume xli – BL, Egerton MS 255 – has the title 'Continuation *of the* Debate upon the report *of the Committee* upon the Booksellers' petition, *from* the last volume'.

[94] Edward Thurlow†* (1731–1806), MP for Tamworth and counsel for Donaldson in *Donaldson v Beckett* (1774) *Cobbett's Parl. Hist.*, xvii, 953.

[be] to the general right of the people of England that the petition was itself [seeking to address]. For in the stating of the petition everything dark and ambiguous and nothing [good]. In the course of the evidence I heard the same kind of art and industry was used to keep the subject in the dark and state nothing particular as the object of the wish of the petition. Upon hearing the whole of that evidence examined, I took the freedom, by no means with the purpose of repealing the Petition but purely for the sake of understanding it myself and putting it in the train for others.[95] To suggest to them that there should be definite line laid down, upon which the examination should proceed to some clear and definite purpose. That single suggestion made in the Committee broke it up.[96] There was no one, either of the honourable gentlemen present, or the agent and solicitors, or of the witnesses as they are called though they are the petitioners themselves. No, no, no. Then it has never been read. One of the petitioners is Scotch[97] because he states himself to have a more material interest in the subject of the petition than any other bookseller in London. It has to be said now to such a boast[98] that after hearing the evidence read, and after hearing that man declare that the present article [is such that] it is one peculiar interest. That did go far enough for me to be able [to know] what was the [peculiar] ground of interest of next and the bound of the complaint that they make to which particular part [was the] subject of it. A relief was proposed, it seemed to be advisable on all hands that the Committee should be put off for a week in order to form a report **{S2}**.

It was put off for a week and at the end of that time they have proceeded just in the same train of evidence, just in the same degree of obscurity, and also of uncertainty as to the purpose for which the petition was framed. I was very happy when a motion was made that it was put in the hands of a gentleman so very learned and able to distinguish [a good] ground. He has stated to you that it is not the case of any particular bookseller ruined by an accident happening to him in the course of his trade, but it is the case of the combined and united booksellers of London. [Their claims] of this hardship which have fell upon them in a body, the House will have occasion to decide whether the case of the combined and united booksellers presents itself to them in a more favourable light than the case of an individual betrayed by the confidence of the judgment passed in a court of law.

[It costs a] large sum of money [for a party to] apply for a petition instead of a public law.[99] I wish the House will all along keep in their idea [the difference] between privilege and public law. Privilege is to be understood as a monopoly, which is fair and wise, upon proper consideration for the public to give to one or more individuals though it was given at the expense of the public. Their means may entitle them to [relief] and the privilege of monopoly may in that respect be just. But when you are about to give a privilege of monopoly: consider you do it at the expense of the public. A privilege of monopoly makes an exclusion to all other artifices to employ their skill and their time and their industry in the same course of trade. As you by granting that privilege bestow upon the individual or number of individuals to whom it is granted a privilege of monopoly also implies another

[95] The shorthand has a repeat symbol, but Joyce has nothing.

[96] *Edinburgh Advertiser*, 11–15 Mar., 166.

[97] Joyce has 'Scott'. The word is written out in full in the shorthand but the final letters could be either 'tt' or 'tch'.

[98] Joyce has 'to be as that'; the shorthand has 'a bt that'.

[99] A private bill required fees, whereas a public bill did not (but there was a fee for lodging the petition itself).

thing. A right on the part of the person on whom it is granted to put what price he thinks fit upon the articles that are comprised in that privilege of monopoly. If, as in the case of property, it is inherent**{S3}** and essential to the property that I should be at liberty to retain or part with it[100] as I please. Privilege of monopoly [has various rights] part of that privilege that I should chose at what price I should part with that monopoly.

The laws of the country having observed that have always laid down these rules to govern the Crown itself before 1623[101] in the property of granting monopolies. In the first place, it was as [the Crown] if they granted to any man a monopoly which had been [free before] **{T29}** the Crown could not do it because the Crown could not [know] the numbers of individuals who before that time were employed in the trade. In the second place, the Crown could not [prevent] no interversion [and] not grant an unreasonable term in a monopoly so as to deprive the other artificers in the same trade at the end of that reasonable term,[102] the exercise of trade in the very article and could not [for that] reason also [prevent the] necessary effect of the monopoly being putting their own price upon the commodity. [But the] public was not subject to that slavery for a longer time than was held to be reasonable. These principles were well known to be laid down antecedent to 1623.[103]

Under[104] the present case does not present to the House either one or the other of these principles upon which and upon which only before the reason and wisdom of the monopoly has been endured in this case. On the contrary, I present to you merely this case that a man having laid out a sum of money upon a title unsound at law and being [mistaken] of his title before judge of the law, finds himself in a worse situation than if he had brought title. A request to the public [asking] that you should put him right at the expense of the public.

I wish I could have heard from the learned gentleman any clear and sound distinction between the case of evictive title: where the authority stands upon the authority of the decision of law and where a subsequent decision overtakes the rule and where the rule overtakes the property. I wish some small distinction [was made to] give [relief] rather through the medium of the monopoly, **{S4}** and at the expense of the public as giving before [its] sold some money to be paid by the public to the person so evicted. The only ground stated to the House of persons being evicted from their title upon which they had laid out a considerable sum of money. Now there are two grounds in which that divides itself in order to maintain the merit of the present mode. The first that of booksellers who were really deceived, as early as 1748,[105] by a hope that the law stood otherwise. In the next place that those who now are in possession by purchase of certain copies as they call them have actually suffered a loss fit to touch the compassion rising from the circumstance of their being so deceived. If gentlemen are nevertheless inclined to take either of these proposals in the gross, if they wish no evidence, if they wish no loss, no history of either to be certain of report, and of opinion, of one of those who ask relief that such has been the case. But it is no more the case with regard to the evidence it does not [appear] to be

[100] Not in Joyce, but in the shorthand.

[101] The year the Statute of Monopolies came into force.

[102] *Darcy v Allin* (1602) 11 Co Rep 84 (77 ER 1260).

[103] Sir Edward Coke, *The Third Part of the Institutes of the Laws of England* (1644), 184.

[104] Joyce has 'in'.

[105] This was the date of the judgment in *Midwinter v Hamilton* (1748) Kam Rem 154; Mor 8295.

any evidence at all. It would have been just as wise, just as sensible, for the House to have believed the petition because the persons interested in the petition said so as it was wise and just to believe the petition because he afterwards said so before the Committee. It is a mockery of an absurd kind, both of wisdom and justice to [rely on this for] your satisfaction. It distresses the House to [have] to act upon information if the information turns out to be of no better value and account than that on the table. If a man pretends to be deceived in that of 1748, or any period of time, it is not possible that my learned friend knows well that upon such a subject as this. I speak merely possible [and it is] not possible that the booksellers should have proceeded upon [a belief in a] right which no one legislature ever gave their opinion upon it. I was asked that question does not stand on the report. No one legislature ever ever[106] nor was there ever a hope in Westminster Hall till it started up all at once in a new-fangled form on the insistence[107] of two judges. With regard to the right that booksellers were supposed to have acted under, I will not be long, not answering any evidence, none before the House. Referring to tests to be found in books, that which **{S5}** they pretend to be the suppliers [of those but,] never was so in fact. It is well known that all the monopoly [claims go] back before Charles II before the King and regulation. [There was a] Ordinance of Parliament in the time of usurpation[108] [which the booksellers] first condemn and afterwards transcribe them in their own [by-laws] and the Licensing Act[109] [followed and] transcribed by order and proclamation. Under this regulation, the council interpreting and the Star Chamber assisting the booksellers and in point of fact securing for them a monopoly. I am not speaking to this as upraiding them as resorting to pure phantoms [rather than the] 14 years. The booksellers know that there was no law which protected them in any part to expect[110] enjoyment **{T30}** of the copyright and the Act of the 8 of Queen Anne in the 10[111] is founded on the petitioners expressly stating to the House that sort of explanation of the Licensing Act of 1694 every man had thought proper at his own pleasure to print the works of every other man whatever.

It happened very remarkably that the very first suit brought in Chancery[112] and before Lord Harcourt[113] was an express decision that there was no copy right in common law. It was brought to the works of Hudibrass[114] printed before that time.[115] Suggested in the bill[116] was that the same principle which guided the legislature to give the right that they

[106]There is a repeat symbol in the shorthand, but Joyce does not repeat any text.

[107]Joyce has 'instance', the shorthand is 'inst' so it could be either word.

[108]In Joyce it is '—...'; *St James's Chronicle*, 24–6 Mar. 1774.

[109]Licensing of the Press Act 1662 (13 & 14 Chas. II, c. 33); Licensing of the Press Act 1664 (16 & 17 Chas. II, c. 7, 8); Licensing of the Press Act 1665 (17 Chas. II, c. 4); Administration of Intestates' Estates Act 1685 (1 Jas. II, c. 17), s. 15. (Its long title makes more sense: An Act for Reviving and Continuance of several Acts of Parliament therein mentioned.) There was a fight over whether to revive it in 1695: Raymond Astbury, 'The Renewal of the Licensing Act in 1693 and its Lapse in 1695', *The Library*, xxxiii (1978), 296.

[110]Joyce has 'except'; shorthand is 'xc'.

[111]Copyright Act 1709.

[112]*Horne v Baker* (1710); H. Tomás Gómez-Arostegui, 'The Untold Story of the First Copyright Suit under the Statute of Anne in 1710', *Berkeley Technology Law Journal*, xxv (2010), 1248.

[113]Simon Harcourt†† (1661–1727).

[114]The various parts were published in 1663, 1664 and 1678: J.L. Thorson, 'The Publication of "Hudibras"', *The Papers of the Bibliographical Society of America*, lx (1966), 418.

[115]'... of ...'.

[116]*Horne v Baker*: TNA, C 5/290/70.

had done by Act of Parliament, would go to protect the right in Hudibrass. A demurer was put in that bill, and it being insisted upon a Bill for discovery[117] and finding of the relief he allowed a demurer of that bill because it proceeded not under the statute of Queen Anne, but upon the principle which had existed in 1700. The answer to the injunction in the court of Chancery is more material for the consideration of the House than my learned friend has stated. It did not show that injunctions were no evidence of law.[118] But no bills filed[119] on common law right either of law or equity **{S6}** by the statute of Queen Anne.[120] Every [bill] was expressly upon the foundation of the Statute. No other whatever. Nor did they [claim in any Bill] that there was such a nonsensical[121] right as that now set up. The first attempt to be argued as late as 1752 [before Lord Hardwick][122] in deference to that time [it is] known he was of a different opinion, but in deference to [the case] argued in 1752 he said if a case had not ground within the statute[123] he would have sent to [law][124] to be decided. [Until] 1759 no measure taken to bring this right in question.[125] Says my learned friend, it must have afforded great right to suspect that there was such a right. How that history should have any influence upon the minds of the booksellers I cannot imagine. If that history is as true as is supposed it is true [there is] every probability [the view] that was made at the[126] time in the profession.[127] The action was supposed to be collusive therefore, the court would send it to all judges of the chamber. The action was found to be collusive therefore the court would not decide at all.[128] In the court but such a measure no man. Taken from the judge of the court. I never heard it was collusive. I was consulted in that

[117]There is a manuscript report of the discovery application in the archives of Lincoln's Inn: William Melmoth's Reports, Lincoln's Inn MS 10, p. 1 [spelling modernised].
Horne v Baker (9 May 1710) Lord Chancellor:
One Bookseller prints another Booksellers Copy, the person injured brings a bill for an injunction to stay his selling, and to discover what has been sold, and what profits defendant has made.
The plaintiff as estre of her husband makes a bill to get copy of Hudibras and sets forth by his bill, that the defendant has printed a new edition of that Book having no right or property in the copy, and therefore it is prayed, that the defendant may be directed to account for the profits of which he has sold off, and may be enjoyed from selling any more.
The defendant demurs generally.
Lord Chancellor: To make the defendant account for the profits of what he has sold, is going too far; for the injury that the plaintiff has sustained ought to be the measure of the damage, & not the profit, which the defendant has made.
Thou as to the Discovery of what books the defendant has sold, and what he has done in respect of his publishing of this Book is in order to recover greater damages at law; now I don't know, that this Court ever went so far: Suppose a trespass was done, would you come here against the trespasser to discover how many Cattle he put in to the land, & what damage he has done! I am not willing to carry this matter so far, especially now the late act of parliament has given another remedy in respect of the property in Copies of Books.

[118]'… injunction … chancery has never brought in controversy was undoubted … a far …'.

[119]Joyce does not have any word for 'filed'.

[120]'…'.

[121]Joyce has 'national'; shorthand is 'nsnl'.

[122]*Tonson v Walker* (1752) 3 Swans 672 (36 ER 1017).

[123]The words from 'he said' to this point are not in Joyce.

[124]The lord chancellor sent the matter to the common law courts: *Tonson v Walker* (1752) 3 Swans 672 at 679 (36 ER 1017 at 1020). This was done because a jury could not be empanelled in chancery.

[125]'In 1759 …'.

[126]Joyce has 'same', but this is not in the shorthand.

[127]'see how … told in …'.

[128]'… though that …'.

case big or little I also fancy myself arguing seriously in the case of Collins.[129] I know he had a great interest in saving the common law right I suppose by [means] that escaped me. The court found it ought to be collusive, still it will not go to the point in hand. The court were not unanimous in their opinion yet they refused to give a unanimous opinion. The Chief Justice was very desirous to inoculate to the world [his opinion] but that he would not have missed an opinion.

In the case [heard in] 1769, Millar & Taylor [we] come upon the opinion of the court. The first that ever had been given either by counsel or judge from that time till it was thrown in question against those who were not [of the booksellers of] London **{S7}**. Those who did not know they had brought the writ[130] of error might have imagined they were deceived by the authority of justice. But those people that knew would not believe him to be so deceived. With regard to the exception in 1759, I have seen letters of theirs[131] which prove they were not deceived and which combining with the evidence as it is called [have] proved beyond contradiction they were not deceived. It also appears from his evidence there were [copies] bought it being considered not as a legal right but as a[n honourary][132] right among booksellers for neither [could it be said it is] worth money. I agree with him. Not worth half the money as if a legal right. I will affirm on the side that it was worth a great deal more money than it ought to be worth for it was [found] standing on this sad[133] combination of tradesmen as ever prevailed to announce the price of a commodity, which ought to have been *juris publica* in [these] public letters [said they had] sent riders to examine the shops of booksellers.

They subscribed £3,140[134] to file bills in Chancery in order to obtain the injunction [against the] booksellers in the country and by that means to support this [a condition] of the combination was this: that all books that were first printed in [London] should not be printed either in Scotland or Ireland [neither should they be] printed by any [other bookseller] they disguised their combination in such a form,[135] **{T31}** wrote circular letters to let them know that they would take the Scotch & Irish editions at the price they sold them to the trade, and give an even in the English edition of the same books, when you have read a circular letter confessed by a man who has been examined by the Committee that he looked upon it to be [a right] and that it was in that view he purchased. Is it not too gross an imposition too imprudent to be suffered[136] side.[137]

{S8} [How can they say they] are deceived when no legislature had given the opinion [on] literary property and when the judgment had been given House of Lords [there should be no] undoing of the papers [in a case] when the law was otherwise. Supposing cases which I did not state, suppose a number of cases that have happened when the rule of law has been

[129] *Tonson v Collins* (1762) 1 Black W 301, 321 (96 ER 169, 180).

[130] Joyce has 'right of error'; a writ of error is a form of appeal: Sir William Holdsworth, *A History of English Law* (1938), i, 201–2, 215–26.

[131] Part IV, The Five Letters.

[132] *Morning Chronicle*, 25–6 Mar. 1774.

[133] For 'sad' Joyce has 'his'.

[134] This may have been £3,150: Part IV, Donaldson's Petition.

[135] Part IV, The Five Letters.

[136] 'On this' is included in Joyce, but not in the shorthand original where there is just 'side'.

[137] '… to be let aside … Lord Mayor'. The lord mayor was John Wilkes†* (1725–97).

one[138] [way]. When convinced have acted [and] states purchased is it possible to state[139] one of these cases with so little pretension to compassion as those before you. [It is] not one of those [cases, which] is not more generally adopted and received among the legislature: with regard to two branches it is a chaos; the idea: confusion. If Mister Scott[140] would on producing his accounts demonstrated before them that having given £500[141] for copy right[142] he not sold a single copy [and so] the whole lost [or at least] £250 lost.

If I could see any specific loss arising to any of these booksellers for having laid out his money in an unprofitable fund I should have something to say. But not one of the evidence goes to that it does not appear at this time that any one of the copies. They[143] ought to have to [prove to the House] that they have actually lost a single shilling before the money given for the purchase. To what are you to apply your compassion? To a united body of booksellers? Compassion has to rouse [sentiment] to die worth a million to marry worth only. If words could move compassion [then] no words so will put [it right]. But being very phlegmatic, convey no kind of idea [of what this] unworthy combined body of booksellers appear to have suffered [believing] entitled to all the copy.[144] Gone through a number of copies former booksellers recompense, they said they never were recompensed and they never gave above 5; on one side of the **{S9}** claim stood £5 on the other? I was desirous of enquiring, I ask a question or two of that kind an anxious petitioner[145] always said. I did not know [which] one of our books [suffered a loss.][146] What is his proposal? Did not know. Not make up any accounts so in the end not a single book that they stated could give any answer. I will tell you who I asked this question though I had not made up my mind. Giving up the expense of the public. I thought it would sound better to the House if the case of common sense were to be proposed. I wish for the sake of common sense that the House might have some ground to state if they had lost the [money] that was all [there was] to that. That was the of a piece with the original petition without having [any][147] title to that compassion upon which alone my learned friend put it. They were determined to trust to his oratory [not any] real ground. Such simple people as himself without any shadow whatever, [they are precluding the public] from them a much cheaper. And having thought of that before, upon a sudden I should have been surprised have considered how to make 2 and 2 make 4. Cast up the sum. They conclude in a very different way. You are to suppose that which is indeed true [for one] to be the case of a certain number of individuals because it is the case of A and B, you are to give that relief with compassion.[148] For A and B to the whole alphabet [that is] all booksellers to be included in a monopoly

[138]Joyce has 'of'.

[139]Joyce has 'of'.

[140]The repeat symbol is used here, but it is not clear what is repeated.

[141]The report, *CJ*, xxxiv, 590, c. i, has a different sum.

[142]This was for Gibson's translation of Camden: *CJ*, xxxiv, 588, c. ii: William Camden (1551–1623) (trans Edmund Gibson* (1669–1748), *Britannia* (Bowyer, 1772) (ESTC: N15692).

[143]Joyce has 'of'.

[144]'£5 … it was to a 15'.

[145]Joyce has 'probably'.

[146]'You give … 40'.

[147]Joyce has 'a' but the shorthand has a blank.

[148]'…'.

because A and B [have suffered]. If there could be any ground my learned friend thought himself obliged to talk of the gross and obnoxious [nature] of the bill. Donaldson[149] my client had printed a certain number of books. He proposed to take them in a partnership in this [trade and] I do believe my client would be very glad to have a reasonable share with the **{S10}** London booksellers [and both parties] *non hasc in*.[150] It was to defend him to a certain point and go no further. Not wish him so well as to encumber **{T32}** him with a [book] monopoly entirely for the sake of giving him a share of it.

I wish gentlemen would explain how monopoly comes to be a more wholesome thing to the trade of books. I know one conceives the amazing announcement of the press if there was one of [these granted] to the booksellers. It would be a shameful announcement of the books I should have given credit to that particular topic.[151] There is a case in which the law allows monopoly for an author for 14 years when the renewal [of copyright is given, the booksellers say they are for a further period][152] under the protection of that case.

Dr. Hawksworth's book[153] sells for 3 guineas; if such trash as that sells for 3 guineas only because it is a monopoly subject to 14 years, it will better books sell for [£500].[154] If make a monopoly [of] 21 [years for] Virgil, Milton, Bacon:[155] every book before being become a monopoly will have the price raised upon it. Will have infinitely a better title [for much less than] 3 guineas.[156] All this under the compassion which [asks] to raise the new foundation. Will they say they have better such and that they will not be worth quite so much as if nobody else was allowed to sell them. This is a question where my learned friend has not pretended [otherwise].[157] With regard to authors, I am inclined to think they are entitled to another sort of [right] than they have at present under the statute of Queen Anne. If [it is] accompanied to any [significant] literary merit. Another side to that difference I can understand[158] but things like this has produced no merit. **{S11}** [I have] not tried to support it [for witnesses who are] not competent. Only in the report affected to be competent. They did not give [any] trouble [and they refused to] deal with me as a man ought. They did not think it worthwhile. They tried you not with impudence it is beyond that. Doesn't for you to protest you had it not. Would not make us as long as the world endures. If they have only to insult the house by bringing a petition which the house would not believe without evidence and then making one of the petitioners rehearse it. I am persuaded it is too bad for the House to come in consistent with any [view upon] wisdom justice or these grounds [as there is nothing] upon which it ought to act.

[149] Alexander Donaldson* (1727–94).

[150] Trans. 'not enforcing'.

[151] 'If I had not to be … was just as … only say word for all'.

[152] Copyright Act 1709, s. 9.

[153] John Hawkesworth (?1715–1773), *An Account of the Voyages undertaken by the Order of His Present Majesty for Making Discoveries in the Southern Hemisphere* (Strahan and Cadell, 1773) (ESTC: N34379).

[154] *Morning Chronicle*, 25–6 Mar. 1774.

[155] John Milton* (1608–74); Francis Bacon*, Lord Verulam (1561–1626); Virgil (Publius Vergilius Maro) (70–19 BC).

[156] '… 300 …'.

[157] '… point'.

[158] Joyce has 'it' after understand.

Mr. Dunning.[159] [With this] subject travelled so long perfectly [through every stage]. It is [unfortunately] in case [in the House of Lords I was on the] wrong [side of the] argument.[160] A question at length decided and finally [resolved], far be it from me to have any intention to distribute these monies. I was not quiet sanguine at [the judgment as] my client however both the court and the client both out of my memory. I wish my learned friend had not been quite so [willing to] recollect he had [argued before]. I will say so much that the circumstance of having [argued] and carrying affection along with the argument is apt to leave some traces behind. That he as well as the learned gentleman conceives he has delivered his mind of these impressions. The learned gentleman rather expressed a regret. Not collected from the evidence in the ground. It was not my fortune to be present at the Committee at the time he was, I wish I had been as fortunate to have attended the Committee in the progress of it. If he had attended the Committee in the progress of it besides getting information upon certain points, he would not answered to the question. The same evidence was put to that Committee that **{S12}** opposite to me afforded complete ground for that motion.[161]

The house already in possession of much the Honourable Gentleman did not attend to the report or it escaped. One told them he did purchase a quantity [of copies that is] literary property £1,200 [he sold] in the month of June last; long before the decision of this question. Sold it to a branch of his own family.[162] He advanced by way of further information [since the decision] that property not part one shilling. Not saleable at the price of a quarter part. Not think it very material to inquire whether the inferences is this witness was contrary in the interest of petitioners. In truth **{T33}** he had parted with their property [his evidence was] naturally included from having once had this property. If any could make it [the witness was] in his form in any other sense just and disinterested. That he was not in the number of petitioners the learned gentlemen did not presume he was [interested] before the forms of the House admitted as a witness. By these forms he was admitted as a witness all evidence when admitted and admissible mistake its notions[163] in the mind was who are to judge? [The question is] can it be possible that [the facts] that which he has stated is true?

If it was true [then] the fact truth and proved but this the case of the petitioners is at least a case of compassion of complaint of a loss because in truth they have just ended one. They do complain of a judgment the cause of that loss. Such complaints ought not to be awkward they know there exists no precedent capable of relieving them. But their case being a case of compassion their loss indisputable. Leaving it to the House to decide whether any relief [be given. They do] not presume to suggest any specific relief to which they conceived themselves to be entitled to. They know too well how little attention would be paid to any relief.

Before them it is true the witness when I was there was not desired to state what books make this literary property **{S13}** what had been bought or sold high prices. If he had been there and put the question I am of the opinion he would have got an answer. It did not

[159]John Dunning† (1731–83), MP for Calne.

[160]*St James's Chronicle*, 24–6 Mar. 1774.

[161]'… half on our … hard question … aware'.

[162]Joyce has 'own form'; *CJ*, xxxiv, 588, c. ii.

[163]Joyce has 'chance', but the relevant letters are 'ntns'.

conceive either the objection. The House were of opinion in this state of the question. The only question whether we are now ripe to say upon this proposition we will be inattentive on the case of compassion in this situation [and allow the House to] give no remedy.

My learned friend will have an opinion to suggest what is a proper sort of relief unless we are all ready to decide this is a case that requires no relief must concur in the motion. It is not simply merely the case of distress or compassion now before. Certain, certain that is a case that requires a reasonable attention upon the part of the House. The gentleman seems to [not care] whether the booksellers have gone on under that [misapprehension]. No further proof than that they have bought that at a great price which is now grown to no value. Parting with their money but by supposing they have proceeded under a degree of witness upon the subject is it so clear that this witness was not a[n exception but] one in a [group] of this that committed it.

My learned friend alluding to the complaints of the that produced the Act[164] of Queen Anne in which petition [they] claim no such property. It may be so. This is equally true and subsequent to that period a different idea got in the minds of that people. We all very well know further no profession of mine who never see any reason to adopt the idea.[165] This I may venture to say without reason to apprehend being contradicted: had these booksellers consulted those who could have given advice. Would have advised that it was not imagination of their own.[166] Consider people of the profession that great man[167] not singular in his opinion show us at the time of our decision of an equal number of the judges of that opinion. In the progress of this opinion it got into other hands [and with a] decision in the Court **{S14}** of Chancery affirmed.[168]

It got to a further length. Long to be returned so generally I believe the learned gentleman not differ from me when I presume to think he was not very sanguine two months ago.[169] Not supposed it would be a fundamental principle of common law at this time. I differ from him I was not as sanguine before my clients. I was sanguine to think the decision was likely to be exposed to little dangers to their costs they have found the contrary. Not a ridiculous idea [to suggest] booksellers ought to be wiser. Naturally suppose they might be more fit to be trusted. They went on to purchase with more evidity, they extend their purchases, they think they would have the final decision upon[170] other which [no more] material than this: state money by their trade. The decision was finally decided, it was therefore in their hands treated a property. The honourable gentleman thinks that material to to be thought is the case. Bearing the terms of the learned gentleman over the way making this broad[171] [undertaking] united and combined. The idea of combination brings to one's **{T34}** imagination that there is something legal in that combination. If any such imputation! But to the conduct of this man, I am not in possession of the secret.

[164] Joyce has this followed by 'of Parliament'. This is not in the shorthand.

[165] '...'.

[166] '...'.

[167] It is presumed the reference is to William Murray†*, Lord Mansfield (1705–93).

[168] 'Johnston and ... affirmed'.

[169] '...'.

[170] Joyce has 'other' followed by 'the'. This is not in the shorthand.

[171] Joyce has 'this hear'; shorthand is that/this 'br'.

Not a single complaint. Learned gentleman not averse to a single complaint.[172] That the title of relief should have decreased [but it] increases if to relieve a single man [is permitted]. That complaint which if coming from a single individual [is good] coming from the whole trade, coming from men knowing no fault. It is the circumstance of that combination that unanimity that entitled them to that relief. It is that that distinguishes them in that case from the actual[173] title, does any man says my learned friend [who] bought without a title [then] apply for relief. No book he was a single man the case did not fall within any of these rules [of] legislative administration to apply readers this bill is not like the case of a single man, it is a sort of case the House, in others instances, have administered relief **{S15}** have an individual asked it. It would just[174] been fit to have given it to such application it will I trust appear to the House.

Every bookseller in London is a loser in some way, as Mr Johnson,[175] his case common with the whole trade all other people who have purchase some sort of property must have purchased at a stable price must have sustained [profit] to equal the loss upon it. It appears to me to be such a one without any imputation of impudence upon the petition without any imputation of impugning upon those who have taken the pains of proposing the terms of great modesty [for] consideration[176] from the House. A bill which is only left to a discussion of the question: what sort of relief? It assumes only more than that the case is entitled to some sort of relief. Have not gone the length of convincing me by this mode of application not given a negative. Remind the House before I sit down, what passed upon this very subject so long since as 4 or 5 or 6 or 7 years.[177] Act of Queen Anne [set out] the ground upon which the legislature thought fit to give relief. It would be important to go into a full discussion of it. Suffices to show that these booksellers were thought to deserve the protection then afforded. In the judgment the same. The case was thought to deserve degree of protection. More property, more interest to [protect] that property. It was [important] to the case of authors and booksellers under the idea the bill I believe was presented during all these successive years in this House. In the last 7 year the Bill obtained the concurrence of this House, the Bill miscarried in the House of Lords for the reason nothing to do with the merit of it. It was there understood to be coupled with something by the rules of Parliament ought not to be coupled with.[178] For that reason the Bill was thrown out in the House of Lords.[179] But for that regulation the booksellers would now have been in possession of a much better right they now look at term in some cases to continue for life, in other cases for a number of years or months. The last of them advanced at last something to which they had [under the] Act of Queen Anne. We may so far avail ourselves of the opinion of gentlemen,[180] when in truth **{S16}** the complaint of no greater

[172]'…'.

[173]Joyce does not have 'actual'.

[174]Joyce has 'have'.

[175]This would be a reference to William Johnston.

[176]Joyce has 'has consider', but this is not in the shorthand.

[177]This means 1734, 1735, 1736 and 1737.

[178]It was said that the Booksellers' Bill 1737 failed because it included a mechanism to refund the universities any duties on paper.

[179]On 10 May 1737: *LJ*, xxv, 111.

[180]'…'.

when they had sustained no loss. Not applying on the ground now. From that time to this and an accident that had baffled the trade know something of [it]. Has not made their case worse than it was in 1737. They were entitled to something so much from me say that [I hope we] will have a disposition to give them. I will to that advantage for the future consideration of this particular petition. So much advantage to the title, so much advantage to the [Booksellers].

What is now under the consideration of the House will at least entitle [them] to bring in [a Bill]. If my learned friend [believes] all that opinion will be evidence to his [side] enough to object, much better to amend it, to improve it, to alter it, not to reject it. Though the case equally is good as when our [petitioners] ask [before] though the case now particularly deserves relief. I trust the House will not send **{T35}** long [delayed relief back] to the public [or] that this ought to stop in the first instance; and that the House is ripe to say it ought not to go further.

Mr. Greaves.[181] I differ from the honourable gentlemen. When a body of people are applying for a monopoly they should give reasons. I should have imagined when the proposal [is a] monopoly [there should be] some introduction to it. I did not find they have done it in that report, particularly inquiring into the losses they have sustained. I could not get the last of the shares.[182] What they give for these shares? I ask if the right to the shelf of classic.[183] [They do] not claim the right [to classics]. It must in some means be independent of the law. Common law against you, you pretend no common law right to that fine edition of the classics. Let me know what you have given for these classics. I could not get any account from them. They said they looked upon the right so settled could not be questioned. Bought to a very great amount. They produced an assignment **{S17}** the excellent Robertson[184] in 1769. In that assignment they particularly were not [limited] how did that remain if no doubt [over] common law right. This certainly was after this solemn decision. Whether they had not heard the troubled views of the bar against it. They said they did not know. I did not find the learned gentleman ever said there was a common law right. I daresay he told me [there was] no common law right. Never took a counsel's opinion on it. Ask another question have you an assignment? Give no account of the books they have bought. Only produced a few assignments [valued merely] in shillings [and a] small share £500. They did not imagine they were answerable with their whole fortune.[185] If those gentleman have lost anything [even] in an ideal way. It is not any proof they have lost anything. Alter the late Act of Parliament are[186] in favour of authority, none in favour of booksellers.

They know they are a very crafty set of men. A few get the most valuable books keep the others dependent upon them. You might now have 200 practising booksellers who would sign a petition and say they would be injured. Relieve these people. Not proper [to] give a monopoly is that to be likely that without giving specific losses. These gentlemen would

[181] William Graves† (?1724–1801), MP for West Looe.

[182] As to shares see Part I: Chapter 5: Public Auctions.

[183] Joyce has '—'.

[184] This was probably for William Robertson* (1721–93), *The History of the Reign of the Emperor Charles V* (3 vols, Strahan, 1769) (ESTC: T71143).

[185] '... it was a case of large'.

[186] Joyce has 'be'.

ask since this judgment had there been any sale. [They said] could not get them since the determination of the House of Lords? Has there been any [for] years. Could not say much how do you know any loss? You might see their property less than before, but there is no instances of it. [Giving a] monopoly in London dangerous principle.

Lord North[187] Today a business of great consequence. To read the Boston Port Bill[188] the third time. As this debate is likely to go on, the House should be appraised of it. If the House chooses to go through this debate now adjourn to tomorrow.

Mr Greaves It does not seem to me any one of the principles that should concur to introduce a monopoly in this **{S18}** particular case. No proof of that before the House. Will take away as much from the other people as you give to them. It is well known if books are tolerably printed point of paper etc no danger of their being broken into on before other people. As to the Scott editions [these are] an incorrect [edition and] nobody [should] admit them in his study.[189]

Solicitor General.[190] I am much less astonished than I have found myself on many occasions. Particular occasion I mean determination on literary property. [When the House is] applying itself to any particular subject should make any proposal appear either very clear or very doubtful. Not surprised at one time, **{T36}** [it was] as clear as the sun [there was a] property common law [in] works of art.

When I have heard a [clever] and ingenious for a man and I am sure he must have persuaded himself that the determination of that question. On the contrary because they had had no loss because they had had no injury in their property that it should now be supposed they had no property in their copy right. To the proposal, certainly a mind against the [right]. Not so absurd. One stands confirmation by the very judgment of Westminster Hall. It is asked what loss is sustained. How injured [enough that] one copy worth less than it was before. One need not require a great a deal of evidence to prove [when a] final judgment of law in favour of his state or against his state. That is precisely the case of the booksellers. Yet it is said they have not sustained any loss. As to the quantity of property engaged in copy right, from the conversation I have heard. I should not think it very material to have detained the Committee on the single question: whether the Bill permit or not on the [report]. That property so very notorious that copy right had been bought and sold as states had been [made]. I ask that the House should take into consideration whether it is possible to regulate this business, so as to promote every public purpose and for the sake of trade at the same time.[191] It may be said what error were they not **{S19}** apprised that there was no such right? Did they not know that the judgment of the Supreme Court of King's Bench was contradicted at the bar? Were they to[192] attend all the coffee houses ask all the students and note takers or come before the House? Whether the determination of the King's Bench should be a point of law.

[187] Frederick North†* (Lord North) (1732–92), prime minister.

[188] It became the Boston Port Act 1774 (14 Geo. III, c. 19). It closed off the port of Boston until the damage caused by the 'Tea Party' was repaid (it was one of the 'intolerable acts').

[189] *Lloyd's Evening Post*, 23–5 Mar. 1774.

[190] Alexander Wedderburn†* (1733–1805), MP for Bishop's Castle, counsel for Beckett in *Donaldson v Beckett* (1774) *Cobbett's Parl. Hist.*, xvii, 953.

[191] '… individual … engage … error'.

[192] 'to' is not in Joyce.

But they are mistaken they are culpable. A gross neglect which makes them unworthy of attention of Parliament. I conceive that very circumstance can be to think this matter worthy of their consideration and the present matter goes no further. I conceive there will be observed a difficulty in giving relief. Will any man for that reason pronounce that for that reason impracticable not permit the bill to be brought in. Go into a Committee and consider the [Bill]. I wish to [address] it upon another account. I do not think it for the interest of literature, for the interest of booksellers in general, for the interest of public at large, that this trade in books should be totally and absolutely free and uncontrolled. It is said people will not buy bad and incorrect editions, which are bad incorrect editions? There must be a degree of sale by the badness of these copies found out after [sale of the book]. The temptation of a cheaper copy though a worse one will be an inducement to many people to purchase. Surely it is important that the trade should be as free as may be. But that proposal may be pushed to a great degree of absurdity. So totally uncontrolled that the benefit may be much subserved by making it so evident. I did not know that the trade of the booksellers should be one of these particular instances.

Whoever undertakes the printing of a book must undertake at one stroke the whole. The profit [even] an equal price upon a book till the whole is sold as fair and ordinary profit is[193] not returned. They pay materials and labour. Not so in the other business for the quantity of materials for the quantity for[194] work used is but equal to the things produced[195] and had on a single sale of it. It makes it unsafe and dangerous to apply a general principle. All that is desired is that the House with so far considers [a bill]. Favourable reception by the House not **{S20}** for the [London] booksellers only be for a [public] another only be for society at large to say if the wisdom of Parliament can regulate this matter. If not the perfect observation if not not set the wisdom **{T36}** of the House to put upon seeing booksellers combine [something so] obnoxious, upon other accounts some of the booksellers are now far from the matter. I am of the opinion the House will not [do such] mischief to the public or danger to individuals.

Col. Onslow.[196] Honourable gentleman [says this a] dark petition [but it is] modesty [itself]. Sir, it must be a pleasure to every man in this house to hear him say we have either power or wisdom. Sir, I attended that Committee. I came in the latter end of the first day. I found only seven or eight of the same way of thinking. The two learned gentleman with flaming swords of law and otherwise drawing the poor booksellers out of the Committee with flaming swords as our forebears out of the garden of Eden.[197] I interfered and begged my learned friend that he would not make short work with the booksellers but let us have another day which he graciously pleased to do.[198] Accordingly we got a little time to [consider] we got a little otherwise though I cannot pretend to set my opinion in law in opposition to the learned gentleman, I will venture to deal in matter of order.

The Honourable Gentleman complains of that Committee. All in irregularity. I never heard anything so disorganised when I came he was putting questions to the booksellers

[193]Joyce has 'as'.

[194]The shorthand has the repeat symbol. Joyce includes no repeat.

[195]Joyce includes 'and they recommend', but there is nothing in the shorthand.

[196]George Onslow†* (1731–92), MP for Guildford.

[197]Genesis 3:24.

[198]There is no record of any contribution from Onslow in the short newspaper reports of the petition committee, day 1.

out of their petition. When petition offers they are obliged to act upon that alone. What right [to] inquire into a trade in general? There is your ground. There is your field. There is your circle. You're to walk in that circle if you go out of that no business can be done. The learned gentleman of the arguments used to day has told you he went out of the petition and therefore the booksellers were wise enough not to give him an answer. I will only state one question. A desire to know whether the booksellers had not entered in a combination, a conspiracy persecute every **{S21}** man who [prints a book] and following that with another. How many crimes they have committed for which they deserved to be hanged? At Guildford, I remember an old fellow say he wanted to go out of the world [he was] 80 [in his] dotage [and accused of] horses stealing. [The old justice said][199] 'I warrant you have stolen many' 'countless [across] years[200] ayn't please your worship' he declares he's desirous of going out of the world.[201] He was hanged sir. I say be over order in the Committee [we had] an exceeding good chairman. Well sir the gentleman argued against monopoly whether the Act of Queen Anne [or otherwise]. Are they not beneficial to the public? If the booksellers are not beneficial to the public, what will become of the poor author? Author will sell the most sell again entitled to a monopoly. In this case a monopoly is absolutely necessary. The next point that the report was made on the opinion of one bookseller.[202] The Committee did not care. The Committee did not give themselves trouble. They could have produced 100. That case was strong, a Johnson not state it against. There is with us there is another. There is £200,000 property set afloat and at the time of the Act of Queen Anne that Act only protected £40,000 now that increased.

The gentlemen then [continued] to examine whether they have not property in the [copies] whether [or] not purchase. Two sorts of literary property. One the author and their assignments, the other [an honorary] agreement among them. But one instance of [a book] being sold that amounted to so small a sum as £50. The learned gentleman next stated that the copy right were now on producing find. Very true these booksellers thought[203] themselves so secure in the [belief]. Copy right is Gentleman though in the revenue arising from their land acres. They had their crop every year but no more than their crop. There is an end of the farm [end of] men, boys and farm. Not for the sake of an uncertain crop, but for the sake of the whole farm. Now the farm is put on there never was a case so much required of compassion and intermission of this House as the present case.

If I know it come to another part, why should we not do it? If crimes rise too[204] strong for the common **{S22; T37}** law. We make an Act of Parliament and make punishment adequate to the crime or is a new decision. I did not argue it was not law but here is a cause where we should interpose and meliorate the common law of the land is necessary to do in one instance is right to punish in another. Stand on good ground better it had been argued that it is an insult to common sense that they come here to impose upon us that they have not the least plea.

[199] *Lloyd's Evening Post*, 23–5 Mar. 1774, p. 287.

[200] Joyce has 'yet', but the shorthand has 'co … y' (y in longhand is 'years' elsewhere).

[201] Joyce omits the words from 'he declares' to here.

[202] William Johnston.

[203] Joyce does not include 'thought'.

[204] Joyce has 'to'.

I did not know that [error] belong to the trade of a bookseller, judges have erred in the first law courts. Judges have erred may not booksellers have erred [in understanding] Queen Anne. When the judges divided in opinion seven on the one side four or five on the other side is not some explanation necessary to have some[205] Act to give relief where the distress upon these people is brought by the decision of Superior Courts? After the judge had given that another way [in the House of Lords] people almost tempted to have gone into the decision, but I will not do it. Gentlemen have gone into that on the one side. I believe it might be replied to it upon another. I who pay a deference to the law and constitution of my country yet for one doubt must [be cast] upon this decision I pay laws of the land a just compliment. I submit to them I have faith I believe it is right but I do not know it is patent grievance law. I do not know law[206] knowledge lying in me.

Ought to feel either the propriety or justice of that decision, I only bow low to submit to it. The booksellers submit to it. All this property which is now set afloat, and which was before thought to be sold and real property is now no longer, is now become material intangible and incorporeal. This is a new argument. The whole argument that prevailed with the King's Bench,[207] the whole argument that prevailed with the judges, it was reserved for some other invisible, intangible incorporeal.[208] That argument I had put against the words of our Statute what should a man give in exchange for his soul?[209]

[Copies] can be protected by the common law **{S23}** of the land. If not so I might burn my Blackstone[210] that tells us the common law of the land. Protects a man in his property and reputation. Now what is a man's reputation?[211] Never very disagreeable, I could find what overtakes all this ancient property. But it is not for the sake of the booksellers whose[212] case I thought an extraordinary hard one but I thought the case of literature in general engage in this question. There are some instances of it upon the letter of a great author of the present [who is] hoping the House will take this matter up and give relief. I will give an instance if deceived. Mr. Mason[213] of Cambridge who has now published a work [he] says after this decision of the House of Lords he had better burn his papers. There are letters of Mister [?]. All hoping we should here plant the tree of knowledge: grabbed up by the roots may grey age and flourish. Therefore I hope will not only come in a Bill proposed the present but I hope gentlemen will attend this bill consider it seriously. Not only with regard to hope of individuals to extend property to consider it seriously for the sake of literature, for the sake of the public.

Mr. Dempster.[214] As it will be my inconvenience to give my opinion again what is called compassion. I asked that question. I think there was a witness under examination,

[205]Joyce has 'some other'.

[206]The shorthand has repeat; Joyce includes nothing.

[207]*Millar v Taylor* (1769) 4 Burr 2303 (98 ER 201).

[208]'if …'.

[209]'… there is something … now think only …'.

[210]This would be a reference to William Blackstone†* (1723–80), *Commentaries on the Laws of England* (4th edn, Oxford, 1770) (ESTC: T57758).

[211]'…'.

[212]Joyce has 'which'.

[213]Probably William Mason* (1724–97). The work is probably *An Heroic Postscript to the Public, Occasioned by their Favourable Reception of a Late Heroic Epistle to Sir William Chambers, Knt. &c* (Almon, 1774) (ESTC: T36167).

[214]George Dempster†* (1732–1818), MP for Perth Burghs.

I very soon found he was a party at the time. The Honourable Gentleman told the very same [thing] accompanied with the inconvenience of being 2 handled. My reason gave a negative, my reason for it is from mere compassion. It is necessary for us to interpose an individual has at his own expense procured a decree in the last Court of [Justice]. Those who are injured come to desirous of exclusive power [so as] to remedy. If a set of booksellers in the trade would determine that by the decree of the court they have suffered an **{T39}**[215] injury. Good God what will come next? Would gentlemen choose that Parliament should be applied to **{S24}** remedy the decrees of a law court. One of the most dangerous [precedents], the most danger of mere compassionate though we give a negative [to the petition] not totally persecuted booksellers. The relief [under the Statute of] Queen Anne coupled with the decision lately happened is safe for [the trade to continue. It] is a proper question for the House to take it up. The booksellers will collaterally [benefit] what will more than compensate the inconvenience that has risen from this decision. The evidence in the Committee. I did not see any clear symptom to decide that the booksellers themselves believe they had a constitutional right. Whether it was not by a combination and subscription in order bring individual booksellers that they had just supported that combination. In consequence of the means practice of that body. So much of the introduction of the property [was for it] to be saleable. For that reason, I wish to put the negative upon this now leaving it open to consideration how far the law of this House is safe.

Mr. Edm*und* Burke.[216] I am very sorry whenever my honourable friend before me resists any case of compassion. It must appear to him very powerful upon the want of justice. I shall endeavour therefore upon this principle to give such satisfaction to my honourable friend, to give such satisfaction to the House, as occurs to me.

Some complaint that honourable gentlemen not any profession[217] is come into the debate.[218] Profession on the one side if not balanced by his great weight[219] another on the other side. Where such differ [I have] diffidence in my opinion.

To have travelled through the several stages, I should have improved by my travel.[220] [I must] of now to enliven one of the two honourable friends, the same to think it a ridiculous thing that no person should come to you for relief until they feel **{S25}** injury. They ask what these booksellers have lost by the final judgment of the House of Lords the state [was] to the public [to] open the trade. All that the public will gain these persons must undoubtedly lose. The loss of advantage of a monopoly. The Honourable Gentleman considers this is a privileged demand of loss of what is attended with no misery.

Convince us no sort of benefit though we imagine that this sort of people who are acute enough. [Those who] are no overseen in this business are calling for a privilege. Argued against them at the same time they hope to draw new advantages from it. Honourable gentleman has asked a question requires a serious solution. How this different, how this differs from any other.[221] When any member states it [when put] out of his [estate to] claim

[215]Joyce has a second 'an'.

[216]Edmund Burke†* (1729–97), MP for Wendover.

[217]i.e., not a lawyer.

[218]'come now …'.

[219]Joyce has 'await'; the shorthand is 'awt'.

[220]'… but deserted by …'.

[221]'… essential'.

property is equal. Cannot they restore the book to the original possessor without taking it out of the hands of the author.[222] No gain wasted in any particular person. Before that great advantage acquired [demonstrate there is] other evidence of monopoly. If there is any question it is acquired in a specific property before that property being [vested in the] author [and] booksellers before that judgment that property ought not to be impeached by this Bill. It is not anything this bill has impeached it. We are not in a stage to do what would be an injustice. But is property really wasted [to give] a public advantage. It is lawful in legislation to compensate and give up one possible advantage for the sake of some other great principle and public advantage. That brings me to the question of property. Ask, he asks, what is the merit of these persons that come here to demand this privilege? Privilege never granted for great personal merit but for public advantage. I agree natural privilege. I agree in setting aside the merit of the party. I state they do not come **{S26; T40}**. Compassion for [a party], compassion connected with principle of public policy. That no persons who commit a great part of their property and trust it to the fate of our laws should be losers by it. If ever there was a principle [for a] legislature to compensate it is this principle. The question is whether these men who have stood in a dangerous natural error upon which I ground the distinction of describe the men who have trusted their property upon the general idea and hope of the laws of their country. I will say whether this was law first[223] [it is] law no longer. Whether a common public error, so respectable an error involved the whole King's Bench except one. [I] engage [with the] learned judges of that profession, I engage in a question which brought the opinion of that profession to the level of this [confusion].

The very learned judges who [considered] the great literary property had been myself the hope that that literary property can be the exclusive perfect powerful right. What then I will put the case [of *name* a] transaction of a lawyer of that name diffusing that profession. Broken the monopoly in it should they send in the coffee house to know whether he is in a violent or popular minister error on such occasion. But the judge who settled that property first[224] delivered that opinion when it is said it might be learned. Will the honourable gentlemen of this profession, will they say their opinion are these judges, there ought to be my guide in a purchase of any literary property. Whatever it is very true, strange evolutions happened in Westminster Hall. There is not a man in this Committee that would not be assured sometime ago, that would not be assured [when that the judgment of the] King's Bench affirmed in the House of Lords. How that happened that persons who [learned in law] persons of the law who either, neither in any[225] metaphysical reasoning supported by so many learned gentleman.[226] **{S27}**[227] I am clear he might have imagined that that opinion which led the majority of the judges of the King's Bench and half the judges of the Lords was a good ground for him to waste his property. It does not appear to me fit for [anyone] except persons just in court[228] Will any man say that found himself on such judge.

[222] '… different nature … in this case …'.

[223] Joyce has '—'; it is 'fi'.

[224] Joyce has '—'.

[225] Joyce has 'a annoy' for 'any'.

[226] 'In much of them … could make it'.

[227] '… of a bed chamber … involve themselves in the bearer of the law … conduct … I leave to nothing more … lord … legal and court … no booksellers …'.

[228] '… overall legal presumption give people …'.

Venture his whole property in it. With regard to judges of the King's Bench after which I mentioned [persons] not presume to [be any different from] the final determination of the House of Lords. It did naturally accord with me one poor idea upon that judgment but when I consider I was to have wasted any part of property [I would] with 10 times have observed the opinion of that bench than any opinion of my own. Yet I have a little travelled take a little turn in a turnpike more than many persons of that close have. I was asked how this monopoly came to merit any encouragement. This differs in my opinion from the general cause of monopoly. It differs totally.

Powerful principle existing naturally in law and reason unless in particular instances make it law and policy [and] common law. Yet there does not exist a country in Europe in which this is not made a monopoly as it is called. It differs from it [as it is] made for [a limited] time. Because a monopoly generally speaking is formed upon this idea: that there are certain things in their own nature public and common which require afterwards some act of the policy to divert from that common right **{S28}** common interest. For instance, the monopoly of corn, the monopoly of paper, the monopoly of imported flax. All these are property as in their individual interest, not as in their specific interest. Therefore no right can belong to them.[229] It does differ in its reason when a thing is an original production of any person that that person should have some way or other **{T41}** of securing to him the profit of that not individual thing but specific thing even when it goes. He ought to have some advantage in it. These differences [are the] common and ordinary nature of a monopoly when any man by force or the craft or power of law. It differs specifically in this case. These people might have imagined they were not guilty of a collusive monopoly when following the opinion they wasted their property in this business, [but those] who wasted it by this business grounded it upon the faith of judges they did not know. I will presume this ground which have induced these judges to give that opinion [the backing] that induced the judges [to reach] that opinion and make people practised in the world and think this ground [secure].

Undoubtedly, a reputable thing for a judge because they only induced him to imagine that the common law was a larger and better thing than the common law could be. So far I am obliged to say in favour of the judge. If not wrong[230] for a judge to be in error is it criminal for these people? I know gentlemen in the profession are affected scared away by general maxims. They say ignorance of fact excuses ignorance of law never ignorance of law and ignorance of fact upon which men have fixed their faith ought not to be misled by it [no person] suffer. The community at large suffers no more than it has done Where a specific [interest is] not taken away and vested in another.

The constant practice of every day to take away that when not the injury in public. The instance [of] an old East India Company under Charles 2nd **{S29}** Charter [come to mind]. Very great doubts upon the legality of this charter could not have the least validity if the law had no [basis]. Lawyers took up that afterwards authority of the East India Company.[231] They did it for money do it you for your justice and compassion.

[229] 'because …'.

[230] Joyce has '—'.

[231] *East India Company v Sandys* (1683) Skinner 223 (90 ER 103).

This has been done before you have a precedent[232] for it. What induced the legislature in 1714[233] to give 14 years for copy.[234] I think there are words in the Act of Parliament pro and con. Sometimes think right or wrong. They admitted something like the property [although] limited [held by] booksellers [they] vested property: were entitled to some security that it was necessary for 21 years. They think under the Licensing Act[235] they had got a property on less ground than the booksellers knew.

Through the Licensing Act to it that secure that property.[236] Whether these people stand in such a situation without any specific injury done to individuals or any [money] give out of the Treasury or preventing a man exercising a trade he did exercise more freely before.[237] You can vest no erroneous opinion of law in [these people] they had been led by the great and most sacred authority in this country.

Mr. Dempster. Degrees of claim.[238] These gentlemen born to a state brought up to a profession he was apprised till he procured a right to do it.[239] For us to attend to [the] industry [and the] possession of a state.

Lord Folkestone.[240] I did not think to trouble the House because I understood there was to be a proposal for a bill. Gentlemen **{S30}** seem to carry drop to extreme. I neither agree with the gentlemen who have spoken on the one side or the other. The assigns of the author are entitled to some compassion since the judgment in 1769.[241] I do not think they are I think the method of giving relief as proposed by the Honourable Gentleman is very exceptionable little. It is not relief for the present Booksellers it is using like the terms of the Statute of Queen Anne. I wish to [propose a] motion wish to give relief than by an amendment. [I move] to leave out the words after the word 'booksellers' [to the end][242] meaning to put in purchasers of copy right since the time [. I propose a] scheme that purchasers within 28 years should have a term allowed them. Approve upon oath the value of the book [and set] price. Should have some advantage price if **{T42}** worth 5 shillings [and subsequently] sold at 5s. 3d. After that term it should be 5 shillings for 14 years then only half of it.

Sir Geo. Savillle.[243] The question is whether these words stand part of the motion. Although in the contention of the noble lord put in other words. By no means inconsistent in putting in these words. Not prepared [to reject it] rather with a way of leaving it in a short state. Whether within the power of the Committee to do it. But I apprehend such a substantial alteration [is permissible, and so] the Committee [is] not impaired to recompense them. No other way. I think the method the noble lord spoke of before struck them as

[232]Joyce has 'privilege'.

[233]This must mean 1710.

[234]Copyright Act 1709, s. 1.

[235]Licensing of the Press Act 1662 (13 & 14 Chas. II, c. 33).

[236]'... only will ... please ...'.

[237]'...'.

[238]'... property ... amount not to be ...'.

[239]'...'.

[240]Jacob Pleydell Bouverie†, Lord Folkestone (1750–1828), MP for Salisbury.

[241]*Millar v Taylor* (1769) 4 Burr 2303 (98 ER 201).

[242]*CJ*, xxxiv, 590.

[243]Sir George Savile†* (1726–84), MP for Yorkshire.

very reasonable. Extremely struck with the objection. Not answered by the Honourable Gentleman (Burke). I agree with Burke in everything he said [but he] left it a little short [he did] not answer. He made a thorough distinction [in the] state. No man come to have it restored by law [of an] opinion of real or [imaginary property] and where it could be restored without hurting property but only interfering with the supposed general property. I have always said the public was a brave gentleman and should do handsomely. A solid object, I say as soon as it was shown to them. Not my own **{S31}** cunning foundation to it. The difficulty here is to make compensation to those who have not happened [to suffer loss and identity those] very innocently have erred with every great man. In the situation of a person who has been evicted [this is] impossible because[244] somebody must lose where others gain. Whether they should be resorted to the case they were in at the expense of particular persons, or whether they should be restored upon the state of the great gentleman I honour so much who I think ought to be so very generous. It meets that in these words if any method can be found of making recompense I know of one without meeting the objection of the honourable gentlemen I think it ought to be done. I think it cannot be done if upon a state of private people.

Mr. Mackworth.[245] I do think what the Honourable gentleman has said is wise with regard to our proceedings in the Committee. We are fully at liberty in the Committee. But not so far at liberty to take every proposal that may be made for the most eligible method of giving relief.[246] The two modes [replace] for one or other I wish to leave the motion as free as possible debate. Join in leaving out the words not prosecute myself in the Committee.

The question was then put:	*Aye*	*50*
That the words stand part of the motion:	*No*	*25*

They went forth.

The main question.

Mr. Rose Fuller. The Honourable gentleman communicated his idea struck me very strong. [He meant Mr Dempster who told him his object and which had great weight with him to make him alter his opinion.][247]

{T43} The question put:	*Yea*	*54*
For the main question:	*Nos*	*16*[248]

At that time divided the House

They went forth

{T149; S234}

Friday April 21.[249]

[244] Joyce has 'before'.

[245] Herbert Mackworth† (1737–91), MP for Cardiff Boroughs.

[246] '… the two modes … for one or other …'.

[247] These square brackets have been added editorially.

[248] *CJ*, xxxiv, 590.

[249] The shorthand suggests 21 Apr., but first reading was on 22 Apr.: this is noted by Joyce.

Booksellers' bill brought in

Mr Dempster.[250] deserve the attention of the House as the bill tended to enact something contrary to the decision of the House of Lords.

{S235} Colonel Onslow. said it did not tend to [overturn] the decree of the House of Lords.[251] If it had he would not have had a hand in it. Sorry one judge did not give an opinion.[252] No means in this Committee so high as to put him above his office. This country required his opinion might have been had with very little trouble. That is the inconsistency of the case. It may have been lost for this reason. Some time or other some law to compel every judge to give his opinion.

Mr. Field.[253] With regard to objections made to altering the judgment of the House of Lords. The foundation upon which I moved it so far from departing from the principle of the decision of the House of Lords, I ground myself on the principle of the decree. I believe no new law is made but is ground on the alteration of some law.

Mr. Dempster. I impute it partly to my own want of apprehension, partly to the noise in the House at the same time the breviate was read. I confess myself as ignorant of the contents as when the bill was brought in. As the bill is meant to give relief, I think it improper to oppose the second[254] reading. But I still do adhere that it is a bill of most uncommon nature. The individual booksellers [who] before the booksellers in London led through all the courts in England and in Scotland at great expense and trouble has dragged at last into the House of Lords where he obtains a decree to carry on his trade. No sooner passed but it is followed by a bill here to restore the law to its ancient footing on which it did not stand but on which the booksellers think it did stand to retain a monopoly. No privilege more dangerous by the supposed interests of both Houses applying for an Act of Parliament for[255] a relief of law refused them. The long day that the petitioners[256] may be heard before their counsel.

It was ordered for Wednesday se'nnight.[257]

Booksellers
Second Reading 10 May

{228} Sir John Dalrymple Counsel against the bill[258] [The Petitioners claim relief which they say] they are either intitled to in point of favour, intitled to in point of publick utility, or intitled to in point of publick Justice. w*ith* respect to the first point of these, when men come to P*arliament* to ask a favour **{229}** no doubt they are intitled to boast of publick merit, bec*ause* the best foundation in a free *country* for publick favour. the Petitioners may

[250] George Dempster.

[251] *Donaldson v Beckett* (1774) *Cobbett's Parl. Hist.*, xvii, 953.

[252] Lord Mansfield.

[253] Paul Feilde.

[254] He must have meant 'first' reading. Indeed, *Cobbett's Parl. Hist.* corrected this.

[255] Joyce omits 'for'.

[256] Joyce has 'privilege'.

[257] 'Sennight' is a week.

[258] Sir John Dalrymple* (1726–1810).

be shy of speaking out what those are, upon that account I will spare their delicacy, & do it for them. we find the petition sign'd by twenty men who h*ave* a large property in Copyright. we confess it [we respected the] others who h*ave* no property in that way. above half of the twenty are proprietors, are the printers of almost the scandalous Newspapers, & Pamphlets of the time.

we find that almost all engage [actively] in that sort of employment: whereas of the various names at the end of our Petition, I am warranted to say not a single man whatever was engag'd in that kind of Traffick. theref*ore* the persons who came to ask the favour of P*arliament* [they] who h*ave* b*een* represented [by these newspapers] as a knot of Pickpockets[259] and their Sovereign, virtuous, & placable, say he is [a terrible] Tyrant. they desire the decree of the King's Bench[260] to be revers'd in part. they desire the judgment *of the* H*ouse* of L*ords*[261] to be [reversed, a court] wh*ich* sometimes they Represent as ignorant of the law, & at other times as the only check upon that Court of King's Bench, which at **{230}** other times they say [it was reasonable to believe.] there is not one of you who has not receiv'd at some time of his life [abuse.][262]

as a publick body traduce, & insult. then come [to this House and they] want to ask a favour: what favour? only a mere bagatelle, only a monopoly at the expence of all the rest of their fellow citizens [that is the same persons] whom they h*ave* b*een* endeavouring to inflame into madness against you. I speak not against the Liberty of the Press. the Liberty of the Press, & the liberty of England must stand, or fall together; God forbid either of them ever should be touch'd. but that is not enough for those Booksellers, Petitioners, the Proprietors of those scandalous papers. it is not enough for them, that they are permitted to commit crimes w*ith* [impunity, they seek to] be rewarded by P*arliament* for doing it. it is not enough for them [to pay a] tribute of our Characters, **{231}** but must they h*ave* the pay [returned and multipled so that they] get a monopoly, get power of fixing the price to whatever [and enable each of them to put his hands in the] pocket of his neighbours. Sir, I think G*entleman* [acted] as I think some must h*ave* felt that there has b*een* a cessation of arms for some little time past in this way of attacking private Characters. but I [will tell you] when that cessation of arms begun, & I will tell them when it will end. it began when the present application to P*arliament* was thought of, & it will end when the fate of this application shall be determind. I observe of late in Newspapers apologies of the publisher for not inserting this, that, & t'other letter of their Correspondents,[263] these letters are not lost, they are laid up in Arsenals again [for the time when] this [bill] is come f*rom* this H*ouse* one way, or another. upon this account if M*embers* w*il*l take my advice, they would read no Newspapers this next summer [it is] advice I will take, for on account of some things that h*ave* dropp'd f*rom* me already no London Newspapers shall enter my walls for three months to come. [If Members] took one advice [may I] give them another. hang **{232}** up this bill 'till the General Election is over. 'till then the Proprietors will be your friends. When this bill is out of suspense, the Lord have mercy upon all Members of both Houses of P*arliament*.

[259] '. . .'.

[260] *Millar v Taylor* (1769) 4 Burr 2303 (98 ER 201).

[261] *Donaldson v Beckett* (1774) *Cobbett's Parl. Hist.*, xvii, 953.

[262] 'if . . . if a man takes place of a rouge . . . reject . . . part a better one. if he . . . he is . . . if he is . . . if . . . if . . . defies you'.

[263] *Morning Chronicle*, 10 May 1774.

I h*ave* b*een* some way curious to know how the blanks of this bill were to be filled up, & for how long a time they were to ask the monopoly: I am [told] they ask the monopoly for 21 years. had they come to me I should h*ave* advis'd [no more than] seven and if the M*embers* of this *country* were as designing [as it appears] they might perhaps h*ave* had [their relief.] my notion is, that as [parliamentary sessions run] f*rom* year to year, so monopo[lies should be sought to run] f*rom* seven years to seven years. the monopoly should be begun f*rom* the first session of the new P*arliament* & end the last session. by wh*ich* means [you're] abused for six years, for the seventh year you would h*ave* rest, the year of the General Election would be a Sabbath to you.

having shewn [this] I [move to the next] branch of the [case. So I address you] upon considerations of publick utility. Sir, when [petitions] for a new law come to P*arliament* the following things [have] to be inquir'd into concerning us: what effect it **{233}** will h*ave* upon the price of the Commodity, what effect it will h*ave* upon the interest of the manufacturers employ'd in that business, what effect it will h*ave* upon the publick revenue, what effect it will h*ave* upon the interests of [letters and authors][264] connected with it, & lastly what effect it will h*ave* upon the Foreign trade of the Kingdom. now, Sir, all these questions may be answered by putting one, that one is, is this bill [today] offerd to be a monopoly, or free trade? if the monopoly is only to one, but it will [be for] five [hundred] I h*ave* mentioned, & [I hope] to shew the H*ouse* that this would enhance the price of books, second, hurt the interest of the Manufactories in that branch of business, third, it would hurt the publick revenue, fourth, it would hurt the interest of Letters, & Authors, & last, it would hurt the interest of Foreign trade, but wh*ich* I confess [is mainly that] f*rom* North America to the West India trade of this Kingdom. w*ith* regard to price, this monopoly, like every other monopoly must rise the price. it must rise the price two different ways. in the first place the Booksellers having the property [in copies] will lay a high price upon **{234}** the new editions wh*ich* they make, bec*ause* they h*ave* the exclusive privilege of printing them. in the next place when the edition of the books is nearly run out, instead of printing new editions for some time, they will lay an additional price upon the remaining copies of the former edition. we well know this to be case now, if any G*entleman* will go into a shop [in it] three fourths of the edition d*isplayed*, the price upon the title page, he will tell [whether] the book almost out print. [If it is, the bookseller will say he] must ask fifteen shillings [and this price even] if to is[265] own brother not give it to you one penny under it. Sir in this second case I am warranted by experience. Harlein Voyages[266] were printed for three Guineas. not to h*ave* cost half the sum. I do not blame the purchaser. the law can be a monopoly to them. they had a right to imburse themselves for the great price they paid. we who are Lawyers feel this greatly. not for [a term of years] but perpetuity. the case of law books are beyond all bounds. I am told the present [petitioners] will not suffer a book to be printed, 'till it pays a tax of 4l'.

One of [the counter-petitioners] Mr [Donaldson[267] is an] honest **{235}** punctilious, honest man, but he paid a high [price due to the] monopoly. I mention facts to shew the H*ouse* what effect such a monopoly may h*ave* in the hands of bad [men; let alone] good men.

[264]Based on the list further down the paragraph.

[265]It is presumed this should be 'his'.

[266]This is a reference to John Hawkesworth's *Voyages*.

[267]*Morning Chronicle*, 11 May 1774.

again w*ith* regard to the intent of manufacturers [it is clear if] you increase the price of commodities, fewer buyers come, less work made, consequently fewer workmen are employd: whereas if you diminish the price, more is bought, more made, consequently more workmen are employ'd. the number of persons employd in this Kingdom in the various branches connected w*ith* printing will merit the attention of P*arliament*. I see in the Petition wh*ich* was presented 1710[268] set forth that of Printers, & the book binders alone, five thousand [were] employd in the City: now if to this we add the number of Printers, & Book Binders employ'd over all the rest of the Kingdom. if to these we add the number of Booksellers all over the Kingdom, if to these we add the number of Manufacturing Printers all over the Kingdom; & if to the whole we add the number of Printers, & [book binders] supported by these different four sets of men, I fancy I shall not go much astray if I say that this H*ouse* is now determining upon **{236}** the interests of an hundred thousand of his Majesty's subjects. if you grant the monopoly you will decrease this number, if refuse the monopoly you will increase this number, as the H*ouse* of L*ords* has d*one*.

this brings me to the interests of the Revenue. wherever this Commodity is made, wherever many workmen are employd, there the revenue must always be increased. this matter of [printing] is a thing that has b*een* [brought to] the attention of the H*ouse* as now the revenue upon Printing is consider'd, I am sorry I can't give a name to it, the reason is this[: inquiries were made] by my direction to know what the tax upon printing was, I find these Booksellers h*ave* friends every where [and so the Treasury gave no answer to our] Petition [so we] never petition the Treasury to get losses.

Sir, if you grant the monopoly askd, you must decrease the publick revenue, if you refuse the monopoly askd, you must increase the publick revenue. next w*ith* respect to Letters, & of Letter'd men: supposing that the interest of [authors] was upon the side of the monopoly, wh*ich* is not the case, yet I think it is not much for the honour of Letters **{237}** to make money the object of letter'd men. for if you do, you will tempt them to write for the mob, not for the wise. this is[, a matter,] if G*entlemen* will reflect [upon the] literary perfection of this age, they will feel the weight of it. Sir, the Greeks, & Romans writ I fancy full as well as we do in the eighteenth century, yet they had no literary property, but what we call literary property, they call fame, & Glory. the [Italians][269] write well, their authors get nothing for writing, bec*ause* the States are so small, & intermix'd w*ith* each other, as soon as a book is publish'd in one State, it is republishd in another. the French give nothing to their authors [but nevertheless] what number of Booksellers, Printers, [and] number of editions of Books they give forth [in these countries.] they exchange w*ith* each others Copies in order to throw the books off their hands: then the other persons [sells] among their Customers. by wh*ich* means letters come to be [circulated] thro' every corner of the Kingdom. I know we shall here be told [to] open a free trade will be opening the door to coarse editions, & thereby throw a distress upon literature. to that argument I will pay **{238}** no [attention.] I hold it mighty cheap [but it] may be first answer'd. shall we by opening the door to coarse editions, will it thence follow that we shut the door against fine ones? competition is the source of emulation, & emulation is the source of perfection in all arts. we in Scotland know this [fact to be true.] the top men in that place are the most

[268] 2 Feb 1710: *CJ*, xvi, 291.

[269] This is clear as the same example was also used before the house of lords: *Pleadings of the Counsel before the House of Lords in the Great Cause Concerning Literary Property* (1774) (ESTC: T90593), 6.

excellent [publishers] but no Englishman ever [was] one of them, for a reason I shall explain presently: sometime ago the [Booksellers] in that c*ountry* made the stroke [and were] persuaded to give premiums for the finest books. I chanc'd to h*ave* in my pocket a Cornelius Nepos[270] [edition from] G*lasgow* [which won][271] a premium out of the [Edinburgh Society and][272] to another a Gold Medal out of our pockets. I believe the G*entleman* enrag'd at the Superiority, printed a book the finest that ever was publish'd on the face of the earth.

Milton.[273] so convinc'd are the Booksellers of this Town, they can't make such a book, or will not make such a book none of them will sell this book. if any G*entleman* should tomorrow go, & ask for G*lasgow* Milton, I will tell him the answer. the Bookseller will tell him [it is] out of print, **{239}** [but they] are incorrect [assuming] no learning in that c*ountry* in short [nothing is] manufacturerd by the Scotch [who are] a designing p*eople* [and] perpetually imposing on the credulous English. in consequence [cannot] get the book. my next answer is this, I should be glad to know where is the harm in coarse editions? upon the plan of this objection there ought not to be a yard of broad Cloth made in England under 16s or a yard of Lower made under 8s. but the Printing trade like every other branch of Manufacturer [should have] coarse books for coarse eyes, & empty pockets, fine books for fine eyes, & full pockets. the coarse Woollen, & Linen manufacture employ ten times the number of poor, send ten times the money into the Exchequer[. I am sure that far] more money goes into the Exchequer upon two hundred *Glasgow* books, than goes in upon two thousand fine London ones. Sir, Lewis the 14th[274] among the follies [he had,] he thought nothing but fine books should be printed in his Dominions. [This meant that] he was oblig'd to bring [into France] fine paper, fine type [and to] give a bond [to the] Printer [yet] few sold [and] the Dutch [on the other hand] **{240}** lay behind them, & assum'd [to print] fine books [and] printed new editions [with] many Manufactures inrichd the State [could] run away w*ith* the trade of France; at a time when the [cost of] literature was in [so high] we in Scotland, thro' the example of the Dutch, printed the New Testament value one Shilling, Thomson's Seasons[275] value three [Shillings,] thousands upon thousands sold to the [publick to the benefit] *of the* revenue. you will always find in the [Scotch] pockets one of Thomson's [Seasons] in one [pocket] one of the New Testaments in the other so that they are doubly arm'd w*ith* prose, & verse. by the first of these books they are taught every thing that is good, by the last they are taught to be content w*ith* their natural situation, to be lovers of nature, & the God of nature. what harm it is in [allowing this to] printing in this fine town, I can't discover?

w*ith* respect to [authors] G*entleman* will [see it is the case] that in this bill no provision made for authors whatsoever. I heard this bill was to give monopoly of twenty one [years] to books to be hereafter publish'd. that would be taking care [of the author but] there is no

[270] As there is only one surviving work it must have been *Excellentium Imperatorum Vitae.*

[271] *Middlesex Journal*, 12–14 May 1774.

[272] This may have been a reference to the silver (not gold) medals awarded for printing in the 1750s and 1760s: Brian Hillyard, 'The Edinburgh Society's Silver Medals for Printing', *Papers of the Bibliographical Society of America*, lxxviii (1984), 295 (Robert Foulis likely won the award for *Cornelius Nepos* in 1761: 319).

[273] John Milton.

[274] Louis XIV (1638–1715), the Sun King.

[275] There were numerous Scottish editions published in the years before 1774. It is not clear which edition is being referred to.

such clause: the only provision **{241}** is for the interest of rich booksellers. the monopoly is to be given to the Proprietors of books already publish'd. ninety nine out of an hundred Petitioners for this bill are the Proprietors. in this next place w*ith* respect to the provision wh*ich* they h*ave* made. I think it is a matter of Mathematical Demonstrations; that is the name I give to the argument I am to use. I repeat it I think it is a matter of Mathematical demonstration, that authors h*ave* an interest against the monopoly here askd: my argument has never got any answer; it is this, the trade of a bookseller like every other trade [means] the Merchant who has a great quantity of old Stock on hand, seldom goes to market to buy new. [A tea merchant does not] go back to China to buy new Teas, whereas had their friends in North America instead of destroying [the crates of tea] better go back to China [to buy more.][276] if you grant the monopoly [then the] stock in the hand of the Petitioning Booksellers [that is] every book of eminence since Henry 8th[277] for to all those books [will be held] either good, or bad. now w*ith* such a stock in their possession as almost the whole books of merit for two hundred years past; will they go to a **{242}** new Author, & pay him an adequate price for his new Stock. on the other hand if you refuse the monopoly ask'd this old stock being taken from him, he must go to Authors to get a new Stock, & those Authors will know they h*ave* a right to an adequate price for them. it is self-evident they h*ave* an interest against the monopoly here askd for: I shall now [move] upon the second branch *of the* argument to shew that the monopoly askd would be contrary to the interest of Foreign trade. I mean chiefly the North America, & West India Trade. I take my information upon this head f*rom* the p*eople* of [Glasgow] who know the publick, & private interest very well. but the argument will apply to every trading Town in England, or in Scotland. the account they give *of the* trade is this, the G*lasgow* Merchants h*ave* great Warehouses in North America, wh*ich* are stored w*ith* goods, which [are sold by agents.] every year [the agents] send over Schemes, that is the list of Goods wh*ich* they desire to be sent out by the return of the Ship. this consists of different branches of manufacture, & great quantities of books. Sir, experience has taught the p*eople* [of Glasgow they must support] manufacture [and trades which] they **{243}** h*ave* establish'd in their own town, & from thence arises all the Grandeur of that City. in the same manner f*rom* experience they h*ave* printed vast numbers of Books not under the Statute of [Anne and outside the] monopoly. a Merchant in [Glasgow][278] goes on the credit of eighteen, or twenty months; his Towns p*eople* [being] manufacturers of the Goods, are Printers *of the* Books, knowing the credit they give[, they] give the same Credit. but if [the North American agent sends] for books f*rom* London, then the Merchant must do one of three things; either keep [a stock from] London pild up ready for being shipp'd off; or second, send to London Booksellers for books, or lastly not send those books to North America at all. if he keeps them ready in [stock] the charge *of the* trade runs away w*ith* the profit *of the* trade: on the other hand if he sends to London, [there is] often no time for comeback, the Ship has saild: or if he does get them, the London Booksellers [will] give but the ordinary credit [of] six months [or] if he makes up the books [in Glasgow he] got credit eighteen, or twenty months. if he neither has them at [hand it means] then the third consequence must follow, that he can't send them to North America; & to the next of his

[276]This was a little over six months after the 'Boston Tea Party' of 16 Dec. 1773; the city was being required to repay the loss caused by the destruction of the tea before the port was reopened: Boston Port Act 1774.

[277]Henry VIII.

[278]*Morning Chronicle*, 11 May 1774.

not sending the interest **{244}** of the Manufacturers are hurt. the [health] *of the* revenue is hurt [when] Printing in North America is [encouraged;] this last consideration is no trifle. the art of Printing is gone to a very great height in that c*ountry*. if you were to grant the monopoly [it] must go to the greatest. [There is] free trade in America [where there is no] monopoly. upon this account had my Lord Somers,[279] & those great men who found'd [the Statute of Anne].[280] one Scholar Secretary of State, another confident to Lord Oxford.[281] had they foresaw any extent to which the North America, & West India trade was to h*ave* gone, I fancy [they would have] limited the monopoly given by that Statute: but had they lived now, & saw the present circumstances of things, the mischief this monopoly would do to the North America, & West India [they] would h*ave* rejected it, w*ithou*t hesitation. Scholars, & Learned [men,] it is very good in their own way, & in their own day, but the interests of Great Britain are very good things, & must not be sacrificed to the imaginary importance of the others.

Sir, if [I am forced to] contradict all the interests I h*ave* recited to the H*ouse*. I know no interest it can serve, but that of **{245}** about fifteen, or twenty booksellers of this Town, above half of whom h*ave* spent their lives, & amass'd fortunes in abusing this H*ouse*, the other H*ouse*, their Sovereign, his [household], his judges, his m*inisters*, & every man of private virtue, & talents in this Nation. in the one Scale, hang these twenty p*eople* in the other scale hang the interests of Great Britain. in other cases a private interest has b*een* made to yield to a publick, but in this case a publick interest is to be sacrificed to a private. I come now to the last branch of argument, wh*ich* is to shew that the Petitioners are not intitled to the bill upon principles of private Justice. their plea upon this head results in this, that they h*ave* misunderstood the law. next I say if they did [there is] no reason why we should [suffer] for their want of understanding. w*ith* regard to the first of these, when this q*uestion* was agitated in the Court of King's Bench, to my [surprise it was put] as a metaphysical, [question, and] as a historical q*uestion* [and not as a] matter of law, [or as a] matter of fact. when that case came into the H*ouse* of L*ords* an honourable M*ember* in this House took a different line, & as my ideas coincided very much w*ith* [his] I did myself the honour to follow him. there we got the history *of the* Law, w*ithou*t wh*ich* I h*ave* always **{246}** thought [there is] no knowing a law. there we got a history that Literary property was an idea unknown among all ancient Nations, unknown among all modern Nations, England alone excepted. that [no better reason was] receivd by the Lawyers, or by the Judges, or by the P*arliament*, or by the [people of Scotland] or by the p*eople* of England, or by the Booksellers, or Authors themselves. upon this historical, [and] liberal, not metaphysical ground we carried that q*uestion*. it would be very improper [for me] to resume the arguments [made before the court but I am] under the necessity of stating an outline to the H*ouse*. the property of booksellers [was] first protected by Patent, this chiefly took place in the reins of Henry the 7th & 8th. but this could not create a misapprehension in the Booksellers of this day having a right [in copies] bec*ause* this Patent shew'd the consciousness of those who took them [believed in] no such right[. Booksellers then] found protection under prerogative alone, not under the common law of their c*ountry*.

[279]John Somers†† (1651–1716).

[280]'state … scholar …'.

[281]Robert Harley†† (1661–1724), 1st earl of Oxford.

The property of Booksellers was next protected by decrees *of the* Star Chamber,[282] & by Proclamations *of the* Privy Council.[283] this took place chiefly in the reign of Queen Elizabeth, James 1.st & Charles 1.st but this could not create any misapprehension **{247}** *of the* law in the present Petitioners. on the contrary [it] shewd that their predecessors knew they had no right [under] Common law, & that they were oblig'd to revert to prerogative [this was] bec*ause* at Common law [they had] no protection. besides they knew very well that [their monopoly] for above a Century past [would be found] to be illegal. the property *of the* booksellers next protected by ordinance of the two house of P*arliament* in 1649.[284] neither could that lead the Petitioners into a misapprehension, for that Ordinance was nothing more than a repetition verbatim of one *of the* decrees *of the* Star Chamber of Charles 1. when the Star Chamber gave the power [of] licensing *of the* King. the H*ouses* took it f*rom* the K*ing*. not to mention not having the three Legislators was against law. the next protection was the licensing act of Charles 2d.[285] that could not tell the Petitioners they had a right from Common law. that act only gave [a form of] property only to some prescribd by that act. in the year 1679 that licensing act expir'd, & continued [in abeyance] 'till the reign of James 2d. so conscious even the Booksellers *of the* age of no right f*rom* Common Law, that during that period [they] never brought an Action [at] Common Law against [persons] pirating their Books.

{248} their next protection was the licensing act of James 2.[286] that could not create any misapprehension, bec*ause* that only gave the [rights but for it] only to last for a limited time. Sir, the licensing expird in the reign of K*ing* William,[287] & God Grant [we should] never allow an abuse *of the* Press [again, its freedom was] revived f*rom* the year 1694 until the Statute of Q*ueen* Anne.[288] the property *of the* Booksellers was protected by the Common law [we are told] notwithstanding wh*ich* so conscious were the Booksellers of that period [there was] no Common law right [they] never brought one single action at Common law against those pirating these books. they knew so well they had no Common law right that five [petitions] after 1694, & four bef*ore* 1701.[289] they came to P*arliament* knowing they had none:[290] but P*arliament* thinking they were not intitled to it, either in point of favour [or otherwise] refused all their applications.

[282] Ordinance Decrees for Reformation of Divers Disorders in Printing and Uttering of Books, 21 June 1566: Arber, *Transcript of the Registers of the Company of Stationers*, i, 322; *The New Decrees of the Starre Chamber for Orders in Printinge*, 23 June 1586: ii, 807.

[283] *Decree of the Star Chamber Concerning Printing*, 11 July 1637 (Robert Barber, 1637).

[284] An Act against Unlicensed and Scandalous Books and Pamphlets, and for Better Regulating of Printing (1649): *Acts and Ordinances of the Interregnum, 1642–1660*, ed. C.H. Firth and R.S. Rait (3 vols, 1911), ii, 245–54.

[285] Licensing of the Press Act 1662 (13 & 14 Chas. II, c. 33); Licensing of the Press Act 1664 (16 & 17 Chas. II, c. 7, 8); Licensing of the Press Act 1665 (17 Chas. II, c. 4).

[286] Administration of Intestates' Estates Act 1685 (1 Jas. II, c. 17), s. 15.

[287] William III (1689–1702).

[288] Copyright Act 1709 (8 Anne, c. 19).

[289] This might have been intended to be four after 1701.

[290] The Bills between 1694 and the Statute of Anne were (1) Bill for the better Regulating of Printing, and Printing Presses (ordered 11 Feb. 1694 (OS) (*CJ*, xi, 228; the Commons rejected the Lords' amendments); petitions lodged: *CJ*, xi, 288, 289 (30 Mar. and 1 Apr. 1695); (2) Bill for the better Regulating of Printing, and Printing Presses (ordered: 26 Nov. 1695: *CJ*, xi, 340; died in committee): two petitions *CJ*, xi, 354 (5 Dec. 1695); (3) Bill for Regulating of Printing and Printing Presses (ordered: 22 Oct. 1696: *CJ*, xi, 567; died in committee); petition *CJ*, xi, 706 (16 Feb. 1696 OS); (4) Bill to Prevent the Writing, Printing and Publishing any News without Licence (1 Apr. 1697: *CJ*, xi, 765; died at second reading); (5) Bill for Better Regulating of Printers, and Printing Presses

the property *of the* Booksellers was next protected by an Act 10th[291] of Q*ueen* Anne; that could not mislead them [as the Act] that told them you shall h*ave* [your] books publishd by the act nineteen years,[292] & no longer. I repeated the words of limitation. I never could find in any Statute f*rom* the reign of Henry 3d.[293] down to the reign of George 3. Sir in 1731 **{249}** the twenty one years monopoly expir'd: what happen'd then? from 1731 'till 1748 so convincd were they of having no right at Common law [they] never brought any action – this is not [everything] in 1734,[294] 1735[295] & 1736[296] they renew'd their application to P*arliament* conscious that f*rom* a Statute alone [would it possible that] they could h*ave* any protection. what sort of a bill was that? let G*entlemen* compare it w*ith* this [current Bill,] that askd twenty one years for Authors, this act asks twenty one for Booksellers.[297] in 1735 they ask'd only seven. w*ith* some modesty then they askd only seven,[298] w*ith* what imprudence they now ask twenty one. w*ith* some feeling for authors, they ask'd twenty one for authors. thus, Sir, this H*ouse* has the conduct of three Parliaments, & of twelve Sessions [as precedent] to direct. the P*arliament* of K*ing* William, that of Queen Anne, & George 2d. in five sessions after 1694, in four after 1705.[299] in three after 1731, that those men came to P*arliament* to ask that very-monopoly, wh*ich* they are now asking f*rom* you. for twelve times it has b*een* refused them, & now they come for thirteen to pester you again. here I stop in the history [of the matter] at 1748: but the G*entleman* who is to speak after me will carry on that history somewhat father. he will shew you one *of the* artifices of **{250}** Stationers Hall [and their perfidious] conduct [leading to the] oppressions of their poor brothers. when they find their poor [brothers suffering] f*rom* their buckling to the rich, when they find [themselves threatened it leads to] oppression of Mr D*onaldson* to whom all of us owe our liberty. what he has said added to what I h*ave* said, the Booksellers did not misunderstand the law, on the contrary they only understood it too well. in the next place supposing they had misunderstood the law [on the matter] as p*eople* may for their want of Common Sense. I believe in the reign of Charles 1. nine tenths [of the counties][300] could not lay

290 (*continued*) (ordered: 7 Dec. 1697: *CJ*, xii, 3; rejected at second reading); (6) Bill to Restrain the Licentiousness of the Press (prepared: *LJ*, xvi, 217: 24 Feb. 1697 OS; never read); (7) Bill for the Better Regulation of Printing and Printing Presses (1st reading: *LJ*, xvi, 358; 4 Jan. 1698 OS; rejected in the Commons 1st reading); (8) Bill for the Better Regulation of Printers and Printing Presses (1st reading: *LJ*, xvii, 22: 22 Jan. 1701 OS; rejected 2nd reading); (9) Bill to Restrain the Licentiousness of the Press (ordered: *CJ*, xiv, 249; rejected on report): petitions: *CJ*, xiv, 323, 338–9 (7 and 15 Feb. 1703); (10) Bill for Better Securing the Right of Copies in Printed Books (petition for private bill: *CJ*, xv, 313 (26 Feb. 1706/7); John Feather, *Publishing, Piracy and Politics: An Historical Study of Copyright in Britain* (1994), 51–63; Ronan Deazley, *On the Origin of the Right to Copy* (Oxford, 2004), 1–29.

291 This is an error as it should be eighth as it must be a reference to the Copyright Act 1709.

292 This must be an error as the Act protected old books for 21 years and new books for 14 years.

293 Henry III (1216–72).

294 3 Mar. 1734 (*CJ*, xxii, 400); report: 12 Mar. 1734 (*CJ*, xxii, 411–12).

295 It may be that this is a reference to activity during the passage of the Booksellers' Bill 1734 as no new petition was lodged.

296 15 Mar. 1736 (*CJ*, xxii, 800).

297 Part IV, Booksellers' Bill 1774, cl. 1; cf. Booksellers' Bill 1737: Parliamentary Archives, HL/PO/JO/2/39, cl. 1 (life plus 21 years).

298 Booksellers' Bill 1735: Parliamentary Archives, HL/PO/JO/2/38, cl. 1 (7 years).

299 The date used earlier for a similar statement was 1701; Cavendish Diary {248}.

300 As to its collection from counties and more generally: M.D. Gordon, 'The Collection of Ship-Money in the Reign of Charles I', *Transactions of the Royal Historical Society*, iv (1910), 145.

on Ship-Money.[301] I ask how a bill would h*ave* b*een* receiv'd by P*arliament* signd by twenty great Lords *of the* Land [stating the] K*ing* [could] not levy Ship-money [Lords] bought Land [and the] Judges h*ave* thought otherwise. [Booksellers] claiming a power to lay on taxes to be applied in law, & to relieve them f*rom* any intolerable suffering [. When] in the reign of James 2. nine tenths [of the] Roman Catholicks [could not take office] and the judges [were asked if this was the law.] Let me suppose the judges had found [differently and that the] seventy two Roman Catholicks **{251}** [who had sworn] upon that faith take place in Office. but the Judges had found the K*ing* had no dispensing power.[302] in consequence of that the £500 penalty [inflicted] twice upon them. their praying the P*arliament* to give a third monopoly to that sufferer f*rom* his misapprehension *of the* law. what would P*arliament* h*ave* thought at that. but I agree [the House needs] to consider two things. the one, who are the contending parties now before you? & the other what is the present state *of the* application to you? Eighty seven booksellers, & Printers of London, that is of one class, the other all the Booksellers, & Printers *of the* rest *of the* Kingdom. these two sets of men h*ave* differd in apprehending *of the* Law. the one thought the law one way, the other thought the law another way. [Now in] London, the opposers *of the* bill h*ave* thought right. now [you are asked to overturn] what they think right [and now] you are desird to give to those who h*ave* b*een* acting against the Law a property they had not; you are desir'd to take f*rom* those who h*ave* b*een* acting according to law a property which they had. you are desir'd to give a monopoly to the wrongdoer, & you are desird to take a free trade f*rom* the righteous doer. that is the state *of the* contending parties before you. how is it to be **{252}** made good? is it to be made good by you in your Legislative capacity reverting decrees pronounced by the other H*ouse* in their J*udicial* capacity. for Mr D*onaldson* supported by one continued spirit [and also] by the many Booksellers of this c*ountry*, & obtaind in support of the Judicature of this c*ountry*. declaration *of the* Lords in his favour, & you by an ex post facto law [are being asked to] rob him *of the* effect of that declaration obtaind in his favour; obtaind in favour of those who[303] [trade freely] the great [bastion] *of the* English Constitution. laws not only [obeyed in fear] but in the reverence wh*ich* men who stand upon those laws pay to them.[304] [The rulings of the other House] are final determinations in this c*ountry*. step not over them. Courts of Justice never by their decree displace your Acts of P*arliament* & you by your Acts of P*arliament* never displace their decrees: each keeps to its own part, neither encroaches upon the other, but now you are desir'd to do for fifteen, or sixteen Booksellers, what for hundreds **{253}** of years even in the heat of parties your Ancestors [never did].[305] on the other hand I h*ave* always thought a Bill should be brought into P*arliament* to regulate this [practice] I first suggested this at the bar *of the* H*ouse* of L*ords*. but I [faced strong] opposition. I made the bill to regulate the effect of that decree [which was a] decree against the consent of the parties. had they come to me I could h*ave* devised such a bill [it is] not such a difficult matter[. Now,] I say it would end in nothing, that

[301] *Rex v Hampden* (1637) 3 State Trials 825 (Ship Money Case).

[302] *Godden v Hales* (1686) 11 State Trials 1165 actually found the opposite; hence the Bill of Rights Act 1688 (1 Will. & Mar. c. 2), art. 1; Dennis Dixon, 'Godden v Hales Revisited – James II and the Dispensing Power', *Journal of Legal History*, xxvii (2006), 129.

[303] … in favour of those who may …

[304] 'Sir, does not … w*ith* one or two Acts of P*arliament*. But that part … never … Courts of Justice'.

[305] '… never … on the other hand … great interest of …'.

shall conclude my argument, w*ith* a consideration to what I ask the attention *of the* House, & wh*ich* I am sure will obtain it: Sir, how can these Petitioners talk of Justice, when they know the injustice wh*ich* this bill is to bring on Scotland. Sir, in that c*ountry* h*ave* no literary property [indeed] the litigation between [Mr Donaldson] & his Antagonists could not affect it: we were "proceed a Jove" we could not be affected by that Judgment. suppose D*onaldson* had lost his cause, a literary monopoly [in England] **{254}** could not have touch'd Scotland. and now we are to suffer much f*rom* his having won his cause [so] had he lost it we could not be affected by the Judgement, but now he has won it, we are to h*ave* an act of P*arliament.* monopoly that we had not bef*ore* [what] an act of Justice [which hurts] many thousands in Scotland. [Parliament should] not change an Act of P*arliament* w*ithou*t evident necessity. what evident necessity is there to protect [the Booksellers'] imaginary loss, you are to lay [a] real loss [upon the people.] I never knew what breach of faith [has occurred] when she took f*rom* the [Stationers Company][306] their arbitrary Jurisdiction. but what made ample amends they gave them £120,000 for a subject not worth £20. it is the fashion *of the* time to [heap blame] upon that c*ountry*. in the reign of Henry 8 all mischief came f*rom* Rome, in the reign of Elizabeth all mischief came f*rom* Spain, in the reign of James 1 all mischief came f*rom* Scotland, in the reign of Charles 2 all mischief came f*rom* France, in the reign of K*ing* William all mischief came f*rom* Holland, in the reign of George 2, all mischief came f*rom* Hanover, in the reign of George 3 the circle **{255}** is turning round, & all mischief comes f*rom* Scotland. where the Needle may point next upon this compass, I confess I can't say, perhaps [I am] altogether displeased to say turning a little more to the West, a little less to the North. Sir, notwithstanding this popular abuse I trust that the English [members] will not violate lightly the laws of that c*ountry*, that country which in the late Wars in Europe, Asia, Africa, & America pound out their blood in [defence] of Great Britain; & when it [comes to it] the inhabitants of that c*ountry* are submissive to Government, to P*arliament* to the Laws. let not G*entlemen* mistake that for a want *of the* Sense of freedom. I fear, I fear a day may come when sons of freedom may call in vain for help, or find it in regions where liberty continually resides, resting upon Mountains, & Ground w*ith* Snows [and] here they reside [and so it has been] in all c*ountry* since the world begun. but even [though] she has b*een* [one with England] she never was conquer'd. I h*ave* now concluded the [Opponent's part] of my argument, tho' not [my own case for] I h*ave* b*een* blamed for selling a book in publick, & private [benefiting from the monopoly] & **{256}** immediately after attacking [the same] monopoly at the bar *of the* House [oh dear] that unfortunate book[307] wh*ich* pleases nobody, & wh*ich* all the world buys. that unfortunate book [requested] by M*embers* & encourag'd by K*ing*'s who desire [that] it was publishd. that book written by one who has not much to hope for, but where he may very well ask [whether it is the case] he has nothing to fear. it is as true as soon as I engaged in this [matter of] literary [property] I called upon Mr. Cadel, & told him, if any stroke fell upon him, whatever he should suffer f*rom* others, f*rom* me he should suffer nothing, for whatever was lost upon that book, should come out of my pocket, not out of his. my reason for mentioning this fact is this [: a] Lawyer's arguments strike w*ith* double force when he is supposed to come f*rom* an honest man; upon that account for the sake of my clients, I h*ave* wip'd off the aspersion, which had I considered my own, I would scorn to h*ave* taken notice of.

[306]This is the most likely as the next sentence links back to the value of literary property.

[307]He published *Memoirs of Great Britain and Ireland. From the Dissolution of the Last Parliament of Charles II, until the Sea-battle off La Hogue* (Strachan, 1771) (ESTC: T145644).

Witness Examined[308]

{257} Mr. Murphy[309] Counsel against the bill. If this H*ouse* is to solder up all the bad bargains made in the Kingdom, your table will be covered w*ith* Petitions & c. the other day a G*entleman* in the Common Pleas recoverd an Estate in possession of a G*entleman* for thirty years, Mr. Tyson of Hackney,[310] that G*entleman* would be very glad to h*ave* himself indemnified, & have his Estate continued for twenty one years. [There was a farce called] Love Alamode[311] [Mr Macklin, the author, did][312] not sell it[. The performance of the] farce taken in Short hand by Gurney,[313] & sold for two Guineas. what happend upon the bill[314] [in the] conference:[315] Mr. Addison[316] one *of the* Member: the words *of the* reasons [for 'vesting' was] disagreeable to your Lordship [was used] bec*ause* Authors, & Booksellers [did not have the right before][317] what followed afterwards? Mr. Pope in three years after sells his Translation of Homer[318] for the Statute time, & as long as he could by the Statute after. (he dwelt a good deal upon the booksellers pretending not to understand the Act of Q*ueen* [Anne] he mentiond their application in 1735).[319]

Mr. Putney[320] wrote to Dean Swift[321] for his opinion upon Literary property. in consequence the bill was brought in [and] passed the H*ouse* [and was] receiv'd w*ith* open arms in the H*ouse* of L*ords*. but afterwards died away on account of duty upon **{258}** paper. I must say it requir'd some Genius to mistake the Statute of Queen Anne. Tonson said he had securd Shakespeare to himself by reducing the price. the poor man [was] obligd to give up his all. almost ready to swear him not to print Shakespeare. [And for] J. Osbourne of Pater Noster Row[322] bought all his copies [to] retire f*rom* trade.[323] I *have* seen him lately [he

[308]The witness evidence is not recorded by Cavendish: see *London Chronicle*, 10–12 May 1774, pp. 450–1.

[309]Arthur Murphy* (1727–1805).

[310]*Tyson v Clarke* (1774) 3 Will KB 541 (95 ER 1201); this was part of a long saga mainly heard in the king's bench (1773/4) 2 Wm Bl 891, 941 (96 ER 524, 556); (1773) 3 Will KB 419, 514, 558 (95 ER 1133, 1201, 1210); (1774) Loft 496 (98 ER 766).

[311]'Love A-La-Mode' was first played in 1759, but first published in 1779: Charles Macklin, *A New Comedy. Love A-al-a-mode in Two Acts* (1779) (ESTC: T119854); W. Matthews, 'The Piracies of Macklin's *Love-à-la-Mode*', *The Review of English Studies*, x (1934), 312.

[312]*Morning Chronicle*, 12 May 1774.

[313]Thomas Gurney* (1705–70).

[314]This must be a reference to the Copyright Act 1709. In Jessé Foot, *The Life of Arthur Murphy, Esq.* (1811), 341–2, there is a transcript of his notes for *Millar v Taylor* which give a similar example.

[315]With the house of lords: 5 Apr. 1710 (*CJ*, xvi, 395–6).

[316]Joseph Addison†† (1672–1719), MP for Lostwithiel and then changed to Malmesbury during passage of the Statute of Anne.

[317]Foot, *Life of Arthur Murphy*, 341.

[318]The first translation by Pope was Alexander Pope* (1688–1744), *The Iliad of Homer* (Lintot, 1715–20) (ESTC: T59731).

[319]Petition report, *CJ*, xxii, 411–12 (12 Mar. 1735); 1st reading: *CJ*, xxii, 431 (26 Mar.).

[320]William Pulteney†† (1684–1764), 1st earl of Bath; letters from Pulteney to Swift, 29 Apr. 1735 and Swift to Pulteney, 12 May 1735: see *The Correspondence of Jonathan Swift*, ed. Harold Williams (5 vols, Oxford, 1965), iv, 327–8, 336–8.

[321]Jonathan Swift* (1667–1745) had been dean of St Patrick's Cathedral, Dublin.

[322]John Osborne (*d.* 1775); tr. 1733–52, 33 Paternoster Row.

[323]Part IV, Goldsmith's Hints {2do}.

became] Sheriff for Buckinghamshire.[324] all the injunctions h*ave* b*een* contradicted [and] not one gave the least ground for thinking of a Common-law right. in 1735 [there was] an injunction Mott against Faulkner.[325] the use they made of it that great part of Pope, & Swifts Miscellanies[326] had b*een* printed more than twenty eight years. Mr. Mott[327] swore he bought the work f*rom* Swift, Pope, Gay, & Arbuthnot[328] forever. he goes on, & says under the Statute of Q*ueen* Anne [common law preseved. In] 1752 a q*uestion* [heard which] involvd in it the old Copyrights, Tonson against Walker[329] for Newton's Milton.[330] [In 1765][331] another injunction by Lord Northington [granted over] three books: at the same time Lord Northington[332] dissolved the injunction as to Thomson's Seasons.[333] [the second Pope's Iliad][334] a third, Hawksworth's Swift[335] set upon the same ground as Newton's Milton, &c: (he mentioned these three cases, & the opinion of the Chancellor, that **{259}** there was no foundation for Common law right.[) Some] excluded f*rom* the Sales [of] books in Quires's[336] cheaper[. So booksellers,] all the Petitioners excepted excluded f*rom* a fair, & open Market. they keep all the Copies, now they complain they are loaded w*ith* them. numbers of books can be produced w*ith* no Patents for fourteen years. the very person f*rom* whom [they] borrowed the idea of Common Law right, he publishd also w*ith* a pamphlet in 1747[337] address'd to the Members of P*arliament* written by the Learned Commentator to Mr. Pope's Works, to whom he left his works.[338] the Learned Commentator says if I could make this my own I should h*ave* a valuable Legacy. the Pamphlet &c [says] he publish'd Pope's Works w*ith* a Patent for fourteen years. what did Millar, & Taylor throw them in? after that they stirrd no more for many years. made a Country Bookseller give up [, buying stock][339] & they put a London title page. they began by fraud [with] Mr.

[324]Osborne was sheriff in 1759–60.

[325]Granted 28 Nov. 1735: TNA, C 33/366, f. 18.

[326]Jonathan Swift, *The Works of Jonathan Swift* (Faulkner, 1735) (ESTC: T52771).

[327]Benjamin Mott (*d.* 1738), Temple Bar.

[328]John Gay* (1685–1732); John Arbuthnot* (1667–1735).

[329]*Tonson v Walker* (1752) 3 Swans 672 (36 ER 1017).

[330]John Milton, *Paradise Lost. A Poem, in Twelve Books with Notes of Various Authors, by Thomas Newton* (Walker, 1751) (ESTC: T133928).

[331]The case is reported as *Millar and Osborne v Donaldson* (1765) 2 Eden 327 (28 ER 924). This report does not mention the books, but there is another longer note of the case in Lord Coalston, *Information for Alexander Donaldson and John Wood* (Edinburgh, 1773) (ESTC: T90591), 70 (as Thomson's *Seasons*, Pope's *Iliad* and Swift's *Miscellanies*).

[332]Robert Henley†* (c. 1708–1772), 1st earl of Northington, lord chancellor.

[333]James Thomson* (1700–48), *The Seasons* (Donaldson, 1761) (ESTC: T220621).

[334]Alexander Pope, *The Iliad of Homer* (Donaldson, 1763) (ESTC: T127161).

[335]Jonathan Swift, *The Works of Dr Jonathan Swift* (Donaldson, 1761) (ESTC: T52743).

[336]This must be a reference to the 'Queen's Arms': *Morning Chronicle*, 12 May 1774; Part IV, Further Remarks {5}.

[337]William Warburton* (1698–1779), *A Letter from an Author to a Member of Parliament Concerning Literary Property* (1747), available in *The Works of the Right Reverend William Warburton*, ed. Richard Hurd (12 vols, 1811), xii, 405–16; Mark Rose, 'The Author in Court: Pope v Curl (1741)', *Cultural Critique* (1992), 197; Graham Dutfield and Uma Suthersanen, 'Pope v Curl (1714) Revisited', in *Forgotten Intellectual Property* Lore, ed. Shubha Ghosh (Cheltenham, 2020).

[338]Alexander Pope, *The Last Will and Testament of Alexander Pope, of Twickenham, Esq, to which is added an inscription wrote by himself* (Dodd, 1744) (ESTC: N19354).

[339]The newspaper reports suggest this is referring to Scottish sellers: *Public Ledger*, 11 May 1774.

Tonson against Collins[340] [which was] a collusive action.[341] the Court saw the fraud [so] would hear no more of it [and] let it sleep again 'till Mr D*onaldson's* circular letter [after he] open'd a Shop in London [in] 1763. then the country Booksellers took heart. not being able to get books, but at a shop [where they] bought them *from* Mr D*onaldson* **{260}** [and they are] equally good. they found a Mr. Taylor, they began w*ith* him for selling the books. when D*onaldson* issued out a [Middlesex][342] bail, no says the Petitioners it must go on [to] Westminster Hall [as so] the matter [was] made up between them, & Taylor. then Mr D*onaldson* w*ith* the Judgment *of the* King's bench publishd Thomson's Seasons.[343] not bring actions of Common Law [but] by injunction. not mean to argue, they go up to the H*ouse* of Lords. [who grant] a decree for him. the last resort is well known. *from* all these circumstances, can they pretend to infer that there was a Common law right. Mr D*onaldson* has a [stand against] all these persons. [At great] expense [to him] in the mean time his books h*ave* b*een* restrain'd by injunction. they in the mean time [had no] monopoly [but seek] to lose his right. the honour would be to him [and] the fifty two London petitioners are excluded *from* the market. they keep these men poor, & their Counsel are instructed to laugh at them for their poverty. in the Publick Advertiser[344] they are chargd w*ith* being the Authors *of the* licentious abuse *of the* Press. Mr. Woodfall[345] is the man who complains &c. Mr. Woodfall **{261}** thinks that p*eople* do not understand any thing *of the* conduct of Newspapers. the Proprietors *of the* Newspapers are the Petitioners for the bill. they can do more to connect the licentiousness *of the* Press than the whole Legislature &c. they may lay their Commands upon Printers. they dine together July, & August, they h*ave* a book, they drink the staining of papers. [When] dining there upon the murderd reputation *of the* year. a man has nothing to do, but to shelter himself in a contempt for them, & their Newspapers.

not dwell upon Mr D*onaldson's* case, it is fully stated in his petition [he had] two very material objections [namely] all the Learning thro' the Kingdom will be attained [and all the] literature of this Kingdom to belong to the Booksellers. if the Learned h*ave* a mind to give an edition *of the* old [books to be] protected by the new Statute. if this bill passes their hands are tied up [they] must ask leave *of the* Booksellers. if the Bookseller gives leave, he must do it at the Bookseller's price. scarce a book in thirty years that does not want notes, & illustrations. would do it as independent men, not as the hirelings of Booksellers. in the course of thirty [years,] laws change. if an Author makes mistakes, are they not to be set right? Anecdotes **{262}** &c. who are to do that? is it not the province of Learned men to do it. are Milton &c wrote for Pater Noster Row only. Milton never never received but one five pound.[346] [In] 1752 [there was a] charity Play for the Grand

[340] *Tonson v Collins* (1762) 1 Black W 301, 321 (96 ER 169, 180).

[341] See *Millar v Taylor* (1769) 4 Burr. 2303, 2327 (98 ER 201, 214).

[342] As to an explanation of the Bills of Middlesex, R. Ross Perry, *Common-law Pleading: Its History and Principles* (1897), 153–4.

[343] James Thomson, *The Seasons* (Donaldson, 1768) (ESTC: T141531).

[344] This was based on the publication of the *Public Advertiser*, 15 Feb. 1774, p. 2; *CJ*, xxxiv, 456, 526–7.

[345] Henry Sampson Woodfall* (1739–1805), 62 Salisbury Court, Fleet Street.

[346] His original assignment is held by the British Library: Add. MS 18861: John Milton's contract for the publication of *Paradise Lost*, 27 Apr. 1667. It is reproduced in Kerry MacLennan, 'John Milton's Contract for "Paradise Lost": A Commercial Reading', *Milton Quarterly*, xliv (2010), 221.

daughter[347] of Milton. upwards of thirty thousand pound made by Paradise Lost. Thomson's Seasons £100, w*ith* a bargain that all amendments should be given to him. not a shilling less than £10,000 made by it. Mr. Tonson's copies; he was induced to leave off trade; five, or six *of the* Petitioners agree to give £10,000 for all his Stock. a secret [meeting where] books sold by Auction. the purchasers are there puffing £23,000 [and] put £13,000 in their own pockets. highest benefit to the publick, if a fair, & open trade. the only thing can keep up the price is a monopoly. we h*ave* seen the London Booksellers driven to lower their books since Mr D*onaldson* one single instance will illustrate. Mr D*onaldson's* Homer; he found eleven volumes £1.13.6 [so] printed it in eight, afforded to sell it in one [part,] he prints a good, correct, neat edition for £1 in eight Volumes. they printed it in seven Volumes at a Guinea. Mr D*onaldson* gives a Homer w*ithou*t any Notes, pocket size at 7s 6d. w*ithou*t notes. **{263}** gave another edition[348] leaving out notes, that containd Greek etymologies [thereby] making a Homer fit for a man of common capacity [at] twelve shillings [although] he has left out two thousand lines. it has forced the London Booksellers to the book of a Guinea. an advantage [to] adopt an argument I h*ave* seen a book of Lord Kaimes,[349] he argues tho' edition should be uncouth, will that do harm to Letters? none at all. he tells this story, [I] went to my cows [and was] glad to see my Gardiner reading upon a Whited brown paper [for] three pence [a copy of] Miller's Gardiners' Dictionary &c.[350] Learning is put within the reach of everybody. the Community is serv'd by it. the first, & greatest objection [to] the Petitioners of London [claiming] the old monopoly [is to] shew we h*ave* not understood the Act of Queen Anne. bec*ause* you will make one as soon as our interest [is granted] we will misunderstand it. we h*ave* bought a Lease hold, we h*ave* bought a freehold: bec*ause* you will consider us as ruind [by it] we h*ave* dealt out large [and given the] booksellers a nullum Tempus[351] against us.

a quarter before 10 O'Clock – adjourned to another day.

13 May 1774
{21} Booksellers Bill
Mr. Field moved to put it off to Monday next

The question *was put:*	*Yeas*	*26*
	Noes	*34*
	The yeas went forth	*8*[352]

Mr. Mansfield[353] in support *of the* bill

[347]There was a charity performance for Elizabeth Foster on 5 Apr. 1750. Samuel Johnson wrote a Prologue: Samuel Johnson* (1709–84), *A New Prologue Spoken by Mr Garrick* (Payne, 1750) (ESTC: T39922). Johnson later claimed that the show raised £130.

[348]Homer, *Odyssey* (Donaldson, 1769) (ESTC: T90526).

[349]This is most likely a reference to Lord Kame's report of *Midwinter v Hamilton* (1748) Kam Rem 154 at 160 (later Mor 8295 at 8300).

[350]This book would be Phillip Miller* (1691–1771), *The Gardeners Dictionary &c* (Rivington, 1731) (ESTC: T59420).

[351]Trans. 'No time runs against the king'.

[352]*CJ*, xxxiv, 752.

[353]James Mansfield†* KC (1734–1821).

The great object *of the* bill is to give to authors who h*ave* not transferred the Copyright &c [. there is a] single thing to be determind on by me, not what [relief is] to be granted in the C*ommittee*, but simply whether the present bill should find its way to the C*ommittee*. the persons who apply to P*arliament* for this bill h*ave* b*een* represented under very odious Colours indeed, h*ave* b*een* calld Conspirators, oppressors, Tyrants, & every possible hard name. tho' a great deal has b*een* said very well [against the bill,] when I say nothing has b*een* proved by it [indeed] these men are said to be accused [of things] by all men [and] I mean by Authors of all denominations &c. I am very happy **{22}** I h*ave* an opportunity of saying this [it is clear] Authors of eminence to be forc'd [by those] not much employed, I don't except the Learned G*entleman* who now appears as Advocate against them, who do not bear testimony to their merit, most warmly wish success to that law the Booksellers ask for. the ground upon wh*ich* they apply for relief is a very plain, & simple one: if the ground is not made out; they are not intitled to what they ask; if the ground is made out, the Justice, & Wisdom of this H*ouse* will not refuse them. laid out £100,000, & they h*ave* d*one* this under a receiv'd [wisdom] not too much to ask *of the* Legislature to give them that property for a time, at least they h*ave* in some instances very dearly bought. it is said they never did believe such a permanent right. if they did not then I admit there is no pretence for this application, on the one hand consider the nature of this trade, or right. if it is made out to the satisfaction *of the* H*ouse* tha't they h*ave* b*een* under this delusion. I flatter myself, they do not pretend [to something] unreasonable. to secure to themselves that property w*ithout* wh*ich* many of them, & their families must be involvd in ruin. something ought to be said to obviate many prejudices. a great deal has b*een* said very ingeniously, **{23}** & elegantly, much to the entertainment of all who heard it. to raise the greatest prejudice in favour to the opposition of this bill: as if the natives of Scotland labour under peculiar disagreeabilities, bec*ause* they belong to that c*ountry*. I know no distinction between one part of this Kingdom, & another. speaking as an Englishman, [who is] much indebted to what she gives, on the other hand I hope Scotland does not much complain for the little she receives in return. as to National prejudice, bec*ause* it may be supposed to affect anybody on this or the other side *of the* Tweed. I am satisfied no such disagreeable [feeling exists] in the resolutions of this H*ouse* &c. will decide upon the matter w*ith* the utmost indifference. – a case that needed such a support must be a wretched one indeed. ask to do something to contradict the decision in the other H*ouse*. to be now so unparliamentary a topick, give it no other answer: it is totally w*ithou*t foundation. it never was, it never could h*ave* b*een* agitated in that place. a decision has b*een* made in the H*ouse* of Lords in its Judicial capacity; declaring what the law is, or considering what the law ought to be.

News papers: I did not expect to hear so much **{24}** severity upon the Subject. one *of the* complaints was that they were not suffer'd to h*ave* a share in one of those News papers. no man can [justify newspapers which] not only attack M*embe*rs & c they do worse, they attack the sacred characters of Authors. not what they h*ave* [yet they are] most barbarously traduced f*rom* day to day; & no man can be more angry upon this account than I am w*ith* those Newspapers. they[354] h*ave* no more to do w*ith* the actual printing *of the* papers, than you, Sir, who sits in that Chair. he never would h*ave* employed men deserving of those invectives he the other day [stated.] besides this, another very heavy one is brought against

[354]Meaning the London Booksellers' petitioners.

them, which applies more naturally to the present case: they are said to be conspirators, entered into combination: to this evidence was calld, 5 Witnesses: what h*ave* they proved? what, h*ave* they combind? who has b*een* present when they enter'd into this combination? what the term? for what purpose carried on? as far as Mr. M*erill's*[355] evidence. what does it amount to? at the time 1756 Copies were circulating about in the hands of Booksellers *of the country*. being so [the] Booksellers [of the] *country* complain'd. the Booksellers in Town committed what was proper **{25}** to be d*one*. they must h*ave* stop'd the sale of every book w*ithou*t making compensation. [they] might h*ave* recovered as far as evidence could reach the person [that they had received a] pirated Copy. having a notion *of the* Law, what did they in fact? the measure Mr M*errill*[356] proves himself is this. instead of pursuing so rigorously, they sent to them [agents,] let us h*ave* all the books [and] pay prime cost, tho' they might h*ave* made them throw them away. no instances of prosecution are produced, but a subscription was set on foot says Mr M*erill* for the purpose. he tells you some were sold in London afterwards w*ith* title pages. not prove Mr. M*erill*. I am sorry for him [it] must hurt his conscience a little [on] this occasion. tells you one *of the* ends *of the* subscription [was] to prosecute, not to pay. suppose [we] prosecute what injury? how difficult to obtain Justice by an action? if any one Bookseller had set about prosecuting himself [it] must h*ave* b*een* his own ruin. [so they] join [the] expense [by way of a] small subscription. the case [is] not at all blameable. but another grievous thing [is] laid to the charge [there were] some Sales they did not admit all the Booksellers. **{26}** who is hurt by this? the persons who come bef*ore* you wanted to buy. suppose [that is] admitted; instead of sixty or seventy who did buy there might h*ave* b*een* many more. to the Publisher it would h*ave* b*een* the same. instead of circulating in a hundred hands [it was] kept in seventy, or eighty. why has it happend that all those who call themselves Booksellers who keep [presses or] shops &c when they [buy books] by Auction. many *of the* persons for whom those sales are held, are not Booksellers, [and at these sales][357] they sell upon Credit as long as three years. why are not Catalogues given to more than those seventy, or eighty? bec*ause* they are the only persons who are able to pay. those G*entlemen* would be very glad to buy upon Credit, but the Sellers would not get the money. this is the amount *of the* five Witnesses, except Buckley.[358] he spoke to a small prosecution, very foolish in itself. two, or three plays of Shakespeare were printed. some G*entlemen* had attend them. [he] thought they had acquird a right in them; I mean that they thought he acted lawfully. what is this to the eighty, or ninety that appears at [the foot of the petition.] I am glad to find that not a single instance of oppression has b*een* **{27}** found[.] so much for the head of conspiracy &c. it was said this bill would be very prejudicial to Authors [and it was] extremely noble minded in him to do it, bec*ause* no author has trusted him w*ith* their works, they are extremely generous. the Booksellers will be very happy to h*ave* any clause inserted in the bill to give a more valuable extent to Authors. but has any evidence b*een* laid bef*ore* you that any Author thinks he shall be injur'd? I, Sir, can tell you,

[355] *Morning Chronicle*, 11/12 May 1774.

[356] John Merill (c. 1731–1801), or his father Thomas Merill (*d.* 1781), Regents Walk, Cambridge; both gave evidence before parliament.

[357] Further Remarks {5}.

[358] Probably George Bulkley, tr. 1774–1811, bookseller, Bridge Street, Chester: *Morning Chronicle*, 11/12 May 1774.

I h*ave* letters f*rom* the most eminent Authors, Dr Robinson[359][, Dr Bettie, Mr Hume, Dr Hurd][360] & others [all] wish for the success of this bill. you will surely believe Authors when they speak, & surely they are capable of judging what is for their advantage. runs to Merchants, & Manufacturers. when you are [hearing] complaints it will be time enough for me to speak to them [like the] revenue [there are] persons sufficiently awake to avoid such mischief [to] Foreign trade [and] Glasgow Foreign trade to America. no Merchant complains [yet we are told] f*rom* one to ten. how a thousand men concerned, fell to three hundred. [claimed by opponents] & their connections. how [do we] know **{28}** what it means [does it] goes to some [issue.] but what are the books this valuable trade consists of? [books] printed in Scotland? no not all. [there are] some f*rom* London. if I am to form conjectures upon this trade, my apprehension is this: it is a trade carried on by pirated books [those] within the protection *of the* Statute of Queen Anne (reads the Letters 1771) as soon as works are printed in England, an Irish edition is imported into Scotland. Dr. Robertson feels this in his History of Charles 5.[361] [These] actions [are] attended w*ith* no prejudicial effects to any men who ought to feel them.

Alexander D*onaldson* [the man] who has freed the art of printing f*rom* Chains. in the first place Mr D*onaldson* is an extreme good Printer, & deserves the thanks, and acknowledgements of every man, bec*ause* he prints very cheaply. but Mr D*onaldson* is modest [sharing] the fault of some of his enemies[; he] assumes less than he is intitled to. a great Editor & Commentator of Homer: for he sells you a translation of Homer [leading] you believe you h*ave* the whole. Pope: but he has found they understood little of Homer, he has w*ith* great ingenuity, & great Critical art, **{29}** greatly abridged those notes. they buy an edition of wh*ich* he is the commentator [and not Pope.]

it would h*ave* b*een* better if he had told the world he had struck out [passages;] in general the World supposed they were buying it w*ith* all the appendages. [pity who] use the book. it will be known in the World what sort of Books [he sells.] I say nothing *of the* paper, or the print [being] some cheaper: wherever they are, they are miserably worse. but Mr D*onaldson* is intitled to your compassion [as] a very much oppressed man. he has had thirteen injunctions [against him] & publishd any books during the time. I should h*ave* had much more compassion, if they had not b*een* all proved upon him by himself thirteen h*ave* b*een* fil'd: the earliest in 1763. dissolved in 1767[362] & w*ith* [more] new bills fild, as new books were pirated. an injunction: he acquiesces: had he answerd no such [injunction and] the consequence would h*ave* b*een* the Chancellor would h*ave* sent the case to a Court of Law [and then] receive its final decision in the H*ouse* of L*ords* in less than a year. no more expense; than a hundred pound. why not hold this Conduct, bec*ause* he thinks the right is against him, & chooses to publish new books, & make advantage of those new books. **{30}** that is the reason why Mr. D*onaldson* has held the conduct [he has] laid out £50,000 in different impressions of books. the consequence will be, by a provision already in the bill [he] will

[359]This should probably be Robertson: *Morning Chronicle*, 16 May 1774. William Robertson, James Beattie* (1735–1803), David Hume* (1711–76), Richard Hurd* (1720–1808).

[360]For the other names see *Morning Chronicle*, 16 May 1774.

[361]Robertson, *History of the Reign of Charles V*.

[362]This must be a reference to *Millar and Osborne v Donaldson* (1765) 2 Eden 327 (28 ER 924). However, the injunction was dissolved in 1765 not 1767.

sell every book he has so printed.[363] he will h*ave* all the profit to be derived f*rom* thence: by wh*ich* he will h*ave* infinite advantage over the London, & York Booksellers, bec*ause* he never paid a Shilling Copyright [fee.] let me state what is the nature of this trade, & then what has passed upon the Subject. you will see whether they h*ave* be*en* under a mistake. whether they h*ave* or h*ave* not f*rom* the nature *of the* Trade, f*rom* the effect of what has passed, they are intitled to the relief they want. this trade [differs from][364] all others for by any book produced [a cost worthy] of great men must be incurrd. for that reason the persons concernd in it must be put to a very great charge. those impressions a great while going away. sometimes twenty, or thirty years. if they are not for a time to be protectd in the enjoyment, it will prevent any [new editions.] the consequence will be w*ith* a little different in the price [and] other impressions will come out. very considerable prices are often given for books that do not sell at all. if the trade **{31}** absolutely open, what would be the consequence? necessarily this, every man who took it into head to print w*ould* be producing the cheapest edition. 'till the market was filld w*ith* coarse editions. how it has be*en* in Scotland since the late decision *of the* H*ouse* of L*ords*.[365] I can read to you f*rom* a Bookseller.[366] he said he [thinks the trade] it is in a most deplorable situation. the late decision will ruin the trade intirely. every petty town has got a printer. nay Shoe makers are become Printers.

Governor Johnstone.[367] [moved] that the Counsel may withdraw. perhaps this may be wrong. the reason when the Counsel so exceedingly conversant in points of Law presumes to read to this H*ouse* a letter w*ithou*t having proved the letter. you are sitting there, & hearing it, I presume I am [not mistaken.] I remember how exceedingly exact the G*entlemen* were on the other side, when the letter came f*rom* Mr M*erill*.[368]

Speaker.[369] The Honourable M*ember* is mistaken, between the Making of evidence: if he don't make it out by legal evidence. we should make strange work if we were to stop Counsel in stating [his case].

Counsel called in.

[James Mansfield KC] I am stating to **{32}** the H*ouse* a letter. the copy of Mr. Creech's Bookseller in Edinburgh. if firmly proved [it will say] every Shoe-maker, & Weaver are become publishers, flushd w*ith* the hope of gain. [Leading to] half a dozen impressions going on together. perhaps ten different impressions of Pope's Homer. a species of literary [agent] go round to [towns and villages to] hawk about their villanous editions. if they make one shilling on a days sale, they think themselves very well rewarded. that this must necessarily be the consequence. the Learned Advocate told you Thompson's Seasons[370]

[363]Booksellers' Bill 1774, cl. 5.

[364]*Morning Chronicle*, 25 Mar. 1774.

[365]*Midwinter v Kincaid* (1751) 1 Pat App 488.

[366]William Creech* (1745–1815), leading Scottish bookseller.

[367]George Johnstone† (1730–87), MP for Cockermouth.

[368]Five Letters.

[369]Fletcher Norton†* (1716–89), Speaker 1770–80.

[370]The reference was probably to this edition: James Thomson, *The Seasons* (Donaldson, 1768) (ESTC: T141531).

were sold for three pence. I wonder any G*entleman* who are Advocates for Authors can support Printers like these. suppose those valuable memoirs should get into the hands of a shabby printer [who will] hawk them [even though] so mutilated, he himself [did] not know we should see the name of Sydney[371] mistaken for the name of [Barillon[372] despite him being one of our] most illustrious Patriots. such is the fare they ought to h*ave* who write for fame [and] posterity. I cant help adding to these editions of cheapness that English books are not so cheap as one would generally wish them to be. some very dear, but I h*ave* a list[373] of many books that are to be had for two shillings a volume. whenever a **{33}** a book is raised to an extravagant price: I don't say [it is] not sometimes the fault in the person who holds it: except in the single case of a book so expensive [it will] not bear reprinting. but that is not a case peculiar to those who h*ave* a Copy right. if a book [is] out of print it rises to a very high price. that is almost the only case you will find books rated to an extravagant price: [there is an] honorary property [which is] certainly not protected by law. any man may invade it if he pleases. [there is] a rule of honour among the trade not to reprint it 'till he has had a sufficient time. does that cast a reflection upon the honour of that trade? does it not prove that they themselves are convinc'd that the trade could not be carried on w*ithou*t it.

Come now to the great ground *of the* present application, that very great property[374] indeed has b*een* invested in this sort of property, wh*ich* will be very much hurt, if not totally lost unless some relief [is] given to them. [I] make an observation in O*rder* to obviate every common fallacy. they tell you [they] desir'd no indulgence, they got their books for a trifle, a dinner [and] not to protect that property. as to the present possessors that proceeded upon a mistake: the present possessors h*ave* bought them by **{34}** Auction. hardly a book that has not passed thro' a great variety of hands. to the present possessor they came at a very dear rate. [great sums of] money that has b*een* expended in the purchase of this Copyright: it is I think a pretty strong proof, if no other, that the G*entleman* were certainly mistaken, that the Booksellers proceeded w*ithou*t any notion of such right. I think those Crafty men did not invest all their property in air, & Moonshine: but besides this, what has passed in [the law] what is the history *of the* subject? I mean not to go into the legal arguments: this is not the place for it. the subject is now decided. the law has excluded f*rom* the Statute of Queen Anne, the Authors, or the purchasers of Authors [who] has not the exclusive right to multiply the copies *of the* book. but what is the state *of the* q*uestion* when printing first made its introduction into this *country*, & the other Countries of Europe it was in many [countries] consider'd as the subjects: the prerogative *of the* Crown endeavourd to secure it to itself. in this *country* many Patents were granted. the exclusive right to print were secur'd by the decrees *of the* Star Chamber. these were followd by orders of P*arliament* then the licensing act, lastly the Statute of Queen Anne. during the time **{35}** that [statute had been found that it] had such weight. you heard little *of the* [history] bec*ause* those who had the security of Patriots, & protected by the arm *of the* Crown found that a stronger protection. that very same, precise right now contended for was then contended for. the

[371]Sir Philip Sidney* (1554–86).

[372]Paul Barillon d'Amoncourt*, marquis de Branges (*d.* 1691). The original clearly referred to a named author and it appears from the *Morning Chronicle*, 16 May 1774 that it was Barillon.

[373]Part IV, Printed Books.

[374]Meaning 'money'.

Statute recites the property of Authors had b*een* invaded.[375] it was a very singular expression. if such property [is false why] had not b*een* [the suit dismissed by the] Courts of Equity. at last in 1759 an action brought,[376] the q*uestion* agitated [and then] argued in the Kings bench [until] a discovery that the action was fictitious [and] prevented a decision being made: but I believe it is now no secret, that the sense of that Court, the unanimous sense of it was in favour of this property. the second time [it was] agitated in 1766, or 1769,[377] then came that decision wh*ich* producd the late appeal. four Judges. three decided in favour, & one against the property. nay even in this last discussion *of the* Subject by the supreme Judicature. five Judges thought clearly in favour *of the* right;[378] & of those who disputed it, two thought it had existence at Common law, but that the Statute of Queen Anne had abrogated it. so that these were seven who decided **{36}** in favour of it as an original right interest in the author, and transferable by him to any person to whom he chose to dispose of it. besides this I h*ave* here in my hands an account of many assignments. Milton in 1680 &c[379] [unidentified in] 1660 in wh*ich* those great men assign their works forever. now, Sir, is it seriously contended that the Booksellers invariably believed they never had any such right. here I h*ave* very clear, & satisfactory grounds for both the Advocates to say they could [claim the booksellers case was] contrary to Common sense. it is not for me in this place to attempt to raise the reputation by any thing I could say of those great, & distinguish'd men who so lately judg'd of that right. I can say of two of them that so long as any esteem can be had in this *country* for genius, literature, taste, so long will their names be had in estimation. if the Booksellers had felt the want of Common sense, they felt that want in the best Company. add one authority more, the great Alexander D*onaldson* for even this distinguish'd man has acted the same way, or else he is an extreme Ideal: if he had thought the [right of it] had b*een* w*ith* him, when the first bill for an injunction was brought against him **{37}** [an answer in] less than a year [for no more than] £100 expence if this is the case, what is there unreasonable in this application. the Booksellers think so as well as Mr. D*onaldson* they h*ave* expended their fortunes. unless this [relief] is some security many deserving men will be injur'd.

in France, & Holland there is such a property in fact, tho' not in name. tho' they apply for a privilege for particular reasons to the State. not understood to confer property, only to give a particular support to it. in France they printed under privilege.[380] it is granted from time to time. it is a thing of course to grant it to the Authors. I don't see particular reasons of state, or interest [or why] great men may not sometimes interrupt it. no publick prejudice; no grievance to private men if the bill should pass. if not a great hardship I may say ruin will fall upon many who h*ave* laid out their money upon what the greatest part of his Majesty's subjects thought perpetual, 'till the late decision[381] thought otherwise. the

[375] Booksellers' Bill, preamble.

[376] *Tonson v Collins* (1762) 1 Black W 301, 321 (96 ER 169, 180).

[377] It is presumed this is a reference to *Millar v Taylor* (1769) 4 Burr 2303 (98 ER 201).

[378] As to the votes see Part I: Chapter 4: Hangs in the Balance.

[379] John Milton's contract for the publication of *Paradise Lost*.

[380] Laurent Pfister, 'Author and Work in the French Print Privileges System: Some Milestones', in *Privilege and Property: Essays on the History of Copyright*, ed. Ronan Deazley, Martin Kretschmer and Lionel Bently (Cambridge, 2010), 115.

[381] *Donaldson v Beckett* (1774) *Cobbett's Parl. Hist.*, xvii, 953.

letters *from* the Authors I h*ave* mentioned, I doubt whether they would be evidence. they h*ave* b*een* in many M*ember*s hands. I read a letter [about the damage to the trade in] Scotland by the importation of Irish books. I **{38}** could produce f*rom* Mr. Johnson[382] &c. but as that is already in the report *of the* C*ommittee* as I don't find any evidence on the other side to impeach it. as the evidence h*ave* not establish'd one fact to the prejudice of those for whom I am concerned[. I need] not trouble [you] w*ith* any evidence, the facts are undisputed between us.

Mr. Hett[383] three different kinds of property. the original right, the right of withholding, or printing, the right or property of printing f*rom* that written Copy as many as he the author; or the purchaser of them shall think fit to print. the third kind annex'd to the printed Copies of this book after it has b*een* printed. he has the right of those copies wh*ich* he had bought, or his assignees. Booksellers are not Lawyers, they might easily mistake the actions of their Ancestors to be agreeable to law. by no means contending that the Judgment *of the* H*ouse* of L*ords* was not extremely right. do not set up one H*ouse* against the other, the determination *of the* H*ouse* of L*ords* was made by them as a Court of Justice, not as a part *of the* Legislature. they may determine this upon a very different matter as Legislators, than what they determine as Judicators. I can appeal to the Journals **{39}** of this H*ouse*. I can appeal to the Statutes wherein this H*ouse* h*ave* altered, extended, varied the rules wh*ich* were bef*ore* established, & laid down by the Common law of this Land. it is an authority wh*ich* the Legislature exercises to vary the Common law. if they did not, what occasion for that authority. Common law wh*ich* determines in all cases. but wherever the Legislature *of the* King*dom* sees either f*rom* a variation of circumstances, or f*rom* the nature of that branch of trade it is necessary to give either a perpetual, or temporal relief to the persons who carry on that trade, that f*rom* inconveniences [caused by a] general rule of Common law respecting them in general. of course may extend their assistance to those particular cases. by the Law of this Land they sold a power, & privileg of selling particular commodities [and it may be said] has not the Legislature in many instances interposed, & given this power. in the Statute wh*ich* is the most strong against monopoly, there is still reserved a right to the Crown to grant to the original inventor of any species of property; a right [and] privilege for a certain number of years.[384] any derogation of a Common law right [permitted] by the Act of P*arliament* [of] K*ing* James 1.[384] Statute against Monopoly, **{40}** it appears that the Legislature did not chose to interfere to put a stop to that, wh*ich* had b*een* bef*ore* term'd, & was termd then a monopoly. w*ith* respect to other sorts of Manufacturers, or branches of trade [the Act] granted [a proviso for any patent] grant for printing.[386] the Legislature at that time consider'd this art of printing a distinct species of property f*rom* any other species of property whatever. G*entlemen* on the other side h*ave* gone f*rom* the allegations *of the* Petition in O*rder* to prejudice this H*ouse* [with talk of] monopoly. [Not] guilty of a

[382] William Johnston.

[383] John Hett, junior counsel for the London Booksellers. The son of a notable bookseller and former treasurer of the Stationers Company 1755–66, he was called by Inner Temple on 12 June 1752 and became a master in chancery in Dec. 1775, resigning in 1792: John Nichols, *Literary Anecdotes of the Eighteenth Century, Comprising Biographical Memoirs of William Bowyer* (1812), iii, 606–7.

[384] Statute of Monopolies (1623) (21 Jas. I, c. 11), s. 6.

[384] For a discussion of the statute's passage and the protection of individual rights, Phillip Johnson, *Privatised Law Reform: A History of Patent Law Through Private Legislation, 1620–1907* (2017), ch. 3.

[386] Statute of Monopolies, s. 10.

breach *of the* Law of this Land by selling their own copies. it is the fair Trade that is intitled to favour, & protection, not the man who invades the real proprietor under the Statute of Queen Anne [.Mr. Donaldson sold books which] were within the protection *of the* Statute of Queen Anne. is this the man who is to stand here as a Patriot, who for the good *of the* publick brings his Shop f*rom* Edinburgh to London[387] [why not stay] at Edinburgh? not content w*ith* not being distrib'd for thirteen years at Edinburgh, sets up a Shop in London; continues to sell the books he had printed at Edinburgh [so will only] h*ave* the costs in the suits against him, wh*ich* suits are dismissed.

{41} *Mr. Mansfield call'd in Mr. Wilkie to prove the Sales*

[**John Wilkie**:][388] the Pyrated books were lodgd in a Press, & sometime after a fire happen'd, & they were destroyed. I fancy they were not insur'd. I did deliver some out by the O*rder* of Mr. Millar[389] &c I don't know for what purpose. never saw any w*ith* London title pages. [There are] a great many Petitioners for the bill. [counter-petitioners] sell Quack Medicines. Mr. M*urphy*[390] charges me w*ith* having desir'd him to quit the Sale, but I don't know that I ever did. the resolution in the year 1759[391] that those who sold Scotch books should not be admitted. many of them h*ave* come since[. now] lock'd up the Ware house Shaftesbury's Characteristicks,[392] several Plays, Rollin's Ancient History.[393] the books were deliver'd out by O*rder of the* C*ommittee*.

Governor Johnstone. [asks] *Counsel, & Witness to withdraw.*

[**George Johnstone**] whether this Witness is a competent Witness? move that his evidence may be struck out *of the* Report, &c.

Sir Rich*ard* Sutton.[394] I second the m*otion*.

Mr. Edmund Burke. It is not Judicial evidence, but evidence for information. it would not [need to be proved unless] the **{42}** information could h*ave* Juridical consequence.

Mr. Dempster.[395] If the evidence [is] not a Petitioner to be admitted [like] Mr Paine, &c[396]

Sir Rich*ard* Sutton. This is an application for a specifick relief, these men expect a specifick relief.

Mr. Charles Fox. [It] is no compensation, wrong to proceed upon Juridical evidence.

Mr. Edm*und* Burke. The suffering party themselves h*ave* been [providing] evidence. if you establish the strict rule of Juridical evidence, & apply it to complaints [entirely] stripped

[387] Donaldson's Petition.

[388] John Wilkie (*d.* 1785), app. 1743–50, tr. 1753–75, bookseller, 71 St Paul's Churchyard; clerk of auctions.

[389] Andrew Millar* (1705–68), app. 1720, Strand.

[390] Arthur Murphy, junior counsel for Donaldson.

[391] Part IV, The Five Letters.

[392] Anthony Ashley Cooper*, 3rd earl of Shaftesbury (1671–1713), *Characteristicks of Men, Manners, Opinions, Times* (?Urie, 1758) (ESTC: T163859).

[393] Charles Rollin* (1661–1741), *The Roman History from the Foundation of Rome to the Battle of Actium* (Knapton, 1754) (ESTC: T121677).

[394] Richard Sutton† (1733–1802). MP for St Albans.

[395] George Dempster.

[396] Described as the governor in *St James's Chronicle*, 15–17 Mar. 1774; accordingly, it would be Edward Payne (*d.* 1794), former governor of the Bank of England.

wholly of evidence. were not the persons on the other side liable to the same objection of Complainants. equal injustice [is caused] not bec*ause* you h*ave* punish'd one man, you are to punish another, but suffer the same identical evidence for the other. [I] appeal to precedent, the last precedent [was applied] in the same case.

Govern*or* Johnstone. I conceived this to be so [accordingly] I did not trouble the H*ouse* w*ith* any arguments. [I will] state the reasons upon wh*ich* I proceeded. the evidence so far f*rom* hurting this cause, is of service to it. if were not for the general rule I had rather proceed. having a particular instance in the case bef*ore* **{43}** you. can a man who is Proprietor in a Navigation give into evidence? the Learned G*entlemen* argued that Mr. Johnson[397] was interested another G*entleman* argued [that it was good] evidence. he was divested of his property. [this is] not the case of Mr Paine[398] [whom] continued in the general Interest.

Mr. Charles Fox. If the man not a Witness bec*ause* ultimately concerned. the interest of every man in England is ultimately concerned in passing of this bill. Mr Brindley[399] said he had parted w*ith* his property.

Mr. Dempster. [We had] better call in the Counsel, & Witness.

Mr. Edmund Burke. When a Witness is calld upon [to prove] an allegation; every body knows it is to decide upon property. but when persons I am [sure it is a] universal practice *of the* H*ouse* whether their own Story of their own sufferings. [to hear them] unless the H*ouse* are of opinion other evidence should be call'd – the evidence *of the* [witness] is not calld to give an account of his own sufferings. whether evidence of detail, or explanatory evidence, you h*ave* constantly receivd it. there would be a want of Justice if you did not. perhaps in some respects they are the only Witnesses. **{44}**

Mr Sawbridge. Moved "that the Counsel be called in now"

Attorney General.[400] For what purpose? the Witness has b*een* examin'd: has stated that interest upon wh*ich* the objection arises. that being stated it comes to the H*ouse* to decide whether Competent Witness. if a competent Witness how [do we] dispose of his testimony. the H*onourable* G*entleman* has moved that his evidence shall be expunged. (no such q*uestion*)

Mr. Cornwall. that the idea *of the* Competence *of the* Judges themselves should be started. but it is competent for the H*onourable* G*entleman* to move, that it appearing to this H*ouse* that the Witness being so, & so, resolvd that he be no longer examined. [His] evidence strike it off. I rise to give no opinion but only to inform them of their proceeding. a shorter way to call in the Counsel if it should occur to G*entleman* &c

Mr. Charl*es* Fox. give this opinion whether the Witnesses be competent, or not. therefo*re*, I hope the H*ouse* understands

Mr Edm*und* Burke. You decide when a person claims a right to print a book, general freedom [to do it] under the law. either they are adverse parties, or they are not. if **{45}** not made unequally appear upon the principle of equality.

Mr. Dunning [I am] not being prepard to reject this bill w*ithout* this q*uestion*.

[397] William Johnston.

[398] He gave evidence before the committee of Linen Manufacture: *London Evening Post*, 15–17 Mar. 1774§; *Gazeteer*, 17 Mar. 1774§; *Baldwin's London Weekly Journal*, 19 Mar. 1774§; *General Evening Post*, 15–17 Mar. 1774§; also see Cavendish Diary, BL, Egerton MS 254, ff. 153–76.

[399] This was probably George Bulkley.

[400] Edward Thurlow.

Attorney General. My Learned friend wishing to step aside f*rom* that parity of Justice, to get aside in the depth, almost in the labyrinth of parliamentary proceedings. he has b*een* desir'd very civilly to give us one, or two instances of that practice [or any practices] wh*ich* has turn'd out directly the contrary way. whether the men who desire to be [given relief will be] vested in the interest of Homer &c. this stands in the same line as the man who says that word lies in common. I desire it may be suffer'd to lie in common. the man who desire to h*ave* a monopoly. if it could be proved that the rules of P*arliament*, that the rules of law were so different. that those p*eople* [who were] excluded as well as included [were] admitted, then the argument would h*ave* had no weight: but as it is as contrary to Common sense, as it is to law [to] expect, that a man w*ith* an interest to himself would give an impartial testimony, so far this H*ouse* has rejected the evidence. that those who are voting for the bill are to vote upon any sort of evidence, are to vote **{46}** upon any legal evidence. I do not carry the idea whether the bill does, or does not suffer by this: I wish [for] Justice *of the* cause to obtain. I h*ave* always said; I h*ave* always acted upon this: at the time I observ'd the proposition in the enormous shape it was produced; I stated to the H*ouse* to a much greater extent, what I was inclind to do for Authors.

Authors [who] h*ave* a degree of merit: I am willing to give large privileges to them as a reward for their labour. but those men to take books that h*ave* long lain common [have] no merit at first in composing,[401] or introducing [to] the World. if the bill is to be carried, I hope it is not to be carried in contempt of all legal Justice. I know no better reason to reject it, than upon that q*uestion*.

Mr. Edm*und* Burke. (repeats) tho' as much for these p*eople* as the other, I will determine the fate *of the* Bill. undoubtedly, bec*ause* it turns upon [not having] any evidence at all. the Learned G*entleman* has rather exercisd his wit, than his [reason] upon this occasion. [these] Copyright, they are a vendible Commodity. we see it is for the publick good, as [a book] is for the good of the Community. **{47}**

Mr. Popham. This man confesses himself a party, theref*ore* an incompetent evidence.

The Speaker declin'd giving his opinion.

Mr. Dempster. I must vote for the competence *of the* evidence.

Mr Ch*arles* Fox. [It is] always my principle not to withdraw any q*uestion* or suffer it to be drawn by the opinion of any body.

Speaker. I wish G*entleman* for their own sakes would content themselves w*ith* speaking once.[402]

The question *was then put That Counsel be called in*	*Yeah*	*73*
The Noes went forth.	*Noes*	*5*[403]

Counsel, & Witness calld in

[John Wilkie][404] The Copy right has b*een* twice sold in some cases.

[401] The typographical arrangement of books has been protected under copyright law since the coming into force of Copyright Act 1956, s. 15 and now the Copyright, Designs and Patents Act 1988, s. 8.

[402] As to the rule, John Hatsell, *Precedents of Proceedings in the House of Commons* (Dodsley, 1781), 64–9.

[403] *CJ*, xxxiv, 752.

[404] No name is given in the MS, but it was the witness being recalled.

Mr. C*harle*s Fox. ask'd his opinion what would be the consequence if the bill made Felony?

Mr. Morton[405] *desird the Counsel might withdraw*

Mr. Ch*arle*s Fox said, it was a q*uestion* constantly ask'd. q*uestion* Navigation. I dont understand why not, the robbery of that should not be made Felony as well as the robbery of any other. I dont imagine one argument why it is not the intention *of the* H*ouse* to make it felony w*ithou*t benefit of Clergy.[406]

{48} *this* question *was proposed by Charles Fox* I shall abide by the q*uestion* not as a ridicule upon the H*ouse*.

Governor Johnstone. [I will] not go against the general sense *of the* H*ouse*. I beg the H*onourable* G*entleman* to consider what will be the consequences *of the* q*uestion*. the impression he would give is fully given w*ithou*t putting the q*uestion*. I should hope he would not put it.

Lord Beauchamp. My wish is the q*uestion* may not be put, I second it in a jocular way to express my opinion. [I do] not wish this q*uestion* should be seriously put.

Mr. Morton moved to adjourn, that the question *might not be put upon the Journals.*

*Mr. Will*iam *Burke. wanted to* have *the* question *divided.*

Speaker. If the q*uestion* is divided, the H*onourable* G*entleman* may put the latter part to the Witness when he comes in.

Mr. Dunning. Putting the q*uestion* will put a degree of ridicule upon the H*ouse*.

Mr. Charl*e*s Fox. The ridicule will fall upon me, not upon the H*ouse* who are exceeding ready, willing, & desirous of bearing it.

Mr. Sawbridge. The ridicule will fall intirely upon himself, no M*ember* will take any part in it. **{49}**

The simple question *that the Counsel be calld in was put, & the Counsel were calld in, & the Witness. Mr Charles Fox askd the same* question.

Answer [**John Wilkie**] I hope I shall be excused giving any Answer to the q*uestion*.

General Craneck.[407] If no other but q*uestion* at this late hour, by wh*ich* [to] throw a burlesque upon our proceedings, I hope the H*ouse* will excuse me if I move to adjourn. *he withdrew the* motion.

Counsel called in.

Mr. Murphy's reply [The booksellers were] not ignorant of Law, but the misconstruction of it. the ground of our argument [is] not intitled to relief: but ignorance *of the* Law does not excuse. we further contend by a variety of Circumstances [they are] arrogating to themselves this property. using every method to establish himself in that right w*ithou*t the

[405]John Morton† (?1714–1780), MP for New Romney.

[406]As to benefit of clergy, A.L. Cross, 'The English Criminal Law and Benefit of Clergy during the Eighteenth and Early Nineteenth Century', *The American Historical Review*, xxii (1917), 544.

[407]John Carnac† (1721–1800), MP for Leominster. For the correction of this name, P.D.G. Thomas, 'Check List of MPs Speaking in the House of Commons, 1768 to 1774', *BIHR*, xxxv (1962), 222.

aid of Law, h*ave* they bought since Millar, & Taylor,[408] if they h*ave* h*ave* they not assignments, & receipts? Mr Johnson was askd at the C*ommittee* he had not time to produce them. the bill has these words, every author of any book, or books [already printed and published,][409] who h*ave* not transferr'd the Copyright &c. why bodies politick are **{50}** here introduced unless to steal in some dominant claim *of the* Stationers Company I can't tell [but what about works] otherwise acquired are they not large comprehensive words? getting as Mr. Gurney:[410] is that property? [What of the] Duchess of Queensbury,[411] & Dr Shebbeare.[412] is it to be acquir'd in that manner? [Is the] purchase of an Author, or his Executor. what after the term the act has explained[413] is that to give a property? [there is] a clause for securing to the [Booksellers] every publication. h*ave* they sufficiently secured that to them? I remember a bill in 1745 brought in,[414] they never did comply w*ith* it. an Anecdote *of the* B*ish*op of Carlisle in his pamphlet.[415] the method, they leave one Volume w*ith* the Press Keeper *of the* Stationers Company. they apply to the Bookseller, give us the four, no, buy all five. there is the edition [in an] advertisement in the London Gazette & c [so] need not comply w*ith* the Statute of Queen Anne. there seems to be [a] proviso of extraordinary fallacy.[416] it professes that if [a copy is] sold for a valuable consideration; for a perpetual Copyright, they wish [for a] further term of years—how far that is property must be left to the H*ouse*.

I **{51}** dont mean to make any objection, when the author has had a fair consideration. [But] no obligation to let the Booksellers h*ave* a further term. [Or upon the] transfer the right. the Author meant only to sell during the time he was possessed of it. why they are to derive the right not f*rom* the Author, but themselves is a bold attempt. the bill in 1737, Mr. Pultney,[417] & Dr. Swift, I h*ave* the Chancellor's Authority to say this clause was drawn by Dr. Swift: "& for as much as the true worth of books is not found out 'till [a considerable Time after the Publication thereof; and][418] Authors may sell their right bef*ore* the true value is known. may put it in [their] power to alter:[419] no Authors were to sell &c except by the last [testament][420] for a longer time, than ten years." All the eminent Authors *of the* Age assisted in that bill. there was a true term for the honour & Interest of Letters. put it in the power of Authors [and so] if he wants to correct, he must h*ave* the Bookseller's leave on his own terms. Mr D*onaldson* has had above an hundred, & fifty *of the* London Booksellers Plaintiffs

[408] *Millar v Taylor* (1769) 4 Burr 2303 (98 ER 201).

[409] Booksellers' Bill 1774, cl. 1: the space in the text is quite short and might not have fitted this phrase.

[410] The shorthand writer Thomas Gurney.

[411] Probably a reference to the duchess seeking to get a licence for John Gay's play 'Polly' in 1728.

[412] Dr John Shebbeare* (1709–88), the satirist, was a common whipping boy.

[413] This should probably be 'expired'.

[414] It became the Continuance of Acts, Act 1746 (20 Geo. II, c. 47).

[415] [Edmund Law* (1703–87)], *Considerations of the Propriety of Requiring Subscription to Articles of Faith* (1774).

[416] Booksellers' Bill 1774, cl. 1.

[417] William Pulteney, earl of Bath.

[418] Booksellers' Bill 1737: Parliamentary Archives, HL/PO/JO/10/2/39, c. 1.

[419] The full wording of the preamble to the clause is 'And forsomuch as the true Worth of Books and Writing is in many Cases not found out till a considerable Time after the Publication thereof; and Authors, who are in Necessity, may often be tempted absolutely to sell and alienate their Right, which they will here have to the original Copies of the Books, which they have composed, before the Value therefore is known, and may thereby put it out of their own Power to alter and correct their Compositions upon mature Judgment and Reflection'.

[420] Booksellers' Bill 1737.

against him in their turns.[421] the clause of indemnification to him is no compensation to him, for the right he is to lose. that he may sell the **{52}** books he had in hand. [he] lay out £50,000, he has not a stock of £50,000 now on hand: he means in the whole course of trade he had it f*rom* 1751 to this time. letters h*ave* b*een* mentioned. we are told respectable Authors are warm upon the occasion: if Authors are warm, I should h*ave* expected to see them at the bar. Hume, & Robertson h*ave* b*een* handsomely rewarded for their works. I believe they meant to sell their works for a perpetual property. I heartily rejoice they had their works. but are they to h*ave* all mankind's books? are they to bind everybody? the conference between K*ing* James the 1st &three Bishops, [to Neale,] B*isho*p of Durham [he said cannot I] take my p*eople*'s money, God forbid [you should, you are the] breath of my Nostrils. [Bishop] Winchester. you h*ave* a right to take my Brother [Neale's] money, he offers it.[422] don't let them make a sweeping clause to take in everybody. if they are satisfied, if Hume has made his [assignment] if Mr [Handel of][423] St George Hanover Square; if Dr. Robertson will provide [copies] is that the sale for Authors? it is the encouragement of Learning [which is] now bef*ore* the H*ouse*.

I hope in preference to any Petition whatever [and wit] says Lord Chesterfield[424] the only property *of the* man who has it. **{53}** my Dictionary says a great Author was not written in the [midst of] obscurity of [other men but] in the shadow of Academicks, Books, &c. Dr. Johnson. they h*ave* not provided [a share of] £49,000, wh*ich* is paid every time it is sold&c &c.

Mr Johnson's second reason [namely that] copies go out of Print. [You reject this and in the] next Session of P*arliament* a bill may be found that may do true honour to Learning.

half an hour after 11 O'clock. Counsel withdrew.

The bill read the second time.

Mr. Field. [I move] that this bill be committed. I think it a case of very great magnitude. the case of many men deservedly interested. how far [to] debate it at this time: [I am] willing to abide by the opinion *of the* H*ouse*. go into your C*ommittee*. the argument against the bill has b*een* against supposed clauses.

Mr. Sawbridge. [I second] to go into the C*ommittee*. I hope [there is] no q*uestion* of adjournment. I hope they will h*ave* the candour to let us go into the C*ommittee*.

Attorney General. [I have been] exceedingly misunderstood if what I said meant to say, the bill wanted weight, & importance to consider. I think it a bill of very considerable **{54}** importance, bec*ause* all that is d*one* is done at the expence *of the* publick. w*ith* regard to candour, & fairness, I don't understand the meaning of it. what am I to get by it. it was

[421] See list of cases at pp 414, n 152.

[422] For a contemporary version of this story, Edmund Waller (1606–87), *The Works of Edmund Waller* (Davis, 1772) (ESTC: T124620), p. vii.

[423] George Frideric Handel* (1685–1759) was the most famous resident of the Square. It is reasonable to assume this is to whom was Murphy was referring.

[424] Speech on the Stage Licensing Bill, in Philip Dormer Stanhope*, 4th earl of Chesterfield (1694–1773), *The Works of Lord Chesterfield* (1838), p. lxviii: 'wit, my Lord, is a sort of property it is the property of those who have it, and too often the only property they have to depend on'.

the only shape in which it could come. it was promised it should come in another shape, they may alter some expressions

moved that the debate be adjournd to monday

Mr. Edm*und* Burke. [I see] two difficulties, whether debate it at this time of night, or whether postpone it at such a time *of the* Session as to make it impossible to decide upon such a q*uestion* of magnitude at all. [it is] a q*uestion* of time the bill is a remedial bill. [Granting] effectual relief, a peremptory, & speedy relief. the property of many men will be impaird, many thousands by our not deciding at this Session. the q*uestion* becomes more difficult by postponing [and so I] would wish to decide to night. the q*uestion* is not to day whether Mr. D*onaldson* is to h*ave* relief &c. (the G*entleman* is determin'd to give [no] proof of Debating it to night by determining not to hear.) I am a Bookseller, Mr. Blackstone lays down £7,000. am I to enter into a dispute w*ith* him whether he has that right to transfer. upon what authority did he give one *of the* two Universities, one *of the* eyes of this *country* that chose **{55}** that G*entleman* as Law Professor [the] perpetual property. if the University was wrong, if the Crown was wrong, that very work was as clear a proof that that law book was the work of a man whose opinion in Law was [so highly held. The] first Copy he sold, reapd a large Harvest. it is a bill of [compassion] not a bill of right. persons who h*ave* portiond their Daughters &c. the Printer is the substitute *of the* Author, one may enjoy the lucrative advantage, the other the mechanical trade of it. the paper wh*ich* says Authors are to write for glory, & Printers print for glory, [is incomplete.] whether you call it glory, or call it money, he as a right to the glory, or money some way, or other. the arguments I h*ave* heard to day, go to the repeal *of the* Act of Queen Anne.

Gov*ernor* Johnstone. I can't conceive how they reconcile going on at this hour, when they were for not hearing of Counsel at six O'Clock.

that the debate be adjournd to Monday.
The question *was then put …* *Yeas* *24*
Noes *39*

The yeahs went forth.
That the Bill be Committed.

Gov*ernor* Johnstone. Since it is the pleasure *of the* H*ouse* to debate the **{56}** principle *of the* bill now. I shall state the reasons why I think it cant be committed; while this bill pretends to do justice to some [it will] do injustice to another.

Commit the bill

Yeas *36*
Noes *10*

The [*yeas*] *went forth.*[425]

Standing Order *that no private bill be committed above stairs.*
Chairman of the Committee.

[425] *CJ*, xxxiv, 752.

Attorney General. [We should] first of all vote, that the Chairman *of the Committee* above stairs is not the Chairman [of Committee for] a private bill. then you are out of O*rder*. the q*uestion* whether referring a private bill to the whole H*ouse* you can dispute w*ith* the Standing O*rder*?

Speaker. If this is the case within that O*rder* it can't be disputed[426] w*ith*.

Col*onel* Onslow. The reason *of the* change in the [order is so] that a private C*ommittee* may not be smuggled

Attorney General. In case of a private C*ommittee* the persons interested may be apprized.

Mr Will*iam* Burke. How is this a private C*ommittee*? one must **{57}** be pleaded in the Courts, the other not[427]

Speaker. Whether the nature *of the* Subject is private, that where all mankind is not concern'd [and] they least expect f*rom* that H*onourable* G*entlemen* to go to an obsolete [rule.] I don't know where the Devil he caught it. the Chairman is answerable for his transgression.

Col*onel* Barre.[428] Whether it has not b*een* usual to do the same? the Standing O*rder* certainly alludes to the C*ommittee* above stairs. (**Speaker** it certainly does.) The next O*rder* that no private bill proceeds upon

Mr. Onslow. [There are] numberless instances in which it has b*een* practis'd.

Committed for Monday *Yeas 35*
Noes [None][429]
The [yeas] went forth. was *2 O'clock*

Mr Charles Fox, & the Attorney General were tellers for the Noes. Fox had been out, but supposing there were not forty, Members, returnd again, & made up forty one.

Monday May 16

...{58}

Order of the *day for Committing the Booksellers' bill*

Mr. Char*les* Fox.[430] applied to the Chair [:] if [it is] not the custom to leave [the chair] bef*ore* committing [with an] exception only when at the end *of the* Session there was not time?

Speaker. I am glad the H*ouse* would still know [the standing orders] w*ith* regard to the letter, it cant mean a C*ommittee of the* whole Ho*use* bec*ause* it gives a week [notice] not in the H*ouse* bec*ause* the Chairman [is] not appointed.[431] I do believe where there has b*een* time to give the notice above, it has b*een* usual. the **{59}** H*ouse* will for the future lay down

[426] This should probably be 'dispensed'.

[427] This is clearly a reference to the Bill, and not the committee: on the point of law, that private bills need to be pleaded, see: *Greswolde v Kemp* (1842) Car & M 63 (173 ER 668).

[428] Issac Barré†* (1726–1802), MP for Chipping Wycombe.

[429] *CJ*, xxxiv, 752.

[430] Charles Fox†* (1749–1806), MP for Midhurst.

[431] 24 Nov. 1699 (*CJ*, xiii, 6).

a rule to regulate their proceedings. I hope notwithstanding any thing that has fallen *from* the Chair, the H*ouse* will enter into a free discussion of this matter.

Mr. Field.[432] The proposition is upon the O*rder of the* H*ouse* upon that ground [and I] take this matter up, & offer the ground why this O*rder of the* H*ouse* should be extended to a case, not now within the O*rder of the* H*ouse*. the objection made, that the spirit *of the* O*rder*, that in Co*mmittee* [it is necessary that] parties should h*ave* notice a Just ground. h*ave* not the parties had notice? Counsel [attended] two days [ago and] as any matter [which is] now fully submitted to the consideration of this H*ouse*. this bill has b*een* a great while in the H*ouse*. what reason there is to establish a new rule in this case[?] now the q*uestion* whether on this particular case you shall lay down a rule not bef*ore* laid down [when the] parties h*ave* had notice [and they] brought their Counsel f*rom* Scotland. I should be glad to know what surprise [is after] a debate on Friday, when that noble manoeuvre was made, that will be fairness to future Ages.

Mr. Ch*arles* Fox. I did not expect after what fell f*rom* you that **{60}** I wanted to lay down a new rule: that it was not your opinion, your memory, & knowledge that in point of fact it always had b*een* adher'd to, except in cases of literal impossibility in point of time. wherever it is the Custom *of the* H*ouse* to dispense [with orders] there will be very soon an end [and] as to the glorious manoeuvre, I will only say, whenever I see a few attempting not only to do an act of absolute injustice that is another q*uestion*. [We were asked] late at night to lay aside the O*rder of the* H*ouse*. I do think it is very right to tell them, that whatever the H*ouse* would h*ave* d*one* [it is] wrong to make a precedent. if the H*onourable* G*entleman* still persists contrary to all rule: when a fuller H*ouse* shall hear that [which has passed,] I flatter myself it will h*ave* a debate.

Mr. Edm*und* Burke. a new mode of commenting, & explaining his meaning. he does not comment upon the Standing O*rder*, but upon your meaning. I should [wish] to adhere to what the Author says. I shall not obtrude the least of my Comment to force it surreptitiously into [a debate taking place] late at night[. When it was raised] that night when all the rest were [in debate we did] not apply to this q*uestion* w*ith* regard to **{61}** the spirit *of the* O*rder* [which] amounts to no more, than that the H*ouse* has dispens'd w*ith* when they found occasion. is not a Standing O*rder*: all comments of Standing O*rder* are not. but when you say the spirit *of the* O*rder* is applied to our proceedings [you show it is] a discretionary rule. [These can be] dispensed w*ith* for discretionary reasons. a discretionary rule [is like a Standing Order,] the only difference is the deference that is to be paid to your memory, & [when dispensing an order] your Learning will give way to the power of your Judgment. I appeal to you whether it has not b*een* dispens'd w*ith*. the reason assign'd, that the bill can't pass thro' the forms. if [against] a standing O*rder* that never could h*ave* b*een* the reason. [It should be] dispensed [with when] the spirit of your common practice is this, that notice should be given, and no surprise [to parties.] three month has this bill b*een* in this H*ouse*. it has given an opportunity [for the opponents to be heard and saying otherwise is] unbecoming his character[. they] brought a whole Wagon load of Petitions f*rom* Glasgow [Dispensing such a] precipitate way of getting rid of business, as well as precipitate way of hurrying it on. the H*onourable* G*entleman* spoke of manaeuvers, of P*erson*'s manaeuvers that night. I must have leave G*entleman* to Judge, whether the Standing O*rder of the* H*ouse*

[432] Paul Feilde.

was violated. if there was a discretionary [rule, should] dispense. as good reason **{62}** for dispensing w*ith* it then, as at any other time. does the evil apply? the evil is want of notice: in this case a standing O*rder* is pleadable against the Standing O*rder* that is pleaded against us. to prevent delay: Judge whether the proceeding has b*een* surreptitious. h*ave* brought the best Witnesses, the ablest Counsel. now I h*ave* d*one* w*ith* the surreptitious proceedings [and now it] must be left to the candour *of the* H*ouse*. if they find [that the] proceeding perverted, let them vote against you quitting the Chair: if not, [we] will not go to throw out the bill.

Attorney General.[433] I should be extremely sorry if upon a q*uestion* like this where the livelihood of Individuals are to be taken in O*rder* to retrench[. Indeed,] among those Individuals [there are objections which] on the one side ought to be met w*ith* the same [objections] upon the other. if the H*ouse* are ready to do it a fairer opportunity could not be offer'd to them to do it by that name: to avow the principle of [fairness and equity and to] call it the name of [justice which] belong to the Subject, where there is great trouble on one side, & great distress on the other side. the q*uestion* is private **{63}** [but] it was for that purpose only the rule was made: a great deal of dispute has b*een* made, whether this should be deemed a standing O*rder*, or discretionary rule. may I be forgiven, & not much laughd at, if I [try to] make a difference between those two words, a standing O*rder*, & discretionary [rule. it is] my poor opinion when this H*ouse* lays down a rule for its proceeding, it becomes a standing O*rder* what a discretionary rule is, I don't know [whether] discretionary arising f*rom* the case. I do understand [that it is adopting a] rule for the perpetual, everlasting Government of our proceedings in all similar cases. [the] rule you h*ave* undertaken to bind your [successors applies] and come to the [effect] *of the* Standing O*rder*. a great deal of pains has b*een* taken [for] benefit [and beneficiary] of this O*rder*. if [it does] not apply to a Co*mmittee of the* whole H*ouse*. if I am to [speak for those] to be deprived of this property [they] are intitled to as much time as other p*eople* h*ave*. I know very well [the order was made] w*ith* great [care.] would take this analogous O*rder* [which] ought to fall [if willed by the] majority. but that is not the present case. the O*rder* is universal, it must h*ave* b*een* meant to be Universal: for **{64}** there never was so [clear a case before the House] as this. that private bill, that the parties interested should h*ave* seven days notice. should be deprived of that, by sending it to the Co*mmittee* above stairs, [needs correcting, but] I won't presume to set your words, or rely on your opinion: it is not becoming to squabble about the words *of the* Chair on any case whatsoever. I take the terms to be universal: why not apply to a bill referd to a Co*mmittee of the* whole H*ouse* as well as a private Co*mmittee*? the answer [is for the] Co*mmittee* above. Chairman no more appointed by the H*ouse*: in that case [it is] no more than the H*ouse* [whereas] above stairs [we] do no more business, than like Chairmen, then adjourn to the week. is there any more difficulty in one sort of Co*mmittee* choosing a Chairman, & giving parties notice, than a Co*mmittee of the* whole H*ouse* choosing a Chairman, & giving parties notice? is there not the same facility of doing it, is there not the same propriety of doing it? wh*ich* I don't urge as matter of equity, in O*rder* to get a ground for having it d*one*. but I urge it as a ground of direct [justice] that the O*rder* should not be dispensed w*ith* [and therefore is put aside as a] discretionary rule. I apprehend it would make the proceedings *of the* Co*mmittee* irregular if they were departed f*rom*. but **{65}**

[433] Edward Thurlow.

you are desired to depart *from* it, bec*ause* all manner of notice has b*een* given antecedent, theref*ore*: the parties ought not to be intitlted to that notice wh*ich* the H*ouse* is pleased to give them. after they h*ave* adopted the necessity, & after they h*ave* sent to the C*ommittee* [I was] surprised to hear that arguments, [there were] peculiar circumstance of a great number [of] parties urged. living so far as Scotland: that I did not imagine would h*ave* b*een* pressed upon the H*ouse* as reasoning for dispensing w*ith* any *of the* notices. but they h*ave* had a great deal of them: let us attend to those *of the* Citizens: they h*ave* had notice that such a bill was brought into the H*ouse*: they h*ave* had notice *of the* principles being produced here obnoxious to their interest, destructive to their way of livelihood. that they h*ave* b*een* able to instruct Counsel to argue against the principle *of the* bill.

that was the reason for suffering the parties to be heard for two long days together by their Counsel, & by their evidence: that brought it to 12 O'Clock at night. at twelve O'Clock at night it was [our duty] to consider those arguments, to digest, & apply that evidence. I had the honour to move the H*ouse* that the debate might be put off to sometime, when [it would be] possible to discuss it. **{66}** the H*ouse* was pleased to be of opinion that that was a proper time to to discuss it: [yet] in the course of arguing that that was the best time to discuss it. I was told that if I would consent to its going to the C*ommittee*. an article of Candour: that the business would proceed as well as if I would debate whether [the Bill should] go to the C*ommittee*, or not. I did say [it was] such a one as the finest understanding might make, but none as the most contemptible understanding could adopt, in [any event] I had the good fortune to be told, not that I look'd upon such kind of candour to be free, but that I look'd upon all candour to be free. that is what is calld height in debate, a man of great capacity gives you what is calld a height. I believe *from* the ingenious, & simple manner in wh*ich* that was produced, that he is perfectly serious, & that he does not perceive there is any of that [required for the] inquiry in the bill I do: I will theref*ore* allow him that part. when [at second reading] it was an article of Candour for me to consent. Whether the H*ouse* were persuaded that twelve was the best time to enter into debate: we did not mean literally that twelve was the best time to enter into debate, but we meant to convey to **{67}** [the House which had] sense enough to apprehend it was not a Subject to be debated at all. only a subject fit for Counsel, & Witnesses.

w*ith* profound respect for the H*onourable Gentlemen* who enter'd into the whole. I don't answer them if you [raise it here] (a word to the wise.) [There is] not debate at all: the event has turnd out a little abortive. there was notice, but came so short: it was denied to the Judges an opportunity of considering what had b*een* said. that is so short, but w*ith* notice [the parties could consider] not only the bill, but particular clauses. you are to go on now upon a spirit of Justice to bind those particular clauses. bec*ause* they had an abortive notice to debate the Standing O*rder of the* bill. this is what you call executing the standing O*rder* not according to the letter, but according to the spirit of them. I know how easily it is to debate spirit of Standing Orders, I think myself well founded to debate upon the letter.

I flatter myself the H*ouse* will not do so vain a thing [as] to go into the several clauses in the teeth *of the* O*rder* wh*ich* has proved the very contrary. we are told [of the] impropriety. [Certain] clauses, I agree **{68}** [but not] merely the principle *of the* bill. nothing but that remains now: whether this property, I often heard the word applied to the claims of Booksellers. to take property [from the public and it] is taken away *from* them w*ith*o*u*t giving them all the notices had b*een* given them bef*ore*. Sir, we h*ave* had a great deal of debate upon previous occasions. the bill has b*een* made for reforming certain [matters and] upon subjects that partook of property. this is [a case with] as much delicacy, as much love of truth, as much love of Justice, & as much compassion to the individuals who are to be rob'd. *of the* Estate wh*ich* the Courts of Justice has decided for them as any one q*uestion* that we was bef*ore* the H*ouse*. not far in that now. the business at present merely upon a construction *of the* O*rder*. I hope we shall h*ave* some opportunity to debate it [so I will] at present confine myself to the O*rder*.

Mr. Edm*und* Burke. rise to exculpate myself f*rom* doing a thing [but] must needs [to be] irregular [. it is true, I] did laugh[, but it was a] laugh of approbation [he] shewed a great wit, great ingenuity. the H*onourable* G*entleman* made such a use [and so] I must be extremely hurt, or laugh at the ingenuity by wh*ich* I suffer'd. he says I **{69}** h*ave* proposed *summa injuria*[434] [this is something] in wh*ich* no man [knows any] better. whether chooses to approve him, or whether chooses to condemn [him] I put it as a [rule yet] he says he [relies on] the spirit of this rule: I am glad that ground is gone. wh*ich* w*as* his concession, & your authority, we are in possession *of the* measure, then we must divide upon the q*uestion of the* letter. [nothing] superiour the H*ouse* [than] over itself in his standing Orders. tho' generally adopted, not universally so: the moment he expresses a rule w*ith* an exception, he expresses a rule w*ith* a discression. the H*onourable* G*entleman* takes an advantage in stating this as a q*uestion* of property on one side. I consider as so many flourishes *of the* H*onourable* G*entleman's* eloquence. I h*ave* no business here upon this point of O*rder*. might lose the C*ommittee* above [stairs. the] C*ommittee* above has b*een* had w*ith* regard to hearing and notice that has b*een* said: oh! but they h*ave* not time to object to the clauses in the C*ommittee*. I h*ave* in my hand a printed paper,[435] if [it does] not indicate notice, it indicates nothing: a sort of brief for debate; in wh*ich* they object to every clause *of the* bill. not only time to prepare for it, but to print it. if they have b*een* taken by surprise, if they think it is a **{70}** a surreptitious bill, they will oppose your going out *of the* Chair. you h*ave* chang'd a general practice, not a common rule. if you like it upon the rule it does not apply upon the practice, if it does not apply upon the equity, & reasonableness *of the* notice; it does not apply upon the general rule. when it comes to the necessity, I believe you will see the difference. men who h*ave* vested their property useful to the republick of Trade, useful to the Republick of Letters. [the opponents] can be considered at best as Thieves that h*ave* escaped Justice. escaped by your laws not being [seen as] enough for creating Justice property. they should be put face to face, when that H*onourable* G*entleman* should not be able to throw a cloud bef*ore* us. we shall see what sort of Justice [whether it is] summum Jus[436] is another name for the summa injuria.[437]

Mr. Field. The Learned G*entleman* did me the honour of a very high Compliment. [He said I] persuaded I did not think those p*eople* had that barefaced iniquity. I do not think they h*ave* [iniquity] at all. there never came into this H*ouse* a case that deserves [relief for] individuals as this does. not able to encounter that H*onourable* G*entleman* in parliamentary hits, & manoeuvres. w*ith* regard to the occasion of it. the candour **{71}** *of the*

[434] Trans. 'supreme injustice'.

[435] This appears to be Further Remarks.

[436] Trans. 'exact law'.

[437] Trans. 'extreme justice is extreme injustice'.

Learned *Gentleman* the candour that I proposed to the H*ouse* was not what the H*onourable Gentleman* says, that it was agreed by the H*ouse* that that was a proper time. just the reverse. I said [something quite different] theref*ore*. I did refer it to the candour of that H*onourable Gentleman*, & others to let it pass on to the C*ommittee* in O*rder* to avoid the inconveniences [from the] defeat the whole bill, that I calld candour, that the Justice *of the* q*uestion* might be answered. the principle *of the* bill, & the other clauses may be debated upon other occasions.

Mr. Ch*arle*s Fox. I rise to make the m*otion* the H*ouse* are in want of. I wish the first of Standing O*rder*s may be read. (4 February 1697)[438] it has happend to me upon this occasion, it has happend to me upon others, when there were points stated that no man can controvert, that point is said to be given [as accepted.] as to the letter of this O*rder*, I never could conceive that my H*onourable* F*riend* nor any other man in the H*ouse* would h*ave* disputed w*ith* me. w*ith* th*e* [standing order] was clearly, that in all private [bill Committees,] the Chairman should give notice a week bef*ore* he sat. I think the only ground of opposition to that would h*ave* b*een* explain'd by practice. in answer to such practice [when has the] Chairman not to give notice, **{72}** a week bef*ore* the committing. are we to judge it by the Spirit [or the letter of the order] utrum horum mavis accipe.[439] the words are [clear in the order] is that the letter, or is it not the letter? (repetition) no man has attempted to establish a distinction between Committees above stairs, & Committees below stairs: the practice has b*een* proved to be contrary to the letter, it is clearly contrary [to the letter] bec*ause* no distinction has b*een* attempted to be made. if contrary to the letter, if contrary to the [spirit] if contrary to the practice I shall take the liberty to make a m*otion*, that this H*ouse* will on Thursday sen'night resolve itself into the same C*ommittee*.

Mr. Will*iam* Burke.[440] If the G*entleman* calld upon you to stop 'till he explain'd something [I understand] this m*otion* can't come on 'till the other m*otion* is made. it is a kind of amendment upon the other motion.

Speaker. It was not surprising to me: he gave notice to the whole H*ouse* what he was going to say.

Mr. Will*iam* Burke. I don't mean [to surprise] the Chair. but [ask] the H*ouse*. know no other word for it. never denied the *Gentleman*.

Speaker. Is it not intended to take the sense *of the* H*ouse* upon **{73}** this business. whether fit to go into the C*ommittee* now, or not. if that is the intention *of the* House. just the same whither you take the sense *of the* H*ouse* upon the m*otion* for me to leave the Chair, or not.

Mr. Ch*arle*s Fox. a word, or two [on the] difference. I conceive two q*uestion*s, first whether according to the O*rder* [not] go into q*uestion*. upon whi*ch* I wish to h*ave* separate divisions? second, Whether we ought to go into the C*ommittee* at all? I appeal to any body's candour.

Mr. Will*iam* Burke. There can be no m*otion* it being after four O' Clock.

[438] The standing order 4 Feb. 1697/8 (*CJ*, xii, 83) reads 'That no Petitions be received after ten o'clock in the forenoon'. However, most of the debate seems to be about another order of 24 Nov. 1699 (*CJ*, xiii, 6), 'That the Chairman of the Committee for any private Bill do not sit thereupon, without a Week's public Notice thereof set up in the Lobby', which was made a standing order on 15 Feb. 1700 (*CJ*, xiii, 333).

[439] Trans. 'take whichever you prefer'.

[440] William Burke†* (1729–98), MP for Great Bedwyn.

Mr. Field. I desir'd that he might explain, bef*ore* I made the m*otion*. I was in possession *of the* H*ouse*.

Attorney General. a new kind of q*uestion* whether the debate is upon the first m*otion* or the other. the O*rder of the* day being read the H*onourable* G*entleman* has now explaind to you; he was about to make a m*otion*. H*onourable* G*entleman* having something to propose, he suffer'd him to proceed. nothing is better known, than the ancient manner of making motions. when suggestions were made, the sense of them collected in the form of a m*otion* irregular propositions were no motions, but it was according to the old form. **{74}** the m*otion* may be, that we may h*ave* leave to make a m*otion* it being after four O'Clock.

Mr. Edm*und* Burke. decorum of proceeding as necessary as O*rder*. it is understood when G*entleman* means to make a m*otion* he is in possession [or] not legal possession [but as a matter of] dicorum, and Civility to each other. if the H*onourable* G*entleman* interrupted him only to h*ave* some conversation on the Subject w*ithou*t giving notice that he would induce a m*otion*. if he does it is in the possession *of the* H*ouse* who shall move. but w*ith* regard to O*rder* why, Sir, does any one believe that you h*ave* assured the H*ouse*, that this does not come w*ith*in the letter *of the* O*rder*. put you in mind, that you h*ave* decided very right. the purport of that Standing O*rder* that names should be stuck up in the lobby. C*ommittee of the* whole H*ouse* [look] first to the spirit, then to the letter. the O*rder of the* day [the House go into] C*ommittee* [the] usual way of opposing [it is] against leaving the Chair [and it is] irregular to go into another O*rder*[. There is no] reason for removing the obstacle, just for formality [yet] formality stands

Mr. Sawbridge.[441] The manoeuvre of today exceeded all manoeuvres that ever were practis'd in the H*ouse* of C*ommons*. You must first move for another day: I will theref*ore* avail myself. I **{75}** do move that you leave the Chair.

Gov*ernor* Johnstone.[442] I apprehend the H*onourable* G*entleman* who spoke last is intirely wrong. that the manner of moving to discharge the O*rder* [at a time] previous to wh*ich* it stands; but upon the day to h*ave* taken it into consideration [is wrong. I] state my reasons why the same substantial Justice induc'd the H*ouse* to make the Standing O*rder* [for the] C*ommittee* above, should induce the same practice in Committees below. has not says the H*onourable* G*entleman* the Counsel b*een* heard. collected all kind of evidence. [no] surprise: does not this mode of reasoning apply, supposing it were to go above stairs. that is not the purpose of making Orders. [It is possible] that you may oppose it upon the general principle; but that you should h*ave* sufficient time even after to collect your evidence, to concert, & consider *of the* clauses. if this is the reason that induced us to make the Standing O*rder*: I am certain the same principle applies now. I think the reasons why the words explanatory were added, that the Chairman should give notice when [the Committees sits]. w*ith* respect to the H*ouse* [considering] private property, they h*ave* left it to the Chairman to give notice. if G*entleman* say it never has b*een* dispensed **{76}** let them argue it upon the footing of precedent, is not that equal to a Standing rule? if there never was a case that demanded it more than the present, I hope the H*ouse* will not dispense even w*ith* its discretionary power at present. but if you do [look at it] this way, you can't give the relief. would you put *of the*

[441] John Sawbridge.

[442] George Johnstone.

bill by such a manoeuvre, when you think such relief ought to be given[? Mr Donaldson] had receivd Judgment in Courts of Law, full damages of expence. I can't conceive how you could stir a step to do Justice. I should be glad G*entleman* would state to me upon what principle they go, to come in w*ith* a bill of compassion for one set of men, w*ithout* offering any recompence to another, who h*ave* be*en* undoubtedly at great expence for recovering general liberty for the p*ublic* of this c*ountry*, &c [having been] successful in a great suit should be [protected from the other who] come in w*ith* a bill. w*ithout* indemnification [to] in some measure ruin them &c. Sir, I am certain I, by my improper conduct the other night lead the G*entleman* into a dilemma. I find the whole blame laid upon me after a vote [to] adjourn the debate. that the debate should not be adjourned: I thought we were really to go into a debate. **{77}** I did not do it by way of manoeuvre. I thought when the H*ouse* had said this debate should not be adjourn'd, that we were to debate it. I did not intend [to suggest] I will give them an answer another time. however I hope the H*onourable* G*entleman* will now enter into the whole *of the* debate. I should h*ave* be*en* as willing upon the q*uestion* for leaving the Chair; but as the H*onourable* G*entleman* [has raised it] I hope he will give some kind of answer. put him in mind of some *of the* arguments. how he can possibly do this act of humanity to one set of p*eople*, & do this act of injustice to the other. next, how he can come to this H*ouse*, & desire a compensation to the London Booksellers, bec*ause* they acted upon the supreme Court of this c*ountry* and limit the Scotch Booksellers, who had the judgment of their c*ountry* in 1748 upon the same q*uestion*. since 1748 upon every book not protected by the Statute of Queen Anne the Scotch Booksellers h*ave* be*en* acting. h*ave* appeal'd to the H*ouse* of L*ords*. the case of Midwinter, Miller, & others[443] against the Printers of Books in Scotland not [protected] by the Statute of Queen Anne [finding] no remedy [at] Common Law; no remedy at Statute Law. another point, Sir, the manner of conducting the case: bringing **{78}** no evidence, selling of assignments, reading letters no evidence. not bringing the persons that they might be cross examined. I should be glad to know what was the reason of doing it. bec*ause* it appears upon the case of Dr. Blackstone,[444] whose assignment I h*ave* since seen. that the assignment [was] first of all the sum not so large instead of £7000 it is £4000. included in that there is above five hundred, & fourteen sells of his work, & as many of his tracts, & three, or four Volumes [there is] above £1400 to be deducted f*rom* this Sum. whether upon the Statute of Queen Anne it is not a good bargain? but the date of this transaction is only about thirteen years ago. there the Booksellers could only act upon that authority f*rom* the date *of the* [decision] to the time *of the* appeal. it was well known an appeal was to be made, if not f*rom* the Court of Chancery here. Court of Quarter Session[445] of Scotland. another matter upon this evidence is this: the declaration of Mr. Samuel Johnson: a case has be*en* publishd [with] General observations upon granting relief upon Literary property.[446] no doubt it went under the strictest examination bef*ore* [being] put into the **{79}** hands *of the* Members of this H*ouse* to induce G*entleman* to think of keeping up this

[443] *Midwinter v Hamilton* (1748) Kame 154; Mor 8295; on appeal *Midwinter v Kincaid* (1751) 1 Pat App 488.

[444] William Blackstone. This is probably a reference to his assignment in relation to *Commentaries on the Laws of England*.

[445] Probably the court of session (while Scotland had quarter sessions created under the commission and instructions to the justices of peace and constables 1661 [Records of the Parliament of Scotland, 1661/1/423] the relevant cases were heard by the court of session).

[446] Part IV, General Observations/Hints {GO4–5}.

monopoly. they h*ave* publishd a fact w*ith* regard to Johnson [that he would] not go on w*ith* his Dictionary. upon seeing this, he wrote to the Counsel at the bar, desird them to contradict it. Mr. Murphy perhaps forgot it: he has put it into my hand, & given me his authority to read it. (reads) "Mr. Johnson send his Compliments to Mr. Murphy, having seen a paper calld general observations &c thinks it proper to inform Mr. Murphy that the story of £500 advancd is utterly, & absolutely false. I h*ave* no complaint to make of fulfilling their bargain, but I never desir'd a subscription." this shews how dangerous it is: these two facts shew how dangerous it is in a matter of this kind to take general declarations w*ithout* producing the regular evidence as in all other cases. I hope G*entleman* will give some account why not produce the evidence. evidence [opened] so wide a case, & closed so short a one, [it was] confirm'd this case different f*rom* any other. not owing to want of abilities [the] able manner in wh*ich* he pleads their cause, not owing to want of abilities in the G*entleman* who assisted him. but owing to the foundation **{80}** *of the* circumstances of the pity, & compassion being wanting, theref*ore* they make a general declamation, that G*entlemen* may not interest [themselves] in particulars. at the same time. I make no doubt, there are certain men among them who do demand pity, & Commiseration. I wish the particular cases had b*een* taken [and heard] & granted them relief. we know in Buckley's case, [there was] a particular act of P*arliament*.[447] I should h*ave* b*een* glad to h*ave* gone as far as [Parliament did then] for a particular term. but bec*ause* there are certain men who deserve pity, that I am not able to give them [relief] under a general bill, we must do essential injury to an individual, & I think great hurt to the publick. I can't say but that I am exceedingly sorry, that in a q*uestion* of this consequence, that not only affect this c*ountry*, but affects Literature throughout the World, I am sorry it has b*een* attended by so thin a H*ouse* in doubt whether forty Members upon a great, & Capital q*uestion*. my reason not to defeat the bill that way if G*entlemen* will point out any lines upon wh*ich* my notions of Justice could be reconcild. it is for this reason of opinion this is a q*uestion* of such consequence, if gave it time for Members to be fully inform'd of it, they would see **{81}** it in a different light f*rom* wh*ich* the H*ouse* has hirtherto seen it: that is one reason I wish for the delay. I don't like that kind of business in defeating by delay

Mr. Sawbridge. keep to the q*uestion*.

Speaker: I wish I could.

Mr. Ambler.[448] If the H*onourable* G*entleman* meant I shall certainly [agree, I do] not know what state of things we were in. at the hottest of this business [and] having alterd your opinion *of the* sense of that O*rder*. wish it might be discussed. I understood we were to go into a debate what was the meaning of that O*rder* it is [unclear] to me, I am satisfied what is the sense *of the* O*rder*. I am exceedingly clear that it right to extend to a C*ommittee of the* whole H*ouse* as well as to a private C*ommittee* upon the reason *of the* thing, & upon the practice; & what the H*onourable* G*entleman* [must do] to shew that order ought not to be put in force now, does not prove it. what he [has] said [about the order] was that [it was a] surprise [to the House] bec*ause* [it should have] had notice. [Counsel] appear at the bar *of the* H*ouse* that goes exactly to the case *of the* C*ommittee* above. is there any case of a C*ommittee* above, if there should be an opposition upon the second reading? whether it

[447] Printing of Thuanus Histories Act 1733 (7 Geo. II, c. 24).

[448] Charles Ambler† (1721–94), MP for Bramber.

was thought **{82}** sufficient by a Weeks notice? I was present when the m*otion* was made to bring in the bill; he grounded it upon compassion [which was] very proper no other ground to stand upon.

Speaker. This is not to the q*uestion*.

Col*onel* Onslow to O*rder* this bill is to fall by delay.

Mr. Ambler. The H*onourable* G*entleman* need not h*ave* put himself in such a passion upon the occasion. I understood [we are not] going into the whole q*uestion* [so I will] say nothing more upon it.

Mr. Dempster.[449] The reason why [this is a] private bill. one fact convinc'd me *of the* necessity [of this being a] private bill. the morning after the last debate, when the H*ouse* had agreed to go into this business today, the Manager *of the* petition told me he was in great distress. Sir the only evidence that was calld [was] the evidence [which was incorrect but] not know how to set the H*ouse* right except by Affidavit. we are precluded by the H*ouse* coming so soon in a C*ommittee* [so] not able to h*ave* them printed, unless we set the presses at work on Sunday.

Mr. William Burke. The Circumstance *of the* Affidavit need not delay the H*ouse* a moment. Mr. D*onaldson* and others might h*ave* b*een* prevaild upon to forego their duty of going to Church. we might h*ave* had Affidavits: we did not receive **{83}** Affidavits. printed Affidavits we ought not to mind.

Mr. Fred*erick* Montague.[450] I rise for information, I was so negligent of my duty as to leave the H*ouse* a quarter of an hour bef*ore* you. a little asham'd of. I understand the H*ouse* did decide that the bill should be committed for today. if so are we not again debating

Sir Geo*rge* Savile. If that O*rder* was contrary to the standing O*rder* [then the] standing O*rder* takes place [but I] unfortunately was out when you gave your opinion. since I h*ave* heard Standing orders [stated] w*ith* great diffidence. I cant conceive how that can be interpreted any other way than going to alter private business. whether that alters the nature of that f*rom* a private business to a publick; it is still a private business, & comes within the Letter of that O*rder* as I conceive. whether w*ith*in the practice. if when they did come into the Company [and] attend its nature. I don't find, but it was [said] if it stood so that in all private [business] the letters *of the* O*rder* [takes precedence over] practice. I don't see any [significance in the] level *of the* ground.[451] there are above that [and below.] I h*ave* five petitions upon this very subject [which] came this morning. would it be proper **{84}** to present them now, or after the committing *of the* bill?

(Speaker. You must dispute of this.).

Mr. Edmund Burke. say a few words, the H*onourable* G*entleman* totally mistakes the fact. rule constantly observed [is different from a rule which] never has b*een* observed [and it] never is observed. upon wh*ich* the conclusion I draw is this, that it is an O*rder* applicable to something else. above observation [whether] within the Letter. whether within the standing O*rder* that is to be observe'd. I put it upon the single issue, if that O*rder* has b*een* [properly] observed [and then whether] any time is proper to present petitions: God forbid all should not be present. God forbid all should not be heard.

[449] George Dempster.

[450] Fredrick Montagu†* (1733–1800), MP for Higham Ferrers.

[451] i.e., whether the committee is above stairs or the whole house.

Mr. Mackworth.[452] not go into the q*uestion*. not love to go into a collateral q*uestion* to argue upon the main q*uestion*. as far as compensation goes [then] just application should be made upon that ground. unjust that a set of men should come to take away a [relief] w*ithou*t any reason assign'd. it is a Common law proceeding *of the* H*ouse* itself: it goes [as follows where] proceedings above when Committees above doubt; they apply to the H*ouse* below **{85}** them. should go to Friday not Thursday sennight that would be within the strict rule *of the* O*rder* unless a reason is given why curtail the Common time: as an honest man I can't[453] it regularly goes to the distance of eight days. if my H*onourable* f*riend* keeps it within that eight days. w*ithou*t method, & O*rder*, & publick bodies [there is] confusion in this H*ouse*. not d*one* it w*ith* a design of delay.

Mr. Char*les* Fox. I understood the H*ouse* would be adjourned on Friday next. O*rder* preserved: that O*rder* wh*ich* no ingenuity can explain. [The] letter, & [notice] not post it up in the Lobby, bec*ause* the votes *of the* House gives the notice: the C*ommittee* might be closed, bef*ore* the notice given in the votes.

Mr. Whitworth.[454] Whether consistent w*ith* the Letter [of the] O*rder*. I think the notice in the votes is sufficient. the notice in the lobby not stuck up for the p*eople* at large. already inform'd by the votes. [the notice is] stuck up, that G*entlemen of the* C*ommittee* may know what day the Chairman is to sit. the Members are all supposed to be present in a C*ommittee of the* whole H*ouse*.

Mr. Popham.[455] [I'm] puzzled between the distinction **{86}** of Standing Orders, & discretionary orders. O*rders* bec*ome* the law *of the* H*ouse* must be complied w*ith*. the H*onourable* G*entleman* has proved all the parties h*ave* not had notice.

Mr. Cholmley.[456] I apprehend the O*rder* w*ithou*t the H*ouse* for information *of the* parties concerned as well as M*embers* votes. the Parties can't h*ave* notice 'till the votes are printed. I don't know whether the votes the other day, are yet printed.

Mr. Whitworth. read the standing O*rder* that no Footman shall be in the lobby &c[457] [not complying with some orders] most dangerous [whereas others are] less dangerous: in this case [we should consider] what is the state *of the* bill? [If it is][458] carried up to another H*ouse* go thro' all the forms & w*ith* [us] already in the middle of May[. It is] commonly understood the Session [will] not last longer than June. justifiable reason for bringing it on now.

Mr. Dempster. Read five words *of the* votes [for a] bill relating to Mr Frazer and Co[459] on this day sen'night resolve itself into a C*ommittee*. I voted against the m*otion* bec*ause* I thought it would destroy the bill &c. &c.

[452]Herbert Mackworth.

[453]The MS has '—'.

[454]Richard Whitworth† (?1734–1811), MP for Stafford. The MS simply has 'Mr' so it could have been Charles. However, it is clear from newspaper reports that Richard was involved in earlier stages, and chaired the committee.

[455]Alexander Popham†* (?1729–1810), MP for Taunton.

[456]Nathaniel Cholmley† (1721–91), MP for Boroughbridge.

[457]15 Nov. 1705 (*CJ*, xv, 26), 'That the Serjeant at Arms, attending this House, do take into his custody all such strangers, as shall presume to come into the Body of the House, or the Galleries, during the sitting of any Committees therein; and that the Lobby, and Stairs coming up to the Lobby, be kept clear of Footmen.'

[458]The MS has '—' indicating the shorthand cannot be deciphered.

[459]*Votes 1774*, p. 338; *CJ*, xxxiv, 558 (14 Mar.); Crown Lands-Forfeited Estates Act 1774 (14 Geo. III, c. 22).

Sir George Savile. Presented the petitions. **{87}**[460]

Mr. Field. I Moved for you to leave the Chair.

Lord Folkestone. surpris'd at the assertion *of the* H*onourable* G*entleman* the other night [on] time of debating. know the time of debating short. in a full H*ouse* only can expect a proper decision [it is] not supposed [there is] any interest to serve, exclusive of that as a M*ember of the* Community at large, exclusive of that as a Representative *of the* publick, whose rights, I always think affected by any species of monopoly. this bill is brought in upon the notion of Literary property. the merits are historical. [Act of] Queen Anne. for encouragement of Learning: in O*rder* [and for that purpose][461] a right establishment &c [for a] limited time. Sir, the Booksellers had in preceding time, partly by propagative [and] Proclamation [of] Star Chamber, a monopoly of books. a monopoly of books of wh*ich* they had tasted the sweets: sorry to part w*ith* them. P*etitioners* said they should h*ave* them for a certain number of years, & no longer: the Booksellers being able to get no more were contented w*ith* it as long as the monopoly continued; wh*ich* was for books bef*ore* that time twenty one years for books after that fourteen &c. what kept books to be common again? Petition P*arliament*. this H*ouse* in **{88}** two instances, & the H*ouse* of L*ords* in another refused to extend their monopoly. what did the Booksellers do then? if [Parliament] not give it us we h*ave* it already. this they asserted: it is f*rom* that time we begin to hear *of the* claims of Literary property at Common law. all the arguments that h*ave* b*een* searchd for, all the records that h*ave* b*een* examin'd [but] not countenanc'd by the authority of any one Lawyer, not countenanced by the authority of any one decision: I know when the q*uestion* became agitated in Courts of Justice [and yet] Lawyers differ about it. it was very excusable for persons whose study was not in the law to differ about it. ignorance *of the* Law does not excuse. [There is] a right answer [in law, for instance,] if the title of my Estate [in question] Judges differ [on its validity][462] yet nobody give me relief. I did move, I took Counsel's opinion upon my estate Counsel's opinion in my favour [yet] still there is a claim to compassion: but give me leave to make this observation I never heard bef*ore* that of all the Lawyers that h*ave* countenanced this claim, not one except Baron Smyth,[463] that is not, or has not b*een* a puisne Judge *of the* Court of King's Bench under Lord Mansfield. he took it up very early; [he][464] argued at the **{89}** bar. I should be apt to think [it strange,] for he would not support his opinion in the H*ouse* of L*ords* [or the] Quarter Session of Scotland.[465] w*ithou*t the twelve Judges the Booksellers got all they could in 1709. when books became to get in common again, by the monopoly upon old books expiring, they petition'd P*arliament* for an extent of that monopoly [but it was] refused [and so they] set the Legislature at defiance: erected a Common law claim; which by the meritorious exertion of an individual defeated. they now come to P*arliament* for an ex post facto law for indemnification. I think they are not intitled [as a trade, as] individuals, as Subjects. it is now bef*ore* P*arliament* to decide upon it. present q*uestion* is material to that purpose.

[460] *CJ*, xxxiv, 757, 16 May.

[461] See Lord Folkestone's Diary.

[462] See Lord Folkestone's Diary.

[463] Sir Sidney Stafford Smyth†* (1705–78).

[464] See Lord Folkestone's Diary.

[465] This is likely a reference to the court of session.

Mr. Field. I beg leave to trouble [you with a] few words upon the subject of this bill. many objections [it will] introduce great publick inconveniences: introduce great monopolies, & attended w*ith* great publick mischief. The N*oble* L*ord* who spoke last has calld upon me to enter into this debate now, wh*ich* he says I declin'd doing the other night: at the same time, I did say I thought the ground of this bill mistaken, & the Justice of this bill **{90}** mistaken. Sir, I shall beg leave to take notice of some *of the* mistakes that I think h*ave* b*een* made w*ith* regard to this. one mistake made w*ith* regard to this has b*een* and we h*ave* b*een* calld upon very earnestly to account for it, that we are said to impeach, & call in q*uestion* the decision *of the* H*ouse* of L*ords*. Sir, the decision *of the* H*ouse* of L*ords* was upon intirely a different ground from wh*ich* this application is now made: the decision *of the* H*ouse* of L*ords* was upon the q*uestion* of what is Common Law, or not Common Law at the instance of that decision. that decision excluded it professly in the Lords, & Judges who debated it, excluded the consideration of all q*uestion*s as to the hardship that might arise f*rom* that q*uestion*. that was not the q*uestion* [for them. The] Legislature was not of a Juridical power [it can consider the] inconveniences arising f*rom* the law as declared by that Judgment. the ground upon wh*ich* I took the liberty to move to bring in this bill was, that by the decision *of the* H*ouse* of L*ords*, that those p*eople* the Booksellers who had possessd themselves of Copyright by purchase, had no other rights in those Copies, but by the Statute of Queen Anne. it appears by the report made by the C*ommittee* that the Petitioners h*ave* for many years [acquired copy rights] in the course of **{91}** their trade: the opinion upon wh*ich* they acted in the course of their trade, that there did such a thing exist as Common law derived f*rom* Authors, by assignment f*rom* Authors in perpetuity, as according to the degree of that assignm*ent*. it appeard that upon that idea in the course of trade, they had for a number of years invested large sums, & a great part of their property in purchases of this kind. I did state upon the first m*otion* of this bill, that this was not an unwarrantable idea in them, an idea of their own raising, & creating, but founded upon such principles as h*ave* b*een* afterwards adopted, not only among the trade themselves, not only the sincerity of their ideas warranted by investing great sums upon it, but warranted by the most solemn decision *of the* first Court of Law in this Kingdom,[466] w*ith* Judges in that Court, & at the head of that Court equal I may venture to say to any that ever sat there. it would not become me to speak *of the* character *of the* great man that presided:[467] his abilities will be rememberd to posterity as a very great Judge, and of as great abilities as I believe ever sat in that place. what I humbly offer'd upon that occasion, if that all the grounds that could induce that Court to adopt the **{92}** idea of that Common Law, was surely excusable in a body of men, not Lawyers, not learned; but who h*ave* contracted their ideas by the usage, & practice they found in the general possession of trade, & in wh*ich* they saw numbers invested their fortunes, & upon the credit of wh*ich* they themselves invested their fortunes. Sir, it was said that admitting this all to be true, that they were really deceived, admitting that, they had ruin'd themselves by venturing [upon a property and] upon the bottom. it is no case of Parliamentary compassion: they stand, or fall by their own errors. many p*eople* h*ave* b*een* ruind in their errors, & particularly a case has b*een* mentiond of [a person] purchasing an Estate upon a bad title. Sir, a person purchasing an Estate upon a bad title, stands I think rather upon a different foundation: the

[466] *Millar v Taylor* (1769) 4 Burr 2303 (98 ER 201).

[467] This is a reference to William Murray, Lord Mansfield, lord chief justice of king's bench.

law of title is known; there are Lawyers professing to settle titles: every man applies to that Lawyer he thinks he can trust: if he applies to no Lawyer, then his own error. [Sir, for an individual,] in that case a case of Compassion, but not a case of general relief. another case has b*een* mentioned, not today; I dont desire to decline any difficulty **{93}** that has b*een* offer'd. a case has b*een* put of a person lead into such a mistake, by his Lawyer giving an opinion upon a case decided in Court of Law, which afterwards [is overturned and so is] not advantageous to [that person.] a cause many years ago bef*ore* [House of Lords involving] Lee.[468] that cause many years after was determind otherwise. is that a case of Parliamentary relief? I do not take upon me to say it was not a case of parliamentary relief. I think great deference ought to be paid to this claim of parliamentary relief that lays by a settled practice, or lays by the Law *of the* Land. to go [now] in the present case, undoubtedly this wh*ich* is now treated as the most ideal of all phantoms, a mere Chimera raised by wicked Booksellers was the Law *of the* Land for several years, f*rom* the time the Judgment *of the* Court of King's bench unappeald to. it was his business not the Booksellers to appeal f*rom* it: it was not in their power, theref*ore* I say f*rom* that time; I look upon it as the Law *of the* Land. I go further, I h*ave* always understood, that when the Lord Chancellor made his decree upon a cause:[469] instead of sending it for [judgment] as a q*uestion* of Law, he sent it decided, & decreed upon it. I understand in **{94}** the H*ouse* of L*ord* he[470] was of a different opinion, & spoke the reversal of his own decree. I understand he gave his reasons that he thought himself bound by the Judgment[471] as it then stood. whether he thought himself bound by that Judgment? I am very well assur'd any Bookseller might h*ave* thought himself bound by that Judgment. whatever was so justified by that Judgment, was the most justifiable error in the course of their trade. the ground upon wh*ich* that Judgment was given must h*ave* b*een* good ground for them to pursue in the course of trade. was a ground for creating a long establish'd practice: & wh*ich* practice I shall submit is a very great ground for the relief in this case: is such as if it was not quite sufficient to make law, was quite sufficient to give a strong idea, & opinion of law [. Sir,] it is said that this was not acquiesced in a great many suits, the suits were brought bef*ore* [the Courts so] why not pursued to the Judgment. Mr Do*naldson* [could have sought judgment and] if the Court of Chancery thought it a Law q*uestion* why not pursued by the Defendant to bring it to a decision; & final hearing? I really do look upon this a q*uestion* of practice so long established, & so long acted under as to stand very much in the **{95}** light of a very long possession. I call it a possession, Sir, it is said all this practice was raised by an illegal combination, now Sir, what is an illegal combination? a combination of obtaining Letters Patent, a combination of obtaining Star Chambers decrees, a combination of obtaining injunctions *of the* Court of Chancery. was this any fraudulent practice of theirs? I dont understand it. I believe the p*eople* under the influence that [these things] did establish a practice. a practice within forty years f*rom* the first use of Printing in this Kingdom, 1503.[472] Star Chamber decrees continued in succession in

[468] Probably an imprecise reference to *Antonius, Son of Count Leslie v James Leslie* (1742) 1 Paton 324 (*LJ*, xxvi, 108); and *Charles Cajetan, Count Leslie v Peter Leslie Grant* (1763) 2 Paton 68 (*LJ*, xxx, 326); Part IV, Glasgow Memorialists {18}.

[469] TNA, C 33/439, ff. 26–7 (16 Nov. 1772).

[470] Henry Bathurst, Lord Apsley†* (1714–94), lord chancellor.

[471] *Millar v Taylor* (1769) 4 Burr 2303 (98 ER 201).

[472] William Caxton (*d.*c.1491) returned to England in around 1476 and set up his printing shop near Westminster Abbey.

a course that was law. could any man say the Star Chamber decrees was not Law? perhaps Mr. Hampden[473] might say [it was not law,] but the Booksellers could not say it was not [law][474] 'till it came to ordinance 1640[475] they establishd the licensing *of the* press. a very improper act. all this put them in possession in fact *of the* exclusive privilege of printing, not in [doubt] so they continued 'till within a few years bef*ore* the act of Queen Anne. [So not] absurd in them to proceed in the idea of purchasing Copyright: the art **{96}** of Printing was not arrived at that heigth then, either for many Printers, or many readers. I h*ave* not b*een* able to raise any one instance *of the* purchasing of copyright. I don't know any antecedent to that of Milton. the receipts of that are in 1679, or 1680. I h*ave* heard a great deal said *of the* combination of Booksellers, & how they impose upon one another: what an infamous thing it is for Booksellers to complain. wants a recompense, & satisfaction. the Bookseller who contracted w*ith* Milton for the Sale of Paradise lost. to give Milton five pounds upon the first edition, five pounds upon the second, & five pounds upon the third[476] only say one word, when he sold his copy upon those terms, he had not an idea *of the* decision [of the Court.] he had not an idea that the first Copy was a gift to the publick, for he sold three editions of it. I h*ave* heard in the history of that book. I h*ave* seen his receipts for the two five pounds. I h*ave* seen the receipt of his Widow for the third wh*ich* was eight pounds.[477] but w*ith* regard to the exhortance of it, Simmons[478] who made this exorbitant purchase, & so far imposed upon Milton, sold it for twenty five pounds. but **{97}** [why pay for] that if not law; in my opinion a very strong ground [based on] the opinion of writers [and the booksellers'] long uninterrupted possession: I don't say it was law; I don't move it in the least idea in opposition to the Judgment *of the* H*ouse* of L*ords.* not possession [in law] but in practice. then, Sir, it is objected, that it is [on the basis] that the ground itself is false ground. the G*entleman* contends that so far as f*rom* their having an idea of this kind, they never had an idea of the kind, it was all imposition upon the world. I shall submit to the H*ouse* in the first place that the prices they h*ave* given [for copies] has b*een* in evidence. some h*ave* given £4000, some h*ave* given six, for the perpetual right of printing; now, Sir, they die. they did not believe it. they must h*ave* had a very strange turn of mind to waste upon a species of property they believed to be no property such sums as they did. A very great [property] no doubt. but it is very certain they all spoke of it. all the assignments of Milton, & of Judge Blackstone are perpetual. theref*ore* not only Booksellers h*ave* b*een* deceived, but Authors h*ave* b*een* deceived. Milton has b*een* deceived. he w*ith* that sense of Liberty, wh*ich* he had, that he **{98}** would h*ave* d*one* it.

I do not conceive that Judge Blackstone would h*ave* d*one* it, I do not conceive that even Sir John Dalrymple would h*ave* d*one* it: if he did, he most certainly w*ou*ld not h*ave* taken £2000 f*rom* a Bookseller, & made a Conveyance forever. and has there never existed [a right] that for a work not his own, but a collection, might as well h*ave* b*een* let alone. upon

[473]Presumably a reference to Thomas Hampden† (1746–24), MP for Lewes.

[474]MS has '—'.

[475]It should be 1647: see Part I: Chapter 4: The Prehistory.

[476]See Kerry MacLennan, 'John Milton's Contract for "Paradise Lost": A Commercial Reading'.

[477]'… editions … eight … twelve'.

[478]Samuel Simmons (1640–87); D.F McKenzie, 'Milton's Printers Matthew, Mary and Samuel Simmons', *Milton Quarterly*, xiv (1980), 87.

the authority of [a poor witness] not deserve the credit. [M. Paul Barillon][479] one *of the* weakest M*inisters* ever employd. if ever any merit [in the man is unclear; but he] greatly contributed to the Revolution by his conduct. greatly misled the Prince he was not to [be praised for uncovering this wrongdoing][480] that is the merit he has receivd his £2000 for. I hope he will make good the promise he himself said he had [that any loss][481] should be his own, not the Booksellers'. I am afraid the Booksellers h*ave* not got a very good reliance upon [the ground as] I wish they may. whatever the foundation of this ground [a] great loss *of the* Petitioners. the means by wh*ich* they h*ave* b*een* lead in may [justify relief.] it will be attended w*ith* great publick inconveniences. that [inconvenience] ought never be sacrificed to the relief prayed for by the Petitioners. Sir, the monopoly is very **{99}** much insisted on. monopolies are odious. the law not suffer monopolies: sure the Law does suffer monopolies: it suffers monopolies every day the very Statute against Monopolies excepts. it allows monopolies. it allows Patents for useful arts, except they be in regard to printing.[482] w*ith* some reason. very particular circumstances attend that, that attends no other. the Printer bef*ore* he can get the price of a single book must print the whole impression. that impression in many books amounts to very large sums £1500, or £2000. those impressions sometimes lie twenty years bef*ore* they are sold off. now [a printer] who is to undertake such a charge, to advance money, to lay by [money in a] trade of that kind, if he has no sort of security [in the copy so he] and other person has to print on. will destroy every Adventure of that sort. he is Adventurer upon that occasion, as the new inventor of a Machine. it must be a total discouragement of all books of value if such sort of editions as coming f*rom* Scotland: are to be permitted to be printed upon brown paper, in O*rder* to undervalue all those other editons[. It is] not a monopoly to h*ave* the sole making [a machine or] any particular kind of Commodity **{100}**

take the case *of the* Stall Booksellers & c one would think the whole merit of printing was to be ingrossed in their hands: one would think it [true.] the Scotch Petitioners say the paper making will be stopd in Scotland. they say a Scotch author will not sell his own work, but carry it to a London Bookseller. I believe there is a secret in that. I believe the London Booksellers happen to give better prices than Edinburgh, or Glasgow Booksellers. one *of the* mistakes generally made is, it is to h*ave* the effect of a total monopoly, & suppression *of the* whole art of printing for twenty one years. it is meant to be confined if not, I hope G*entleman* will assist in framing clauses, that it should not be extended to give right to any Bookseller, or Printer beyond what they h*ave* a right f*rom* authority: much less f*rom* Shakespeare, Beaumont, & Fletcher[483] &c. every work of our Nation antecedent to 1679. let us a little consider this calamitous condition *of the* Edinburgh, & Glasgow Printers, & those G*entleman of the* Stalls of London, & Westminster, that they can't get a book: there is not a Classick Greek, or Latin book they are not at full liberty to print in the most elegant & beautiful editions. this bill I hope will be an encouragement to them to turn their heads

[479]The French ambassador to England from 1677 to 1688. The relevant book is Sir John Dalrymple, *Memoirs of Great Britain and Ireland. From the Dissolution of the Last Parliament of Charles II, until the Sea-battle off La Hogue* (Strahan, 1771) (ESTC: T145644).

[480]The reference to the £2,000 means it must be referring back to Sir John.

[481]Cavendish, Dalrymple {255–6}.

[482]Statute of Monopolies, s. 10.

[483]William Shakespeare* (1554–1616), Sir John Beaumont* (1584–1627) and Phineas Fletcher* (1582–1650).

that **{101}** way. [They may print] elegant edition of Books [which] perhaps more valuable than those your London, & Westminster Booksellers are[. They can print from the] whole fund of Classicks: does not the whole fund of Learning in Europe lie open to them? France, Italy, Spain? every Country in Europe. (here he paused a good while.)

Sir, I h*ave* said something *of the* extent of Booksellers expence in printing: I might add to this the great expence they are at in purchases f*rom* Authors. I should think it never can be looked upon as greatly detrimental to Learning, that such encouragements are given. I h*ave* heard many great sums h*ave* be*en* given to Authors. I h*ave* seen accounts w*ith* regards to the publishing of Shakespeare. p*eople* who h*ave* wrote notes I h*ave* seen accounts to the amount of £2800 give to different Editors only. is it for the benefit of Learning, or not for the benefit of Learning that those prices should be given. G*entleman* say this rises the price of Books: I should conceive that it beneficially rises the price of books. most undoubtedly the man who gives £2000 for the copy of his book, & is at the expence of making an expensive edition can't upon the same terms print, as the man who gets a copy, & prints it off w*ithou*t paying **{102}** anything for it. you h*ave* heard this is the trade. I h*ave* seen a Catalogue of Irish books. Ireland does not fall within this law. they h*ave* produced every Copy they sell w*ithou*t paying any thing for it. You h*ave* heard accounts *of the* Traffick between Ireland, & Scotland of printing books. you had a Letter: it is said not legally proved: this is not the Subject of legal, & exact proof. I do think if a person receiv'd a letter from Mr H*ume*[484] [it would be doubted.] everybody knows they print books in Ireland. the Learned G*entleman* at the bar complain'd most loudly, that those books are printed in Ireland, sent over to Scotland. run on them, they can't sell their own books. the books they themselves h*ave* printed in London are not saleable in Scotland. is it not for the encouragement of Learning, that encouragement should be given to men who print fairly, to men who print honestly? another thing, purchase the Copy, they want to make alterations, & editions: where will they make their amendments. when those books get into Mr. Donaldson's hands. like Pope's Homer: there is hardly an Author they purchased a book of, that they h*ave* not given almost as much as the first price for alterations, & editions.

{103} I am extremely ashamed [to have] taken up so much time, I am extremely ashamed [to have] spoke disjointedly. the litigation of this cause [means I have] not spoke so correctly, if any thing I h*ave* omitted, I shall be glad after [to adding my thoughts] not trouble you long. but we are now in this stage of this bill. it is not a bill in its compleat form. every objection that goes to correction, & amendment it is open [to make] if G*entlemen* see what particular turn [needs making.] I spoke w*ith* much reserve. whatever is against the principle *of the* bill I hope I h*ave* answered: if I h*ave* omitted any thing I shall be glad to submit my thoughts. never had any connection w*ith* those p*eople* the first accident threw me into it.

a great deal said upon the utility [and] the unfairness *of the* proceedings in the C*ommittee*. I take a good deal of shame to myself to h*ave* heard this thing not to h*ave* said any thing to justify myself. I do venture to say nothing passed unfair, or lending in the least to conceal evidence. G*entleman* propos'd q*uestion* other G*entlemen* opposed them. I always calld upon the M*ember* who put the q*uestion* after others objected. I always calld upon him to vote, or divide, they never did vote, or divide, they never took the sense *of the* C*ommittee*. one was particularly mentioned: he **{104}** seem'd to mention it as if a want of candour. a q*uestion* he

[484] David Hume.

ask'd: I call'd upon him at the time, he said no, he would not put the q*uestion*. was carried on w*ith* as much decency, & fairness as any thing I ever saw. I will take it upon me, I endeavourd to conduct myself by the reference *of the* H*ouse* & by the Petition by [the question] referd to the consideration *of the* C*ommittee*.

Mr. Charles Fox. Sir, take up the H*ouse* very shortly upon this occasion, for having endeavourd unsuccessfully to persuade G*entlemen* to claim [my side] shall hardly attempt to persuade them to abandon [it now.] right of p*eople* very materially concernd [by the] retrospective [nature of the Bill.] what the H*onourable* G*entleman* said divided into two parts. [One part is a claim for compensation for an idea of the common law][485] the other when any compensation can be given to them wh*ich* is manifest injustice to others. as to the first part, their right to compensation. very short. what has the greatest weight w*ith* G*entleman* is the decision *of the* Court of King's Bench.[486] the first observation if that is the ground of compensation: the first consequence arises f*rom* thence, that such compensation should be given since the decision of **{105}** the Court of King's Bench I must beg leave to observe, that this Judgment *of the* Court of King's Bench in 1769, not longer ago than that. if I had not known that I should h*ave* thought it was taken to be the law of this c*ountry* so long. any G*entleman* who had not recollected that, would h*ave* fancied that the wisdom *of the* decision *of the* H*ouse* of L*ords* never had b*een* appeald to. that is not the state *of the* q*uestion*. even as to the uninterrupted possession, as to the claims of this [it is] so far f*rom* being the q*uestion* [as] no such right imagin'd[, the Petitioners] came w*ith* a Petition to the other H*ouse* [claiming] no law for protecting our rights. how happen'd [they did] not attempt their rights by prosecution. there I hold that proposition of its being uninterrupted &c is false, as that it is the law of this c*ountry*: that argument for compensation intirely gone [as the] opinion *of the* King's Bench can't extend to any but such copyrights that h*ave* b*een* purchas'd since 1769. if so the pretence for committing [the bill has] not now [been proved.] compare it to purchasing Lands upon false titles[. For any] conveyance well known [purchasers] take the opinion of Lawyers [and] abide **{106}** [by it. It is] certainly true to a certain degree. but when you h*ave* consulted [Counsel who gives a] false opinion [on title] that is possible [then] G*entleman* say at least you must h*ave* taken the opinion of Lawyers. does it appear that any of those Pretenders to Copy right did take the opinion of Lawyers. I shall take it for granted f*rom* what I h*ave* heard that they never did take the opinion of Lawyers: why did they not take the opinion of Lawyers. suggest the petitioners reason, bec*ause* they could suggest that he would upon [opining that they were] under no deceit whatsoever[. Not] deceived the first observation when p*eople* take the prices for Copyright, p*eople* take no Copyright. when they say not give £4000 if he had not known it to be perpetual, would he ascertain the difference? answer that work was worth it for fourteen years. they took the chance of perpetuity against nothing. they took that [chance] the very instant Sir John Dalrymple's book [was published with the] universal sale of it. I should imagine whoever has bought it for £2000 will probably w*ith*: the Statute of Queen Anne get their repayment. as far as I could collect there were other ways **{107}** [of] protecting their property. by the mode of Combination. whoever has heard what we h*ave* already heard, may be ripe to

[485] *Middlesex Journal*, 14–17 May 1774.

[486] *Millar v Taylor* (1769) 4 Burr 2303 (98 ER 201).

say, that [no deception] to the person purchasing Copyright to maintain that by means of Combination[;no] doubt [it is] illegal. there*fore* I say give them that [combination which] will account for his purchasing such copies: that he was not deceived in his opinion. it is not proved that they ever did misconceive [before the decision of the] King's Bench.

not for a Bookseller to deny that to be law; I did not say it was for a Bookseller to deny that to be law. to adopt that to be law 'till there was an appeal. the person who was to h*ave* b*een* the appellant [did not appeal] no inference could be drawn f*rom* that, it stood upon the same circumstance as other decisions *of the* K*ing*'s Bench, not appeald f*rom*. so much I h*ave* said w*ith* regard to the point, whether there is any [need to] compensate at all.

the manner of compensation [has] two objects[. first,] publick utility against monopoly, & another the H*onourable* G*entleman* has touchd very little upon [he] has totally forgot that he has b*een* deaf when it has b*een* stated by other G*entleman*. if he had [heard] I don't see how [he can] go on **{108}** w*ith* this bill. the other point the injustice d*one* to individuals. the H*onourable* G*entleman* goes to the utility *of the* present monopoly in regard to Learning. first observe that utility goes only perspectively.[487] if any utility in a publick loss, that utility would only go to make this a perspective bill, to those who in future should purchase no encouragement to any person who is now writing. so far to utility. glad to see that. no more concerns me to h*ave* imputed to me, than any wish to discourage literary merit. [the Bill] as far as goes to encouragement wh*ich* has nothing to do [with authors] if [any] further encouragement given to Authors rather of opinion it ought that must be d*one* by amending Queen Anne's [Statute to apply] perspective[ly.] no injustice to be d*one* to any man. I may buy as well as Mr. Wilkie[488] no injustice d*one* to any individual.

now I come to the last, & most important point of injustice d*one* to individuals: allowing the two first propositions deserve compensation [and providing] publick utility. I shall still see no such cause of compassion. not know such publick utility as is states to arise: I deny both. but suppose I allow these would justify this bill. **{109}** not a Justification, bec*ause* A is in a state of Compassion relieving A then B's property should be sacrificed. that is a doctrine of Compensation, I never heard breachd in this H*ouse* 'till now. whenever heard [it] reprobated. it is not B. that is to pay that compensation, it is the publick that is to pay, that compensation. taxes ought to be laid upon the subject [to make] such compensation. it ought not be on one individual, or sett of Individuals who are to pay for the generosity *of the* publick, & the utility *of the* publick also: wh*ich* is the case of Mr Donaldson for one [but] others in that predicament rightly conceive [that as they] succeed [before the courts the matter finish.] he has told [that by going to court has] robb'd himself of his own property. it is not [just.] I h*ave* stated bef*ore* by very unjust means kept out of what he is allowed to be his property. [for] twenty [years now and for] twenty years longer. the case of an individual so clear, that his property as directly concernd in it [and it cannot be given] w*ithou*t taking it out of Mr D*onaldson's* pocket, & others in the same predicament of Mr D*onaldson* the q*uestion* after all comes to be considered is this: first of all, whether in the case of **{110}** composition [. I] attempt to disapprove [this point; and secondly] whether allowing the two first cases [is just and] whether the property of an individual, Mr D*onaldson* and others ought to be given to the satisfaction of publick utility.

[487] This should probably be prospectively.

[488] John Wilkie.

Col*onel* Onslow. I undertook this cause when it was falling: when it had no friend, but myself, & when it had very able opponents. I h*ave* carried it the length it has gone. I hope the H*ouse* will allow me a little time upon the subject. I had framed a regular form of defence upon this day, but the Learned Baronet at the bar put every thing so much out of my head, that I hope the H*ouse* will indulge me to confine myself upon the observations I made upon the Learned Counsel. It was among the best I heard against this bill, that we were told that the Booksellers of London, & Westminster should not be intitled to any favour bec*ause* they had libelled both Houses of P*arliament*, & their Sovereign. how it could enter into the mind of man, that a British P*arliament* should be composed of such narrow-minded persons, who would not do Common Justice in one case, upon the supposition that one part had erred in another case. is beyond my reason to comprehend. or f*rom* what principle of **{111}** law, Justice, policy, or equity, that the Learned G*entleman* drew that argument, is not for me to comprehend. an argument of that there sort when it proceeds f*rom* any person whatever is shocking, but when it proceeds f*rom* the Robe, & the Gown it is hideous. Sir, it has b*een* said, that they are not to comply w*ith* the petition *of the* London Booksellers bec*ause* they request a monopoly. for the trade of a Bookseller in some instances a monopoly is necessary, it is necessary for the encouragement *of the* Author. if he can't go down to Fleet Street, & sell his copy to the best advantage, there will soon be an end of Authors. theref*ore* it affects Authors, & Literature in general, if a monopoly in such a case is not complied w*ith*. Sir, the Learned G*entleman* pleaded that it was bad policy to make money the object of Learned men. Sir, use h*ave* studied the same f*rom* the Ancients. it is very true Poets wrote for fame formerly wh*ich* I believe would be very disagreeable to the Poets *of the* present day. the Lawyer's then pleaded for fame: but tho' the Lawyers pleaded for fame at that time, yet according to their abilities, according to their pleadings they got into the principal Posts *of the* Government *of the* State by it. they got both power, & emolument. Sir, the Learned G*entleman* himself took the middle way: he took some fame, & some **{112}** money. as long as there is a friend of Liberty in this c*ountry*, & as long as the name of Russel, & Sydney[489] are revered, so long the name of that Learned Counsel will not be forgot. & every body knows that the Learned Counsel did sell his work for a very good price, & I beg leave at this time to make an observation upon that. I think a very fair one. a Judge may be of one opinion, & when asked as a Counsel, he might h*ave* pleaded what was not his real opinion. Sir, the Learned Counsel did exceedingly right in saying all he did say.

as a Scotch, & national cause he was in the right in saying what he did. but I shall put the case of Sir John Dalrymple selling his book, & taking a large sum of money, ag*ainst* what he said when he was pleading at the bar. when he sold his copy, he conveyed, all he said at the bar was only to serve his Client. Sir, it has b*een* said that the booksellers h*ave* asked a monopoly for books f*rom* the time of Henry the 8th how could this be asserted? this bill says only the copy right of Authors, or their assigns. Sir, another argument, the second best I h*ave* heard, was, we should be favourable to his Client the Scotch Booksellers, bec*ause* the Scotch saved us in the last war,[490] bec*ause* they now keep us f*rom* anarchy, & confusion, & **{113}** bec*ause* every other great advantage this c*ountry* has to expect is f*rom* Scotland, & Scotland only. the Counsel put it upon that ground why this H*ouse* should not oppress a

[489] Sir Philip Sidney; it is not clear which Russell is being referred to.

[490] The Seven Years War (1756–63).

Scotch Bookseller. if any body had replied to that, & said, why you had two rebellions. why, Sir, I am above that, it is a wrong way of arguing. this making it a Scotch cause has b*een* one *of the* worst ways to support it.[491]

when I saw Mr Adams[492] attacked, I attended in every division, bec*ause* I thought he was prosecuted for his c*ountry* (a laugh.) it is very true, Sir, let us see how different a ground I will take f*rom* that Learned Counsel, & how impartial I mean to be, & how much I am willing to serve North Britain. I beg leave to observe to the H*ouse* that I h*ave* Copies of Letters f*rom* the greatest Authors of that c*ountry*, & perhaps the greatest Authors of any c*ountry* in Europe. I h*ave* copies of Letters f*rom* Hume,[493] Robertson, Dr. Beattie, & others, expressing their earnest wish that the London Booksellers may be protected. the Learned Baronet tells us will you to injure the Scotch, no, I will go to serve Scotland. there shall be literary property there. the G*entleman* say, we can print cheaper at Glasgow, than at London, why should we be deprived *of the* benefit of our national situation. I allow their argument is an ostensible **{114}** one. if we will establish Literary property in Scotland, wh*ich* is not now, & they can print cheaper than us, they can afford to pay their own Authors better than we can, & they will h*ave* the monopoly of all the new books, & it will be a detriment to the London Booksellers. consider it in the light *of the* Learned G*entleman* I say it is the greatest interest of North Britain to h*ave* this bill, bec*ause* now there is no literary property there. I think it will be a very great acquisition to Scotland. but Sir, this was not what was wanted. good as this would be to Scotland no, Sir, the p*eople* did oppose this bill f*rom* that c*ountry*. no, Sir, it was the monopoly of Fleet Street. the English Booksellers has paid the Scotch Author. what is the case? after giving four, or five thousand G*entlemen* come, & say no we will take half now we h*ave* paid our Countrymen. I should never h*ave* made it a Scotch cause. the Learned Counsel has put every thing else out of my head. they want John Bull to pay the Authors. a very odd sort of a G*entleman* who has fallen asleep. America pulls him by the nose, the North Briton gives him a twinge. ut Iugulent homines surgunt de nocte Latrones, ut te ipsum serves, nonne expergisceris?[494] shall we never be **{115}** awake? shall we never pursue our own interest? it has b*een* said this bill will act as an ex post facto law against Mr Donaldson. I deny that, for the account given in evidence, every day he is going on printing: & by this bill he will h*ave* a right to the sale of those books he is printing at the expence of [the London booksellers] to sell those books to the amount of £10,000 so that he will be amply compensated where he has b*een* attacked for books out *of the* Statute. I must observe, there has b*een* a compromise: one was a term of years: it is nothing to the present q*uestion* when we come to the C*ommittee* we will talk *of the* compromise. then says Mr Donaldson you are to pay me for all the expence of those thirteen suits.[495] a pretty modest request. in six of them he has b*een* cast w*ith* costs. in three now going on, I understand is for books protected by the Statute. I take it, a dead certainty against him: it ought to be. there is a

[491] In the MS 'support it' is underlined with a question mark.

[492] This is a reference to John Adams (1735–1826), later 2nd president of the USA, during the passage of the Massachusetts Government Act 1774 (14 Geo. III, c. 45).

[493] Only Hume's letter remains: Hume to William Strahan, 1 Mar., in *Letters of David Hume*, ed. J.Y.T. Greig (2 vols, Oxford, 1932), ii, 286–7 (no. 496).

[494] Horace, *Epistles*, bk 1, ch. 2, verse 32; trans. 'Rogues watch by night the traveller to enthral; And will not you awake to save you all?'.

[495] See pp 89 n. 205

glorious uncertainty in the law. says Mr Donaldson come into my proposal for a certain term of years. pay all expenses – make friends – agree in the bill. Sir, very great stress has b*een* laid that the English Booksellers, poor fellows, they are the most stupid blockheads in the world; they h*ave* not understood what Lord Mansfield could not understand, **{116}** what the majority *of the* Judges could not comprehend, w*ith* all their misconceptions h*ave* had the imprudence, & assurance to come to this H*ouse* to ask for relief. & this is the way these p*eople* h*ave* b*een* treated. every act has b*een* made use of to distress them. they h*ave* b*een* traduced for their imprudence in coming to this H*ouse* for redress when they h*ave* b*een* deceived where a great many h*ave* b*een* deceived, & when they h*ave* paid great sums of money for Copyrights. this is a case of compassion. tho' it immediately follows the decision *of the* H*ouse* of L*ords*. yet does not controvert that decision, it does not overthrow that decision. pray, Sir, what is all the Statute Law, but an amelioration *of the* common Law *of the* Land. why do many acts of P*arliament* begin w*ith* "whereas great inconveniences h*ave* arisen f*rom* the law as it now stands." do we sit here for no other purpose but to tax the p*eople*? I think the most glorious privilege, the most glorious power this H*ouse* h*ave* is that of redressing the grievances *of the* p*eople* wherever we can. Sir, upon the whole of this case you h*ave* the sanction of great authority. the cause of Literature depends upon it: for who will digest? who will compile great works confess they are to be paid for their Labour. if that is not the case, Booksellers will not be able to pay their Authors. we h*ave* not the spirit in this *country* **{117}** to work for nothing. we must be paid. tho' I love, and honour the army, if you take away the pay f*rom* the army I should not be fond of going to the West Indies. not even the Church. there is not such spunk in the Sons of Zebudee[496] you would not h*ave* a very large attendance here. I leave the whole of this matter now thinking that as my Learned friend has told me my fire was dead, my zeal has b*een* abated [so I do not wish to] break his heart. that does not lessen any eagerness. I love to comfort the Widow, the desolate, & oppressed. there will be a number of families, if they h*ave* not relief f*rom* this bill, starving. Mr Donaldson will h*ave* very ample compensation. his expense £1000 —he has b*een* wrong six times in the nine. I think the Booksellers h*ave* a right to the favour they ask, notwithstanding they h*ave* traduced you, & me.

Sir Richard Sutton. There is one point I wish could be cleared up to our satisfaction. the H*onourable* G*entleman* who moved you leaving the Chair told us, the bill may be altered in the C*ommittee*. now, Sir, tho I wish myself to give relief, who do think that many of them, tho' some may h*ave* known better, many of them h*ave* b*een* ignorantly drawn in. I am satisfied w*ith* that mode of a **{118}** term. to the prejudice of those now intitled to it. is so prejudicial to Justice, it is impossible to speak upon it. I apprehend that mode is pinned upon us. this bill is brought in under an O*rder* to grant them a further term. it is impossible w*ithou*t a fresh O*rder* to alter that mode. this is a practice *of the* H*ouse* I am not acquainted w*ith*. I should be much obliged to you to clear up that point.

Speaker. The bill must be brought in in pursuance *of the* leave.

Mr. Field. With regard to the idea of injustice to the Counter petitioners if this bill gives a relief. By a new term it affects the interest of the Counter petitioners, & deprives

[496] Zebedee was the father of James and John, two of Jesus's Apostles.

them *of the* right. w*ith* regard to the idea[497] of their right, it is the right of all the World. w*ith* regard to a work [and they] claim a protection [it] was not open to them: that is at the time the author sold the identical work. an Author writes a book: while it is in his hands, he undoubtedly has the sole disposal of it. in O*rder* to publish it, he contracts w*ith* the Bookseller for the sale of it. at that time no man has a right to it. every man has a right to print—but Printers had not at the time Mr Pope, or Judge Blackstone since **{119}** [they gave a right so] no other Printer has a right to print that work. these are p*eople* that under that under the idea that the Author had a right over that particular work; give him a price for being the sole printer of that particular work [the booksellers] h*ave* given that price, you shall enjoy this for a perpetuality: the publick h*ave* taken that away [the counter petitioners] obtaind that victory, may surety out of their generosity give you a term as a part of what they h*ave* recovered the whole, they may give you a poor man that wh*ich* you cant afford to be w*ithou*t but wh*ich* they can afford to be w*ithout*. says the H*onourable Gentleman* you take that away f*rom* them. I do not call it taking it away f*rom* them, bec*ause* no other was in possession. all who h*ave* entered into possession are attended to in this bill. I am not making a speech, Sir, but explaining the ground of this bill. I will take it upon the ground *of the* Statute of Queen Anne. what does that Statute do? every body that supports the decision *of the* H*ouse* of L*ords* says, that at the time of making the Statute of Queen Anne, no such thing existed as Copyright at Common Law. the Judges, & Lords who argued against the decision *of the* Court of King's Bench tell you that act declares, & shews the Legislature had **{120}** no idea then [but] some p*eople* h*ave* a little doubted that the act spoke two Languages: that there is room to think they were not so clear in that proposition: at the same time not so clear the other way to declare [the law.] I take it upon the argument *of the* decision *of the* H*ouse* of L*ords*. they say the act clearly decides against literary property. how did the P*ublic* stand [in respect of] that case? the Authors, & Printers of Books apply to the H*ouse* for legal protection. they stand in the light of having for ages b*een* in actual possession *of the* exercise of that exclusive right[in copies.] The Legislature are applied to in the eighth of Queen Anne. what is the act they made. I say they stood then in that light of having no right to apply to P*arliament* to exclude the rest *of the* Trade in such books as our present application is for, that is, books purchased, but not f*rom* Authors. what is the provision of P*arliament*? in this first place, that act extends both to books already printed, & to books hereafter to be printed. but the provisions are totally distinct, & upon different ground. the books to be printed comes within the purview *of the* Act of P*arliament* for encouragement of Learning. G*entleman* say it is no encouragement to Learning to give a privilege to books already **{121}** printed. it is the very object I mean, & this bill goes to them. we are told we take away the publick enjoyment of that right. you exactly did in the same manner as by this bill. you invaded the private right of all printers who were then in possession *of the* right. I desire to know the distinction of that case f*rom* the present, only in this, that that act does not take into consideration [already] printed Books. this bill has provision for every hardship of that case. I beg leave now upon this ground to say how the Legislature look'd upon the exercise of that valuable right of those honest, good Printers that ought not to be deprived *of the* right of publishing that wh*ich* was quite in common. they brand it w*ith* the name of [purchases they had made in] the preamble [but they are] taking that wh*ich*

[497] The MS suggests 'idea' is inserted for 'identity', but identity is not crossed out.

other p*eople* had bought. by making a profit of what was due to the other. I intended to h*ave* mentioned this, but was in some degree of confusion. – it is a principle that ought to be met w*ith*. I never meant to flinch f*rom* that part *of the* argument. d*one* upon the principle of this. I say the Legislature has d*one* things *of the* like kind – the 8th year of K*ing* George 2. an act for the encouragement of engraving.[498] now that act **{122}** does not go full to the present case. that act looks into futurity. it gives encouragement for new inventions in engraving. a monopoly for a further term of fourteen years in imitation *of the* second clause *of the* 8th of Queen Anne. but I would follow that by another act, wh*ich* is the seventh of George 1st.[499] that act recites, Sir, the ill practices made use of by engravers notwithstanding the other act, & you see how the Legislature has all along looked upon Artists taking the inventions of others, & making an use of them for their own benefit wh*ich* others had paid a consideration for. this Act of George 1, recites the hardship of persons encroaching [on others works] but there is one particular that goes precisely, & in point to the great object of Justice of this case, it is a strong parliamentary precedent. Sir, it is the cause w*ith* relation to Mrs. Hogarth. she lodgd a petition, wh*ich* I h*ave* out *of the* Journals[500] laid bef*ore* the H*ouse*, when the general bill was in P*arliament* for encouraging the art of engraving. – extending the provision *of the* first act. she petitioned the H*ouse* setting forth that her husband &c (see the petition)[501] in consequence of that there was a special provision in the bill (see the clause wh*ich* Mr Field reads.)[502] so, Sir, it gave the term for **{123}** invention, not fourteen years, but for twenty years: after the first term of fourteen years had expired, & the rest *of the* Trade had gone into the printing of it. there is a clause likewise to save those who h*ave* d*one* it

Sir Richard Sutton. The H*onourable Gentleman* has intirely misunderstood part of my argument. I conceive taking away the right is an injury, as well as taking away the possession. I apprehend the act of Queen Anne gave a protection to living Authors where they had no kind of protection at that time, whereas now there is a reasonable protection for the encouragement of Authors.

Lord Beauchamp.[503] I do not mean to follow the Learned G*entleman* through the whole of his argument respecting the act of Queen Anne, but will confine myself to what he said last relative to Mr. Hogarth. that Statute stands upon a very different predicament. it was a specifick remedy for another case. it was grounded upon the very extraordinary merit of her Husband. the Legislature knew the extent of its operation. it [related to] no third person either in the case of Mr Buckley[504] who published an edition of Thuanius[505] – yet the Legislature f*rom* the ingenuity *of the* man, made a Statute **{124}** vesting an extraordinary

[498] Engraving Copyright Act 1734 (8 Geo. II, c. 13).

[499] This is clearly a mistake as it is a reference to the Engraving Copyright Act 1766 (7 Geo. III, c. 38).

[500] 14 May 1767 (*CJ*, xxxi, 359–60).

[501] There is an asterisk here and on the opposite page in the manuscript is the following text "no Engraver ever had an idea of any property, but what is given by that Statute. the case *of the* Engravers was one *of the* greatest grounds of argument against the Booksellers (reads) Petitioner's chief support arises & c (reads the petition)".

[502] Engraving Copyright Act 1766, s. 3.

[503] Francis Seymour Conway†* (1743–1822), MP for Orford.

[504] Samuel Buckley, the bookseller.

[505] Jacques Auguste de Thou (1553–1617), *Jac. Augusti Thuani Historiarum sui temporis Tomus primus* (Buckley, 1733) (ESTC: T98490).

term on him[506] on account of his particular merit. w*ith* an additional clause to make the importation of it highly penal. if there had b*een* any thing of that sort, I should h*ave* b*een* a ready advocate for the bill. if cases of hardship are brought bef*ore* the H*ouse* the Legislature provides for them. the present bill does not discriminate in any degree. it confounds those who h*ave* made large fortunes by Copyrights, w*ith* those, if any such there are who are in the King's Bench, having purchased Copies that were reduced to a small value, that is my objection to the bill. unless I hear arguments more convincing I never can consent to saddle the publick w*ith* a new monopoly injurious to the publick, as well as individuals who h*ave* b*een* overborn by the monopoly. I think it the most imprudent demand after the practices they h*ave* b*een* guilty of. It gives me some pleasure the H*onourable* G*entleman* looks upon this decision *of the* H*ouse* of L*ords* as a victory for the publick. I always look'd upon it in that light. I lookd upon monopolies [as odious] yet a monopoly of Literary property [is] the only sort of monopoly, that should subsist in this *country*. I h*ave* read many works wrote upon that Statute penn'd in the wisest manners to the purpose it was intended, to answer **{125}** the purpose of encouraging Learning. a preamble if it does not create a new right, it was a very extraordinary one indeed. if any right prexisted in Common Law. no favour to D*onaldson* that by Statute that right should exist no longer. it never was made for the encouragement of Booksellers. the merit of booksellers, & the merit of Authors stands in a very different situation, tho for the purpose of arguing this bill, G*entlemen* h*ave* attempted to blend the two together as if you could not separate them. the Legislature were so cautious not to put them in the hands *of the* booksellers, that there was a clause to fix the price of books[507] [which was repealed][508] in the late reign, is a [example of the] exposition *of the* Wit the Legislature had at the time of passing that Statute. the case of Scotland is alluded to. the H*onourable* G*entleman* thinks the Counsel made a National cause of it: I think the case of Scotland an exceeding hard one, if we pass the present act w*ith* the further extension *of the* monopoly. you subject the Kingdom of Scotland to a further extent of that right, bec*ause* it was deemed the Common law existed in this *country* wh*ich* never existed there at all. as a British M*ember* of P*arliament*, I rise up to enter my protest against that particular hardship. the H*onourable* G*entleman* seemed to beat a Learned Baronet w*ith* **{126}** some degree of [hardship when] printing was extended in the Kingdom of Scotland. I think that argument cuts the opposite way. he said presses had b*een* multiplied in Falkirk—if a number of p*eople* having faith in the late determination *of the* H*ouse* of L*ords* h*ave* gone into the printing branch, will you by an ex post facto law oblige those p*eople* to renounce the blessings in wh*ich* they h*ave* lately gone. surely they are intitled to the protection *of the* Law. what faith can there be in the subjects of England, if one day the Court of King's Bench determin'd one way, then the Supreme Judicature set that determination aside, then the Legislature to begin afresh to extend this monopoly. Sir, in my opinion the Booksellers *of the* City of London are exceeding safe f*rom* a variety of circumstances. they are placed in the seat of Learning, & there resort of Learned men. a variety of circumstances will ever hinder the bookseller in the c*ountry* will hinder the Booksellers of Scotland f*rom* entering into the printing business. there are sufficient branches of trade sufficient to occupy them – one branch of trade should

[506] Printing of Thuanus Histories Act 1733 (7 Geo. II, c. 24), vesting right of printing in Samuel Buckley for 14 years.

[507] Copyright Act 1709 (8 Anne, c. 19), s. 4.

[508] Importation Act 1738 (12 Geo. II, c. 36), s. 3.

not be the peculiar favourite of this H*ouse.* to extend monopolies when they increase trade may be serviceable. I do conceive that the present bill can in no shape be moulded so as to answer the purpose I throw out.

{127} Sir, let the particular circumstances of each case be stated to the H*ouse*, & I shall be very ready to give a particular remedy. that is a bill as much for the relief *of the* Heirs, & [successors] of Mr. Thompson[509] who afterwards found his way to a seat in this H*ouse* as to any Bookseller who may be the subject *of the* present conversation, I shall vote, Sir, for your leaving the Chair.

Mr Jollifee.[510] The opposition to this bill has b*een* so ably treated by the N*oble* L*ord*, & the H*onourable* G*entleman* on the other side *of the* H*ouse* who always speaks w*ith* a peculiar degree of ingenuity whenever he takes the pains to consider the Subject. It is highly impertinent in me to attempt to give my sentiments upon the Subject but I am so averse to the longer continuation *of the* monopoly, wh*ich* has too long already subsisted to the great prejudice *of the* publick, I cant help entering my protest against it, & stand forth to declare how sincerely I am averse to it. if it was meant to give relief to Authors: if they were asking for peculiar encouragement, no man would go further than I would, no man would be more ready to lend his aid upon such an occasion, than I myself. Authors are a very great ornament to every c*ountry* by them the actions of great men are perpetuated. w*ithou*t them fame after this life would be no more. but, Sir, the object *of the* present bill is to vest **{128}** in Booksellers, it says in Authors, tho' they seem to h*ave* very little concern in it. it vests in the Booksellers an absolute right to vend books for a limited time, wh*ich* time is to be mentioned in the bill. Authors can't themselves receive the least benefit, or advantage f*rom* it. the only inducement that can make Authors anxious that booksellers may make a tolerable advantage of that wh*ich* he has sold to them. I believe that all books of any real consequence now in print. are sold to some Bookseller. the Authors cant receive the benefit. the Booksellers may. the greatest pretence that has b*een* made for this bill is that the Booksellers h*ave* bought at great prices copy rights, & h*ave* not receiv'd an adequate price for them. has any such fact b*een* stated an evidence was brought to prove that £49,000 had b*een* invested some time, or other in literary property. he never attempted to prove that any one person was a loser. he never stated the original sums given: never told you what was the loss when those books came to be sold, or if the terms were expired – fourteen, or even eventually twenty eight. he never told you what would be the loss. Sir, it has b*een* much insisted upon that if every person who is suffered to print had not the sole right to print, incorrect editions would be perpetually printed: and the Learned Counsel at the bar said we should h*ave* **{129}** the name of Sydney[511] instead of [another author] we should h*ave* the worst of actions attributed to the greatest of [authors.] if incorrect editions were published I am clear they could never sell. it was then said that all kinds of books that is books both good, & bad, printed w*ith* a bad type, & upon bad paper would go out into the world. I should be exceeding glad: every body would h*ave* an opportunity of reading books (now) too high for men of moderate Fortune. I h*ave* tolerable good eyes, I would read any

[509]This was a reference to Richard Tonson† (*d.* 1772), MP for New Windsor 1768–72, son of Jacob Tonson: *Morning Chronicle*, 21 May 1774.

[510]William Jolliffee†* (1745–1802), MP for Petersfield.

[511]Sir Philip Sidney.

book, printed upon paper no better than News papers are printed upon, w*ith* a type no better, than a balad. Sir, it is undoubtedly right that Authors should h*ave* a certain time to enjoy the sole right of their own labour, they ought to receive a consideration for the part they h*ave* taken. w*ith* that idea patents are granted to persons for any new inventions. w*ith* that idea the Legislature in Queen Anne's time granted to Authors an absolute term of fourteen years, & an eventual one of twenty eight. it has b*een* stated that all men who are Authors of any eminence h*ave* sold the copy right to the Petitioners. it is fact, & very right it should be so. they are men of great property as Booksellers, they are the persons who can best afford to run the risk *of the* Sale of Books. **{130}** but, Sir, the only argument I h*ave* heard advanced by Counsel, or advanced by *Gentleman* in favour *of the* bill is, that the London Booksellers bought their copy rights under the idea that there was a perpetual right vested in the Authors themselves. now I beg leave to say that I apprehend no such idea could possibly h*ave* entered into the minds *of the* Booksellers in the year 1640 was the first time that copy right began to be established. they continued the sale of Copy rights under the licensing act[512] to 1691.[513] by the Revolution the prerogative *of the* Crown being curtailed, it was necessary for the Booksellers to apply to P*arliament* & they did apply to P*arliament* for relief in 1709.[514] P*arliament* granted them a term for twenty one years. that term expired in 1731. they applied again, P*arliament* refused it. P*arliament* adopted the idea wh*ich* I trust this H*ouse* will do. they rejected the petition, bec*ause* they thought it would continue the monopoly they thought already had subsisted too long. I trust this H*ouse* will do so upon this occasion.

Gov*ernor* Johnstone. The matter of fact to wh*ich* I rise to speak is this, it has b*een* asserted by an Honourable M*ember* whom I don't see in my eye, who generally gives the H*ouse* so much pleasure when he rises, that in the causes against Mr Donaldson **{131}** that he had b*een* condemned in costs upon six. now I don't know where he has got this information; but I am authorized to say it is not so. that he has prevailed as yet in every cause that has b*een* brought against him. I asserted that before upon hearing the H*onourable* G*entleman* assert the contrary; I did inquire again. if my information is improper; I shall state f*rom* whom I had it. Sir, he has prevailed in every one suit. there are two now depending for Yorick's Sermans,[515] & for Shenstone.[516] I stated it the other night. but as it is not the same attendance, I shall state it again, not in hopes of altering the H*ouse* yet it will lead to the q*uestion* being better understood w*ithou*t any [need] of a division in a full H*ouse* – supposing the Statute of Queen Anne requires particular observation, as the name *of the* author, & other things, & suppose no such man existed, you must not condemn him, 'till you hear his plea. w*ith* regard to Shenstone's works, if he says not

[512]Licensing of the Press Act 1665 (17 Chas. II, c. 4) was extended by the Administration of Intestates' Estates Act 1685 (1 Jas. II, c. 17), s. 15.

[513]The Act actually expired in 1695.

[514]Copyright Act 1709.

[515]*Becket & Others v Donaldson* (1771) (bill: TNA, C 12/1042/11). The book in question may have been *The Sermons of Mr Yorick* (1770) (ESTC: N24107); *Whiston & Others v Donaldson* (1771) (TNA, C 12/64/26). This case was about Sherlock's *Sermons*, but it is the most likely candidate. The sermons of Yorick were actually by Laurence Sterne: Lansing van der Heyden Hammond, *Laurence Sterne's Sermons of Mr. Yorick* (New Haven, CT, 1948).

[516]*Dodsley v Donaldson* (1770–3) (bill: TNA, C 12/1321/36). The relevant work was William Shenstone, *The Works in Verse and Prose of William Shenstone, Esq* (3 vols, 1768, 1770) (ESTC: T92448).

one thing, but what has b*een* publish'd bef*ore* in Dodsley's Collection, & Magazines[517] he may be

Col*onel* Onslow. In points of this nature we can only speak f*rom* our Instructions. I was informed so. that I give the G*entleman* my word, & honour. the H*onourable* G*entleman* does not mean that I made it. I was informed of it in the Court of requests.[518] I shall **{132}** take it very ill if I h*ave* b*een* misinformed. as to Shenstone, & Yorick it is very likely they may get off some such quibble.

Mr. Field. I rise to a fact, The evidence of Mr. Wallis[519] mentioned the names *of the* thirteen suits in Chancery. he said in several of those suits the injunctions were continued. if that is gaining a suit, I don't know.

Gov*ernor* Johnstone. It is f*rom* Mr. Wallis I had the facts, except in two [suits] in favour of Mr Donaldson.

Mr. Dempster: I observe the H*ouse* extremely impatient, yet I hope they will accept my apology, if I say a few words to this most extraordinary bill. the beauty of this H*ouse* is there is nothing so easy as to bring in a bill: & the beauty of it likewise is, when any thing violent, any thing strong is brought in, there is nothing so easy as to get it out again. I rise to speak relative to the parallel he draws between the act of Queen Anne, & the present bill prayed for. in the act of Queen Anne it was necessary to give twenty one years. the Author might h*ave* published his work, & bef*ore* he could h*ave* reaped any benefit, he might instead h*ave* b*een* deprived of that benefit. had any **{133}** Author enjoyed any term of fourteen years bef*ore* –permit me to say I h*ave* felt great uneasiness during this bill. we seem to be a Court of Appeal, not in a Legislative capacity. Judging upon the decision *of the* other H*ouse* wh*ich* has b*een* decided upon the soundest principles, more than upon prejudice – to sacrifice a monopoly – I can't help stating some *of the* evidence upon your paper. it appears they h*ave* pushed this monopoly too far. no books has escaped them. there is no Printer that is not under their lash. as to religious books, the publication of them has b*een* punished in the most severe manner. it was given in evidence above Stairs that a poor Bookseller published the Pilgrim's Progress[520] [which I] never read. it is a book of great piety. it was wrote by John Bunyan, to wh*ich* these was not the least title pretended. the Bookseller was threatened w*ith* the tenor, not of a decision but the tenor of a Chancery suit. the poor man was forced to deliver up every Copy. he had no compensation. we h*ave* had an evidence at the bar frightened out of his senses, frightened out of his flesh. a poor, unhappy, miserable spectre.

[517]Robert Dodsley (1704–64), Pall Mall. As to his magazines, see James Tierney, 'The Museum, the "Super-Excellent Magazine"', *Studies in English Literature, 1500–1900*, xiii (1973), 503; as to his collection of poems and plays, see M.F. Suarez, 'Dodsley's "Collection of Poems" and the Ghost of Pope: The Politics of Literary Reputation', *The Papers of the Bibliographical Society of America*, lxxxviii (1994), 189; Donald Eddy, 'Dodsley's "Collection of Poems by Several Hands" (6 vols), 1758 Index of Authors', *The Papers of the Bibliographical Society of America*, ix (1966), 9; Thomas Dabbs, 'The Rise and Fall of Dodsley's Old Plays', *Studies in Language and Culture*, xx (1994).

[518]For an introduction to these local courts, W.H.D. Winder, 'The Courts of Requests', *Law Quarterly Review*, lii (1936), 369; William Cornish, Patrick Polden *et al.*, *The Oxford History of the Laws of England* (Oxford, 2010), 851–7.

[519]Part I: Chapter 3: Second reading.

[520]John Bunyan* (1628–88), *The Pilgrim's Progress from this World, to that which is to come* (Ponder, 1678) (ESTC: R12339).

I never saw any thing like except Romeo's Apothecary.[521] w*ithou*t notice, the man said he had no notice of it, he was served w*ith* two bills in Chancery **{134}** he had a wife, & family to maintain, himself just set up. they at last compounded the matter. he gave up the books: they were not paid for. he gave up the Copper Plates, these he was paid for. they made him ask pardon for what he had d*one* in this manner, they settled this legal prosecution. there was a joint purse made for the purpose. these are practices it is impossible for us to countenance.

not the case *of the* Scotch Booksellers, but a few wealthy Monopolists in this c*ountry*. I do assent there is not the least shadow of proof upon your papers of any man reduced to beggary upon these proceedings – men who all grown fat upon this monopoly. if they do sustain a loss [the London Booksellers] are best able to sustain it. having said this I do hope this will be the last time you will have the trouble of painful long sittings in that Chair. the last time I hope we shall ever hear any more of that Subject.

At 25 minutes after 9 the House divided.[522]

The numbers for the Speakers leaving the Chair:	*57*
Against:	*26*

Mr. Whitworth then took the Chair in the Committee.

{135} Mr. Field proposed 14 years—**Mr. Harris**,[523] said, there was another body of men as well as Booksellers, Authors. I am afraid, he said, this clause will lessen all terms [so protection is] shorter. if that Authors sell for seven years, he would have a right for fourteen. I either object to this clause, or wish to have some other provision.

Mr. Field then referred **Mr. Harris** to another part of the bill as satisfactory.

Governor Johnstone. Suppose a man has sold his whole right to a Bookseller [and he is now] dead [and] within three elapsing you give a term of 11 years more to the Bookseller wh*ich* ought to return to the author.

Mr. Edmund Burke. When an Author dies, the act of Queen Anne has made no provisions – all we do is that fourteen years be substituted instead of that perpetuity.

Mr. Mackworth. I should be glad to know whether any particular Sum was given upon the idea of a perpetual right. if not you fill up the blank with fourteen years. which is too much. under that idea I shall move an amendment to that. I move seven – this was opposed by **Mr. Burke**, & **Mr. Field**, & was dropped – **{136}**

Mr. Harris proposed to h*ave* ten Copies deliver'd to the British Museum –

[521] The apothecary who gave Romeo a sleeping draft which made him appear dead: *Romeo and Juliet*, Act V, scene 1.

[522] *CJ*, xxxiv, 757.

[523] James Harris†* senior (1709–80), MP for Christchurch.

Mr. Pulteney.[524] In what respect is this clause better than the Act of Queen Anne which is evaded?

Mr. Field There is a notice that seven days

Mr. Pulteney. They should forfeit the privilege unless they gave the books. the books will never be delivered.

Solicitor Gen*eral* Wedderburne. If there is a common attention to look over the Copy it can not be evaded. you may as well make a bill that everybody should h*ave* a compleat Copy who buys from a Bookseller.

Mr. Harris. Besides Authors, there are the p*eople* of England: it would be right to make all books of the last Century totally free.

Solicitor General.[525] Every book he can derive a title from, the Author is provided for by this act. to draw a point of time would be unjust. those books not derived from titles are Common property as free as air, should be the subject of a different act. running limitation. at present we are giving relief to those under titles, no matter how ancient the title. the Poets of the age of Queen Elizabeth **{137}** [provided they have] title, the title to Milton can be produced. that the first property sold for £15. the transmitted property is now very considerable.

Mr. Harris. Bacon, and Spencer.[526] Bacon has been claimed by the Millars, Thompson has claimed the right in Spencer an hundred years back.

Col*onel* Onslow. They got somebody to write the life.

{141}

Thursday May 19th 1774

The H*ouse* was very thin, & the Booksellers bill came on.

Mr. Dempster said, it was a reversal of the decree of the H*ouse* of L*ords*.

Mr. Cavendish,[527] *sai*d if that were the case the H*ouse* of L*ords* might by a determination prevent this H*ouse* from ever bringing in a bill to alter the Common law.

Mr. Dempster then observing the thinness of the H*ouse* decided **{142}** the H*ouse* might be reckoned. which was done, and there were forty members – **Mr. Stewart**[528] gave a clause to **Sir Rich*ar*d Sutton**, to give the Scotch Booksellers leave to print. it being objected to, he said, I did not mean they should print books to send to England to be sold, but to be sold in Scotland. there is not one single book that will not now be claimed. some Booksellers have agreed to it, but have since altered their opinion.

Mr. Field[529] said, it was against the principle of the bill—

At this time there happened not to be forty members present, and some little disturbance was heard in the lobby, which arose from **Mr. Char*les* Fox** proposing **Lord Beaucchamp** not to go into the H*ouse* of wh*ich* **Mr. William Burke** made a complaint to the H*ouse*. I saw, said he, a M*ember* stopping a G*entleman* coming into the H*ouse* he not only does not do his own businesss, but prevents others.

[524] William Pulteney† (1729–1805), MP for Cromarty.

[525] Alexander Wedderburn.

[526] Francis Bacon; Edmund Spenser* (*d.* 1599).

[527] Henry Cavendish†* (1732–1804), MP for Lostwithiel.

[528] Probably John Stewart† (c. 1723–1781), MP for Arundel.

[529] Paul Feilde.

Sir Richard Sutton. Whether he detained him by force, or by persuasion?

Mr. William Burke. There is nothing more violent than the persuasion of an ingenious man. I desire the opinion of the Chair –

{143} Speaker. I can have no opinion of this.

Mr. Field. This bill is to be exprobated per fas et nefas[530] –

he was going on when **Mr. Demspter** desird the H*ouse* might be again told–**Mr. W*illia*m Burke** told the Speaker he should send for Members: but however upon telling the H*ouse* there were not 40 in: & the H*ouse* was adjourned of course –

[27 May 1774]
{159}
Booksellers Bill

{160} Mr. Cha*rles* Fox: The q*uestion* is simply this *of the* Proprietors part Petition for the bill, part against it. the one desire it f*rom* a case of compassion – the party against it, says I thought I had a legal right, so far my claim is as good as my adversary. it has turned out I had a right, I desire I may not be kept 14 years more. this has gone to the third reading w*ith* a total disregard to precedent, w*ith* a total disregard to the O*rders* of private bills. first the letter, then the practice. neither the taking the letter, nor the practice, nor even any Idea *of the* Spirit coming up to their intention. they chuse to knock in the head a rule of P*arliament* in O*rder* to go to this business, great care has b*een* taken to bring it into as thin a H*ouse* as possible. 40 M*embers*: they wish'd to h*ave*, there is not one member in my own opinion but must be against such Robbery. as much has b*een* said about counting the H*onourable* G*entlemen* **{161}** if ever in any case it is right, I think in most cases, it is when peculiar pains were taken – they were disappointed, for fear of having too many hearers they were too few [and it] may happen again, whether in this day, at this time of year, the H*ouse* will send it up to another H*ouse* of P*arliament* – arguments are used for the sake of talking, not for the sake of making any impression upon any body. the ground they went upon was the Opinion *of the* booksellers in Common law. they were in wilfull ignorance. there was a clause offere'd the other day to take Scotland out *of the* bill.[531] such was always the decision in Scotland. they are to be deprived of th*at* right never disputed in th*at* c*ountry* and at last decided in their favour, they are to be deprived of it bec*ause* some booksellers – they had b*een* misled in to a mistake of their Right. the book sellers of Scotland are to be taxed in O*rder* to compensate **{162}** the Booksellers of England.

Mr. S. Fox[532] spoke against the bill upon the same ground as his Brother –

Mr. Dempster, was up to speak, but **Mr. W*illia*m Burke** desird to H*ouse* might be cleard, **Mr. Dempster** then spoke as follows –

I can't find fault w*ith* my H*onourable* f*riend* for moving to clear the H*ouse* bef*ore* I spoke. I can't see how he gained any thing by it. I am rather further f*rom* the close of wh*ich* I meant to say than I should h*ave* b*een*. I am one of those who never in publick or in private chuse to do any thing ungentlemanlike – having just secur'd to his breaking up the H*ouse*, he said, I rise up for the last time solemnly to enter my protest against the most abusive

[530] Trans. 'for right or wrong'.

[531] See Part I: Chapter 6: Saving and Exclusion.

[532] The abbreviation is unclear, but it is clear that it is a reference to Stephen Fox† (1745–74), MP for Salisbury.

purpose P*arliament* has ever been applied to for. I could h*ave* patience to debate it to the end *of the* Session. if my strength could hold it out. Donaldson has received **{163}** a decree. in February he obtained it, was put into the legal right, into the Exercise of it. he was engaged in publishing many books, wh*ich* is not the work of a minute, th*at* bill provides for books only th*ose* are printed, not printing. another very material point, they are giving relief to the book-sellers upon the Idea of property – I apprehend the book-sellers who h*ave* bought M*essrs* Millars and Tonsons[533] book, may h*ave* part refunded to them. this bill is intended to give a Monopoly of one *of the* articles of Trade th*at* ought to be the most free. when the Act of 2nd[534] Anne passed, so cautious P*arliament* were at th*at* time; th*at* least authors should make use of temporary privilege only. to [protect] against the publishing, th*at* they inserted a clause in th*at* bill authorising the Lord Chancellor to regulate, and fix the price at wh*ich* those books under monopoly were to be sold.[535] if any thing can justify monopoly it is such a Clause as **{164}** this, otherwise great extortion might be raised upon the publick several years after this Clause was repealed.[536] I believe the law now passing continues th*at* Act. you will h*ave* the Statute of Queen Anne extended 14 years longer over all book, and the subject put into a worse condition than he hitherto has b*een*. Sir, I beg pardon – having troubled the H*ouse* so long, I am perfectly sincere in this. I look upon the injustice done to Scotland *of the* most glaring kind, as to the injustice to an individual, I don't insist upon the one so much as the other [Parliament] may induce to alter the law of Scotland, but no reason should induce this H*ouse* by an ex post facto law –

Lord Beauchamp. With respect to the mode in wh*ich* this bill has b*een* opposed. I don't conceive in the Opinion of any one man th*at* th*at* G*entleman* has b*een* guilty of ungentlemanlike behaviour. I **{165}** saw it not a fortnight ago in the case *of the* West Indian loan bill.[537] it is justifiable when there is little hope of it being discussed by a fair, and impartial Jury, none remain but those solicited f*rom* personal solicitation. it is a bill totally new and unprecedented in its nature. a bill (depending the suits) the most flagrant [and there is] no motive but th*at* the London Booksellers h*ave* more friends in this H*ouse*, and are more likely to h*ave* their interest attended to than the book-sellers of Scotland. this is a precedent th*at* ought to be resisted in the first instance. p*eople* with*ou*t doors – h*ave* no remedy but th*at* of Complaint, it is paying a compliment to one set of men at the expense *of the* other. it is subversive *of the* first principles of Justice. I did not attend the Co*mmittee* in its progress, it assumes more than it contended for – praying further time to compensate lost [property] a clause to extend to rights purchased, or otherwise acquired, by which **{166}** you will open the widest door – the right *of the* Stationers Company is attack'd – the Attorney General coming at this moment into the H*ouse* his Lordship concluded by saying, I am glad to see th*at* learned G*entleman*, I flatter myself his Arguments will h*ave* some weight –

[533] Andrew Millar; Jacob Tonson (1714–67), app. 1729–31, tr. until 1767, Strand.

[534] This should be the Act of 8th Anne (the Copyright Act 1709).

[535] Copyright Act 1709 (8 Anne, c. 19), s. 4.

[536] Importation Act 1738 (12 Geo. II, c. 36), s. 3.

[537] It became the Legal Rate of Interests Act 1774 (14 Geo. III, c. 74); 19 May 1774 (*CJ*, xxxiv, 774).

The Speaker then put the q*uestion* th*at* this bill be read a third time[538]

Yeah:	*40*
Noes	*22*
The Noes went forth:	*18 Majority*

PARLIAMENTARY DIARY OF LORD FOLKESTONE (LATER EARL OF RADNOR)

Wiltshire History Centre: Parliamentary diaries of the second Earl Radnor, MS 1946/4/2F/1/3.
{NP} marks the start of a new page in the manuscript notebook; the pages are unnumbered.

March 24th 1774[539]

On a Motion for a Bill for the Relief of Booksellers by granting in them the Copies of Books for a Term, spoke as follows.

Sir, I really did not think of troubling you on this occasion because I thought a Proposition for the Relief of these Booksellers, which an honourable Friend of mine, who is not now in his Place (Sir Richard Sutton) had drawn up, was that which the worthy Chairman of the {NP} Committee on their Petition (M: Feilde)[540] would have adopted, & which I would have given my assent to, because it was just, & reasonable; for this present Motion I can not: Sir, it is upon this occasion, as I have observed it upon many others that Gentlemen fond of their own Ideas have carried them to an extreme; I neither agree with those who think the Assignees of Authors (for it is in that Light the Booksellers ought to be considered here upon this Occasion) ought to have the Relief that is contended for on one side, nor that they ought to have no Relief, as is contended on the other: I think they clearly are entitled to Relief since the Judgment of the King's Bench in 1769:[541] though to make difficulties in the manner of administering Relief I would consent to carry it to a longer Period, but not {NP} by vesting the Copies, & nothing on Monopoly, but by allowing an additional demand over, & above the intrinsic value of the Books, which value shall be ascertained before Commissioners, to the Purchase Money is fairly reinstated[542] to them; To meet there loses, I should move to leave out the words such time[543] to vesting the Copies, in order to insert the words "purchasers of Copy-Rights within a limited Time", if this paper in the question I must vote against the Relief as proposed.

Seconded by Sir Cecil Wray.[544]

On the Division for the Continuance of the first words

Ayes: 50. Tellers. Mr: Sawbridge, & Mr. Feilde.

538 *CJ*, xxiv, 788.

539 Cavendish, {S29–30}.

540 Paul Feilde.

541 *Millar v Taylor* (1769) 4 Burr 2303 (98 ER 201).

542 This word is unclear.

543 This does not fit the motion made, and the word before "time" is unclear.

544 Sir Cecil Wray† (1734–1805), MP for East Retford.

Nos 25. Tellers. Folkestone. & Mr. Graves.
On the Main Question[545] in the Minority.
Ayes. 54 Tellers, Mr. Burke, & Mr. Whitworth.
Noes 16. Tellers. Mr. Thurlow Att*orney* Gen*eral*, & Mr: C. Fox.

{NP} **May 13th 1774.**
On a Motion to adjourn the further Hearing of Council upon the Bill for relief of Booksellers, spoke as follows,

Sir, I cannot agree with the Hon*ourable* Gentleman (M: Feilde) who has proposed to postpone this business, because we have at present an open day, & we hear by Experience the Difficulty there is of finding one at this Time, for we sat [illegible] last night a full hour & half on this very Question.

A short time afterwards spoke again, I mean shortly to answer the noble Lord (L: Beauchamp), who was he an Agreement to take Place, of having the Council tonight, & adjourning the Debate on the Bill 'till another day: The certain Consequence of that will be the House will be forced to rise from want of 40 Members, & therefore thou' I by no reason mean to engage to push the Debate to-night, I am {NP} likewise desirous of being understood that I make no Engagement that I will not-push it.
In the Division[546]
Ayes 26. Tellers: Mr: T. Townshend, & Mr: P Feilde.
Noe 34. Tellers, Folkestone, & Mr: Yorke.

On a Motion for Council to be called in (withdrawing an Exception taken to a Witness) spoke as follows,

Sir, I presume to think myself upon for the Decision of any Question upon this Bill at large, but I am sure if I may be allowed the Exception so though a Member of Parliament as to decide one question by one Vote upon another; I certainly shall vote differently upon this Occasion from the Ho*nourable* Member (Mr: C. Fox)[547] who understands this Question as decisive on the Bill, at the same Time that I have reason to think we shall not differ much on the main Question if that was before us.

On the Division in the Majority,[548]
Ayes 5.
Noes 73.
On a Motion to adjourn the debate on the Question of Commitment to be Monday in the Minority,
Ayes 24. {NP}
Noes 89.
On a Motion to commit to Bill in the Minority.[549]

[545] *CJ*, xxxiv, 590.
[546] *CJ*, xxxiv, 752.
[547] Charles Fox.
[548] *CJ*, xxxiv, 752 (the votes are reversed in Folkestone's diary).
[549] *CJ*, xxxiv, 752.

Ayes 36.
Noes 10.

May 16th 1774[550]

On a Motion for Mr. Speaker to leave the Chair to go into a Committee upon the Booksellers Bill, spoke as follows,

Sir, as the Hon*oura*ble gentleman (M: Fielde) who has made this Motion, addressed the House on Friday last with so extraordinary a Proposition, as that the Bill required a debate, but it was then too late to debate it, I must suppose he meant the debate on it should be in this stage, & I therefore said to object to your leaving the Chair: Sir, I am not sure that my worthy[551] Motion can be objected to – for an opposition to this Bill, I have, I can have no Interest except that of a Member of the Community, & a Representative of the Public, whose rights I always think impeded by a Monopoly. The Merits of this Bill may I think be called Historical, for it is brought in in consequence of the late total[552] annihilation of the imaginary property of Copy Right at common law: the Statute of Queen Anne,[553] which has been so much talked of of late was expressly enacted for the Encouragement {NP} of Learning, & for that Purpose created an extraordinary Property in books to certain Persons for a limited Time; that reason & years antecedent to that by years of Regal[554] Proclamations, Proceedings in the Star Chamber, the Licensing Act, & other such Methods the Booksellers has tasted the sweets of a Monopoly, which they earnestly wished to again, the Act declares in an unusually precise, emphatical manner, that they shall have it for 14 years, and <u>no longer</u>: as they could get no longer Term they sat down for the present contented, but as some of the Copies began to come into common again, which they did upon an average about 20, or 25 years after, they began to grumble anew, & petitioned for an Extension of their Monopoly; Parliament, this House in two, the House of Lords in a third Instance denied it them. What then was to be done? Nothing was easy, what you will not give us, we have at Common Law already. And from this Time we begin to hear of these sort of Claims; that in all the arguments that have been heard, all the Records that have been examined upon this Occasion, there {NP} does not appear Previous to the determination of the King's Bench in 1769[555] the authority of a single Lawyer, or the decision of any one Court to continuance it: that, Sir, I see it with he objected that since, when it did come into Litigation, the question was formed so intricate by Lawyers, it was a very excusable Error in the Booksellers - Ignorance, on what is the same in Effect this construction of the Law is no Excuse. I admit the answer is a trite one, but I must contend it is complete. The Title of my Estate is in Question; the Judges differ upon the Validity of it, but in the End I am ejected; yet I took Council's opinion, & that opinion was in my Favour: yet no one would think of giving me a parliamentary Relief, thou' I have at last at the Credits of the Booksellers to plead, for they confess they never took any either generally, or specially but let me make one Reservation that I do not know has been made on those Judges who gave their voices

[550] Cavendish, {87–9}.
[551] This word is unclear.
[552] This word is unclear.
[553] Copyright Act 1709.
[554] The word is unclear.
[555] *Millar v Taylor* (1769) 4 Burr 2303 (98 ER 201).

in favour of Copy Right. There is {NP} not one of them except my Lord Chief Baron Smythe,[556] who either is not, or has not been a puisne Judge under my L: Mansfield.[557] Sir, it is well known L: Mansfield took up this Idea early, it was a favourite one with him, he argued it at the Bar, & and "quo semel est imbuta recens servabit odorem Testa diu",[558] I say diu, for from the Effect we may Judge it now gone, for L: Mansfield would not support his opinion in the House of Lords. In short, this is the Case the Booksellers got all they could in the years & when their great advantage of that Monopoly was over, they repeatedly petitioned Parliament for further Advantages.[559] Parliament was repeatedly informed, they then made up a Right in defiance of the legislature, which they have till lately supported by Combinations, conspiracy, threats, & every species of Tyranny but which has at last been overturned, & baffled by the spirited, & I think mountainous Exertions of an individual (M: Donaldson), now they come petitioning for an ex post facto justification of their {NP} past Conduct, & an Indemnification from the Consequences of it. In the of that[560] intended I have no wish to deny it, & I hope the House will negative this Bill in the present stage.

On the Division[561]

Ayes 57.

Noes 26.

[556] Sir Sidney Stafford Smyth.

[557] William Murray, Lord Mansfield.

[558] 'The jar will long retain the odour of the liquor with which, when new, it was once saturated.' Horace, *Epistles*, bk. 1, ch. 2, verses 69–70. Thanks to Dr Laurence Totelin for assistance with identifying the origin of the classical quote.

[559] See Part I: Chapter 4: The 1730s.

[560] This word is unclear.

[561] *CJ*, xxxiv, 757.

PART III: NEWSPAPER REPORTS

Introduction

This Part comprises all the known reports of the parliamentary debates on the Booksellers' Bill in the London, Edinburgh and Glasgow newspapers and monthly magazines. It also includes the reports in John Debrett's *Debates*[1] and Cobbett's *Parliamentary History*. In total the reports in 23 publications are represented. It therefore provides a complete picture of the parliamentary debates as they would have been seen by those who were not present in the chamber.

The Sample

The majority of the newspapers represented here form part of the Burney Collection held by the British Library and are now digitised. The following are taken from the collection: *Baldwin's Weekly Magazine*, *The Craftsman or Say's Weekly Journal*, the *Daily Advertiser*, the *Gazetteer and New Daily Advertiser*, the *General Evening Post*, the *London Evening Post*, the *Middlesex Journal*, the *Morning Post*, the *Public Advertiser*, the *Public Ledger* and the *St James's Chronicle*. The collection is not complete. For instance, there are very few issues of *Baldwin's Weekly Magazine* and the *Morning Post* remaining for the relevant dates, and the *Public Ledger* also has limited availability.

Apart from the Burney Collection, the British Library has a complete collection of the *Caledonian Mercury*, the *London Chronicle*[2] and the *Edinburgh Advertiser* for 1774. The first of these has been digitised as part of the British Newspaper Archive, but the other two are only available as original documents. The Guildhall Library in London has the complete collection of the *Lloyd's Evening Post* for 1774. The National Library of Scotland has a complete collection of the *Edinburgh Evening Courant* for the relevant year.[3] The other collections of debates (Debrett's *Debates*, Cobbett's *Parliamentary History*, the *London Magazine*, the *Scots Magazine* and the *Gentleman's Magazine*) are available in numerous libraries and have been digitised.

[1]John Debrett, *History, Debates, and Proceedings of both Houses of Parliament of Great Britain* (7 vols, Debrett, 1792), vii. There was nothing included in John Almon, *The Debates and Proceedings of the British House of Commons* (11 vols, 1766–75), xi.

[2]The Burney collection includes the *London Chronicle*, but it is incomplete and some relevant issues are not included.

[3]It does not have the *Edinburgh Advertiser* for 1774 however. The British Library has some issues of the *Edinburgh Eventing Courant* for 1774, but the collection is patchy and includes only a couple of relevant issues.

Ownership

The newspapers each took a particular stance on the merits of the Bill. This can be reflected at the simplest level by indicating that most Scottish newspapers were against the Bill and most English newspapers were in favour. The proprietorship and the target readership therefore influenced the coverage. Table 1 sets out the named proprietor of each newspaper, but it must be noted that the ownership might be held in 'shares' and only the named proprietor is listed below. Next to each publication is the abbreviation which will be used throughout this Part and Part IV (Table 1).

Table 1: *Proprietors of Contemporary Newspapers and Periodicals*

Paper (Abbreviation)	**Proprietor**[4]
Annual Register (AR)	James Dodsley* (1724–97)
Baldwin's Weekly Magazine (BW)	Henry Baldwin* (1734–1813)
Caledonian Mercury (CM)	John Robertson (1739–82)
Craftsman or Say's Weekly Journal (CR)	Charles Say (*d.* 1775), app. 1735–43, tr. 1749–75
Daily Advertiser (DA)	Matthew Jenour (*d.* 1774), tr. 1724–74
Debrett's Debates (DB)	John Debrett* (*d.* 1822)
Edinburgh Advertiser (EA)	James Donaldson* (son of Alexander) (1751–1830)
Edinburgh Evening Courant (EC)	Alexander Kincaid* (1710–77)
Gazetteer and New Daily Advertiser (GZ)	Charles Say
General Evening Post (GP)	John Bew tr. 1774–95
Gentleman's Magazine (GM)	David Henry* (1709–92)
Lloyd's Evening Post (LLP)	William Nicoll tr. 1761–93
London Chronicle (LC)	John Wilkie (*d.* 1785), app. 1743–50, tr. 1753–75
London Evening Post (LNP)	Robert Page (no further information)
London Magazine (LM)	Robert Baldwin (*d.* 1810), tr. 1746–1810
Middlesex Journal (MJ)	William Griffin (*d.* 1803), tr. 1748–1803
Morning Chronicle (MC)	William Woodfall* (1745–1803)
Morning Post (MP)	John Williams tr. 1761–1810
Parliamentary History (PH)	Published later
Public Advertiser (PA)	Henry Sampson Woodfall* (1739–1805)
Public Ledger (PL)	Francis Newbury (*d.* 1780), tr. 1765–80
Scots Magazine (SM)	Alexander Murray and James Cochran tr. 1739–82
St James's Chronicle (SJC)	Henry Baldwin

[4]It was common (although not uniform) practice for the publishers to include their names on the front or back page of the newspaper; also see Arthur Aspinall, 'Statistical Accounts of the London Newspapers in the Eighteenth Century', *EHR*, lxiii (1948), 228.

It has already been explained how newspapers copied parliamentary reports from each other, and this often meant that the perspective put forward might not follow its usual stance even though when being copied it is possible to slightly change the slant of a particular report.

Multiple Versions of Debates

There are multiple reports of each stage of the Bill, but the copy of a report (with minor variations) might appear in numerous different papers. It was also possible for a paper to run two different reports of the same debate. For instance, the report of the first day of second reading of the Bill (10 May) was reported in 14 different publications. There were only ten different reports however and four publications carried two different reports of the debate. At the other end of the scale, 12 newspapers[5] reported on the second day of the petition committee, but there were only two versions of a report used across those publications. Table 2 demonstrates the extent and scale of reliance on a limited number of reports. Each publication is listed with the version of the report it covered (the version numbers used below). Some publications carried two different versions (where two numbers are listed) and some simply have a short note (marked N) about the debate (for example, the debate will be held or was held) and some have both notes and debates. Where the number is emboldened it is believed to be the original source of the text (or where text has been copied from elsewhere, but it has been substantially developed). Where there is no report of a debate there is a dash and where the relevant issue is missing it is marked with an M.

Presentation of the Debate

The wide-scale use of the same report means that a single text can be used to represent the reporting in many different newspapers. The names of speakers have been reproduced in bold (and misspellings have not been corrected).[7] Any difference between reports based on the same original version are marked, except where the change is an alternative spelling or abbreviation, the capitalisation of a letter or different punctuation (it was common for semi-colons to be used in one paper where a full stop was used in another for instance). In each case, the spelling and punctuation of the earliest version is used (the version in bold in Table 2). All modifications, additions and excisions from that version are marked by use of square brackets indicating in which versions the text is, or is not, included. Where versions are embedded then the outer square brackets have been emboldened. For example, the following text is one of the most complicated sections due to the high level of minor variations between versions and it comes from the Petition Committee, Day 2: 16 March:

> [Not LM2: He finished his Evidence at Four o'Clock, when the Committee seemed perfectly satisfied with his Account, and adjourned to] [Not DA/SJC/LM1/LM2: This] [PA/LC/LLP: Morning] [GP/CM/EC: day] at Twelve o'Clock precisely] [DA/SJC/BJ: Yesterday morning] [PA/GP/LLP/CM/EC: when it] **[**[PA/LLP/CM: is] [GP/EC: was] expected Mr. Wilkie and several others [PA/LLP: will] [GP/CM/EC: would] be examined.**]**

[5] The *London Magazine* published the report twice over the year.

[7] In particular, Paul Feilde's name was spelt in a variety of ways.

Table 2: *The Various Versions of the Debates Published*

	28 Feb. Pet	8 Mar Pet Com	15 Mar Bac Pet	16 Mar Pet Com	17 Mar Pet Com	24 Mar Pet Rep	22 Apr 1R	26 Apr Don Pet	4 May 2R adj	10 May 2R	13 May 2R	16 May Bill Com	19 May Bill Rep	20 May Rep	26 May 3R	2 Jun HL 1R
							London Daily and Tri-Daily Newspapers									
Daily Advertiser	5	N	4	1	1	N	N	Nx2	N	N	N	**9** N	2 N	N	—	N
Gazetteer	5	—	5	—	N	**6**	**4&N**	—	Nx2	**9** N	5 N	**8**	**5**	**2**	N	N
General Evening Post	**1&5**	2	1	1	1	1 N	4	N	N	1 N	1&5	2	4	2	1	1 N
Lloyd's Evening Post	1&5	2	—	1	1	**3**	2 N	**1**	Nx2	4	3	2	**3&7**	3	1	2 N
London Chronicle	**3&5**	2	1	1	1	3	2	1&N	N	1 & 2	5	2	**2**	2	1&N	1 N
London Evening Post	1	2	—	—	5	9	4	N	N	**10**	N	**7**	5	2	5	2 N
Middlesex Journal	**2&5**	N	**3&4**	**2**	**2** **N**	7	1&N	—	N	**3** N	5	**3**	**4**	2	**2**	**1** N
Morning Chronicle	**4**	2	**1**	Nx2	**3&6**	**1&9** N	**1**	N	Nx2	**1&2** N	**1&5** N	**1, 5 & 6** **N**	**1**	N	**5** Nx2	**5** N
Morning Post	5	M	—	M	M	**7**	M	M	M	M	M	M	M	M	M	M
Public Advertiser	5	**2**	—	**1** N	**5**	**4** N	**5**	N	Nx2	N	**3** N	4	**7**	**3**	N	**2**
Public Ledger	M	—[6]	—	M	**1**	M	**2**	N	M	**4** N	M	**2**	M	M	M	N
St James's Chronicle	—	2	**2**	1	5	2	**3**	N	N	**6**	**2**	**4**	**6**	N	**3**	2

(*Continued*)

Table 2: *Continued*

	28 Feb. Pet	8 Mar Pet Com	15 Mar Bac Pet	16 Mar Pet Com	17 Mar Pet Com	24 Mar Pet Rep	22 Apr 1R	26 Apr Don Pet	4 May 2R adj	10 May 2R	13 May 2R	16 May Bill Com	19 May Bill Rep	20 May Rep	26 May 3R	2 Jun HL 1R
London Weekly Newspapers																
Craftsman	5	—	5	—	N	6	4	—	N	9	5	7	5	2	N	N
Baldwin	M	M	M	1	5	M	M	—	M	M	M	M	M	M	M	M
London Monthly Magazines																
Gentleman's Magazine	1	—	—	—	—	—	—	—	—	—	—	—	—	—	—	—
London Magazine	5&**6**	1	—	1 × 2	1 × 2	3	2	—	—	4	2	1	4	—	5 N	N
Scottish Newspapers and Periodicals																
Caledonian Mercury	1&5	N	1	1 N	1&6 N	1	4	N	N	1&**5**	2	2	1	2	1	1&**4** N
Edinburgh Advertiser	1&5	**1**	2	N	**4**	**5**	3&**6**	—	N	2&**8**	**4**	2	1	1	1	N&**3**
Edinburgh Evening Courant	1&5	1&2	1	1	1&4	3	4	1	N	1 N	5	2	1	2	1	2
Scots Magazine	6	N	—	N	—	**8**	**7**	**2**	—	**8**	**6**	**10**	—	N	**4**	1
Collections of debates																
Annual Register	1	—	—	—	—	—	—	—	—	—	—	—	—	—	—	2
Debrett's Debates	—	—	—	—	—	10	—	—	—	—	—	—	—	—	—	—
Parliamentary History	6	—	—	—	—	3	2	—	—	1&2	1	1	—	—	1	1

[6]There is no coverage in the issue of 10 or 12 Mar., but 11 Mar. is missing.

Accordingly, none of this text is in the second version in the *London Magazine* (LM2). The text of the *Public Advertiser* can be picked out as follows:

> [Not LM2: He finished his Evidence at Four o'Clock, when the Committee seemed perfectly satisfied with his Account, and adjourned to] [Not DA/SJC/LM1/LM2: This] [PA/LC/LLP: Morning] ~~[GP/CM/EC: day]~~ at Twelve o'Clock precisely] ~~[DA/SJC/BJ: Yesterday morning]~~ [PA/GP/LLP/CM/EC: when it] **[**[PA/LLP/CM: is] ~~[GP/EC: was]~~ expected Mr. Wilkie and several others [PA/LLP: will] ~~[GP/CM/EC: would]~~ be examined.**]**

Whereas the *St James's Chronicle* reads as follows:

> [Not LM2: He finished his Evidence at Four o'Clock, when the Committee seemed perfectly satisfied with his Account, and adjourned to] ~~[Not DA/SJC/LM1/LM2: This] [PA/LC/LLP: Morning] [GP/CM/EC: day] at Twelve o'Clock precisely]~~[DA/SJC/BJ: Yesterday morning] **[**~~[PA/GP/LLP/CM/EC: when it] [PA/LLP/CM: is] [GP/EC: was] expected Mr. Wilkie and several others [PA/LLP: will] [GP/CM/EC: would] be examined.~~**]**

And the *Edinburgh Evening Courant* like this:

> [Not LM2: He finished his Evidence at Four o'Clock, when the Committee seemed perfectly satisfied with his Account, and adjourned to] [Not DA/SJC/LM1/LM2: This ~~[PA/LC/LLP: Morning]~~ [GP/CM/EC: day] at Twelve o'Clock precisely] ~~[DA/SJC/BJ: Yesterday morning]~~ **[**[PA/GP/LLP/CM/EC: when it ~~[PA/LLP: is]~~ [GP/CM/EC: was] expected Mr. Wilkie and several others ~~[PA/LLP/CM: will]~~ [GP/CM/EC: would] be examined.**]**

In most cases the variations are only a single word or phrase being added or omitted in a much longer report, rather than the multiple variations in this example. Therefore, save for a few passages the text is easy to follow. The purpose of showing these variations is to demonstrate the very minor changes made between publications; indeed, that text was copied even where it now seems odd to keep the original wording (for instance there is often reporting of things happening in the future when the date of publication for the later newspaper means the relevant date has already passed). However, it also demonstrates how small the changes made were as well as the likely source of the report. For instance, the extract above likely originated in the *Public Advertiser*[8] but the editor of the *Edinburgh Evening Courant* probably copied the debate from the *General Evening Post* as it includes all the variations in that publication.

By following the variations, it is possible to work out the most likely source a newspaper used for each report. However, as before, if a variant was followed by numerous papers, it is possible that it was not the originating paper which was copied by an editor of the later edition even where variants are copied exactly. Table 3 sets out the likely newspaper copied for each report subject to that caveat. Where a newspaper is marked with '★★★' it is believed to be an original report and where it is marked with '###' it is believed to be an original note; otherwise, the likely source is marked. Where multiple versions of a debate were published the sources are marked in numerical order.

[8]See Table 2.

Table 3: *The Apparent Original Source of the Debates Published*

	28 Feb. Pet	8 Mar Pet Com	15 Mar Bac Pet	16 Mar Pet Com	17 Mar Pet Com	24 Mar Pet Rep	22 Apr. 1R& Pet	26 Apr. Don Pet	4 May 2 Radj	10 May 2R	13 May 2R	16 May Bill Com	19 May Rep Adj	20 May Rep	26 May 3R	2 June HL1R
London Daily and Tri-Daily Newspapers																
Daily Advertiser	LEP	###	★★★	PA	LLP	###	###	###	###	###	###	★★★ ###	LC ###	###	—	### ###
Gazetteer	Vote	—	★★★	—	###	★★★	★★★ ###		###	★★★ ###	GP ###	★★★	★★★	★★★	MC#	DA
General Evening Post	★★★ GZ	PA	MC	PA	PL	MC ###	GZ	PL	LC	MC PL#	MC	PL	MJ	GZ	LC	###
Lloyd's Evening Post	GP	PA	–	PA	PL	★★★	PL ###	★★★	### LC	★★★ PL	PA	PL	★★★ PA	PA	LC	PA ###
London Chronicle	★★★ PA	PA	MC	PA	PL	LLP	PL	LLP	###	MC	MC MC	PL	★★★	GZ	★★★ ###	MJ ###
London Evening Post	GEP	PA	—	—	PA	MC	GZ	DA	###		###	★★★	GZ	GZ	MC	PA
Middlesex Journal	★★★ MP	###	★★★	★★★	★★★ ###	MP	MC ###	—	—	★★★ ###	MC	★★★	★★★	GZ	★★★	★★★ ###
Morning Chronicle	★★★	PA	★★★	### ###	★★★ ★★★	★★★ ★★★ ### ###	★★★ ###	###	###	★★★ ★★★ ###	★★★ ★★★ ###	★★★ ★★★ ###	★★★	###	★★★ ### ###	★★★ ###
Morning Post	PA	—	—	—	—	★★★	—	—	###	—	—	—	—	—	—	—
Public Advertiser	★★★	★★★	—	★★★ ###	★★★	★★★ ###	★★★ ###	###	###		★★★ ###	SJC	PA	★★★	###	★★★
Public Ledger	—	—	—	—	★★★	—	★★★	###	—	★★★ ###	—	★★★	—	—	—	###
St James's Chronicle	—	LC	★★★	DA	PA	★★★	★★★	###	###	★★★	★★★	★★★	★★★	###	★★★	PA

(*Continued*)

Table 3: *Continued*

	28 Feb. Pet	8 Mar Pet Com	15 Mar Bac Pet	16 Mar Pet Com	17 Mar Pet Com	24 Mar Pet Rep	22 Apr. 1R& Pet	26 Apr. Don Pet	4 May 2 Radj	10 May 2R	13 May 2R	16 May Bill Com	19 May Rep Adj	20 May Rep	26 May 3R	2 June HL1R
London Weekly Newspapers																
Craftsman	GZ	—	GZ	—	GZ	GZ	GZ	—	GZ	GZ	GZ	LNP	GZ	LC	GZ	DA
Baldwin	—	—	—	DA	PA	—	—	—	—	—	—	—	—	—	—	—
London Monthly Magazines																
Gentleman's Magazine	LLP	—	—	—	—	—	###	—	—	—	—	—	—	—	—	—
London Magazine	★★★ DA	LC	—	DA	DA	LC	—	—	—	PL	SJC	MC	MJ	—	MC ###	—
Scottish Newspapers and Periodicals																
Caledonian Mercury	GP LLP	-	MC	GP ###	MCx2 ###	MC	GZ	###	### SJC MC	★★★ GP	SJC	LC	MC	LC	LC	GP ★★★ ###
Edinburgh Advertiser	LNP LLP	★★★	SJC	—	★★★	★★★	★★★ SJC	—	###	★★★ LC	★★★	LC	CM	★★★	LC	★★★ ###
Edinburgh Evening Courant	GP LLP	EA PA	MC	GP	LLP EA	LLP	GZ ★★★	LLP	LC	GP ###	GP	GP	CM	—	GP	LLP
Scots Magazine	LM	###	—	—	—	★★★	★★★	★★★	###	★★★	★★★	★★★	—	###	★★★	MJ
Collections of debates																
Annual Register	GM	—	—	—	—	—	—	—	—	—	—	—	—	—	—	LM
Debrett's Debates	—	—	—	—	—	★★★	—	—	—	—	—	—	—	—	—	—
Parliamentary History	LM2	—	—	—	—	LC	LC	—	—	LC	LC	MC	—	—	LC	LC

Thomas suggests that in the early period of parliamentary reporting it was the *London Evening Post* which was the primary source of so many reports and the *London Chronicle* and *General Evening Post* printed only pirated copies. He goes on to say that in 1773 the *London Evening Post* or the *Gazette* were the original sources and these were then widely copied by the other papers, with papers like the *Morning Chronicle* being mere copyists. A year later, as can be seen from Table 3, this was no longer the case.[9] Indeed, it can be seen that the Woodfall brothers, Henry at the *Public Advertiser* and William at the *Morning Chronicle*, were providing some of the most widely copied reports, with Francis Newbury at the *Public Ledger* also putting in a very good show.

While there are some publications which almost exclusively copied from one source (*Craftsman* from the *Gazetteer*), the general practice for contemporary publications appears to be to copy from a variety of sources. However, the same source is often widely copied for a particular debate, therefore suggesting that the 'best' report was selected, rather than necessarily routinely reproducing material from one particular publication. In relation to the later publication, Cobbett's *Parliamentary History*, it has been said that it largely came from Debrett's *Debates* and the *London Magazine*.[10] However, as is evident, a substantial amount of that work in fact came from the *London Chronicle*, and even some of it from the *Morning Chronicle*. Overall, it appears that all newspapers had some form of original coverage (although much could not really be called reporting), but there were some favourites.

Presentation of the Petition: 28 February 1774

Version 1: *General Evening Post*, 26 February–1 March; *London Evening Post*, 26 February–1 March; *Lloyd's Evening Post*, 28 February–2 March, 202; *Edinburgh Evening Courant*, 5 March; *Caledonian Mercury*, 5 March; *Edinburgh Advertiser*, 4–8 March, 147; *Gentleman's Magazine*, March, 137; *Annual Register*, 97.

Mr. Alderman Harley[11] presented a Petition from the booksellers of London, & c. setting forth that many of them [Not LNP/EA: would] [LNP/EA: shall] be ruined by the late decision in the House of Lords,[12] unless some relief was given them.

Mr. Sawbridge[13] seconded the motion [GP/LNP/EC/CM/EA:, saying,] [LLP/GM/AR: in which he said, that] by a decision in the year 1769, in favour of Copy Right, many of the booksellers had laid out their whole fortunes in that article, which right had now been taken from them by the determination of the Upper House; and if some redress was not given them, many families would be totally ruined.

[GP/EC/CM: The petition was read and referred to a Committee. A motion was next made that there should be laid before that House: "A list of the entries and transcripts in

[9] P.D.G. Thomas, 'The Beginning of Parliamentary Reporting in Newspapers, 1768–1774', *EHR*, lxxiv (1959), 628, 631.

[10] P.D.G. Thomas, 'Sources for the Debates of the House of Commons, 1768–1774', *BIHR*, special supp. iv, (1959) p. x.

[11] Hon. Thomas Harley†* (1730–1804), MP for London; in the *General Evening Post* and *Caledonian Mercury* the names are given as H–Y and S–dge.

[12] *Donaldson v Beckett* (1774) *Cobbett's Parl. Hist.* xvii, col. 953.

[13] John Sawbridge†* (1732–95), MP for Hythe.

the register-books of the Company of Stationers, with the [GP/CM: date][EC: dates] of such entries, and of all books to the copies whereof any claims are now made, with the names of the person's claiming title thereto.']][14] [LLP/GM/AR: It was referred to a committee.]
[EA: **Mr. Graves**[15] moved, that a list be laid before the house, of all the copies in which right was claimed, and by whom.

The petition was referred to a committee.]

Version 2: *Middlesex Journal*, 26 February–1 March.

A petition brought up by **Mr. Alderman Harley** from the London Booksellers, setting forth the great hardships they labour under from having depended on decisions in the courts of law relative to copy rights, and praying to bring in a bill to ascertain and establish their right.—Seconded by **Mr. Sawbridge**, and leave given; upon which **Mr. Graves** moved, that a list be laid before the House of all the copies in which right was claimed, and by whom.

Version 3: *London Chronicle*, 26 February–1 March, 207–8.

A petition was brought up by **Mr. Ald Harley** from the London Booksellers, setting forth the great hardship they labour under from having depended on decisions in the courts of law relative to copy rights, and praying to bring in a bill to ascertain and establish their right.

Mr. Sawbridge seconded the motion saying by a decision in the year 1769, in favour of Copy Right, many of the booksellers had laid out their whole fortunes in that article, which right had now been taken from them by a late determination; and if some redress was not given them, many families would be totally ruined.

Mr. Graves moved, that a list be laid before the House, of all the copies in which right was claimed, and by whom.

Version 4: *Morning Chronicle*, 1 March.

Yesterday several of the most eminent booksellers presented a petition to the House of Commons for leave to bring in a bill for the better securing of their copy-rights, &c. The same was read and referred to a committee. A motion was next made that there should be laid before that House 'A list of the entries and transcripts in the register books of the Company of Stationers, with the dates of such entries, and of all books to the copies whereof any claims are now made, with the names of the person's claiming title thereto.'

Version 5: Booksellers' Petition text.

***Votes 1774*, pp. 245–6;[16] *Public Advertiser*, 4 March; *Lloyd's Evening Post*, 2–4 March, 215; *Daily Advertiser*, 5 March, *Gazetteer*, 5 March; *Morning Post*, 5 March; *London Chronicle*, 3–5 March, 218; *Middlesex Journal*, 3–5 March; *General Evening Post*, 3–5**

[14] *CJ*, xxxiv, 513 (28 Feb.), discharged 2 Mar.: 525.

[15] William Graves†* (?1724–1801), MP for West Looe.

[16] The *Votes* (VT) is likely to have been the source of all versions of the petition and so its text is included here.

March; *Edinburgh Advertiser*, 4–8 March, 148; *Edinburgh Evening Courant*, 9 March; *Caledonian Mercury*, 9 March; *Craftsman*, 12 March; *London Magazine*, 151–2.

[VT: A Petition of the Booksellers of *London* and *Westminster* on Behalf of themselves and others, Holders of Copy Right, was presented to the House, and read setting forth,] [Not VT/GZ/GP/CT: The following is] [Not VT: the [DA/LM: Substance of the] Petition of the Booksellers of London and Westminster on Behalf of themselves and others, Holders of Copy Right, which was presented to the House of Commons last Monday by **Mr. Alderman Harley** [Not VT/DA/LM:, and seconded by **Mr. Alderman Sawbridge**, and read;]] [PA/MP/DA/LC/MJ: setting forth,] [LLP/DA/EA/EC/CM/LM: It sets forth,] [GZ/GP/CT: sets forth,] that, by an Act passed in the Eighth Year [Not MP/MJ: of the Reign] of Her late Majesty Queen *Ann*, for the Encouragement of Learning, by vesting the Copies of printed Books in the Authors and Purchasers of such Copies, during the Times therein mentioned, the Authors or Proprietors of such Books as had been then printed were to have the sole Liberty of reprinting and publishing the same, for the Term therein mentioned; and that the Petitioners have constantly apprehended, that the said Act did not interfere with any Copy Right that might be invested in the Petitioners by the Common Law; and have therefore, for many Years past, continued to purchase and sell such Copy Rights, in the same Manner as if such Act had never been made; and that the Petitioners were confirmed in such their Apprehensions, in regard that no Determination was had, during the [Not MP: Period] [MP: term] limited by the said Act, in Prejudice of such Common Law Right; and the same was recognized by a Judgment in the Court of King's Bench, in *Easter Term*, 1769;[17] [Not DA/LM: and] that, in Consequence thereof, many Thousand Pounds have been, at different Times, invested in the purchase of ancient Copy Rights, not protected by the Statute of Queen *Ann*, so that the Support of many Families does in a great Measure depend upon the same; and that, by a late Decision of the House of Peers,[18] such Common Law Right of Authors and their Assigns hath been declared to have no Existence, whereby the Petitioners will be very great Sufferers, through their former involuntary Misapprehensions of the Law; and therefore praying the House, to take their singularly hard Case into Consideration, and to grant them such Relief in the Premises as [VT/GP/PH: to] the House shall [Not DA/EA/EC/CM/LM: seem] [DA/EA/EC/CM/LM: see] meet.

[PA/MP/MJ: Likewise] [PA/LC: the House ordered that there be laid before them a List and Transcript of the Entries in the Register Book of the Company of Stationers, with the respective Dates of such Entries of all Books to the Copies whereof any Claims are now made, with the Names of the Persons claiming Title thereto.] [LC: This order has been discharged.][19]

Version 6: *London Magazine*, 619; *Scots Magazine*, 530; Cobbett's *Parliamentary History*, xvii, cols 1077–8.[20]

[LM: The following petition of the booksellers of London and Westminster, on behalf of themselves and others, holders of copy right, was presented to the House of Commons

[17] *Millar v Taylor* (1769) 4 Burr 2303 (98 ER 201).

[18] *Donaldson v Beckett* (1774) *Cobbett's Parl. Hist.* xvii, col. 953.

[19] *CJ*, xxxiv, 525 (2 Mar.).

[20] The text of the petition for this version is probably based on the *Votes*, or in the case of the PH the *CJ*.

by **Mr. Ald Harley**, setting forth,] [SM: The judgement was pronounced on the 22d of February,[21] and on the 28th of that month, a petition of the booksellers of London and Westminster, on behalf of themselves and others, holders of copy-right, was presented to the Commons by Ald. Harley, setting forth,] [PH: Mr. Alderman Harley presented a Petition from the booksellers of London and Westminster, on behalf themselves and others, holder of Copy-Right, setting forth,] that, by an act [Not SM: passed in the 8th] [LM: year of the reign of her late majesty] [PH: of] [Not SM: Queen] [SM: 8°] Anne, for the encouragement of learning, by vesting the copies of printed books in the authors and purchasers of such copies during the times therein mentioned [SM: it was enacted, That from and after the 10th of April 1710]; the authors or proprietors of such books as had been then printed were to have the sole liberty of reprinting and publishing the same for [Not SM: the term therein mentioned; and] [SM: twenty-one years, to commence from the said 10th of April 1710, and no longer;] that the petitioners [Not SM: have] constantly apprehended, that the said act did not interfere with any copy right that might be invested in the petitioners by the common law, and [Not SM: have] therefore, for many years past [SM: they] continued to purchase and sell such copy rights, in the same manner as if such act had never been made; [Not SM: and] that the petitioners were confirmed in such their apprehensions, in regard that no determination was had, during the period [Not SM: limited by the said act] in prejudice of such common law right, and the same was [SM: actually] recognized by a judgment [Not SM: in] [SM: of] the court of King's Bench, in Easter Term, 1769;[22] [Not SM: and] that in consequence thereof, many thousand pounds have been, at different times invested in the purchase of ancient copy rights, not protected by the statute of Queen Anne, so that the support of many families does in a great measure depend [LM/PH: upon][SM: on] the same; and that, by a late [SM: solemn] decision of the House of Peers, such common law right of authors and their assigns hath been declared to have no existence, whereby the petitioners will be very great sufferers, through their former involuntary misapprehensions of the law; [Not SM: and] therefore praying the house to take their singularly hard case into consideration, and to grant them such relief in the premises as [SM/PH: to] the House [Not SM: shall] [SM: should] seem meet.

[PH: **Mr. Harley** moved, that it be referred to a committee.]

[LM/PH: **Mr. Sawbridge** seconded the motion, saying, by a decision in the year 1769, in favour of copy right, many of the booksellers had laid out their whole fortunes in that article, which right had now been taken from them by the determination; and if some redress was not given them, many families would be totally ruined.]

[SM: This petition was referred to a committee, and upon a motion by Mr Greaves, it was ordered, that there should be laid before the House a list, and transcript of the entries in the register-book of the company of stationers, with the respective dates of such entries, of all books to the copies whereof any claims were made, with the names of the persons claiming. But this order was afterwards discharged]. [PH: A committee was appointed accordingly.]

[21] In *Scots Magazine* there is then '[233, 7].'

[22] *Millar v Taylor* (1769) 4 Burr 2303 (98 ER 201); in the *Scots Magazine* there is then '[xxxi. 716. Xxxii. 453]'.

Notes

***Gazetteer*, 3 March: Mr. Greaves**[23] acquainted the House, that on account of the variety of objects which must necessarily come under the cognizance of the Committee appointed to enquire into the petition of the London booksellers, which, he said, would give employment to twenty clerks, and require twenty days close investigation, he moved, That the order might be discharged, which was agreed to.[24]

Petition Committee, Day 1: 9 March

Version 1: *Edinburgh Advertiser*, 11–15 March, 166; *Edinburgh Evening Courant*, 16 March.

Wednesday the committee of the House of Commons went upon the petition of the London booksellers, the aim of which is to get a new monopoly from this date, for all books to which they pretend a right. Only one witness[25] was examined, who said he has paid above ten thousand pounds for copy-rights in many books which were now without the protection of the statute of Queen Anne.[26] He was asked what profits he had gained from these purchases, whether he had lost upon the whole, or [EA: on] any particular article, and what assignments there were from the authors. To these questions he either could give no answers, or declined it. He was then told that perhaps he might have gained considerably by these purchases, and unless he could specify a loss upon the whole, there was no good reason to ask for relief: but supposing he had been a loser, the duty which parliament owed to the public would make them consider well of the matter before they granted a dangerous monopoly, which would be in effect, to repeal the statute of Queen Anne. The witness was then asked if he had purchased any shares in the classics *in vsum Delphini*.[27] He answered in the affirmative, and mentioned among others, Horace and Virgil. He was then told that if the booksellers were so foolish as to traffic in that way, and combine against the public, they had themselves to blame, and could expect neither relief nor protection from the legislature. The **Attorney General**[28] observed, that if an hundred such evidences were produced, who would only answer such questions as were for them, and conceal what were against them, the committee behoved to report the petition not supported by proof; he therefore moved to discharge the committee, and was seconded by **Mr. Graves**. **Mr. Walpole**[29] moved to adjourn the committee till next Wednesday, when the London booksellers might be able to produce more evidence, which was agreed to.

[23] This is a typographical error for William Graves.

[24] Order discharged, 2 Mar; *CJ*, xxxiv, 525.

[25] William Johnston (*d.* 1804), app. 1743–48, tr. 1745–73, 16 Ludgate Street. He retired in 1773, although he seems to have been the stationer to the board of ordnance later.

[26] Copyright Act 1709 (8 Anne, c. 19).

[27] The Delphin classic, which was a collection complied for the Dauphine in the 1670s: J.E. Sandys, *A History of Classical Scholarship* (3 vols, Cambridge, 1908), ii, 292–3; *The Oxford Companion to the Book*, ed. M.F. Suarez and H.R. Woudhuysen (2 vols, Oxford, 2010), ii, 663.

[28] Edward Thurlow†* (1731–1806), MP for Tamworth.

[29] Hon. Richard Walpole† (1728–98), MP for Great Yarmouth.

Version 2: *Public Advertiser*, 10 March; *London Chronicle*, 8–10 March, 240; *General Evening Post*, 8–10 March; *London Evening Post*, 8–10 March; *Morning Chronicle*, 11 March; *Lloyd's Evening Post*, 9–11 March, 234; *St James's Chronicle*, 10–12 March; *Caledonian Mercury*, 14 March; *Edinburgh Evening Courant*, 14 March (Second Account); *London Magazine*, 619.

[PA/GP/LNP/LLP/CM: Yesterday Morning] [MC: Wednesday morning] the Committee [Not LNP: who were appointed to take into Consideration the Petition of the Booksellers of London and Westminster, [Not LC/SJC/LM: on Behalf of themselves and others,] Holders of Copy Right, met in one of the Committee Rooms [Not LC/SJC/LM: adjoining to the House of Commons]] [LNP: appointed to consider the petition of the booksellers of London and Westminster, on behalf of copy right, met], and **Mr. Alderman Harley**[30] being in the Chair, several Persons were examined [Not LNP: in order] to prove the Allegations in the Petition; but the **Attorney General**[31] and **Mr. Graves** thought there [Not LC/SJC: was] [LC/SJC: were] not [Not LLP: sufficient] Proof [PA/MC/LLP: enough], [Not LNP: therefore they] [LNP: and] were for having the Committee discharged; but [Not SJC: **Mr. Walpole**] [SJC: **Mr. Wallace**][32] said, that if there was not sufficient Evidence before them now, they might adjourn over to another Day, and then [Not LNP: the Committee] [LNP: they] might have such Evidence [Not LNP: laid before them] [LLP: before them] as would enable them to go on; the Committee then [Not LNP/LLP: agreed to adjourn over] [LNP: adjourned] [Not LLP: to Wednesday next] [LLP: till Wednesday next.]

Notes

***Middlesex Journal*, 8–10 March**: The Committee for taking into consideration the copy right of booksellers, have adjourned till next Wednesday. It is reported, that a longer term will be allowed to the London booksellers, and which will be the only relief that can be granted to them.

***Daily Advertiser*, 11 March**: The Booksellers Petition, respecting Copy Right, will be reconsidered next Wednesday.

***Scots Magazine*, 530**: The committee met on the 9th March, Ald. Harley in the chair …

Bach and Abel Petition presented: 15 March

Version 1: *Morning Chronicle*, 16 March; *London Chronicle*, 15–17 March, 262; *General Evening Post*, 15–17 March; *Caledonian Mercury*, 19 March; *Edinburgh Evening Courant*, 21 March.

A Petition, signed by John Christian Bach and Frederic Abel,[33] on behalf of themselves and others, was presented yesterday to the House of Commons, setting forth, "that doubts had

[30] Thomas Harley.

[31] *General Evening Post, Caledonian Mercury* and *Edinburgh Evening Courant* have A—y G—l, G—ves and W–lp–le instead of the names in full.

[32] James Wallace† (1729–83), MP for Horsham.

[33] Johann Christian Bach* (1735–82); Karl Friedrich Abel* (1723–87), both composers.

arisen relative to the act of the 8th of Anne[34] respecting copy-right, as it had been doubted whether musical compositions came within the letter of the act;[35] and therefore praying to be relieved by that honourable House."

Version 2: *St James's Chronicle*, 15–17 March; *Edinburgh Advertiser*, 18–22 March, 179.

... a Petition was presented from Messrs. Bach and Abel, in Behalf of themselves and several others, Composers and Proprietors of Books of Music, setting forth, that Doubts having arisen, whether, by an Act of the 8th of Queen Anne, the sole Right granted by the said Act, extends to the Author of any Book, Writing, or Composition in Music; and praying, that they may have such Relief as to the House shall seem meet.— The said Petition was referred to the Committee appointed to take into Consideration, the Petition presented by the Booksellers of London and Westminster.

Version 3: *Middlesex Journal*, 15–17 March.

... a petition was presented, from the authors of composition musick, praying, that if a bill should be brought into the House, relative to prolonging the time for Literary Property in Booksellers, beyond the time in the Statute of Queen Ann, that the said act might extend to the authors of Musical Compositions.

Version 4: *Daily Advertiser*, 17 March; *Middlesex Journal*, 15–17 March (Second Account).

A Petition was presented to the Lower Assembly on Tuesday last, by Mess. Bach and Abel, on Behalf of themselves and several other Composers and Proprietors of Books, Works, and Compositions in Musick, relative to their Right in such Works; which was referred to the Committee to whom the Petition of the Booksellers is referred.

Version 5: *Gazetter* 18 March and *Craftsman*, 19 March.

See Petition Committee, Day 3, 17 March.

Petition Committee, Day 2: 16 March

Version 1: *Public Advertiser*, 17 March; *London Chronicle*, 15–17 March, 264; *General Evening Post*, 15–17 March; *Daily Advertiser*, 18 March; *Lloyd's Evening Post*, 16–18 March, 258; *St James's Chronicle*, 17–19 March; *Baldwin's Weekly Journal*, 19 March; *Caledonian Mercury*, 21 March; *Edinburgh Evening Courant*, 21 March; *London Magazine*, 153 (First Account) and 619–20 (Second Account).

[34] Copyright Act 1709.

[35] The application of the Statute of Anne to musical compositions was confirmed in *Bach v Longman* (1777) 2 Cowp 623 (98 ER 1274).

[Not LM2: … the committee met who were appointed to take into Consideration the Petition of the Booksellers of London and Westminster, and others, Holders of Copy Right, in one of the Committee Rooms, when] [LM2: The committee again met,] **[**Not DA/SJC/BJ/LM1: M. Paul Feilde, Esq;[36] [Not LM2: was] in the Chair, [Not LLP: in the room of Mr. Alderman Harley,][37] when**]** Mr. Johnson,[38] Bookseller, in Ludgate-street, was examined for near three Hours [Not DA/SJC/BJ/LM1: by Mr. Edmund Burke, the two Mr. Onslows, Mr. Dunning, Mr. Montagu, Mr. Sawbridge, Mr. Stewart, Mr. Whitworth, Mr. Fuller, Mr. Walpole, Mr. Graves, and Lord Folkstone,][39] [Not LLP/SJC/BJ/LM1: when] he gave the Committee a very clear and substantial Evidence; [EC: and] told them that he had laid out 12,000l. in Copy Right, which would fetch last Year about 9000l.[40] [Not LLP: and] [LLP: but] now by the [DA/SJC/BJ: late] Determination of [Not DA/SJC/BJ/LM1: the House of Lords,][41] [DA/SJC/BJ/LM1: a Great Assembly] was not worth [Not DA/SJC/BJ: the] [DA/SJC/BJ: a] fourth Part of it: [PA/GP/LLP/CM/EC: He said the Money which he laid out was a Fortune which was left to his Son, on which Account][42] [LC/DA/SJC/BJ/LM2: and that] [LM1: that] he would never have laid out that Sum if he thought he had not been authorised by the Common Law Right. [Not LM2: He finished his Evidence at Four o'Clock, when the Committee seemed perfectly satisfied with his Account, and adjourned to] **[**Not DA/SJC/LM1/LM2: This [PA/LC/LLP: Morning] [GP/CM/EC: day] at Twelve o'Clock precisely**]** [DA/SJC/BJ: Yesterday morning] **[**[PA/GP/LLP/CM/EC: when it] [PA/LLP/CM: is] [GP/EC: was] expected Mr. Wilkie[43] and several others [PA/LLP: will] [GP/CM/EC: would] be examined.**]**

Version 2: *Middlesex Journal*, 15–17 March.

A Committee was appointed to hear evidences in the case of the Booksellers of London and Westminster, concerning literary property, and they adjourned to one of the Committee Rooms.
{separate entry}
The Committee for taking into consideration the Petition of the London Booksellers, have as yet come to no determination: an opinion prevailed that the Booksellers wanted perpetuity: but **Mr. Whitworth** moved that ten years be allowed for what has expired,

[36]Paul Feilde† (1711–83), MP for Hertford.

[37]Thomas Harley.

[38]William Johnston. The spelling of his name varied in reports: *Daily Advertiser/ St James's Chronicle/ General Evening Post/ Caledonian Mercury/ Edinburgh Evening Courant/ London Magazine* (both versions) have Johnston; all others have Johnson.

[39]Edmund Burke†* (1729–97), MP for Wendover, Col. George Onslow†* (1731–92), MP for Guildford, George Onslow†* (1731–1814), MP for Surrey, John Dunning†* (1731–83), MP for Calne, Frederick Montagu†* (1733–1800), MP for Higham Ferrers, John Sawbridge, MP for Hythe, Richard Whitworth† (?1734–1811), MP for Stafford, Rose Fuller†* (?1708–1777), MP for Rye, Richard Walpole, MP for Great Yarmouth, William Graves, MP for West Looe and Lord Folkestone† (1750–1828), MP for Salisbury. It is not clear which Mr Stewart attended.

[40]*CJ*, xxxiv, 590.

[41]*Donaldson v Beckett* (1774) *Cobbett's Parl. Hist.* xvii, col. 953.

[42]*CJ*, xxxiv, 590.

[43]John Wilkie, 71 St Paul's Churchyard. He also acted as clerk to the Booksellers' public auction which is why he gave evidence.

which was afterwards reduced by **Mr. Burrell**[44] to seven years; and this day the Committee will come to some resolution.

Notes

***Morning Chronicle*, 16 March**: The petition of the Booksellers of London and Westminster will be farther considered this day before a private committee at the House of Commons.

***Public Advertiser*, 16 March**: This Day the Committee are to meet according to their last Adjournment in one of the Committee Rooms, to take into Consideration the Petition on Behalf of the Booksellers of London and Westminster, and other Holders of Copy Right; when, it is expected, several of the Booksellers will be examined before the Committee in Support of their Petition.

***Morning Chronicle*, 17 March**: The Committee of the House of Commons, who are enquiring into the merits of the Booksellers' Petition, sat yesterday for some hours, and adjourned to this day.

***Caledonian Mercury*, 19 March**: The petition of the Booksellers of London and Westminster, will be farther considered this day, before a private committee at the House of Commons.

{second entry}

You will, no doubt, be desirous to know, what is likely to become of the Booksellers bill. They both gave in a Case to the committee for their consideration. The inclosed Observations on that case, wrote by Mr. Murphy, was this day delivered to the House, on the part of the Scots Booksellers. Thurloe[45] seems resolved to oppose it to the last; and it is the general opinion here, that the bill will be rejected—It is said that several Authors are likewise to petition the House.

***Scots Magazine*, 530**: The committee met on the 9th of March, Ald. Harley in the chair; and had sundry other meetings; to one of which an account was given in of money laid out at public sales for copy-right, which amounted to 49,498l. 5s exclusive of what had been sold by private contract.

Petition Committee, Day 3: 17 March

Version 1: *Public Ledger*, 18 March; *Lloyd's Evening Post*, 16–18 March, 263; *Daily Advertiser*, 19 March; *General Evening Post*, 17–19 March; *London Chronicle*, 17–19 March, 270; *Caledonian Mercury*, 23 March; *Edinburgh Evening Courant*, 23 March (First Account); *London Magazine*, 153 (First Account) and 620 (Second Account).

[Not CM/LM1: … the committee appointed for a further hearing of the Booksellers petition met in the great Committee Room, when Mr. Johnson,[46] Bookseller, underwent [PL/LC/LM2: a long] [LLP/DA/EC: a second][47] [GP: another] examination [Not DA: by Lord Folkstone, Mr. W.

[44] Peter Burrell† (1723–75), MP for Totnes.

[45] Edward Thurlow.

[46] *General Evening Post/Daily Advertiser/London Magazine* (both versions) have Johnston throughout.

[47] The *Lloyd's Evening Post* refers back to the earlier report: 'see p. 258'.

Burke, Mr. Sawbridge, Mr. Harris, Mr. R. Whitworth, Mr. Crofts, Right Hon. G. Onslow, [Not LLP/EC: Col. Onslow,] Mr. Dempster &c.[48]]] [CM: In the examination of Mr Johnson before the Committee to whom the London booksellers petition was referred,] [LM1: When Mr. Johnstone, bookseller, underwent a second examination] A question was put to him whether he ever knew of any prosecution being carried on against Printers or Bookseller for PIRACY? He answered in the affirmative; [LLP/DA/EC/LM1: that] he himself had prosecuted two persons[49] and had convicted both; the one about eighteen years ago, the other not five [Not LLP: years] since, for a book entitled "HUMPHREY CLINKER,"[50] which was not only reprinted in Edinburgh, but the Pirates had prefixed his (Mr. Johnson's) name to the [Not LM2: books][LM2: book], so that the original and copy could not be distinguished one from the other.

[Not LLP/EC/LM1: **Mr. Dempster** asked,] [LLP/DA/EC/LM1: Being asked] in whose name the [Not CM/LM2: prosecutions] [CM/LM2: prosecution] were carried on? and whether the expences were paid out of any fund of the Company or Society of Booksellers? [Not LLP/DA/EC/LM1: The question was strongly objected to by several Members as improper. Mr. Johnson answered,] [LLP/DA/EC/LM1: he answered] "that in both his own cases he had been at the sole expence, and he believed it was customary for every other person to do the same."

[Not LLP/DA/EC/LM1/LM2: **Mr. Onslow** said, "the question ought not to be recorded: that a question might as well be put to a person, whether he had not been guilty of that for which he [PL/LC/CM: deserved] [GP: ought] to be hanged."**]** [PL/GP/LC/CM: He said, he remembered only one instance where such a question was put, which was at Guildford, where an old Justice in his dotage asked an old foolish criminal that was brought before him for horse stealing, "whether he had not likewise been guilty of stealing COWS, CALVES, and SHEEP?" To which the Culprit replied, "Yes, an't please your Honour, I have."]

[Not DA/LM1: **Lord Folkestone**] [DA/LM1: One of the committee] desired to know whether the last Prosecution of Mr. Johnson was on the STATUTE, or for COPY RIGHT?

Mr. Johnson replied, on the STATUTE, for the Book had not been printed more than four years.

Mr. Wilkie[51] delivered in an account of money laid out at public sales for Copy Right, which amounted to 49,981*l*. 5*s*[52] [PL: 0*d*.] exclusive of what had been sold by private contract.

[48] In the *General Evening Post* these were anonymised to F—ne, B—ke, S—dge, H—s, W—th, C—fts. O—w, D—ster and W—th: Lord Folkestone, William Burke†* (1729–98), MP for Great Bedwyn, John Sawbridge, MP for Hythe, James Harris†* (1709–80), MP for Christchurch, Richard Whitworth, MP for Stafford, Richard Croftes† (c. 1740–1783) MP for Cambridge University, Col. George Onslow, MP for Guildford, George Onslow, MP for Surrey, George Dempster†* (1732–1818), MP for Perth Burghs.

[49] It is not clear what is meant here. He had been a co-plaintiff in numerous chancery suits: the earliest one recorded is *Dodsley v Kinnersley* (1759), TNA, C 12/496/2.

[50] A version was printed in Salisbury by Benjamin Collins of Silver Street, almost at the same time as William Johnstone's edition: F.B. Newman, 'Consideration of the Bibliographical Problems Connected with the First Edition of "Humphrey Clinker"', *The Papers of the Bibliographical Society of America*, xliv (1950), 340. The Edinburgh version is less clear.

[51] John Wilkie.

[52] *CJ*, xxxiv, 590.

Mr. Barlow,[53] Solicitor for the Booksellers, delivered in the opinion of the Court of King's Bench in 1769,[54] likewise the Decree of the House of Lords. [Not LLP/EC/LM1: A Petition was then presented to the Committee from the Composers of Music.

Mr. Augustine Greenland[55] was about to be examined, but as he was instructed only to inform the Committee that the Musical Composers entertained a doubt whether they had or not the same claim to a Copy Right as Booksellers.

Mr. Burke,[56] and several other Members said, "they should report this Petition to the House with the other, but could say nothing as to any facts being proved, only that the Petitioners entertained doubts"

George Onslow requested the Committee to come to some resolution of reporting their opinion to the House, as the House was impatient for want of Members to on with their other business.]

[Not DA/LM1: **Mr. R. Whitworth**] [DA/LM1: It was] then moved, "That the Committee [Not LLP/DA/EC/LM1: would] [LLP/DA/EC/LM1: should] [Not LM2: then] adjourn and make their Report to the House that they had examined the Petition, and that the allegations had been proved." The Question was put and agreed to. The Committee then broke up, [Not LLP/DA/EC/LM2: and proceeded to the House.] [LLP/DA/EC: and the Report is to be made to the House the beginning of next week.] [LM1: and the report was agreed to be made to the House].

Version 2: *Middlesex Journal*, 17–19 March.

Yesterday the committee appointed to examine the allegations set forth in the petition of the Booksellers, and others holders of copy right in London and Westminster, met in the large committee room, when Mr. Johnson, Bookseller, was examined by several members, to which he gave very concise and proper answers. He was questioned, whether he ever knew any person to be prosecuted for pirating author's works? he replied yes; he himself had prosecuted two, one about eighteen years ago, the other about four or five years past, for a book which he printed, and the Booksellers of Edinburgh reprinted in his name, so that it was hard to distinguish the original from the copy; he said he had obtained a verdict against both. He was asked whether this last action was for *Copy Right*, or on the *Statute*? he said it was on the statute, for the book had not been printed more than four years, the title of which was "Humphrey Clinker". **Mr. Dempster** desired to know if the Booksellers prosecuted at their own expence, or whether by combination? The question was strongly objected to by Mr. Whitworth, Mr. Sawbridge, the Right Hon. George Onslow, Mr. Onslow, Mr. William Burke, &c. as improper for the witness to answer. **Mr. Onslow** told a humorous story of an old Justice at Guildford, and a person that was brought before him for stealing a horse; he said, the Justice asked the old fool of a criminal whether he had not likewise stole *cows* and *sheep*? The man being tired of his life replied, "Yes, and please your honour, I have." He

[53] Robert Barlow was an attorney at Conduit Street and Bedford Row: *Browne's General Law-list* (2nd edn, Whieldon and Co., 1777) (ESTC: T085768), 11.

[54] *Millar v Taylor* (1769) 4 Burr 2303 (98 ER 201).

[55] An attorney at Newman Street and Oxford Street in London: *Browne's General Law-list*, 22.

[56] Edmund Burke.

said that that and this question of the honourable gentleman (Mr. Dempster) was the only two he ever remembered to have heard put for a man to condemn himself.

Mr. Wilkie produced an account of Copy Right bought at public sales, which amounted to forty nine thousand, nine hundred, and eighty one pounds five shillings, exclusive of what had been purchased by private contract.

A petition was referred to the committee from the authors of Composition-musick; but Mr. A. Greenland, who appeared as agent for the petitioners, said he was only commissioned to inform the committee, that the authors of Composition-musick entertained a doubt of their right of copy. The committee broke up at three o'clock, and are to make their report to the House.

The principal persons who examined the witness in favour of the petitioners were, Mr. Whitworth, Mr. Sawbridge, Mr. W. Burke, the Right Hon. George Onslow, Colonel Onslow, Mr. Crofts, &c. Against the London Booksellers, Lord Folkstone, Mr Dempster, &c.

Version 3: *Morning Chronicle*, 19 March.[57]

During Thursday's enquiry into the merits of the petition of the booksellers by the committee of the House of Commons, **Mr. Dempster** offered a question of the following import: "Whether Mr. Johnston (then on his examination) knew of any private combination of booksellers instituted at any time to prosecute those who printed upon either of the parties forming that combination." **Colonel Onslow** with great spirit objected to this question. He said it was every way improper to be put, as it could not safely be answered. "It reminds me (says he) of a circumstance which happened some time since at Guildford. An old fellow was brought before a justice of the peace, then in his dotage, on a charge of sheep-stealing. The justice mumbled out," "What, you are an old trader this way; I suppose you have stolen many a sheep, many a calf, and many an ox, in your time?" "Yes, an't please your worship," replied the man. Such a question, continued the Colonel, could only have been put by a dotard, and answered by a man equally foolish and weary of existence. This pleasantry had its effect, and in the general laughter, its personal tendency (altho' the Colonel evidently meant not to direct it personally) was overlooked. **Mr. Dempster** with that candour and decency which particularly mark his character, withdrew his question.[58]

[57] It begins with the following commentary: 'During the sitting of the Committee appointed by the House of Commons to enquire into the merits of the Booksellers petition, praying relief respecting their copy-right, it has been a matter of great doubt whether they would even procure a report in their favour. Mr. G—s, Lord F—e, Mr. D—r, the A—y G—l, and a few other Members, openly declared themselves enemies to their petition, and have stood forth professedly as advocates for those, who having no property in copy-right, find it their interest that Booksellers should be a kind of Arabs, and that property should rather accrue from prosperous pillage and plunder, than from any conscientious tenure derived from an equitable bargain and sale. How the general sense of the Commons will turn out is at present a mystery, but it is notorious, that the Members abovementioned have rather appeared as counsel for the pirates, (for such, in the eye of reason and common sense those who take away an equitable interest will be, however they may be warranted by a legal decision) than men desirous of disavowing any previous knowledge of the matter before them, and willing to trust to the evidence adduced on their enquiry.'

[58] It is followed by: 'It is a notion, of all others the most ill-founded, that books will be cheaper from the effect of the late decision respecting copy right in the House of Lords. The fact is notoriously otherwise. If booksellers can buy for a certainty only fourteen years right, and eventually twenty-eight years right of an author, they must raise the price of the work purchased in proportion to the shortness of their statutory tenure. The public will consequently be greatly incommoded, and the price of books, now without reason complained of as extravagant, will natural be most considerably encreased.'

Version 4: *Edinburgh Advertiser*, 18–22 March, 182; *Edinburgh Evening Courant*, 23 March (Second Account).

On Wednesday and [EA: yesterday] [EC: Thursday] the committee of the House of Commons, on the petition of the London booksellers, again examined Mr. William Johnstone, when several questions were put to him by Lord Folkstone, Mr. Graves, Mr. Dempster, Mr. Burke, the two Mr. Onslows, Mr. Dunning, Mr. Montague, Mr. Sawbridge, Mr. Stewart, Mr. Whitworth, Mr. Fuller, Mr. Walpole, &c. The committee agreed to report the state of the evidence that had been laid before them, to the House of Commons. The amount of the evidence is, that the London booksellers have laid out large sums in purchasing copyrights in books, many of which being printed more than 28 years, are, by the late judgment of the House of Peers, without the protection of the statute of Queen Anne. They therefore want, that the legislature should give them a new *monopoly* from this period, for all these old copies; although the fact will turn out; that the London booksellers [EA: have] [EC: had] gained considerably by these purchases, taking them *in cumulo*.[59] If a bill shall be ordered in, the Scots booksellers, printers, paper-makers, &c. should immediately petition the House of Commons to be heard by counsel against it, and write to their members to oppose it, as the bill which the London booksellers now want, would be highly prejudicial to trade, as well as to the public in general [EA:, books being already abundantly dear, without creating a new monopoly.]

Version 5: *Public Advertiser*, 18 March; *St James's Chronicle*, 17–19 March; *London Evening Post*, 17–19 March; *Baldwin's Weekly Journal*, 19 March.

Yesterday Morning, between Twelve and One o'Clock, the Committee met [Not LNP: in one of the Committee Rooms according to their Adjournment of Yesterday,] [LNP:, pursuant to their adjournment,] **Paul Feild**, Esq; in the Chair, to consider [Not LNP: farther] [LNP: further] the Petition of the Booksellers of London and Westminster, on Behalf of themselves and others, Holders of Copy Right, when Mr. Johnson was again examined relative to the Purchase of Copies, and was asked several other Questions by the Committee in Support of the Petition, and likewise if it was not the general Opinion of Persons that Copy-Right would go in favour of the Booksellers; he said, Yes; and likewise if it had, whether Copies would not have [PA/LNP: raised][SJC/BJ: raisen] in their Price? he said, Without Doubt. Mr. Wilkie was next examined, and asked a few Questions; the Committee then seemed perfectly satisfied that the Petitioners had proved their Allegation set forth in their Petition; the Question was then put by the Chairman, that he report to the House that the Committee had examined the Matter of the said Petition, and found the same to be true, which was carried unanimously, and the Chairman ordered to report the same to the House, which is expected to be on Monday next.

Version 6: *Morning Chronicle*, 18 March; *Caledonian Mercury*, 21 March.

[MC: Yesterday Mr. Johnson underwent a long examination before the committee of the House of Commons appointed to enquire into the merits of the Booksellers petition for

[59] Trans: 'in a heap' (meaning all together).

relief respecting their copy-right. The members who chiefly questioned the examinant were, Mr. Graves, Lord Folkstone, Mr. Dempster, Colonel Onslow, the Hon. George Onslon, Mr. William Burke, Mr. Harris, Mr. Sawbridge, Mr. R. Whitworth, and Mr. Stewart.] After Johnston's answers to the variety of questions put to him, were all taken down by the clerk of the committee, written proof of the decision in the court of King's Bench,[60] the determination [MC: in][CM: of] the House of Lords,[61] and the immense sums paid at different sales of Copy-right by public auction, were exhibited. **Mr. Feild**, the Chairman, then put the question, "whether the different allegations of the petition appeared to have been sufficiently proved by the evidence the committee has heard?" it was carried in the affirmative *nem. con.*[62] and the Chairman was ordered to report the same to the House of Commons, as soon as they had gone through the merits of the petition of Mess. Bach and Abel touching the property in musical copyright, whether it was affected by the 8th of Queen Anne.

Notes

***Middlesex Journal*, 15–17 March**: A Committee was appointed to hear evidences in the case of the Booksellers of London and Westminster, concerning literary property, and they adjourned to one of the Committee Rooms.

***Gazetteer*, 18 March** and ***Craftsman*, 19 March**: Yesterday the Committee appointed to consider of the petition of the London Booksellers, touching copy-right, closed their examination, and are to make their report this day or Monday. The petition of Mess. Bach and Abel was likewise taken into consideration, but no person appearing before the Committee to give evidence, they agreed to report the facts as therein stated to the House generally.

***Caledonian Mercury*, 19 March**: The petition of the Booksellers of London and Westminster, will be farther considered this day, before a private committee at the House of Commons.

Petition Report: 24 March

Version 1: *Morning Chronicle*, 25 and 26 March; *General Evening Post*, 24–26 March; *Caledonian Mercury*, 28 March and 2–4 April.

Mr. Feilde,[63] Chairman of the Committee [MC/CM: of the House of Commons,] appointed to enquire into the truth of the allegations contained in the Booksellers petition, praying relief respecting Property in Copies, gave in the report at the table; it was read immediately by the Clerk, and contained the substance of the examination of Mr. Johnston,[64] formerly a bookseller on Ludgate-hill, Mr. Wilkie,[65] clerk to the public sales of copies, and the Agent

[60] *Millar v Taylor* (1769) 4 Burr 2303 (98 ER 201).

[61] *Donaldson v Beckett* (1774) *Cobbett's Parl. Hist.* xvii, col. 953.

[62] Unanimously.

[63] Paul Feilde. In the *General Evening Post*, the names were anonymised: F—lde, S—b—dge. A—ney G—ral, D—nn—ng, S—tor, G—ral, O—low, D—ster, B—ke, F–stone and S—v—l—e.

[64] William Johnston.

[65] John Wilkie.

to the booksellers; the former of whom proved, that in the year 1748 he had purchased of the executors of Mr. Clarke[66] a quantity of copies for a valuable consideration, and that it had been the custom of the trade ever since to buy and sell copies under an idea of a Common Law right, which idea had uniformly prevailed in their minds, and was a few years since entirely confirmed to them by the solemn adjudication in the Court of King's Bench in the case of Millar and Taylor;[67] that he had expended a very considerable sum in purchasing copies; that a few years since he might have sold them for nearly the value he gave for them; and that he had transferred his right in them last year to his son, as a transfer of great value. Mr. Wilkie proved that since the year 1755, 45,000l.[68] and upwards had been expended in the purchase of copies at public sale. The Agent to the booksellers proved the decision in the King's Bench, and the late final one in the House of Peers.[69] The report concluded with a relation of Mess. Bach and Abel's adduced evidence, touching their petition respecting musical copy right. As soon as the Clerk had done reading, Mr. Feilde rose up and spoke for some time on the subject; he first assured the House, that after a long investigation of the merits of the petition, the committee conceived the allegations to be sufficiently supported; he then explained the grounds on which the petitioners stood, informed the House that they were a respectable body of men, the booksellers of London and Westminster, that they complained [MC/GP: not] of the late decision so fatal to them, but as they had though a natural and defensible error laid out very large sums in purchasing that [CM: to] which they had for the first time learnt by the House of Lords decision [MC/GP: to have] [CM: they had] no legal title, they appealed to the compassion of the House, and prayed for such relief as they in their wisdom should think meet to grant them. [MC/GP: Mr. Feilde said he had received a paper from some persons who differed from him in sentiments, and termed the petitioners "Men obstinate in error, and wilfully deaf to conviction."[70] This severe description he amply obviated, and after going a good deal into a defence of the measure adopted by the booksellers, he produced a motion which was read by the Speaker, and was contained in the following words:

> "That leave be given for a bill to be brought in] [CM: After going a good deal into a defence of the measures adopted by the booksellers, he moved for leave to being in a bill] for the relief of Booksellers and others, by vesting the copies of printed books in the purchasers of such copies from authors, or their assigns, for a time therein to be limited."[71]

Mr. Sawbridge[72] immediately rose, and after observing upon the distress in which the petitioners stood involved, and the justness of their appeal to the compassion of the House, he seconded Mr. Feilde's motion.—**The Attorney General**[73] then in a long speech took

[66] John Clarke (*d.* 1746), tr. 1722–46, Royal Exchange.

[67] *Millar v Taylor* (1769) 4 Burr 2303 (98 ER 201).

[68] *CJ*, xxxiv, 590.

[69] *Donaldson v Beckett* (1774) *Cobbett's Parl. Hist.* xvii, col. 953.

[70] See Part IV: Case Observations.

[71] *CJ*, xxxiv, 590.

[72] John Sawbridge.

[73] Edward Thurlow.

the adverse side of the question, arraigned the conduct of the Committee, and declared that what had been read as the report was no matter of evidence, but merely the opinion of an interested party. He took much pains to throw an odium on the petitioners and to defeat the desired effect of their prayer: he thanked the honourable member who brought in the report, for having informed the house, that the petitioners were the *united* and *combined* Booksellers of London and Westminster; it was, he said, a very just description, for the petition was the dark, unintelligible, stupid prayer of a combination of tradesmen, to procure a legal but an odious monopoly, prejudicial to the public interest, and of infinite mischief to many individuals. From the moment of their beginning this work, they had, he observed, clearly seen how necessary it was to make the matter as unfathomable to the House as possible; they had during the sitting of the Committee conducted the enquiry in such an intricate, inexplicable manner that no light was thrown on the subject, and when the Committee rose, they were to the full as wise as when they sat down. He had endeavoured in vain to get an insight into the affected distress of the petitioners, but their interest taught them to conceal the true state of the case; he had warned them in the Committee of coming before the House in that manner, and had in vain endeavoured to draw from them real matter of evidence, but when the proper question was put by him to one of the petitioners he was answered, "That the Petitioner was not prepared to speak to that question," he had therefore moved to have the petition discharged, but [MC/GP: that] the rest of the Committee begged more time, and then got ready what was now brought in, but which he never would consider as evidence, but as a mockery of a report, a mere echo of the petition, as something worse than imprudence. Had one man, through an error in judgment, expended his estate in purchasing a matter which a decision in a court of law taught him to conceive a legal property, prayed relief, he should have been inclined to grant it; but here the united and combined body of Booksellers asked for a privilege, and not a public law; and their plea of ignorance respecting a Common-law Right, was a mere pretence; they had not been led into a deception by the judgement of the Court of King's Bench,[74] they knew that the lawyers to a [MC/GP: man] [CM: person], were of a different opinion, and they should have consulted the lawyers; but they knew very well that the idea of a Common-law right could not be maintained, and they bought off Taylor,[75] and sent to every country Bookseller, offering to exchange their own London printed books for such pirated editions as they might have on their hands. The present request was an impudent insult to the House; if a person was evicted, by a final decision, in a Court of Justice, out of an estate which he had foolishly purchased without a sufficient title, what would Parliament think of his applying to them to give him a good title to that which did not belong to him. Copy-right was necessarily *publici juris*; and the extravagant price put upon Hawkesworth's Voyages[76] by the booksellers, shewed how injurious to the public an exclusive monopoly was. Books [CM: were] since the decision of the Court of King's Bench, [MC/GP: had] risen in price most shamefully. If [MC/GP: the] [CM: this] monopoly now impudently demanded by the combination of the booksellers [MC/GP: was allowed, what might not the price of books rise to?] [CM: what might they not rise to?] If Hawkesworth's

[74] *Millar v Taylor* (1769) 4 Burr 2303 (98 ER 201).

[75] Robert Taylor tr. 1717–79, Berwick-upon-Tweed.

[76] John Hawkesworth* (?1715–73), *An Account of the Voyages undertaken by the Order of His Present Majesty for Making Discoveries in the Southern Hemisphere* (Cadell, 1773) (ESTC: T74465).

trash fetched Three Guineas, Milton, Locke, Bacon,[77] and the most admired writers, would fetch Five Hundred. It had been discovered by the Committee that the Classics were, by the booksellers, termed Honorary Copy-right, and that they had entered into a dishonest combination to support this honorary copy-right [MC/GP: as the property of the rich men] [CM: among the rich men] of the trade; sending threatening letters [MC/GP: round] to all the country[78] booksellers to frighten them from printing upon them, and raising a subscription to prosecute and harass the lesser people of [MC/GP: the] trade, and prevent the Public from having books at a reasonable price. The petition was a deceit; and to those who came as strangers to the matter might excite compassion, especially as the Honourable Member had so ably opened the business in favour of the petitioners, by declaring "that by the late decision, they who were a few months since worth many thousands, were now worth nothing." This, he said, might [MC/GC: have] had its effect even [MC/GP: on] [CM: upon] him, had he not known the matter fully, and [MC/GP: from] being of a phlegmatic constitution, apt to look at words merely as words. The Booksellers, to strengthen their request had agreed to take his client, Mr. Donaldson, into their combination, and as far as he could judge of his client, he did not conceive he had the smallest objection to partake of the benefits of a lucrative monopoly, but although he rejoiced that he had gained his cause in the late decision, he did not wish him quite so well as to desire that he might partake of the monopoly prayed for. After giving an account of his conduct as counsel for Collins [MC/GP: in the case of Tonson and Collins][CM: and Tonson],[79] and endeavouring to prove that the booksellers all along, [MC/GP: from the publication of Homer down to the publication of Hawkesworth,] knew that there was no Common Law Right; he repeated that their present conduct was an impudent attempt to acquire a monopoly, and objected to the motion.— **Mr. Dunning**[80] then rose, and informed the House that he had travelled through every stage of the question, and had unfortunately been employed on the wrong side in the late hearing and decision in the House of Lords,[81] but that he meant not to disturb the manes of that suit; the suit and the parties were now off his mind, and he sincerely wished his learned friend who spoke last had also not quite so well remembered his client; but arguments, he observed, which had been laboriously pursued and founded on ingenuity and fiction at the bar, in support of a client's interest, were apt to leave a few traces behind them. His learned friend had affected to conceive that the petitioners were not deceived by the judgement of the King's bench in 1769.[82] This was rather an extraordinary supposition, for it was very natural for Booksellers, as well as other people, [MC/GP: on hearing] [CM: to imagine that] a title adjudged by a bench of Judges, in the highest of the Law Courts below, to be strictly legal, to suppose [MC/GP: that] they were warranted and secured in purchasing under that title; it was a very [MC/GP: easy] [CM: natural] error, and one into which the petitioners did not alone fall, for many others were swayed by it, and confirmed in opinion that a Common Law right in copies did exist. This being admitted, the conduct of the petitioners was in his opinion by no means [MC/GP: impudent] [CM: imprudence], nor any way forward.

[77]John Milton* (1608–1674), John Locke* (1632–1704), Francis Bacon* (1561–1626).

[78]See Part IV, Five Letters.

[79]*Tonson v Collins* (1762) 1 Black W 321 (96 ER 169).

[80]John Dunning.

[81]*Donaldson v Beckett* (1774) *Cobbett's Parl. Hist.* xvii, col. 953.

[82]*Millar v Taylor* (1769) 4 Burr 2303 (98 ER 201).

The petitioners had, by a decision, which no man was certain would have happened, and which, on the contrary, many men conceived would not have happened, sustained a very great loss; that which they had given a valuable consideration for, and which they had every reason to look on as their property, was changed from a substance to a shadow. Mr. Johnston had proved very satisfactorily before the Committee, that he had expended his fortune in Copies, and that previous to the determination of the House of Lords, he had transferred those copies to his son for a valuable consideration. His case was singularly hard, and therefore it was the most proper to be laid before the House. With regard to the *united* and *combined* body of Booksellers, his learned friend had taken up the chairman of the Committee's idea in a much broader point of view than he meant it. The petitioners could not be construed as an illegal combination of tradesmen begging an injurious and [MC/GP: odious] [CM: divers] monopoly; the late decision had distressed a whole trade, and therefore a whole trade very properly applied to Parliament for some relief in a loss they had sustained from a very natural and a very accountable error. Their petition was decent, their whole conduct strictly modest and respectful; they did not [CM: even] chalk out to the House any mode of relief favourable to themselves, [MC/GP: and] [CM: or] injurious to others; they humbly submitted their [MC/GP: entire] case to them, and prayed only such relief as the House should think proper to grant. Nor was this mode of proceeding without a precedent, the same had been [MC/GP: more than] once adopted since the passing of the 8th of Queen Anne,[83] and much greater relief had [MC/GP: at one time] been agreed to be granted by that House (altho' the bill failed for peculiar reasons in the House of Lords)[84] than was now asked, and without there existing a tythe of the plea the present petitioners were now, unfortunately for them, enabled to make. There could surely exist no stronger reason for denying a request of the nature stated in the petition now, than there was then. [MC/GP: As to denying relief, merely because the petitioners were numerous, it was wholly a new argument. If one distressed man was an object of compassion, surely a number of distressed men were much more so. And if the ruin of an individual deserved prevention, the ruin of a great number was immediately deserving of rescue.] After a variety of arguments in favour of the petitioners, Mr. Dunning concluded with hoping that the House would [MC/GP: not reject the petition, but] give such relief as appeared to them most proper.[85]

Mr. Graves[86] complained greatly of the committee, and the partial conduct of the enquiry; he said he had received no other answer to the several pertinent questions he had put to the Examinant than "he could not tell," and replies equally evasive. That he had endeavoured to sift the matter to the bottom, but the [MC/CM: petitioners][GP: petitioner] were determined he should gain no [MC: instruction] [GP/CM: instructions] by his questions. He had repeatedly asked what loss the trade had suffered by the late decision, but never heard from Mr. Johnston, that he could prove the loss of a single shilling by the alteration

[83]Copyright Act 1709 (8 Anne, c. 19).

[84]It related to the duty on paper.

[85]*Morning Chronicle*, 25 Mar., ends here, with 'Sketches of the speech of Mr. Graves, Mr. Dempster, and Lord Folkestone, who spoke *against* the motion, and of the Solicitor General, Colonel Onslow, and Mr. Burke, who spoke *for* it, to-morrow.' *Caledonian Mercury*, 28 March, also ends at this point, with 'Mr Graves, Mr Dempster, and Lord Folkestone, spoke against the motion; and the Solicitor-General, Colonel Onslow, and Mr Burke, for it. The debate upon this motion lasted near three hours, and on a division, there appeared for the question 50, against it 25.' Graves' speech is in *Caledonian Mercury*, 30 Mar.

[86]William Graves. In the *Caledonian Mercury* the names are anonymised as 'G—ves' and 'A—ney G—ral'.

of the price of Copy-right, since the Lords reversed the decree. The petitioners were desiring the legislature to grant them a monopoly; monopolies were always odious, generally unnecessary, particularly so in the present case, which could only tend to enhance the price of books, and prove an injury to the public, as well as the lesser kind of booksellers, two hundred of whom were now ready to supplicate the House against the intended bill, and to shew that the opulent men of the trade, by a combination among themselves, always crushed and kept under such booksellers as were not so rich as themselves. As far as he could judge, without any parliamentary security, a bookseller who was honest and assiduous, might exercise his trade with great safety and success; if a man printed a good and valuable edition of a book, no other bookseller would venture to print upon him; and he had nothing to fear from Scotland, for the Scotch editions were so badly printed, so very incorrect, so scandalously defective both in their paper and [MC/GP: their] type, that no gentleman would admit one of them into his library. In the course of the Committee, there had not turned up one Iota of evidence to support the petition; to talk of relief and remedy where there was no loss or damage, was ridiculous and absurd: he therefore joined his learned friend [the Attorney General][87] in putting his negative upon the motion.[88]—**Mr. Solicitor General**[89] replied to Mr. Graves, and began with observing, that it was somewhat surprising to hear it affirmed that the petitioners had suffered no loss; there might possibly have been no sale of copies since the decision of the House of Lords, and therefore no positive proof could be adduced; but he flattered himself the House would conceive, that any person who purchased an estate under a title warranted by the solemn decision of the highest Law Court in Westminster Hall, and who by a future and final decision, destroying the validity of that title, had been evicted of the estate, was an object of compassion, and had really suffered an obvious and material loss, and therefore merited such a parliamentary remedy as seemed most consonant with the general welfare of the Public. With regard to the observation that the gentlemen of the bar were of a different opinion from the Judges of the Court of King's Bench, who determined in favour of the Common-Law Right in the case of Millar and Taylor in 1769, and the conclusion drawn from the observation, they were of the most extraordinary nature he ever had heard. In the first place it was entirely a new doctrine, that the opinions of the bar were more to be relied on than the solemn decisions of the bench; and even allowing for the sake of argument that they were so, how were the Booksellers to procure the sentiments of all the Counsel? Were they to make themselves masters of their opinions, by formally laying a brief before every barrister? Or were they to run from coffee-house to coffee-house, leave no accommodation house to an inn of court unvisited, and in conversation learn the opinion of all who were [MC: and] [GP/CM:, or] meant to be lawyers, from the youngest students to the oldest practitioners? The idea was in the highest degree repugnant to reason and possibility. Three out of four Judges,[90] men of acknowledged skill in their profession, one of them the brightest of its ornaments, had fully, by argument, convinced not only the booksellers, but at least half the

[87] The square brackets are in the original.

[88] *Caledonian Mercury*, 30 Mar., ends here; the solicitor-general's speech and beyond is in the issue on 2 Apr.

[89] Alexander Wedderburn†* (1733–1805), MP for Bishop's Castle, solicitor-general 1771–8; *Caledonian Mercury* has S—tor G—ral, G—ves, O—low, At—ney G—ral.

[90] William Murray†*, Lord Mansfield (1705–93), Sir Richard Aston†* (1717–78), Sir Edward Willes†* (1723–87); dissenting judge Sir Joseph Yates* (1722–70).

public, that a Common-Law Right did exist; and even in the late decision, the opinion of the great luminary of the law, was supported nearly by half the number of the Judges. Were therefore the petitioners to doubt the opinion of the Court of King's Bench, and to have recourse to counsel? If any answer insufficient had been given in the Committee to the honourable member who spoke last, a future opportunity of enquiry would offer, and he might then make himself more perfectly acquainted with the real merits of the petitioners plea. In answer to one objection strongly urged, he (the Solicitor General) could not but observe that the person examined by the Committee, was not a party interested; he had some months, previous to the determination of the House of Lords, parted with his Copies to his son,[91] he was therefore an impartial, but a most intelligent witness. His answers to the questions put to him were proper and elucidatory. With regard to Scotch editions being imperfect, he begged the House to remember, that the imperfections of any edition were not discoverable on the purchase of one book, a whole edition of it might be sold off before the errors of it were generally known, or the work reprobated and denied admission into the libraries of the learned. The sale of an entire edition (however its faults might prevent the sale of a second) might do infinite mischief and disservice to an honest trader. The argument, therefore, that any man who printed correctly and elegantly, might print safely, would not hold. It was to be remembered likewise, that bookselling differed essentially from all other trades. The moment a bookseller printed one sheet, he made himself liable to the expences of a whole, numerous edition. His profit arose from an equal proportion set on each book, and he was not reimbursed his principal, nor that fair interest every trader had a right to expect, till the whole impression was sold. By the determination that there was no Common-Law Right for a perpetuity in copies, many heads of families, many widows, and many orphans, found themselves removed from that state of provision in which they had every reasonable excuse for thinking themselves secured. They now asked not half so much as the House had many years back consented to allow them; their request was reasonable, their mode of offering it perfectly modest, and he did not doubt but the humanity and justice of the House would join in support of the motion.—**Colonel Onslow**[92] rose next, and declared, that although he would not venture to argue points of law with the learned members on the opposite bench, [the Attorney General and Mr. Graves][93] yet he thought himself a competent judge of order with any member. On that ground therefore he arraigned the conduct of the Attorney General and Mr. Graves; they had both been out of order, in the Committee, by asking such questions as were foreign to the petition; they had attempted to enquire into the general state of the trade, a matter entirely out of the question; for every petition pointed out a peculiar circle of enquiry, within which the committee it was referred to, were necessarily confined; and such questions as were put out of it, no examinant was obliged to answer. The honourable gentleman who spoke last but one, had openly confessed, by what he had just said, that the whole line of his conduct in the Committee was out of order, every question he had stated having been foreign to the allegations of the petition; indeed he and his learned friend [the Attorney General][94] had endeavoured to drive the witnesses from the Committee with their flaming arguments, in

[91] See Part IV, Petition Committee Report, *CJ*, xxxiv, 590 c. i.

[92] George Onslow, MP for Guildford.

[93] The square brackets are in the original.

[94] The square brackets are in the original.

like manner as the two angels drove our fore-father Adam with their flaming swords out of the garden of Eden.[95] Others had likewise endeavoured to confound the witness by asking improper questions; one of them had offered to ask him, "Whether the trade had not entered into a combination to prosecute all who printed any of the works they claimed a property in." Upon which the Colonel said he had directly added, that if that question was suffered to be put, he certainly would follow it by another, viz. "Whether the witness, and every person present, had not repeatedly committed crimes for which they deserved to be hanged." [The Colonel then repeated the story of the horse-stealer at Guildford, which he had told in the committee room.][96] As to the observation that the Booksellers had reaped profits by many of their copies, which they would not disclose; the case was exactly the same with the possessor of a farm. Because by his industry and care he raised a good and advantageous crop, was it to be said he suffered no loss when his farm was taken away? If the value of his crops for a number of years possession of the farm turned out superior to the original cost of the farm, it did not at all diminish his right in the farm, nor could it be brought forward as an argument to prove that he sustained no loss in being deprived of the farm. The Colonel said that, as a good subject, he owed an implicit submission to the executive power of his country; he had great faith, and he believed the decision of the House of Lords was founded in justice; but altho' he bowed with submission to it, his opinion was, previous to the decision of the Lords, very different from that which they had decisively given. A new fangled argument had been spun by the Lawyers in the House of Lords, they had experienced that plain sense and sound reasoning were against them in the Court of King's Bench, they therefore had conjured up new matter for the Court of Appeal. The immateriality, inherency, intangibility, and incorporeality of Literary Property, had been wisely talked of; even upon such subtle grounds he thought he could put a case in point. In the Bible it is said, "What shall a man take in exchange for his Soul,"[97] now it was to be presumed that a man's soul was immaterial, intangible, and incorporeal; so likewise was his reputation, and if a man's reputation was not his property he would burn his Blackstone,[98] for he had taught him that it was. Considering the case candidly, the petitioners had been no further criminal than in having fallen into a mistake, and even Judges had erred; was it therefore wonderful that booksellers should mistake? they had been deceived, and under that deception they had risqued their fortunes in the purchase of Copy-right. Booksellers and printers were sometimes obnoxious to government, but they were subjects, and had a right to participate those advantages the constitution allows to subjects in general; their case was exceedingly hard; he was well informed that the most respectable living authors thought it so, and that it merited the compassion of the House.—[99] **Mr. Dempster**[100] rose to explain what the honourable member alluded to in regard to the question intended to be put in the Committee room. He informed the House that he was the person who offered it; he came into the Committee, and imagining they were examining a witness, he offered a question tending to discover whether the booksellers had not formed a combination among

[95] Genesis 3:24.

[96] The square brackets are in the original.

[97] Mark 8:37.

[98] William Blackstone (1723–80), *Commentaries on the Laws of England* (Oxford, 1765–9) (ESTC: T57753).

[99] *Caledonian Mercury*, 2 Apr., ends here. Dempster's speech is in *Caledonian Mercury*, 4 Apr.

[100] George Dempster. *Caledonian Mercury* has D—ster, B—rke. F—stone and S—v—l—e, F—lde.

themselves [CM: tending] to prevent their printing upon each other, but finding that they were only taking the opinion of a party, he withdrew his question; when the honourable member was pleased to tell the jocular story he had now repeated, and which had lost none of its jocularity, altho' what was generally considered as an ugly circumstances, had attended it, viz. the being twice told. He owned he was so unfortunate as to differ exceedingly in opinion [MC: with] [GP/CM: from] the two honourable gentleman who had spoke last, for he was entirely adverse to the motion, and thought that the interference of parliament, as a remedy to a legal decision in the supreme court of justice, was wholly repugnant to usage and custom, and that an *ex post facto* law should on no account be granted. In the present case a Common-law right had been maintained on the one side, and denied on the other; an individual had at an infinite expence made that public which in its nature was a common right, but from which the public had been long debarred. At the moment that he arrived at the goal to deny him the profits he had a right to from his gaining the race, was impolitic, was unjust: the petitioners desired a monopoly at the expence of the public; they prayed for a grant of estate belonging to others, which ought not to be allowed them. Their appeal was to the compassion of the House, the grounds of compassion were alarming and dangerous, for he always thought the greater the objects of compassion, the more wary those should be who had the power to relieve; he therefore hoped the motion would not be carried.—**Mr. Burke**[101] spoke next, and began by observing that as the subject was now clear of that dogmatical cloathing given it by the honourable gentlemen in office, he would say a few words on it. As had been observed, it would certainly be both impolitic and unjust to remedy one man's loss at another's expence; but if the line of distinction was drawn, and it was found that either an individual or a number had through an error in judgment, not peculiar to themselves, suffered a manifest loss, and that such loss could be remedied without any peculiar or general injury, it would be perfectly consonant with sound policy, strict justice, and immemorial custom to grant relief. Parliament had in cases of this kind frequently interfered, and the present petitioners fell under this description. Their error was the error of the sages in the law, and the learned of all ranks; a great and able lawyer now upon the bench, whose writing had taught the world what the law of the country was,[102] and who would be held in high esteem as long as Englishmen entertained a trace of either law or justice, had sold his works to a bookseller, under a firm persuasion that there existed a Common-law right for authors to dispose of their productions forever; that an author had a right in perpetuity, was his idea when he disposed of his book; and he had maintained the same idea when giving his opinion on the question in his judicial capacity. When such characters thought that there was a perpetual right, were booksellers to be branded with the names of crafty knaves, under a supposition of their knowing better than the Judges, and blinding the eyes of the world? The lawyers would allow that there was some excuse for ignorance of fact, but none for ignorance of law; and yet the present case proved that the maxim was more severe than just; and that, like all general rules, it was not without its exceptions. Monopolies had been mentioned; and it had been urged, that monopolies, of all kinds were odious; the position was generally true; but frequent instances could be cited to prove, that in particular cases monopolies were useful and necessary: in

[101] Edmund Burke.

[102] William Blackstone, author of *Commentaries on the Laws of England*, appointed justice of king's bench 1770.

his opinion, that now prayed for was strongly so. If the right was suffered to remain open, anarchy and confusion among the trade must be the consequence, and a multitude of incorrect, wretched editions, would pour in upon the public. [MC: Mr. Burke took occasion, frequently in his speech, to laugh at the Attorney General and the Courtiers, and was sarcastically humorous upon all who were connected with the Ministry.] After a variety of pertinent observations in favour of the petitioners, [MC: he] [GP/CM: Mr. B—ke] concluded with declaring that they were proper objects of parliamentary compassion, and that their prayer was rational, modest, and proper.—**Lord Folkstone** said he thought the petitioners deserved some relief, but not in that extent which had been hinted at; he therefore moved to amend Mr. Feild's motion, by leaving out all the words after "Booksellers and others." This he said would afford room for his adding some new terms; if this amendment was carried, he should go hand in hand with the bill; if not, he should oppose it.—**Sir George Saville**[103] spoke a few words upon the subject, observing that there was not a gentleman in the world for whom he had so great a regard as the gentleman called the Public, he was a very worthy and a very honest gentleman; and as he was a very rich, he hoped he would prove a very generous gentleman, and assist the petitioners, by granting them relief under proper restrictions. The question[104] was then put, [MC/GP: the original motion carried, and the amendment negatived, by the divisions mentioned in [MC: yesterday's paper.][105] [GP: in the first page of this paper.] [CM: and carried.]

Version 2: *St James's Chronicle*, 24–26 March.

At Half after Three, **Mr. Feilde**, Chairman of the Committee appointed to enquire into the Allegations contained in the Petition of the London Booksellers, and to state the same to the House, reported the Opinion of the Committee thereon. The leading Facts were, that Mr. Johnston, one of the Witnesses examined, had entered into the Bookselling Business in the Year 1748, at which Time he succeeded one Clark, to whose Assigns he paid the Sum of 3000l. for his Interest in certain Copy rights; that in June 1773, he quitted Business, and disposed of several Copies to his Son, to the Amount of 9000l.[106] which if now brought to Market, would not fetch a Quarter the Sum; that a general Idea had prevailed, that Purchase; thus made conveyed an exclusive common Law Right to the Purchaser; that the Trade in general were still further confirmed in this Opinion by the solemn Determination in the Court of King's Bench, in the Case of Millar and Taylor; that trusting particularly to this Decision, as well as the almost universal Opinion that such a Right did exist, Sums to a very great Amount had been laid out in Purchases of this Nature, which Mr. Wilkie, another Witness, proved, amounted to the Sum of 45,000l. within the last nineteen Years, at public Sales or Auctions only, exclusive of private Contracts; and, that the Booksellers laid no

[103] George Savile†* (1726–84) MP for Yorkshire.

[104] *CJ*, xxxiv, 590.

[105] The *Morning Chronicle* ends with '[*The Public are requested to read the above not as an exact account of the debate on the subject, but as a mere skeleton of the arguments urged on the occasion; the writer is conscious of the impossibility of an auditor's carrying away the arrangement of the arguments, or the exact phraseology, used by the speakers; he submits it to this readers as the substance of the debate, but he does not venture, like his brethren, to call it a perfect report of what was said on the occasion.*]'

[106] *CJ*, xxxiv, 590.

Claim to an exclusive Right to the printing the Classics, but an honorary one, founded on a general Consent among themselves, not to re-print on each other.

After the Clerk had finished reading the Report, **Mr. Feilde** rose and informed the House, that the Committee, after giving all the Attention a Subject of such Importance deserved, were fully satisfied of the Truth of the Allegations contained in the Petition; that, as to the Mode of Relief, he should not, in this Stage of the Business, pretend directly to point it out, but he conceived, that vesting the Copies for twenty-one Years in the several and respective Proprietors would not be deemed unreasonable, or be supposed to exceed what they were justly entitled to; that it was certain the Law had already declared they had no Right, to the Justice and Wisdom of which he was as willing to subscribe as any Man; and that, consequently, any Claim, not directed to the Compassion of the House, was now clearly out of the Question. He then entered into an historical Detail of the several judicial Proceedings, had on the exclusive Right of Authors and their Assigns, from the Year 1751, when it was first questioned, to the late final Determination in the House of Peers, and concluded with observing, that every progressive Step taken throughout led to confirm the Booksellers in those Errors they were at length so fatally convinced of. He then moved, that Leave be given to bring in a Bill for Relief of Booksellers and others, by vesting the Copies of printed Books in the Purchasers of such Copies, from Authors or their Assigns, for a Time to be limited.

Mr. Sawbridge. The Hon. Gentleman who has made the Motion has so fully and ably submitted to your Consideration the Necessity there is for the Relief now proposed, that I shall not trouble or take up the Time of the House in giving my Reasons why I am of the same Opinion. I shall avoid, therefore, entering into any Investigation of the Subject, and only rise to second the Motion.

Mr. Attorney General. What is the Intention of the present Motion? Only to inform us, that the Party now applying have been in the Possession and Exercise of a Right to which they were by no Means entitled; that they have been evicted by due Course of Law, and that they now come to Parliament to desire us to reinstate them in their Usurpation. Were this Principle followed and indulged, on the present Occasion, what would be the Consequence? Why, that every Man who, through Imprudence, had made a foolish Bargain, or Injustice had held what he had no Right to, would resort to us for Redress on being evicted. But I suspect there is more Art than Folly in this Application, and more Impudence than either; but I trust it is too gross to have its desired Effect. The Petition and the Report are nearly of the same Complexion, dark, unintelligible, and stupid; and are both supposed precisely on the same Ground. A Body of Men come to this House for Relief, and one of this Body, without any other Proof whatever, gives us the Information on which we are to proceed and determine. They come to us to procure—what? A legal, but an odious Monopoly, at the Expence of the public Interest. Their Impudence has, indeed, been only exceeded by their Insolence; they have attempted to impose on the House, but I trust that no great Argument or Investigation will be necessary to prove that two and two make four. These Men now come desiring a Privilege. Upon what their Pretensions are founded, I must confess, I am at a Loss to discover. For my Part I know of no just Grounds on which a Monopoly ought to be granted but two; that is, in the Case of an original Invention, that cannot intrench on the Rights of others, where the Public may be benefited but cannot be injured; and where the Public, on vesting a Benefit in an Individual or a Body of Men, receive, in Return, a general Advantage. The first cannot be so much as pretended in the present Instance; and as to the second, so far from the Publick being benefited by this exclusive Privilege, the extravagant Prices demanded on that very Ground shew to a Demonstration how very injurious such an exclusive Privilege has been. For Instance, Hawkesworth's Trash sells for Three Guineas on this very Account. Great Stress has been laid on the Sums expended in the Purchase of those Copy Rights, and the Assurance that the Purchasers imagined they had from the Common Law. Now I contend that both these are no better than mere Pretences; for Milton received but Five Pounds out of Fifteen he agreed for for the Copy of Paradise Lost,[107] under the Pretence that the Sale did not answer; and Dr. Robertson[108] was obliged on a recent Occasion, to make an Assignment of a Tenor never before desired in such Transactions, which was the most indubitable Proof that the Booksellers, who purchased the Work alluded to, did not think themselves so secure as they, among the rest, would now endeavour to make us believe.

Mr. Dunning. I have travelled through every Stage of the Question, as well as my learned Friend, but was unfortunately engaged on the wrong Side of the Question. I would not have any Thing which passed on that Occasion now brought forward, but with it to be totally forgotten; and I am sorry to have it in my Power to observe, with some Degree of Justice, that a deal of the Oratory employed on that Occasion, seems now to have returned on us with redouble Force. My honourable Friend affects to think that the Petitioners have not been deceived by the Judgment of the Court of King's Bench;[109] but I would appeal to his own Knowledge of Clients in general, if that be not rather an unnatural Supposition; for leaving out of the Prescription the general Sentiments of Lord Hardwicke,[110] as often as the Question came before him, I believe he can be hardly ignorant what an Effect a Determination of the highest of our Law Courts might be supposed to have on Persons looking on such a Decision in their Favour, to be in a great Measure final. However fertile my learned Friend may be in devising Modes of Abuse, suited to the supposed criminal Ignorance of the Petitioners in Matters of Law, I am far from thinking their Conduct so very reprehensible. If they fell into an Error, it was a very excusable one; it was on a Point in which all the Judges of England were divided in Opinion. As to the Competency of the Witness, to whose Evidence my worthy Friend has objected, I know of none so competent to give Testimony as he, who not being immediately interested in the Event, has it in his Power to draw from Sources of Information unknown to others standing in a similar Situation. Mr. Johnston[111] is no longer a Bookseller, no longer interested in the Success of this Bill; his Testimony is therefore both competent and unimpeachable.

Mr. Greaves. I attended the Committee above Stairs with all possible Assiduity, and cannot help observing, that the Evidence given there was far from being satisfactory. I pressed to know the Amount of the Sums paid for Copies, to whom paid, and looked for the Assignments that might be supposed to accompany them, but could not get a satisfactory Answer to any one Question I put. General Assertion were made, but not on any specific

[107] See Kerry MacLennan, 'John Milton's Contract for "Paradise Lost": A Commercial Reading', *Milton Quarterly*, xliv (2010), 221.

[108] William Robertson* (1721–93). For a summary of his historical writings see David Womersley, 'The Historical Writings of William Robertson', *Journal of the History of Ideas* (1986), 497.

[109] *Millar v Taylor* (1769) 4 Burr 2303 (98 ER 201).

[110] Philip Yorke†† * (1690–1764), lord chancellor 1737–56.

[111] William Johnston.

Case stated, which could lay a Foundation sufficient to support the Contents of the present Petition.

Lord North. I do not mean to interrupt the Business now before the House, but wish to know, if Gentlemen mean to prosecute the present Debate; because, if they do, I shall move to put off the Order of the Day, for the third Reading of the Boston Port Bill[112] till To-morrow. No Answer was given, and the Debate continued.

Colonel Onslow. Some of the great Oracles of Order, on the other Side, like the Angel with the flaming Sword, attempted in the Committee to prevent us from entering the Garden. New Doctrines have been broached, concerning the Incorporeality, Immateriality, and Intangibility of Literary Property, but, though a Soul be immaterial, we have very good Authority to believe, it may be exchanged; for Christ says, What shall a Man get in Exchange for his Soul? So that a Thing which is neither tangible, corporeal, or material, may be given in Exchange for a Thing which has these several Qualities. Two learned Gentlemen have spoken of the Committee above Stairs, but, considering what passed there, and who were the Actors, I think they might have been silent. Their Conduct put me in Mind of an old Surrey Justice, who, on a Culprit being brought before him, cried, "You Rogue, you Villain, I suppose you have been an old Offender, what Thefts have you been guilty of?" I have stole Cows, Horses, and Sheep, please your Worship. The Fellow was hanged on his own Confession, and it appeared afterwards, that he took this Method of getting rid of a Life already become too burdensome to him to be worth keeping.

Mr. Sollicitor General. My learned Friend seems extremely angry with the Petitioners, on Account of their real or affected Ignorance of the Event of the Literary Property Decision in the other House. For my Part, I cannot see their Conduct in that very criminal Light. Nor can I perceive how they could have acted otherwise than they did, unless they searched all the Coffee-Houses in the Neighbourhood of the Temple, and collected the Opinions of the several Students frequenting them; for it cannot be denied but they had previously taken the Opinion of the most eminent of the Profession, and had likewise a Determination of the Superior Court in their Favour, as well as the implied one of the Court of Chancery by the several Injunctions which had been granted from that Court.

Mr. E. Burke. The learned Member over the Way has been very eloquent on the many evil Consequences arising from Monopolies, but I cannot see that one of his Arguments apply in this Case, because, in granting what he justly in one Sense terms a Privilege, no one Person whatever will be injured. In this Sense then, though it may partake in some Points of the Qualities that distinguish a Monopoly, it will in the only essential Difference, that of public or private Injury, totally differ from a Monopoly.

Mr. Dempster. The Honourable Gentleman, Colonel Onslow, has told us a very humorous and witty Story, but it wants one of its greatest Recommendations to such a Claim, that of Novelty (alluding to the same Arguments made Use of by him in the Committee above Stairs). Another Hon. Gentleman (Mr. Burke) contends, that no Man can be injured by our granting the Prayer of the Petitioners. Is this really the Fact? or has a Man at a very uncommon Expence and Trouble, resisted what he deemed a public Injury and Injustice, and what the Event clearly proved to be so; and shall he, after all this Trouble, be precluded from reaping any Benefit from it by an *ex post facto* Law?

[112]It became the Boston Port Act 1774 (14 Geo. III, c. 19).

Lord Folkstone. I must confess that I cannot subscribe to the Ideas entertained on either Side of the House; for, though I think the Conduct of the Petitioners was extremely ambiguous, obscure, and unsatisfactory, it is pretty evident that they are entitled to every Aid in our Power; so that it has no Retrospect further back than the Determination of the Court of King's Bench. I do therefore move, that the Remainder of the Motion, after "others" be left out, and "Purchasers within a Time limited" inserted in their Stead. The Question being put on this Amendment, it passed in the Negative; Ayes 25, Noes 50. The Question was then put on Mr. Field's original Motion, which passed in the Affirmative, Ayes 54, Noes 16.

A Bill was accordingly ordered to be brought in, and the House rose at Half past Six.

Version 3: *Lloyd's Evening Post*, 23–25 March, 287; *London Chronicle*, 24–26 March, 292; *Edinburgh Evening Courant*, 30 March; *London Magazine*, 620–2; Cobbett's *Parliamentary History*, xvii, cols 1086–9.

… **Mr. Feilde,**[113] **[**Not PH: Chairman of the Committee appointed to hear evidence in support of the Petition of the Booksellers of London and Westminster, [LC/LM: and other holders of copy-right] made his report, which was, that the Committee had examined evidence, and found the facts stated to be true.**]** [PH: reported from the Committee, to whom the Petition of the booksellers of London and Westminster, on behalf of themselves and others, holders of copy-right; and also the Petition of John Christian Bach, and Charles Frederick Abel, on behalf of themselves and several other composers and proprietors of books, works, and compositions in music, were severally referred; that the Committee had examined the matter of fact contained in the first-mentioned Petition; and had also examined the matter of the second-mentioned Petition; and that that Committee had directed him to report a state of the facts contained in the first-mentioned Petition, and also the matter of the second-mentioned Petition, as it appeared to them, to the House; and he read the Report in his place.][114]

Mr. Feilde said a great deal in favour of the Booksellers as to the hardship of their case, and [LLP/EC: that] [LC/LM/PH: how] they had been led astray by the decision of the Court of King's-bench in 1769;[115] he concluded with [Not PH: making a Motion, "That leave be given to bring in a Bill for the relief of the Booksellers, and other Holders of Copy-right, and to allow them a further limited time for their sole property in Copyright."] [PH: moving "That leave be given to bring in a Bill for relief of booksellers, and others, by vesting the copies of printed books in the purchasers of such copies from authors or their assigns, for a time therein to be limited."] [LLP/EC: —**Mr. Sawbridge** immediately rose, and after observing upon the distress in which the Petitioners stood involved, and the justness of their appeal to the compassion of the House, he seconded **Mr. Feilde's** Motion.]— **The Attorney General**[116] [LC/LM/PH: was against the booksellers; he] said, they were a set of [LLP/EC: monopolizers] [LC/LM/PH: impudent monopolizing men], that they [LM/PH:

[113] *London Chronicle* has Mr Paul Feilde.

[114] The Report from the *CJ* was then inserted into *Cobbett's Parl. Hist*; see Part IV: Petition Report.

[115] *Millar v Taylor* (1769) 4 Burr 2303 (98 ER 201).

[116] *London Chronicle/London Magazine* called him Mr Attorney General and *Cobbett's Parl. Hist.* Mr Attorney General Thurlow.

had] combined together and raised a fund of upwards of 3,000l.[117] in order to file Bills in Chancery against any person who should endeavour to get a livelihood as well as themselves; that [Not LM: although] they had purchased Copies from *Homer* [PH: down] to *Hawkeworth's* voyages, [LLP/EC: the latter book] **[**LC/LM/PH: which [LC/PH:, he said,] was very low indeed, [LC/PH: that] Hawkesworth's book, which**]** was a mere composition of trash, sold for three guineas by their monopolizing; [Not LM: And] [LM: he] observed, that the Booksellers were highly censurable for not having taken Council's opinion whether they had a right in Copies or not, and not to rely solely upon the decision of the Court of King's Bench. He said, they had not proved any thing in the Committee, neither did he think they had any claim to the protection of the House. [LC/LM/PH: He was exceedingly severe on the Booksellers of London throughout the whole of his speech, and much in favour of Donaldson.]—**Mr. Dunning**, **[**LC/PH: in a [LC: very long and] masterly speech,**]** answered [LC/LM/PH: all] his objections [LLP/EC: and asked,] [LC/LM: said,] Were the Booksellers [LM/ PH:, he said,] to [LLP/EC: dance] [LC/LM/PH: go dancing] about town, to all the Coffee-houses and Inns of Court, to ask Attornies' Clerks, whether a decision in their favour in the Court of King's Bench was binding or not? No: They relied solely on the opinion of Lord Mansfield,[118] [Not LM: whom] [LM: whose advice] they thought superior to any other [Not LM: advice] they could receive. He entered very fully into the merits of the Booksellers' Case, mentioned a number of instances in their favour, and said, that his honourable and learned Friend [Not PH: (Mr. Thurloe)] not a month since, was of opinion [LC/LM/PH: that] the London Booksellers were in the right; but since the decision of the House of Lords, and [Not PH: that] Mr. Donaldson had become his Client, he had changed his opinion.—**Mr. Greaves** [LC/LM/PH: spoke much against the Booksellers; he] said, he had attended the Committee, and found that the person who was examined as a witness was a party concerned; that he had put a considerable number of questions to him concerning what the Booksellers had lost by the late final determination of the House of Lords, but he could get no direct answers; that it was shameful to allow a monopoly in books; they might as well allow a monopoly of any thing else; that monopolies always enhanced the price of goods; that [Not PH: as to] being fearful of being undersold by the Booksellers of Edinburgh, [LLP/EC: it] was idle, for no person would purchase an Edinburgh book when he could get an English one, for the Scotch editions were generally incorrect, and not fit for a Gentleman's library.—**The Solicitor General**[119] [LLP/EC: in answer said, that] **[**LC/LM/PH: answered him very smartly; [PH: he] said, [LM: that] as to**]** no persons [Not LM/PH: would buy] [LM/PH: buying] [LLP/EC: Scotch Editions] [LC/LM/PH: a Scotch edition], because [Not LM: they were] incorrect, was a mistake, for persons must buy them before they could find out the faults, and [LC/LM/PH: that] the lowness of [Not LC/PH: the] price was a great temptation; [LC/LM: said] as to the Petitioners being reprehensible for not having taken Council's opinion, [LLP/EC: it] [PH: that] was idle [PH:, for,] as the Hon. Gentleman (Mr. Dunning) had said, Were they to enquire of an Attorney when they had the opinion of the first Judge in the Kingdom? [LLP/EC: He said the Attorney General] [LC/LM/PH: He was extremely close upon the Attorney General,] [LC: whom][LM/PH: who,] he said, could not be serious in what he had alledged; that as to the

[117]See Five Letters.

[118]William Murray, Lord Mansfield, chief justice king's bench, 1756–88.

[119]*London Chronicle/London Magazine* have Mr Solicitor General and *Cobbett's Parl. Hist.* has Mr Solicitor General Wedderburn.

witness being a party concerned, he was not, for he had proved to the Committee that he had sold the Copy Right he had bought for 12,000l. to his son for 9,000l. and that by the late decision in the House of Lords it was imagined it would not now sell for 4,000l.[120]—[LC/LM/PH: **Col. Onslow** said he would inform the House, the reason why Mr. Johnson,[121] the witness, did not answer the questions, it was because they were improper; that he was present in the Committee at the time the questions were asked, one of which was, "Have not the Booksellers entered into a combination to prosecute any person that shall reprint their works?" He said, he told the Committee then, that if the member insisted on his question he should put one, which was, "How many acts in your life have you committed for which you deserve to be hanged?" He said he only remembered one instance of such a question being put, which was at Guildford, where an old fool of a criminal was brought before an old fool of a justice for horse-stealing; the justice, who was in his dotage, said to the criminal, "I suppose you have many time stolen cows and calves as well as horses, an't you?" The criminal being tired of his life, but not having resolution enough to put an end to his existence, replied, "Yes, an' please your Honour." The consequence he said was, the man was hanged. He afterwards told another humorous story of the Committee driving the witness out of the room with a flaming sword, like the Angels driving out Adam from the garden of Eden. He spoke much in favour of the Booksellers, and said he heartily wished they might have relief.

Mr. Dempster said, the Hon. Gentleman alluded to him, as the person who asked the improper questions; that, however improper the questions might be, he believed they were true; [Not PH: that] he really thought the Petitioners had not the least right to expect any relief from the House, for that Mr. Donaldson had, at a prodigious expence, obtained a verdict in his favour from the first Court of Law in the kingdom, and that it was cruel, [LC/PH: to] [LM: in] the highest degree, to endeavour to wrest that verdict out of his hands.**]** **Mr. E. Burke**[122] [LLP/EC: in his speech] [LC:, in a long and spirited speech] [LM: in a long speech], set forth the absurdity of the arguments [Not LLP/EC: that had been] urged against the Petitioners; he said, there could not be a clearer proof of the justice of their cause, or a stronger reason for them to think themselves right, than Judge Blackstone's selling his book to a Bookseller for a large sum, and afterwards maintaining the opinion of the Bookseller's right to Literary Property. He spoke [Not LM: much] in favour of Blackstone's Commentaries, which he said were now, and always would be esteemed; and when the Booksellers had the opinion of so able a Judge on their side, he thought they had a just right to imagine themselves secure in purchasing a Copy Right. He was exceedingly [LLP/EC: sarcastic] [LC/LM/PH: smart] on the Attorney General, who, he said, now, was an ornament to the Bar, and he made no doubt, from his conduct, but he would soon become an ornament to the Bench [LC/LM: (meaning the Treasury Bench)]. He spoke much in favour of the Booksellers, and said he should give his hearty consent to a Bill being brought in.—**Lord Folkestone** said, he did not mean to oppose the Bill in this early stage, but he should move for an amendment to the Motion, [LLP/LC/EC/LM: which was, that after the words, "Copy Right," be inserted, "who shall have purchased, within a certain time to be limited." **Sir George Savile** made an objection to the amendment, though he said, he did not see but it was a very necessary step to be

[120]The *London Magazine* has 3,000l.

[121]*London Magazine* has Johnston.

[122]'Edmund Burke' in *Cobbett's Parl. Hist.*

observed: that he had weighed the matter within [LLP/EC: himself] [LC/LM: him], and found that it would require the utmost of their attention.— The question was then put, that the amendment stand part of the Motion: for it 16; against it 54. The original Motion was then put: for it 51; against it 25. The Bill was ordered in accordingly.**]** [PH: by leaving out from the word "others" to the end the question, and inserting "purchasers of copy-rights, within a limited time."

The question being put, that the words proposed to be left out stand part of the question; the House divided. The Yeas went forth.

Tellers.

YEAS	Mr. Feilde Mr. Ald Sawbridge	50
NOES	Lord Folkestone Mr. Graves	25

So it was resolved in the affirmative. Then the main question being put, That leave be given to bring in a Bill; the House divided. The Yeas went forth.

Tellers.

YEAS	Mr. Burke Mr. Whitworth	54
NOES	Mr. Attorney General Mr. Charles James Fox	16

So it was resolved in the affirmative.]

Version 4: *Public Advertiser*, 25 March.

… at Three o'Clock **Paul Feilde, Esq**; brought up the Report from the Committee who were appointed to enquire into the Petition of the Booksellers of London and Westminster, and other Holders of Copy Right; when the Clerk of the House having read over the said Report, containing the Evidence of Mr. Johnston and Mr. Wilkie, **Mr. Feilde** then got up and explained to the House the Nature and Necessity there was for some Relief being given to the Petitioners; went through the Whole of their Case; shewed plainly that it was a Matter in which the House ought to give them Relief; that a few Months ago they had great Property in Copy Right; but since the Determination of the House of Lords, they were worth nothing; he concluded with making a Motion for Leave to bring in a Bill for the Relief of the Booksellers and others for a limited Time. **Mr. Alderman Sawbridge** got and said that his Honourable Friend had entered so largely upon the Subject that he should content himself by seconding the Motion. **The Attorney General** then got up, and spoke warmly against the Motion, entered largely upon the Statute of Queen Anne; and to shew they had never no Common Law Right; he then entered upon the Examination of Mr. Johnston; said that Parliament would never give Relief to one single Man who pretends that he has sustained a Loss. What Loss? Has it ever been proved before the Committee what Loss? No: But a Set of artful Men combine together, and send about to the Booksellers in the Country to take the Scotch Editions of Books from them on Purpose to sell their own. He concluded, by saying he should be totally against the Bill. **Mr. Dunning** then got up, and answered him in every Particular, shewed that they were not a Set of Men in Combination together; for that Word would imply something bad in it: He said he wished his worthy Friend had but considered that he had no Client in this Case. My worthy Friend asks, what Loss have they sustained? undoubtedly the Booksellers thought two Months ago, and by the Determination of the Court of King's-Bench, that they had a great Property in their Hands, and now they have none; therefore that is the Loss which they now apply to this House for Redress. **Mr. Graves** got up and answered Mr. Dunning; he said as to the Scotch Editions of Books they were so imperfect that no Gentleman would have them appear in his Library. **Lord North** then got up and said, he did not rise to oppose the Motion, only to acquaint the House, that as it was intended for the Boston Port Bill to be read a third Time, and as this Question seems to take up some Debate, he wished that Gentleman would put it off till To-morrow, which was agreed to.

Col Onslow then got up, and entered very fully into the Hardships of the Petitioners, and spoke very strongly in their Favour. **Mr. Dempster** got up next, and spoke against the Motion. **Mr. Burke** spoke next, and entered very fully into all the Arguments that had been used against the Motion, said that the Booksellers went by the Authority of the Court of King's Bench, and was they afterwards to take Opinion of Council to know whether their Decision was right, but now they have had it decided against them, they only desire such Relief as this House thinks proper. One of our Judges has sold to the Booksellers that great Book of the Laws of England, and certainly he knows what the Common Law Right is.

Lord Folkstone then got up just to leave out Part of the Motion, and to add some other Words, when the Question being called for, the Speaker put, Whether the latter Part of the Motion should be left out? when the House divided, Noes 50, Ayes 25; then the Motion was put as it stood first, when the House divided, Ayes 54, Noes 16. A Bill was then ordered in upon the said Motion, and the House broke up at Quarter past Six, and adjourned to this Day.

Among the Gentlemen who divided for the Booksellers were, Mr. Feilde, Geo. Onslow, Col. Onslow, Mr. Grey Cooper, Solicitor General, Mr. Dunning, Sir Charles Whitworth, Mr. Whitworth, Mr. Martin, Mr. Baker, Mess. Crosby, Sawbridge, Oliver, Harley, the Lord Mayor, two Burkes, General Carnac, Mr. Van, Mr. Montague, Mr. Fuller, and Mr. Cavendish.

A noble L—d, who took a great Lead in the Affairs of Literary Property, was asked his Opinion of Mrs. M—y's 'Modest Plea for the Property of Copy Right: I think, replied his L—p, *it is a Copy of the Lady's Countenance*. That is very probable, said a Gentleman who stood by, and I do not wonder since that is the Case, that she should be desirous of converting her *Copy-hold* into Free-*hold*.

Version 5: *Edinburgh Advertiser*, 25–29 March, 197–8.

Yesterday, **Mr. Field**, chairman to the committee, appointed to take into consideration the petition of the booksellers of London and Westminster, made a report to the House of Commons. After the evidence laid before the committee was read, Mr. Field explained the ground on which the petitioners stood: He informed the House, that the combined booksellers of London and Westminster were a respectable body; that they had laid out large sums of money on that, in which, by the late decision of the House of Lords, they were informed for the first time they had no property; and that now they appealed to the compassion of the house for relief in their present distressed circumstances. He therefore moved for leave to bring in a bill "for the relief of booksellers and others, by vesting the copies of printed books, in the purchasers of such from authors or their assigns, for a time therein to be limited." **Mr. Sawbridge** seconded the motion.

The **Attorney General** declared, that what had been read as the report of the committee was no matter of evidence, but merely the opinion of an interested party. He thanked the honourable member who brought in the report, for having informed the House, that the petitioners were the *united* and *combined* booksellers of London and Westminster: it was, he said, a very just description, for the petition was the dark, unintelligible prayer of a combination of tradesmen; to procure a legal but an odious monopoly, prejudicial to the public interest, and of infinite mischief to many individuals. The booksellers saw how necessary it was to make the matter as unfathomable to the house as possible, and had conducted the inquiry in so intricate a manner, that no light was thrown on the subject, and the committee when they rose, were fully as wise as when they sat down. He had endeavoured in vain to get some insight into the affected distress of the petitioners, but their interest taught them to conceal the true state of the case; for, when he asked one of the petitioners a proper question, he was answered, *That the petitioner was not prepared to speak to that question*. The booksellers had laid much weight upon the decision of the King's Bench, in the cause Millar against Taylor; had they consulted the lawyers, they would have paid no attention to it, as all the lawyers to a man were of opinion, that that decision was erroneous: the booksellers themselves were conscious of it, as they had bought off Taylor from bringing an appeal. It appeared from the evidence, that the petitioners had *combined* and *united* into a subscription to harass all the country booksellers, to hinder them from printing all books in which they thought proper to claim a property even the classics, they maintained before the committee, were their *honorary copy-right*. The petition was an insult upon the house; for if a person had been so foolish as to purchase an estate without a sufficient title, and was evicted out of that estate by a final decision in a court of justice, what would parliament think of his applying to them to give him a good title to that which did not belong to him?

Mr. Dunning took the opposite side of the question, he said, that the error the petitioners had fallen into was a natural one; that their case was peculiarly hard, as they had been led into that error by a solemn decision adjudged by a bench of judges, in the highest of the law-courts below. That it was absurd to think that the booksellers would consult lawyers, after having the opinion of Lord Mansfield, to whom alone they trusted, and whom they thought superior to any other advice they could receive.

Mr. Graves said he attended the committee, and found the person examined as a witness, a party concerned; that he had put a considerable number of questions to him, concerning what he had lost by the late decision, but could get no direct answers. He thought it shameful to allow a monopoly in books, as they might as well allow a monopoly in any thing else. The inevitable consequence of which would be to enhance the price of the commodities so monopolized.

The debate continued about three hours, when on a division there appeared 50 for the question, 25 against it.

The speakers *for* the question were, Mr. Feild, Mr. Sawbridge, Mr. Dunning, the Solicitor General, Col. Onslow, and Mr. Burke. *Against* it, the Attorney General, Mr. Graves, Mr. Dempster, Sir George Saville, and Lord Folkstone.

Version 6: *Gazetteer*, 25 March; *Craftsman*, 26 March.

At half after three **Mr. Field** brought up the report from the Committee, to whom the Petition of the London Booksellers, respecting copyright, was referred, and the same being delivered in at the table, was read by the clerk. It contained several particular facts, respecting sums of money being paid for copies, and of their comparative value before and since the late determination of the House of Lords on the subject of literary property, which was stated to have decreased in a proportion of four to one. Besides this general information, the report contained a great number of questions put to Mr. Johnston, the principal evidence examined by the Committee. The report concluded with desiring relief in the usual terms.

Mr. Field then prefaced a motion he intended to make for entering into a general view of the affair in its several stages before the several Courts of Judicature; expatiated largely on the very great hardships the petitioners must suffer if denied relief by Parliament, and relied much on the very melancholy consequences in which families, widows, and orphans, must inevitably be involved, if their properties, should be thrown in common among the public at large.

He was answered by the **Attorney-General**, who arraigned the ignorance of the London booksellers, in trusting their property on so precarious a security, and their impudence in applying to Parliament for relief from the consequences of blunders they had artfully or obstinately been the occasion of themselves.

Mr. Dunning answered his leader with great abilities, and shewed, in a very masterly manner, that if the booksellers had fallen into an error, they were not so much to blame, as they shared the imputed ignorance in common with some of the most able and eminent sages of the law.

Mr. Greaves observed, that he had attended the Committee above stairs, and that among the numerous questions he put, and which led to the only true ground on which the present application could be supported, he never received one precise nor direct answer.

Mr. Solicitor-General next spoke, and answered very fully and satisfactorily many of the objections made by the two learned gentlemen on the other side.

Colonel Onslow gave a very entertaining account of the conduct of several gentleman above stairs, and of the immateriality, *inherency*, and incorporeality of literary property. He was very strenuous in behalf of the petitioners, and while on his legs kept the House in a loud laugh.

Mr. Burke was very ingenious on the same side, and shewed that there was a great difference between a monopoly which entrenched on other people's right, and that by which no person suffered.

Mr. Dempster answered Mr. Burke against the petitioners.

The following motion, first made by Mr. Field, was at length put, "That leave be given to bring in a bill for the relief of booksellers and *others*, by vesting of printing books in the purchasers of such copies from authors, or their assigns, for a time therein to be limited."

Lord Folkstone said, that he disagreed with both sides of the House; for as on one hand he thought the booksellers were deserving of the commiseration of Parliament, so on the other he could not think them entitled to any security for purchases made further back than the year 1768, the time the Court of King's Bench gave the determination in their favour: he therefore moved, that the remainder of the words, after *others*, should be left out, and the following substituted in place of them, "purchasers within a time limitted:"

And the question being put, the House divided, Ayes, 25, for the amendment; against it 50.— This made room for the original motion, which caused a second division; Ayes 54, Noes 16:— A bill was accordingly ordered to be brought in.

Version 7: *Morning Post*, 25 Mar; *Middlesex Journal*, 24–26 March.

… until half past three o'clock, when **Mr. Field**, Chairman of the Committee appointed to hear evidence in support of the Petition of the London Booksellers made a report to the House, that they had examined into the Petition, and found the allegations there set forth to be true; he then made a short speech in favour of the booksellers and concluded with making a motion that leave be given to bring in a bill for the relief of the booksellers and other holders of copy right &c.

Mr. Attorney General, in a long speech, arraigned the conduct of the London booksellers; called them a set of impudent monopolizing men that wanted to engross the whole of the trade to themselves, and spoke much in favour of Mr. Donaldson, who, he said, at a vast expence, had obtained a final decree from the first tribunal in the land.

Mr. Greaves seconded him, and was extremely severe on the booksellers, who, he said, had not answered any question that had been asked them on the Committee.

Mr. Dunning, in a long and spirited speech, set forth the whole of the proceedings, and answered the Attorney-General in a very masterly manner.

The Solicitor-General spoke much in favour of the booksellers; and said, that whatever opinion his honourable friend the Attorney-General harboured now, that before the decision of the Lords, he was of opinion, that the booksellers had a right to perpetuity; he was very severe on the Attorney-General.

Mr. Onslow spoke much in favour of the booksellers; and related several stories with a deal of humour; was very severe on the conduct of Mr. Dempster in the Committee for asking improper questions.

Mr. Dempster, in a short speech, said, he thought the measure was wrong; that Mr. Donaldson had gained a decree, and it was not just now to take it away.

Mr. E. Burke spoke a long time in favour of the booksellers, and was exceedingly humorous throughout the whole of his speech.

The other speakers for the bill were Sir Geo. Saville, &c. Against it Lord Folkstone, &c.

Lord Folkstone proposed an amendment to the motion, which was for it to extend only to such owners of copy-right as had purchased within a limited time back. On a division for the original motion, 54 against 16; on a division for the amendment, 25 against 51.

Version 8: *Scots Magazine*, 530–1.

On the 24th of March **Mr Paul Feilde**, chairman of the committee in the absence of Ald. Harley, reported, that the committee had examined evidence, and found the facts stated to be true; and, after saying a great deal in favour of the petitioners, moved, That leave be given to bring in a bill for the relief of the booksellers, and other holders of copyright; and to allow them a further limited time for their sole property in copyright.—**The Attorney-General**, on the other hand, was very severe on the London booksellers: he said, they were a set of impudent monopolizing men, and had combined to raise a fund of upwards of 3000l. in order to file bills in chancery against any person who should endeavour to get a livelihood as well as themselves.—**Mr Dunning**, in his answer, said, that his honourable and learned friend [Mr Thurloe], not a month since, was of opinion that the London booksellers were in the right, but since the decision of the House of Lords, and that Mr Donaldson had become his client, he had changed his opinion.[123] **Mr Mansfield**[124] said, that the subscription entered into by the London booksellers, was for the purpose of indemnifying country-booksellers who had ignorantly bought pirated editions, the real proprietors names being falsely prefixed, by buying from them the books they had so bought. **Lord Folkstone** proposed an amendment, after "copyright" to insert, "who shall have purchased within a certain time to be limited." But the question being put, That the amendment stand part of the motion? it passed in the negative, 54 to 16. The question on the original motion was then put, and carried, 51 against 25. A bill was ordered in accordingly.

Version 9: *Morning Chronicle*, 24 March (Second Account); *London Evening Post*, 24–26 March.

Yesterday a report was made to the House of Commons from the Committee to whom the Petition of the Booksellers of London and Westminster, was referred, and the matters of fact which came out upon the examination stated to the House, after which it was moved for leave to bring in a bill "for the relief of Booksellers and others by vesting the copies of printed books in the purchasers of such copies from authors, or their assigns, for a time therein to be limited;" a debate arose, which held near three hours, and on a division, there appeared for the question 50, against 25; there was a trifling amendment which passed in the negative, 54 to 16.

Version 10: Debrett's *Debates*, vii, 76–83.

Mr. Feilde reported from the Committee, to whom the petition of the booksellers of London and Westminster, on behalf of themselves and others, holders of copy-right; and also the petition of John Christian Bach, and Charles Frederick Abel, on behalf of themselves and several other composers and proprietors of books, works and compositions in music, were severally referred; that the Committee had examined the matter of fact contained in the first-mentioned petition; and had also examined the matter of the second-mentioned petition; and that the Committee had directed him to report a state of the facts contained in the first-mentioned Petition, and also the matter of the second-mention petition, as it appeared to them, to the House; and he read the report in his place; and afterwards delivered it in at the Clerk's table; where the same was read.

[123]The *Scots Magazine* then has '[This shows the propriety of a resolution of our general assembly in 1751 [xiii. 258.], That no member of assembly or commission should act as counsel before those courts.]'.

[124]It is not clear who Mr. Mansfield is referring to, unless it is the London Bookseller's Counsel and his submissions during the Petition Committee.

A state of the matter of fact contained in the first-mentioned petition, is as follows; viz.

[*The Report of the Petition Committee is then set out in full*]

And the question being put, That the words proposed to be left out stand part of the question;

The House divided.

The yeas went forth.

Tellers for the Yeas	Mr. Feilde Mr. Alderman Sawbridge.	50
Tellers for the Noes	The Lord Folkestone, Mr. Graves.	25

So it was resolved in the affirmative.

Then the main question being put, That leave be given to bring in a Bill for Relief of Booksellers, and others, by vesting the copies of printed books in the purchasers of such copies from authors or their assigns, for a time therein to be limited;

The House divided

The yeas went forth.

Tellers for the Yeas	Mr. Burke Mr. Whitworth.	54
Tellers for the Noes	Attorney General, Mr. Charles James Fox.	16

So it was resolved in the affirmative.

Ordered, That Mr. Feilde, Mr. Alderman Sawbridge, Mr. Solicitor General, Mr. Dunning, Mr. Burke, Mr. Alderman Harley, and Mr. Harris, do prepare, and bring in the said Bill.

Notes

***Morning Chronicle*, 24 March; *Public Advertiser*, 24 March**: This day Mr. Field will report to the House from the Committee who were appointed to enquire into the petition of the booksellers of London and Westminster, that they had examined the said petition, and found the facts to be true, when it is expected a bill will be ordered in upon the said report.

***Daily Advertiser*, 25 March**: Proceeded on the Report of the Committee relative to the Petition of the Booksellers. Ordered in a Bill, on a Division 50 against 25; and an Amendment 54 against 16.

***General Evening Post*, 24–26 March**: Proceeded on the report of the Committee relative to the petition of the booksellers. A long debate ensured. Ordered in a bill, on a division 50 against 25; and an on amendment 54 against 16.

***Morning Chronicle*, 29 March**: A counter petition is prepared and signed by the stall booksellers, in order to be presented to the House of Commons, against the bill for the relief of the booksellers holders of copy-right.

Mr. Fielde, Mr. Sawbridge, the Solicitor General, Mr. Dunning, Mr. Burke, Mr. Harley, and Mr. Harris, are ordered to prepare and bring in the bill for relief of booksellers and others, by vesting the copies of printed books in the purchasers of such copies from authors, or their assigns, for a time therein to be limited.

First Reading: 22 April

Version 1: *Morning Chronicle*, 23 April; *Middlesex Journal*, 21–23 April.

Yesterday the Booksellers bill was presented by **Paul Field, Esq;** and read a first time. Mr. Field, and **Colonel Onslow**, spoke for a short time upon it, when **Mr. Dempster** rose, and begged that it might meet with the attention of the House, as it [MC: was] a very extraordinary measure to follow so closely after the determination of the House of Lords,[125] he hoped therefore every member would maturely weigh its consequences, and that the petitions against it might be fully heard. The second reading is ordered for Wednesday se'nnight.

A petition from some London Booksellers was also presented against the bill, and counsel are to be heard for and against the same on the day above mentioned.

A petition from some booksellers in Edinburgh, and another from Glasgow, were presented against it.

[MC: The Booksellers Bill, after stating the purport of the 10th of Queen Anne, observes that it hath been a prevailing opinion with Booksellers and others, that authors and their assigns had by the Common Law, independently of the act of Queen Anne, the sole right of printing and re-printing Copies of their works; and that the said act was not intended to take away or abridge any such right; and in consequence of this opinion, many of them have from time of time invested the whole, or the greatest part, of their fortunes in the purchase of such Copy Rights, on which the support of them and their families at this time doth in a great measure depend.

After this it recites the late reversal of the decree in their favour, and points out the ruinous consequences that may ensue from it.

The enacting clause are to give authors of books already printed, or those who have purchased or acquired the Copy-right of books already printed, the sole and exclusive right and liberty of printing such books for a term to be limited; and that if any other Bookseller, Printer, or Person whatsoever, from and after a certain day, shall print, or import, or cause to be printed or imported any such books, without the consent of the proprietor thereof, or, knowing the same to be so printed without the consent of the proprietor or proprietors thereof respectively, shall sell, or cause to be sold, any such books without such consent, then such offenders shall forfeit certain penalties, and also forfeit for every sheet which shall be found in their custody, either printed, printing or published, a modus to be limited

[125] *Donaldson v Beckett* (1774) *Cobbett's Parl. Hist.* xvii, col. 953.

by the act, part of it to go to the King, and the other part to any person that shall sue for the same.[126]

The bill then ordains that the holders of Copies shall register the names of their Copies in the Hall book of the Company of Stationers,[127] regulates the mode of doing it, and provides that nothing in the act shall extend to prevent any persons from selling such impressions or copies of any books as shall have been actually printed and published before the passing of the act,[128] and might have been lawfully sold by such persons in case this act had not been made; and also, that nothing contained in it shall extend or be construed to deprive any Authors, who shall not before the passing of this act have sold, or for a valuable consideration disposed of their whole right or interest in or to the Copies of any books so printed and published, to the Printers or Publishers thereof respectively, of any right or interest in or to such Copy or Copies, or power of reprinting the same, which they had or were intitled to before the passing of the act, or might or ought to have enjoyed in case the act had not been made.

The bill reserves the Patent Rights in the Universities;[129] and enacts that if any person resident in Scotland, shall incur any of the penalties,[130] they shall be recoverable by any action before the court of sessions in that kingdom.]

Version 2: *Public Ledger*, 23 April; *London Chronicle*, 21–23 April, 392; *Lloyd's Evening Post*, 22–25 April, 388; *London Magazine*, 622–3; Cobbett's *Parliamentary History*, xvii, cols 1089–90.

[Not LC/PH: **Mr. Feilde** presented the Booksellers Bill] [LLP: the substance of which,][131] [LM: which] [LLP/LM: after stating the purport of the 10th of Queen Anne,] [LLP: is,] [LM: observes] That it hath been a prevailing opinion with Booksellers and others, that Authors and their Assigns had, by the Common Law, independently of the Act of Queen Anne, the sole right of printing and re-printing Copies of their Works; and that the said act was not intended to take away or abridge any such right; and in consequence of this opinion, many of them have from time of time invested the whole or the greatest part of their fortunes in the purchase of such Copy Rights, on which the support of them and their families at this time doth in a great measure depend.

After this it recites the late reversal of the Decree in their favour, and points out the ruinous consequences that may ensue from it.

The enacting Clauses are to give Authors of books already printed, or those who have purchased or acquired the Copy-right of books already printed, the sole and exclusive right and liberty of printing such books for a term to be limited; and that if any other Bookseller, Printer, or Person whatsoever, from and after a certain day, shall print, or import, or cause to be printed or imported any such books, without the consent of the Proprietor thereof,

[126] Part IV, Booksellers' Bill, cl. 1.

[127] Booksellers' Bill, cl. 2.

[128] Booksellers' Bill, cl. 5.

[129] Booksellers' Bill, cl. 7.

[130] Booksellers' Bill, cl. 8.

[131] This summary of the Bill is either copied from, or from the same source, as Version 1. It is quite possible this is just a straight copy from the Bill's brevet.

or, knowing the same to be so printed without the consent of the Proprietor or Proprietors thereof respectively, shall sell, or cause to be sold, any such books without such consent, then such offenders shall forfeit certain penalties, and also forfeit for every sheet which shall be found in their custody, either printed, printing or published, a Modus to be limited by the Act, part of it to go to the King, and the other part to any person that shall sue for the same.

The Bill then ordains that the holders of Copies shall register the names of their Copies in the Hall book of the Company of Stationers, regulates the mode of doing it, and provides that nothing in the Act shall extend to prevent any persons from selling such impressions or copies of any books as shall have been actually printed and published before the passing of the Act, and might have been lawfully sold by such persons in case this act had not been made; and also, that nothing contained in it shall extend or be construed to deprive any Authors, who shall not before the passing of this Act have sold, or for a valuable consideration disposed of their whole right or interest in or to the Copies of any books so printed and published, to the Printers or Publishers thereof respectively, of any right or interest in or to such Copy or Copies, or power of reprinting the same, which they had or were intitled to before the passing of the Act, or might or ought to have enjoyed in case the act had not been made.

The Bill reserves the Patent Rights in the Universities; and enacts that if any person resident in Scotland, shall incur any of the penalties, they shall be recoverable by any action before the Court of Sessions in that kingdom.**]**

[LC: **Mr. Feilde** presented the bill for vesting the copy right in Authors and their Assigns, for a time to be therein limited] [PH: Mr. Feilde presented the Bill to the House.] **[**PL/LC, which was read a first time, but] [LM: While] [PH: Whilst] [LM/PH: the bill was reading] [Not LLP/PH: the House being vociferous,]**[**Not LLP: **Mr. Dempster**[132] [Not PH: got up, and desired the House to be attentive,] [PH: called the attention of the House to it,] as this was a Bill to reverse a Decree of the Supreme Court of Judicature in this kingdom**]**

[PL/LC/LLP: Mr Dempster] [LM/PH: He then] presented a Petition from the Country Booksellers against the [Not LM/PH: London Booksellers] Bill.

Lord Frederick Campbell[133] [Not PH: likewise] presented a Petition from the Booksellers of [Not PH: the city of] Glasgow against the Bill **[**Not PH: of the London Booksellers, both which Petitions were ordered to [PL/LLP: lay] [LC/LM: lie] on the table.**]**

[LLP: The above Bill was read a first time; before which, Mr. Dempster got up, and desired the House to be attentive, as this was a Bill to reverse a Decree of the supreme Court of Judicature in this kingdom]

Col. Onslow said, he was astonished to hear any person make such a declaration, [LM: as had Mr. Dempster] [PH: as Mr. Dempster had done] for the Bill was not founded on any such principles: [PL/LC/LLP: that] it had not any connection with the decree: that he should be far from espousing the Bill was it meant for that purpose: that he held what the Lords did to be the law of the land; but it was no new thing for an application to be made to the Commons for redress against laws, when they were particularly hard and cruel; that he firmly believed there would have been no occasion for [Not LM/PH: this] [LM/PH: the] Bill, had the Judge, who was silent on the occasion in the Lords, [PH: (lord Mansfield),] delivered his

[132] George Dempster.

[133] Lord Frederick Campbell† (1729–1816), MP for Glasgow Burghs.

opinion; he said, it was what he ought to have done; [Not PH: that] by their opinions people were to be guided; [Not PH: that] for those purposes they had large salaries, and [Not LLP: no one][LLP: none] of them ought to be above their office.

Mr. Feilde [Not PH: said, he] agreed with the Hon. Gentleman, that, had [Not LLP: that][LLP: the] [PH: learned] Judge given his opinion, this Bill would not now have been before the House; but, on account of a trial in the King's Bench,[134] the Booksellers had laid out great sums in copy right, so much, that unless some relief was given them, they must inevitably be ruined; that as to this being a Bill to reverse a decree of the Lords [PH: that] was entirely wrong, which the Hon. Gentleman would see, was he to look into it.

Mr. Dempster said, the Bill was only meant to serve a few individuals; that many persons had signed the Petition for it through fear, threats, &c. that the case of Mr. Donaldson,[135] was extremely hard; he had been dragged through all the Courts of Law both in this kingdom and Scotland, and at last to the House of Lords, where he obtained a decree [Not LLP: for] to carry on his business in the way which he always had done.[136] That this Bill was not meant to restore the Law concerning copy right as it formerly stood, but as the individual Booksellers of London thought it stood; he said, he should not oppose the order for the [Not PH: second] [PH: first] reading, but would undoubtedly attack it whenever it was read a second time, and hoped that some time would be given for the perusal of the Bill [Not PH: before the second reading].

[Not PH: Mr. Feilde said he had no objection, and proposed next Wednesday se'nnight, which was agreed to.]

[PH: The Bill was ordered to be read a second time on the 4th of May.]

Version 3: *St James's Chronicle*, 21–23 April; *Edinburgh Advertiser*, 26–29 April, 266–7 (Second Account).

[SJC: Petitions were likewise presented from certain Booksellers in London and Westminster, in behalf of themselves and Brethren in the Country, as likewise from the Printers and Booksellers of the City of Glasgow against the intended Bill, "for vesting the Copies of printed Books in Purchasers of such Copies from Authors or their Assigns for a Time therein to be limited."

As soon as the Petitions were read, **Mr. Feilde** presented the last-mentioned Bill, which was read a first Time.] [EA: The bill for relief of the Booksellers of London and Westminster, being read, **Sir Laurence Dundas**,[137] **Lord Frederick Campbell**, and **Mr. Dempster**, presented petitions from the Booksellers of Edinburgh, Glasgow, and London, against the said bill.]

Mr. Dempster. For my Part, the House has been so extremely disorderly, that I have not been able to collect a Syllable of the Contents of the Bill now read. I would with that the House had paid more Attention to a Bill [EA: of the greatest consequence] which is meant to defeat a Decree of the Supreme Court of Judicature in this Country.

[134] *Millar v Taylor* (1769) 4 Burr 2303 (98 ER 201).

[135] Alexander Donaldson* (1727–94).

[136] *Donaldson v Beckett* (1774) *Cobbett's Parl. Hist.* xvii, col. 953.

[137] Sir Lawrence Dundas† (c. 1710–1781), MP for Edinburgh.

Colonel Onslow. I am surprised to hear the Honourable Gentleman behind me (Mr. Dempster) conceive that the Bill proceeds on any such Grounds. I should be far from standing up as an Advocate for it if that were the Case. On the contrary, the Persons who are intended to be relieved by this Bill, are fully satisfied of the Wisdom and Justice of that Decision. It is not of the Law, but the Hardship of that Law, that they complain, and now come to seek a Mitigation from this House, in the first Instance, and from the very noble and august Body who determined it, in the second. I am pretty firmly persuaded, that there would have been no Need of the present Application, had the Judge who was silent in the other House [SJC: delivered his Opinion. It was his Duty to have done so.] [EA: on whose judgment the booksellers risked so much, delivered his opinion. It was his duty to have given an opinion on one side or other, and the neglecting to do so, was a manifest breach of his duty.] Judges are paid by the Public, and should render those Services attendant on their Office; and I should be glad to see a Law passed to oblige them to a strict Performance of their Duty.

Mr Feilde. I imagine the Honourable Gentleman (Mr. Dempster) has not properly considered the Contents of the Bill, or else he could not have so totally miscomprehended it. It is not meant to impeach or overturn the Determination of the other House. It proceeds chiefly to remedy an Evil occasioned by a Judgement of the Court of King's Bench, by which the Booksellers have been induced to lay out large Sums of Money, in the Purchases of Copy Rights, and by which, unless some Relief should be given, many of them must be inevitably ruined.

Mr. Dempster. I do not mean to oppose the Bill in the present Stage, or to debate or enter into its Merits till the second Reading; yet, I think, this House, who have at all Times discouraged Monopolies of every Sort, should be very cautious in the present Instance, in granting one, to the Emolument of a few interested Individuals, who have used every Effort to gain an exclusive Privilege to the Oppression of the rest of the Persons concerned in the same Business. It is said that the Decision alluded to is not meant to be impeached, but, in my Opinion, by what I could collect of the Contents of the Bill, it goes directly to that Purport, as it supposes a Right in common Law previous to the Statute of Queen Anne, and suppose the Right defeated only by that Statute. [EA: I would earnestly recommend it to the House to give that attention which the magnitude of the bill deserves. The case of Mr. Donaldson is extremely hard, he has been interrupted in the exercise of a right, to which, as the event proved, he was legally entitled; he has been dragged through all the courts of law both in this kingdom and in Scotland, and at last to the House of Lords, where he obtained a decree to carry on his business in the way he had always done; yet a bill is now brought in to hinder him from reaping the benefit he has derived from it, and has so justly merited, after a loss of so much time and trouble, attended with a very heavy expense.]— The Bill was ordered to be read a second Time on Wednesday Se'nnight, and, was ordered to be printed.

Version 4: *Gazetteer*, 23 April; *General Evening Post*, 21–23 April; *London Evening Post*, 21–23 April; *Caledonian Mercury*, 27 April; *Edinburgh Evening Courant*, 27 April; *Craftsman*, 30 April.

Mr Feild[138] brought in a bill for vesting the copy-right in authors and their assigns, for a time therein to be limitted. The bill was read; a motion being made for reading it a second time **Mr. Dempster** observed, that on account of the noise, confusion, and inattention of the House, he was yet to learn what it contained. He said, he looked upon it to be a matter of much greater consequence than it might seem on a transient view, as it was meant to give relief against an express determination of the Supreme Court of Judicature.[139]

Colonel Onslow replied, that it was by no means intended to impeach that solemn decision; that the justice and equity of it were unquestionable; that, however, there was one circumstance attending it, which rendered the case of the booksellers extremely hard, which was, the silence of one of the Judges,[140] on whose judgment they had risqued a very considerable part of their property; that, in his opinion, such a silence deserved severe reprehension; that a Judge's place being an office, required the discharge of a duty, for the execution of which they were paid by the public; that declining to give an opinion on one side or other, was a manifest neglect of that duty; and wished that a law was passed to compel to a faithful and punctual discharge of it.

Mr. Feild observed, that the Honourable Gentleman behind him (Mr. Dempster) had entirely mistaken the grounds on which the bill proceeded [GZ/LNP: on]; that the question was not what is now law, or what was always so, but simply whether, the petitioners being in a mistake, deserved relief, considering the causes which led to that mistake.

Mr. Dempster said he should not then enter into the merits of the question, reserving his objections for the second reading; but he recommended earnestly to the House to give the question that attention a matter of so much magnitude deserved, and at the same time, while they were busily employed in contemplating one side of the question, not totally to overlook the other. Here (says he) is a man interrupted in the exercise of a right to which, as the event proved, he was legally entitled; he is dragged to every Court in both kingdoms, and is at last brought before the supreme Judicature in the nation, and has it there established by a solemn adjudication in his favour, yet a bill is brought in to preclude from any benefit he may [GZ/LNP/CT: desire] [GP/CM/EC: derive] from it, after a waste of so much time and trouble, attended with a very heavy and ruinous [GZ/LNP/CT: an] expence. Mr. Dempster desired that a reasonable time might be allowed for the second reading, and that the bill might be printed, which were agreed to, and the bill was ordered to be read a second time on Wednesday sen'night. and to be printed.[141]

A [LNP: very well framed and judicious] petition was presented by Mr. Dempster from several Booksellers in the Cities of London and Westminster, against the said bill, in behalf of themselves and the Booksellers concerned in the country trade, previous to its being brought up and read; as likewise [Not LNP: another by Lord F. C—bell][142] from those of the City of Glasgow, praying to be heard by Counsel. [EC:; and a third by Sir Laurence Dundas from those of the city of Edinburgh, to the following purpose:

138 In the *General Evening Post* the names were partially obscured: F—ld, D—ster, O—low, J—s (Judges).

139 *Donaldson v Beckett* (1774) *Cobbett's Parl. Hist.* xvii, col. 953.

140 Lord Mansfield.

141 The remaining part of the *Gazetteer* is obscured but the *Craftsman's Weekly Journal* usually copied it verbatim, so it was almost certainly included.

142 Only the *Caledonian Mercury* has the name Lord F. Campbell.

'That the petitioners observe, that leave is given to bring in a bill for the relief of the booksellers of London, Westminster and others, by vesting the copies of printed books in the purchasers of such copies from authors, or their assignees, for a time to be therein limited; and the petitioners are informed that the aim of the London booksellers, since the failure of their late attempt to gain a dangerous and perpetual monopoly at common-law, is now to obtain an exercise, for a limited time, of the same exclusive privilege beyond the terms of the act of Queen Anne. That in the paper-mills alone about Edinburgh, many hundreds of persons are employed; and the booksellers, book-binders, and printers, are still most numerous, who will all be most materially affected, and some of them ruined by the consequences of the bill, should it pass into a law. Few compositions, proven of Scots authors, are published originally in Scotland; and the petitioners have hitherto lived chiefly by re-publishing, when permitted by the act of Queen Anne, and their business must be given up altogether if any further monopoly is conferred upon the London booksellers. Literary property at common-law, never existed even in idea in Scotland. The attempt made some time ago to introduce it, was received with universal disapprobation; and was, after a full discussion of its merits, over-ruled by a judgment of the supreme court. The petitioners, in consequence of the established law of the country, have laid out great sums of money in printing books not within the protection of the statute of Queen Anne, stocks of which books they have now on hand, and many now printing; and they cannot but think their situation extremely hard, if they, who have been all along exercising their undoubted legal rights, are to be subjected to vexations law-suits, and many of their families to be ruined by a law made *ex post facto*. The petitioners, for these, and other reasons, pray that they may be heard by counsel against the bill of the London booksellers, and be allowed a reasonable time to send their witnesses to London for proving all facts material to their petition.'

These petitions were severally read, and counsel allowed to be heard for and against the bill on Wednesday se'nnight, when it is ordered to be read a second time.]

Version 5: *Public Advertiser*, 23 April.

… at Three o'Clock **Paul Feild, Esq**; presented to the House the Bill for Relief of Booksellers and others by vesting the Copies of printed Books in the Purchasers of such Copies from Authors, or their Assigns, for a Time therein to be limited. The Speaker then took the Bill and read some Part of its Contents to the House, which sets forth, That an Act made and passed in the 8th Year of her late Majesty Queen Anne, intituled, An Act for the Encouragement of Learning, by vesting the Copies of printed Books in the Authors or Purchaser of such Copies during the Time therein mentioned; it was amongst other Things enacted, that from and after the 10th Day of April 1710, the Authors of any Book or Books then printed, who had not transferred to any other the Copy or Copies of such Books, Share or Shares thereof, or the Bookseller or Booksellers, Printer or Printers, or other Person or Persons, who had purchased or acquired the Copy or Copies of any Books or Books in order to print or reprint the same, should have the sole Liberty of printing such Book and Books for the Term of Twenty-one Years, to commence from the 10th of April 1710, and no longer: And whereas it hath been a prevailing Opinion with Booksellers and others, that Authors and their Assigns had by the Common Law, independently of the said Act of Queen Anne, the sole Right of printing and reprinting Copies of their Works, and that the said Act was not intended to take away or abridge any such Right; and in consequence of this Opinion many of them have from Time to Time invested the Whole or the greatest Part of their Fortunes in the Purchase of such Copy Rights, on which the Support of them and their Families at this Time doth in a great Measure depend. And whereas it hath lately been adjudged in the House of Lords, that no such Copy Right in Authors or their Assigns doth exist at common Law; in consequence whereof Purchasers of such Copy Rights must be great Sufferers by their Misapprehension of the Law in respect thereof, and many of them likely to be involved in Ruin unless they shall obtain the Aid and Assistance of Parliament:—

"May it therefore please your most excellent Majesty, that it may be enacted, and be it enacted by the King's most excellent Majesty, by and with the Advice and Consent of the Lords Spiritual and Temporal, and Commons in this present Parliament assembled, and by the Authority of the same, That from and after the," then comes the Blanks in order for the Committee to fill up the Time it is to be taken from, and Number of Years, as they think proper. The Bill being read a first Time, **Mr. Dempster** got up and said, that he should not oppose the Bill's being to be read a second Time, but as it was a Thing of great Consequence, he hoped that the House would attend to it, and therefore begged that the second reading, might be put off for some Time, in order that the Petitioners might be heard by their Counsel against the Bill; he said that they had been at a great Expence in bringing it to the House of Lords, and no sooner obtained their Decree there, but they are followed close at the Heels with another Bill to this House; he was answered by **Colonel Onslow** and **Mr. Feild**, who related the Situations the Booksellers were in, and Mr. Feild moved for the Bill to be read a second Time on the 4th of May next; which was agreed to.

Version 6: *Edinburgh Advertiser*, 22–26 April, 261–2.

A bill was presented, and read a first time, for the relief of the booksellers of London and Westminster, and others, by vesting the copies of printed books in the purchasers of such copies, for a time, to be therein limited.

Sir Laurence Dundas presented to the Commons, a petition from the booksellers, printers, paper-makers, and book-binders in Edinburgh; setting forth, that the petitioners observe, that leave is given to bring in a bill, for the relief of the booksellers of London, Westminster, and others, by vesting the copies of printed books in the purchasers of such copies from authors, or their assignees, for a time, to be therein limited; and the petitioners are informed, that the aim of the London booksellers, since the failure of their late attempt to gain a dangerous and perpetual monopoly at common-law, is now to obtain an exercise, for a limited time, of the same exclusive privilege beyond the terms of the act of Queen Anne. That in the paper-mills alone about Edinburgh, many hundreds of persons are employed; and the booksellers, book-binders, and printers are still more numerous, who will all be most materially affected, and some of them ruined by the consequence of a bill, should it pass into a law. Few compositions even of Scots authors, are published originally in Scotland; and the petitioners have hitherto lived chiefly by re-publishing, when permitted by the act of Queen Anne, and their business must be given up altogether if any further monopoly is conferred upon the London booksellers. Literary property at common-law, never existed even in idea in Scotland. The attempt made some time ago to introduce it, was received with universal disapprobation; and was, after a full discussion of its merits, over-ruled by a judgment of the supreme court. The petitioners, in consequence of the established law of the country, have laid out great sums of money in printing books not within the protection of the statute of Queen Anne, stocks of which books they have now on hand, and many now printing; and they cannot but think their situation extremely hard, if they, who have been all along exercising their undoubted legal right, are to be subjected to vexatious law-suits, and many of their families to be ruined by a law made *ex post facto.* The petitioners, for these, and other reasons pray, that they may be heard by counsel against the bill of the London booksellers, and be allowed a reasonable time to send their witnesses to London for proving all facts material to their petition.

Lord Frederick Campbell presented a petition from the booksellers, printers, paper-makers and bookbinders in Glasgow; setting forth, that many of them would be ruined if the bill of the London booksellers should pass into a law, and praying to be heard by counsel against it.

A petition was presented from several booksellers in London and Westminster, setting forth, that the bill of the booksellers of London and Westminster would, if passed into a law, be highly injurious to them, and praying to be heard by counsel against it.

These petitions were severally read, and counsel allowed to be heard for and against the bill on Wednesday se'nnight, when it is ordered to be read a second time.

Adjourned to Monday.

Version 7: *Scots Magazine*, 531.

Mr Feilde presented the bill April 22. and it was read a first time.—**Mr Dempster** desired the House to be attentive, as this was a bill to reverse a decree of the supreme court of judicature in the kingdom. **Col. Onslow** said, that he held what the Lords did to be the law of the land, but it was no new thing, to apply for redress against laws when they were particularly hard and cruel; that he believed there would have been no occasion for this bill, had the judge who was silent in the House of Lords, [Lord Mansfield, who did not give his opinion as a judge, and did not speak as a Peer],[143] delivered his opinion, which he ought to have done; that by their opinions people were to be guided, that for those purposes they had large salaries, and that no one of them ought to be above their office. In this **Mr Feilde** agreed with the Colonel.—The bill was ordered to be read a second time on the 4th of May; at which time counsel were allowed to be heard for the petitioners against the bill, and also in favour of the bill.

Notes

***Gazetteer*, 22 April; *Craftsman*, 23 April**: This day the booksellers bill will be presented to the House of Commons.

***Morning Chronicle*, 22 April**: Yesterday a petition from Edinburgh was presented to the Lower House against the Booksellers, and ordered to lie on the table till the bill shall be brought in.

***Daily Advertiser*, 22 April**: Read and referred a Petition from the Booksellers at Edinburgh, against that of the Booksellers of London. Ordered to lie on the Table.

[143]Square brackets in the original.

***Public Advertiser*, 22 April**: A Petition from Edinburgh was presented and read against the Petition of the London Booksellers, which was ordered to lie on the Table till the Bill is brought in.

***Lloyd's Evening Post*, 20–22 April, 383**: Yesterday a Petition from the Booksellers of Edinburgh was presented to the House of Commons, against the Bill ordered in, in favour of the London Booksellers, to secure their property after having purchased it.

***Daily Advertiser*, 23 April**: Read a first Time, the Booksellers of London Bill. Ordered to be read a second Time on Wednesday Se'ennight, and Counsel to be heard for and against the said Bill.

***Middlesex Journal*, 21–23 April**: Yesterday a petition from Edinburgh was presented to the House of Commons, and read against the petition of the London Booksellers, which was ordered to lie on the table till the bill is brought in.

***Gentleman's Magazine*, 188**: The booksellers bill for the security of literary property was read the first time, and ordered to be read again on Wednesday the 4th of May, when counsel is to be heard on both sides.

Donaldson Petition: 26 April

Version 1: *Lloyd's Evening Post*, 27–29 April, 405; *London Chronicle*, 28–30 April, 414; *Edinburgh Evening Courant*, 4 May.

[LLP/LC: The following is the Petition of Alexander Donaldson, Bookseller, in St. Paul's Churchyard, London, which was presented to the House of Commons last Tuesday by **Governor Johnstone**,[144] and read;] [LLP: it sets forth] [LC: setting forth,] [EC: Mr Donaldson's petition, which was presented to the House of Commons yesterday se'nnight by Gov. Johnstone, and read, sets forth,] that the Petitioner has seen a Bill brought in upon the Petition of certain Booksellers of London and Westminster, for vesting the Copies of printed Books in the Purchasers of such Copies from Authors, or their Assigns, for a time therein to be limited, and should the said Bill pass into a Law, a very dangerous Monopoly will be thrown into the Hands of a few wealthy Booksellers, to the great Detriment of the Public, to the Injury of Letters, and the utter Ruin of the inferior Booksellers both in Town and Country, and therefore praying that the Statute of Queen Anne, which was expressly made for the encouragement of Learning, may not now be altered, or suspended, for the Encouragement of the London Booksellers only, and that the Petitioner may be heard by his Counsel against the Bill now depending.

The House ordered, that the said Petition do lie upon the Table until the Bill be read a second time, which [LC/LLP: is fixed for the 4th of May next, and Council to be admitted] [EC: was fixed for this day, and counsel] to be heard at the same time for and against the said Bill.

Version 2: *Scots Magazine*, 531.

[144]George Johnstone†* (1730–87), MP for Cockermouth.

A petition of Alexander Donaldson bookseller in London [and likewise in Edinburgh][145] was presented April 26. praying, that the statute of Q. Anne, which was expressly made for the encouragement of learning, might not now be altered, or suspended, for the encouragement of the London booksellers only; and that he might be heard by counsel against the bill. Which was allowed.

On an application to the annual committee of the Royal Boroughs of Scotland, by the booksellers, printers, &c. in and about Edinburgh, the press of the committee sent a letter to all the boroughs, April 14. signifying, that the committee were unanimously of opinion, that the subject-matter of the bill aforementioned, was of great consequence to this country, and to many of the royal boroughs in particular; and therefore begging of them to apply immediately to their members, to use all their interest in opposing the bill's passing.

Notes

***Daily Advertiser* 27 April; *London Evening Post*, 26–28 April; *London Chronicle*, 26–28 April, 406**: Received and read a petition from Alexander Donaldson, against the London Booksellers bill, which was ordered to lie on the Table until the bill is read a second Time, and then Counsel to be heard for and against the same.

***Public Advertiser*, 27 April**: A Petition was presented to the House and read from Alexander Donaldson, Bookseller, against the Bookseller Bill, which was ordered to lie on the Table till the Bill is read a second Time, and Council to be heard on both Sides.

***Public Ledger*, 27 April; *General Evening Post*, 26–28 April**:[146] Governor Johnstone presented a petition from Mr. Alexander Donaldson, against the Bill of the Booksellers of London and Westminster, now depending, which was read, and ordered to lie on the table.

***Morning Chronicle*, 27 April**: Mr. Donaldson presented a petition yesterday to the House of Commons against the Booksellers, which was ordered to lie on the table 'till the second reading of the bill.

***St James's Chronicle*, 26–28 April**: A Petition of Alexander Donaldson, Bookseller, was presented to the House against the Bill for vesting the Copies of printed Books in Authors, or their Assigns. The Petition was order to lie on the Table, to be taken up at the second Reading of the Bill, and the Petitioner to be then heard by Counsel, if he shall think fit, against it.

***Caledonian Mercury*, 2 May**: Mr. Alexander Donaldson's petition, mentioned in our last, was presented to the House of Commons by Governor Johnston.

Second Reading Adjournment: 4 May

***Edinburgh Advertiser*, 6–10 May, 291**: **Sir Geo Saville** presented a petition from the booksellers of the city of York, in behalf of themselves and other country booksellers, against the bill for "vesting the copies of printed books, in the purchaser, of such copies,

[145] Square brackets in the original.

[146] *General Evening Post* has 'J—stone'.

from authors or their assigns, for a time therein to be limited". Ordered, that the petition do lie on the table, till the second reading of said bill.

...

The second reading of the booksellers bill was deferred till Tuesday next: To stand the first order for that day.

***Caledonian Mercury*, 9 May**: The other orders of the day were then disposed of, and the Booksellers bill was ordered to be read a second time, and counsel heard on both sides, on Tuesday next.

Yesterday, a petition was presented by the booksellers of the city of York, in behalf of themselves and other country booksellers, against the bill for "vesting the copies of printed books, in the purchasers of such copies from authors or their assigns, for a time therein to be limited." Ordered, that the petition do lie on the table, till the second reading of said bill.

Notes

***St James's Chronicle*, 30 April–3 May; *Caledonian Mercury*, 7 May**: To-morrow is the Day fixed for the second Reading of the Bill for Relief of Booksellers in the Affair of [CM: the] Copy-Right when it is thought the House will be crowded with Members.

***Morning Chronicle*, 4 May; *Caledonian Mercury*, 7 May**: The second reading of the Booksellers bill stands for [MC: this day][CM: tomorrow] in the House of Commons, when counsel are to be heard for the bill, and likewise for the petitioner against the bill.

***Public Advertiser*, 4 May**: This Day comes on in the House the second Reading of the Bill for Relief of Booksellers, and Others, by vesting the Copies of printed Books in the Purchasers of such Copies from Authors or their Assigns for a Time therein to be limited; when Counsel will be heard for and against the Bill.

***Gazetteer*, 4 May**: And to read a second time the Bill for vesting copy-rights in the Purchasers of such Copies from Authors and their Assigns, for a time therein to be limited.

***Lloyd's Evening Post*, 2–4 May, 423**: And to read a second time the Bill for vesting copy-rights in the Purchasers of such Copies from Authors and their Assigns, for a time therein to be limited; and to hear Council for and against this last Bill.

***Gazetteer*, 5 May; *Craftsman*, 7 May**: The booksellers bill deferred till Tuesday next.

***Public Advertiser*, 5 May; *Middlesex Journal*, 3–6 May**: The Booksellers Bill was put off on account of the American Bill[147] coming on, and no Person was admitted into the Gallery.

***Morning Chronicle*, 5 May**: The second reading of the Booksellers' bill is put off till a future day.

***Daily Advertiser*, 5 May**: Deferred the second Reading of the Booksellers Bill.

***London Evening Post*, 3–5 May**: Deferred the second reading of the booksellers bill to Tuesday next, when counsel will be heard on both sides.

***London Chronicle*, 3–5 May, 432; *General Evening Post*, 3–5 May; *Lloyd's Evening Post*, 4–6 May, 428; *Edinburgh Evening Courant*, 7 May**: The other orders of the day

[147] What became the Massachusetts Government Act 1774 (14 Geo. III, c. 45); see *CJ*, xxxiv, 702.

were then disposed of, and the Booksellers bill was ordered to be read a second time, and Counsel heard on both sides on Tuesday next.

***Scots Magazine*, 531–2**: A petition of the booksellers, printers, and bookbinders, of York, was presented, May 4. praying, that the statute 8° Ann. as lately explained by the House of Lords, might stand in full force, and be neither amended or extended; and that they might be heard by counsel against the bill. The petition was ordered to lie on the table till the second reading of the bill; which was put off from the 4th till the 10th of May.

Second Reading: 10 May, First Day

Version 1: *Morning Chronicle*, 11 May; *London Chronicle*, 10–12 May, 450–1;[148] *General Evening Post*, 10–12 May; *Caledonian Mercury*, 16 May (First Account); *Edinburgh Evening Courant*, 16 May; Cobbett's *Parliamentary History*, xvii, cols 1090–4.

[MC/LC: … about four o'clock, the Petition of the Booksellers of Glasgow, and the Petition of the Booksellers of London [MC: against the Booksellers Bill] [LC: who have no copy-right, against the bill of the Booksellers, who have,] were read, after which **Sir John Dalrymple**[149] was heard on behalf of the Counter Petitioners; Sir John began with] [GP/CM/EC: The order for the day for hearing Counsel on the Booksellers bill was called for and read. The Counsel were called in, and Sir John Dalrymple opened the cause as Counsil for the petitioners against the bill. He began with] [MC/GP: endeavouring to inflame the minds of the House, by] [PH: The said Bill was read a second time. The Petitions against the Bill were then read, and the counsel for the petitioners were heard. Sir John Dalrymple appeared on their behalf. He began with] declaring that a large number of the men who had signed the petition for the bill, were proprietors of those infamous news-papers which had traduced the Sovereign, and abused the members of [Not EC: each House] [EC: both Houses] of Parliament. He dwelt much upon this idea, and was by no means sparing of his severities on the Booksellers, positively asserting that they entirely governed the news-papers; and that after having in the most bare-faced and scandalous manner abused every gentleman present, and every person in existence, the old for not being young, the young for not being old, the poor for not being rich, and the rich for not being poor: after having called a man a scoundrel if he accepted a place, and a fool if he resigned it; after having vented every calumny which impudence and ignorance could give birth to, he said they [Not LC/PH: now came] [LC/PH: came now] and asked favour from the very objects of their abuse. Of late he owned there had been an alteration in the public prints, and scandal and traduction had less prevailed; he would inform the House the reason why there was such a cessation of abuse, where it began, and [Not EC: when] [EC: where] it would end. It began as soon as the present bill was thought of, and it would end as soon as it was disposed of. He advised the members to throw out the bill for that reason; for while the Booksellers had the bill in pursuit, they would keep the newspapers free from scandal, and every man might read them with safety. At any rate, he would wish the House to grant the monopoly prayed for, for seven years only, by

[148] The witness evidence in the *London Chronicle* and replicated in *Cobbett's Parl. Hist.* appears to be copied from the *Public Ledger* (Version 4).

[149] Sir John Dalrymple* (1726–1810).

which means the term would expire a year before the next general election but one, and they might in the parliament after, grant a fresh monopoly for seven years more; by such a measure, the members would be sure [Not EC: of being] [EC: to be] abused only for six years at a time. If they granted the bill, he would advise them to read no [Not EC: newspaper] [EC: newspapers] all the summer, to avoid seeing themselves traduced. For his part, on account of what he had then said, he had ordered that no English newspaper should come within his doors for three months. [Not CM: After a great deal more of this sort of foreign matter,] Sir John [CM: then] went into the history of the statute of Queen Anne; insisted on it that the Booksellers well knew from the passing of that act; that there was no Common Law Right, and therefore their plea of having been deceived by the determination in the Court of King's-bench was exceedingly fallacious and groundless. He contrasted the bill prepared under Dr. Swift's auspices,[150] with the present one; spoke of the different requisitions of each, gave the Petitioners the title of monopolists, talked of the general bad tendency of [CM: all] monopolies; [MC/GP/CM/EC: instanced the law patent, which he declared was held by Mr. Strahan,[151] an acquaintance of his, and a man of unimpeachable probity, and yet that the addition of four shillings in the pound was put on the expence of printing law books;] [LC/PH: and] what abuse might not be made of monopolies [MC/GP/CM/EC: then], if in the hands of unjust men? He had himself in the House of Lords first mentioned a new bill, but he meant a bill of compromise, and not a bill of opposition. If the petitioners had applied to him, he would have drawn [PH: up] an unobjectionable bill, which could not have failed of success. [MC/GP/CM/EC: After mentioning Mr. Strahan,] he justified the extravagant price of Hawkesworth's Voyages,[152] although he [MC/GP/EC: most illiberally] abused the petitioners; [Not CM: and having vented many ill-natured [MC/GP/EC: and unjust] observations on them,] [CM: and having spoke some time longer on the same subject;] he described the state of the Counter Petitioners, enlarged on their unfortunate situation, and was extremely copious on the merits of his client Mr. Donaldson. He entered into a description of the mode of trading in Glasgow, particularly their exportation of books, for which he declared they gave eighteen or twenty months credit, whereas if they sent to London for English editions, they could only obtain six months credit. The present application, he said, was contrary to all law and all usage. In the worst of reigns it never had been attempted to alter and destroy the effect of a decision of a supreme court of law.[153] That the House, by granting the present Bill, would sanctify an *ex post facto* law, which was by no means the proper object of legislation. He had observed, he said, that, it was ever the fashion to ascribe the ill of the times to some particular country. In the reign of James the First all the ill came from Scotland; in the reign of Charles the First all the ill was supposed to come from Spain; in that of Charles II., all the ill came from France; [LC/PH: in that of William all the ill came from Holland;] in the reign of George the Second, all the ill came from Hanover, and now the circle seemed to have come round, and all the ill [Not EC: came] [EC: comes] from Scotland again. He could not conclude, he said, without clearing up a point respecting himself. It was generally found, that the arguments of a counsel went a great way, especially if he was an honest man. It had been thrown out against him, that after having sold the copy of a book, which had the

[150] Booksellers' Bill 1737; Jonathan Swift* (1667–1745).

[151] William Strahan* (1715–85).

[152] John Hawkesworth, *An Account of the Voyages*.

[153] *Donaldson v Beckett* (1774) *Cobbett's Parl. Hist.* xvii, col. 953.

misfortune universally to displease, although it was universally read; which had been said to have been printed under the patronage of Kings and ministers, although it was never seen by either 'till it was printed; of this book[154] he was charged with having sold the perpetual and exclusive right of multiplying the copy for 2000l and immediately afterwards, taking an active part, to destroy the value of the very property which he had so disposed of. This insinuation was, he said, as false as it was scandalous; for that immediately after the decision in the House of Lords he went to Mr. Cadell[155] and told him, that if any loss accrued from the event of the decision, he would sustain it himself, and would not suffer it to fall on Mr. Cadell.

[LC/PH: Sir John concluded, with informing the House, that he should call in some witnesses.

The first witness was Mr. Merrill, senior. of Cambridge,[156] who proved that he had, in [LC: the year] 1759, received two letters from J. Whiston,[157] a Bookseller, purporting that a Committee of London Booksellers was appointed to prosecute the sellers of pirated editions; he talked of two more letters, which he said would shew the House the iniquitous practices of the Booksellers of London, who had combined against the Scotch and Country ones; but as he could not produce the originals, nor tell what was become of them, the House would hear no farther from him.

The next person was his son,[158] who being asked the same questions as his father, would not speak positively to any thing he was asked, particularly if he did not know that Scotch books were bought by the London Booksellers, who printed a new title page purporting them to be English editions.

The next was Mr. Murray,[159] who was asked a considerable number of questions by Mr. Murphy, one of the counsel for the petitioners, and cross questioned by **Mr. Mansfield**, most of his answers seemed rather favourable to the cause of the London Booksellers.

The next was [PH: a] Mr. Fox,[160] who spoke a considerable time; but as most of it was hear-say evidence, it was not attended to.

The next was Mr. Bulkley,[161] who was but a young Bookseller, and was asked but few questions.

The chief thing they all seemed to complain of was, not being admitted to the Booksellers sales, which, they said, were held at the Queen's Arms in St. Paul's Church-yard, and Globe

[154] Sir John Dalrymple, *Memoirs of Great Britain and Ireland. From the Dissolution of the last Parliament of Charles II, until the Sea-battle off La Hogue* (Strahan and Caddel, 1771) (ESTC: T145644).

[155] Thomas Cadell* (1742–1802), app. 1758–65, tr. 1766–93.

[156] Thomas Merrill (*d.* 1781), tr. 1736–81, 3 Trinity Street, Cambridge (he received a letter: see Five Letters).

[157] John Whiston* (1711–80), tr. 1767–75; as to the letter see Five Letters.

[158] Thomas Merrill (c. 1731–1801); he traded as Thomas and John Merrill and then later with his brother as Thomas and Joseph Merrill.

[159] Probably John Murray (1745–93), 32 Fleet Street. He had been born in Edinburgh so he might have been seen as potentially sympathetic.

[160] William Fox tr. 1773–83, 128 Holborn Hill; later a very active abolitionist: Timothy Whelan, 'William Fox, Martha Gurney, and Radical Discourse of the 1790s', *Eighteenth-Century Studies*, xlii (2009), 397. He also provided a statement, see Part IV, Further Remarks.

[161] It is unclear who this might be. The most likely is George Bulkley tr. 1774–1811, Bridge Street, Chester.

Tavern in Fleet-street;[162] that they had known instances of Country and Scotch Booksellers being turned out from those sales: But, on cross examination, it appeared they had been turned out for misdemeanours, for breaking through the rules observed at sales, &c.

There appeared among the persons who had signed the different petitions against the bill, Weavers, Old Cloths-folks, Chandler's-shop men and women, a person who keeps the stall upon the wall in Parliament-street, &c. The House was almost a scene of laughter during the whole of the evidence, which was very long.

After these evidences, Mr. Wallace,[163] Solicitor for Mr. Donaldson, was called in, who stated, that it had cost Mr. Donaldson 1000l. in thirteen different Chancery suits, which had been brought against him by the London Booksellers, but on explanation and cross examination, it appeared, that many of those suits were for printing books that were protected by the Statute of Queen Anne, two in particular Shenstone's Works and Yorick's Sermons.**]**

[MC/GP/CM/EC: **Mr. Murphy**, the other Counsel for the Counter Petitioners, then examined the two Mr. Merrills of Cambridge, Mr. Murray of Fleet street, Mr. Fox of Holborn, Mr. Wallis, Mr. Donaldson's Solicitor, [MC: and Mr. Buckley, a poor bookseller] [GP/CM/EC: &c.]; endeavouring to deduce from their several testimonies such evidence as would prove that the Petitioners for the bill had entered into an illegal combination many years since to oppress the Counter Petitioners; that they excluded them from their sales; that they menaced them with prosecutions; that [CM: Mr.] Donaldson had been harassed and put to one thousand pounds expence in defending thirteen suits, which the Petitioners brought against him; and many other instances of their conduct; all which were meant to paint them as unworthy of the relief prayed.

A bookseller from Glasgow[164] was then examined by Sir John Dalrymple; his evidence was in support of Sir John's observation respecting the mode of the exportation trade of Glasgow.

Mr. Murphy afterwards spoke for an hour and a half against the bill. [MC: We have neither time nor room now even to hint at is arguments; the substance of them shall be given To-morrow.][165]

The House rose a quarter before ten, and the further hearing of Counsel on the Booksellers Bill is ordered for Friday.**]**

[LC: After he had finished, Mr. Murphy, another Counsel for the Petitioners against the bill, made his remarks on the evidence, which in general were pretty shrewd; however, as well as the nature of the case would admit of, he at the latter part was particularly severe on

[162] Globe Tavern and Coffee House, Fleet Street, and Queen's Arms Tavern, St Paul's Churchyard: Bryant Lillywhite, *London Coffee Houses: A Reference Book of Coffee Houses of the Seventeenth, Eighteenth and Nineteenth Centuries* (1963), 234–7, 461–4, nos 466, 1032.

[163] Albany Wallis of Wallis and Parker, Norfolk Street, Strand: *Browne's General Law-list*, 1777 (ESTC: T085768) – where his first name does not appear, only the name of the partnership, but it does appear in the version of 1887: ESTC T085770.

[164] This was William Smith tr. 1760–82, Glasgow West Side, Salt Market (see Version 5).

[165] The *Morning Chronicle* ends with 'We May hereafter give such observations as naturally arise on what we heard yesterday. We shall now only remark that Sir John Dalrymple has either been misinformed respecting the news-papers and the Booksellers connection with them, or the soreness occasioned by the unwelcome truths they have spoke respecting Sir John and his productions, had determined him to retaliate and abuse somebody in his turn, no matter whether that somebody merited his severity, or whether what was said by way of retaliation had the least relation to truth; certain it is that he began his speech with a matter totally groundless, and continued in a maze of error.'

the news papers in general; he attempted to shew the House, that the Bookseller made it their business to keep no Printer employed, but what would traduce any person's character.

After he had finished his remarks, **Mr. Feilde** moved, that the father hearing of Counsel on the said bill be deferred until Friday next, which was agreed to.

The House broke up at ten o'clock, and adjourned to this day.]

Version 2: *Morning Chronicle*, 12 May;[166] *London Chronicle*, 12–14 May, 457–8; *Edinburgh Advertiser*, 17–20 May, 314; Cobbett's *Parliamentary History*, xvii, cols 1094–5.

[LC/EA: Among other arguments made use of by **Mr. Murphy**, on Tuesday last in favour of the Counter-petitioners, respecting the booksellers bill were the following:]

[MC/LC/EA: Mr. Murphy,] [PH: After he finished, Mr Arthur Murphy, another Counsel for the petitioner against the Bill, made his remarks on the evidence. He] began with observing, that the Bill prayed for, was a very extraordinary attempt to defeat the laudable and successful endeavours of an individual, to obtain common justice; the plea urged by the petitioners, he affirmed, was repugnant to every principle of law; that there was no maxim more general; no maxim so notoriously inviolable as that the ignorance of the law could not be urged or received as a palliative, or an excuse; the petitioners, he observed, were remarkable for mistaking the law; two of them, some time since, employed one Gurney,[167] a short-hand writer from the Old Bailey, to take down a farce universally approved of, and much followed: this farce was called *Love A-la-mode*; and Mr. Macklin,[168] the author of it, found it his interest to keep the copy in his closet, and not to publish it; but two of the petitioners taking a liking to it, accommodated Mr. Gurney with a convenient seat in the shilling gallery of the theatre, on one of the nights on which it was acted; and in a periodical publication, the first act was soon afterwards retailed. Mr. Macklin remonstrated [MC/LC/EA: to] [PH: with] the two petitioners on the illegality of their conduct, and the unfairness of pirating an unpublished copy; the only answer he could get was, that it was their property; they had purchased it of Mr. Gurney for two guineas, and therefore they had a right to print it. Mr. Macklin applied to the Court of Chancery,[169] an injunction was immediately granted by Ld. Northington, and that injunction was made perpetual by the Lords Commissioners of the Great Seal in 1770. At length, therefore, the petitioners were convinced that they had mistaken the law. A case in point occurred to him; a few days [MC: since] [LC/EA/PH: ago] Mr. Tyson, the legal claimant to an estate, brought his action of recovery against Mr. Clarke,[170] who had been in 30 years undisturbed possession of it, the matter was tried in the Common Pleas, where the claim was made good, and the jury gave a verdict for the claimant; there could be no doubt but Mr. Clarke would be very glad to obtain an act of parliament giving him 14 or 21 years further possession. If a bill, immediately granting relief to those who had bought an estate, which was clearly discoverable to have no title, passed into a law, the table of the House

[166] Begins with '*Substance of Mr. Murphy's arguments in favour of the Counter-Petitioner, respecting the* BOOKSELLERS *Bill*.'

[167] Thomas Gurney* (1705–70).

[168] Charles Macklin* (?1699–1797).

[169] *Macklin v Richardson* (1770) Amb 694 (27 ER 451).

[170] It was in fact in the king's bench: see *Tyssen, Lord of the Manor of Hackney v Clarke* (1774) Loft 496 (98 ER 766); 3 Will KB 541 (95 ER 1201); it was heard on 4 May at a grand assize.

would be loaded perpetually with petitions of a similar nature with that of the Booksellers, and the whole business of the session would be to remedy the losses incurred by ignorance and folly.[171] [MC: But he could not help following Sir John Dalrymple, in most positively asserting, that the plea of the petitioners was fallacious; that they never dreamt of a Common Law Right, that the decision of the King's Bench, in the cause of Miller and Taylor, did not deceive them; and that knowing there was no Common Law Right, they had deferred a final decision as far as they possibly could. To prove this, he instanced the mode of obtaining the statute of Queen Anne, recited a great part of the Chancellor's speech in the House of Lords respecting it, and like wise what he had said relative to the attempt to obtain the act which Dean Swift[172] had drawn up, and which was so very warmly received in the two houses, that each member contended who should give it most countenance. It was true, he said, that one great genius had misconceived the question, and supposed that a Common Law Right did exist, but he was certain that the same reasons which governed the opinion of the noble Lord he alluded to, had no sway on the minds of the petitioners; it required some abilities to mistake the law so widely, there must have been an ingenuity in the train of thinking, which the petitioners could not be supposed to possess, they were perfectly aware of their having no other protection than what the statute of Queen Anne gave them, and for thirty-one years they had by various artifices maintained a monopoly unwarranted by law, prejudicial to many individuals, and diametrically opposite to the public rights of mankind. From the evidence of the two Merrils, although only two of the four letters sent to them could be produced, it was plain the petitioners entered into an illegal combination, and opened a boundless measure of subscription to support them in oppressing the poorer and the helpless part of the trade; it was plain also that their sales at the Queen's Arms and Globe Tavern, were not fair open sales, but that they excluded whom they chose from them; and from the evidence of Bulkeley, it was clear how unmercifully they dealt with those over whom they conceived they were superior. How contrary was their conduct with those whom they feared? Osborne of Paternoster-Row some years since printed an edition of Shakespeare, and published proposals for many other books. The petitioners did not prosecute him, they bought off his stock, and made it worth his while to retire from business, and that very John Osborne had lately been Sheriff of Buckinghamshire.[173] With regard to Mr. Johnston's evidence,[174] and his reply, "that he always conceived there was a Common Law right," he wishes to know whence he drew his conception, he was sure he could not draw it from any injunction which had been granted. To prove this assertion he

[171]The *London Chronicle* finishes with 'The rest of Mr. Murphy's arguments were nearly to the same purport as those made use of by Sir John Dalrymple; for which see our last, p. 450. The arguments urged against the Booksellers for excluding particular persons from their sales, are exceedingly futile and nugatory. It was proved, by the witnesses examined last Tuesday, at the bar of the House of Commons, that the Petitioners had turned two or three persons notorious for selling pirated editions out of their sale rooms. As the Petitioners urge, and truly urge, that they did really conceive a common law right to exist, it was as natural and as honourable for them to exclude a notorious pirate from their company, as it would be for a set of honest Tradesmen to refuse keeping company with a notorious Highwayman.'

[172]Jonathan Swift, dean of St Patrick's Cathedral, Dublin.

[173]John Osborne (*d.* 1775), tr. 1733–52, 33 Paternoster Row. He was sheriff in 1759: *The Victoria History of the County of Buckingham* (1925), iii, 101–2.

[174]William Johnston. His evidence is summarised in Part IV, Petition Committee Report.

instanced the cases of Motte and Faulkner,[175] and Walker and Tonson,[176] went into all the Chancery cases, repeated what Baron Eyre had said in the Upper House concerning Lord Hardwicke's opinion on the matter,[177] and the large Q marked by his Lordship in his notes, recited the history of the collusive suit between Tonson and Collins,[178] and came down to the determination in the Court of King's Bench, declaring that the petitioners never would prosecute a determinate, firm minded man that they would not attack Donaldson, because they knew he was not easily to be moulded to their purpose, but that they attacked Taylor for selling what Donaldson printed. That they knew the determination of the King's Bench, was directly opposite to the opinion of the whole Bar; that they bought off Taylor, and would not till the last necessity, bring the question to a final issue; that they had harassed Mr. Donaldson with thirteen suits, and after having put him to the expence of 1000l. to obtain justice, they now came and petitioned parliament that they who had been acting unjustly for 31 years, might be warranted in the same conduct for 21 years longer, at the expiration of which term, he did not doubt they would pray for a further monopoly; that it was exceedingly cruel to deprive Mr. Donaldson of what he had with so much spirit, so much pains, and so much expence, obtained for himself and his brethren. He mentioned Mr. Donaldson's having published three several editions of Pope's Homer, and urged, that the petitioners having, in consequence, printed a cheap edition, was a proof how beneficial to the public the laying printing open would be. To support this idea, he told a story of a gentlemen[179] finding his gardener reading a sixpenny number of Miller's Gardener's Dictionary,[180] printed in an ordinary manner, which, he said, was at once a proof that the middling and lower ranks of people would be enabled to read, and buy books, if the trade was open, while the sale of the better editions would not be at all injured. He took an opportunity of seconding Sir John Dalrymple's attack on the news-papers; the petitioners, he insisted, could do more than Kings, Lords, and Commons; that they could silence them in a moment, for that they might discharge their printer, if he did not implicitly obey their will; the mode was, he said, in summer for the proprietors to have a buck at Richmond, or Hampstead, they cared only for their dividend, and minded not what libels their printer put in the paper. In the present case, he charged the petitioners with falsehood and partiality; they, in the Public Advertiser,[181] accused the Counter Petitioners of being the venders of the licentious publications, when not one counter petitioner either printed, published, or was concerned in a newspaper; and yet, though they accused them so falsely, they refused to insert an answer to the accusation, and abused them afresh. But there was no end to their calumny, it was therefore the wisest way for every man, however insignificant, to hold them in contempt: after having, by a variety of invectives against them, shewed that *he* did not think them beneath his notice; he returned to his encomiums on Mr. Donaldson, in which he was as exceedingly lavish, as he had been laboriously severe on the news-papers.

[175] *Mott v Faulkner* (1735), TNA, C 11/2249/4 (pleadings).

[176] *Tonson v Walker* (1752) 3 Swans 672 (36 ER 1017).

[177] See Baron Eyre's judgment in *Donaldson v Beckett* (1774) *Cobbett's Parl. Hist.* xvii, col. 953 at 973, where he mentions the 'Q'.

[178] *Tonson v Collins* (1761) 1 Black W 301 (96 ER 169).

[179] The gentleman had been Henry Home, Lord Kames* (1696–1782).

[180] Philip Miller* (1691–1771), *The Gardeners Dictionary &c* (Rivington, 1731) (ESTC: T59420).

[181] Letter from AZ, *Public Advertiser*, 4 May§.

He told a story of a sale, by which the petitioners cleared some thousands; said that they had got 10,000l. by Thompson's Seasons,[182] and four times as much by Milton; at length, he concluded with hoping that the Bill would not be passed into a law.][183]

[PH: After he had finished his remarks, **Mr Feilde** moved, That the farther hearing of counsel be deferred till the 13th, which was agreed to.]

Version 3: *Middlesex Journal*, 12–14 May.[184]

Being employed on behalf of the Petitioners against the bill, and Mr. Donaldson, I shall beg leave to begin by observing, that the Petitioners for the bill consist of 20 Booksellers who really purchase copies, and of seventy-two others who never bought any: And, Sir, I must father observe, for throwing the matter into the clearest light, that the only principles upon which it is possible they should apply to you, are either as a matter of favour, as benefitting the public, or as a matter of justice to their situation; first, Sir, let us consider their plea as asking a favour. Half the twenty booksellers are either printers or proprietors of three fourths of the news papers which daily deal out such plentiful abuse upon you, upon every one of you, upon the Lords, and upon the Sovereign; all possible means are taken to blacken the character of every man who has a seat in this House; if a member is with the Court, he is a knave; if in opposition, factious; if he takes a place, he is a villain; if he refuses it, a fool; act how you will, and do what you will, nothing can shield the most virtuous character from the most envenomed attacks, yet these are the men who now come to you petitioning for a favour; if it is said that the proprietors of a paper have it not in their power to direct what shall and what shall not be printed, I deny it. What is their conduct? They meet at Hampstead or at Richmond to divide the price of all the murdered reputations of the quarter. What is their conversation over their buck, their claret, and their delicacies? *The Editor is very severe on such a one—those letters were confounded hot, he will go soo far—never mind,* replies another, *the paper tells, and as long as that is the case all goes well.*

These fellows by opening their mouths could put a stop to calumny, but no, they will not, they gluttonize on abuse, it is their food, their support, yet these are the men who now come to ask a favour of you truly. From what I have already said, I am clear how they will treat me, and I am determined no English newspaper shall enter my doors for three months to come, and I would advise you all as the best revenge, not to read a newspaper for a twelvemonth.

[182]James Thomson* (1700–48), *The Seasons* (Millan and Millar, 1730) (ESTC: T143907) (the first season, Winter, had been published in 1726).

[183]This was followed by a comment: 'One side of a question is always good, says a correspondent, till the other is heard. From the evidence of a number of imperfect witnesses, and the laboured harangues of two Lawyers, who are immediately interested in opposing the Booksellers Bill, as bad a colour is put on the Petitioner and their conduct as art and inveteracy can possibly paint. When the Counsel on the side of the Petitioners are heard, it probably will appear that the real fact is, those who were exceedingly dirty have endeavoured to make themselves appear less foul by throwing mud on other people. Mr. Murphy on Tuesday last, at the bar of the House of Commons, asked a person whom he had just called, how long he had been a witness. We should naturally wonder how such an odd question should occur to Mr. Murphy, if we did not recollect that a considerable part of the business of an Old Bailey Sollicter, consists in a previous examination and settling of evidence; and there, "How long have you been a witness? To what points are you ready to swear? Do you think you can stand a cross-examination in the proof of an alibi", are proper and necessary questions. The question therefore was a very natural one, the mistake only lay in the time and in the place.'

[184]The headline is '*Sir* John Dalrymple's *speech against the Booksellers petition, at the Bar of the House of Commons on Wednesday last.*'

Next, Sir, let us enquire into their next plea, public good. They ask you for a monopoly for twenty one years to come, which is, in other words, to put an immense sum into their pockets out of those of all the rest of the community: A very modest request truly! What will be the consequence? Why they will be able so much longer to keep up the price of books as high as they please; to cut off their purchases of authors, having so much old stock to trade in, and to prevent the printing cheap editions for the benefit of trade and exportation. They have affected to consider their own interest as that of authors; but no demonstration can be clearer than the interest of the latter being promoted by refusing them. Take from them their old stock, which consists of every thing printed from the days of Henry VIII. to the present time, and they will throw their money into new purchases, and thereby advance the interest of authors. Then, Sir, as to cheap editions, with what face can any set of men demand a right of preventing them! Why should there not be cheap and rough editions of books, that suit the pockets of poor men, as well as Paternoster-Row editions; that are plentifully stocked with margin, and large types for rich men! By means of cheap Scotch editions ten times the number of men are employed, and the Exchequer receives ten times as much as from the London finer editions. The manufacturers of broad cloth might with as much reason petition you to prevent all fabrics under 18s a yard. But, Sir, I beg to let the House know, that there is a very great trade from Glasgow to the West Indies and North America in printed books, which, if this bill passes, will suffer materially, and that is an object of commercial importance which ought not to be sacrificed to such a set of men. I cannot but smile, Sir, at one argument which has been pretty much insisted upon, that Scotch editions are so beggarly that no gentleman would buy them.[185] But, Sir, such editions are printed in Scotland as never appear in England, for the London Booksellers take care you shall never see them. There was a premium for fine printed books in Scotland—Glasgow and Edinburgh were the rivals. There was printed at the latter a Cornelius Nepos[186] (here it is) of such superlative beauty, that nothing could equal it but a work produced from Glasgow; they were so equal, that we gave the medal to Edinburgh, but its value also to Glasgow. The latter piqued at this, set to work and produced a book, such as one as I venture to say never appeared in any country under Heaven; I mean the Glasgow Milton: but that Milton is never to be met with in the London shops.

Lastly, Sir, let me consider the plea of granting their request as a matter of justice; nothing can be clearer, from that historical deduction which I entered into before the House of Lords, and in which I had the honour of assisting a great law officer now in the House; nothing could be clearer from a variety of transactions, than the booksellers knowing they had not a common law-right, from their never trusting it. Numerous were their purchases in which they bought for the statute period of Q. Anne, therefore to assert that they were deceived and drawn unintentionally to mistake the case, is an absurdity. (*He quoted many cases too tedious to mention.*)

Upon the whole, Sir, I must conclude, that their petition is entirely unsupported upon the ground of favour, of public good, and of justice; they can have no other foundation to come upon.—As a matter of favour, it can only be asked in return for abusing you: as a matter of public good, they can apply only by reason of doing public mischief; and as a

[185] See Cavendish, Graves {S18}.

[186] Cornelius Nepos (c. 110–c. 25 BC), *Excellentium Imperatorum Vitae.*

matter of justice, they must petition for it at the expence of commons sense, and in defiance of general right.

Version 4: *Public Ledger*, 11 May; *Lloyd's Evening Post*, 9–11 May, 447; *London Magazine*, 623.

[PL/LM: The order of the day for hearing Counsel on the Booksellers Bill was called for and read. The Counsel were called in, and] [LLP: Yesterday Council was heard before the House of Commons against the Booksellers Bill.] **Sir John Dalrymple** opened the cause as Council for the Petitioners against the Bill, in a long [PL:, dull, and laboured] speech, the [PL/LM: first] [LLP: former] part of which was [PL/LLP: entirely] taken up in illiberal invectives against the licentiousness of the Press. He said the Booksellers who had signed the Petition for the Bill were chiefly proprietors of public News-papers: [PL/LM: that they were a set of the most despicable of all beings, for they blasphemed their God, ridiculed their King, Lords, Commons, Judges, and every public Character in the Kingdom;] that no private Character was secure from them; that they had indeed been a little still since their Bill was in agitation, but he would pledge himself to the House, that as soon as their Bill was decided, either way, they would immediately let loose all their venom against both Houses of Parliament (he was going to be called to order several times, but some of the Members desired he might go on). **[**PL/LM: The rest of his speech was a [PL: mere] jumble of absurdities, which even the enemies to the Bill could not but [PL: evidently] allow.**]** He attempted to shew how hard Mr. Donaldson's case was, and concluded with [PL/LM: informing the House that he should] [LLP: requesting the House that he might] call in some witnesses.

The first [PL/LM: witness] was a Mr. Merill, senior, who [PL/LM: proved] [LLP: said] that he had, in [PL/LM: the year] 1759,[187] received two letters from [PL/LM: J.] [LLP: Mr.] Whiston, [PL/LM: a] Bookseller, purporting that a Committee of London Booksellers was appointed to prosecute the sellers of pirated editions; he talked of two more letters, which he said would shew the House the iniquitous practices of the Booksellers of London, who had combined against the Scotch and Country ones; but as he could not produce the originals, [PL/LM: nor tell what was become of the them,] the House would hear no father from him.

The next person was his son, who being asked [PL/LM: the same questions as his father, was rather more conscientious, and would] [LLP: similar questions, could] not speak POSITIVELY to any thing he was asked, particularly [PL/LM: if he did not know] [LLP: whether he knew] that Scotch books were bought by the London Booksellers, who printed a new title page purporting them to be English Editions.

The next was [PL/LM: a] Mr. Murray, who was asked a considerable number of questions by **Mr. Murphy**, one of the Council for the Petitioners, and [LLP: was] cross questioned by **Mr. Mansfield**, most of [PL/LM: his] [LLP: whose] answers seemed rather favourable to the cause of the London Booksellers.

[PL/LM: The next was a Mr. Fox, who spoke a considerable time; but as most of it was *hear-say* evidence, it was not attended to.

The next was a Mr. Bulkley, who was but a young Bookseller, and was asked but few questions.

[187] The *London Magazine* has 1739, but this is clearly a typographical error.

The chief thing they all] [LLP: Some other questions were asked; but the chief thing the Petitioners] seemed to complain of was, not being admitted to the Booksellers sales, which, they said, were held at the Queen's Arms in St Paul's Church-yard, and Globe Tavern in Fleet-street; that they had known instances of Country and Scotch Booksellers being turned out from those sales. But, on cross examination, it appeared they had been turned out for misdemeanours, [PL/LM: for] [LLP: or] breaking through the rules observed at sales, &c.

There appeared among the persons who had signed the different Petitions against the Bill, Weavers, Old Cloaths-folks, Chandler's-shop Men and Women, a person who keeps [PL/LM: the] [LLP: a] Stall upon the wall in Parliament Street; &c. [LLP: &c.] The House was [PL: almost a] [LLP: one] [LM: a] scene of laughter during the whole of the evidence, which was very long.

After these evidences, Mr. Wallace, Sollicitor for Mr. Donaldson was called in, who stated that it had cost Mr. Donaldson 1000l. in thirteen different Chancery suits, which had been brought against him by the London Booksellers, but on explanation and cross examination, it appeared, that many of those suits were for printing books that were protected by the Statute of Queen Anne, two in particular, SHENSTONE'S and YORICK's Sermons.[188]

After he had finished, **Mr. Murphy**, [PL: another] [LLP: the other] Council for the Petitioners against the Bill, made his remarks on the evidence, which in general were [PL/LLP: pretty] shrewd; [PL: however, as well as the nature of the case would admit of,] **[**PL/LM: he at the latter part was particularly severe on the News papers [PL: in general], and condemned Mr. Woodfall, Printer of the Public Advertiser in particular; he attempted to shew the House, that the Booksellers made it their business to keep no Printer employed, but what**]** [LLP: and concluded, as his brother Council began, with invectives against the London Booksellers, as Proprietors of News Papers, who would, he said, employ no Printers but such as] would traduce any persons' character.

After he had finished his remarks, **Mr. Feilde** moved, that the father hearing of Council on the said Bill, be deferred until Friday next, which was agreed to.

Version 5: *Caledonian Mercury*, 16 May (Second Account).

Yesterday, came on the Literary Property affair in the House of Commons. The counsel on both sides being called to the bar, **Sir John Dalrymple**, on the part of the Scots Booksellers and Printers, opened the pleadings with an excellent speech; the plan of which was the shew, That the petitioners for the bill were entitled to no favour in any point of view—neither from their own merits—from considerations of public utility—nor from private justice. Each of these heads he reduced to proper subdivisions. He illustrated them all in a spirited and masterly manner; shewed the extensive bad consequences of the bill in many striking points of view; handled the Booksellers very severely, setting them in a most odious and contemptible light; and through the whole, in this usual way, he so mingled wit with argument, and ridicule with serious facts, as tended at the same time to divert and to convince; and it is said here of the H. of C. that they like to be diverted, and that often more is to be expected from their good humour than from their convictions. After finishing, he

[188] *Beckett v Donaldson* (1771), TNA, C 12/1942/11 – it might have been Laurence Sterne* (1713–68), *Yorick Serman* (1769) (ESTC: T14764); *Dodsley v Donaldson* (1770–3), TNA, C 12/1321/36 – William Shenstone, *The Works in Shenstone* (Donaldson, 1770) (ESTC: T182532).

was asked, If he meant to examine any evidences? To which he answered, That there were evidences in waiting, and that his brother Murphy was to examine them. By the English evidence it was meant to prove,

1. "That the booksellers sales of copies were not (as Mr Johnson had asserted in his evidence) open and free to every person who kept shop or sold a book; but that only a select number, agreeable to the learning junto, were admitted, and whom they previously invited by sending them catalogues; and that it any came to whom catalogues had not been sent, they were turned out the room". This was to be proved more or less by all the witnesses.
2. "That, in contradiction to their pretended mistake of the law, these London booksellers never had any real conviction of the existence of a right at common law." This was to be proved partly by Mr Murphy, who had often heard many of themselves speak to that purpose; and partly by Mr Osborne, who printed Shakespeare upon them,[189] and issued proposals for an edition of Chamber's dictionary at 30s. and whom they could not stop from going on, but by a composition with himself, viz. by buying up all his stock at his own price, and giving him a handsome annuity. But Mr Osborne could not be got.
3. "That in consequence of their conviction of having no right at common law, they entered into an unlawful and oppressive combination against all the rest of their brethren in trade through the kingdom; and raised a large subscription to vex and weary out, by groundless but expensive law-suits, all who should be refractory or disobedient to the injunctions of this usurping junto." This was to be particularly proved by four letters from Whiston and Wilkie, to Merril and son at Cambridge, in which the whole scheme is laid open. These letters had been given by old Merril to Mr Donaldson, who engrossed them in a pamphlet concerning Literary Property, which he published in the year 1764.[190] The originals of two of these Mr Donaldson preserved, but the other two (which are the most material) were lost; and in order to supply the loss by evidence, the Merill's were summoned up from Cambridge.

On the above points, five witnesses were examined. There remained a sixth, viz. Mr John Bell in the Strand.[191] He was however set aside, and then it came to the turn of the Edinburgh evidence; he was accordingly called down from the gallery, to attend at the door; but in the mean time it was moved, that no more evidence *should* be heard. Upon this Sir John Dalrymple (who in one part of his speech laid rather too much stress upon the trade of Glasgow with America and the West Indies) begged he might be allowed to bring in only one witness from that place, whom he would dismiss in five minutes. This was Mr William Smith, who was to have been called only as an auxiliary to the Edinburgh evidence, if necessary, in one question relating to the export-trade of Glasgow. But Sir John's request was complied with; Mr Smith was called in, examined upon the above single point, dismissed in five minutes; and this paltry piece of evidence is all that has been, or is to be, heard from Scotland. After finishing the evidence, the other counsel, **Mr Murphy**, arose and made his speech. When he ended, it was moved, and carried, that the further hearing

[189] This is probably William Shakespeare, *Works of Shakespeare* (9 vols, John Osborn, 1747) (ESTC: N26023).

[190] Alexander Donaldson, in *Some Thoughts on the State of Literary Property* (1764) (ESTC T049411).

[191] John Bell (1745–1831) traded at Exeter Exchange, Strand.

of the cause should be adjourned till Friday; and then the counsel on the other side will have the advantage of coming fresh to the bar, and reinforced no doubt with new matter. Sir John is to reply.

Version 6: *St James's Chronicle*, 10–12 May.

The Order of the Day being read for the second Reading of the Bill for vesting the Copies of printed Books in the Purchasers of such Copies from Authors or their Assigns for a Time therein to be limited, Counsel for and against the Bill were called in, and the Bill was read a second Time, on which **Sir John Dalrymple**, Counsel for the Counter Petitioners, opened his Clients Cause, and, in a very tedious and laboured Harangue, vented all the Spleen he had been collecting since the Publication of his political Atlantis on the Persons for whom Relief is intended by the Bill, and whom he pleased to confound, or rather identify, under the Name of the Printers of London News-Papers. His Discourse throughout was little else than a most bitter Invective against News-Paper Publications, and all the Malice, Falsehood, and Scandal, he was pleased to charge them with, he very charitably laid to the Account of the London Booksellers.—The Narrator must so far go out of his Way as to observe, that he imagined Sir John's Age, Experience, and Decency, would have taught him to have carried himself with more Respect towards the August Assembly whom he addressed. But allowing that he was justified in throwing off every Habiliment of the Scholar, the Gentleman, and the Man of Honour, to appear in the genuine brazen Armour of an Advocate, the Narrator would ask him by what Rule of Law did he argue upon Facts not proved or assented to on the other Side? and, supposed they had, what Rule of Law authorized him to argue upon Facts, neither stated nor deducibly implied in the Petitions of his Clients? or by what Rule of Justice or Equity did he make a criminal Accusation against the Party litigant, in a Matter of Property, in which the very Persons who were to determine were likewise the Persons supposed to be injured?— But enough of Sir John, he is sufficiently known to have a profound Knack at *Story Telling*.

Five Witnesses were then severally examined to prove a Monopoly formed in, and supported by, a preconcerted, steady, uniform System of Combination, aided by Seclusion and Oppression; but their Testimony sell entirely short of what it was slated to prove. **Mr. Murphy**, the other Counsel on the same Side, followed his Leader in Sentiment, as well as Order of Succession, and waded through a tedious Detail, the much greater Part of which had fallen from the Lord Chancellor and Judges in the House of Lords, concluding in a most scurrilous Invective on News-papers, Printers, Publishers, and Booksellers. It being Ten o'Clock when Mr. Murphy finished, **Mr. Feilde** moved to adjourn the further Consideration of the Business till Friday.

Version 7: *Edinburgh Advertiser*, 13–17 May, 309.

On Tuesday in the House of Commons, the order of the day was read for taking into consideration the bill for granting a new monopoly in copy-rights in books, for old copies, wherein the terms allowed by the statute of Q. Anne are expired. **Sir John Dalrymple** as counsel for the booksellers of Glasgow, opened the debate, and showed, that the present application was contrary to all law and usage, as even in the worst of times it had never been attempted to destroy the effect of a decision of a supreme court, by an *ex post facto* law.

He contended, that the petitioners for the bill were entitled to no favour in any point of view, either from their own merits, from considerations of public interest, or from private justice. Each of these heads he reduced to proper subdivisions; he illustrated them all in a spirited and masterly manner, and shewed the extensive bad consequences of the bill in many striking points of view. Five witnesses were then examined, viz. Mess. Merrils, of Cambridge, Mr. Murray, and Mr. Fox, booksellers in London, and Mr Wallis,[192] Attorney, whose evidence went chiefly to prove the oppression exercised by the London booksellers; and that in consequence of a conviction of their having no common law-right in book property, they entered into an illegal and oppressive combination against all the rest of their brethren in trade throughout the kingdom, and raised a large subscription to harass and vex by litigious and expensive law-suits, all who should be disobedient to the injunctions of this usurping junto. After the witnesses were examined, **Mr. Murphy**, one of the counsel against the bill, spoke for an hour and a half, and made many sensible remarks upon the evidence. It being near ten o'clock, the house adjourned the further consideration of this affair to this day.

'This day the House proceeded to examine witnesses, and hear counsel father, and the house was left sitting thereupon, and like it sit late.'

Version 8: *Scots Magazine*, 532.

Accordingly the bill was read a second time May 10. and counsel heard upon it then and on the 13th.—**Sir John Dalrymple**, on behalf of the counter-petitioners, said, That a large number of the men who had signed the petition for the bill, were proprietors of those infamous news-papers which had traduced the sovereign, and abused the members of each house of parliament. He dwelt much upon this idea, and was by no means sparing of his severities on the booksellers; positively asserting, that they entirely governed the news-papers; and that after having, in the most barefaced and scandalous manner, abused every gentleman present, and every person in existence, the old for not being young, the young for not being old, the poor for not being rich, and the rich for not being poor; after having called a man a scoundrel if he accepted a place, and a fool is he resigned it; after having vented every calumny which imprudence and ignorance could give birth to, he said they came now and asked favour from the very objects of their abuse. And Col. Onslow having said, that "a learned counsel certainly thought, there was such a thing as copy-right, when he sold his History for 2000 l.;[193] yet he, lawyer-like, at the bar went from his own opinion in behalf of his client;" Sir John said, he could not conclude without clearing up a point respecting himself. It was generally found, that the arguments of a counsel went a great way, especially if he was an honest man. It had been thrown out against him, that after having sold the copy of a book, which had the misfortune universally to displease, although it was universally read; which had been said to have been printed under the patronage of kings and ministers, although it was never seen by either till it was printed; of this book he was charged with having sold the perpetual and exclusive right of multiplying the copy for 2000l. and

[192] As he was Donaldson's attorney, the spelling is more likely to be correct in the paper his son edited. Accordingly, it is almost certainly Wallis and not Wallace. Indeed, the law lists include no Wallace, but do include a Wallis.

[193] The *Scots Magazine* then has '[xxxv.140]'.

immediately afterwards taking an active part to destroy the value of the very property which he had so disposed of. This insinuation was, he said, as false as it was scandalous; for that immediately after the decision in the House of Lords,[194] he went to Mr Cadell, and told him, that if any loss accrued from the event of the decision, he would sustain it himself, and would not suffer it to fall on Mr Cadell.

Version 9: *Gazetteer*, 11 May; *Craftsman*, 14 May.

At five o'clock the order of the day for the second reading of the Bookseller's Bill being read, the counsel were called to the bar; **Sir John Dalrymple** and **Mr. Murphy**'s counsel against it, and **Mr. Mansfield** and **Mr. Hett** in favour of the bill. Sir John opened the cause on the part of his clients in a long laboured speech, composed chiefly of a phillipic on the London news-paper printers, whom he took for granted, by a peculiar figure of his own, to be the very same persons with those intended to be relieved by the bill, and a tedious fulsome panegyric on the King, Lords, and Commons, and the said Sir John Dalrymple himself.

Five witnesses were then called, who proved very little more than that they were neither holders nor owners of copy-rights; that some of them dealt in old books, and smuggled Irish ones; that other were turned, or feared to be turned out from the booksellers sales at the Queen's Arms in St. Paul's church-yard, and the Globe in Fleet-street; and that one of them in particular was detected in pirating some of Shakespeare's plays, and felt the iron hand of power. **Mr. Murphy** next proceeded in his argument, which lasted for an hour and a half; what he said was little better than a trite detail of what was argued at the bar of the House of Lords, and Sir John's abuse of the printers thrown into another form. **Mr. Mansfield** was proceeding to reply, when **Mr. Field** moved, that the further consideration should be postponed till Friday.

Version 10: *London Evening Post*, 10–12 May.

At five o'clock the order of the day for the second reading of the bookseller's bill being read, the council were called to the bar; **Sir John Dalrymple** and **Mr. Murphy** as counsel against it, and **Mr. Mansfield** and **Mr. Hett** in favour of the bill. Sir John opened the cause on the part of his clients in a long laboured speech, Some witnesses were then called. Mr. Murphy next proceeded in his argument, which lasted for an hour, and a half. Mr. Mansfield was proceeding to reply, when **Mr. Field** moved, that the further consideration should be postponed till Friday.

Notes

***Daily Advertiser*, 11 May; *Edinburgh Evening Courant*, 14 May**: Read a second Time the Bill for the Relief of the London Booksellers; Counsel was heard for and against the Bill. Expected to sit late.

[194] *Donaldson v Beckett* (1774) *Cobbett's Parl. Hist.* xvii, col. 953.

***Morning Chronicle*, 10 May**: This day the Booksellers argument comes on in the House of Commons, which is expected to take up most part of the day.

***Gazetteer*, 10 May**: This day the second reading of the Booksellers bill will come on in the Lower Assembly, when long and very warm debates are expected.

***Public Ledger*, 10 May; *General Evening Post*, 7–10 May**: The great question concerning Literary Property, in consequence of the Booksellers Petition, will be argued in the House of Commons this day at two o'clock.

***Middlesex Journal*, 7–10 May**: This day came on in the House of Commons, the bill for relief of booksellers and others, by vesting the copies of printed books in the purchasers of such copies from authors or their assigns, for a time therein to be limited, when Counsel will be heard for and against the said bill; and yesterday morning cards were delivered by Mr. Donaldson to all the Members to attend the House.

Second Reading: 13 May, Second Day

Version 1: *Morning Chronicle*, 16 May;[195] *London Chronicle*, 14–17 May, 465–6;[196] *General Evening Post*, 14–17 May;[197] Cobbett's *Parliamentary History*, xvii, cols 1095–1103.

[MC/LC: **Mr. Mansfield**][198] [PH: The House proceeded to the further hearing of counsel upon the said Bill. Mr. *Mansfield* was heard in favour of the bill. He] **[**MC/LC/PH: opened his speech with a description of the purport of the Bill, its tendency to relieve the petitioners, and give a further time to authors than the term allotted by the [MC/LC: 10th] [PH: 8th] of Queen Anne: he then entered upon a reply to the objections advanced by the counsel for the counter-petitioners.**]**[199] [LC/PH: in substance as follows:]

"MY clients, Sir, have been treated by the learned gentlemen of the other side, with every term of reproach which their ingenuity could frame; they have held them up as oppressors of their poor brethren, as members of an illegal combination, and as men ever ready to put in practice any thing, however cruel, however criminal, if it promoted, or was likely to promote, their own interest; witnesses have been called to prove these assertions, but after a long examination it has been found impossible to adduce one tittle of evidence to support the matters alleged against the petitioners; on the contrary, those who have been examined

[195] The *Morning Chronicle* opens with the paragraph '*As the state of Letters in every country is an essential matter, and well deserves the notice of the historian, we were as circumstantial as possible in reporting the arguments of the Bar, the Judges, and the Peers which governed the late Decision in the House of Lords. From the same principle we are more minute on the progress of the* Booksellers Bill *than we usually are upon private Bills*. Account of Counsel's Arguments, Examination of Evidence, and Debate in the House of Commons on Friday. There is also an account which combines second reading with committee: see Committee, Version 6.'

[196] *London Chronicle* begins with 'ARGUMENTS *made use of by* MR. MANSFIELD, *in Behalf of the* LONDON BOOKSELLERS BILL, *on Friday last in the* HOUSE of COMMONS.'

[197] The *General Evening Post* begins with '*The Substance of Mr.* MANSFIELD's SPEECH *at the Bar of the* HOUSE *of* COMMONS, *on Friday Night last, in Favour of the* BOOKSELLERS.'

[198] James Mansfield† (1734–1821).

[199] The *Morning Chronicle* then includes the following: '[As it is extremely awkward to give a long speech in the third person, we shall take the liberty to use the first; not presuming to advance that what follows is given as the identical words, or that it contains the exact arrangement of the arguments used by Mr. Mansfield, but merely offering it as the substance of his speech.]'

at your bar, have rather established than destroyed their merit; Mr. Merril,[200] indeed, did not fully speak his mind; Mr. Merril knew, Sir, that the subscription entered into by the petitioners was for the purpose of buying up such Scotch editions of those copies which they conceived to be their property, and which the country booksellers had ignorantly taken from the piratical printers; the petitioners might have put the country booksellers to great expence, by commencing prosecutions; instead of that, Sir, they were unwilling to trample on the fallen, they raised a purse to indemnify those who had got Scotch editions, and out of this purse they paid them for those editions; this, Sir, was their oppression, this was their cruelty. The learned advocate has gone a great way to support his clients; he has drawn Scotland into the scrape, and has brought one bookseller from Glasgow[201] to prove the magnitude of the export trade of that city. This evidence, Sir, told you that of late years that city exported books to the amount of 10,000l. per annum. I desired he might be asked who were the exporters? He told us, the booksellers of Glasgow. He was asked how many? and I expected to have found that 1000 persons dealt for the enormous sum of 10l. a year each, but the witness says only a few; and when asked if those few dealt for 10,000l. he says they and their connections. Now, Sir, "their connections" is, I confess, a happy expression, though somewhat unintelligible. Does the witness mean the butcher, the baker, the draper, the taylor, the hosier, the barber, and the washerwoman of the booksellers he alludes to? for I presume they are all connected with them? The witness told you that the Glasgow merchants exported some London books, and some of [MC/LC/GP: those] [PH: these] he confessed were pirated editions with the names of the London booksellers affixed to their title pages."

An attempt has been made to insinuate that the petitioners are nationally prejudiced against the Scotch booksellers; Sir, I will not think so degradingly of this House as to suppose that the Members of it can be influenced by any prejudice; distress is of no country; this House will only consider if the petitioners are men in distress, and if they find them so, as I trust they will, they will doubtless grant them relief.

Another matter urged against the petitioners is, that they are proprietors of the news-papers. Some of the petitioners, Sir, have shares in the public prints, so have several country gentlemen, but they have no more to do with the printing and direction of those papers than you, Sir, sitting in your chair. I do not wonder at the learned Advocate's being loud in reprehending the news-papers; no language can be too severe, too opprobious for them, Sir; they not only attack the characters of King, Lords, and Commons, but [MC/LC/GP: Sir,] they have the insolence to traduce authors and their productions; even that learned, that admired volume, that prodigy of historical merit, the Memoirs of Great Britain, [PH: by sir John Dalrymple,][202] has not escaped their malice; Sir, they have dared to question the veracity of that renowned historian, and after such daring, can any thing too virulent be urged against them?

A further objection made to my clients is, that they have excluded the counter-petitioners from their sales at the Queen's Arms, and Globe Taverns. You have learnt by the evidence examined to this point, that those they did exclude were notorious for selling pirated edi-

[200] Thomas Merrill (*d.* 1781) and John Merrill (c. 1731–1801), Regents Walk, Cambridge.

[201] William Smith.

[202] Dalrymple, *Memoirs of Great Britain and Ireland.*

tions; and, Sir, I will tell you a further, and the true reason for excluding the counter-petitioners; the sales are upon credit from three months, to three years; now if the [MC/GP: poorer] [LC/PH: poor] part of the trade were admitted, as the sales are by auction, they might bid and bye[203] to a large amount, they might make immediate advantage of their purchase, and when the day of payment came, the proprietor of the sale might look in vain for his money; the keeper of a chandler's shop might have quitted trade, and the retailer of books on a wall might have moved his quarters.

A great argument has been made by the gentlemen of the other side of Mr. Donaldson's public spirit, of his great patriotism, and the abundant scale of his merit: Sir, sinking as that scale is with its weight, I will contribute to its preponderation; Patriot Donaldson, Sir, has still greater attributes, [MC: that] [LC/GP/PH: than] his counsel have given him, he is not only as they have described him, an excellent printer, and an admired bookseller, but, Sir, he is more, he is the rival of the famed Eustathius,[204] he is, Sir, an editor and a commentator; he has refined upon the edition of Pope's Homer, published by the poet himself,[205] by expunging no less than 23,851 lines from the notes; [MC/LC/PH: these] [GP: those] lines, Commentator Donaldson thought unnecessary, and therefore he left them out of the edition I now hold in my hand;[206] perhaps, Sir, mean spirits may say, that it would not have been less honest, if he had specified in the title what was omitted, and given the unwary purchaser some intimation of the disappointment he was to meet with in perusing the book, but the fact is as I have stated it.

It has been strongly contested on the side of the counter petitioners, that the petitioners were not at all mistaken respecting the non-existence of a common law right, and that the decision of the King's Bench[207] did not deceive them. Sir, from the immense sum, full one hundred thousand pounds, expended in copy-right, it is evident that they did misconceive, and I do not wonder at it, when I recollect that the highest court of law in Westminster Hall, equally misconceived it, and that five of the judges, when giving their opinion in the House of Lords,[208] immediately previous to the late determination were also of the same sentiments; but, Sir, I will add to these, a still greater authority, the authority of commentator Donaldson: for, Sir, it follows naturally that he either was very ill advised, or that he and his advisers thought all along that there did exist a common law right, otherwise, instead of his being harassed with thirteen suits, he need only have been troubled with one. It was in his power, Sir, to have put in his answer, and brought the question to a final decision within the space of one year, and at the small expence of one hundred pounds; this is a fact not to be disputed, Sir, and it is evident from this great patriot, this learned commentator's pursuing a different line of conduct, that he did not dream that he was warranted in printing the books he published, but that he thought it worth his while to print on, and snatch up such advantages as he could gain previous to the possibility of the copyholders being able to get proof sufficient to ground a prayer to the Court of Chancery for an injunction. The prosecutions then so tremendously stated, were all of Donaldson's seeking, he had nobody

[203] Corrected to 'buy' in *London Chronicle*, *General Evening Post* and *Cobbett's Parl. Hist.*

[204] Eustathius of Thessalonica (c. 1115–c. 1195), famed for among other things his commentaries on Homer.

[205] Alexander Pope* (1688–1744), *The Odyssey of Homer* (Lintot, 1725–6) (ESTC: T67134).

[206] This is *The Odyssey of Homer* (Donaldson 1763) (ESTC: T125952).

[207] *Millar v Taylor* (1769) 4 Burr 2303 (98 ER 201).

[208] *Donaldson v Beckett* (1774) *Cobbett's Parl. Hist.* xvii, col. 953.

to blame for them but himself, and it is evident he thought as well as the petitioners, that there did exist a Common Law Right; besides this I have in my hand an authority* which will, I doubt not, be admitted on the other side. It is a letter, Sir, from a great author to a learned judge,[209] complaining of the piratical practices of Scotch and Irish booksellers. This proves that the petitioners alone were not without reason jealous of the Scotch printers. This letter speaks the language of [MC: of] the heart, it describes things as they are, it wears no artificial dress; it differs, Sir, exceedingly from the light in which the learned Advocate on the other side has painted the printers of Glasgow; it records not their glory, it only speaks of their peculation.

It [MC/GP/PH: has] [LC: hath] been urged that laying the trade of printing open, would be of service to letters, and of service to the public. I deny both positions; and I have by me letters of Mr. Hume, Dr. Hurd, Dr. Robinson, Dr. Beattie,[210] and other writers of established reputation, containing the warmest wishes to the petitioners, lamenting the late decision of the House of Peers, as fatal to literature, and hoping that the Booksellers might get speedy relief. To prove that laying printing open would be a public service, the learned Advocate has told you that he saw an edition of Thompson's Seasons[211] sold for three pence in Scotland; considering the price of paper, of types, and the manual labour, you, Sir, will judge what sort of an edition this must have been. Sir, authors must shudder at what may happen to their works, if the printing trade continues open. Ignorant and careless printers may totally reverse their meanings, and destroy the force of their arguments. I tremble, Sir, for the fate of the learned author of the Memoirs of Great Britain; may not his work be mutilated, transposed, and altered; may we not hereafter see the name of Barillon substituted for that of Sidney;[212] and may not the infamous creature of a Minister be held up as the most disinterested and able patriot this country ever knew. Sir, if the trade continues open, not only Authors but Booksellers and Printers will suffer; already is the destruction of some of the latter working. I have information here that there are now in the press in Scotland no less than [MC/GP: twelve] [LC/PH: five or six] different editions of [MC/GP: Young's Night Thoughts][213] [LC/PH: Young's Works]; this, Sir, is the copy of a letter from Mr. Creech,[214] [MC/GP: printer] [LC/PH: bookseller] in Edinburgh, he says that in every little town there is now a printing press, coblers have thrown away their *awl*, weavers have dismissed their shuttle, to commence printers. The country is over-run with [Not GP: a][GP: any] kind of literary packmen, who ramble from town to town selling books. In the little [LC/PH: inconsiderable] town of Falkirk there is now [MC/GP: an edition of Young's Night Thoughts in the press; there are two in Berwick upon Tweed, two in Edinburgh, two in Glasgow, two in Dumfries, two in Aberdeen, and one in Stirling.] [LC/PH: set up a printing press, and [LC: that] there are several

*Original footnote: A letter sent some time since from Sir John Dalrymple to Judge Blackstone.

[209] William Blackstone.

[210] David Hume* (1711–76), Richard Hurd* (1720–1808), William Robertson (the name is correct in everything other than the *Morning Chronicle*), James Beattie* (1735–1803).

[211] James Thomson, *The Seasons* (Auld, 1772) (ESTC: T85315).

[212] Paul Barillon* d'Amoncourt, marquis de Branges (1630–91), French ambassador to England 1677–88; Algernon Sydney* (1623–83).

[213] Edward Young (1683–1765). The series began with *The Complaint, or Nights on Life, Death and Immortality* (1742) (ESTC: T20819) and additional 'nights' were published thereafter with the Eighth and the Ninth Night being published in 1745.

[214] William Creech* (1745–1815), Edinburgh.

editions of the same book carrying on in Berwick upon Tweed, in Edinburgh, in Glasgow, in Dumfries, and in Aberdeen.][215] The continuing printing an unrestrained trade will be of infinite mischief; it is a trade of so peculiar a nature that it can be compared to no other; it must be governed by rules of its own, and it must of necessity be restrained within some compass. Mr. Donaldson has no right to say that this bill is injurious to his interest, he has already every advantage a reasonable man can wish: this bill does not preclude the sale of his large stock; he tells you he has expended 50,000l. in printing, this bill ensures him a sale, and ensures likewise that he shall have no competitor in the market; is not this a real and a substantial benefit? The Petitioners, Sir, have every plea to urge in their behalf; but their claim to relief is so self-evident that I shall not trouble the House with a long examination of witnesses; when my learned co-adjutor concludes his argument, I shall only call one evidence to prove that their petition is incontrovertibly true.

[MC/GP: **Mr. Hett**[216] then rose, and inferred from the various settlements consisting of Copy Rights made by different families, that the petitioners really did entertain an idea of the existence of a Common-Law Right; he corroborated what Mr. Mansfield had said respecting the possibility of Donaldson's bringing the matter to an early and almost immediate issue if he had thought he was maintaining a legal right; he observed that although the advocate on the other side had spoken so warmly in the behalf of the Scotch Printers and the London Counter Petitioners, that he had trusted neither the one nor the other with the publication of his work; Mr. Hett concluded with warmly urging the plea of the Petitioners, and hoping they would be relieved.][217] [LC/PH: Mr. Hett, the other Counsel for the London booksellers, coincided with Mr. Mansfield, and concluded with warmly urging the plea of the Petitioners.]

[MC: **Mr. Mansfield** was then called upon by the Speaker for his witness, when Mr. Wilkie[218] was brought to the Bar, and questioned as follows:

Question. How long have you been in trade?
Answer. I have been in business upwards of 16 years.
Question. How long have you acted as Agent for the London booksellers?
Answer. Nineteen years.
Question. Please to inform the House what sum of money has been laid out in Copy Right during that time.
Answer. I gave in a written account to the gentlemen of the Committee above stairs of the sum of 49,981l. which I extracted from papers then in my possession; and besides this sum of 49,981l. there have been many sales to large amount; but as I am not in possession of the Sale Papers, I cannot speak positively to the sums; but from the best of my recollection, it cannot be less than fifteen or sixteen thousand pounds more.
Question. Can you give any guess what proportion of this 65,986l. is old Copy Right, not protected by the statute of Queen Anne?
Answer. I should think three-fourths, if not more.

[215] The only edition printed in Scotland in 1774 was in Edinburgh: Young, *The Complaint: or, Night-thoughts, on Life, Death, and Immortality* (Darling, 1774) (ESTC: T165469).

[216] John Hett, junior counsel for the London Booksellers.

[217] The *General Evening Post* ends at this point.

[218] John Wilkie.

Question Do you know any or all the persons who have signed the Counter Petition?

Answer. Yes, Sir, I know some of them.

Question. Are they persons who have served any regular apprenticeships to the business of a bookseller, and in what light or estimation are they looked upon among the trade, and what is the nature of their business?

Answer. I have seen the list of their names, they are all, a few excepted, sellers of books on walls, at the corners of streets, and at the doors of alehouses.

Question. What is the rule observed by you in inviting booksellers to sales?

Answer. It is my business, when I am employed by any of my brethren to act for them, who make sales, to invite the booksellers by a printed catalogue, which is generally delivered two days before the sales.

Question. Some of the Counter-Petitioners that were examined last Tuesday, I think, said the sales were confined to a few booksellers only; pray, is that the case?

Answer. No, Sir. I frequently have sent out upwards of sixty or seventy catalogues, seldom less than that number; and I don't recollect ever being desired to omit inviting any person but such as had not made their payments regular.

Question. By what you have now said, I suppose you give long credit at these sales?

Answer. Yes, Sir, three, six, nine months, and so on to three years; and it would be very hazardous for the proprietors of those sales to sell their books to some of the persons who have signed the Counter-Petition.

Question. It has been said by the Counsel on the other side, that of the 85 persons who signed the Petition, only 20 of them had property: what answer can you give to that?

Answer. I have looked over the list, and do not remark above nine out of the whole but what have considerable property in Copy Right.

Mr. Murphy then cross-examined the witness:

Question. I desire that the witness may inform the House, whether he did not sign a circular letter in 1759,[219] and send it to the country Booksellers at the instance of a committee?

Answer. Yet, Sir, I believe I did.

Question. Was this the letter you signed?

[Letter read by the evidence.][220]

Answer. I think that was the substance of the letter. I did not compose it, I only signed it as agent to the Committee.

[Letter read by the Clerk of the House.]

Question. Was it not the intention of the Committee to prosecute out of a common purse, such Booksellers as had Scotch editions.

Answer. No, Sir, the association of the London booksellers was not set on foot for the purpose of prosecuting the booksellers in the country, as the elder Mr. Merrill informed you last Tuesday, but in order to relieve the country Booksellers a subscription was made to pay all such Booksellers who had bought any pirated books through mistake, which was often done, as the pirates printed books with the proprietors names at the bottom.

Question. I desire that the witness may say who composed the committee?

[219] See Part IV, The Five Letters.

[220] All the square brackets in the questioning are in the original.

Answer. Mr. Millar, Mr. Tonson, Mr. Ward, and I believe Mr. Rivington;[221] it consisted of about five or fix, and most of them are dead.

Question. Does the witness know what became of the books received from the country booksellers?

Answer. I engaged a warehouse to put them in.

Question. What became of them after they were lodged in the warehouse you mention?

Answer. I delivered some of them by order of the committee, but the greater part were burnt by the fire which happened at London House.

Question from Governor Johnston, [Counsel ordered to withdraw.]

Is the witness possessed of any Copyright, and what?

Answer. I have a shade in Boyer's Dictionary, Bailey's Dictionary, Glasses Cookery, Stanhope's Paraphrase, Maitland's History of London, Tatler, &c.[222]

Witness ordered to withdraw.]

[LC/PH: **Mr. Mansfield** was then desired by the Speaker to produce his witness, when Mr. Wilkie was called to the bar and asked several questions, to which he gave very clear and satisfactory answers. The substance of his information was as follows, in reply to the questions put to him, viz. That he had acted 19 years as Agent for the London Booksellers, that during the said time the sum of 65,986l.[223] had been laid out in purchasing copy right; three fourths of which, if not more, he imagined was protected by the statute of Queen Anne. That he had seen a list of the names of the Counter-Petitioners, who are all, a few excepted, Sellers of Books on walls, at the corners of streets, and at the doors of alehouses. That when he is employed to make sale for his brethren, he invites the Booksellers by a printed catalogue, which is generally delivered two days before the sales. That he frequently sent sixty or seventy catalogues, seldom less than that number; and never omitted inviting any person [LC: of][PH: in] the trade, but such as had not made their payments regular. That the credit given to the purchasers at the said sales was three, six, nine months, and so on to three years; and it would be extremely hazardous for the proprietors of those sales to sell their books to some of the persons who have signed the counter petition. The Counsel in favour of the Counter Petitioners having said, that of 85 persons who signed the London Booksellers petition only twenty of them had property; Mr. Wilkie declared, that all, except nine, had considerable property in copy-right. Upon a cross-examination Mr. Wilkie's replies to the questions put to him gave the House the following information:— That in 1759 he signed a circular letter to the Country Booksellers at the instance of a Committee of the London Booksellers, who had entered into an association, not for the purpose of prosecuting the Country Booksellers, as the elder Mr. Merrill had informed the House on the Tuesday before; but in order to relieve the Country Booksellers a subscription was made to pay all such

[221] Jacob Tonson* the younger (1714–67), Andrew Millar* (1705–68), Caesar Ward* (1710–59), James Rivington* (1724–1802) – although the reference might have been to his brother and partner John Rivington (1720–92).

[222] Abel Boyer* (1667–1729), *The Royal Dictionary* (Clavel, 1699) (ESTC: R27810); Nathan Bailey* (1691–1742), *An Universal Etymological English Dictionary* (Bell, 1721) (ESTC: T87493); Hannah Glasse* (1708–70), *The Art of Cookery, Made Plain and Easey* (Ashburn, 1747) (ESTC: T79545); George Stanhope* (1660–1728), *A Paraphrase and Comment upon the Epistles and Gospels* (W.B., 1705–9) (ESTC: T123666); William Maitland* (c. 1693–1757), *The History of London* (Richardson, 1739) (ESTC: T100091); *Tatler* (Addison & Steele, 1709–11) (ESTC P1919).

[223] This is clearly an error: see Petition Committee Report, *CJ*, xxxiv, 590, c. ii.

Booksellers who had bought any pirated books through mistake, which was often done, as the Pirates printed books with the proprietors names at the bottom. That the Committee was composed of Mr. Millar, Mr. Tonson, Mr. Ward, and he believed Mr. Rivington; it consisted of about five or six, most of whom are dead. That he engaged a warehouse to put the books received by the Country Booksellers in. That he delivered some of them by order of the Committee, but the greater part were burnt by the fire which happened at London House.

The Counsel were then ordered to withdraw, and Mr. Wilkie was asked if he possessed any copy-right, and what? He answered that he had shares in Boyer's, Bailey's, and Dyche's Dictionaries, Maitland's History of London, Tatlers, and many other capital books. He was ordered to withdraw.]

A debate then ensued respecting the competency of his evidence, **Governor Johnstone**[224] objected to its admission, and desired it might be expunged from the book, as the witness was evidently interested in the event of the bill. **Mr. Burke**[225] answered the Governor, and observed that the sort of evidence necessary to the present question needed not juridical competency, it was merely evidence of information; and information could only be gathered from an interested party; he supported his observation by instancing the case of Mr. Payne,[226] a witness on the linen bill, and added that the House were wrong in admitting the evidence on Tuesday. **Mr. Charles Fox**[227] replied to Mr. Burke, and said it was true where the tendency of a bill was to further the public interest, the evidence given at the Bar needed not juridical competency, but as the present bill was to give a private compensation, it required evidence nicely competent. Mr. Fox was supported by **Sir Richard Sutton**[228] and several others. **Mr. Dempster**[229] said that if the witness was not a petitioner, he conceived his evidence perfectly admissible. [MC: The strangers were ordered to withdraw, and] a debate of an hour ensued; upon the division, however, there were 75 for the competency of Mr. Wilkie's evidence, 9 against it. When he was again at the Bar, **Mr. C. Fox** proposed that the witness be asked "whether it was his opinion that if the invasion of Copy Right was deemed felony without benefit of clergy, it would be for the benefit of the public;" the ludicrousness [MC: and absurdity] of this question occasioned fresh cavil. The counsel and witness were again ordered to withdraw, **Mr. Dunning**[230] hoped the honourable Member would not urge so absurd a question, **Mr. Burke** solicited his withdrawing it, **Mr. W. Burke**[231] mentioned the complex nature of it, **Mr. Turner**[232] spoke on the same principle, **Mr. Walsh**[233] and **Mr. Moreton**[234] hinted that they would move the question of adjournment if it was not withdrawn; **Mr. C. Fox**, however, persisted in desiring it to be put. The

[224] George Johnstone.

[225] Edmund Burke.

[226] Edward Payne (*d.* 1794), governor of the Bank of England 1771–3.

[227] Charles Fox†* (1749–1806), MP for Midhurst.

[228] Richard Sutton† (1733–1802), MP for St Albans.

[229] George Dempster.

[230] John Dunning.

[231] William Burke.

[232] Charles Turner† (?1727–83), MP for York.

[233] John Walsh†* (1726–95), MP for Worcester.

[234] John Morton† (?1714–80), MP for New Romney. There is no record of any of these speeches in Cavendish.

witness and counsel were again called in, and it was put, when Mr. Wilkie [MC: begged leave to decline answering it.] [LC/PH: said, he hoped the honourable House would excuse him from answering the question; which was almost unanimously agreed to.] His examination was then closed, and **Mr. Murphy**[235] [MC: rose] [LC/PH: arose] to reply to what had been urged [MC: on the side of] [LC/PH: by] the Petitioners, [MC: Mr. Murphy denied that Mr. Mansfield had proved any thing by Mr. Wilkie's evidence, he claimed him as a witness on his side, expressed his wonder that no other person had been called to the Bar, and returned to his former argument, positively declaring that the Petitioners could not be said to have mistaken the law, but that a charge of wilful misconstruction of the law lay against them. Mr. Murphy denied the competency of Mr. Johnston's evidence before the committee, related the private history of Mr. Johnston's quitting business, and declared that it Dr. Robertson, Dr. Heard, Mr. Hume, and Dr. Beattie, accorded with the present bill, and gave up their claim to any interest in their productions, they had no right to give up that of other people. Mr. Murphy recited the old story from Waller[236] of James the First, talking to the Bishops of Winchester and St. Davids,[237] and repeated the reply of the latter; he concluded his speech with an extract from Dr. Johnson's preface to his Dictionary of the English Language.[238] As soon as Mr. Murphy had finished, a debate arose whether the bill should be committed, or whether the House should be adjourned. **Mr. Field** opened the debate with moving that the bill be committed, allowing that there were several objectionable passages in the bill, but hoped the Gentlemen would let it be committed, and in an after stage correct it. **Mr. Sawbridge** seconded this motion, and begged the Gentlemen who were adverse to it to use candour, and accede to the present motion. **Mr. Attorney General** rose to answer this request. He said he really did not know what gentlemen meant by candour. The gentleman might as well ask him be a fool. As the bill was to take away the rights of the public, he certainty should oppose it; he knew from the first enquiry of the committee above stairs, that no other bill than such a one as the present would be brought in, or could be brought in, although he was informed a very different one was designed to be brought in. If gentlemen meant to enter into a debate now, he could not help saying it was exceedingly indecent, he should therefore move for the adjournment of the House.] [LC/PH: As soon as Mr. Murphy had finished, a debate arose whether the Bill should be committed, or whether the House should be adjourned.] **Mr. Burke** [MC: then] spoke in favour of the Petitioners for some time, he instanced the sale of Blackstone's Commentaries,[239] "If [MC/LC: (says he)] [PH:, said he,] the University of Oxford, one of the eyes of this kingdom, chose him the Professor of Laws,[240] allotted him the task of instructing youth in the most important of all studies; if the King afterwards appointed him to distribute justice and interpret the laws, if *he* sold his copy, was it for a bookseller to question his title? but this is only one instance out of many; the

[235] Arthur Murphy* (1727–1805).

[236] Edmund Waller* (1606–87). It was mentioned in *The Works of Edmund Waller*, ed. Percival Stockdale* (1736–1811) (Davies, 1772) (ESTC: T124620), p viii, but the story itself was not promulgated by Waller in any work.

[237] For the story, see Cavendish {52}.

[238] The most recent full edition of the dictionary was Samuel Johnson, *Dictionary of the English Language* (3rd edn, Stathan, 1765) (ESTC: T83962).

[239] William Blackstone, *Commentaries on the Laws of England* (4th edn, Oxford, 1770) (ESTC: T57758).

[240] He was appointed the first Vinerian professor of English law on 20 Oct. 1759.

petitioners have sustained a loss, they are men in distress, the question is, what sort of relief we ought to grant; the learned advocate has told us, that glory is the only reward sought by the Scotch Booksellers, let them have their glory [MC/PH:, and] let the Petitioners have property, we will not quarrel about terms." Mr Burke was for committing the bill: **Governor Johnstone** answered him, and said, his arguments all cut double. **[**MC/LC: **Mr. Feilde** and **Sir Richard Sutton** also spoke. The House at length divided, when there appeared for the adjournment [MC: 24] [LC: 34], against it 39.**]**[MC: A debate then ensued, **Governor Johnston** spoke against the bill, he said it was evidently an injury to Mr. Donaldson and the other Counter Petitioners. He acquitted the Petitioners of the charge of directing the news-papers, said, he was above any national influence, but upon the pure conscientious principles of equity and justice, he thought the bill ought to be thrown out. **Mr. Charles Fox** took the same side of the argument as Governor Johnstone had done. He was exceedingly vehement against the Petitioners, said they had by an illegal monopoly enjoyed the rights of Mr. Donaldson for 31 years, and now they desired legislature to give them a further enjoyment for 21 years longer. The Petitioners were, he said, wallowing in wealth, and had not the least claim to the relief they prayed. **Mr. Onslow** rose to correct a part of Governor Johnston's speech, which **Governor Johnston** explained, and shewed that Mr. Onslow had misconceived him. Upon the House dividing on Mr. Fielde's motion, the ayes were 36, the noes 10; so the commitment was carried.] [LC: Another debate then ensured at length the House divided on Mr Field's motion for committing the bill for Monday; the ayes were 36, the noes 10; so the commitment was carried.] **[**MC/LC: Just as the House was preparing to rise, [MC: the **Attorney General**][241] [LC: a great Law Officer] attempted to defeat the labours of the day, by a manoeuvre as unexpected as curious. He ordered the clerk to turn over to the Journals of March 1697,[242] wherein it is made a standing order. That seven days notice of every private bill going through the House, shall be posted up in the Lobby, by order of the Chairman of said Committee. In this he had two views, either that the House could not get over the standing order, or that there would not be members sufficient to constitute one; but the question being put, it appeared that there were just 40 members present, 35 of whom were against the Seven Days Notice, and 5 for it. The bill was accordingly committed for Monday.**]**

[PH: Then the question being put, That the Bill be committed; the House divided,
The Yeas went forth.[243]

	Tellers.	
YEAS	Mr. Feilde Mr. Wilbraham Bootle	36
NOES	Sir George Savile Sir Richard Sutton	10

So it was resolved in the affirmative.

[241] Edward Thurlow.

[242] It should be *CJ*, xiii, 6 (24 Nov. 1699).

[243] *CJ*, xxxiv, 752.

A motion was then made, That this House will, upon Monday, resolve itself into a Committee of the whole House, upon the said Bill; the House divided.
The Yeas went forth.

Tellers.

	Tellers	
YEAS	Mr. Cavendish Mr. Whitworth	35
NOES	Mr. Attorney General Mr. Charles James Fox	None

So it was resolved in the affirmative.]

* A letter sent some time since from Sir John Dalrymple, Judge Blackstone.

Version 2: *St James's Chronicle*, 12–14 May; *Caledonian Mercury*, 18 May; *London Magazine*, 623–4.

At a Quarter after Six, the Order of the Day for the second Reading of the Booksellers Bill being read**, Mr. Field** moved, that as it was so late in the Day, and the Matter to be considered was of so much Importance, that it might be deferred till Monday. **Lord Beauchamp**[244] attempted to mend [SJC/CM: the Motion,] [LM: this motion] by moving, that the Counsel should be now heard, but that the Debate should be put off for the above Day. **Colonel Barre**[245] observed, that he should dissent from both Propositions, as in all Probability, if the present Opportunity was permitted to escape, the Matter would not be again discussed in so full a House. The Question being at length put on Mr. Field's Motion, it passed in the Negative, there being but 26 Ayes, to 34 Noes. The Counsel were accordingly called in, and Messrs. Mansfield and Hett heard in Favour of the Bill, and the former having stated some Letters and other Matters relative to Sales of Copy Right, he was called upon from the Chair to produce Evidence of them. Mr. Wilkie was called in and examined. When the Counsel had finished their Interrogatories, he was asked by Governor Johnstone, whether he had any Copy-Right Property? and the Witness answering he had, and at the same Time enumerating the several Copies he had Shares in, a Question arose, whether he was a competent Witness, and after a long Altercation, in which [LM: almost] every Person present [SJC/CM: almost] bore a Part, **Mr. Cornwall**[246] framed a Motion for expunging his Evidence, and the Sense of the House being taken on it, there appeared for the Motion, 24, against, 39. Mr. Wilkie and the Counsel being again called in, **Mr. C. Fox** [SJC/CM: propounded the following Question to him, in Substance: Whether Persons invading Copy-Right, ought not be prosecuted as Felons and convicted without Benefit of Clergy? This gave Birth to another Wrangle, which lasted above an Hour, and Mr. C. Fox still adhering to his Question, refused, though pressed from every Side to give it up; answering humorously,

[244] Francis Seymour Conway, Lord Beauchamp†* (1743–1822), MP for Orford.

[245] Issac Barré†* (1726–1802), MP for Chipping Wycombe.

[246] Charles Cornwall† (1735–89), MP for Grampound.

that he was not ready to recede, as the House well knew, the Consequences of which came home personally to him on a recent Occasion. In order that so extraordinary a Question should not appear in the Journals, the House agreed to divide upon that Part which orders the Counsel to be called in, for which there was 173 Ayes, and only Nine Noes. On the Return of the Members, Mr. Wilkie[247] was again called in to answer Mr. Fox's Question; to which he replied, he did not know.—**Mr. Murphy** being then heard in Reply, it was Twelve o'Clock before he finished.] [LM: proposed, that the witness be asked, "Whether it was his opinion, that if the invasion of copy right was deemed felony without benefit of clergy, it would be for the benefit of the public?" The ludicrousness of this question occasioned fresh cavil. The counsel and witness were again ordered to withdraw. **Mr. Dunning** hoped the honourable member would not urge so absurd a question; **Mr. Burke** sollicited his withdrawing it; **Mr. W. Burke** mentioned the complex nature of it; **Mr. Turner** spoke on the same principle; **Mr. Walsh** and **Mr. Moreton** hinted, that they would move the question of adjournment, if it was not withdrawn. **Mr. C. Fox**, however, persisted in desiring it to be put. The witness and counsel were again called in, and it was put, when Mr. Wilkie said, he hoped the House would excuse him from answering the question, which was almost unanimously agreed to. His examination was then closed, and **Mr. Murphy** arose to reply to what had been urged by the petitioners. As soon as Mr. Murphy had finished, a debate arose, whether the bill should be committed, or whether the House should be adjourned.

Mr. Burke spoke in favour of the petitioners for some time: he instanced the sale of Blackstone's Commentaries: "If (says he) the university of Oxford, one the eyes of this kingdom, chose him the professor of laws, allotted him the task of instructing youth in the most important of all studies—if the king afterwards appointed him to distribute justice and interpret the laws, if *he* sold his copy, was it for a bookseller to question his title? But this is only one instance out of many: the petitioners have sustained a loss, they are men in distress, the question is, what sort of relief we ought to grant. The learned advocate has told us, that glory is the only reward sought by the Scotch booksellers. Let them have their glory, and let the petitioners have property: we will not quarrel about terms." Mr. Burke was for committing the bill, **Gov. Johnstone** answered him, and said his arguments all cut double.]

The Gentlemen who pressed the Affair in the Beginning, now wanted to decline the Combat; and after a long Debate, **Mr. Fielde** having moved to commit the Bill for Monday, **Mr. Attorney General** moved to adjourn, and the Question being put on Mr. Feidle's Motion, the House divided, Ayes 36, Noes 10; so the Commitment was carried. When the House was just preparing to rise, the **Attorney General** attempted to defeat the Labours of the Day, by a Manoeuvre as unexpected as curious. He ordered the Clerk to turn [SJC/CM: over] to the Journals of March 1697,[248] wherein it is made a standing Order, That seven Days Notice of every private Bill, going through the House, shall be posted up in the Lobby, by Order of the Chairman of [SJC/CM: the] [LM: said] Committee. In this he had two Views, either that the House could not get over the standing Order, or that there would not be Members sufficient to constitute one; but the Question being put, [SJC/CM: it appeared that

[247] John Wilkie.

[248] This is a reference to 4 Feb. 1697/8 (*CJ*, xii, 83), but this does not relate to the rule that there must be seven days' notice, which was resolved on 24 Nov. 1699 (*CJ*, xiii, 6). Further, the journals refer to the version of the standing order made on 18 Jan. 1708 (*CJ*, xvi, 63), although the order was renewed again on 5 Mar. 1722/3 (*CJ*, xx, 161).

there were][LM: there appeared to be] just 40 Members present, 35 of whom were against the seven Days Notice, and five for it. The Bill was accordingly committed [SJC/CM: for Monday], and the House [SJC/CM: rose precisely] [LM: arose] at Three Quarters past One o'Clock.

Versions 3: *Public Advertiser*, 16 May; *Lloyd's Evening Post*, 13–16 May, 463.

[PA: At Six o'Clock the Order of the Day was read,] [LLP: On Friday, on the Order] for the second reading of the Bill [PA: for Relief of Booksellers and others, by] [LLP:, in the House of Commons, for] vesting the Copies of printed Books in the Purchasers of such Copies from Authors or their Assigns, for a Time therein to be limited; [PA: when] [LLP: being read,] **Mr. Field** [PA: got up and] moved for its being put off till This Day, [PA: as it was so late in the Day,] [LLP: it being late,] which was objected to by the Opposers of the Bill, when the Question being put the House divided for putting it off, Ayes 26, Noes 34. The Counsel then being called in, **Mr. Mansfield** [PA: got up and] spoke for the Bill for near two Hours in a most able Manner, and answered all that Sir John Dalrymple had said in Favour of the Petitioners, against the Bill, and upon the illiberal Abuse which he had thrown out against the London Booksellers: He went through the Whole of the Evidence that had been examined against the Bill, and shewed, [PA: plainly] that they were a Set of Men that never had Copy Right, and therefore could be no Losers, and yet [PA: pretend to come to this] [LLP: came to that] House complaining that they should be greatly injured if this Bill was to pass. He then begged Leave to read a Letter [PA: to the House, which he was sure that the Gentlemen of the other Side would disprove the Authority of; it was a Letter to] [LLP: sent some time since from Sir J.D. to] Judge Blackstone, complaining of the pirating of Books in Scotland and Ireland, and that the Author had ordered a Prosecution against them, [LLP: as being] to the great Detriment of the fair Trader: Whilst the Letter was reading the whole House was fixed upon [PA: Sir J— D—, as it was his own Letter which he sent himself.] [LLP: Sir J.D] Mr. Mansfield then read a Letter from Mr. Creech, Bookseller, at Edinburgh, [PA: which gave] [LLP: giving] an Account, that since the Decision of the House of Lords the whole Place was in Confusion, every one had turned Printer and Publisher of pirated Books, even Shoemakers, Coblers, and Weavers. He then produced [PA: a Book of Homer, printed by Donaldson, (to shew the Matter the Public were imposed and cheated by these pirated Books) which wanted above 300 Lines of the Notes. He then produced Letters from Dr. Robertson, Hurd, Beattie, &c. to shew their general Approbation of the Bill, and wishing them Success. He concluded with] [LLP: letters from Mr. Hume, Dr. Hurd, Dr. Robinson, Dr Beattie, and other Writers of established reputation, containing their warmest wishes for the Petitioners, lamenting the late decision of the House of Peers, as fatal to Literature, and hoping that the Booksellers might get speedy relief. He made] several Observations on Mr. Donaldson's Conduct [PA: upon this Business, and hoped sincerely] [LLP: who, he observed, was very ill advised, or thought all along that there did exist a Common Law Right, otherwise, instead of his being harassed with thirteen suits, which costs him above 1000l. he need only have been troubled with one, as it was in his power to have put in his answer, and have brought the question to a final decision within the space of one year, and at the small expence of 100l. and concluded with hoping] that the Bill would pass into a Law, as several innocent Persons had been drawn in to lay out their Money in a perpetual Copy Right, which they thought they were intitled to by the common Law, and the Opinion they had entertained of the Determination of the Court of King's Bench.

[PA: Mr ——] [LLP: **Mr. Hett**] then followed Mr. Mansfield, and went thro' all the Arguments; [PA: said that tho' it appeared that Mr. Donaldson had been at] [LLP: and observed, that great part of Mr. Donaldson's] 1000l. [PA: Expence] [LLP: Expences] in 13 Injunctions in the Court of Chancery and other Law Suits, [PA: yet a great Part of that Money was entirely his own seeking, he] [LLP: was for] having printed Shenstone's Works, and Yorick's Sermons, which were protected by the Statute of [PA: Queen][LLP: Q.] Anne. [PA: Mr. Hett spoke for an Hour.] Mr. Wilkie then was called to the Bar, and gave an Account how the different Sales were managed; he said that he gave Catalogues to all Booksellers that were thought to have Property enough to pay when they purchased any Share, and no one was ever excluded but those who could not pay, as their Credit was from three Months to three Years. Governor Johnstone then asked him whether he had Copy Right, he said yes; he was then ordered to withdraw, and [PA: Governor Johnstone][LLP: the Governor] got up and said he was not a proper Evidence, he being deeply concerned in this Bill, and therefore his Examination ought to be struck out. This occasioned a warm Debate, when the House divided that he was a proper Evidence; Ayes 75, Noes 9. **Mr. Murphy** then replied to the Whole of the Evidence; as soon as he had finished a Debate ensured upon the Commitment of the Bill, [PA: when] [LLP: and] the Attorney-General moved for an Adjournment [PA: and the House;] [LLP: of the House; when there were] Ayes 24, Noes 39. The Motion for the Bill's being committed for this Day was [LLP: then] made, and after a long Debate the House divided, Ayes 35 to no Noes, they being gone out excepting the two Tellers, in Hopes that [PA: that] they would not have had 40 Members in the House, but with the Speaker there were just the Number. The Bill was then ordered to be committed for this Day, and the House broke up at past Two o'Clock [PA: in the] [LLP: on Saturday] Morning.—The Speakers were for the Bill the two Mr. Burkes, two Mr. Onslows, Mr. Field, Mr. Sawbridge, and Mr. Harris. Against the Bill the Attorney General, Governor Johnstone, Sir William Sutton, Mr. Charles Fox, and Mr. Dempster.

Version 4: *Edinburgh Advertiser*, 17–20 May, 317.

On Friday the House of Commons went into a committee on the bookseller's bill; **Mr. Mansfield**, and **Mr. Hett**, counsel for the bill, spoke for a considerable time. Mr. Wilkie, bookseller in London, was examined: He was asked, if he was a proprietor in copy-right? he replied in the affirmative; **Governor Johnstone**, **Mr. Charles Fox**, **Sir Charles Sutton**, and several others objected to his evidence. A debate of an hour ensured, and the question was put, and carried for the admissibility of Mr. Wilkie's evidence, who was again called in and examined. A letter from Mr. Creech,[249] bookseller in Edinburgh, was produced and read, in favour of the London booksellers, and against the booksellers of Scotland; setting forth, That since the late decision of the House of Peers, the whole trade of printing and bookselling in Scotland was gone into confusion; that coblers had thrown away their awls, and weavers dismissed their shuttles, and commenced printers, &c.—But as Mr. Creech, although in London at the time, did not chuse to be examined on the contents of the letter, it was not admitted as evidence.* **Mr. Murphy** then replied against the bill. A warm debate ensured, **Mr. Field** and **Mr. Sawbridge** moved, that the bill might be committed,

[249] It appears extracts of the letter were sent to the editor, but he would only publish the entire letter: *Edinburgh Advertiser*, 31 May–3 June, 349§.

allowing that there were several objectionable passages in the bill, but hoped the gentlemen on the other side would act with candour, and alter them at a future stage of the bill. **Mr. Attorney General** said he did not know what the gentlemen meant by desiring them to act with candour, and commit the bill; as it was to take away the rights of the public, he would oppose it in every stage, that it was exceedingly indecent to enter into a debate of so much importance at that late hour when the house was so thin, he would therefore move to adjourn. **Mr. Burke** spoke for committing the bill, and was answered by **Governor Johnstone**. The House then divided, for the adjournment 24, against it 39. A fresh debate arose, **Governor Johnstone** and **Mr. Charles Fox** spoke against the bill, and **Mr. Onslow** for it. **Mr. Fox** was exceedingly violent against the petitioners; said they had by an illegal monopoly enjoyed the rights of other people for 31 years, and now they desired the legislature to give them a further enjoyment for 21 years longer. The petitioners were, he said, wallowing in wealth, and had not the least claim to the relief they prayed for. It was then carried to commit the bill for this day, and the house rose at two o'clock on Saturday morning.

This day the house proceeded, when the debate lasted till 12 o'clock at night, several votes were put, the blanks filled up, and the bill ordered to be reported on Thursday.

The principal speakers for the bill, were Messrs. Feild, Sawbridge, Burke, W. Burke, and Gen. Carnac; against the bill, Lord Folkstone, Attorney General, Gov. Johnstone, Sir Wm. Sutton, Mr. Cha. Fox, Mr. Dempster &c.

---

* It is remarkable that Mr. Creech is now printing the English Poets in 40 Volumes, which, if the late decision of the House of Peers had not been obtained, is a direct infringement on the property of the London booksellers; and even the terms allowed by the statute of Queen Anne, to the proprietors of many of these works, and not expired.

Version 5: *Morning Chronicle*, 14 May; *Middlesex Journal*, 12–14 May; *London Chronicle*, 12–14 May, 464; *General Evening Post*, 12–14 May; *Gazetteer*, 16 May; *Edinburgh Evening Courant*, 18 May; *Craftsman*, 21 May.

[MC: At five o'clock yesterday the order of the day was read in the House of Commons, when the further hearing of Counsel respecting the Booksellers bill standing first, counsel were called in, and **Mr. Mansfield**] [MJ: Then came on the Booksellers bill; Mr Mansfield pleaded their cause with infinite wit, great sagacity, and uncommon happiness in throwing off all the imputations of Sir John Dalrymple. He read a letter of Sir John's to Judge Blackstone, complaining of the villainous piracies of the Scotch Booksellers of Glasgow, in printing cheap editions of the Commentaries and his own Memoirs: A most compleat refutation of his argument in defence of Glasgow. He produced letters of Dr. Robertson, Mr. Hume, Dr. Hurd, Mr Beate, &c. shewing their approbation of the bill, and in a word, went through the whole argument in a most masterly manner.] [LC: At five o'clock the House of Commons went into the further hearing of Counsel respecting the Booksellers bill; Counsellor Mansfield,] [GP/GZ/EC/CT: Then came on the Booksellers Bill; Mr. Mansfield, as Counsel,] **[**Not MJ: spoke for an hour and [Not LC: a] half in favour of the Petitioners; he was followed by **Mr. Hett** on the same side.**]** Mr. Wilkie was then examined in support of the petition for the bill. **Governor Johnston**[250] asked the witness if he possessed any Copy-right, being answered in the affirmative, he desired the Counsel might withdraw, when he objected to the admission of Mr. Wilkie's evidence; this objection gave rise to a warm debates[251] respecting its competency on which the House divided, Ayes 75, Noes 9. Mr. Wilkie was then again called to the bar, and cross examined by **Mr. Murphy**; after which, Mr. Murphy replied to the Counsel for the Bill. As soon as Mr. Murphy had finished, a fresh debate [Not MJ: ensured][MJ: enived], which lasted some time; at length, the Attorney General moved to adjourn; the House, after a short argument, divided upon the question, when the numbers were 24 for the adjournment, 39 against it. Governor Johnston, Mr. Fox, Mr. Onslow, and the Attorney General then spoke; at half after one the question was put for committing the bill, [Not MJ: the House again divided, and the numbers were 35 to nothing, the four Tellers and the Speaker making a House.] **[**Not MJ/CT: The bill stands committed for [MC/LC/GP/EC: Monday.] [GZ: this day.]**]**

[MC: We shall give a more particular account of this matter in Monday's Paper.[252]

The principal speakers yesterday were Mr. Feilde, Mr. Sawbridge, Mr. Burke, Mr. W. Burke, and General Carnac, for the bill; Lord Folkstone, Mr. Attorney General, Governor Johnston, Sit William Sutton, Mr. Charles Fox, Mr. Dempster, & c. against it.]

[LC: The principal speakers yesterday were Mess. Fielde, Sawbridge, Burke, W. Burke, and Gen. Carnac, for the bill; Lord Folkstone, Attorney General, Governor Johnston, Sir William Sutton, Mr. Charles Fox, Mr. Dempster, &c. against it.

[MJ: After several divisions and long debates, which lasted till past one o'clock this morning, the bill was committed for Monday next, by a majority of 36, against 10.]

Version 6: *Scots Magazine*, 532.

In answer to Sir John, **Mr Mansfield** said, "I do not wonder at the learned advocate's being loud in reprehending the news-papers no language can be too severe, too opprobrious for them, Sir: they not only attack the characters of King, Lords, and Commons, but, Sir, they have the insolence to traduce authors and their productions; even that learned, and admired volume, that prodigy of historical merit, the Memoirs of Great Britain,[253] has not escaped their malice: Sir, they have dared to question the veracity of that renowned historian; and after such daring, can any thing too virulent be urged against them?—It is evident, that the counter-petitioners, as well as the petitioners, thought that there did exist a common-law right: I have in my hand an authority which will, I doubt not, be admitted on the other side. It is a letter,* Sir, from a great author to a learned judge, complaining of the piratical practices of Scotch and Irish booksellers. This proves, that the petitioners alone were not without reason jealous of the Scotch printers. This letter speaks the language of the heart, it describes things as they are, it wears no artificial dress; it differs, Sir, exceedingly from the light in which the learned advocate on the other side has painted the printers of Glasgow; it records not their glory, it only speaks of their peculation."—After the pleadings were

[250] *General Evening Post* has 'J—stone', 'A—ney-G—ral', 'F–x' and 'O–slow'.

[251] It is corrected to 'debate' in *London Chronicle, Gazetteer, General Evening Post, Edinburgh Evening Courant*, and *Craftsman*.

[252] *Morning Chronicle*, 16 May.

[253] The *Scots Magazine* then has '[xxxv. 140]'.

finished, there was a long debate; which issued in two questions: 1. Whether to adjourn? which passed in the negative, 39 to 34. 2. Whether to commit the bill for Monday? which carried, Ayes 36, Noes 10.

---

* A letter sent some time since from Sir John Dalrymple, to Judge Blackstone.

Notes

***Morning Chronicle*, 13 May**: This day the further hearing of the Booksellers Petition comes on in the House of Commons, when Counsel for the bill will be heard.

***Gazetteer*, 13 May**: And for the second reading of the bill vesting the copies of printed books in the purchasers of such copies from authors, or their assigns, for a time therein to be limited.

***Public Advertiser*, 14 May**: At Eight o'Clock the House was left sitting hearing Council on the further Proceedings on the Booksellers Bill.

***London Evening Post*, 12–14 May**: Proceeded to hear further counsel on the booksellers petition.

At half after one the question was put for committing the bill, the House divided, and the numbers were 35 to nothing, the four Tellers and the Speaker making a House. The bill stands committed for Monday.

***Daily Advertiser*, 16 May**: On Friday Night the Booksellers Bill was taken into Consideration in the Lower Assembly, which continued sitting till Three Quarters past One o'Clock on Saturday Morning, when the Bill was committed for this Day, on a Division 36 against 10.

Committee of the Whole House: 16 May

Version 1: *Morning Chronicle*, 18 May; *London Magazine*, 624–7; Cobbett's *Parliamentary History*, xvii, col. 1103–9.

[MC: As soon as the order of the day was read last Monday, for the House to go into a Committee on the Booksellers Bill, **Mr. Charles Fox** rose, and begged leave to say a few words previous to Mr. Field's motion; he said he hoped the House would not hear so indecent a motion as that for committing the bill; a learned friend of his, had on Friday evening ordered the Clerk to refer to the journals for a standing order made Feb. 1697, which declared it a resolution of the House, that no private bill should from that time be committed untill eight days notice had been pasted up in the Lobby.[254] After this he did not conceive the House could go into a committee without violating the unvaried practice of parliament. The whole business of the present bill, he observed, had been conducted in a manner so irregular, so party-like and so unfair, that he thought it necessary to oppose in every manner and in every stage, a bill founded upon a most inequitable principle, a bill calculated to continue a monopoly exceedingly injurious to a number of individuals; he therefore rose to controvert the resolution of a few members at a late hour,

[254]This is inaccurate: the correct standing order is at 24 Nov. 1699 (*CJ*, xiii, 6).

for he could not call them a house. The order he conceived spoke directly against the bill's being now committed, and he called upon the Chair to determine the meaning and customary use of the order in question. **The Speaker**[255] immediately expressed his satisfaction that the House would come to a proper understanding of the order; according to the letter of which he declared the House might now go into a committee, as the order had frequently been dispensed with by the committees below stair, but never by those above.]

[LM: The order of the day was read for going into a committee upon the booksellers bill. **Mr. Feilde** arose; but **Mr. C. Fox** desired he would sit down while he mentioned to the House a few words. He began, saying,] [PH: The order of the day being read for going into a committee upon the bill. **Mr. Charles Fox** rose. He began with saying, that] **[**LM/PH: he hoped [LM: that] [PH: the] House would not be guilty of such imprudence as to act contrary to a standing order, which [LM: says] [PH: said], that no private Bill [LM: shall] [PH: should] be committed until eight days after the second reading. He mentioned the manner in which the business was conducted on Friday night and Saturday morning last, saying, [LM: they hurried it] [PH: it was hurried] through by a few *people*, for he could not call them a *House*; for on the division they were obliged to count the four *tellers* and *Speaker* to make forty. He was exceedingly severe on the booksellers in general, and concluded [LM: making a motion][PH: with moving], that the bill be committed for Thursday se'nnight.**]**

[LM: He was seconded by the **Attorney General**,[256] who spoke a considerable time against the booksellers; said,] [PH: The **Attorney General** seconded the motion. He said,] **[**LM/PH: they came and asked a favour of the House, under a pretence that *authors* would be benefited, which he denied; for it was meant entirely for the benefit of a few individual booksellers, who ruled the whole trade. He said, the members who were for the bill seemed to triumph, but he was sure it was in a wrong cause; and that if they went into a committee on [LM: the bill] [PH: it] *then*, it was contrary to the express standing order of the House, and [LM: contrary] to all rules of justice.**]**

Mr. Burke [MC/LM: answered Mr. Fox, and] observed, that there was a material difference between a standing order and a discretionary rule. This, he said, was a discretionary rule, made for a discretionary reason, and might be dispensed with for a discretionary purpose. He entered into all the various logical distinctions between the one and the other, clearly shewing that the former was of a fixed indispensable nature, the latter framed for occasional purposes, and might, without any difficulty, be waved as occasion required. With regard to the bill, he declared it was founded upon the *summum jus*, and nothing could controvert it but *summa injuria*.[257]

Mr. Field [MC: spoke next, and] remarked that the manoeuvre practised at the close of the debate last Friday evening was, indeed, a most glorious, a most admirable manoeuvre, and he hoped it would be handed down to future ages.

The **Attorney General** [MC/LM: then rose, and] said he did not really conceive the difference between a standing order and a discretionary rule. When the House entered a Rule in their books, he thought it was to be a maxim of parliament not to be departed from. As to the manoeuvre spoken of as so glorious a matter, it was a fair, regular proceeding; the

[255] Sir Fletcher Norton†* (1716–89).

[256] Edward Thurlow.

[257] Trans: 'extreme justice' and 'extreme injustice'.

gentlemen in favour of the bill had desired him to use candour on the occasion; to which he had replied, that he should as soon give up his senses; this reply had been twisted to another meaning, and they had related his answer as a declaration that all candour was folly; this was, he said, what men of genius called a hit; and he was frequently the subject of these hits, and the laughter they created. The argument of the *summum jus* was what scholars termed a sounding argument. It was, indeed trusting more to sound than sense to say, that the *summum jus* of the Counter-Petitioners was properly opposed by the *summa injuria*, in which the bill had its foundation. [MC: He spoke severely against the Petitioners, and the principle of the bill.]

Mr. Burke[258] [MC: very laughably] replied to the Attorney General, and said, that no man living knew better how to give such hits than the learned gentleman himself, as he had fully proved by the notable reversion of his application of the terms *summum jus* and *summa injuria*. He confessed he had worn a risible countenance which was provoked by the wit and ingenuity of the leaned gentleman who spoke last; laughter, he observed, was of different kinds, and one was a complimentary sort. [MC/LM: With regard to the glorious manoeuvre it was an absolute star; but he must own it was *stella insperata*[259] which the Speaker had caused very properly to set.] He would not now enter [MC/LM: fully] into [MC/PH: a] defence of the bill, or the plea of meriting compassion, which the petitioners had, but he conceived he could not only give satisfactory proof of that, but could also prove that the counter-petitioners, whom the learned gentleman spoke so highly of as parties who were about to lose their right, were no better than thieves who had escaped justice. Mr. Burke again asserted that the order ought not to be attended to. He shewed that the cause of its being made was, that the parties who were interested in a private bill might not be taken by surprize. This could not be now said to be the case; the counter-petitioners had enjoyed every benefit arising from delay. The bill had been near three months in the House. A Counsel had found time to travel, he would not say post-haste, for that was beneath the gravity of the profession; but he had found time to go to Glasgow and return to town with a whole waggon load of Scotch arguments. These arguments had been doled out at the bar; two long days had been spent in hearing learned pleaders state the merits of the counter-petitioners; they had examined several witnesses, and appeared perfectly satisfied with their evidence. It could not be urged that the opposers of the bill had not fully understood the whole of the subject; nay, it was evident that they knew every clause in the bill, for he had in his hand a series of observations and objections to every single clause. The counter-petitioners had, therefore, every advantage they could reasonably desire; and as a part of the order, [MC: viz] the pasting up notice in the lobby, had never been followed respecting Committees below stairs, so he conceived the whole of it was inapplicable, and might be dispensed with on the present occasion.

Mr. Dempster[260] [MC/LM: rose and] said there was an absolute necessity for the [MC/LM: order's] [PH: order] being enforced, for he had been assured by the counter-petitioners, that part of the evidence offered on Friday was groundless, which they could prove by affidavits.

[258] Edmund Burke.

[259] Trans: 'unexpected star'.

[260] George Dempster.

Governor Johnstone[261] [MC: then spoke to the question; he] said, he conceived that the order held equally with respect to committees below, as committees above stairs: that the pasting up notice of the former was unnecessary, as the printed votes gave sufficient warning. The Governor declared, he was sorry he had misconceived the meaning of the supporters of the bill last Friday, for when the question for adjournment was carried in the negative, the plain common sense of the matter told him, that the bill was necessarily to be debated, and he entered into debate accordingly. Speaking of the little confidence to be placed in the printed hints, [MC/LM: &c.] put into the members hands in the lobby,[262] he said it had been urged by some writers of hints and observations, that Dr. Johnson had received an after gratification from the booksellers who employed him to compile his Dictionary; this, was a groundless assertion, for he had in his hand a letter from Dr. Johnson, which contradicted it; he then read the letter,[263] in which the Doctor denied the assertion, but declared, that his employers fulfilled their bargain with him, and that he was satisfied. The Governor then [MC: declared,] [LM/PH: said] that the honourable gentleman, (Mr. Burke) who on Friday last mentioned 7000l. as the price paid by one of the petitioners for the copy of Blackstone's Commentaries,[264] was mistaken. The sum paid, as appeared by the original assignment, which he had seen, was 4,000l.[265] out of which the purchaser received stock in printed books, &c. to the amount of 1400l. so that the nett receipt of the seller was only 2600l. which the Governor conceived even within the term allowed by the statute of Queen Anne, the buyer might get back. After stating this particular, Governor Johnstone went into a recapitulation and enlargement of those arguments against the Bill which he urged on Friday. [MC: The Governor spoke very fully in opposition to it.]

Mr. Fox [MC/LM: rose again, and after persisting] [PH: persisted,] that both the spirit and the letter of the order were against the commitment of the bill, [MC/LM: he] [PH: and] moved, "that this House do enter into a committee on the [Not PH: Booksellers] Bill next Thursday se'nnight."

Mr. Mackworth[266] [MC/LM: rose next, and said, that he] thought the petitioners deserved some relief, but could not see that the present bill was such a one as deserved the countenance of the ligislature; with respect to the order in question, he saw no reason why it should now be dispensed with, but he thought that Friday next should be substituted in Mr. Fox's motion, for Thursday se'nnight.

Mr. Fox rose to explain that as the House adjourned next Friday for the holidays, Thursday se'nnight was the first open day.

Mr. Whitworth[267] said the notice pasted in the Lobby was merely a notice to the Members, not to the public.

[MC: **Mr. Popham** said a few words in favour of Mr. Fox's motion.]

[261] George Johnstone.

[262] See note in Part I: Chapter 2.

[263] See Cavendish {79} for the contents of the letter.

[264] William Blackstone, *Commentaries on the Laws of England* (Oxford, 1765–9) (ESTC: T57753).

[265] Cf. the figure of £3,000 was reported from the petition committee: Petition Committee Report, *CJ*, xxxiv, 588, c. ii.

[266] Herbert Mackworth† (1737–91), MP for Cardiff Boroughs.

[267] Richard Whitworth.

Mr. Sawbridge, Mr. W. Burke, and **Mr. Burke**,[268] said that Mr. Fielde's motion ought to be put prior to Mr. Fox's, for that out of the civility which ever prevailed in that house from one gentleman to another, Mr. Fox had been allowed to speak what he said would only be a few words previous to Mr. Fielde's motion, although that gentleman was on his legs to put his motion.

Mr. Fox said, it was *utrum horum mavis*;[269] for that both motions would have the same effect.

[MC/LM: The strangers were ordered to withdraw, and it was carried against Mr. Fox's motion.] [PH: Mr. Fox's motion was rejected.] A debate then ensued, whether the Speaker should leave the chair. **Lord Folkstone** opened it with a speech against the bill; his Lordship began with stating the law-history of the act of Queen Anne, and tracing the conduct of the petitioners from the year 1709 to the present time, the whole of which he urged as a proof that they never did misconstrue the law. His Lordship observed, that Lord Mansfield, at a very early period of his life, was employed as counsel for the petitioners, the idea of the existence of a common law right was a favourite idea with his Lordship, and he could not but remark, that most of the Judges who gave their opinion coincident with Lord Mansfield's sentiments, had been puisne Judges in the Court of King's Bench. His Lordship disclaimed any other motive [MC: for] [LM/PH: of] his opposition to the bill than a necessary parliamentary consideration of the rights of the public, which consideration now obliged him to object to the bill.

Mr. Fielde [MC/LM: spoke next, and] entered [MC/LM: very] diffusively into the principle of the Bill, and its tendency. He shewed, from a variety of historical facts, that the petitioners were mistaken, and that they did not wilfully misconstrue the law. He said that the assignment from Blackstone, the assignment of Milton,[270] and the assignments of Mr. Hume, Dr. Robertson, and Dr. Beattie,[271] were all expressly *for ever*. This sufficiently proved that those celebrated writers thought there was a perpetuity. Milton especially, that great friend to liberty, would never have let such an assignment go out of his hands, if he had entertained a contrary sentiment. The booksellers [MC/LM:, he said,] were not those oppressors of authors which they had been described. They not only paid liberally for copies, but they frequently gave an author as much for corrections and additions as they originally paid for the first copy. He instanced, among other proofs of the Booksellers liberality, the purchase of Dalrymple's Memoirs,[272] a book which, in the most barefaced manner, traduced the noblest of all characters,[273] upon the testimony of such a wretch as Monsieur Barillon, the weakest and most unable Minister ever employed by a bad King. He did not venture to assert, that a determination of the Court of King's Bench could make the law, but he would positively declare, that it was very likely to induce the petitioners to misconceive the law. The matter prayed for was not a monopoly. He only wished the relief to be for such copies as the petitioners had really purchased and could shew assignments for: this, therefore, would leave an ample field for Mr. Donaldson and the Scotch booksellers to exercise their ingenuity,

[268] John Sawbridge, William and Edmund Burke.

[269] Trans. 'whichever they prefer'.

[270] MacLennan, 'John Milton's Contract for "Paradise Lost"', 221.

[271] David Hume, William Robertson, James Beattie.

[272] Dalrymple, *Memoirs of Great Britain and Ireland*.

[273] In the *Memoirs* it was claimed that Algernon Sydney took bribes from Paul Barillon.

and produce elegant editions of a variety of learned authors. All the classics, Bacon,[274] and many of our best old English writers would remain open. But while the interest of the counter-petitioners was under consideration, it surely was worth while to consider that of the petitioners; many books which they had purchased of authors had not paid in the time limited by the 8th of Queen Anne. The principle of the bill was a compassionate one; it relieved those who merited relief; and, therefore, he hoped it would pass into a law.

[MC: **Mr. C. Fox** spoke with great warmth and ability against the bill; he said the grounds of argument divided themselves under three heads; the one, the justice of the plea of the petitioners; the second, the degree of relief necessary and proper to be given; and lastly, how far any relief would affect the property of individuals. With regard to the first, he totally denied that the petitioners had proved their plea; he recurred to the state of what had been called literary property at the expiration of the licensing act,[275] quoted the substance of their petition to Parliament for the act of Q. Anne, in which they pleaded, that having lost the security they had till that time enjoyed, they were absolutely *starving*, and unable to provide for their families; they prayed therefore for some relief. The Parliament listened to their petition, and relieved their distress. Did this shew a consciousness of any common law right? He further asserted that they never had been warranted in so thinking, as it appeared they never had taken counsel's opinion upon it. With regard to the determination of the King's Bench,[276] it was notorious that the learned in general exclaimed against it; and even allowing the plea of the petitioners, it only proved, that those who purchased since 1769, were entitled to relief. Under the second head, he went into the difference between a gift of public property and a gift of the property of individuals. If the petitioners had made good their plea of loss, let an adequate sum be voted for them; but without proof, they had no right to expect any. He then endeavoured to shew that the relief prayed for was an extension of an odious and injurious monopoly; that from the late final determination in the House of Peers,[277] it was evident the Petitioners had for 31 years enjoyed the right of the Counter Petitioners, and they now came and asked to have their monopoly continued for a longer time; an honourable Gentleman had called the Counter Petitioners thieves, if they were so, they were like the learned Gentleman's countryman in the play, they had robbed themselves, and stolen their own property. Mr. Fox professed the warmest wishes to the promotion of literature, and the welfare of authors; but as he conceived the present bill was not likely to serve the cause of either unless in a prospective sense, he opposed it, and denied either the truth of the Petitioners plea, the propriety of the relief prayed, or that any relief could be granted without materially injuring the Counter Petitioners.]

Colonel Onslow [MC/LM: then rose, and] confined himself to answering Sir John Dalrymple's arguments, against the force of which he said he would pit the Baronet's opinion before the late decision, when he sold his [MC: Memoirs] [LM/PH: own Memoirs for 2000l. yet lawyer like he pleaded against his own opinion.] What he had urged at the Bar respecting the Greeks and Romans writing only for fame, he said [MC: it] was very true, but it was

[274] Francis Bacon, Lord Verulam.

[275] Administration of Intestates' Estates Act 1685 (1 Jas. II, c. 17), s. 15. This act revived the Licensing of the Press Act 1662 and it lapsed at the end of the next parliamentary session, seven years after 20 June 1685 (14 Mar. 1693).

[276] *Millar v Taylor* (1769) 4 Burr 2303 (98 ER 201).

[277] *Donaldson v Beckett* (1774) *Cobbett's Parl. Hist.* xvii, col. 953.

also true that the Lawyers of that day were wont to plead without fees. Lawyers of this day took a middle path, they were glad to have some money as well as some fame; without pay soldiers would not fight, and without it the clergy had not *spunk* enough to pray. As to the talk of its being a national question, it might be urged against the advocate's pleading in favour of Scotland, that Scotland had two rebellions,[278] but he would not offer so unmanly an observation. [LM/PH: He had letters from Hume, Beattie, Robertson, &c in favour of the Bill.] The abuse of the newspapers, and the assertion that the Petitioners reviled the Members, was an insult to the understandings of the House to suppose they would on so partial a ground deny justice to the injured. The Colonel warmly took the side of the Petitioners, and said the House sat for other purposes than taxing the subjects; their most glorious prerogative was that of affording relief to the distressed.

Sir Richard Sutton [MC/LM: declared, he] really wished those of the Petitioners, who were injured might be relieved, but he could not but object to the present bill, as it tended to establish a monopoly, and materially injure the property of the Counter-Petitioners.

Mr. Fielde rose to explain [MC/LM: some of his arguments, and to remove some of the objections of Mr. Fox and Sir Richard Sutton.] [MC: He said he heartily joined in allowing that the decision of the House of Lords was the triumph of the public; the public had then gained a victory; and] [LM/PH: He said] it was only now prayed that having acquired a large estate, they would grant a short lease of a small part of it. The matter obtained was the acquisition of the public, not particularly of the Counter-Petitioners; the latter, therefore, would not be injured by the legislature's granting the relief prayed, nor was such a matter without a precedent: the Widow Hogarth had in the 8th of the present King been favoured with [LM/PH: a] relief of a similar kind.[279] Mr. Fielde painted the distress of the Petitioners in a very forcible light, and shewed that the bill prayed for was not at all injurious to Mr. Donaldson or the London Stallmen.

[MC: **Lord Beauchamp** began with declaring that he was exceedingly happy to hear the Honourable Gentleman call the decision of the House of Lords the triumph of the public; it was a very true description, the public in that decision triumphed over one of the most injurious monopolies ever known in this kingdom. The petitioners had, as an honourable member had related, been reaping the fruits of the Counter Petitioners right for 31 years,[280] and they now had the impudence, wehn the claim of the Counter Petitioners was clear and certain, to ask a further enjoyment of an estate to which they notoriously had no title. The case of the Scotch Printers had been ridiculed, it surely was an object worthy of attention. It had been said there was a printing press in Falkirk, and that many editions of Young's Night Thoughts[281] were in the press. Falkirk, he supposed, was a small town, but if so many new adventurers had embarked in the printing trade, were they to be ruined by the present bill, which precluded their present labours from coming to market. Some of the petitioners might deserve relief, but the whole did not. It was an effort of the underserving to screen

[278] It is not clear which of the various Jacobite risings are being counted here. The major risings since the Act of Union 1706 (6 Anne, c. 11) were in 1715 and 1719, led by the deposed James II, and the rising of 1745 led by Bonnie Prince Charlie.

[279] Engraving Copyright Act 1766 (7 Geo. III, c. 38), s. 3.

[280] It is not clear where the reference to 31 years comes from. The protection for old works under the Copyright Act 1709 (8 Anne, c. 19), s. 1 expired 53 years earlier; Donaldson entered business 26 years earlier; it may have been a reference to *Tonson v Walker* (1752) 3 Swan 672 (36 ER 1017).

[281] Edward Young, *The Complaint, or Nights on Life, Death and Immortality* (1742–5).

themselves behind those who had real merit. It did not discriminate, it ought therefore to be rejected, and he thought it his duty to put in his protest to it]

[LM/PH: **Lord Beauchamp** spoke [LM: a considerable time] against the booksellers, and entered [LM: very] minutely into the whole of the business, [PH: He] stated a considerable number of objections why the bill should be thrown out, and concluded with saying, as he found the bill was meant to persecute one party, and benefit another, he should give his hearty negative against it.**]**

Mr. Jolliffe[282] rose next, and in a dry manner recapitulated some of the arguments urged against the bill by Mr. Fox and Lord Beauchamp. He paid the former a great compliment on his abilities, and joined with him in objecting to the bill, declaring he thought the public would be benefited if books were printed on paper as ordinary as that of a newspaper, and on types as wretched as those with which halfpenny ballads were printed.

[MC/LM: At half after nine the house divided, when the numbers were 57 for the speaker's leaving the chair, 26 against it. The House then chose **Mr. R. Whitworth**[283] chairman of the Committee, and filled up the several blanks. The further time allowed to the holders of copies, without the benefit of Queen Anne, [MC: is] [LM: was] 14 years.**]** [LM: from January 4, 1774.] [MC: The third reading is appointed for to-morrow.]

[PH: The House divided. The Noes went forth.

Tellers.

YEAS	Mr. George Onslow Mr. William Burke	57
NOES	Mr. Charles James Fox Mr. Dempster	26

So it was resolved in the affirmative.]

Version 2: *Public Ledger*, 17 May; *London Chronicle*, 14–17 May, 471; *General Evening Post*, 14–17 May; *Lloyd's Evening Post*, 16–18 May, 467; *Caledonian Mercury*, 21 May; *Edinburgh Evening Courant*, 21 May; *Edinburgh Advertiser*, 20–24 May, 321–2.

The order of the day [Not LLP: was] [LLP: being] read for going into a Committee upon the Booksellers Bill. **Mr. Feilde**[284] arose, but **Mr. C. Fox**[285] desired he would sit down while he mentioned to the house a few words; he began, [LLP: by] saying, that he hoped that House would not be guilty of such imprudence as to act contrary to a standing order, which says, that no private Bill shall be committed until eight days after the second reading; he mentioned the manner in which the business was conducted on Friday night and Saturday morning last, saying, they hurried it through by a few PEOPLE, for he could not call

[282] William Jolliffee†* (1745–1802), MP for Petersfield.

[283] Richard Whitworth.

[284] The *General Evening Post* and *Edinburgh Evening Courant* used F—lde, A—ney G—ral, D—ster, B—ke, S-vile, F—stone, F-x, S—ton, B—champ, J-liffe and W—worth.

[285] The *Edinburgh Advertiser* just has Mr Fox.

them a HOUSE, for on the division they were obliged to count the four TELLERS and SPEAKER to make forty; he was exceeding severe on the [EA: London] Booksellers in general, and concluded with making a Motion, that the Bill be committed for Thursday se'nnight.

He was seconded by the **Attorney General**, who spoke a considerable time against the Booksellers; said they came and asked a favour of the House, under a pretence that AUTHORS would be benefited, which he denied, for it was meant entirely for the benefit of a few individual Booksellers, who ruled the whole trade; he said the Members who were for the Bill seemed to triumph, but he was sure it was in a wrong cause, and that if they went into a Committee on the Bill THEN it was contrary to the express standing order of the House, and contrary to all rules of justice.

Mr. Dempster said it was highly improper to go into the Committee then; that he had been informed that several of the Petitioners against the Bill had heard [PL/GP/LLP/EC: Mr. Wilkie's] [LC/CM/EA: the] evidence [LC/CM/EA: given] on Friday last, which was directly contrary to truth; that they were ready to make affidavit of it, but could not have time if the Bill was committed then.

[Not EA: **Mr. E. Burke** was exceedingly pleasant [PL/GP/LLP/EC, yet severe,] on the Attorney General, for finding out such a manoeuvre to evade the business being settled.**]** [EA: These gentlemen were supported very ably by **Mr. Mackworth** and **Governor Johnstone**.]

Mr. Fielde was [PL/GP/LLP/EC: likewise very severe, both on Mr. Fox and the Attorney General, and was much] for the House going into a Committee THEN.

A [Not EA: pretty] warm debate ensured, whether the standing Order affected a Committee of the whole House, as well as a Committee above stairs; but on the Question being put on Mr. C. Fox's Motion, it passed in the negative.[286]

Sir George Savile then presented several Petitions from the Booksellers of York, Knaresborough, &c. against the Booksellers Bill depending.

{Some other matters were then dealt with in the *Public Ledger/ General Evening Post/ London Chronicle/ Edinburgh Evening Courant* reports before returning to the Booksellers' Bill}

Mr. Fielde then moved, "that the Speaker do NOW leave the Chair, in order that the House may resolve itself into a Committee of the whole House upon the Booksellers Bill". He was seconded by **Mr. R. Whitworth.**[287]

Lord Folkstone then arose and, [Not GP/EC: in a long masterly speech,] spoke much against the London Booksellers, and stated to the House many objections why the Bill should not pass into a Law.

Mr. C. Fox [Not LLP: next arose,] [LLP: spoke next,] and was exceeding warm against the Booksellers [Not EA:, said they] [EA: and entered into the argument with great accuracy and force of reasoning; he said the booksellers] came to Parliament for relief in a cause which they had brought [PL/GP/EC: upon][LC/LLP/CM/EA: on] themselves by their own foolishness; that he should not be against granting those relief, who REALLY had sustained a loss, but the Petition was signed by many who never had Copy Right, nor [Not EC: ever][EC: never]

[286] *CJ*, xxxiv, 757 (there was no division).

[287] The *Edinburgh Advertiser* has Whitworth only.

were injured in the least; he said, the chief complaint on the side of the Booksellers was, that they had been led astray by the opinion of Lord Mansfield in 1769;[288] he should have no objection in the least to grant such persons as had suffered since that time, redress, but he did not see that the Bill then in dispute was meant for any such purpose, it was entirely intended to benefit one set of men at the ruin of another.

[EA: The booksellers pretending [*to act for the benefit of*][289] authors but now they had thought proper to lay aside that specious mask and appear in their proper colours.

The present bill, he said, was a monopoly of the worst kind, for it invaded the rights of the public, without any original claim, power or authority whatever. He remarked, if the promoters of the bill were serious in their professed intentions of serving authors, it was evident, that protecting future purchases, by an additional term to the statute of Queen Anne, would alone answer that end effectually; and that no grounds whatever could be stated, nor case made, sufficient to balance the manifest injustice of diverting out of the public that right, which every man is legally entitled to, to print and publish all works not protected by the statute, and transferring it into the hands of a few overgrown monopolists, whose principal argument for relief is, that they have usurped a property to which they never had the most distant colour of right, and come now to parliament to confirm them in their unjust usurpation.]

Mr. Fielde then [Not EC: arose] [EC: rose], and in a speech of [Not EA: near] an hour, entered into the whole of the Bill and the Clause depending, and spoke very much in favour of the Booksellers of London and Westminster, and said, that Mr. Blackstone, selling the Copy Right of his Commentaries,[290] and Milton selling the Right of his Paradise Lost[291] for a perpetuity, plainly proved that those great men entertained an opinion that there was such a thing existing as Copy Right at Common Law.

Colonel Onslow next arose, and, [PL/GP/LLP/EC: in a speech of full an hour,] spoke much in favour of the Bill, **[**Not LLP/EA: and was extremely severe on the speech of Sir John Dalrymple at the Bar. He said, that *learned* Council certainly thought there was such a thing as Copy Right, when he sold his [PL/GP/EC: infamous trash] [LC/CM: history] for 2000l. yet he, Lawyer like, at the Bar went from his own opinion in behalf of his Client.**]** [Not LLP: He said, the Bill would be of service to the Scotch Booksellers, as it would establish a Copy Right in Scotland, which they had not now, and they would be better able to pay the Authors of their own Country; he said he had letters in his pocket from Hume, Beattie, and Robinson,[292] all which seemed to express a desire that the Bill might pass.] [PL/GP/EC: He was exceedingly severe on the Lawyers, Army, Church, &c. He said formerly the Lawyers used to plead, the Soldiers fight, and the Churchmen pray for FAME; yet he would be bound to say, there was not now any Lawyer that would plead without money; that if you took away the Soldier's pay, the Devil may fight for him; and as for the Sons of the Clergy, they had not SPUNK enough to preach one Sermon gratis] [LC/CM/EA: He added;] [LLP: and said,] [LC/LLP/CM/EA: that as the law, army and clergy did not plead, fight, or preach for fame only,

[288] *Millar v Taylor* (1769) 4 Burr 2303 (98 ER 201).

[289] The bottom line of text was trimmed when producing the newspaper and this is the only known copy. The text in italics is editorially suggested.

[290] William Blackstone, *Commentaries on the Laws of England* (Oxford, 1765–9) (ESTC: T57753).

[291] John Milton, *Paradise Lost* (Simmons, 1667) (ESTC: R9505).

[292] This was probably meant to be Robertson (only the *Public Ledger* has Robinson).

it could not be expected authors should give up their time and their labour for fame alone, without any pecuniary consideration.]

[PL/GP/EC: **Sir R. Sutton** spoke a few words against the Speaker leaving the Chair.]

[Not EA: **Lord Beauchamp** spoke a considerable time against the Booksellers, [PL/LC/LLP/CM: and entered very minutely into the whole of the business,] stated a considerable number of objections why the Bill should be thrown out, and concluded with saying, as he found the Bill was meant to persecute one party, and benefit another he should give his hearty negative to it.**]**

[EA: **Lord Beauchamp** chiefly replied to the arguments made use of by Mr. Fielde. He observed that the cause of a few persons who were real sufferers by the late decision of the other House, was artfully blended with that of others, whose claim by no means stood on the same ground; that to such as stood in the former predicament, no man would be readier to grant every reasonable relief than himself; that this idea perfectly coincided with the conduct of parliament in respect to Mrs. Hogarth;[293] that specific cases required specific remedies, it not being at all reasonable that one indiscriminate measure should be dealt out to all. He likewise insisted, that the present application was not only unreasonable but it was to the last degree impudent, no one fact being stated above or below stairs, which at all supported the principle or objects which the bill had manifestly in contemplation. He should therefore give his hearty negative. **Sir Richard Sutton**, **Governor Johnson** and **Mr. Joliffe** spoke against the Bill.]

[PL/GP/LLP/EC: **Mr. Joliffe** spoke [PL/LLP: a short time, but much to the purpose,] against the Booksellers.**]**

[PL/GP/LLP/EC: The Question was then called for, and on the House dividing there appeared for the Motion 57, against it 26.

The House then formed itself into a Committee] [LC/CM: At half after nine the House divided on the question whether the Speaker should leave the Chair, which was carried in the affirmative; the ayes were 57, the noes 26. The House then went into a Committee (Mr Whitworth in the Chair) on the bill] [PL/LLP:, Mr. R. Whitworth in the Chair, and the blanks of the Bill were filled up, and the Bill ordered to be reported; the Bill to commence from the 4th day of June, and the term to be for 14 years. After which the House adjourned until this day.] [GP/EC: on the bill (Mr Whitworth in the chair)] **[**LC/GP/CM/EC: and filled up the blanks; the additional term [LC/CM: of years] given to the holders of copy right [GP/EC:, with the benefit of the Statute of Queen Anne, being fourteen years] [LC/CM: not protected by the Statute of Queen Anne is fourteen years]. Near an hour was spent in regulating the mode of entry in the Hall books of the Stationers' Company, and the volumes to be delivered of each copy. At length all the clauses were gone through, and the Speaker took the chair, when the report was [GP/EC: made, and the third reading ordered for Thursday next.][294] [LC/CM: ordered to be made on Thursday next. The bill to commence from the 4th day of June.] After which the House adjourned ...]**]**

[EA: A few minutes before ten, the House went into the committee, and Mr. Whitworth, chairman, having read the preamble and several enacting clauses of the bill, they were agreed to, after several short conversations on each. The first blank, relative to the term of an

[293] Jane Hogarth* (née Thornhill) (*d.* 1789).

[294] This is incorrect and it was the report ordered to that day (Thursday next being 26 May).

exclusive privilege, given to the proprietors of copy-right not protected by the statute of Queen Anne was filled up with the words "Fourteen years." As soon as the chairman had gone through and filled up the blanks, **Mr. Harris**[295] observed, that there were certain ancient authors who were the glory of this country; that he thought their works, as they tended to inspire the noblest sentiments of liberty, and conveyed the most useful knowledge, and taught the most important truths, should be free. Spenser, Hooker, Bacon, Locke and Milton,[296] were the persons he had chiefly in contemplation, those works, he hoped, no person would contend for an exclusive privilege of printing or publishing. He therefore acquainted the committee, that, he would, with their permission, bring up a clause for leaving all publications whatever in common, which were printed or published previous to the present century. This motion was strongly objected to by **Mr. Solicitor General**.[297] He said, it directly went against the principle of the bill, which was that of giving an exclusive privilege to publish all books for which assignments could be proved from the author; that among those mentioned, the works of Milton for one, had, it appeared, been transferred or assigned regularly from hand to hand to the present proprietors; and, that for this reason, he must resist any such proposition, as being entirely repugnant with the professed intentions of the bill, and to avowed motives on which it proceeded.

The question being put for bringing up Mr. Harris's clause, it passed in the negative.[298] The bill was then ordered to be reported on Thursday, and the House broke up precisely [?] at 11 o'clock, and adjourned to this day.

The bill to commence from the 4th day of June 1774.

The only speakers for the bill were Mr. Fielde, Mr. E. Burke and Col. Onslow, the gentlemen on that side chusing rather to resort to the powerful doctrine of *numbers* then to the force of *argument*.

The speakers against the bill were Lord Folkstone, Lord Beauchamp, Attorney General, Sir Geo. Saville, Sir Richard Sutton, Governor Johnstone, Mr. Dempster, Mr. Charles Fox, Mr. Popham, Mr. Joliffe, Mr. Harris, Mr. Ambler, Mr. Mackworth &c.]

Version 3: *Middlesex Journal*, 14–17 May.

Lord *Folkestone*. I am against your quitting the chair, Mr. Speaker, because I am an enemy to the principles of the bill. I think the booksellers have no pretence for the favour they are now asking. I shall not attempt to reason upon the nature of property, because I think it a question merely historical: the common law slept, I suppose, during the exertions of prerogative: the Star Chamber, the Licensing Act, and the 8th of Anne,[299] which expressly gives the twenty-eight years, *and no longer*. That act, besides the future publications, gave them twenty years in those already in their possession; when that twenty years were near expiring, they came to parliament, but both House repeatedly rejected their petitions, and their case slept for some years; after which, came their opinion of a common law right,

[295]James Harris.

[296]Edmund Spenser* (1553–99), Richard Hooker* (1554–1600), Francis Bacon, John Locke, John Milton.

[297]Alexander Wedderburn.

[298]*CJ*, xxxiv, 757.

[299]Copyright Act 1709 (8 Anne, c. 19).

arising from trials in which they obtained injunctions; I think therefore, Sir, the pretence that they knew not the law, is merely a pretence, and ought not to be taken notice of here.

Mr. *Field*. That the booksellers really suppose they had a right at common law, is a part of the present argument, which has been so fully and so clearly proved, that I think it would be impertinence to go into it so amply, as a direct answer to what the noble Lord has urged, would require; but, Sir, the point which appears to make the greatest impression from what I heard in the first debate of this day, is giving them a monopoly by taking away the property of other people; now, Sir, one would think that the poor booksellers of Edinburgh and Glasgow could, if this bill passes have no more trade, must be struck out of all their employment: but let it be remembered, Sir, that this act gives a right to no more than the booksellers can prove they purchased the copies of from the authors, and no copy-right has been traced father than 1679 or 1680, which was that of Milton's Paradise Lost; now, Sir, all books before that period will be open to the printing of all men, and therein are the best books in the English language, Shakespeare, Spencer, Bacon, Johnston, Beaumont, Fletcher,[300] and many others, the Classics are also open to all the world; there is farther, all the learning of the rest of Europe, France, Spain, Italy, Germany, Holland, all which, Sir, may surely prove sufficient employment for the presses of Scotland.

Mr. *Charles Fox*. I think, Mr. Speaker, that the principles of this bill are so unjust and so useless, that I cannot give my vote for your leaving the chair. Let us consider, Sir, the arguments in their favour, which are most common, and upon which the greatest stress is laid; their asking this compensation for their having made such large purchases under the idea of a common law right, is not a motive to be urged at present, because it is a matter of particular debate in the committee, when the term is examined that ought to be given them, supposing any term should be granted, and, Sir, as I conceive from the title of the bill, that the relief they ask for must go in that form, and as that form is inconsistent with justice to others, I am against going to the committee at all. This is a point, Sir, which demands serious attention; if in consideration of their having expended large sums thus to the benefit of the public, they have a right to a compensation, the public ought to pay that compensation; lay taxes on that public that has received the benefit in order to raise the compensation, but as to making individuals pay for the compensation of which the world at large has received the benefit, it is such a mode of making the recompence as appears to me to be contrary to every principle of common justice and common sense; A. suffers by serving the public, he comes to parliament for a compensation, will parliament make the public pay that compensation, or will she take it from the pocket of B? This is stating the case fairly; you cannot grant the recompence asked by the booksellers, without taking what they ask immediately from the pockets of Mr. Donaldson, and other petitioning booksellers against the bill.

Next, Sir, let us consider the plea that granting their request will prove an encouragement to learning: here, Sir, the advocates for their cause change their ground, and confound two very different pleas: this makes it a prospective bill, whereas the purport and preamble shew, that they ask relief only for what is past, for distress that is come upon them from want of security to the property already in their hands. Keep these ideas distinct; if the friends of the bill want to give a farther encouragement to learning, I will agree in the idea, for I am sure

[300]William Shakespeare* (1564–1616), probably Ben Jonson* (1572–1637), Francis Beaumont* (1584–1616), John Fletcher* (1579–1625).

there is not a man in the House who wishes better to the cause of literature than myself. Let them make this the principle of their bill, and ask a longer period to authors in future, I may agree with them, though not in the duration of their term; but as to pretending, as in the present case, that authors in future transactions with booksellers will fare the better, because the booksellers in former transactions with other authors have now fresh encouragement, to suppose that that will do six-pennyworth of good to learning is an affront to common sense. Keep therefore the ideas distinct; this bill can be no encouragement to authors, can be of no benefit to learning; it is preposterous to assert it, it is contrary to the petition of the people themselves.

Upon what principle therefore, Sir, is this bill demanded? Not, I have shewn, as an encouragement to authors and learning, for it goes not to the future. Not upon the plea of public utility, because the compensation then should be paid by the public, and not by individuals. Upon what then does it depend? Upon nothing rational; the principles are false, and the bill ought not to be committed.

Colonel Onslow's Speech, in Answer to Sir John Dalrymple.

Mr. Speaker, with permission of the house, the mode in which I shall give my sentiments upon the present bill will be, to make some observations upon what fell from the learned Baronet the other day at the bar of the house, for his speech surprized me so much that it put everything else out of my head. That gentleman, Sir, thought proper to lead the way in making this a Scotch question; he ran into it so much, that I am persuaded he hurt his cause by it not a little. The first reason why we should not favour the booksellers was a very extraordinary one indeed—because they are proprietors of some news-papers we should not do justice, because a few of them may have been accessary to the abuse we have met with! therefore we are to deny justice to the whole body!— A strange way of reasoning indeed!

Next, Sir, we ought not to pass an act which will injure some piratical booksellers in Scotland. Why? Because the Scotch fought for us in the last war. This was actually the learned council's argument—the very words he used! extraordinary ones I thought them! and very little deserving attention. If one is forced—dragged in this manner into national questions, one must say something in reply. It is true they fought for us, Sir, —but did they not owe it us?—Did they not fight against us?—Had they not two rebellions?

Then Sir, we are told, that allowing authors to write for gain is a prejudice to literature. —I deny it. Profit, as well as fame, ought to follow the exertion of great abilities. I honour the army as much as any man—but I doubt our ranks would be wonderfully thin if honour was all that was gotten. It is the same in the navy—the law—and I much question whether there is *spunk* enough in the clergy to preach for nothing. Upon the whole, Sir, I think the arguments against the bill are nugatory, and prove, in no respect the points for which they are brought.

Version 4: *St James's Chronicle*, 14–17 May; *Public Advertiser*, 18 May.

The Order of the Day being read for the House to go into a Committee on the Booksellers Bill, **Mr. C. Fox** opposed the Order as being totally irregular, because it militated against two Standing Orders of the House, one of which expressly ordains that no private Bill shall go to a Committee, without eight Days previous Notice posted up in the Lobby. He maintained his Opinion with great Ability, and were not the House eager to avoid the Question, it is more than probable that the Friends of the Bill would not have got rid of the Objection for some Hours longer. **Mr. Fox** was supported by the **Attorney General, Mr. Mackworth,** and **Governor Johnstone**. **Mr. Fox** at length moved, that the Bill be committed for [SJC: Thursday] [PA: To-morrow] se'nnight. This afforded Matter for a Debate, which continued from five till Eight o'Clock, when the Question being put it passed in the Negative without a Division.

This gave Birth to another Motion, which was that the Speaker do now leave the Chair. The Principle of the Bill, with its several operative Inconveniences, were now very fully discussed on the Part of Opposition by **Lord Beauchamp, Lord Folkstone. Mr. C. Fox,** and one or two others, and very ably replied to by **Mr. Fielde**.

Mr. Fielde then moved that the Speaker do now leave the Chair, which brought on a Debate that continued till within a Quarter of Ten o'Clock, when the Question being put, the House divided, Ayes 37, Noes 26.

Lord Folkstone opened the Debate, but advanced nothing new on the Subject. He was replied to by Mr. Fielde, who made use of several very ingenious Arguments in favour of the Bill, particularly relative to the Intent and Construction of an Act of the late King, for securing to Engravers an exclusive Property in their Designs and Inventions for a certain Number of Years. He instanced besides, the Case of Hogarth's Widow, who, when the Act last mentioned was continued in 1764, had an express Clause inserted therein for her Benefit,[301] which gave her an exclusive Right of publishing her late Husband's Works for twenty Years.

Mr. C. Fox spoke against the Bill with great Accuracy and Force of Reasoning. He said, that it was a Monopoly of the worst Kind, for it invaded the Rights of the Public, without any original Claim, Power, or Authority whatever. He remarked, if the Promoters of the Bill were serious in their professed Intentions of serving Authors, it was evident, that protecting future Purchasers, by an additional Term to the Statute of Queen Ann, would alone answer that End effectually; and that no Grounds whatever could be stated, nor Case made, sufficient to balance the manifest Injustice of divesting out of the Public that Right which every Man is legally entitled to, to print and publish all Works not protected by the Statute, and transferring it into the Hands of a few over-grown Monopolists, whose principal Argument for Relief is, that they have usurped a Property to which they never had the most distant Colour of Right and come now to Parliament to confirm them in their unjust [SJC: Usurpation] [PA: Usurpations].

Colonel Onslow spoke a considerable Time in Favour of the Bill, and was heard with the usual Attention and good Humour.

Lord Beauchamp chiefly replied to the Arguments made Use of by Mr. Fielde. He observed that the Cause of a few Persons who were real Sufferers by the late Decision of the other House, was artfully blended with that of others, whose Claim by no Means stood on the same Ground; that no such as stood in the former Predicament; no Man would be readier to grant every reasonable Relief than himself; that this Idea perfectly coincided with

[301] Engravers' Copyright Act 1766 (7 Geo. III, c. 38).

the Conduct of Parliament in respect of Mrs. Hogarth; that specific Cases required specific Remedies, it not being at all reasonable that one indiscriminate Measure should be dealt out to all. He likewise insisted, that the present Application was not only unreasonable but it was to the last Degree impudent, no one Fact being stated above or below Stairs, which at all supported the Principle or Objects which the Bill had manifestly in Contemplation. **Sir Richard Sutton**, **Governor Johnstone**, and **Mr. Joliffe** spoke on the same Side; and **Mr. Harris** on the other.

A few Minutes before Ten, the House went into the Committee, and **Mr. Whitworth**, Chairman, having read the Preamble and several enacting Clauses of the Bill, they were agreed to, after several short Conversations on each. The first Blank, relative to the Term of an exclusive Privilege, was filled up with the Words "Fourteen Years." As soon as the Chairman had gone thro' and filled up the Blanks, **Mr. Harris** observed, that there were certain ancient Authors who were the Glory of this Country; that he thought their Works, as they tended to inspire the noblest Sentiments of Liberty, and conveyed the most [SJC: useful Knowledge, and taught the most] important Truths, should be free. Spenser, Hooker, Bacon, Locke and Milton, were the Persons he had chiefly in Contemplation, whose Works, he hoped, no Person would contend for an exclusive Privilege of printing or publishing. He therefore acquainted the Committee, that he would, with their Permission, bring up a Clause for leaving all Publications whatever in common, which were printed or published previous to the present Century. This Motion was strongly objected to by **Mr. Solicitor General**. He said, it directly went against the Principle of the Bill, which was that of giving an exclusive Privilege to publish all Books for which Assignments could be proved from the Author; that among those mentioned, the Works of Milton for one, had, it appeared, been transferred or assigned regularly from Hand to Hand to the present Proprietors; and, that for this Reason, he must resist any such Proposition, as being entirely repugnant with the professed Intentions of the Bill, and to the [SJC: avowed] [PA: above] Motives on which it proceeded.

The Question being put for bringing up Mr. Harris's Clause, it passed in the Negative. The Bill was then ordered to be reported [SJC: on Thursday] [PA: Tomorrow] and the House broke up precisely at 11 o'Clock [SJC:, and adjourned to this Day.]

Additional:

[SJC: A Correspondent says, when the young Orator[302] asked Mr. Wilkie, the Bookseller, in a certain Assembly with a Sneer, whether Persons invading Copy-Right ought not to be prosecuted as Felons, and convicted without Benefit of Clergy? Mr. Wilkie answered, with the greatest Simplicity, he did not know clearly who ought to be prosecuted as Felons, and convicted without Benefit of Clergy.]

Version 5: *Morning Chronicle*, 17 May (Second Account).

At five o'clock yesterday the Order the day was read in the House of Commons, for the House to go into a Committee on the Booksellers bill. A debate arose between Mr. Fox,

[302]Charles Fox.

Mr. Burke, Mr. Feild, Mr. Attorney General, Mr. Sawbridge, Mr. Dempster, Mr. Mackworth, Governor Johnstone, Mr. R. Whitworth, and Sir George Saville, respecting the application of the standing order of Feb. 1697. "That no private bill should be committed till eight days notice had been posted up in the Lobby," to the present matter. After a variety of arguments, it was settled. A warm debate then ensured, in which Lord Folkstone, Mr. Field, Mr. Fox, Sir Richard Sutton, Lord Beauchamp, and Mr. Jollyffe spoke; at half after nine the house divided on the question, whether the Speaker should leave the chair, which was carried in the affirmative, the ayes were 57, the noes 26. The House then went into a Committee (Mr. Whitworth in the chair) on the bill, and filled up the blanks, the additional term of years given to the holders of Copy-Right with the benefit of the statute of Queen Anne is fourteen years. Near an hour was spent in regulating the mode of entry in the Hall-books of the Stationers' Company, and the volumes to be delivered of each copy. At length all the clauses were gone through, and the Speaker took the chair, when the report was made, and the third reading ordered for Thursday next; a more particular Account of which will be given in tomorrow's paper.

Version 6: *Morning Chronicle*, 16 May (Third Account).[303]

This day the father consideration of the Booksellers' bill comes on before a Committee in the House of Commons, when a certain number of years, as a further limited time to be given to those who have purchased Copy Right, will be proposed to the Committee, and which is imagined will occasion very warm debates.

The several divisions on Friday night and Saturday morning relative to the Booksellers' business not being rightly understood, the following may be depended upon.

On Friday last the Order of the day was read in the House of Commons for the further consideration of the Booksellers' bill, and for the second reading thereof. A motion was then made to adjourn the further hearing till Monday next, Ayes 26, Noes 34. Counsel were then called in and heard for some time, and ordered to withdraw. It was then moved to call them in again, Ayes 73, Noes 5: they were called in and further heard, and having concluded, a motion was made to commit the bill, upon which a debate arose and lasted for some time; it was then moved to adjourn the debate thereof till Monday, ayes 24 noes 37: the question was afterwards put, that the bill be committed, ayes 36, noes 10; and the last question put was, that it be committed for Monday, ayes 35, noes 0.

Version 7: *London Evening Post*, 14–17 May; *Craftsman*, 21 May.

About five o'clock the order of the day for the House to go into a committee on the booksellers bill, being read, the former question, relative to the standing order of the 4th of February, 1697, which obliges the Chairman, on every private bill, to give eight days previous notice, by an order stuck up in the Lobby, of the commitment of such bill, produced a debate which continued for two hours. **Mr. C. Fox** moved, that the Speaker should not leave the Chair, and that the bill stand committed for Thursday se'nnight; but the question being put, it passed in the negative without a division.

[303]This account in the *Morning Chronicle* relates both to the committee and the earlier second reading.

[Not CT: Another motion was made, that the Speaker do now leave the Chair, which gave rise to a fresh debate that continued till near ten o'clock, when the question being put, the House divided, ayes 57, noes 26. The House then went into a committee, Mr. R. Whitworth in the Chair.

The House then formed itself into a committee, Mr. R. Whitworth in the Chair, and the blanks of the bill were filled up, and the bill ordered to be reported; the bill to commence from the 4th day of June, and the term to be for fourteen years. After which the House adjourned until this day.

The principal speakers in favour of the bill were, Mr. Fielde, Colonel Onslow, Mr. E. and Mr. W. Burke, and Mr. R. Whitworth. Against it, Governor Johnstone, Lord Folkstone, Lord Beauchamp, Mr. Joliffe, Sir Richard Sutton, Mr. Mackworth, Mr. C. Fox, and Mr. Attorney General.][CT: The House then formed itself into a Committee on the bill (Mr. Whitworth in the chair) and filled up the blanks; the additional term given to the holders of copy-right, with the benefit of the statute of Queen Anne, being fourteen years. Near an hour was spent in regulating the mode of entry in the Hall-books of the Stationers' Company, and the volumes to be delivered of each copy. At length all the clauses were gone through, and the Speaker took the chair, when the report was made, and the third reading ordered for Thursday next.]

Version 8: *Gazetteer*, 18 May.

On Monday, when the House of Commons went into a Committee on the Booksellers bill, the blanks were filled up. The additional term of years given to the holders of copy-right, with the benefit of the statute of Queen Anne, is fourteen years. Near an hour was spent in regulating the mode of entry in the Hall-books of the Stationers Company, and the volumes to be delivered of each copy. At length all the clauses were gone through, and the Speaker took the Chair, when the report was ordered to be made tomorrow.

Version 9: *Daily Advertiser*, 18 May.

On Monday the London Booksellers Bill was again taken into Consideration in the Lower Assembly; at Half past Nine, the Assembly divided on the Question, whether the President should leave the Chair, Ayes 57; Noes 26. The House then went into a Committee on the Bill, and filled up the Blanks. It is said, that the additional Term proposed to be given to Holders of Copy-Right, not protected by the Statute of Queen Anne, is 14 Years. Regulations were made for the Mode of Entry in the Hall Books of the Stationers Company, and the Number to be delivered of each Copy. After all the Clauses were gone through, the Report was ordered to be made on Thursday next. It is said the Bill is intended to commence from the 4th of next Month.

Version 10: *Scots Magazine*, 532–3.

The order of the day being read May 16. for the House to resolve itself into a committee; after debate, in which Colonel Onslow said, he had letters in his pocket from Hume, Robertson, and Beattie, all which seemed to express a desire that the bill might pass, it was carried, 57 to 26, that the Speaker should leave the chair. In the committee the blanks were filled up. The additional term given to the holders of copy-right not protected by the act of Q. Anne was fourteen years, and the act was to commence from June 4. 1774.

Notes

***Daily Advertiser*, 17 May**: In a Committee of the whole House proceeded on the Booksellers Bill. Expected to sit late.

***Morning Chronicle*, 21 May**: Lord B—p, in his speech, last Monday, against the Booksellers bill, took an opportunity of reflecting on the late Mr. Tonson's family, and said that one of them had got a seat in the House of Commons,[304] where most rich monopolists at last got a seat. Did his Lordship, says a correspondent, mean to sneer at men of business in general, who have become senators? or is his Lordship seriously of opinion, that a set of whey-faced lordlings are more proper to represent a commercial people than merchants, or those whose connections in trade render them more competent judges of commerce, than sprigs of fashion possibly can be?

Report – Aborted: 19 May

Version 1: *Morning Chronicle*, 20 May; *Caledonian Mercury*, 23 May; *Edinburgh Advertiser*, 20–24 May, 325; *Edinburgh Evening Chronicle*, 25 May.

When the order of the day was [MC/EA/EC: yesterday read] [CM: this day read,] [EA/EC: in the House of Commons], **Mr. Stewart**[305] moved, that the following proviso should be inserted in the Booksellers Bill, "Provided always, and be it enacted, that nothing herein contained shall prevent the booksellers of that part of Great Britain called Scotland, from printing and vending in Scotland all such books as they could have legally printed and vended before the 1st of March, 1774."[306] This clause Mr. Stewart contended was a fair and equitable insertion, for as the Common Law of Scotland differed essentially from that of England, and as it had ever been held, that Printers in Scotland might print any books not protected by the statute of Queen Anne, (which he proved [MC/CM: by instancing their printing the Tatlers[307] as soon as possible after their first appearance in England, and] by various determinations of the Court of Session[308] in that kingdom). It would be exceedingly cruel and unjust to take away by the present bill, that right which the Printers of Scotland ever enjoyed. And as there were in Scotland at least 5000 persons properly brought up to the printing trade, those persons and their families must be inevitably ruined, if nothing but the Classics were left for them to print. The allowing of this Proviso was only letting the law of that kingdom remain in that state which it [CM/EA/EC: had] hitherto [MC: had] done, and which the nature of things required.

[304] Probably a reference to Richard Tonson† (*d.* 1772), son of Jacob Tonson the younger; although William Baker† (1705–1770), MP for Plympton Erle 1747–68, married Jacob Tonson's daughter Mary.

[305] Probably William Stewart† (1737–97), MP for Wigtown Burghs.

[306] *CJ*, xxxiv, 775.

[307] *Tatler* (Addison & Steele, 1709–11) (ESTC: P1919).

[308] *Midwinter v Hamilton* (1748) Kames 158; *Millar v Kincaid* (1751) 1 Pat App 488.

While this point was debating, **Mr. Dempster**[309] came in and counted the house, when there not being 40 members, business was necessarily put a stop to, and the members came away.

[MC/CM: This is the second manoeuvre practised by the opposers to the bill, and was [MC: effected] [CM: affected] by **Mr. Charles Fox**'s staying in the Lobby and persuading his friends not to go in. It is imagined [MC: the booksellers bill] [CM: it] will be the first business [MC: this day…] [CM: tomorrow…]**]**

Version 2: *London Chronicle*, 19–21 May, 486; *Daily Advertiser*, 21 May.

… the Order of the Day was read, to receive the report of the Booksellers Bill; and it was moved that the following clause be added to it, "Provided always, and be it enacted, that nothing herein contained shall prevent the Booksellers of that part of Great Britain called Scotland, from printing and vending in Scotland all such Books they could have legally printed and vended before the 1st of March 1774." But a motion was made to count the number of Members in the Assembly, and there being not forty present, the business was put off till yesterday.

Version 3: *Lloyd's Evening Post*, 18–20 May, 479.

This day the Report is to be received in the House of Commons on the Booksellers Bill, with respect to the temporary security of Literary Property; when the following Clause will be tendered to be added to it, viz "Provided always, and be in enacted, that nothing herein contained shall prevent the Bookseller of that Part of Great Britain called Scotland, from printing and vending in Scotland all such books that they could have legally printed and vended before the 1st of March, 1774."

Version 4: *Middlesex Journal*, 19–21 May; *General Evening Post*, 19–21 May; *London Magazine*, 627.

The order of the day for receiving the Report of the Booksellers Bill was next called for, but on **Mr. Field's**[310] rising to speak in favour of the Bill, **Sir George Saville** and **Mr. C. Fox**[311] went out of the House.

The question was then called for by the enemies of the Bill, whether the Report should be received or not; and on counting the Members there appeared but thirty-seven.

The Committee broke up directly for want of a sufficient number of Members, and adjourned [MJ/GP: to this day].

Version 5: *Gazetteer*, 20 May; *London Evening Post*, 19–21 May; *Craftsman*, 21 May.

The order the day was then read for receiving the report on the Booksellers bill. **Mr. Feilde** moved for leave to bring it up, which being opposed, the question was put, and the House

[309] George Dempster.

[310] *General Evening Post* has F—lde, Sa—le and F–x rather than full names.

[311] Paul Feilde, Sir George Savile, Charles Fox.

going to divide, when it was discovered that there were not forty Members in the House; the Speaker consequently adjourned to this day, when the preference of all the friends of the bill is expected.

Version 6: *St James's Chronicle*, 19–21 May.

The other Order of the Day being read for receiving the Report on the Booksellers Bill, the Report was offered to be made, when a Member suspecting that there were not a sufficient Number to constitute a House, the House was counted, by which it appeared no more than 25 Members were present, on which the Speaker adjourned till Tomorrow.

Version 7: *Public Advertiser*, 20 May; *Lloyd's Evening Post*, 18–20 May, 477.

At Six o'Clock the Order of the Day was read to receive the Report of the Booksellers Bill, and a Clause was offered to the Bill; but a Motion was made to count the Members, and their appearing not 40 [PA: Members][LLP: Present], the House broke up [LLP: immediately], and the Business was put off till this Day.

Notes

***Daily Advertiser*, 20 May**: Left sitting on the Bill relative to Literary Property.

Report: 20 May

Version 1: *Edinburgh Advertiser*, 20–24 May, 325.

The Commons agreed the booksellers bill, ordered to be engrossed and read a third time the 27th curt. when great debates are expected. This bill has been chiefly carried through by the city members and their friends, and if it should pass the House of Commons, there is little doubt but it will be rejected in the Upper House, where the bills of 1735 and 1737[312] brought in by the booksellers expired. The clause proposed that this law should not extend to Scotland, as no common law-right had ever been pretended there, was rejected. If this bill passes into a law, several thousand people in Scotland will be immediately set idle, which will be attended with the worst consequences in the present state of the country. Very few Scots members attended the house while the bill was going on; **Governor Johnstone**[313] and **Mr. Dempster**[314] were very active in opposing it.

[312]Booksellers' Bill 1735: Parliamentary Archives, HL/PO/JO/10/2/38; Booksellers' Bill 1737: HL/PO/JO/10/2/39.

[313]George Johnstone.

[314]George Dempster.

Version 2: *Gazetteer*, 21 May; *London Chronicle*, 19–21 May, 488; *Middlesex Journal*, 19–21 May; *General Evening Post*, 19–21 May; *London Evening Post*, 19–21 May; *Caledonian Mercury*, 25 May; *Edinburgh Evening Courant*, 25 May; *Craftsman*, 28 May.

Mr. Feilde[315] [GZ/MJ/GP/EC: at length] [LC/CM/CT: then] brought up the report on the Booksellers bill, which meeting no opposition, was agreed to, and ordered to be engrossed, and the third reading appointed by motion of **Mr. R. Whitworth**[316] for Friday next.

Version 3: *Public Advertiser*, 21 May; *Lloyd's Evening Post*, 20–23 May, 481.

Mr. Feilde brought up the Report of the Bill for Relief of Booksellers and others, by vesting the Copies of printed Books in the Purchasers of such Copies from Authors or their Assigns for a Time therein to be limited; and there being no Opposition to the Report, the Bill was ordered to be ingrossed, and to be read a third Time on Friday next.

Notes

***Morning Chronicle*, 21 May**: The Booksellers bill was reported yesterday in the Lower Assembly, and ordered to be ingrossed; the third reading is fixed for Friday next.

***St James's Chronicle*, 19–21 May**: Booksellers Bill reported, and ordered to be engrossed, and to be read a third Time on this Day Se'nnight.

***Daily Advertiser*, 23 May**: On Friday in the Lower Assembly, the Report on the Booksellers Bill was brought up, which meeting with no Opposition, was agreed to, ordered to be engrossed, and the third Reading appointed for Friday next.

***Scots Magazine*, 533**: Mr Feilde gave in report May 20; which was agreed to, and the bill was ordered to be ingrossed.

Third Reading: 27 May

Version 1: *London Chronicle*, 26–28 May, 512; *General Evening Post*, 26–28 May; *Lloyd's Evening Post*, 27–30 May, 505; *Caledonian Mercury*, 1 June; *Edinburgh Evening Courant*, 1 June; *Edinburgh Advertiser*, 31 May–3 June, 347; Cobbett's *Parliamentary History*, xvii, cols 1109–10.

… the order of the day, for the third reading of the [Not PH: booksellers bill was] [PH: bill being] [Not EC: called] [EC: talked] for [LC/GP/CM/EC: aloud.] [EA: in the House of Commons, when]

Mr. Charles Fox [Not PH: arose] [PH: rose], and exclaimed vehemently against [Not PH: the bill] [PH: it]; he said, he had already troubled the House very much upon the subject, but he could not let so infamous, so pernicious, [Not PH: and] so flagrant a Bill, pass through any stage without opposing it; that it was entirely meant to compensate a set

[315] The *General Evening Post* and *Edinburgh Evening Courant* have F—dle and W—worth.

[316] Richard Whitworth.

of men, who had been guilty of error through wilful ignorance, for they never had applied to Counsel to know if they really had a claim to copy right, well knowing that if they had, Counsel would have told them they had not; that in this situation the petition for the bill stood. The compensation was likewise to be paid by Mr. Donaldson, and other Booksellers, who really were in the right; [Not PH: that] he was astonished how any person could [Not LLP: have the assurance, supposing the bill should pass that House, to] carry it to the Lords, [Not LLP: for it was as downright and barefaced a robbery as ever was committed;] [PH: he said,] that he, and others of the same way of thinking, had been accused of making glorious manoeuvres against the bill; that the friends [Not EA: to][EA: of] the bill had likewise been [LC/CM/EA/PH: cautious] [GP/LLP/EC: curious], for they knew that so infamous a bill would not bear consideration, and therefore had hurried it on through every stage in a shameful manner, never wishing to have more than forty Members, [Not PH: (sufficient to constitute the House)] well knowing that one man of a thinking and unprejudiced opinion would be apt to throw out such lights as would entirely damn the cause; they had therefore generally conducted their business with a thin House, but unluckily for them they had made their House once too thinn, for they had not Members sufficient to constitute a House; **[**Not EA: he rallied [PH: them] much on their bad Generalship,**]** and said he should give his hearty negative to [Not PH: it.] [PH: the Bill.]

[LC/CM/EA: **Mr. Stephen Fox**[317] spoke greatly against the bill's passing. The question was then going to be put, and the gallery was cleared, when **Mr. Dempster**[318] and **Lord Beauchamp** also spoke against the bill;] [GP/EC: Mr S. Fox next arose, and spoke a few words against the bill. Mr D—ster then arose, and also spoke against the bill.] [LLP: Mr. S Fox, and Mr. Dempster also spoke against the Bill.] [PH: Mr. Stephen Fox spoke greatly against the Bill.] **[**LC/CM/EA: the question was then put, that [LC/CM/EA: this] [PH: the] bill be read a third time when the House divided, ayes 40, noes 22. The bill was then read a third time, and passed,**]** [GP/LLP/EC: The gallery was ordered to be cleared, and in about ten minutes the House divided: for the bill 40; against it 22.] [PH: the question was then put, that the bill be read a third time when the House divided. The Noes went forth.

Tellers.[319]

YEAS	Mr. Feilde Mr. Wilbraham Bootle[320]	40
NOES	Mr. Charles James Fox Lord Beauchamp	22]

[317] Stephen Fox† (1745–74), MP for Salisbury.

[318] George Dempster.

[319] *CJ*, xxxiv, 788.

[320] Richard Wilbraham Bootle† (1725–96), MP for Chester.

[LC/CM/EA: and Mr. Feilde ordered to carry it [LC/EA: to] the Lords to desire their concurrence.] [LLP: It was accordingly read the third time, and carried up to the House of Lords.] [PH: So it was resolved in the affirmative; and the Bill was accordingly read the third time.]

Version 2: *Middlesex Journal*, 26–28 May.

At five o'clock the order of the day was read for the third reading of the Bill for relief of Booksellers and others, by vesting the copies of printed books in the purchasers of such copies from authors, or their assigns, for a time therein to be limitted, when **Mr. Feilde** got up and moved for the Bill being read a third time, when the Speaker was just going to put the question; but **Mr. Charles Fox** got up add said, that he could not suffer the Bill to pass without saying something upon the occasion. He said that this Bill was meant only to relieve certain persons, who had mistaken the law, and laid out their money for a pretended right, which they had no title to, and which the petitioners against the Bill thought they had a right and title, and since been determined that they had, and now by this Bill you take away the right from one who had it, and give to the other who had it not; besides they have been in possession for these 20 years past, and now by this Bill you are giving them fourteen years more; and, Sir, when I think of the shameful manner that this Bill has been carried in so thin Houses, not above forty Members to attend it, and now so late in the Sessions as we are in, is the reason why I shall be against the third reading of the Bill. **Mr. Cavendish**[321] then got up just to read to the House a letter that he received in the morning to desire his attendance at the House on this Bill, and that there were never more than forty Members attended the House on the occasion, which he said was absolutely false, as he remembered that there was a division where there were upwards of 70 divided in favour of the Bill.[322] **Mr Stephen Fox** then got up and spoke greatly against the Bill's passing. The question was then going to be put, and the gallery was cleared, when **Mr. Dempster** and **Lord Beauchamp** also spoke against the Bill; the question was then put, that this Bill be read a third time; when the House divided; ayes 40, noes 22,[323] the Bill was then read a third time, and passed, and Mr. Field ordered to carry it to the Lords to desire their concurrence.

Version 3: *St James's Chronicle*, 28–31 May.

… **Mr. Feilde** moved for the Order of the Day, for the third Reading of the Booksellers Bill.

Mr. C. Fox. I cannot sit silent and see such a Bill go to the other House without expressing my hearty Disapprobation of it. What are the Grounds this Bill proceeds on? A Set of Men, mistaken or not; for Argument Sake, let us suppose they were, since the Injunction in the Court of Chancery, come to us for Relief, that is, after being in Possession of what they had no Right to for twenty Years, they come to us to countenance them in their Robbery for fourteen Years longer. What is the Case on the other side? Persons who

[321] Henry Cavendish†* (1732–1804), MP for Lostwithiel.

[322] There was a division during second reading (counsel being called in) where there were 78 votes (*CJ*, xxxiv, 752) and 83 votes on whether the House should go into committee (757).

[323] *CJ*, xxxiv, 788.

had been kept from the Enjoyment of their Right, who have appealed to the Laws of their Country and have obtained a Decision[324] in their Favour, are now to be unjustly deprived of the Fruits of it by an *ex post facto* Law. But if the Bill be contrary to every Rule of Justice, if it be repugnant to every Notion of common Equity, and injurious to Individuals, the Manner it has been forced through this House has not been less parliamentary or more indecent; at the latter End of a Session, in remarkably thin Houses, and scarcely Members sufficient to constitute a House attending. But supposing we were to take this Bill as a Matter only of private Concern; Mr. Donaldson is interrupted in the Exercise of a private Right, he appeals to the Laws of his Country, they decide in his Favour. What then does this Bill do? It determines at once, that what was a few Days since Right and Justice, shall in few more be the very Reverse. I shall mention but two more Circumstances, which plainly shew its true Complexion. Whatever Pretence there might be for a common Law Perpetuity in this Part of the Island, no such Thing was ever thought of in Scotland. It is true, an Attempt was made there, but it miscarried; yet this Bill, for partial and private Purposes, extends the Law thither with out any reasonable Grounds whatever. The other Circumstance I would allude to, is the Clause offered by a very Honourable Member (Mr. Harris.) who was one of the warmest Advocates of the Bill. He proposed, that the exclusive Privilege contented for should go no further back than the Commencement of the present Century; but the Promoters of the Bill acted perfectly uniform and consistent, for they rejected it.—**Mr. S. Fox**, **Mr. Dempster**, and **Lord Beauchamp** spoke on the same Side, but the Question being put, the Bill was passed by a great Majority.

Version 4: *Scots Magazine*, 533.

On reading the order of the day, May 27. for the third reading of the bill, **Mr Charles Fox** exclaimed vehemently against it: he said, that he was astonished how any person could have the assurance, supposing the bill should pass that House, to carry it to the Lords; that the friends of the bill knew, that so infamous a bill would not bear consideration, and therefore had hurried it on through every stage in a shameful manner, never wishing to have more than forty members, (sufficient to constitute a House); but unluckily for them, they had made their House once too thin, for they had not members sufficient to constitute a House. **Mr Stephen Fox**, **Mr Dempster**, and **Lord Beauchamp**, also spoke against the bill: but the question being put, That this bill be now read a third time? it carried, Ayes 40, Noes 22. The bill was then read a third time, and passed; and Mr Feilde was order to carry it to the Lords.

Version 5: *Morning Chronicle*, 28 May; *London Evening Post*, 26–28 May; *London Magazine*, 627.

[LM: 27 May][325] … the order of the day was read [MC: in the House of Commons] for the third reading of the Booksellers bill, and upon the question being put, whether the bill

[324] *Donaldson v Beckett* (1774) *Cobbett's Parl. Hist.* xvii, col. 953.

[325] This is misdated, as it was 26 May. This probably comes from the fact it was reported in the *Morning Chronicle* a day late.

should pass, a short debate arose, after which the House divided, ayes 40, noes 22;[326] the bill was carried to the House of Peers [MC/LNP: on Tuesday next] [LM: and there thrown out—to the *great injury* both of authors and booksellers.]

Notes

***Morning Chronicle*, 26 May**: To-morrow the third reading of the Bookseller's bill comes on, according to order, in the Lower Assembly: it is expected to be warmly debated.

***London Chronicle*, 24–26 May, 504**: Tomorrow the third read of the Booksellers will come on in the House of Commons.

***Public Advertiser*, 27 May**: This Day comes on the third Reading of the Booksellers Bill.

***Morning Chronicle*, 27 May; *Gazetteer*, 27 May; *Craftsman*, 28 May**: This day the third reading of the Booksellers bill come on in the House of Commons.

***London Magazine*, 251**: the London booksellers bill was read a third time in the House of Commons, and passed without a division.[327]

First Reading (House of Lords): 2 June.

Version 1: *Middlesex Journal*, 2–4 June, 1; *London Chronicle*, 2–4 June, 534; *General Evening Post*, 2–4 June, 1; *Caledonian Mercury*, 8 June; *Scots Magazine*, 533–4; Cobbett's *Parliamentary History*, xvii, cols 1400–2.

[MJ: Yesterday, agreeable to the order of the day, the House of Lords entered into debate on the Booksellers Bill, and, after a short discussion, the House divided on a motion being made for the bill to lay on the table till that day two months; which was carried in the affirmative by 21 to 11.] [LC: On Thursday in the House of Lords came on] [GP/CM: Yesterday at half past three o'clock come on in the House of Lords,] [LC/GP/CM: the first reading of the bill for relief of Booksellers and others, by vesting the copies of printed books in the purchasers of such copies from Authors or their assigns, for a time therein to be limited.] [SM: The first reading of the bill in the House of Lords came on June 2.] [PH: The order of the day being read for the first reading of this Bill,]

Lord Denbigh,[328] [Not SM: stated] [SM: said], [Not LC/PH: in a long speech,] that the very principle of the bill was totally inadmissible, and that it was not necessary to call witnesses, or to make any enquiry into a bill that violated the rights of idividuals, and affronted that House; and therefore moved, that the second reading [Not PH: should] be put off [PH: to that day] [GP/CM/SM: for] two months.

Lord Lyttleton[329] was for its being read a second time, and said, that he had letters from Dr. Robertson, Mr. Hume, &c.[330] in favour of the bill, and that the price the Booksellers

[326] *CJ*, xxxiv, 788.

[327] There was a division, see *CJ*, xxxiv, 788; this was corrected in the later record in the *London Magazine*, see Version 5.

[328] The *General Evening Post* used partial anonymised names rather than giving them in full: Lord D—bigh [Basil Fielding, 6th earl of Denbigh (1719–1800)], Lord L—ton, Lord C—cellor, Lord C—den and Lord M—field.

[329] Thomas Lyttelton†, 2nd Baron Lyttelton (1744–79).

[330] David Hume, William Robertson.

gave for Hawkesworth's Voyages[331] was [GP/CM: a] proof that they did believe they had a common law right. [LC/SM/PH: That this bill was not to repeal that decision[332] which the House had come to, but to relieve men who had laid out about 60,000l. in copy right since the year 1769.]

The **Lord Chancellor**[333] observed, that the Booksellers never could imagine that they had a common law right, for that all the injunctions were on the statute, except that of Lord Hardwicke's[334] in 1752,[335] which Lord Hardwicke granted on condition that the cause should be tried at common law, but that the Booksellers would not venture on it; nor did they ever bring any action thereon till lately in the cause of Miller and Taylor.[336] His Lordship observed, that his late decision on the ground of the common law right[337] had no reference to his own private opinion, for in that judgment he was necessarily governed by the prior one in the Court of King's Bench, and was obliged to decree according thereto; but that he was satisfied there never did exist a common law right, and that the Booksellers were not mistaken on that head: that the monopoly was supported among them by oppression and combination, and that there were none of their allegations, nor any part of the bill, required further inquiry.

Lord Cambden[338] said, that they never could suppose a common law right, for that it was first supported by Star-chamber decrees; that when they obtained the act of [Not CM/SM: 8] [CM: 8th] [PH: the 8th of] [Not SM: Queen Anne,][339] [SM: 8° Ann.] they could not suppose it; for the advantage and security of that act were far short of what the common law afforded them, had their claims been defensible on that ground; that on the expiration of the monopoly in 1731,[340] they could not fall into such a mistake, for they applied to parliament for an extension of the monopoly in the years 1735, 6 and 7. That he really could not compliment those gentleman who had espoused that opinion, by supposing that it was a case in the least doubtful, for that he had always considered it as the clearest and most obvious that could possibly be; that during his practice in the law, he always found the gentlemen of the profession universally against it. That it was asserted in the bill that it was a prevailing opinion that a common law right did exist; that if they meant that such an opinion prevailed among others than Booksellers, he would venture to say there [MJ/LC/SM: was][GP/CM/PH: were] 50 to 1 against it; and with respect to Booksellers, he had ground to say that many London Booksellers were not of that opinion; that all the Country Booksellers, and those of Ireland, Scotland, and America, were against it; that he could not but think this attempt an affront on the House, for that they having determined between the contending parties, that one of them had usurped for forty years, the rights that did not belong to them, and that the other party had been injured and deprived of their rights;

[331] John Hawkesworth, *An Account of the Voyages*.

[332] *Donaldson v Beckett* (1774) *Cobbett's Parl. Hist.* xvii, col. 953.

[333] Henry Bathurst††*, Lord Apsley (later 2nd Earl Bathurst) (1714–94).

[334] *Scots Magazine* and *General Evening Post* do not have 's.

[335] *Tonson v Walker* (1752) 3 Swans 672 (36 ER 1017).

[336] *Millar v Taylor* (1769) 4 Burr 2303 (98 ER 201).

[337] *Donaldson v Beckett* (1772), TNA, C 33/439, ff. 26–7.

[338] Charles Pratt†* (1714–94). *Cobbett's Parl. Hist.* spells him Camden.

[339] Copyright Act 1709 (8 Anne, c. 19).

[340] The time the 21-year period granted by the Copyright Act 1709, s. 1 expired.

[MJ/LC/SM/PH: That] this present preceeding contradicted the whole of that principle, and reversed the state of the parties; that it treated the latter as thieves and pirates, and the first as oppressed and injured, and deserving of having the possession of others taken from them for their particular emolument: that the monopolizing Booksellers had robbed others of their property; for that printing was a lawful trade, and, without all manner of doubt, therefore they had a property in it; consequently thus to deprive Printers of the subject on which they might lawfully exercise their trade, was robbing them of their property; that they had maintained this monopoly by most iniquitous oppressions, and exercised it to the disgrace of printing; that they were [MJ/GP/CM: unrighteous] monopolists, and if the line of justice and equity were drawn, it would be that those who had deprived others of their right for a series of years, should make compensation to all those they had injured by such [MJ/GP/CM: iniquitous] conduct.

[LC/SM/PH: His Lordship said further, that if the bill had stated what particular set of men had been injured, and what loss they had sustained, they might have had some favour shewn them; but in the present state they could have none. He concluded with hoping that their Lordships would reject the bill.]

[LC/GP/CM: At half past four o'clock] **[**Not MJ/SM: the question was put, for putting [LC: it off] [GP/CM: off the bill] [PH: off the second reading] for two months, when the House divided, contents 21, not contents 11.**]** [LC/GP/CM: The bill therefore is [LC: dropt] [GP/CM: thrown out], after all the [Not CM: expence and] trouble that the booksellers have been at.**]** [PH: The Bill was therefore dropt.] **[**Not MJ/SM: Lord Mansfield did not attend the House [LC/GP/CM: of Peers] [GP: upon][LC/CM/PH: on] the occasion.**]** [SM: The question being put, That the second reading be put off for two months? Came out thus: Contents 21, Not contents 11. So the bill was dropt.—Lord Mansfield was not in the House.]

Version 2: *Public Advertiser*, 3 June; *Lloyd's Evening Post*, 1–3 June, 525; *London Evening Post*, 2–4 June, 1; *St James's Chronicle*, 2–4 June; *Edinburgh Evening Courant*, 8 June; *London Magazine*, 298–9; *Annual Register*, 125–6.

[PA/LLP/LNP/SJC … at Half past Three o'Clock,] **[**Not EC: came on in the [LLP: said] House [Not LLP: of Lords], the first reading of**]** [EC: … the House of Lords read a first time] the Bill for Relief of Booksellers and others, by vesting the Copies of printed Books in the Purchasers of such Copies from Authors or their Assigns, for a Time therein to be limited; when **Lord Denbigh** got up and spoke greatly against the Bill, said it was nothing else but encouraging a Monopoly, and therefore he should move, that the first Reading of the Bill be put off for two Months.[341] **Lord Lyletton** answered him, and went through all the Objections that were started by his Lordship; he said that this Bill was not to repeal that Decision[342] which the House had come to, but to relieve Men who had laid out about [Not LM/AR: 60,000l.] [LM/AR: 600,000l.] in Copy Right since the Year 1769. The **Lord Chancellor** then got up, answered him, and entered fully into the Arguments made Use of by his Lordship [Not LM/AR:, and] [LM/AR: he] stated several Cases relative to the Injunctions in the Court of Chancery, and concluded for the Bill being put off for two Months. **Lord Lyttleton** then

[341] The motion was put off to the second reading (and not the first reading which had already been given): *LJ*, xxxiv, 232 (2 June).

[342] *Donaldson v Beckett* (1774) *Cobbett's Parl. Hist.* xvii, col. 953.

got up and replied to the Chancellor. **Lord Camden** then [Not LLP/EC: rose] [LLP/EC: arose] and spoke for some Time against the Bill; [LM/AR: he] said that if the Bill had stated what particular Set of Men had been injured, and what Loss they had sustained, they might have had some favour shewn them; but in the present State they could have none. He stated many Objections to the Bill; and concluded with hoping that their Lordships would reject the Bill.

[Not LM/AR: At Half past Four o'Clock] [LM/AR: After about an hour's debate,] the Question was put, for putting it off two Months, when the House divided, Contents 21, not Contents 11. The Bill [Not SJC/LM/AR: therefore is] [SJC/LM/AR: is therefore] [Not LLP/EC: thrown out] [LLP/EC: dropt], after all the Expence and Trouble that the Bookseller have been at.

Lord Mansfield did not attend the House of Peers upon the Occasion.

[EC: The following is a List of the PEERS who voted for THROWING out the Bill.

The Dukes of Bolton, and Roxburgh; Earls of Denbigh, Gower, Sandwich, Jersey, Spencer, Northington, Oxford, Radnor, Abercorn, Loudon, and Roseberry; Viscounts Weymouth, Falmouth, Say and Sele; Lords Camden, Ravensworth, and Montague; the Bishops of St Asaph, Litchfield and Coventry; in all twenty-one. The Chancellor spoke against the bill, but did not vote.

List of the PEERS who voted for COMMITTING the Bill.

The Dukes of Northumberland, and Portland; the Marquis of Rockingham; Earls Carlisle, and Fitzwilliam; Viscounts Dudley, and Torrington; Lords Bruce, and Lyttleton; the Archbishop of Canterbury, and Bishop of Chester: in all eleven.]

Version 3: *Edinburgh Advertiser*, 3–7 June, 356–7.

Yesterday the London booksellers received a total defeat in the House of Lords, where their unjust claims and illegal usurpations expired together. The bill for vesting in the London booksellers, a monopoly for fourteen years, of all the literature of the kingdom, since the invention of printing, being read, the Right Hon. the **Earl of DENBIGH** presented a petition from Alexander Donaldson bookseller in St Paul's church-yard,[343] setting forth the injustice and oppression of the bill; the high insult it was to that honourable house, and the great hardship and loss it would be to the community in general, and to the petitioners in particular: after the petition was read, **Lord Denbigh**, in a long speech, stated, that the principles of the bill were totally unadmissible; and maintained, that it was not necessary to call witnesses, or to make any inquiry into a bill that violated the rights of individuals, and which was a high affront to that house. His Lordship therefore moved, that the second reading should be on that day two months.

Lord LYTTLETON hoped the house would permit the bill to be read a second time now. He said he had letters from Mr. Hume, Dr Robertson, &c. compassionating the case of the London booksellers. If the bill was allowed to proceed, the booksellers would produce evidence to the house in support of their allegations, and the high price they gave for Dr. Hawkesworth's voyages, was a proof that they were deceived, and purchased in dependence on a common-law right.

[343]See Part IV, Donaldson's House of Lords Petition; there is no record in the *LJ* of the petition ever being presented.

The **LORD CHANCELLOR** observed, that the booksellers never could imagine that they had a common-law right, for that all the injunctions granted by the Court of Chancery were upon the statute, except that of 1752, which Lord Hardwick granted, on an express agreement of the parties, that the cause should be tried at common law; but that the booksellers never ventured to bring an action, notwithstanding their pretended perpetual property was daily invaded, till the year 1769; that his decision in favour of the common-law right had no reference to his own private opinion; that he was necessarily governed by the prior judgment of the King's bench, and was obliged to decree according thereto but he was satisfied there never was a common-law right, and the booksellers were not mistaken on that head; that the monopoly was attempted to be supported by means of combination and oppression, and there were none of their allegations, or any part of the bill that deserved further inquiry.

Lord CAMDEN said that the booksellers never supposed a common-law right—a right which they first supported upon *Star-chamber* decrees! that when they solicited the act of Queen Anne, they did not believe they had any such common-law right, because the advantage and security they obtained by that act was far short of what the common law afforded them had their claims been defensible on that ground, that upon the expiration of the monopoly in 1731, they could not imagine they had a common-law right, for they made application to parliament for a new act in the years 1734, 1736 and 1737, which would have been very absurd if they had enjoyed a right at common law. That he could not even compliment the gentlemen that espoused that opinion, by supposing it a case in the least doubtful, for he always considered it as the clearest and most obvious that could possibly be; that during his practice in the law, he always found the gentlemen of the profession universally against it. It was asserted in the bill, that it was a prevailing opinion, that a common-law right did exist; if they meant that such opinion prevailed among others than booksellers, he would venture to affirm there were 50 to 1 against it; and he had good grounds to say that many of the London booksellers themselves, were of opinion that there was no common-law right. All the country booksellers were against it, as well as those of Ireland, Scotland, and America. This bill he looked upon as a gross insult, and affront to that house, who had determined between the parties, that one of them had usurped for forty years, the rights that did not belong to them, and that the other party had been deprived of these rights, had been oppressed, had been injured; that the present bill contradicted the whole of that principle; that it reversed the state of the two parties; denominated the latter to be thieves and pirates, the former to be injured. That this bill took away their rights from those persons who had been oppressed, and gave them to the oppressors, as a reward for their unjust usurpations. That the monopolizing booksellers, who had robbed the public and their brethren, supported this monopoly, by the most iniquitous oppression, and, if the line of justice was drawn, those unrighteous monopolists who had deprived others of their rights for a series of years, should make a compensation to all they had injured by their iniquitous and oppressive conduct. The question being then put, the second reading of the bill was delayed for two months, on a division, 21 against 11, and the bill was consequently rejected.

List of the PEERS *who voted for* THROWING *out the Bill*

The Dukes of Bolton and Roxburgh; Earls of Denbigh, Gower, Sandwich, Jersey, Spencer, Northington, Oxford, Radnor, Abercorn, Loudon and Roseberry; Viscounts Weymouth, Falmouth, Say and Sele; Lords Camden, Ravensworth, and Montague; the Bishops of St Asaph, Litchfield and Coventry; in all twenty-one. The Chancellor spoke against the bill, but did not vote.

List of the PEERS *who voted for* COMMITTING *the Bill*

The Dukes of Northumberland, and Portland; the Marquis of Rockingham; Earls Carlisle, and Fitzwilliam; Viscounts Dudley and Torrington; Lords Bruce, and Lyttleton; the Archbishop of Canterbury, and Bishop of Chester: in all eleven.

Version 4: *Caledonian Mercury*, 6 June.

… their Lordships took into their consideration, the bill for relief of certain Booksellers of London and Westminster. At same time was presented by **Lord Denbeigh**, a petition from many of the Booksellers of London and Westminster, and another from Mr Alexander Donaldson Bookseller in London, both complaining of the hardships they, and many others, would suffer, should this bill pass into a law.[344] The debates was opened by **Lord Denbeigh**, who spoke for near half an hour against the bill. The **Lord Chancellor**, **Lord Camden**, &c. spoke on the same side. **Lord Camden** was very warm. He said, that the London Booksellers, so far from being entitled to any further monopoly, ought to be obliged to refund part of their unjust gains during the time they had usurped a property, after it expired by the act of Queen Anne. **Lord Lyttelton** spoke twice or thrice on the other side. The question being put by my Lord Chancellor, the House divided, and it carried, 21 to 11, that the bill be read the second time this day two months, which is the same as throwing it out. Three of the Bishops voted against, and two in favour of the bill.

Version 5: *Morning Chronicle*, 3 June, 2.

Yesterday the Order of the Day was read in the Upper Assembly for the first reading of the Booksellers' bill, and the same having been read by the Clerk, **Lord Denbigh** rose up and spoke for some time against the bill, and moved that it might be read a second time on that day two months. He was answered by **Lord Lyttleton**, who was for the bill. **Lord Camden** then got up, and spoke strongly against the bill. The **Lord Chancellor** also spoke against the bill. The House then divided, and the Contents for its being read on that day two months were 21, and the Not Contents 11.

[344]There is no record in the *LJ* of these petitions being presented to the House.

Notes

***Morning Chronicle*, 1 June**: Yesterday the Booksellers bill was presented to the Upper House, and ordered to be read a first time to-morrow, and the Lords to be summoned.

***Daily Advertiser*, 1 June**; ***Gazetteer*, 2 June; *London Chronicle*, 31 May–2 June, 526**: Ordered the Lords be summoned for Thursday, on the first Reading the Booksellers Bill.

***Lloyd's Evening Post*, 27–30 May, 511**: The first proceeding on the Bookseller Bill in the House of Lords, will come on to-morrow, when we hear Mr. Donaldson will petition to be heard by Counsel.

***General Evening Post*, 31 May–2 June**: This day the first reading of the booksellers bill was to come on in the Upper House, when a warm debate is expected.

***Middlesex Journal*, 31 May–2 June**: The Booksellers bill was presented to the House of Lords, yesterday, by Mr. Feilde, Mr. Burke, Col. Onslow, &c.

***Public Ledger*, 2 June**: Read a first time the Booksellers Bill, relative to Literary Property, and after a debate, the Bill was rejected on a division 21 against 11.

***Daily Advertiser*, 3 June; *Gazetteer*, 4 June; *Craftsman*, 4 June**: Read a first Time the Bill in Behalf of the London Booksellers, for the Security of Literary Property; after a short Debate the Bill was rejected, on a Division 21 against 11.

***Edinburgh Advertiser*, 31 May–3 June, 349**: Tomorrow the booksellers' bill will be read a first time in the House of Lords. There is now good reason to expect that it will be thrown out at the second reading.

***Caledonian Mercury*, 4 June**: This day was presented to the House of Peers, by Mr Field, the Bill for relief of certain Booksellers of London and Westminster, who had purchased copyright since the 1769. The bill was appointed to be read the first time on Thursday next, when the whole Lords are to be summoned to attend. It is generally thought the bill will be thrown out.

Division Lists

***Middlesex Journal*, 4–7 June; *London Evening Post*, 4–7 June; *London Chronicle*, 7–9 June, 546.**

***Gazetteer*, 4 June and *Morning Chronicle*, 4 June** (only noting the Archbishop of Canterbury was in the minority).

Also in ***Edinburgh Advertiser*, 3–7 June, 356–7; *Edinburgh Evening Courant*, 8 June** (see Version 2 and 3)

PART IV: PETITIONS, CASES AND PAPERS

The bibliography for each of the petitions, cases and papers is provided beneath its heading.

'Petitions' means it is included in *Petitions and Papers Relating to the Bill of the Booksellers, now Before the House of Commons* (ESTC: T197640) [Copies held at: Cambridge University and Oxford University, The Bodleian]; with Further Remarks: ESTC: T197622 [Copies held at: Oxford University, The Bodleian; McMasters University; Beinecke Rare Books at Yale University; Eighteenth Century Collection Online]. Page numbers for relevant papers are based on those in that document. The summary of the petitions set out in the Votes and the Commons Journal are not reproduced here unless they are the only available source.

Note on Transcription

Some of the material exists with multiple variants. If something is only in one version it will be in square brackets with the version identifier (e.g. '[MC: petition]') and if there are variants these will be in square brackets in version order (e.g. ['petition/petitioning'] where petition is in variant 1 and petitioning is in variant 2). In a few places there are differences in variants and these are individually marked with a version identifier.[1] However, variations in punctuation, font (e.g. italics) and spelling are not recorded and that from the first source is used. Where something was reproduced in a newspaper then the same abbreviations are used as in Part III. Finally, where an original document includes a footnote, this is marked in the text and the footnote itself is included at the end of the text.

Booksellers' Petition[2]

'Petitions' {3–4}; *CJ*, xxxiv, 513; *Votes 1774*, pp. 245–6 (28 Feb.); *Middlesex Journal*, 23–6 Apr.; *London Chronicle*, 23–6 Apr., 397; *Edinburgh Advertiser*, 29 Apr.–3 May, 148; *Caledonian Mercury*, 2 May; *Morning Post*, 24 Apr. (cutting in Bodleian Library).

{3} *To the Honourable the Commons of* Great Britain, *in Parliament assembled,*

The Humble PETITION of the BOOKSELLERS of LONDON and WESTMINSTER, in behalf of themselves and others, Holders of Copy-Right,

[1] A different approach has been adopted for the Booksellers' Bill.

[2] *Middlesex Journal* and *London Chronicle* have this, preceded by 'As the subject of Literary Property has been very partially represented in the public prints, and at present seems to be but partially understood, we shall, for the information of our readers, lay before them the petitions and grounds of complaints from the different parties; by which means every person may be able to form a better judgment, and with more certainty deliver their respective opinions on this important matter, than thy can be supposed to do from the partial representation of individuals'.

SHEWETH,

THAT, by an act of parliament, passed in the eighth year of the reign of her late Majesty Queen Anne, entitled, "An act for the encouragement of learning;" by vesting the copies of printed books in the authors and purchasers of such copies during the time therein mentioned,[3] it was, amongst other things enacted, that, from and after the 10th day of April, 1710, the authors or proprietors of such books as had been already printed should have the sole liberty of reprinting and publishing such books for the term of 21 years, to commence from the said 10th day of April, 1710, and no longer.[4]

That your petitioners have constantly apprehended, that the said Act of Parliament did not interfere with any copy-right that might be invested in your petitioners by the common law; and have therefore, for many years past, continued to purchase and sell such copy rights in the same manner as if such act had never been made.

That your petitioners were confirmed in such their apprehension, in regard that no determination was had during all that period, in prejudice of such common law right; and the same was actually recognized by a judgment of the court of king's bench, in Easter term, 1769.[5]

That, in consequence thereof, many thousand pounds have been at different times invested in the purchase of ancient copy-rights, not protected **{4}** by the Statute of Queen Anne, so that the support of many families, in a great measure, depend upon the same.

That by a late solemn decision of the House of Peers[6] such common law right of authors and their assigns hath been declared to have no existence, whereby your petitioners will be very great sufferers thro' their involuntary misapprehension of the law.

Your petitioners therefore most humbly pray this Honourable House to take their singularly hard case into consideration, and to grant them such relief in the premises as to this Honourable House shall seem meet.

(Signed by eighty-seven persons.)

Bach and Abel's Petition

CJ, xxxiv, 562; *Votes 1774*, p. 346 (15 Mar.).

A Petition of *John Christian Bach*, and *Charles Frederick Abel*,[7] on Behalf of themselves and several other Composers and Proprietors of Books, Works, and Compositions in Music, was presented to the House, and read;

Taking Notice of the Petition of the Booksellers of *London* and *Westminster*, on Behalf of themselves and others, Holders of Copy Right; and reciting Part of an Act, made in the Eighth Year of the Reign of Queen *Anne*, for the Encouragement of Learning, by vesting the Copies of printed Books in the Authors or Purchasers of such Copies; and Setting forth,

[3] Copyright Act 1709 (8 Anne, c. 19).

[4] Copyright Act 1709, s. 1.

[5] *Millar v Taylor* (1769) 4 Burr 2303 (98 ER 201).

[6] *Donaldson v Beckett* (1774) *Cobbett's Parl. Hist.*, xvii, col. 953.

[7] Johann Christian Bach* (1735–82); Carl Fredrick Abel* (1723–87).

That a Doubt has arisen, whether the sole Right granted by the said Act, to the Author of any Book or Books, extends to the Author of any Book, Writing, or Composition in Music: And therefore praying, That Provision may be made, for obviating such Doubt; and that they may have such Relief in the Premise as to the House shall seem meet.

Booksellers' Case

Bodleian Library (two copies): (Vet.) 2581.c.5(2) and MS Carte 207.

The CASE of the Booksellers of *London* and *Westminster*

By an Act of Parliament passed in the 8th Year of Queen *Anne*, intitled "An Act for the Encouragement of Learning, by vesting the Copies of printed Books in the Authors and Purchasers of such Copies, during the Times therein mentioned;" after reciting that Printers, Booksellers, and other Persons, had of late frequently taken the Liberty of printing, reprinting, and publishing, or causing to be printed, reprinted, and published, Books and other Writings, without the Consent of the Authors or Proprietors of such Books and Writing, to their very great Detriment, and too often to the Ruin of them and their Families; it was among other Things enacted, "That from and after the 10th Day of *April* 1710, the Authors or Proprietors of such Books as had been already printed, should have the sole Right and Liberty of reprinting and publishing such Books for the Term of 21 Years, and no longer."[8]

By another Clause in the said Act, it is provided, "*That nothing therein contained should be construed to extend either to prejudice or confirm any Right which the Universities, or any Person or Persons had, or claimed to have, to the printing or reprinting any Book or Copy already printed, or thereafter to be printed.*"[9]

From the Clause, as well as the Recital, it was conceived, that the Act did not affect or take away the Common Law Right supposed to be vested in the Authors of Books, and their Assigns, in Perpetuity; and therefore the Booksellers continued to purchase the perpetual Copy-Rights of Books, in the Manner they had been accustomed to do before the passing of the said Act.

The present Petitioners, confirmed in that Opinion by several Injunctions granted by and out of his Majesty's High Court of Chancery, and by a Decision of the Court of King's Bench about Five Years ago,[10] have, under those Sanctions, and with a full Persuasion and Confidence that they were purchasing a real and permanent Property; not limited as to the exclusive Enjoyment of it to any particular Period, bought, at public Sales and otherwise, at very high Prices, **{2}** the Copy-Rights as well of Books not within the Protection of the said Statute of Queen *Anne*, as of Books which were then protected by the Penalties of that Act, to the Amount of many Thousand Pounds; and have actually printed many Copies of such Books which now remain unsold, the Printing and Paper of which, exclusive of the Consideration paid for the Copy-Right, have also cost them many Thousand Pounds.

[8] Copyright Act 1709, s. 1.

[9] Copyright Act 1709, s. 9.

[10] *Millar v Taylor* (1769) 4 Burr 2303 (98 ER 201).

But by a late solemn Decision of the House of Peers,[11] the before supposed Common Law Copy Right in Books has been declared to have no Existence; by which Determination, the Petitioners, the greatest Part of whose Fortunes are invested in such Property, will, unless they obtain some Relief from Parliament, be very great Sufferers, and many of them and their Families be reduced to unavoidable Distress.

The Petitioners beg leave also humbly to observe, That they are the more excusable for their Misapprehension with respect to the Common Law Copy Right to Books in Perpetuity, as a *Majority* of the learned Judges gave their Opinions in the House of Lords,[12] that such Right existed *prior* to the Statute of Queen *Anne*, and many of them declared their Opinions, that such Right was not taken away by that Statute.

Many of the Books which the Petitioners so purchased the supposed Copy-Right in, and have since printed under such mistaken Notion, are large and voluminous, and have a very slow Sale; so that it must be many Years before a sufficient Number are sold to repay them the Expence of Paper and Print only.

Literary Property having been compared to mechanical Invention, it may not be improper to observe, that the Money arising by the Sale of *single* Orrery, Clock, or other Piece of Mechanism,[13] always amounts to much more than the Expence of the *Materials* and *Manual Labour* employed in making it; and the Maker is repaid the Costs of Materials and Labour, and also a Profit thereon, if he sells but one ONLY. But it is the Reverse with respect to Books; for the *mere* printing of one Copy *only*, would cost above a hundred Times the Price for which it is sold; and whenever another Copy should be printed off, the same Expence would be incurred. It is therefore *necessary*, in order to enable the Bookseller to sell each printed Copy at the customary Rate, to print off a considerable Number at one Impression, uncertain of the Demand there will be **{3}** for them; and the Bookseller cannot in any Instance be repaid the Expence of the *Printing, Paper*, and *Advertising*, till he has sold the greater Part of the Impression: For till that is done, he cannot receive back any Part of what he has paid for the Copy Right of the Book, or any Interest or Profit upon the Money he has advanced.

In a Case nearly similar to that of the Petitioners, the Legislature, to encourage the Art of Engraving, and to secure to the Proprietors of Maps and Prints, the Enjoyment of the Profits thereof, did, by an Act of Parliament made in the 8th Year of King *George* II. grant them the exclusive Right of printing off and selling the same, for the Term of 14 Years;[14] and, by another Act made in the 7th Year of his present Majesty's Reign, for an absolute and unconditional Term of 28 Years.[15] The Petitioners would here beg leave to observe, that the Expence of Plates, Paper, and printing of Maps or Prints, is trifling when compared to the Expence of an Impression of a Book, Maps or Prints may be printed off from the

[11] *Donaldson v Beckett* (1774) *Cobbett's Parl. Hist.*, xvii, col. 953.

[12] As to the vote, Ronan Deazley, *On the Origin of the Right to Copy* (Oxford, 2004), 194–209; H. Tomás Gómez-Arostegui, 'Copyright at Common Law in 1774', *Connecticut Law Review*, xlvii (2014), 1; H.B. Abrams, 'The Historic Foundation of American Copyright Law: Exploding the Myth of Common Law Copyright', *Wayne Law Review*, xxix (1983), 1167–71.

[13] In the previous session, a prize had been given to John Harrison for his timepieces (connected to assessing longitude): Supply Act 1773 (13 Geo. III, c. 77), s. 29. For more details, Phillip Johnson, *Parliament, Inventions and Patents* (2018), 538, PRZA 15.

[14] Engraving Copyright Act 1734 (8 Geo. II, c. 13), s. 1.

[15] Engraving Copyright Act 1766 (7 Geo. III, c. 38), s. 7.

same Copper-Plate in small Numbers, and as the Demand for them arises, the Plate lasting for many Years: Whereas, as soon as a few Sheets of a Book are worked off, the Type with which they have been printed, must of Necessity be separated for the Purpose of printing other Sheets of the same Work.

The Petitioners, therefore, encouraged by the known Equity of the British Legislature, and the Protection it has already afforded and extended to the Proprietors of Maps and Prints, humbly hope that, as a necessary Relief to them in their present unhappy Situation, *such farther limited Term for the sole reprinting of such Books as are not protected by the Statute of Queen Anne, and such Enlargement of the Term given for new Publications by that Act*, will be granted to the Petitioners, as shall be thought just and reasonable.

Case Observations

Arthur Murphy, *Observation on the Case of the Booksellers of London and Westminster* (ESTC: T16365); *Caledonian Mercury*, 21 Mar. 1774.[16]

OBSERVATION ON THE CASE OF THE BOOKSELLERS of LONDON and WESTMINSTER

Case. IT is asserted, that the Booksellers conceived there was, independent of the Statute of *Queen Anne*,[17] a *Common Law Right vested in the Authors of Books, and their Assigns,* in PERPETUITY, and that they have therefore *continued to purchase* the *perpetual Copy-Right of Books*, in the Manner they had been accustomed to do before the Passing of the said Act.

Answer. It is certain that Booksellers, from the Time when they lost the Protection of the *Licensing Act*, 1694, strained every Nerve to turn the *Bye-Laws* of the Stationers Company[18] into the *Common Law of the Land*; but the Idea, they very well know, was rejected by PARLIAMENT, when the *Act of Queen Anne* took place. From the *Journals* of the House of Commons, and the CONFERENCE had with the Lords[19] upon the Subject of the Bill then depending, the Petitioners might, at all Times, see that both Houses conceived that they were *then creating a new Right*, and VESTING the same in Authors and the Purchasers of Copies.

But though the Point was perfectly clear, it is certain that the Booksellers have endeavoured ever since, by *Combination* among themselves, and by various Efforts, to engross the

[16]The version in the *Caledonian Mercury*, 21 Mar. 1774, is preceded by the following paragraph: 'As mentioned formerly, that the London Booksellers had given in to the House of Commons, a petition, craving relief from the late decision of the House of Peers, in the great cause of Literary Property. The matter was referred to a committee, to whom the London Booksellers gave in a printed *case*, setting forth their pretended grievances in consequence of that decision. The following *Observations* on that Case, wrote by Arthur Murphy, Esq; were, on Tuesday last, distributed among the members of that committee. As the issue of the present application is of the last importance to learning, as well as to the interest of all the Printers and Booksellers in Great Britain (a few in London excepted), we imagine most of our readers will be pleased to have a short state of the arguments on both sides laid before them.'

[17]Copyright Act 1709.

[18]The former, made on 17 Aug. 1681, the latter on 14 May 1694: reproduced in D.F. McKenzie and Maureen Bell, *A Chronology and Calendar of Documents Relating to the London Book Trade, 1641–1700* (3 vols, Oxford, 2005), ii, 288–91; iii, 169–74.

[19]*CJ*, xvi, 395 (5 Apr. 1710).

Copies of all printed Books, ancient and modern, old and new, as well in Instances where they had a colourable Assignment from the Author, as where they had none; that is to say, PARADISE LOST,[20] for which they can shew the Author's Receipt for 5*l*.[21] and SHAKESPEARE'S Works, for which they can show no Receipt at all.

If OBSTINACY IN ERROR, even where CONVICTION was to be had, and a Desire to MONOPOLIZE where *no Right* existed, can now be offered as a *Plea of Merit*, the Petitioners have every Advantage that can be derived from those Sources.

The Entries made since the 8th of Q. *Anne*,[22] in the Stationers Register, plainly shew that the Protection of that Act was what the Booksellers relied upon. Soon after the Statute, LINTOT,[23] an eminent Bookseller, purchased *Pope's Homer*, for 14 Years, and as long *after as the Author could assign*, by the Act of Queen *Anne*.

It is notorious, that *John Osborne*,[24] late of *Paternoster Row*, printed an Edition of SHAKESPEARE'S Works, as a Copy *that lay in common*: Upon that Occasion, the Booksellers did not venture to claim an exclusive Right by Law or Equity, but, to avoid the Question, compromised with OSBORNE, and bought up the Copies which he had printed, for a Pension, which, it is said, he enjoys at this Hour.

Motte purchased the Miscellanies of *Pope, Swift, Gay*, and *Arbuthnot*, in the Year 1727, *for ever*; and yet, in 1735, when he filed an Injunction Bill[25] against *Falkener* for printing the same, the Title, which he made **{2}** to the High Court of Chancery, was a *Right under the Statute of Queen* Anne, to the *sole printing thereof* for the Term of FOURTEEN YEARS.

Many of the Booksellers, who now petition, have been so far from conceiving that they had a *perpetual Copy-Right*, that they have, when the Term granted by the 8th *Anne* was elapsed,[26] republished their Books under a *Patent-Privilege for 14 Years longer*. Of the Books printed in this Manner, the following will serve as Instances: WATT'S Works,[27] STACKHOUSE'S History of the Bible,[28] POPE'S Work,[29] &c.

Case. It is said that the PETITIONERS have bought at *publick Sales* the Copy-Right of Books, *protected and not protected by the Statute*, to the Amount of many THOUSAND POUNDS.

[20] The first edition was John Milton* (1608–74), *Paradise Lost* (Samuel Simmons, 1667) (ESTC: R9505).

[21] Kerry MacLenna, 'John Milton's Contract for "Paradise Lost": A Commercial Reading', *Milton Quarterly*, xliv (2010), 221.

[22] Copyright Act 1709 (8 Anne, c. 19).

[23] Bernard Lintot* (1675–1736), app. 1690–1700, bookseller, between Temple Gates. There is a claim by Lintot for Alexander Pope's *The Iliad* on 4 June 1715: *The Records of the Stationers' Company 1554–1920* (1986) and *Literary Print Culture – The Stationers' Company Archive, 1554–2007* (Adam Matthew, 2017), Register of Entries of Copies, 1710–46 (TSC/1/E/06/08, p. 225); reel 6. However, it records ownership, but not the length of the title. The first edition was *The Iliad of Homer*, trans. Alexander Pope (1720) (ESTC: T14924).

[24] John Osborne (*d.* 1775), tr. 1733–52, bookseller, 33 Paternoster Row.

[25] *Benjamin Mott v Arthur Betteworth and George Faulkner* (1735): TNA, C 11/2249/4.

[26] The 21 years granted expired on 9 Apr. 1731.

[27] Thomas Watt, *Grammar Made Easie* (Kincaid, 1772) (ESTC: N2627), includes details of a Scots patent, which was granted in 1708 and had long expired.

[28] Thomas Stackhouse* (1681/2–1752), *A Compleat History of the Holy Bible* (Austen, 1742–4) (ESTC: T101782), includes details of the patent.

[29] Alexander Pope* (1688–1744), *The Works of Alexander Pope* (Millar, 1764) (ESTC: T5442), includes details of the patent.

Answer. Their Sales were not always PUBLIC:— When the Copies of the late *Andrew Millar*[30] were disposed of in 1769, the Auction was confined to a *select Number of Booksellers*, as appears by the printed *Catalogue* now existing,[31] and none were admitted but such as had *Cards* for that Purpose. In particular, *Alexander Donaldson* wished to attend the Sale, but had Notice that it would be disagreeable. Upon other Occasions, Persons, who had Cards of Admission, were turned out of the Room, for REASONS BEST KNOWN TO THE PETITIONERS: It certainly was not for the Interest of the Seller, that Persons who might desire to become Purchasers should be excluded.

It may be further observed, that the first Attempt of the Booksellers, upon the Ground of a *Common Law Right*, was in a *collusive Action* between *Tonson* and *Collins*[32] *of Salisbury*, about the Year 1759. The Court of King's Bench detected the Fallacy; and though the Point had been argued, no Judgement was given, on Account of the Fraud upon the Court.

The second Attempt of the Booksellers was in the Case of *Millar* v. *Taylor*, argued in the *King's Bench*, 1768. And though that Cause began in earnest, it ended *collusively*; for a Writ of *Error was brought*; two Persons now in *London* were Security for the *Plaintiff in Error*, but TAYLOR was practised upon to discontinue the same.

Case. It is said, that the Petitioners are excusable for their MISAPPREHENSION, as a Majority of the LEARNED JUDGES were of Opinion in the HOUSE OF LORDS,[33] that such Right existed prior to the Statute Queen *Anne*.

Answer. In 1734, 5, 6, 7, the Booksellers prayed of the Legislature an Extension of the Term given by the 8th of *Anne*, without pretending a prior Right at Common Law. They were, therefore, under no *Misapprehension*; and in the House of Lords six of the Judges were *decisively* of Opinion, that the Decree against *Donaldson* ought to be reversed:[34] To those six may be added the Authority of the late Sir JOSEPH YATES, Lord CAMDEN, and the Lord HIGH CHANCELLOR.[35]

If the *Writ of Error* in *Millar* v. *Taylor* had proceeded, there would have been SIX of the learned Judges against TWO in the Exchequer Chamber, and of Course the Judgement of the *King's Bench* would have been reversed.

Case. It is customary to *print off* a considerable Number of Books at one Impression; and when one *Orrery is made*, the Expence, Labour, and Materials of *another*, must all begin again.

Answer. The Argument of Petitioners seems to be this, Because they can work at a more expeditious and less expensive Rate than the Author of *mechanical Inventions*, they are therefore intitled to *Privileges*, which have never been extended to those who work under greater Disadvantages.

[30] Andrew Millar* (1705–68), app. 1720, tr. 1728–68, The Strand; also see Adam Budd, *Circulating Enlightenment: The Career and Correspondence of Andrew Millar*, 1727–68 (Oxford, 2020).

[31] A copy still exists: *A Catalogue of the Copies and Shares of Copies of the Late Mr Andrew Millar* (1769) (ESTC: N490136); this is replicated and annotated in Budd, *Circulating Enlightenment*, Appendix 4.

[32] *Tonson v Collins* (1761) 1 Black W 301 (96 ER 169).

[33] *Donaldson v Beckett* (1774) *Cobbett's Parl. Hist.*, xvii, col. 953.

[34] TNA, C 33/439, ff. 26–7.

[35] Charles Pratt†* (Lord Camden) (1714–94); Henry Bathurst†* (Lord Apsley) (1714–94); Sir Joseph Yates* (1722–70).

{3} Case. It is said, that an *absolute and unconditional* Term of 28 Years is granted to *Engravers* of Maps and Prints, by 7th of his present Majesty.[36]

Answer. The 7th of his present Majesty is not a *retrospective Act* to give 28 Years in Works which had been already published; but the Act looks forward, and the *Term is given* to the *Inventors and Designers* in all such Works as they shall design and publish from and after the first Day of *January*, 1767.

Case. The Petitioners say, that they have purchased Copies to the Amount of *many thousand Pounds.*

Answer. The late Mr. *Tonson* and *Millar* left at least 300,000*l.*[37] made in the Trade of Bookselling; and the Petitioners do not set forth how much they have already benefited by the *Monopoly* which they have hitherto exercised.

Case. The Petitioners pray a *further Term* for the sole reprinting of such Books as are not protected by the Statute of Queen *Anne.*

Answer. Those Books are dear enough already, in consequence of a MONOPOLY: If the Term be extended, the Price will continue as high as ever, whereas the Consequence of a free and open Trade, will be a Competition, to print as well and as cheap as possible.

Case. The Petitioners pray an Enlargement of the Term given for *new Publications* by the 8th of Queen *Anne.*

Answer. If they mean for the Time to come, it would be *decent* on their Part to let Authors apply to the Legislature for themselves. But if it be the Intent of the Petitioners to request an Enlargement of the Term of 14 Years, in Books already sold to them by Authors now living, *the Mask is dropt*, and the Aim of the PETITIONERS is to gain from Parliament more than they have bought, to the PREJUDICE of the AUTHOR, whom, in the Argument at the Bar of the HOUSE OF LORDS, they affected to be desirous to serve.

By the 8th of Queen *Anne*, the sole Right of *printing and reprinting any Book*, which had not been published before that Act, is granted to the AUTHOR AND HIS ASSIGNS for 14 Years, to commence from the Day of first publishing the same, and *no longer*:

Provided always, that after the Expiration of the said Term of 14 Years, The sole Right of printing or disposing of Copies shall *return* to the AUTHORS thereof, *if they are then living*, for another Term of 14 Years.[38]

It is observable, that the first Term is given to the AUTHORS AND HIS ASSIGNS: The SECOND TERM is granted to the AUTHOR ONLY:[39] The Omission of the Word ASSIGNS in the second Term, the Booksellers conceive to be a Bar to their Pretensions; and therefore, out of Compassion to their *Wives and Children*, they now pray that they may be let into the Enjoyment of a second Term of 14 Years: But it is hoped the Legislature will recollect that Authors may have *Wives and Children* too, and that, The *Reversion* of the Work, at the End of 14 Years, granted by a Clause, so guardedly drawn up by the great Lord SOMERS,[40] will not now, in favour of the Bookseller, be taken from the Man of LABOUR and INVENTION.

[36] Engraving Copyright Act 1766 (7 Geo. III, c. 38), s. 7.

[37] Their wills are TNA, PROB 11/940/163 and PROB 11/928/110, but no figures are included. Budd also includes an annotated copy of Millar's will: *Circulating Enlightenment*, Appendix 1.

[38] Copyright Act 1709 (8 Anne, c. 19), s. 11.

[39] Copyright Act 1709, s. 1.

[40] John Somers†† * (1651–1716), he was the lord president in council in 1709–10.

Remarks on the Booksellers' Petition[41]

Yale, Beineke Rare Books (ESTC: N472540); *Edinburgh Advertiser*, 29 Mar.–1 Apr., 201.

[Variant 1: Remarks on the Booksellers' Petition (RP); Variant 2: *Edinburgh Advertiser* (EA)][42]

[RP: REMARKS ON THE BOOKSELLERS PETITION.

AS a Literary Monopoly is certainly very pernicious; so it is a very dangerous Example to Society, that a Body of Tradesmen should have been allowed to prosecute such a Cause, in Opposition to an express Act of Parliament, in Hope of being supported by a dispensing Power, which our Constitution does not allow to the King himself.

The Booksellers, after having been defeated in their open Endeavours to set aside an Act of the Legislature,[43] now betake themselves to Artifice; and in a most humble Petition to the House of Commons, are making lamentable Moan Of the Ruin which they pretend is brought on them, by the late Decision of the House of Lords.[44] [EA: AS the claim of a LITERARY MONOPOLY appears to be a very pernicious claim, so it is certainly an example very dangerous to society, that any set of men should be allowed with impunity, to support such a cause, in direct opposition to an express act of parliament, and to endeavour at the establishment of a dispensing power, which our kings have attempted in vain.

Some booksellers, after having ineffectually endeavoured to set aside and disannul an act of the legislature, are now attempting to set forth tragical representations of the ruin and calamity which they pretend the late decision of the House of Lords will bring on them and their families.] [RP: And] after having strained every Nerve [RP:, and used every Contrivance,] to enjoy their Monopoly, in Despite of Parliament; they are now very modestly applying to them for a legal Right to enjoy what they have long [illegally exercised/exercised illegally] to the great [prejudice/detriment] of the Public. They have tasted too long the Sweets of [RP: unjust] Gain, to have any Inclination to part with it, if by Combination, [RP: Mis-representation,] or any other Means, a Possibility remains of enjoying it.

Whilst their Cause was depending I was silent: But now [that/when] the most solemn Adjudication has corroborated my Sentiments, I will beg Leave to make a few Remarks on their Conduct and their Cause.

Having purchased [these/some] pretended Rights of Publication, they now expect to be secured in them, for no other Reason but because they have bought them; although the Persons of whom the [Purchases were/purchase was] made had no [Property in/legal right to dispose of] them. [Are/Is] then the Legislature [and/or] the Public to [guarantee/be the guaranty of] every Bargain, however vague, or however it may militate with general or municipal [Law?/laws!] [EA: If I buy a house that the possessor has no right to sell, must

[41] The Remarks on the Booksellers' Petition are marked RP and the *Edinburgh Advertiser*, 29 Mar.–1 Apr. 1774, p. 201 are marked EA].

[42] The text is preceded by the following: "*To The* Printer of *the* Edinburgh Advertiser, Sir,"

[43] This is a reference to *Donaldson v Beckett* (1774) *Cobbett's Parl. Hist.*, xvii, col. 953; and *Millar v Taylor* (1769) 4 Burr 2303 (98 ER 201).

[44] *Donaldson v Beckett* (1774) *Cobbett's Parl. Hist.*, xvii, col. 953.

the PUBLIC indemnify me? If the tradesman with whom I deal, lets his shop, and sells the customers to his successor, shall the successor say, he has bought my custom, and bring an action against me if I leave his shop?] Various vague kinds of Property are daily sold amongst us, and for valuable Considerations, that can [only be considered/be considered as RIGHTS, but] as Chances or Advantages that are bought and sold with all the [Risks/hazards] to which they are subject; and cannot be secured to the [Purchasers/purchaser, either] on Principles of Law or Justice. [EA: After the tradesman has paid a valuable consideration for the trade of his shop, his neighbour, by superior knowledge, or diligence in his profession, may deprive him of the whole; and yet such conduct will be neither illegal nor immoral.] But the Case in Question [has the least Pretence of any to the claimed Protection; for/can least of any claim a particular exemption, as] an Act of the Legislature has laid down with Precision the Rules by which [the Trade/it] shall be conducted; [has/they have] vested the Property [EA: claimed] for a limited [Term/Time], and [EA: have] expressly declared it shall exist no longer: [Therefore if they purchased/If trademen therefore purchased it] with a View of enjoying it longer, they purchased [EA: it] with a View of enjoying it in Defiance of the Legislature: If they purchased during the Dependance of this Cause, they purchased on Speculation, like Gamblers in the Alley:[45] And it was never before imagined that such [Speculations/speculators] deserved [Protection from the Law, and an Indemnification from the Public./to be protected by the law, or indemnified by the public.]

[The principal Claimants to a Right in Copies are a few Men of large property. These Men/There are only a very FEW men of large property, who are the principal claimants to a right in copies; these men,] though before possessed of a great Number, yet in expectation of this Cause being decided in their Favour, have been [purchasing/engrossing] still more [EA: and more]. These are the Men who have raised so much Clamour about the Loss [EA: which] they shall sustain by the Determination of the first Court of Justice in [the Kingdom/this kingdom].[46] And yet after all, if [these Men were to produce an Account of the great Gains they have illegally made by these Copies, it would /they could be prevailed upon to produce a just state of their gains, as well as their losses, it would then] appear that the Estates they possess have mostly been made by this Traffic; and now they are very angry [that/because] they can no longer [enjoy/engross] so advantageous a Monopoly. For it should be remembered that when these Gentlemen talk of losing, they mean that from the exorbitant Gains which have already been made by the Exercise of this illegal Claim, they had good Reason to conclude (and indeed it cannot well be questioned) that they should make still more, if the Monopoly were continued to them; and that by the Decision of the House of Lords, they are deprived of such flattering Views. [EA: But] That few can be real Losers, will appear from considering that most Purchasers of Copies are reimbursed by one impression; and if they are not reimbursed by two, I am informed they account it a dear Purchase. [RP: And if we farther consider, that Copy-Rights sell low after an Impression is printed, and are most valuable when a Book is out of Print, and on the Eve of a new Impression, it is impossible that the real Loss can, except in a very few Cases, be considerable.] That some [RP: young] Men may have imprudently bought a few [RP: Shares

[45] Exchange Alley – a reference to stock jobbers. As to the views of stock jobbers around the time, Huw Bowen, '"The Pests of Human Society": Stockbrokers, Jobbers and Speculators in Mid-Eighteenth-Century Britain', *History*, lxxviii (1993), 38.

[46] *Donaldson v Beckett* (1774) *Cobbett's Parl. Hist.*, xvii, col. 953.

of] Copies by which they may be Losers is [EA: very] possible; but if young Men with small Fortunes have been deeply [engaged/concerned] in such a Traffic as this, [RP: while the Cause was depending,] they have been very imprudent indeed; and I cannot think that the Public ought to secure them from the Loss.

But if they are to enjoy Copy-Rights, merely because they have presumed to buy and sell them, it will establish the most [ridiculous/rediculous] Claims. The [*Delphin Classics*/classics IN USUM DELPHINI][47] are considered by them as very valuable Copy-Rights, and are sold amongst them for [large/considerable] Sums. Shall a London Bookseller be allowed an exclusive Right to *Horace* or *Virgil*? Or have they any better Right to the Notes and Illustrations made at the Expence of the King of *France*? Many of the valuable Copies they Claim, stand in the same Predicament: And I believe they derive from the Authors but few of the old Copies; though the Names of Authors may be used as the Stalking-[horse/horses] to their Designs. It has indeed been affirmed by their Counsel, "that [nobody/no person] ever thought of a Bookseller's Claim but as derived from the Author;" yet these Cases prove that his Clients have not only thought of it, but have long claimed and enjoyed many Copies (I believe by much the greater Part) without [once asking or thinking of the Question,/thinking or inquiring] "whether they were derived from the Authors or not." If then they are [RP: by an Act of Parliament] to be secured in the Possession of Copies, [for no other Reason but/merely] because they have been bought and sold amongst them; the Establishment of such Claims as these must take Place. And if [Parliament shall establish such Claims only as can be proved/only such Claims are allowed, as they can prove] to be derived from Authors, it will be an acknowledgment of [EA: the justice of] an Author's Claim to a Perpetuity, a Claim which has been solemnly adjudged to have no Foundation. For if an Author has a Claim beyond the Time limited by the Statute, he [must have a Claim/certainly has a claim to it] for ever.

But if [the Parliament shall establish the Claim on either Ground, the Claimants will obtain their Purpose. For though/it is established in either form, it will serve their purpose, for tho'] it is generally believed that they can [deduce/trace] from the Authors but few of the old [Copy-Rights/copies]; yet it will be impossible to [discuss any particular Claim,/try any one of them] without printing an Impression, and standing the event of a Law-Suit; [in which/and then] perhaps they [may/will] produce a Proof, [EA: and] ruin [the Defendant/their opponent], and [by that Means, for want of a Negative Proof in the Hands of their Opponents,/at the same time] have quiet Possession of a Multitude of other Copies, for which they can produce no Proof [: Because their Title cannot be controverted but by the same expensive and litigious/, but not one of them can be ascertained but by the same expensive and vexatious] Process.

Therefore [their Petition cannot deserve a moment's Consideration, till they/before their Petition can possibly deserve a moment's attention, they ought to] give in an Inventory of the Copies they Claim,[48] and the Origins from whence they [derive such Claim/are derived]. And every [Person that has/man who] signed the Petition, ought to [produce/give in,] on Oath, his List of Shares, when and where Bought, the Sums paid for them, the

[47] For an explanation of the collection, J.E. Sandys, *A History of Classical Scholarship* (3 vols, Cambridge, 1908), ii, 292–3; *The Oxford Companion to the Book*, ed. M.F. Suarez and H.R. Woudhuysen (2 vols, Oxford, 2010), ii, 663.

[48] Originally a list was ordered by parliament (*CJ*, xxxiv, 513, 28 Feb.) but the order was discharged (*CJ*, xxxiv, 525, 2 Mar.).

Number of Books he has received in Consequence thereof, what [such Books/they] cost Printing, and at what rates they [were/are] sold. But I find they are very unwilling to produce [such an Account; for this/these particulars, and the only hope of their friends is to prevent such an order taking place as it] would entirely refute the Allegations of their Petition, and shew that they have made large Fortunes by [this/an] illegal Monopoly. They say it would take up [RP: too] much Time to make out [such an Account. To make out their Claims indeed,/ these particulars; with respect indeed to deriving their claims from the authors, THAT] I believe would [be a Work of/take up an] infinite [Time and Labour/labour and time]; but as to the other Particulars, they [may/might] be easily ascertained; and if it would serve their Cause, [EA: it] would [be soon/have been now] ready for the Inspection of the House: But [such an Account ought to be produced, for surely such/whatever hard labour it might require, it certainly ought to have been done, for] an unjust and pernicious Monopoly, [ought/should] not [RP: to] be continued on [their vague Representations./ the vague reasons contained in a petition.]

Most of the Persons that have signed the Petition have very little Interest in Copies: But [Hand-bills/printed invitations] were dispersed, [EA: most] earnestly pressing them to meet [EA: their brethren] at the *Devil* (*Tavern*)[49] on an Affair of the utmost Consequence to the Trade: At the *Devil* they assembled accordingly; a Speech was made on the Good of the Trade; they signed [RP: the Petition] because they were told it was for the Good of the Trade: Those Magic Words among Tradesmen, like the War-whoop among [EA: the] Savages, Invigorate and Unite.

Let *them* consult the Good of [their Trade/the trade], but I trust that the Legislature of this Kingdom have a more important Object for *their* Consideration, [THE GOOD OF THE PUBLIC/I mean THE PUBLIC GOOD], which is often [EA: found to be] incompatible with the private Views of Individuals.

[EA: I am SIR,
Your humble servant,
VERITAS]

Farther Strictures

Farther STRICTURES on the Booksellers PETITION, Yale, Beinecke Rare Books (ESTC: N472540).

Farther STRICTURES on the Booksellers PETITION.

ALTHOUGH the Petitioners have asserted that they shall sustain great Loss by the late Decision;[50] yet only a very small Number of them are materially affected by it: Many, who have very little or no Interest therein, having signed that Petition through Fear or Friendship or from other Motives.

They are now seeking redress from Parliament, on Pretence of their having bought Copy-Rights under a Supposition of their being a Perpetual Property by Common Law. Yet the

[49] 2 Fleet Street. During the 1770s, Thomas Longman* (1730–97) and others ran a literary society for booksellers at the Tavern: Henry Curwen, *A History of Booksellers, the Old and New* (1873), 86.

[50] *Donaldson v Beckett* (1774) *Cobbett's Parl. Hist.*, xvii, col. 953.

following Particulars fully prove that Booksellers never did purchase Copy-Rights on such a Supposition.

About the Year 1640, we find they began to buy Copies. From that Year to 1694, they purchased under the Protection of the Ordinances of Parliament, the Licensing Act, and the Prerogative of the Crown. To answer the Arbitrary Purposes of the latter, they were invested with extraordinary Privileges and Powers: And under that Protection (though not granted them for such Purposes) they claimed, bought, and sold Copy-Rights. But when the Revolution took Place, and the Licensing Act expired,[51] this Property vanished, and their Copy-Rights ceased. In this Situation they never thought of a Common Law-Right; but applied to Parliament as their only Resource. And as it was manifest that they had been induced to make those Purchases on the Protection afforded them by the Licensing Act, which was then expired; and by the Prerogative of the Crown, which was then limited by Law: The Parliament in 1709 granted them an exclusive Right for 21 Years; with a Limitation in these express Words, *and no longer*.[52] Would not any Man conclude that no Possibility of Dispute remained, when so clear a Line was drawn by the Legislature for conducting this Monopoly. But the Increase of Literature in the present Century,[53] rendered a Monopoly of it an important Object: So that on the Expiration of the exclusive Right in 1731,[54] the Booksellers of that Time having made large Fortunes by it, they (like the Booksellers of our Day) were desirous of its Continuance; and accordingly in 1734, 5, 6 made Applications to Parliament; but they totally failed in every Attempt. They had not yet acquired an Idea of a Property founded on the Common Law; but contended themselves (as the Booksellers now will if they fail in the present Attempt) with Endeavours to retain their exclusive Right, in Defiance of the Legislature. They still presumed to call themselves Proprietors; they stigmatized other Editions as Piratical: But as they printed Books cheap and good in Comparison of the present Practice; they met with very little Opposition in their Monopoly till the Year 1746 or 7. About that Time Mr J. Osborne, a Bookseller of Property in Paternoster-Row, having quarrelled with his Brethren, began printing very correct and cheap Editions of some of their pretended Copies of which his small Shakespeare was one.[55] Him they found Means to induce (it is said by an Annuity of 200l.) to quit Business. During this whole Transaction they appear not to have thought of a legal Claim: and it is impossible, they could soon after fall into such a Mistake, with that Transaction recent in their Memories. By this plain State of Facts it fully appears, that from the Expiration of the Licensing Act in 1694 to the Time when the late Litigations[56] were set on Foot, Booksellers never set up a Claim to a Common Law-Right: Nor could they possibly purchase

[51] Licensing of the Press Act 1662 (13 & 14 Chas. II, c. 33); Administration of Intestates' Estates Act 1685 (1 Jas. II, c. 17), s. 15.

[52] Copyright Act 1709 (8 Anne, c. 19), s. 1.

[53] William St. Clair, *The Reading Nation in the Romantic Period* (Cambridge, 2004), 455, suggests that between 1700 and 1750 there were an average of 500 new titles published p.a. in England, which rose to 600 between 1750 and 1789. For some cautionary comments about the data in St. Clair's appendices, particularly Appendix 6, see T.F. Bonnell, 'When Book History Neglects Bibliography: Trouble with the "Old Canon" in The Reading Nation', *Studies in Bibliography*, lvii (2005–6), 243–61.

[54] The term of 21 years under Copyright Act 1709 started on 10 Apr. 1710.

[55] William Shakespeare, *The Works* (Osborn, 1747) (ESTC: N26023).

[56] This is likely to be a reference to the series of cases commonly known as the 'Battle of the Booksellers': Deazley, *On the Origin of the Right to Copy*, ch. 5.

Copy-Rights with a View to any other legal Protection, than the Statutory Right of the 8th of Q. Anne. Yet it is very certain that during this Period they did presume to buy, sell, and share Copy-Rights, that were not within the Protection of the that Statute. It is plain therefore that they did by Combination and Artifice maintain their Monopoly in Defiance of the Law.

From the Commencement of the late Litigations, when they first set up their Claim of a Property at Common Law, to its final Determination by the late Decision of the House of Lords,[57] they might probably buy Copy-Rights on a Supposition of the possibility of Succeeding in their extraordinary Claim. But in this, they can only be considered as Speculators, buying and selling a Property to which they had then first set up a Claim, the existence of which was at the very Time contested. And although three of the Judges of the Court of K.B. Gave Judgment in their Favour;[58] yet as that Judgment was strongly opposed by Sir Jof. Yates,[59] and as it was well known there would be an Appeal from it to the House of Lords;[60] they could hardly (in such Circumstances) imagine that they had a Common Law-Right. Therefore they bought and sold only on Speculation; and just as their Hopes or Fears preponderated. We do not find that any other Monopolists have ever pretended to Claim their exclusive Privelege after the Expiration of the Term granted them:[61] But have quietly resigned their Pretensions, and allowed the Advantage to lie perfectly open to the Public. Therefore the Booksellers in so combining, have set an evil Example to other Monopolists: And having been protected by the Statute in an exclusive Right for a limited Term, and after the expiration of that Term attempted to continue the Monopoly, and by Combination to prevent the Public receiving the Benefit of its expiration; presuming to buy and sell Shares of such Monopoly after such expiration; and prosecuting a Suit at Common Law in Support of it; have certainly committed a very great Offence.

Farther, some Opulent Booksellers by their Influence can greatly promote or obstruct the Sale of most new Publications; so that other Booksellers cannot venture to Purchase new Works of any Consequence: And therefore most Copies are first purchased by a few rich Monopolists. After these have made exorbitant Profits by them, then the Copies are sold in Shares to other Booksellers in order to strengthen the Interest. By which Means the Trade of purchasing Original Copies continuing in so few Hands, they by Combination may easily keep other Booksellers and Authors so ignorant of the Value of new Copies, and the Profits made by them, as to engross the chief Benefit to themselves, to the great Detriment of Authors. If an Author publishes his Work himself, or sells it to a less Considerable Bookseller; the Rich Monopolist will impede the Sale, injure the Author or Ruin the Bookseller who made the Purchase.

Other Booksellers when they thought themselves freed from the litigious and vexatious Practices of their Opulent Brethren, and were rejoicing in Hopes of following their Business

[57] *Donaldson v Beckett* (1774) *Cobbett's Parl. Hist.*, xvii, col. 953.

[58] Sir Richard Aston* (1717–78), Sir Edward Willes† (1723–87), William Murray†*, Lord Mansfield (1705–93).

[59] Sir Joseph Yates.

[60] It is not clear this is right, as the appeal brought was by writ of error: *Millar v Taylor* (1769) 4 Burr 2303 at 2408 (98 ER 201 at 257).

[61] In fact, this is misleading, as letters patent for inventions had been extended beyond the 14-year term by acts of parliament (albeit at the time of the Booksellers' Bill it had been a number of years since it had last happened, but numerous patents were extended the next year, 1775): Phillip Johnson, *Privatised Law Reform: A History of Patent Law through Private Legislation, 1620–1907* (2017), ch. 8.

securely either in printing Editions of their own, or selling cheap and saleable Editions printed by others, are at this Juncture surprized by a fresh attempt, to render their Case more grievous, because irretrievable. And if their Opponents succeed they must be content with the pittance of Profit allowed them, and that Pittance liable to be diminished, or totally withdrawn. This will most capitally affect Booksellers in the Country; who by reason of their Distance from the Capital and from each other cannot join to complain.

Finally, since the printing and selling any Books, after the expiration of the Term given by the Statute, is by the late Decision of the Lords declared to be the natural Right of the Public; it is hoped that the Legislature will not deem it Reasonable to take away that Right, in favour of a few Booksellers, who have already made large Fortunes by this illegal Monopoly.

The Author of these Remarks is firmly persuaded that he is engaged on the Side of Truth and Justice; and that such a Cause is best to be supported by keeping distinct those particular Points on which the Cause materially depends; he has therefore avoided the Question of Literary Property, as not affecting the present Case; the Mask is thrown aside, and Booksellers now appear in their proper Persons.

The only Ground on which they can Support their Application is, 1st, That when they purchased Copy-Rights, the persuasion of those Copy-Rights being acknowledged Property at Common Law, was their Inducement to make such Purchases. 2d, That the Courts of Law gave them sufficient Ground to form such an Opinion. 3d, That notwithstanding the Profits they have already made and will make by their Copies, yet they will be considerable Losers on the whole. 4th, That the Loss will be so Considerable and Universal as to justify the depriving the other Booksellers and Printers of Great-Britain of their natural Rights, and continuing the Monopoly. Now if they fail in establishing any one of these Propositions, the whole of their Pretensions must fall to the Ground; yet the Author cannot but think that the Negative of all of them is very evident: And indeed the Petitioners themselves have not attempted to make out any one of them. They present a Petition to the House of Commons, full of general Assertions; and instead of bringing Volunteer Evidence in Support of them; they abuse in the Newspapers, those who enquire into them; and don't spare even those Members of the House who call for Evidence. Nay, these Men have the controul of the very important Liberty of the Press: for while they insert Daily their own abusive Paragraphs and gross Absurdities,* their Interest with the Printers of the Newspapers (the most expensive and expeditious Vehicles of Intelligence) prevents Detection, by suppressing the Animadversions of their Opponents.

* A Paragraph was industriously inserted in several News-papers,[62] threatening the Public, that if the Monopoly was not given them, they would advance the present enormous Prices of Books still higher, during the Term allowed them by the Act.

[62]The relevant publications were: *Middlesex Journal*, 17–19 Mar. 1774; *Gazetteer*, 19 Mar. 1774; *Morning Chronicle*, 19 Mar. 1774: 'It is a notion, of all others the most ill-founded, that books will be cheaper from the effect of the late decision respecting copy-right in the House of Lords, the fact is notoriously otherwise. If Booksellers can buy for a certainty only fourteen years right, and eventually twenty-eight years right of an author, they must raise the price of the work purchased in proportion to the shortness of their statutory tenure. The public will consequently be greatly incommoded, and the price of books, now without reason complained of as extravagant, will naturally be most considerable encreased.'

Petition Committee Report

CJ, xxxiv, 588–90 (24 Mar.); John Debrett, *The History, Debates and Proceedings of Both Houses of Parliament* (Bew, 1792) (ESTC: T32171), vii, 76–83; *Cobbett's Parl. Hist.*, xvii, cols 1078–86.

{*CJ*, xxxiv, 588; *Cobbett's Parl. Hist.* xvii, col. 1078} Mr. *Feilde* reported from the Committee, to whom the Petition of the Booksellers of *London* and *Westminster*, on Behalf of themselves and others, Holders of Copy Right; and also the Petition of *John Christian Bach* and *Charles Frederick Abel*, on Behalf of themselves and several other Composers and Proprietors of Books, Works, and Compositions in Music, were severally referred; That the Committee had examined the Matter of Fact contained in the First-mentioned Petition; and had also examined the Matter of the Second-mentioned Petition; and that the Committee had directed him to report a State of the Facts contained in the First-mentioned Petition, and also the Matter of the Second-mentioned Petition, as it appeared to them, to the House; and he read the Report in his Place; [CJ: and afterwards delivered it in at the Clerk's Table: Where the same was read.]

A State of the Matter of Fact contained in the First-mentioned Petition, is as follows; *viz*.

It appeared, that by an Act of Parliament, passed in the [Eighth Year of the Reign of her late Majesty/8th of] Queen *Anne*, intitled, "An Act for the Encouragement of Learning, by vesting the Copies of printed Books in the Authors and Purchasers of such Copies, during the Times therein mentioned," it was, amongst other Things, Enacted, That, from and after the 10th {CJ, 588, c ii} Day of *April* 1710, the Authors or {*Cobbett*, 1079} Proprietors of such Books as had been already printed, should have the sole Liberty of re-printing and publishing the same for Twenty-one Years, and no longer:[63] Then your Committee proceeded to examine,

Mr. *William Johnston*,[64] who had formerly been a Bookseller, but had left off Business; who said, He entered into Business in [CJ: the Year] 1748, and left it off in *June* last; during which Time, he attended all the Capital Sales of Copy Rights: That, on his first entering into Trade, he purchased the whole Stock of Books and Copy Right of Mr. *John Clarke*,[65] for which he paid near £.3,000; above One Half of which Sum was for Copy Right: That the Sales are open to the whole Trade; but he never knew any but Booksellers apply to be admitted; that, from that Time, he continued to purchase Copy Right to the Amount of near £.10,000 more; and believed Three-fourths of the Books in Trade had his Name, as Part Proprietor, especially the Old Copies; the Rights to which are expired, according to the Act of Queen *Anne*: That many of them had been printed above Twenty-eight Years; and that he never imagined the Act of Queen *Anne* interfered with the Common Law Right; and it was most undoubtedly the general Idea of the Trade, before the late Judgment in the House of Peers,[66] that the Booksellers had a perpetual Right in the Copies they had purchased of Authors, and their Assigns, by the Common Law; and, if any Doubts had

[63] Copyright Act 1709, s. 1.

[64] William Johnston (*d.* 1804), app. 1743–8, tr. 1745–73, bookseller, 16 Ludgate Street.

[65] There was a John Clarke (*d.* 1746), tr. 1722–46, based at the Golden Ball, St Paul's Churchyard: *London Evening News*, 15–17 Mar. 1744.

[66] *Donaldson v Beckett* (1774) *Cobbett's Parl. Hist.*, xvii, col. 953.

entertained before the late Determination of the Court of King's Bench,[67] that Judgment would certainly have removed them.

Being asked, Whether he did not Claim a Copy Right in some of the Editions of the Classics in *usum Delphini*? he said, No such Right was ever claimed, so as to exclude any other Person who chose to print them: That he had purchased the Right of printing in Part some of those Classics; but never supposed that Right protected by any Law, nor considered it in any other Manner than as the Purchase of an honorary Right; which he explained to be a Maxim held by the Trade, not to re-print upon the First Proprietor: That, in the Sum of £.12,000 mentioned to be paid by him for Copy Rights, some Shares in the Classics in *usum Delphini* are included; but to the best of his Recollection such Shares do not amount in the Whole to £.100.

Being examined as to the Book called *The Tatler*,[68] he produced Sir *Richard Steele*'s[69] Assignment of the Copy right; and said, He had heard that the *Tatlers* {*Cobbett*, 1080} were originally published in Numbers as Newspapers.

Being examined as to his Title to a Share in *Cambden's Britannia*, he said, He never heard of, or saw, any Assignment from *Cambden*; that it was Bishop *Gibson*'s Edition of *Cambden*, of which he purchased the Share; that he knows not what Bookseller first printed *Gibson's Cambden*; and has bought many Shares in Books without looking into the Title.

That the Purchase Deed does not specify any Assignment from *Cambden*, nor was it requisite; that *Cambden*'s original Work was in *Latin*, and translated by Doctor *Gibson*, afterwards Bishop of *London*; that he believes there were two or three Editions printed of that Translation, and one particularly within these Four Years,[70] from a corrected Copy of the late Bishop, which Edition cost the Booksellers £.800, and the Edition before that, was eighteen Years in selling off; that the Consideration given to Mr. *Scott*,[71] for the Copy with the said Corrections, was only a few Copies of the Book, for Presents to his Friends; that he never heard there was any Assignment from *Cambden*, but has always understood that the Translator of any Work, is protected in the Right to his Translation by the Common Law.[72]

That had he imagined a Common Law Right not to exist, he should not have laid out so large a Sum on a precarious Title; nor did he recollect ever to have heard the Common Law Right talked of, till agitated in the {*CJ*, 589} Court Of King's Bench;[73] that they always took Assignments from those of whom they purchased, which they supposed to be Assignments

[67] *Millar v Taylor* (1769) 4 Burr 2303 at 2408 (98 ER 201 at 257).

[68] The *Tatler* began in 1709 and ended in 1711: collected as *Tatler* (Addison & Steele, 1709–11) (ESTC: P1919).

[69] Sir Richard Steele* (1672–1729) was the founder of numerous periodicals, including *The Spectator*. *The Guardian* was a short-lived publication from 12 Mar. 1713, lasting for 176 issues, until 1 Oct.: *The Guardian* (Tonson, 1713) (ESTC: P1756).

[70] The recent edition referred to would be *Britannia* (Bowyer, 1772) (ESTC: N15692); the first translation was *Britannia* (Collins, 1695) (ESTC: R12882), which was reprinted in 1722 (Matthews, 1722) (ESTC: T144701), 1730 (Knapton, 1730) (ESTC: N15690, N43508) and 1753 (Ware, 1753) (ESTC: T145183).

[71] George Scott, app. 1758–65; tr. up to 1777, the son-in-law of Edmund Gibson* (1669–1748), published the translation in 1772.

[72] While there had been a hint in *Burnet v Chetwood* (1721) 2 Mer 441 (35 ER 1008) that translations *might* be protected, it was only confirmed in *Wyatt v Barnard* (1814) 3 Ves. & B. 78 (35 ER 408).

[73] *Millar v Taylor* (1769) 4 Burr 2303 at 2408 (98 ER 201 at 257).

of the Common Law Right; and he produced an Assignment of the *Guardians*, from Sir *Richard Steele.*

That he never heard of either Common Law or Statute Right being inserted in an Assignment, but supposes and always understood, that when a Man sells all his Right and Title for ever, it means a Common Law Right, independent of any Statute; and that is the Idea on which the Trade has always acted in purchasing Shares of Copy Rights; and that he never saw a Term of Years mentioned in an Assignment: That he purchased his Share in the *Guardians*, at *Tonson*'s Sale, the 18th of *August* 1767,[74] and Sir *Richard Steele*'s Assignment [CJ: is] in 1713, and that he had never met with any Interruption in that Right, since he purchased it.

That he never saw or heard of any Assignment, where the Second Term of Fourteen Years, {*Cobbett*, 1081} mentioned in the Act of Queen *Anne*, was reserved to the Author;[75] but that undoubtedly he gets more Money for his Copy for Twenty-eight Years, than he would for Fourteen, and sells the Chance of the Reversion, when he assigns it for ever:[76] That all the Assignments he has ever seen, ancient and modern, run in general to the Bookseller and his Assigns, for ever; and some of them go so far as to bind themselves, their Heirs and Executors, to protect the Purchaser, his Heirs, and Executors, in the full and free Enjoyment of such Copy Right for ever: And he produced to your Committee, the Assignment of Doctor *Robertson*[77] to *Andrew Millar*, of the History of *Scotland*; which appeared to be of that Form.

Having mentioned several other Books of which he had purchased Shares, and, among others, *Dryden*'s[78] and *Locke*'s[79] Works, he said, He had no Assignment of Mr. *Dryden*, but bought it at Mr. *Tonson*'s Sale (and one of the Assignments at Mr. *Tonson*'s Sale was produced)— That he had never seen an Assignment of Mr. *Locke*'s Works, and never heard any Question about it before; but he really believes there was an Assignment, which Belief he founds upon the Practice of the Trade; for that the Person selling was never required to shew or deliver up the Original Assignment; for in the Purchase of this Property, they never inquire into the Title, if they have an Opinion of the Seller.

That it is always presumed, in the Course of Trade, that a long Possession of Copy is a Proof of Title from the Original Author; that Sums to a very large Amount have been laid out upon this Presumption; and that he, in particular, should never have laid out so large a Sum as he had done, if he had entertained any other Idea of it; and that he never inquired into the Length of Time that the Seller had been in Possession of the Copy, in case he thought the Vender to be an honest Man.

Being asked, Where a Copy Right is divided into many Shares, where a Person might learn the several Proprietors of those Shares? he answered, That when a Book is reprinted,

[74] *A Catalogue of the Copies and Shares of Copies of the Late Mr Andrew Millar* (1769) (ESTC: N490136); this is replicated and annotated in Budd, *Circulating Enlightenment*, Appendix 4.

[75] Copyright Act 1709, s. 1.

[76] Copyright Act 1709, s. 11; Lionel Bently and J.C. Ginsburg, '"The Sole Right … Shall Return to the Authors": Anglo-American Authors' Reversion Rights from the Statute of Anne to Contemporary U.S. Copyright', *Berkeley Technology Law Journal*, xxv (2010), 1475.

[77] William Robertson* (1721–93), *History of Scotland, 1542–1603* (Millar, 1759) (ESTC: T78971, T78970).

[78] John Dryden* (1631–1700).

[79] John Locke* (1632–1704).

the general Rule of the Trade is, that the Man who has the largest Share makes up the Account, and every Person claiming a Share in that Work gives in his Claim, and has his Proportion according to his Share; so that any Person wanting to know who are concerned in such a Work, by applying to the Person who makes up this Account, may get the Information; and the Person who makes up these Accounts {*Cobbett*, 1082} sends written Summonses to all whom he knows to be concerned.

That he knows of no Prosecution at Common Law, against any Person either in Town or Country, for printing any Book unprotected by the Statute of Queen *Anne*; that such Books have been printed, but there was a much easier Remedy [that/than] an Action at Law, for by filing a Bill in Chancery, the Booksellers always obtained an Injunction, and by the Answer given the Bookseller could ascertain the Damage he had sustained, as the Defendants were obliged to declare the Number they had printed: That he never made Use of this Remedy {*CJ*, 589, c ii} but once, which was in the Case of printing the *Pilgrim's Progress*, written by *John Bunyon*, which was printed by one *Luckman* of *Coventry*;[80] who delivered up all the Books, paid the Expences, and promised never to offend again: That this Affair was made up by private Agreement, *Luckman* made the Proposal, and the Witness accepted of it: That the Title he set up to the *Pilgrim's Progress*, was by Purchase of the Stock of *Clarke*[81] aforesaid, among which was assigned to the Witness, by *Clarke's* Executor, the Whole of the Copy of the *Pilgrim's Progress*, but he did not look into the Title which *Clarke* had to it; and that he can suggest no other Reason for *Luckman*'s delivering up the Copies and paying the Expences, than that he thought he was doing an unlawful Act: That it is the Custom of the Trade, as he always understood, to prosecute Offenders, in Cases of Piracy of Copies, at their own private Expence; and that the Witness himself prosecuted at his own Expence in Two Instances, the first about Eighteen Years ago, and the other about Three or Four.[82]

That he never consulted any Counsel in making the Purchases of Copy Right, but laid out his Money, upon the general Opinion of the Common Law Right.

Being asked, Whether, in the course of Trade, the undisturbed Possession of a Copy Right, by any Bookseller, has not been deemed such a Presumption of an Assignment from the Original Author, as to warrant Persons to lay out their Money in the Purchase of it? he said, He always was of that Opinion, and never would have laid out the Sum he did, if he had had any other Idea of it.

That when an Author chuses originally that his Name should be concealed, no other Proof than Possession can be had of his Assignment; or if the Author chuses to make a voluntary Present of his Work to {*Cobbett*, 1083} a Bookseller, it would appear very inconsistent to ask such a Thing; and upon the Prevalence of such Presumptions, original Assignments are not always carefully kept, and transmitted from Hand to Hand, as Titles, when the Transaction has been a long Time past, the Nature of the Trade not admitting of it.

[80]Thomas Luckman (*d.* 1784), app. 1744. The book was John Bunyan* (1628–88), *The Pilgrim's Progress* (Sketchley and Luckman, 1769) (ESTC: T58376).

[81]John Clarke, South Entrance Royal Exchange.

[82]It is not clear to which cases he was referring. He was a co-plaintiff in four chancery lawsuits: *Dodsley v Kinnersley* (1761) Amb 403; *Rivington v Donaldson* (1771) (TNA, C 12/1323/15); *Beckett v Donaldson* (1771) (TNA, C 12/13219); *Osbourne v Donaldson* (1765) 2 Eden 327 (28 ER 924).

That, had a Doubt existed in the Mind of the Witness of the Principle of the Common Law Right, it would have been entirely removed by the frequent Injunctions granted, unappealed from, and submitted to; and he certainly should have been the more inclined to lay out his Money in Copy Right, and to have given larger Sums for such Purchases, upon the Authority of such Injunctions.

Being asked, If he knew any One Injunction which turns upon the Claim of Common Law Right, independent of the Statute? he said, He recollected but One, and that was *Tonson* and *Walker*,[83] in regard to *Milton's Paradise Lost*:[84] That he never took a Lawyer's Opinion of the Common Law Right, because he thought it unnecessary; and never heard the Question agitated till it came into the Court of King's Bench, and then Three, if not Four, of the Judges were clear as to the Common Law Right; there were Two Causes agitated in that Court, One, *Tonson* against *Collins*,[85] when Three Judges sat there, Two of whom are dead, and One retired (Mr. Justice *Dennison*, Sir *Michael Foster*, and Sir *Eardly Wilmot*)[86] and the Opinion of the Court then was in Favour of the Common Law Right; and in the Case of *Millar* and *Taylor*,[87] in the Year 1769, a Judgment was obtained in Favour of such Right: That, in the said Case of *Tonson* and *Collins*,[88] the Court of King's Bench did not proceed to Judgment, because (as he hath been informed within these Two or Three Days, and collects from Sir *James Burrough*'s Reports)[89] Lord *Mansfield* declared, in giving Judgment in the Case of *Millar* and *Taylor*, that the Reason of the Court's not proceeding to Judgment, in the Case of *Tonson* and *Collins*, did not arise from any Difference of Opinion in the Judges of that Court, but because they understood that it was a collusive Action.

{*CJ*, 590} That, upon his quitting Business, he assigned his Property in Copy Rights to his Son, on Condition he should be jointly bound with himself to pay all his Creditors; who, not doubting of the Validity of the Security, readily consented to it. Upon which the Copy Rights were valued by Messers. *Longman* and *Cadell*,[90] Two Booksellers of the {*Cobbett*, 1084} first Reputation, at between 8 and £.9,000; and the Witness believes they would have sold for that Sum in *June* last, when he quitted Business; but that since the Determination in the House of Lords[91] they would not sell for a Fourth Part of that Sum; and had there remained a Doubt in the Mind of the Witness of a legal Property in those Copies, exclusive of the Statute of Queen *Anne*, he should never have involved a Son, who had a genteel Fortune left him by his Grandfather, to take them as a Security for any Debts the Witness owed.

That if Relief is not granted in the present Session of Parliament, so many Books will be printed, both in *London* and the Country, as will make it impossible to grant the Sufferers Redress, without Injury to the other Publishers.

[83] *Tonson v Walker* (1752) 3 Swan 672 (36 ER 1017).

[84] John Milton, *Paradise Lost* (Walker, 1751) (ESTC: T133928).

[85] *Tonson v Collins* (1762) 1 Black W 301 (96 ER 169).

[86] Sir Thomas Denison* (1699–1765), Sir Michael Foster* (1689–1763), Sir John Eardley Wilmot* (1709–92).

[87] *Millar v Taylor* (1769) 4 Burr 2303 (98 ER 201).

[88] *Tonson v Collins* (1762) 1 Black W 301 (96 ER 169).

[89] It had not yet been reported: see reference in *Millar v Taylor* (1769) 4 Burr 2303 at 2354, 2407, 2400 (98 ER 201 at 229, 253, 258).

[90] Thomas Longman, Thomas Caddell* (1742–1802); also see Charles Longman, *The House of Longman, 1724–1800* (1936).

[91] *Donaldson v Beckett* (1774) *Cobbett's Parl. Hist.*, xvii, col. 953.

Being asked, What had reduced the Value of the Copy Rights, between the Time of his purchasing them and transferring them to his Son? he said, That many Circumstances contributed to reduce the Value of Copies: Most Books are capable of Improvement, in all Arts and Sciences; that a Copy this Day may be worth £.500, which, in a Twelvemonth, may not be worth £.5; because other Works of a like Nature come out with Improvements which render the old Books on the same Subject of no Value; and a new Edition of a Work, with Improvements, after the Purchase made, lessens the Value of the Copy for a Time.

Being asked, Whether, when Booksellers buy a Copy Right, they [don't/do not], at the same Time, buy all the Copies then printed off? he said, They frequently do, and frequently not; but they never re-print any Copy under that Predicament, until the Books remaining are sold off.

Being asked the Question, he said, That when he sold his Property in Copy Right to his Son, it was known among the Trade, that there was an Appeal depending[92] before the House of Lords, upon the Point,[93] Whether there was any Literary Property at Common Law? but that the Witness, and the Trade in general, was so well confirmed by the Determination of the Court of King's Bench, that he thought there was little or no Risque at all; for, that had such a Doubt existed in his Mind, he could have sold that Property some Years ago, for nearly as much, if not the Whole, it cost him. And that he knows not of any Sale of Copy Rights derived under Authors at Common Law, since the Determination in the House of Lords; nor of any within Six Months previous to that Decision, except his own.

{*Cobbett*, 1085} Being asked, Whether, in his Opinion, if Relief is not granted in consequence of this Application, there is not a Danger of valuable Books being out of Print, from a dread of Competition by the Multitude of Copies that may be printed by different Booksellers, in different parts of the Kingdom? he said, That would certainly be the Consequence as to elegant Editions.

That he thinks, a Month before the late Decision in the House of Lords, he could have disposed of his Property in Copy Rights for a very inconsiderable Loss.

Being asked, Why it was not the Custom of those who are possessed of Copy Right, to enter them in the Books of the Stationers Company?[94] he said, He could only answer for himself, that he never thought the Penalties prescribed by the Act of the Eighth of Queen *Anne*[95] were worth contending for, as a much shorter and more complete Relief might be had, by filing a Bill in Chancery; that the Trade of a Booksellers is circumscribed by no Law, nor any Bye-Law of the Stationers Company; and every Man that pleases may set up in the Business, without an Hour's Servitude to the Trade; {*CJ*, 590, c ii} and the Wholesale Booksellers in *London*, solicit the Country Booksellers, to supply them with Books.

Then the Agent for the Petitioners produced to your Committee, Copy of a Judgment of the Court of King's Bench, in the Cause of *Millar* against *Taylor*, in the Seventh Year of

[92]The appeal was started by the lodging of the petition on 10 Dec. 1772: *LJ*, xxxiii, 476.

[93]This would have been *Donaldson v Beckett* (1774) *Cobbett's Parl. Hist.*, xvii, col. 953.

[94]As to the proportion registered, at a later period (1815–42) see *Libraries and the Book Trade*, ed. Robin Myers, Michael Harris and Giles Mandelbrote (New Castle, DE, 2000), 51–84.

[95]Forfeit, destruction, and one penny per sheet (half to the crown and half to the finder): Copyright Act 1709, s. 1.

the Reign of His present Majesty, in the Year of our Lord 1766; whereby it appeared, that *Millar* recovered against *Taylor* 1*s*. Damages, and £.60 Costs.[96]

Mr. *John Wilkie*,[97] Clerk to the Booksellers Public Auctions, produced to your Committee, an Account, whereby it appeared, that the Sum of £.49,981 5s had been laid out at such Public Auctions, since the Year 1755, in Money for Copy Rights; in which Account the Money laid out by private Contracts, is not included. Then,

There was produced to your Committee, Copy of a Judgment of the House of Lords, upon the Appeal of *Alexander Donaldson* and *John Donaldson*, and the Answer of *Thomas Becket, Peter Abraham De Hondt, John Rivington*, and others, Respondents;[98] whereby it is ordered and adjudged, by the Lords Spiritual and Temporal, in Parliament assembled, that the said Decree complained of in the said Appeal be reversed.

In Support of the Allegations of the Second mentioned Petition,

Mr. *Augustine Greenland*,[99] informed **{***Cobbett*, 1086**}** your Committee, That Doubts have arisen, whether the Right granted by the Act of the Eighth of Queen *Anne*, to the Authors of Books, extends to the Authors of Books or Compositions in Music: That Mess. *Longman, Lukie*,[100] and Company, and one *Thoroughgood*,[101] have published the Compositions of Masters in Music, apprehending such Compositions were not within the Intention of the said Act of the Eighth of Queen *Anne*; but that the Witness had not taken the Opinion of Counsel upon it.

Committee Evidence Observations

Observations on the Evidence given before the Committee for proving the Allegations in the Booksellers Petition, 'Petitions' {12–18}.

{12} *OBSERVATIONS on the EVIDENCE given before the COMMITTEE for proving the Allegations in the Booksellers Petition.*

ALTHOUGH a witness before the *House of Commons* cannot be examined on oath; yet the solemnity of the circumstance, and the important consideration, that by such evidence the legislature is guided in framing the laws for the community, would naturally lead us to expect the strictest adherence to truth: And every departure from it will be viewed in the same light as if such evidence was given in a court of judicature. Nay, in this case, the testimony of one person was intended for the foundation of a bill that must materially affect us as a literary, free, and commercial people; surely then we had the justest ground to expect

[96] *Millar v Taylor* (1769) 4 Burr 2303 at 2309 (98 ER 201 at 205).

[97] John Wilkie (*d*. 1785), app. 1743–50, tr. 1753–85, bookseller, 71 St Paul's Churchyard.

[98] *Cobbett's Parl. Hist*., xvii, col. 953.

[99] Augustine Greenland, attorney, Newman Street and Oxford Street, London: *Browne's General Law-List* (2nd edn, Whieldon and Co, 1777) (ESTC: T85768), 22.

[100] Lukey was a music seller in partnership with Thomas Longman, app. 1745–52, tr. 1754–96. The shop was based at the 'Harp and Crown' at 26 Cheapside.

[101] This was Henry Thorowgood, music seller, 6 North-Piazza, Royal-Exchange: Frank Kidson, *British Musical Publishers* (1900), 131 (he may have moved location by 1770 so this might not have been his address at the material time).

a plain, open, and candid state of facts. How far that witness has answered this expectation will appear.

He says, *he attended all the sales of copy-right from* 1748 *to last June; that those sales are open to every man who sells books, and no man of the trade is excluded.* The contrary to this is known to every *Bookseller.* Fifty of the trade have signed the counter-petition, not one of whom are allowed that privilege. No *Country Bookseller,* no, not those of *Oxford* or *Cambridge,* are allowed at their capital sales to bid for a share, even of so much as a *Delphin Classic.* A man of substance, who was thirty years in the business, was never admitted but once. Not only are many refused admittance, but, after invitation, if any bulky trader thinks proper to object to them, they are turned out, sometimes three or four at a time. One was turned out because it was reported he had sold a copy of a pirated edition of *George Barnwell;*[102] another, because it was said he was in possession of a Scotch printed book; and another, because they did not like his method of trade; some, **{13}** because they could be easily crushed, and others, because they could not. A bookseller of credit is ready to prove that admission was denied him because he refused to pay 5*l.* for it, and to be bound in a penalty of 500*l.* not to print any book claimed by them. And indeed, exclusion from or admission to those sales has been the principal engine employed by them to defend their monopoly.

The witness[103] talks very pompously of a common-law right; he says, *that he understood, and that it was the general idea of the trade, that the act of the 8th Queen Anne interfered not with that common law right,* yet afterwards he was forced to own *that be never heard the common law right talked of among them, or mentioned at any sale of copy-rights, until it was agitated in the Court of K.B.* he says, *that had he supposed a common law right did not exist, he would not have laid out so largely on a precarious title;* yet owns *he made the purchases without inquiring into the common law title,* or indeed into any title whatever.[104] He claims a property in *Bishop Gibson's Camden,*[105] yet knows not of any assignment from either *Camden* or the *Bishop.* He claims a share in *Locke's* Works;[106] yet being asked if he ever heard there was an assignment from *Locke,* he appears to be surprized at such a strange question, and declares *he never heard it asked before*: and adds, that *he never knew, in all the purchases he ever made or was concerned in, that the person selling was required to deliver up,* or even to *shew, the original assignment.* He says, he has a property in three-fourths of the books in the trade; and owns that they have been pirated; yet he never knew of a prosecution at common law against any of the offenders. The reason he gives for which is, that, by filing a bill in Chancery, they always got an injunction. One would imagine that this mode of proceeding was very familiar with them: Yet this man who claims property in three-fourths of the copies, and has been in the trade twenty-five years, being unfortunately called on to name the books on which he has proceeded in this his favourite method, replies, that he never attempted it but on one, *The Pilgrim's Progress.*[107] And what is very remarkable, this only copy that he attempted to defend, he had no claim to, even if the question of an *Author*'s claim to a perpetuity had been established: for being asked what

[102] George Lillo, *The London Merchant* (J. Gray, 1731) (ESTC: T41160).

[103] William Johnston.

[104] *CJ*, xxxiv, 588–9.

[105] William Camden* (1551–1623), *Britannia*, trans. Edmund Gibson (3rd edn, Ware, 1753) (ESTC: T145183).

[106] John Locke.

[107] The first edition was John Bunyan, *The Pilgrim's Progress from this World* (Nath Ponder, 1678) (ESTC: R12339, R27237).

is his claim, he informs us that *the executor of one Mr. Clark assigned him a list of copy-rights, of which this was one*: and although, as he says, they assigned him the whole copy-right; yet an assignment from the *Author* was never thought of, but deemed quite superfluous by these *worthy Gentlemen*. Nor, indeed, is there the least shadow of a proof that the *Author* ever sold it at all. But I grant it is not without reason he is so fond of this mode of proceeding, for it answered his purpose effectually: he says the *Country Bookseller* whom he prosecuted, terrified at the thoughts of a law-suit, "*delivered up all the copies, paid the expences, and promised never to offend again*." Yet this witness says he never so much as *threatened any Man*. I am somewhat loth to give the name to this transaction which it so evidently deserves. But if an action will not lie for the redress of this injury, I heartily with it would.

One bookseller was repeatedly threatened for printing *Joe Miller's Jests*;[108] but on his promising to reprint it no more, they graciously forgave him. No less than four booksellers were harassed by them for selling a *Song Book* in which was inserted some *Songs* taken from a play: although that is the usual method of forming such collections; and the same songs were accordingly inserted in similar publications, by some of the petitioners themselves; and had before been published even in magazines. Nay these very songs were purloined by the author of the play from prior publications. This affair cost one of the defendants *four* **{14}** *score pounds*, and contributed to make another a bankrupt. A poor printer was run to the expence of 117l. only for printing a play. And indeed the object of these prosecutions have been usually to prevent the sale of the most trivial articles, such as *a jest book, a song book, or a play*, unless they had been previously purchased of them. Their attempts were founded on the ignorance and poverty of those whom they attacked: and accordingly the terms of accommodation were different with different people, for the same pretended offence. Those who were poor they deprived of their property without any compensation whatever: but of one man, whom they could not intimidate because he had substance as well as spirit to support the contest, they bought the copies without hostility. Let the publick judge from these facts what dependence the booksellers had on a legal claim: and let the following case be withal considered, in which, having law on their side, they prosecuted it with rigour. A young bookseller happened to buy a few pirated books; and although he repeatedly offered the prosecutors to make affidavit, that when he bought them he was totally ignorant of their being prohibited by law, that he would not have bought them if he had known it, and that he never before was possessed of pirated books to the value of 20s. and further offered to give security never to buy or sell any in future; yet all these circumstances were pleaded in vain: They prosecuted him;[109] but not on their pretended common law right, not on the Statute of Queen Anne, but they multiplied actions on a penal statute, not enacted in favour of authors or booksellers, because that the most oppressive mode of proceeding. It cost him at last about 100l. and during the litigation, they insulted him with menaces of 1500l. expence, and utter ruin. Of these and many other similar facts proof is ready. Various other oppressions have they been guilty of, well known in the trade, though legal proof of them may not be so easily obtained.

These transactions thoroughly explain the reason why these *Gentlemen* think it quite superfluous to inquire about assignments from *Authors*. By means of splitting copies into

[108] The first edition of this was Joe Miller (1684–1738), *Joe Miller's Jests or the Wit Vade-melum* (Reid, 1739) (ESTC: T124768).

[109] It has not been possible to identify any details.

shares, they have so interwoven their interests that they are become a powerful combined body; and have found it very easy to intimidate the ignorant and the poor: They have rung the changes on *pirates, proprietors, injunctions, and exclusion from the sales*; and in *them* they have found sufficient security to make their purchases without regard to *authors* or to *law*. And indeed it is a most alarming consideration, that a great part of the evidence of the witness is introduced to discountenance every inquiry whether they derive from *authors* or not. In order to obtain an exclusive property in *every* copy which they have *claimed, bought*, and *sold* amongst them, merely on that account: he says, when a *bookseller* is in possession of a copy, and offers it to sale, they consider possession, merely as such, a sufficient ground to purchase: And do not consider how long the seller has been in possession if they think him an *honest* man: And that they always consider each other as *honest* men is evident, for he declares he never knew an instance of the seller being required to produce an assignment from the *author*; and says, the *undisturbed possession of a copy-right by a bookseller is deemed a presumption of an assignment from the original author.* It is unfortunate that he forgot himself so much in the beginning of his evidence as to give up the *Delphin Classics* as being only honorary copies: For though there is no absolute proof that *John Bunyan*,[110] or *Lewis XIV.*[111] did sell to the *London* booksellers the *Pilgrim's Progress*, or the *Delphin Classics*; yet, as they have had undisturbed possession, **{15}** that ought to be deemed a presumption, that such assignments were actually made, though not now at hand to produce; for he informs us the nature of the trade will not admit of preserving the original assignments.

But the truth is, the distinction of honorary and other copies was only a device in order to pass muster: for those he calls honorary copies are sold indiscriminately with others, without any distinction, and for as valuable considerations, in proportion to their size, as almost any copy-rights whatsoever; nay, this very man drops his distinction by owning he had them as well as the others by *conveyance*. But, indeed, I will venture to affirm, that all old copies were, before the late litigations, never considered by them in any other light than as *honorary* copies, in their prostituted sense of that word. The word *honour* must certainly have a very extensive signification to be applied to such transactions as these. But however, it is only *London* booksellers for whom they claim the privilege of assuming copy-rights to themselves by re-printing imported books. Mr. *Richardson*[112] some years ago raised a great clamour against the *Dublin* booksellers charging them with a breach of honour in re-printing his novels in *Ireland*. Thus their ideas of *honour* suddenly change on being applied to a *London* or *Dublin* bookseller.

If an author does not sell his copy, these gentlemen seem to infer that the copy does not thereby become common, but is the property of the bookseller who published the first edition: although the author never made a deed of gift, or ever appeared to have any such intention.

He says, it was the common opinion of the booksellers that they had a perpetual right, That the opulent *London* booksellers had an intention to enjoy their monopoly for ever, if they could possibly support it by combination, oppression, or any other means, is very true: And that they gave more for shares of old copies when they found out the method

[110]John Bunyan, the author of *Pilgrim's Progress*.

[111]Louis XIV (1638–1715), king of France, 1643–1715.

[112]Joseph Richardson (*d.* 1763), app. 1748, tr. 1759–63, 26 Paternoster Row; as to the incident see R.C. Cole, *Irish Booksellers and English Writers 1740–1800* (1986), 64.

of bringing injunctions on books to which they had no right, and to which their legal title had never been established. But that booksellers did ever, in reality, believe that they had an indisputable legal claim to a perpetuity in their copies, is what few will credit. The success they met with in terrifying the poor booksellers and printers, by the forms of law, encouraged them at length to push the matter rather too far: They had called themselves *proprietors* so long, that they began to hope the courts of law, nay the legislature itself, would not be so impolite as to contradict them; they had the temerity to bring their cause to a legal discussion; and by a concurrence of particular circumstances, they had some small prospect of success. But when their cause came to be fully investigated, and finally determined, their claim was rejected with the indignation it deserved.

It is with an ill grace such men as these plead for compassion: It is hoped the legislature of this kingdom will rather have compassion on the poorer booksellers, and not leave them at the mercy of their opulent oppressors, deprive a number of people of a lawful trade whereby they may support themselves and families, and countenance an imposition on the public, in order to gratify a junto of *honorary* monopolists. They affect to make a rueful clamour of their loss and calamitous situation. As to real loss, this only witness pretends to nothing like it. He has long claimed those copies, received the advantage of many editions, and has undoubtedly long since re-imbursed himself with large profits. And although he claims property in three-fourths of the books in the trade; yet when asked that material question, by which copies he has not been compensated; he **{16}** mentions only two; yet these gentlemen are not content to escape with the gains of successive harvests with impunity, for oppressing their poorer brethren, and for imposition upon the publick.

Through the whole of his evidence, he appears very fearful of coming to particulars. When he is asked for a list of the copies he claims, he replies, that he did not think it necessary to bring one: and truly he had not time to make one out; though it can hardly be imagined it would have required an hour's time. Yet cautious as he is, enough may be gathered from his evidence to confirm the general opinion, that they have a right to but very few of their copies, even on the ground of the judgment of the court of King's Bench. And yet had that judgment been confirmed, it would have screened them effectually. No assignments ever produced, no titles ever made out, but locked up in obscurity, they would have possessed their claims undisturbed.

Perhaps he may say, though he has himself reaped profit, yet his son will be a considerable loser, having so recently made the purchase. There is something very remarkable in this transaction. He says no copy-rights were sold within six months preceding the decision except his own: Yet this man declares, he should have thought himself unworthy of existence had he not been of opinion that his son had an *undoubted permanent property in them*. It is very odd that he and his son should have no doubt of the permanency of this property, when they knew the appeal was depending; and when he knew, as appears by his own account, that this commodity had not been marketable for six months before. He informs us that this 9000l.[113] copy-right was valued by two gentlemen of the first reputation in the trade: yet it afterwards comes out, that he set the value himself, and asked them if they thought he had over-rated them: He says; without making an exact calculation, they answered no. He does not indeed say they made any calculation whatever: Nay it does not appear that he

[113] *CJ*, xxxiv, 590.

even shewed them a list: for when he is asked for a list of his copies, he says he had not time to make one out: which surely implies that he had not one in his possession. But perhaps it was mislaid; perhaps lists of copies, and assignments from authors may be equally difficult to preserve. Yet after all, that so valuable a property should be sold at such a time, under such circumstances, and in such a manner, is a little strange. But it may be said this was a transaction between a father and a son, and should not be examined with critical precision. It is somewhat singular that he should choose to quit business, and sell all his stock, at this peculiarly critical period. I wish (unless it was too great a secret) he had informed us of his motives for taking such a resolution, in the midst of a flourishing trade, and as capable of managing it as ever. The world will certainly pity him: as it must undoubtedly be an inconceivable grief to him to have been the innocent cause of bringing his son into such a situation: especially since he tells us, he could have disposed of his copies with very inconsiderable loss, even within a month preceding the decision. Surely so affectionate a father will not take advantage of an unexpected accident, but consider that himself ought to bear the loss, who has received the profit.

He infers from *Lord Mansfield's* words, that in the case of *Millar* against *Collins*,[114] the judges were unanimous in favour of literary property. His Lordship's words prove it not: for although it was not on account of any difference of opinion, but because a collusion is discovered, that judgment was not given; yet such a difference might exist; or the judges might be unanimous on the other side: indeed **{17}**, so far were they from having resolved on their judgment, that they ordered the case to be referred to the Exchequer Chamber for the opinion of the twelve judges: And it is generally supposed that Sir J. E. *Wilmot*[115] (the only surviving puisne judge, who was then on that Bench)[116] is against the perpetuity. But whatever was the opinion of the judges at that time, it could not influence booksellers in their purchases; for it is not pretended that any mention of that opinion had been made till *Lord Mansfield* touched upon it, as above, in 1769, in the case of *Millar* against *Taylor*;[117] and it does not appear that this chosen witness himself never understood his Lordship's words to be declarative of such unanimity till the very day preceding his examination.

It appears, from this gentleman's evidence, that authors have always been induced by booksellers to assign together with the first term, the second term of fourteen years given them by the clause[118] inserted in their favour by that patron of learning and merit, the great *Lord Sommers*.[119] To be sure, it cannot absolutely be said, that booksellers give nothing for the reversion of the second fourteen years; but I believe it would hardly turn the scale in a bargain. Booksellers buy with a view to immediate profit; and do not attend to such remote and uncertain contingencies. And if an author was first to sell his copy for fourteen years, and immediately afterwards offer the reversion of the second term for sale, he would soon be convinced of the truth of what I say. The legislature, by inserting that clause, did, no

[114]This must mean *Tonson v Collins* (1762) 1 Black W 301 (96 ER 169).

[115]Sir John Eardley Wilmot.

[116]He was chief justice of common pleas from 20 Aug. 1766 and resigned on 24 Jan. 1771: *Judges of England*, x. 1.

[117]*Millar v Taylor* (1769) 4 Burr 2303 (98 ER 201).

[118]Copyright Act 1709, s. 1.

[119]John, Lord Somers.

doubt, intend to incite authors to aim at permanent reputation, and that they should reap, in the decline of life, the reward of their literary labours. Had parliament intended that the whole should have been the subject of immediate sale, they never would have made such a nugatory distinction, but have added two or three years to the first term, which would have answered the purpose, I believe, much better. If then booksellers compel authors to sell the reversion by refusing to purchase on any other terms, they greatly injure them: And if they persuade them that it is for their advantage to sell both terms together, they grossly deceive them: For although an author cannot reap any considerable advantage by the sale of the second term,[120] with the first; yet many works, when their reputation is established, will afford their authors a comfortable support; and when the work is well known by a sale of fourteen years, the author will not be necessitated to dispose of the second term, from an apprehension of the booksellers suppressing the work, and obstructing its sale. And I am persuaded that, were copies sold according to the meaning of that act, for only fourteen years, and then to return to authors, it would be more advantageous to them than a perpetuity to be disposed of by them on the first publication.

Kindness to authors has long been the foible of booksellers; and whether they feed them or starve them, it is all for their good. They have, for twenty years past, been eagerly prosecuting suits at law, raising contributions, disbursing large sums of money, and practising numberless artifices, all to defend the rights of AUTHORS. And now they are canvassing among *Authors*, persuading them, that it is *their* interest to concur with and countenance the *present attempt*, and yet *Authors* have, in reality, no more concern in it than *Taylors*.

The act of the 8th of Queen Anne[121] was framed, introduced, and passed, upon mature consideration, by men who will ever be accounted ornaments to this nation and to literature. The principles on which it is founded are wise and just, and, with a few amendments, it may, without extending the monopoly, **{18}** be rendered far more beneficial to authors than all this *tender anxiety* of their *generous patrons*, the *Petitioning Booksellers*.

Goldsmith's Hints

Hints upon the Booksellers' petition written by the late Dr Goldsmith, in 'Petitions'.

{18} *The following HINTS upon the Booksellers Petition were written by the late Dr. GOLDSMITH.*[122] *The Editor makes no Addition to the Text, but subjoins a few Notes.*

1*mo*, The booksellers, in the 8th of Queen Anne, made the same complaints for an extension of their rights in old copies that they do at present, and they obtained redress, being granted 21 years in their old copies, while they had but fourteen in the new.[123] They now again petition for a further right in many of the same old copies, having had twenty-one years in them already. They may thus go on petitioning eternally.*

[120] That is, the right granted by Copyright Act 1709, s. 11.

[121] Copyright Act 1709 (8 Anne, c. 19).

[122] Oliver Goldsmith (1730–4 Apr. 1774).

[123] Copyright Act 1709, s. 1.

2*do*, The booksellers alledge that they bought copy under a notion of its being perpetual property. This is not true. Their claims have been almost perpetually in litigation. Thomas Osborne,[124] a bookseller, in the year 1749, printed Shakespeare, Milton, and some other copies, that were exclusively claimed by other booksellers, but they dared not come to a trial with him. They bought up some of his copies, and allowed him a pension for his profits in the rest.

3*tio*, The booksellers alledge that, in consequence of the decision and decree in their favour in the King's Bench, in the year 1769,[125] they have been induced to make large purchases which are now reduced of no value. This is false. The great quantity of purchase was at Tonson's and other sales before that decree; and so far were copies from being enhanced in their value after the decree, that, at Millar's sale, which followed soon after, some actually sold worse. The truth is, many of the capital booksellers, who are now the principal petitioners, had made a fraudulent purchase at Tonson's sale, previous to the public auction, and thus puffed up the price of the copies upon the little booksellers, and so pocketed the surplus.†

---

*This is a very just and important observation. When the booksellers claims were settled by parliament, in 1710, it was, no doubt, as little expected then that they would revive them 50 years after, as any person can now affect to think they will not again revive them hereafter; and if the present bill should pass, their claims may be extended beyond the term to be limited, and resume them with, at least, as much probability of success as at present. Some future lawyers may treat an act of the present parliament with little ceremony. The murmurs of the present London booksellers may, by their successors, be heightened into loud execrations of the late decision, they may stigmatize it without ceremony, as cruel, and attribute it to the jarring feuds and private pique of lawyers, revive the cause, in hope of receiving that justice then that was before denied them; and perhaps present another petition, humbly confiding in the justice and mercy of a future parliament.

†There is *another* circumstance of this transaction, with which the Doctor was unacquainted, but is well known among the trade, although *the nature* of it required that it should be kept as *secret* as possible.

{19} 4*to*, The petition comes before the House as from all the booksellers. About two-thirds of them have signed it; but (except in one or two instances) not above eight or nine wealthy men, who are grown rich enough to despise those learned men, by whom they have acquired their fortunes, are actually concerned.

5*to*, The possessing an unjust monopoly for a series of years, and the employing many fraudulent means to prevent the discussion of a pretended right, are wretched claims to the compassion of parliament.

6*to*, There are many booksellers and printers actually employed at present, particularly in the country, in printing those copies which the legislature have given them an undisputed right in. What must become of these if the London booksellers obtain a continuance of their monopoly? We must not shew compassion to one set of men whose claims to pity are fallacious or doubtful* at the expence of others whose claims are certain and undisputed.

7*mo*, Where do their claims begin, or end? If they are to have a longer term in all books which they have purchased at each other's sales, then the persons who have, at a large expence, purchased the Delphin Classics have as good a right to compassion as the purchaser

[124] This should be John Osborne: see Part I: Chapter 4: The Honorary Monopoly.

[125] *Millar v Taylor* (1769) 4 Burr 2303 (98 ER 201).

of Stackhouse,[126] or Dyche's spelling book.[127] The one paid his money for what he supposed to be copy as well as the other, and nobody will say the publisher of the Delphin Classics has any colourable claim.

8*vo*, The booksellers talk of ruin, but they know better. In fact, that species of trade which they possess by occupancy will still continue to be theirs in a great measure. Their first right in the Delphin Classics was by occupancy, and they have continued in the undisturbed possession of it ever since. Most of the copies which they now possess will still continue to be theirs without rivalship. That aid which they have hitherto given and will continue to give each other, will sufficiently place them above compassion, without any assistance from parliament.

9*no*, The principal operation of the late decision in the House of Lords[128] will be to set the country printers and booksellers at work in printing school books, such as spelling-books, and some other small, but necessary, publications; and it is but just to give country tradesmen their share in every branch of commerce.[†]

10*mo*, The booksellers affect, in their petition, to espouse the interest of authors. Nothing can be more opposite to the interest of modern literature than the tenor of their request.

To these arguments may be added, the unusual method of attempting, by an *ex post facto* law to reverse a judicial decree, and which most probably the legislature will never submit to.

---

[*]Neither the nature nor merit of their claims are in the least doubtful, and the Doctor would hardly have used so tender an expression, had he been acquainted with all the secrets of the trade, and lived to see the farther discussion of this question.

[†] It is to be hoped, if the bill depending does not pass, the late decision will be attended with more important consequences; it certainly will, unless the booksellers actually possess that power which they boast, *of being able to give law to the trade*; but, certainly, a competition, advantageous to the public, will be introduced, and, even if they do what they boast, *viz*. Undersell every one that prints against them, still the public will reap the advantage; and at the least they will be necessitated to print *better*, if not cheaper, editions of old copies than they have hitherto done.

Edinburgh Booksellers' Petition[129]

'Petitions' {7–8}; *Public Advertiser*, 25 Apr.; *Caledonian Mercury*, 27 Apr. (*CM*); *CJ*, xxxiv, 665 and *Votes 1774*, pp. 523–4 (21 Apr.).

[Variant 1: 'Petitions' (Pet) and the *Caledonian Mercury* (CM); Variant 2: *Public Advertiser* (PA)]

{7} *To the Honourable the Commons of Great Britain, in Parliament assembled,*

[126]Thomas Stackhouse, *A Compleat History of the Holy Bible* (1st edn, Edlin, 1733) (ESTC: N55521).

[127]Thomas Dyche* (*d.* 1727), *A Guide to the English Tongue* (1st edn, 1707) (ESTC: N6605).

[128]*Donaldson v Beckett* (1774) *Cobbett's Parl. Hist.*, xvii, col. 953.

[129]There are two variants of the petition, albeit the differences are very minor. The first was published in 'Petitions' and in the *Caledonian Mercury*, the second was in the *Public Advertiser*. The *Caledonian Mercury* includes the opening words 'The following is the petition mentioned in our book as having been presented to the House of Commons, on Thursday last, by the Right Honourable Sir Lawrence Dundas, on behalf of the Booksellers, &c of Edinburgh.'

The Humble PETITION of the BOOKSELLERS, PRINTERS, and others (whose Dependence is on the Trade of BOOKSELLING and PRINTING) residing in the City of EDINBURGH,

[SHEWETH, / setting forth that the Petitioners observe]
THAT your petitioners observing, from the votes of this Honourable House,[130] that[131] leave has been given to bring in a bill for relief of the booksellers in London, Westminster, and others, by vesting the copies of printed books in the purchasers of such copies from authors, or their assigns, for a time to be therein limited, and being informed that the aim of the London booksellers, since the failure of their late attempt to gain a dangerous and perpetual monopoly at common law, is now to obtain an exercise for a limited time of the same exclusive privilege, beyond the terms of the act of Queen Anne, and to the great prejudice of [Not PA: your] petitioners, they think it their duty to submit to the [Not PA: Honourable] House, That the special indulgence prayed for by the London booksellers, will, if granted, be highly injurious to the rights of all who, in this part of the kingdom, are concerned in bookselling, the paper manufacture, the art of printing, and other branches therewith connected. [PA: and that]

In the paper-mills alone, belonging to this city, there are many hundreds of persons employed;[132] and the booksellers, bookbinders and printers [here/there] are still more numerous, who will all be most materially affected, and some of them ruined by the consequences of the bill, should it pass into a law, and should it prevent them from reprinting English books when the terms of the act of Queen Anne are expired. Few or no compositions, even of Scotch authors, are published originally in Scotland.[133] [Your/and the] petitioners have hitherto lived chiefly by republishing, when permitted by the act of Queen Anne; and their business must be given up altogether if any further monopoly is conferred upon the London booksellers.[PA: and that]

Being at a distance from the capital, they have no means of knowing with certainty the nature of the relief which is prayed for by those who have applied for the bill; but if, from the supposed hardship of a particular case, or the consideration of a single inconvenience, [this/the] House should be led into a general measure of enlarging the terms of the statute, [PET/CM: they beg leave to say, that] such an extension of the monopoly will be the ruin of many families in Scotland, as well as prejudicial to the community at large.

[Your petitioners will be forgiven to add,/and] That literary property at common law never existed even in idea in Scotland. The attempt, [PA: made] some time ago [Not PA:, made] to introduce it into Scotland, was received with universal disapprobation; and after a full discussion of its merits, was over-ruled by a judgment of the Supreme Court.[134] The petitioners have, in consequence of the established law of their country, and inveterate*

[130] *Votes 1774*, p. 401.

[131] *Public Advertiser* opens with 'The following is the Petition of the Booksellers, Printers, and Others, whose Dependence is on the Trade of Bookselling and Printing, residing in the City of Edinburgh, which was presented to the House of Commons, and read; setting forth that …'. It then continues from this point.

[132] See further, A.G. Thomson, *The Paper Industry in Scotland 1590–1861* (Edinburgh, 1974).

[133] Richard Sher, *The Enlightenment and the Book: Scottish Authors and their Publishers in Eighteenth-Century Britain, Ireland, and America* (Chicago, IL, 2006), chs 4–6. It should be remembered that many leading London Booksellers were Scottish, including Andrew Millar and William Strahan.

[134] *Donaldson v Beckett* (1774) *Cobbett's Parl. Hist.*, xvii, col. 953.

usage, expended large sums of money, in the printing of books which were not within the protection granted by the 8th of Queen Anne, **{8}** and in the materials for printing. They have stocks of these books upon hand, and many are now printing; and if they are to be exposed to search and seizure by the London booksellers, and to vexatious prosecutions before the courts of law, for exercising what they have all along considered to be their undoubted legal right, and all this in consequence of a law made *ex post facto*, they cannot but think their situation extremely hard.

[They beg leave to say, That they/and that the Petitioners] know no merit on the part of the London booksellers to entitle them to such an undue [preference/reference]; and far less are they conscious of having committed any crime which [Not PET: should] draw upon them those severe forfeitures which will ensure upon the law now proposed. [They must therefore humbly pray/and therefore pray], that [they/the Petitioners] may be heard by counsel against the bill, and that a reasonable time may be allowed to send their witnesses to London for proving all facts material to their petition.

[Not PA: And your petitioners shall ever pray.]

[PET: (Signed by 26 Persons.)][135]

[PET: *Constant].

London Stallholders' Petition

'Petitions' {4–5}; *Middlesex Journal*, 23–6 Apr.; *London Chronicle*, 23–6 Apr., 397–8; *Edinburgh Advertiser*, 29 Apr.–3 May, 273–4; *Caledonian Mercury*, 2 May. *CJ*, xxxiv, 668 (22 Apr.)

[Variant 1: 'Petitions' (Pet) / Variant 2: *Middlesex Journal*, 23–6 Apr.; *London Chronicle*, 23–6 Apr., 397–8; *Edinburgh Advertiser*, 29 Apr.–3 May, 273–4; *Caledonian Mercury*, 2 May]

{4, p. 273} *To the Honourable the Commons of Great Britain, in Parliament assembled,*

The Humble PETITION of sundry BOOKSELLERS of LONDON and WESTMINSTER, in behalf of themselves and their Brethren in the Country,

SHEWETH,

THAT a petition having been presented to this Honourable House, purporting to be the petition of the booksellers of London and Westminster, we, who are also booksellers of London and Westminster, humbly beg leave to represent to this Honourable House the injustice of their pretensions, and the calamitous situation in which we, and a very great number of country booksellers, shall be involved, if their desires be complied with.

Although the former petitioners have asserted that they shall sustain great loss by the late decision of the Lords,[136] yet it is only a very small number of them who are materially affected by that decision, many that have very little or no interest therein having signed

[135] The *Public Advertiser* has at the end 'The said Petition is ordered to be taken into Consideration the 4th May, when the Bill will be read a second Time.' In the *Caledonian Mercury* it is followed by a letter to the annual committee of the royal burgh on the Booksellers' Bill.

[136] *Donaldson v Beckett* (1774) *Cobbett's Parl. Hist.*, xvii, col. 953.

that petition through fear or friendship, or from other motives. From similar motives many others have declined signing this petition, although they deprecate with us the establishment of the monopoly. But your petitioners, moved by a sense of the duty they owe to the public, as well as to themselves and families, presume to lay their grievances before this Honourable House.

Your petitioners humbly hope they shall be indulged in stating the following facts, which, in their humble opinion, prove that the booksellers never could purchase copy-rights on a supposition of their being property at common law.

About the year 1640 we find they began to buy copy-rights. From that year to 1694,[137] they purchased, under the protection of the ordinances of Parliament, the licensing act, and the prerogative of the crown. To answer the arbitrary purposes of the latter, they were invested with extraordinary privileges and powers; and under that protection (though not granted them for such purposes) they claimed, bought, and sold [copy-rights/copy right] But when the revolution took place, and the licensing act expired, this property vanished, and [their **{5}** copy-rights/the copy-right] ceased. In this situation, they never thought of a common law right; but applied to parliament as their only resource. And as it was manifest that they had been induced to make these purchases on the protection afforded them by the licensing act, which was then expired, and by the prerogative of the crown, which was then limited by law, the Parliament, in 1709, granted them an exclusive right for twenty-one years, with this express limitation, that they should have it *no longer*.

Your petitioners would have thought that no possibility of dispute remained, when so clear a line was drawn by the legislature for conducting this monopoly. But the increase of literature in the present century rendered a monopoly of it an important object, so that on the expiration of the exclusive right in 1731,[138] those who had made large fortunes by it (like the booksellers of our day) were desirous of its continuance. Accordingly, in 1734, 5, 6, they made applications to parliament, but totally failed in every attempt. They had not yet acquired an idea of the common law giving them a property, but contented themselves (as the present booksellers will, if they fail in their attempt) with endeavours to retain their exclusive right, in defiance of the legislature. They still presumed to call themselves proprietors, they stigmatized other editions as piratical; but as they printed books cheap and good, in comparison of those printed now, they met with very little opposition in their monopoly; till the year 1746 or 7. About that time Mr. J. Osborn, a bookseller of property in Pater Noster Row,[139] having quarrelled with his brethren, began printing very correct and cheap editions of some of their copies.

They found no resource but tempting him, by bribery, to quit his project. About the year 1750, they found means to induce him (it is said, by an annuity of 200l.) to quit business. During this whole transaction they appear not to have thought of a legal claim. And it is impossible that, while this transaction was recent in their memories, they should fall into a mistake. Your petitioners humbly apprehend, that from this plain state of facts, it fully appears, that from the expiration of the licensing act in 1694 to the time when the late litigations were set on foot, booksellers never set up a claim to [common law

[137]When the Licensing of the Press Act 1662 (13 & 14 Chas. II, c. 33) expired in 1694: Administration of Intestates' Estate Act 1685, s. 15.

[138]It expired on 9 Apr. 1731: Copyright Act 1709, s. 1.

[139]John Osborne.

rights/a common law right]; nor could they possibly purchase copy-right with a view to any other legal protection than the statutory right of the act of the eighth of Queen Anne. Yet it is very certain, that during this period they did presume to buy, sell, and share, copy-rights, that were not within the protection of that statute. And therefore it is plain, that they did by combination and artifice maintain their monopoly in defiance of the law. From the commencement of the late litigations, when they first set up their claim of a property at common law, to its final determination by the late decision of the House of Lords, they might possibly buy copy-rights on a supposition of the possibility of success in their extraordinary claim. But in this, your petitioners humbly apprehend they can only be considered as speculators, buying and selling a property to which they had then first set up a claim, the existence of which was then in contest. And although three of the judges of the court of king's bench[140] gave judgment in their favour, yet as that judgment was strongly opposed by Sir Joseph Yates, and as it was well known there would be an appeal from it to the House of Lords, they could hardly (in such circumstances) imagine that they had a common law right. Therefore they bought and sold only in speculation, and just as their hopes or fears preponderated.**{6}**

Your petitioners cannot find that any other monopolists have ever pretended to claim their exclusive privilege, after the expiration of the term granted them;[141] but have quietly resigned their pretensions, and allowed the advantage to lie open to the public. Therefore your petitioners humbly apprehend, that the booksellers, in so combining, have set an evil example to other monopolists; and that having been protected by the statute in an exclusive right for a **{EA274}** limited term, and after the expiration of that term, attempted to continue the monopoly, and by combination to prevent the public receiving the benefit of its expiration, presuming to buy and sell shares of such monopoly, after such expiration, and prosecuting a suit at common law, in arrogant contempt of an express act of the legislature, have been guilty of a very great offence. And your petitioners trust, that it will not seem meet to the wisdom of this Honourable House, to reward such evil conduct, by a continuance of their monopoly.

Your petitioners humbly beg leave further to represent, that some opulent booksellers, by their influence, can greatly promote or obstruct the sale of most new publications; so that other booksellers cannot venture to purchase new works of any consequence, and therefore most copies are first purchased by a few rich monopolists. After they have made [PET: most] exorbitant profits by them, then the copies are sold in shares to other booksellers, in order to strengthen the interest; by which means, the trade of purchasing original copies continuing in so few hands, they, by combination, may easily keep other booksellers and authors so ignorant of the value of new copies, and the profits made by them, as to engross the chief benefit to themselves, to the great detriment of authors. If an author publishes his work himself, or sells it to a less considerable bookseller, the rich monopolists will impede the sale, injure the author, or ruin the bookseller who made the purchase.

Your petitioners cannot rest unconcerned, while, at the moment when they found themselves freed from the litigious and vexatious practice of the opulent booksellers, and were

140 *Millar v Taylor* (1769); Lord Mansfield, Sir Richard Aston and Sir Edward Willes gave judgment in favour.

141 But see the Printing of Thuanus' Histories Act 1733 (7 Geo. II, c. 24), which gave exclusive rights outside the Copyright Act 1709, and it was also possible to extend a patent by private act: Johnson, *Privatised Law Reform*, ch. 8.

rejoicing in the hope of being enabled to follow their business securely, either in printing editions of their own, or selling cheap and saleable editions printed by others, at that very time their adversaries should attempt to render their case more grievous, because irretrievable; for if they succeed, your petitioners must be content with the pittance of profit they please to allow them, and that pittance itself at mercy; this will most capitally affect booksellers in the country, who, by reason of their distance from the capital, and from each other, cannot join to complain.

Finally, your petitioners beg leave humbly to represent, that it appears by the late decision of the House of Lords, that they have an undoubted right to print any books after the expiration of the term given by the statute. And although the rights of individuals ought to give way to the public good; your petitioners trust that it will not seem meet to this Honourable **{LC398}** House, that they be deprived of that right, and the public burthened with a monopoly, merely to gratify a few booksellers, who have already made large fortunes by such illegal monopoly.

Your petitioners therefore cast themselves on the wisdom, humanity, and justice of this Honourable House, and humbly pray that the bill may not pass, and that they may be heard by counsel against the same,

[PET: (Signed by 52 persons.)]

Glasgow Booksellers' Petition

'Petitions' {8}; *CJ*, xxxiv, 668 (22 Apr.).

To the Honourable the Commons of Great Britain*, in Parliament assembled,*

The PETITION of the PRINTERS and BOOKSELLERS of the City and University of GLASGOW,

HUMBLY SHEWETH,

WE, the printers and booksellers of the city and university of Glasgow, having in former times, without giving just cause, been put to great expence by the groundless and unlimited claims of some booksellers in London, heard with great pleasure of the solemn trial and final decision of the claim of right at common law by the House of Peers, assisted by the twelve judges of England.[142] Since that wise and just decision, your humble petitioners have observed, with concern, that a few booksellers in London, under the name of the booksellers of London and Westminster, have brought in a bill before this Honourable House for an exclusive privilege of printing books that are without the statute of the 8th of Queen Anne,[143] for a limited time; and for a further extension of right beyond what is granted to authors and their assigns by that act. Your petitioners view this bill as a general hurt to the united kingdoms, and particularly to Scotland, as it will give the booksellers of London a monopoly of trade over that kingdom, which they could not have enjoyed,

[142] *Donaldson v Beckett* (1774) *Cobbett's Parl. Hist.*, xvii, col. 953.

[143] Copyright Act 1709.

although the late decision of the House of Peers had been in their favours. And as your petitioners will be much hurt, if not ruined, should this bill pass into a law, they pray to be heard by counsel at the bar of the Honourable House.

(Signed by 27 persons.)

Donaldson's Petition[144]

'Petitions' {9–12}; *Middlesex Journal*, 3–5 May; *Caledonian Mercury*, 9 May; *Edinburgh Advertiser*, 3–6 May, 284–5; *Edinburgh Evening Courant*, 7 May; *CJ*, xxxiv, 679 and *Votes 1774*, pp. 554–5 (26 Apr.).

[Variant 1: 'Petitions'; *Caledonian Mercury (CM)*; *Edinburgh Advertiser*, *Edinburgh Evening Courant*; Variant 2: *Middlesex Journal (MJ)*]

To the Honourable the Commons of Great Britain, *in Parliament assembled,*

The Humble PETITION of ALEXANDER DONALDSON, Bookseller in St. Paul's Church-yard, LONDON,

SHEWETH,

THAT your petitioner has seen a bill, which has been brought into this Honourable House, upon the petition of certain booksellers of London and Westminster, for vesting the copies of printed books in the purchasers of such copies from authors, or their assigns, for a time [PET/EA/EC: therein to be][CM: to be therein][MJ: therein] limited.

The hardships that must befal your petitioner, should this bill pass into a law, are so very peculiar, that he humbly craves leave to submit his case in all its circumstances to the wisdom and the justice of this Honourable House.

Your petitioner embarked in the trade and business of a bookseller in the year 1750, at Edinburgh, soon after the determination of a cause carried on there by one Midwinter, Andrew Millar and others, against the Scots booksellers, in which cause the Court of Session[145] decreed against the claim of the London booksellers, upon the statute of the 8th of Queen Anne.[146] In consequence of that decision, your petitioner had no room to doubt but that the term of twenty-one years, for all books printed and published before the 8th of Queen Anne, was the utmost extent of the monopoly granted in such copies, and that, in all copies printed and published since that statute the right of the assigns of the author was determinable at the end of fourteen years; the said copies being at that period to return to

[144]The *Edinburgh Advertiser*, *Edinburgh Evening Courant* and *Caledonian Mercury* include the following immediately before the petition: 'The following is the petition presented to the House of Commons on Tuesday se'ennight, by GOVERNOR JOHNSTONE, which was read, and ordered to lie on the table till the second reading of the Booksellers Bill, and counsel allowed to be heard.' The *Middlesex Journal* includes the following immediately before the petition: 'As we have already inserted the London Booksellers Petition to the House of Commons for an extension of their Literary property, with the counter-Petition, in favour of the public, we shall now lay before our readers Mr. Donaldson's Petition, which, it is supposed, will throw more light on the merits of this subject that has hitherto appeared'.

[145]*Midwinter v Hamilton* (1743) Kam Rem 154; Mor 8295.

[146]Copyright Act 1709.

the authors thereof,[147] if they were then living. Your petitioner, however, did not wilfully act upon his own conceptions of law, but consulted some of the ablest advocates both in England and Scotland, who confirmed him in his opinion, that literary property depended entirely upon, and was wholly regulated by, the statute of Queen Anne.

Your petitioner therefore entered very largely into the bookselling business. He purchased several original works from authors of distinguished merit, such as Lord Bankton, Lord Kames, David Hume, Esq;[148] and others; and he also reprinted a great number of old and valuable books, not protected by the statute, affixing his name to all his editions, and advertising them openly, without any suit or action by the London booksellers, for thirteen years. In the course of his trade your petitioner has not expended less than fifty thousand pounds, and he is warranted to say that the publick [PET/EC/MJ: have][CM/EA: has] been much benefited by his very extensive undertakings, as he sold, at moderate prices, several books, which were either very scarce in England, or held up by the arts of the London booksellers at a very unreasonable rate.

In the year 1759, your petitioner, who then resided at Edinburgh, found that a combination of the London booksellers was formed and carried on with the most arbitrary spirit, in order to work a total suppression throughout England of all books whatever printed in Scotland. Threatening letters were every where circulated in the name of some principal booksellers in London, with intent to terrify the country booksellers, who were told, in a tone of menace, that all books **{10}** printed in Scotland were an actual piracy, and that those who dealt in such copies would be liable to severe [prosecutions/persecutions] and heavy damages in consequence thereof. In the letters so circulated it was allowed to the country booksellers to expose to sale no editions whatever, except such as were printed in London. The alarm was spread wide through the country; and a subscription of no less than 3150l. was declared to have been actually made for the purpose of supporting an illegal conspiracy of all the opulent booksellers in London.

Your petitioner was determined that he would not submit to oppression: Accordingly, in 1763, he established a shop in London for the purpose of vending his own editions,[149] and with intent to shew the country booksellers that such trade was well warranted by the laws of the land.

From the year 1763, to the late determination in the House of Lords,[150] on the twenty-third of February last, your petitioner has had to struggle with the united force of almost all the eminent booksellers of London and Westminster. No less than eleven suits in Chancery[151] were carried on against him, besides actions in the Court of Session, for the exercise of a legal right in printing books, at prices the most easy to the publick, which were not protected by the statute of Queen Anne. In the variety of suits in which he [has been/was] involved, above one hundred of the most opulent booksellers[152] in London and

[147] But it could be extended by a further 14 years: Copyright Act 1709, s. 11.

[148] Andrew McDouall* (Lord Bankton) (1685–1760), Henry Home* (Lord Kames) (1696–1782), both judges of the court of sessions, and David Hume* (1711–76).

[149] 48 St Paul's Churchyard, London.

[150] *Donaldson v Beckett* (1774) *Cobbett's Parl. Hist.*, xvii, col. 953.

[151] See p 8, n 206.

[152] According to H. Tomas Gomez-Arostegui, *Register of Copyright Infringement Suits & Actions from c. 1560 to 1800* (2009), this is an exaggeration: there were 45 different plaintiffs and a 46th, the Stationers' Company. The

Westminster have, in their turn, been plaintiffs against your petitioner: But he was resolved not to yield to a monopoly most unjustly claimed: It was his fixed purpose that the law should be finally settled in the Supreme Court of the kingdom. That he has at length accomplished this point is now his crime with the London booksellers; but he humbly conceives that his honest efforts against a powerful combination will not subject him to the censure of this Honourable House, where he hopes the rights of the subject will never want protection.

Your petitioner, during the last eleven years, has been put [to/at] very heavy expences, and has undergone much trouble and anxiety: And now, after having made it appear that he always acted with due deference to the laws made for the regulation of literary property, he has the mortification to see the victory, which he obtained with great risk and labour, ready to be snatched out of his hands by the very people who have been hitherto guilty of oppression, and yet hope for a [further/future] time in which they may act the same over again.

Your petitioner begs leave to submit, that the clause in the bill now depending, which provides that any person or persons may continue to sell impressions or copies of any book or books already printed and published,[153] will not be an adequate saving for your petitioner and several other booksellers in the country and in Scotland: The clause, on the contrary, will open a door for much mischief, and the difficulty of satisfying the London booksellers as to the point of time, when such books were printed, will leave your petitioner and others liable to a variety of suits, in which, from what has already past, he has no reason to think the opulent booksellers of London will be sparing. And moreover, your petitioner has been hitherto struggling for a general right to supply the community at large with books at a moderate price; and now that he has succeeded in an undertaking [MJ: so] perfectly just, he submits, that to take that right from him in favour of the old monopolizers, may have a tendency to discourage the subject from contending in future against those who have grown rich by illegal practices, and the arts of combination.

{11} Your petitioner begs leave to observe, That it is in a great measure owing to his perseverance and industry, that the London booksellers have, of late years, given to the publick commodious and cheap editions of several useful and valuable books, which before were kept up at a very unreasonable price.

152 *(continued)* plaintiffs were Peter Abraham De Hondt, tr. 1760–76; Edmund Baker (c. 1723–1774), app. 1738; Samuel Baker (1712–78), app. 1726, tr. 1739–78; Elizabeth Baldwin (*d.* 1776), tr. 1748–50 then as Elizabeth Stevens tr. 1768–76; Henry Baldwin* (1734–1813), app. 1749–56, tr. 1759–1803); Richard Baldwin* (c. 1691–1777), app. 1708–16, tr. 1726–70; Thomas Beckett tr. 1760–86; Thomas Caddell* (1742–1802), app. 1758–65, tr. 1766–93; Thomas Caslon (*d.* 1783), app. 1742–9, tr. 1750–83; Thomas Caxton (no details); William Clarke (*d.* 1795), app. 1742–50, tr. 1750–93; Robert Collins (*d.* 1786), app. 1750–7, tr. 1750–86; Stanley Crowder (d 1798) app. 1742–9, tr. 1755–89; Thomas Davies* (c. 1712–1785), tr. 1730–75; Catherine Davey tr. 1763; Charles Dilly* (1739–1807), app. 1756–63, tr. 1765–1801; Edward Dilly* (1732–79), app. 1756–63, tr. 1765–1801; James Dodsley* (1724–97), tr. 1759–97; Thomas Field (*d.* 1794), app. 1746–53, tr. 1755–92; Robert Harefield tr. 1771; Lacy Hawes (*d.* 1775), app. 1740–7, tr. 1745–75; John Hinton (*d.* 1781), app. 1732–9, tr. 1739–81; James Hodges app. 1718–26, tr. 1732–55; William Johnston; George Kearsley* (1739–60), app. 1753–60, tr. 1758–90; Bedwell Law (*d.* 1798), app. 1745–53, tr. 1756–98; Thomas Longman; Thomas Lowndes (1719–84), tr. 1751–84; Andrew Millar; Thomas Osborne (1704–67), app. 1728, tr. 1728–67; William Owen (*d.* 1793), app. 1733–40, tr. 1748–93; Thomas Payne (c. 1717–1799), app. 1734–42, tr. 1742–90; Thomas Pote (*d.* 1794), app. 1748–54, tr. 1763–94; John Richardson app. 1726–40, tr. 1769–74; Joseph Richardson; William Richardson app. 1748, tr. 1761–99; Charles Rivington* (*d.* 1790), app. 1746–53; John Rivington* (1720–92), app. 1735–42, tr. 1742–75; John Roberts (*d.* 1776), tr. 1764–76; George Robinson* (1736–1801), tr. 1763–97; William Strahan* (1715–85), app. 1738, tr. 1739–85; John Whiston* (1711–80), tr. 1767–75; Benjamin White* (c. 1725–1794), tr. 1757–75; Robert Wilkins app. 1747, tr. 1763–94; Henry Woodfall* (1739–1805), app. 1754; and the Company of Stationers.

153 See below, Booksellers' Bill 1774, cl. 5.

He submits, that the consequence of a free and open trade in printing and publishing [must /most] inevitably be an emulation [PET/MJ: among][CM/EA/EC: amongst] the booksellers to print in the neatest manner, and at the most moderate prices; whereas, should the bill pass into a law, a very dangerous monopoly will be thrown into the hands of a few wealthy booksellers, who have [PET/MJ: already] enjoyed the fruits of usurpation, and will, no doubt, make the best use of the further time now expected, by continuing such prices as will best answer their thirst of gain, to the great detriment of the publick, to the injury of letters, and the utter ruin of the inferior booksellers, both in town and country.

Your petitioner further submits that it will appear from the practice of the London booksellers, that they did not, for a series of years, entertain an idea of a common law right, though the contrary is now pretended. It is indeed true, that, by combination among themselves, they hoped to turn all the antient literature of the kingdom, into, what they call, *Honorary Property*, in the same manner as they have done with the *Delphin Classics*:[154] But their having already made large fortunes by such old copies cannot be a reason for continuing in their hands a pernicious monopoly.

It is also submitted, when the London booksellers pretend that they shall be great sufferers, if the monopoly of twenty-one years granted by the statute of Queen Anne[155] is not now renewed, that they ought to set forth what sums have been paid by each of them [respectively/respectfully] for their old copies, how long they have been in possession, and what profits have been made: But a discovery of this kind is avoided, for the purpose of concealing that they have already gained infinitely more than they ever paid to the author or his assigns.

It is further submitted, that when an enlargement of the term of fourteen years granted by the same statute of Queen Anne [Not MJ: is expected by the London booksellers, in prejudice to the living author, who, by the same statute,] is intitled to a second term of fourteen years,[156] they ought to set forth the agreements between them and their respective authors, that it may be seen whether the sale of a perpetual right at common law was in the contemplation of the author, and whether an adequate price for such perpetual right has been given by the bookseller: But this is also avoided, because they are conscious that, in all such purchases, their method has been to calculate upon one, or two editions at most, for their reimbursement; and of every book which is worth reprinting at the end of fourteen years, it may be truly said that the booksellers have gained their original purchase-money, eight, or ten, or, perhaps, twenty times over.

Your petitioner therefore submits, that the pretence **{EA285}** of hardship upon the booksellers is without foundation: They cannot shew that they have been losers by the old copies, in which they have long exercised an undue monopoly; and for the works of living authors, if they have not been greatly overpaid by the success of those copies during a term of fourteen years, it will be no loss to them, if they never reprint such unprofitable works: If they have been overpaid, it will be no hardship upon them, should those works now return to their respective authors, [agreeably/agreeable] to the intent and spirit of the act of Queen Anne.

[154] The Delphin classic, which was a collection complied for the Dauphine in the 1670s: J.E. Sandys, *A History of Classical Scholarship* (3 vols, Cambridge, 1908), ii, 292–3; *The Oxford Companion to the Book*, ed. M.F. Suarez and H.R. Woudhuysen (2 vols, Oxford, 2010), ii, 663.

[155] Copyright Act 1709, s. 1.

[156] Copyright Act 1709, s. 11.

{12} Your petitioner begs pardon for so long an intrusion upon the patience of this Honourable House, and only craves leave to add, that he has, at this very time, a large sum invested in books actually printed, [PET/MJ: and] that he is engaged in a variety of new editions, now actually at the press, (the expence of printing the same being in a great measure already incurred), and which, when finished, as he proposes in the most correct and elegant manner, will cost him several thousand pounds. Many of the printers and booksellers in the country of England and in Scotland are in the same situation. If therefore any inconvenience must arise from the late determination, he humbly hopes that this Honourable House will not think it just that the loss should fall upon those who have obeyed the law, while the opulent booksellers, who have grown rich in defiance of an act of parliament made for the regulation of their trade, shall, by false glosses and mere colours, excite an unmerited compassion, and be, perhaps, rewarded with an extension of a monopoly, which has hitherto subsisted by all the arts of illegal combination.

Your petitioner therefore most humbly prays that the statute of Queen Anne, which was expressly made for the encouragement of learning, may not now be altered or suspended, for the encouragement of the London booksellers only; and that your petitioner may be heard by his counsel against the bill now depending.

ALEX. DONALDSON

Petition of Booksellers of York

CJ, xxxiv, 698; *Votes 1774*, p. 597 (4 May).

A Petition of the Booksellers, Printers, and Bookbinders, of the City of *York*, was presented to the House, and read; Setting forth, That the Petitioners observe, by the Votes, that Leave has been given to bring in a Bill, for the Relief of some Booksellers in *London* and *Westminster*, by giving them an exclusive Privilege, for a further limited Time, of re-printing Books, not protected by the Act of the 8th of Queen *Anne*;[157] which Bill, if passed into a Law, will be highly detrimental to the Community at large, as well as particularly injurious to the Petitioners, and to all Country Booksellers, Printers, And others, dependent on those Branches of Business, who have heretofore been greatly hurt by the Monopoly of Books unlawfully exercised by the *London* Booksellers; And therefore praying, That the Statute of the 8th of Queen *Anne*, for vesting Copies in Authors, &c. may stand in full Force, as lately explained by the House of Lords, and be neither amended or extended; and that the Petitioners be heard, by Counsel, against the said Bill being passed into a Law.

Remarks on Donaldson's Petition

Remarks on the Petition of Mr Alexander Donaldson and other, against the Petition now depending in Parliament for affording Relief to the Booksellers of London and Westminster in Literary Property, Bodleian Library, (Vet.) 2581 c.5 (2).

[157] *Votes 1774*, p. 597; now see *CJ*, xxxiv, 513 (28 Feb.).

REMARKS ON THE PETITONS of Mr. *Alexander Donaldson* and others, against the Petition now depending in Parliament for affording Relief to the Booksellers of *London* and *Westminster* in LITERARY PROPERTY

THE Petitions against the Relief which is humbly supplicated from the Wisdom of the Legislature, in Literary Property, are four in Number; one from Mr. *Alexander Donaldson*; another from a Set of People stiling themselves Booksellers in *London* and *Westminster*; the third Petition comes from a Body of Men said to be dependent upon the Press in *Edinburgh*; and the fourth is called a Petition from the Printers and Booksellers of the City and University of *Glasgow*.

The first Assertion in Point, which Mr. *Donaldson* hazards in his Petition, is "That having been sufficiently advised that Literary Property depended wholly upon the Statute of Queen *Anne*, he printed a *great Number* of old and valuable Books not protected by the Statute and in the Course of his Trade has expended no less than 50,000l. by which the *Public* have been *much* benefited, as he sold at moderate Prices several Books which were either very scarce, or held up by the Art of the *London* Booksellers at a very unreasonable Rate." —Mr. *Donaldson* has *not* published many valuable old Books; he has published but *very few*, and these are not only shamefully executed upon bad Paper, but they are unpardonably incorrect, scandalously mutilated, and, what is still more extraordinary, they are to the full as dear as the *London* Editions, if either the *Size*, or the *Manner* of Printing, is to determine, as it does in every other Work, their typographical Value with the Reader.

Mr. *Donaldson* affirms, in his next Paragraph, "That in the Year 1759 the *London* Booksellers formed a Combination with a most *arbitrary Spirit*, to work a total Suppression throughout *England* of *all Books whatever* printed in *Scotland*." —In Answer to this Assertion, the *London* Booksellers declare, that they have given every possible Encouragement to Books originally published in *Scotland*, the Property of *Scotch* Booksellers; and they beg Leave to mention as Instances, *Ruddiman's Rudiments,*[158] *Mackenzie on Health,*[159] *Gordon's Accomptant,*[160] *Hutchinson's Philosophy*,[161] and the *Medical Essays*.[162] They could extend the Catalogue much farther; but the few Authors mentioned will serve as amply as a thousand, to teach the Dispassionate what kind of Credit is due to Mr. *Donaldson's* Word, when he solemnly asserts, that all Books *whatever*, which were printed in *Scotland*, underwent an indiscriminate Proscription from the Booksellers of *London*.

To render his Assertion on the foregoing Head additionally striking, Mr. *Donaldson* says, "That circular Letters of a *threatening* Nature, were sent to all the Country Booksellers, to intimidate them from selling *any* Books but such as were printed in *London*."— No Falsehood is so dangerous as that which is connected with some Degree **{2}** of Truth.— Several *Scotch* Editions of Books appearing in 1759, which the *London* Booksellers, as the

[158]Thomas Ruddiman* (1674–1757), *The Rudiments of the Latin Tongue* (Freebairn, 1714) (ESTC: T86953).

[159]James Mackenzie* (?1680–1761), *The History of Health* (William Gordon, 1758) (ESTC: T58746).

[160]George Gordon, *The History of our National Debts and Taxes* (M. Cooper, 1751) (ESTC: T85632).

[161]Francis Hutcheson* (1694–1746), *A System of Moral Philosophy* (Foulis, 1755) (ESTC: T99472).

[162]Thomas Percival* (1740–1804), *Essays Medical and Experimental* (Johnson, 1767) (ESTC: N8407).

Law was *then* understood, deeming to be Piracies, Letters of Caution were sent to the Country Booksellers; and the principal Parties concerned in such Books as were attacked, thought it prudent, with the Advice of Counsel, to raise a Subscription of 600l. to defray the Expences attending the different Prosecutions necessary to protect their Property. There was nothing criminal in this Design.—If, however, their defending themselves by a Subscription is to be considered a real Act of Persecution, the Charge does not come with a very good Grace from Mr. *Donaldson,* as he cannot deny that his own Expences were defrayed by a Subscription of *Scotch* Booksellers.

Mr. *Donaldson* insists through his Petition, "That he has been an incredible Sufferer by supporting, what the Decision on the late Appeal, has proved to be the Law of the Land." He has suffered also for invading the Law, where he found it repugnant to his Interest; for, besides the Suits in which he engaged to defend the Right of printing and vending every Book *unprotected* by the Statute of Queen *Anne*, he incurred Suits in Chancery for printing and vending Books, such as *Sterne's Sermons,*[163] *Shenstone's Works,*[164] and others, which *he knew* to be *protected.*

The more the Petition of Mr. *Donaldson* is examined, the more Occasion there will be to admire the Dexterity with which he suppresses some Circumstances, and improves upon others. Having passed over his Piracies in a most judicious Silence, he peremptorily claims the positive Merit of reducing the Price of Books. Now the Truth really is, that a Reduction took place in the Price of valuable Books previous to Mr. *Donaldson*'s commencing Business.—*Clarke*'s and *Tillotson's Sermons;*[165] for instance, the *Spectators,*[166] *Guardians,*[167] and *Tatlers,*[168] *Rollin's Ancient History,*[169] *Spencer's Works,*[170] *Milton's*, and many other Authors of distinguished Reputation, were sold upon the most moderate Terms before Mr. *Donaldson* began Trade; and even at this Moment, the Writers just named though printed infinitely better than Mr. *Donaldson's* Editions, are sold by the *London* Booksellers upon lower Terms, notwithstanding his disinterested Labours for the Benefit of the Community.

Mr. *Donaldson* is exceedingly offended with the Purchasers of Copy Right on account of the large Fortunes which he supposes they must have acquired in the Course of their Trade; yet if Property is criminal, what must he have acquired who printed so extensively, without purchasing any Copy Right at all?—The Idea of a Common Law Right in Copies, he treats as the artful Invention of the interested, to gloss over the Views of their Avarice. Let the Idea be just or unjust, it certainly was Law, till the House of Lords determined the Question

[163]Laurence Sterne* (1713–68), *The Sermons of Mr Yorick* (Faulkner, 1760) (ESTC: T14719).

[164]The first volume of his works was William Shenstone* (1714–63), *The Works in Verse and Prose* (Dodsley, 1764) (ESTC: T92444).

[165]Samuel Clarke* (1675–1729), *One Hundred and Seventy Three Sermons on Several Subjects* (Powell, 1734) (ESTC: T105019). There are a wide range of sermans by John Tillotson (1630–94) published. These began during his lifetime, and collections of various sorts continued: for instance, *Sermons on Several Subjects and Occasions* (Ware, 1742) (ESTC: T137449).

[166]*The Spectator* ran from 1711 to 1715: (Buckley and Tonson, 1712–15) (ESTC: N24116).

[167]*The Guardian* ran from 12 Mar. to 1 Oct. 1713: (Tonson, 1713) (ESTC: P1756).

[168]*The Tatler* began in 1709 and ended in 1711: (Addison & Steele, 1709–11) (ESTC: P1919).

[169]Charles Rollin* (1661–1741), *The Roman History from the Foundation of Rome to the Battle of Actium* (Knapton, 1754) (ESTC: T121677).

[170]Probably Edmund Spenser* (c. 1552–1599); his works were published during his lifetime and continued thereafter: for instance, *The Works of Spenser* (Tonson, 1750) (ESTC: T134659).

otherwise, on the 23d of *February*,[171] and the Booksellers as certainly considered it such, from the Multitude of their Assignments, not only *subsequent*, but *antecedent* to the Statute of Queen *Anne*. – Nay, one of the Judges[172] recently sold the Property in his own Works *for ever*, which it is presumable he would not have done, but upon a Conviction that there was a Common Law Right.— The very respectable Personage alluded to, is universally reverenced for consummate Abilities in his Profession; and his Opinion of the Common Law Right was previously confirmed by a solemn Adjudication in the Court of the *King's Bench*.[173] — If, therefore, Mr. *Donaldson*, from the Period of this Adjudication, undertook such a Variety of Works as must amount to several thousand Pounds, he proceeded wilfully against what was, at *The Time*, known to be the declared Law of the Land, and consequently has nothing to blame but his own Temerity.— He could undertake no Work of consequence *since* the Determination of the Peers, without undertaking it deliberately at his Peril, because the London Booksellers petitioned the House of Commons for Relief within a Week after that Decision; of course there can be no Comparison in the Severity of their different Cases. The Booksellers paid a valuable Consideration for their Copies, Mr. *Donaldson* paid no **{3}** Consideration for his Copies, and the Booksellers therefore humbly hope that the Wisdom as well as the Equity of Parliament will think them proper Objects of Relief: The Counter-Petitioners exclaim against the present Solicitation, as an Attempt to introduce an *ex post facto* Law; yet the Booksellers flatter themselves that the Nature of the Case will sufficiently extenuate such a Circumstance, since they could not apply for a Remedy to any Grievance, till the Grievance actually existed.

The Counter-Petition from a Body of People stiling themselves sundry Booksellers of *London* and *Westminster*, is presented on Behalf of the Subscribers, *and on Behalf of their Brethren in the Country*.— Yet it is remarkable, that it neither contains the Name of *any one Country Bookseller* whatever, nor any Bookseller of Eminence in Town. These Gentlemen, nevertheless, who in all Likelihood have not a single Shilling existing in Copy Right, are to be totally undone if Relief is benignantly extended to Persons essentially interested.— Opposing this Class of Counter-Petitioners therefore, merely as Individuals, to the Petitioners for Relief, the simple Question is, Which are most entitled to Consideration, the mistaken Purchasers of Property sanctified by Law till the late Decision of the Peers, or those who probably never possessed any Literary Property at all? —The Goodness of Parliament afforded Relief in the Case of Mrs. *Hogarth*, who obtained a Term of Twenty Years in her Husband's Copper Plates,[174] upon representing the Hardships she laboured under; and the Booksellers humbly hope, that the Indulgence shewn to her, will not be denied to a considerable Community who have so large a Property at Stake.

The Counter-Petitions from *Edinburgh* and *Glasgow* are drawn up in much the same Spirit of Candour, as the Counter-Petition from *London* and *Westminster*; the Subscribers also to the former, are with very few Exceptions, nearly as important as the Subscribers to the latter. The Counter-Petitioners of *Edinburgh* take up the Question upon Grounds of national Policy, and assert, "That if the *London* Booksellers are relieved, the *Scotch* Booksellers will be much injured: that their Paper Manufactory will be greatly affected, the Art of Printing

[171] It was actually on 22 Feb.: *LJ*, xxxiv, 32.

[172] Presumably William Blackstone†* (1723–80).

[173] *Millar v Taylor* (1769) 4 Burr 2303 (98 ER 201).

[174] Engraving Copyright Act 1766 (7 Geo. III, c. 38), s. 3.

will receive a mortal Wound, and every Branch connected with it, will be proportionably prejudiced, to the material Detriment of the Revenue."—Let it be granted for Argument Sake, that the *London* Booksellers, under the peculiar Hardships of their Case, are favoured with the Relief which they solicit: Let it be supposed that the *Scotch* Counter-Petitions are built upon the Basis of the most positive Facts, that the Printing and Paper Manufactory of *Scotland* must be greatly affected, and that Numbers must of consequence be plunged into Distress.— Yet even upon *this* Ground, the Good of the comparative *Many*, should be consulted in Preference to the Welfare of the comparative *Few*.— If granting the Relief will injure Hundreds in *Scotland*, the Denial of it will be the Ruin of Thousands in *England*.— The various Manufacturers dependent on the *English* Press, multiply at least in a tenfold *Ratio* to those dependent upon the Press in *Scotland*. The Revenue, besides, accruing from the first is infinitely superior to that arising from the latter; so that, even in a political View, the Counter-Petitions are weak and indefensible.

The Counter-Petitioners affect a great Regard for the Benefit of Authors;—yet the Authors of Character are *entirely* against their Application to Parliament; a Circumstance which the *London* Booksellers observe with singular Satisfaction, because it is a Proof no less forcible in favour of the Relief they solicit as Traders, than a Testimony honourable to their Reputation as Men.

London Booksellers' Considerations

Considerations in behalf of the Booksellers of London and Westminster petitioning the Legislature for Relief (ESTC: T89001). [Copies held at: British Library, Harvard University, Houghton Library; Yale University, Beinecke Rare Books/ Eighteenth Century Collection Online]

CONSIDERATIONS
In behalf of the
BOOKSELLERS of London and Westminster,
petitioning the Legislature for Relief.

AS the important question of Literary Property has been so recently decided before the Supreme Judicature of the kingdom,[175] it would be unbecoming to enter upon the grounds which originally led the Petitioners to imagine that they had a perpetuity in Copy Right.— The House of Peers, to whose decision they submit with the most profound veneration, has convinced them of their mistake; and they now only hope that the authority of what was considered law, which gave so long a sanction to their error, together with the peculiar hardship of their case, may be admitted to operate in their favour for relief.

It is with unspeakable concern, the Petitioners find an idea sedulously inculcated by their opponents, that their present supplication for relief, is an opposition to the late decision of the Peers.—So gross a misrepresentation of the fact must manifestly shew, that the most unwarrantable arts are practised to prejudice the Petitioners.—Men may be just objects of parliamentary tenderness, in cases where they have no legal right to redress; and the wisdom

[175] *Donaldson v Beckett* (1774) *Cobbett's Parl. Hist.*, xvii, col. 953.

of the British Peers will sufficiently distinguish between a daring oppugnance to their just determination, and an humble appeal to their known humanity.

The opposition to the relief solicited, is grounded on the following allegations:

First—That it will secure a monopoly to the Petitioners, who have already acquired large fortunes.

To this the Petitioners reply, that the Bookselling Business is by no means the very advantageous trade which some people may possibly conceive it—Nor are the Booksellers, when compared with other tradesmen, in the least remarkable for their opulence.—In fact, *what property they are possessed of, is chiefly invested in copies, and in large impressions of books now lying unsold in their warehouses*, which they have printed, from time to time, to the amount of many thousand pounds.

The Petitioners for relief beg leave to observe, that the sale even of the best Authors is neither so rapid as their opponents represent,* nor is a **{2}** literary copy in the least like a mechanical invention, though it is so often compared to one. The purchase money of a *single* orrery, a clock, or any other piece of mechanism, always amounts to much more than the expence of the materials and manual labour employed in making it, and the seller has a reasonable profit if he disposes solely of *one*.— But the case with respect to books, is diametrically the reverse—the mere printing of a single book (if books were to be printed copy by copy, just as they were called for) would cost more than an hundred times the price at which it is sold; it is therefore necessary, in order to enable the Bookseller to sell *each particular book*, at a reasonable rate, to print off a large number at one impression; and as it is in proportion to the number which he sells, not to the high value which he sets upon *each particular book*, his profits are to arise, it is always his interest to make his prices as low as possible. Let the opposers of the bill for relief say what they will, it is a notorious fact that a Bookseller cannot, in *any* instance, be repaid the *bare* expence of *paper, printing and advertising*, till the greatest part of the impression is sold.—The unprejudiced will therefore think what a number the Bookseller must sell, where he has a large sum to pay also for the *copy*, and then conclude, as the sale *after all* is *uncertain*, whether the bookselling business can, in the nature of things, be so very lucrative a profession as it is represented.

In a case nearly similar to that of the Petitioners for relief, the Legislature, to encourage engraving, by an Act made in the 8th year of George II. granted the proprietors of maps and prints, an exclusive term of 14 years;[176] and by another Act passed in the 7th year of his present Majesty, the proprietors obtained an absolute unconditional term of 28 years.[177]—Yet the expence of plates, and printing either prints or maps, is trifling when compared to what must be expended on the edition of a book.—Maps or prints may be printed off, from the same copper-plate in small numbers, as the demand for them arises, since the plate will last for many years.—But as soon as a few sheets of a book are printed, the types must of necessity be separated, and upon every new edition require of equal necessity to be re-composed.

The second objection to granting the relief is, That it will keep up the price of books, greatly to the injury of the Public.—This cannot be; because for the reasons already given, the Booksellers profit depends upon the *number* of any work he sells, not upon the *price* of each particular book; and long before Mr. Donaldson's commencing business, the Petition-

[176] Engraving Copyright Act 1734 (8 Geo. II, c. 13), s. 1.

[177] Engraving Copyright Act 1766 (7 Geo. III, c. 38), s. 7.

ers reduced the price of valuable books.—Clarke's and Tillotson's sermons, for instance, the Speculators, Guardians, and Tatlers, Rollin's Ancient History, Spencer's works, Milton's, and many other Authors of distinguished character, were sold upon the most moderate terms; and continue to be so, even upon lower terms than Mr. Donaldson's, though their editions are greatly superior to those printed by him.

{3} It is said, in the third place, That if relief is granted to the Petitioners, learned men will be prevented from improving their works, to the great injury as well of science, as of their own reputation.—It is much more reasonable however to suppose, that men of learning will be deterred from improving their works, if the denial of the relief which is humbly supplicated, leaves their fame an easy prey to the inroads of ignorance or avarice.—In all the books printed by the opponents of the Petitioners, not one improvement has been made.—On the contrary, Mr. Donaldson, the principal, in Pope's Homer, has omitted above 23,000 lines[178] of what the Author judged absolutely necessary for the elucidation of his work, and yet sells it as the genuine publication of Mr. Pope, without giving any hint whatever to the purchaser, of so extraordinary a mutilation.—Far different has been the conduct of the Petitioners.—There are few instances of a new edition of any living Author's work being printed, without submitting it to his correction and improvement.—For though a Bookseller at first buys an Author's absolute right, yet he pays him for the revising every edition, whenever necessary; and in this business of correcting (as most works are capable of some improvement) Authors have frequently received as much, in process of time, as their original copy-money amounted to.—Many books, such as Dictionaries and Lexicons, are a continual expence to the Printer, because every edition must be carefully corrected; and the Petitioners can make it appear, that, over and above their first copy-money, near 12,000l. has been expended in improving works of distinguished merit.—Yet they are represented as enemies to literature, and learning is to sustain an irreparable injury if they are favoured with relief.

The mode of their application likewise is a fresh object of complaint —They are accused of seeking relief by an *ex post facto* law; yet they humbly hope, that the nature of their case will extenuate this circumstance, since they could not petition for a remedy to any grievance, till the grievance actually existed.—Mrs. Hogarth, when relieved, was relieved by an *ex post facto* law.—The wisdom of the Legislature was not to be diverted by any want of popularity in the mere *name* of the act, from attending to the hardship of her case; and neither the art of engraving, nor the public good, have been in the least affected by that gracious extension of Parliamentary Benevolence.

It is finally objected, "That if the London Booksellers, who gave a large price for their copies, are relieved, the Scotch Booksellers, who gave no price for copies *at all*, will be much injured; that their paper manufactory will be greatly affected, the art of printing will receive a mortal wound, and every branch connected with it, will be proportionably prejudiced, to the material detriment of the revenue."—Let it be granted for argument sake, that the London Booksellers, under the peculiar hardships of their case, are favoured with the relief which they solicit: Let it be supposed that the Scotch Counter-petitions are built upon the basis of the most positive facts; that the printing and paper manufactory of Scotland must be greatly affected; and that numbers must of consequence be plunged into distress.—Yet even

[178] It is not clear to which edition this refers, but he printed a two-volume set: Alexander Pope, *The Illiad and Odyssey of Homer* (Donaldson, 1767) (ESTC: T154179). His other versions of the works were longer.

upon *this* ground, Which should be first consulted, the good of the comparative *many*, or the welfare of the comparative *few*?—If granting the relief will injure hundreds in Scotland, the denial of it will be the ruin of thousands **{4}** in England.—The various manufacturers dependent on the English Press, multiply at least in a tenfold *ratio*, to those dependent upon the Press in Scotland. The revenue, besides, accruing from the first, is infinitely superior to that arising from the latter; so that, even in a political view, this objection is wholly indefensible.

The Booksellers of Scotland in their petitions complain, that the encouragement to men of learning in London, almost entirely confines the original printing of every Scotch Author's works to this capital; they nevertheless, with the same breath, call the Booksellers of London, *oppressors* of genius, and represent the very rewards bestowed on writers of merit, as an absolute injury to the advancement of literature.

With a similar degree of consistency, the Booksellers of Scotland affect a great regard for the interest of Authors; — yet Authors of the first character entirely disapprove of their opposition: Dr. Hurd, Dr. Robertson, Dr. Beattie, David Hume, Esq;[179] and others, not only entertain an advantageous idea of the Petitioners, but even think that the interest of letters will be materially affected, unless their prayer is granted by the Legislature.—This is a circumstance which the Petitioners observe with singular satisfaction; because it is a proof no less forcible in favour of the relief they solicit as traders, than a testimony honourable to their reputation as men.

{11} *To prove this assertion, a list of capital Authors is printed and given with the present Case, by which it appears (that among *very* many others) an edition of

Addison's works, in 4 volumes 4to, has been on sale –	33 years,
Ainsworth's Dictionary, 2 vols. folio, – –	22
Ditto, 4to, though so universally used in schools, –	12
Dr. Clarke's works, 4 vols. folio, – –	26
Ditto's Sermons, 11 vols. 8vo. – –	24
Ditto, 8 vols. 8vo, – – – –	18
Ditto, 11 vols. 18vo, – – – –	25
Tillotson's works, 3 vols, folio, – –	23
Ditto, 12 vols. 8vo, – – –	16
Ditto, 12 vols. 18vo, – –	25

[Continued on **{2}**] By the List alluded to, it moreover appears, that the Petitioners, though charged with printing no good books of easy purchase, for the lower orders of the people, have consulted the convenience of *all* orders, in the different sizes of their publications; but from this they claim no merit whatever, because it is as much their interest to accommodate their prices to the pockets of the humblest, as of the highest rank in the community.

Glasgow Memorialists

Robert Foulis, *Memorial of the Printers of Glasgow* (ESTC: T174653) [Copies held at: Glasgow University Library; The National Archives; Columbia University (two copies); University of Michigan]

[179]Richard Hurd* (1720–1808); James Beattie* (1735–1803) (his most famous works at the time being *An Essay on the Nature and Immutability* (1770) and *The Minstrel* (1771)); William Robertson (his notable works at the time were *The History of Scotland 1542–1603* and *History of the Reign of the Emperor Charles V*); David Hume.

MEMORIAL
OF THE
PRINTERS AND BOOKSELLERS OF GLASGOW,
MOST HUMBLY ADDRESSED TO THE HONOURABLE
THE HOUSE OF COMMONS,
ASSEMBLED IN PARLIAMENT,

Occasioned by a PETITION, given in by Booksellers of London, for a New Act to lengthen out the Monopoly further than the act of Queen Anne; and thereby to frustrate the extensive good effects of the late Decision of the House of Peers[180] to England, and put Scotland in a worse situation than hitherto with respect to this matter.

HONOURABLE GENTLEMEN,

YOUR Memorialists are deeply sensible how unfit they are to address, with propriety, the wise and potent Representatives of the people of Great Britain, and of the whole British empire: but being fully persuaded, that there is a compleat concurrence of general national interest with the intention of the present memorial, they are thereby emboldened to lay their thoughts before each Member of the Honourable House. This they esteem an indispensable duty to their country; and their address comes from them with the less impropriety, as they must be involved themselves in the confusion, that a further extension of the monopoly must introduce.

Some of your Memorialists have had access to see, in part, the management of London booksellers since the year 1739; but they can never be certain that every thing they have heard is true; nor, what they know to be true, can they prove, at so remote a distance of place and time, when parties are gone off the stage. These circumstances are **{2}** the less to be regretted, as perhaps the facts themselves may not be deemed very important, and are only meant to unfold the real history of the transferring of literary property, by a few instances. We shall begin with the works of Lord Bacon.

It is not probable that this great man ever received any money from booksellers for his works. The first editions are decently but frugally printed. Before Mr. Millar[181] printed his edition,[182] they were collected and republished, in four volumes in folio, and were become property. Whether this property arose from first occupation, the progress of the writs must show. Mr. Millar gave one hundred pounds to the undertakers of the former edition for their assignment; and to the separate proprietors of the Life of Henry VII.[183] he gave as many copies of the whole at his own neat expences, as was due to them from the proportion that Life bore to the whole. Here is then one instance of a property erected by mutual consent, without any authority of law. Nor was it Mr. Millar's opinion, at that time, that any court would have forced him to the compliance he chose; but that compliance was more for his interest, as it secured his possession, and freed him from all rivals. To give

[180] *Donaldson v Beckett* (1774) *Cobbett's Parl. Hist.*, xvii, col. 953.

[181] Andrew Millar.

[182] Francis Bacon* (1561–1626), *The Works of Francis Bacon* (Millar, 1740) (ESTC: T52745).

[183] This had not been published as a separate edition for over 100 years, the last one being Francis Bacon, *The Historie of the Reigne of King Henry the Seventh* (Young, 1641) (ESTC: R11984)

his edition an advantage, he engaged Mr. Mallet to write a life of Lord Bacon,[184] which would have been useful had it contained any illustrations of Lord Bacon's philosophy, or of his methods of inquiry into nature; but as it is, it served to bring the edition under the protection of the act of Queen Anne. This life cost Mr. Millar a hundred pounds; and all Lord Bacon's works, excluding his Life of Henry VII. cost no more. Whence this difference of the value of new and old property? If the property of each of these were equally ascertained by law, nothing would be a greater disgrace to human understanding than the comparative price of these two properties; and your Memorialists think, he must be very ingenious indeed, who can reconcile this undervaluation of Lord Bacon to a Property by common-law.

As Lord Bacon[185] pointed out the way how discoveries in nature were to be made, so the honourable Mr. Boyle[186] reduced his theory to practice; and spent his life, and the rents of a large estate, in experimental philosophy and chemistry, and in the most honourable benefactions for encouragement of all kinds of merit, and for the promoting of every species of public good. This great man's works had been twice epitomized, **{3}** and had been translated into Latin by foreigners,[187] but the originals lay neglected; when Mr. Millar formed the design of collecting and printing them together, and prefixing a new life of Mr. Boyle before his works[188]. No bookseller pretended to hinder Mr. Millar in the execution of this undertaking; and the design procured him the favour and patronage of the Earl of Orrery; and afterwards, as a reward of his merit in the execution, Lord Orrery made him a present of his manuscript, consisting of Letters addressed to his Son,[189] of which he sold ten thousand copies,[190] soon after publication. All this is honourable for Mr. Millar; but now the works of the honourable Mr. Boyle, given as a free donation to his country, are claimed as private property; and, in the expected petition, may be applied for as a proper subject for a new monopoly.

Milton's prose-works were in the same neglected situation when Mr. Millar collected them together. The subjects, for the most part, occasional and temporary. They were read by few; and, without the great name of the author of Paradise Lost, few of them could excite the curiosity of the public: for it is true of most of them what the author says, that on such subjects he had only the use of his left hand. These prose-works of Milton, with his life by Mr. Birche,[191] are also erected into a property.

Harrington's works,[192] being occasionally the subject of conversation in a company of men of letters, at Glasgow, were thought worthy of being republished, because of

[184]David Mallet* (c. 1705–1765), *The Life of Francis Bacon* (Millar, 1740) (ESTC: T73603).

[185]Francis Bacon, *Francisci de Verulamio, Summi Angliæ Cancellarii, Instauratio Magna* (1620) (ESTC: S122428).

[186]Robert Boyle* (1627–91).

[187]Probably Samuel de Tournes (1669–1752), who translated various of Boyle's works.

[188]Robert Boyle, *The Works of Robert Boyle* (Millar, 1744) (ESTC: T4460).

[189]John Boyce* (5th earl of Orrery) (1707–62), *Remarks on the Life and Writings of Dr. Jonathan Swift, Dean of St. Patrick's, Dublin, in a Series of Letters from John Earl of Orrery to his Son, the Honourable Hamilton Boyle* (Millar, 1752) (ESTC: T80862).

[190]It went through numerous editions in quick succession: ESTC: T109334, T80855, T80861, T80864.

[191]John Milton, *A Complete Collection of the Historical, Political, and Miscellaneous Works of John Milton* (with 'A Life' by Thomas Birch) (Millar, 1738) (ESTC: T135481).

[192]James Harrington* (1611–77). The first collection was *The Oceana and Other Works* (Darby, 1700) (ESTC: R9111).

his valuable and concise accounts of antient republics, and of the republic of Venice, besides the merit of many of his political observations. A gentleman present, connected by friendship with Messrs. Smith and Bruce,[193] then booksellers in Dublin, proposed to write to them to give out proposals for printing Harrington by subscription,[194] and that the company present would promote the subscription among their friends. This was agreed to by all, and the proposals were accordingly published. A very worthy clergyman being present, eldest brother to Mr. Andrew Millar, wrote to his brother Mr. Andrew what had passed concerning Harrington, as a piece of literary news; who being of opinion that the undertaking would be profitable, published proposals, the same day that they were published at Dublin, the only difficulty was, how to make Harrington a property, that is, **{4}** how to secure his works from being reprinted, or imported by any other person. Mr. Millar got notice of two old ladies, grand-nieces of Mr. Harrington, to whom he gave thirty pounds for an assignment of Harrington's works: and thus they are erected into a property, and not without generosity as to the price on Mr. Millar's side, who might have made it ten, or perhaps five pounds, as all was clear gain to the ladies. But how comes this disproportioned value, that a large folio, of the works of so original a genius, and so bold, as to plan a new government for his country, disagreeable to the Usurper because it would have put an end to his power, and to most others, because inferior to the British constitution? Mr. Millar used to give a hundred guineas for a new popular play: what makes the price of the last so great, and the other so small, is the security of an act of parliament, and the number of purchasers for a new play to be found in London.

We do not mean to reflect on this bold and most industrious undertaker, his memory merits the respect, and even the gratitude of many of the learned, and the thanks of the public for many capital republications. His conducting them prudently for his own interest, was accompanied with great zeal for the combined interest of stationers and booksellers.

Your Memorialists humbly hope the Legislature will think, that the common interests of Great Britain are not to be offered up in sacrifice to a single corporation; and that the Honourable House of Commons will think themselves called to support the statute, as connected with their own dignity, the high honour of the House of Peers, and the general interest of learning through the whole extent of the British dominions.

The accident of situation having thrown almost the whole authors of Great Britain and Ireland into the possession of the London booksellers, whenever they saw there was any appearance of printing becoming more extensive in the kingdom, they were alarmed, and exerted themselves to suppress it in every quarter. In subservience to this intention, the fiction of a right by the common-law of England was invented: we presume to call it a fiction, because it has been found so, upon a full investigation, by the highest court of justice in Great Britain.

The long vexatious process they raised against the Scots booksellers, **{5}** they lost by an unanimous decision, first of the Lords of Session in Scotland,[195] and then of the House

[193] John Smith (*d.* 1771) and William Bruce (1702–55), tr. 1725–37; *The Irish Book in English, 1500–1800*, ed. Raymond Gillespie and Andrew Hadfield (Oxford, 2005), 372; Mary Pollard, *A Dictionary of Members of the Dublin Book Trade, 1550–1800* (2000), 60–1, 532–4.

[194] James Harrington, *The Oceana and Other Works* (Reilly, 1737) (ESTC: T128623).

[195] *Midwinter v Hamilton* (1743) Kam Rem 154; Mor 8295.

of Peers,[196] Lord Hardwick[197] being chancellor. In this cause the doctrine of common-law-right was probably first put into writing. The opinions of some ingenious English counsellors, composed at great length, without facts, were read to the Court of Session; which, so far as we remember, did not affirm that it was the practice of the law of England in the case of books, but endeavoured to prove, by analogical reasoning, that it ought to be so.

Sir Dudley Rider,[198] then Attorney-general, as some of us were informed at the time, gave a contrary opinion, against the common-law right, and perfectly conformable to the present decision of the House of Peers, but which the pursuers prudently suppressed. If your Memorialists have been misinformed, the company of stationers may, perhaps, have his opinion still preserved in his own hand; or if they have been mistaken in any facts relative to the great authors before-mentioned, the proprietors, who have purchased them at Mr. Millar's sale, will be able to set them right by a compleat progress of writs, or title-deeds.

The honourable Mr. Hume Campbell,[199] afterwards Lord-Register for Scotland, gave his opinion, in writing, for the defenders, by whom he was consulted.

The right honourable Mr. William Grant, Lord-Advocate for Scotland, afterwards Lord Preston Grange,[200] who pled in court for the common-law-right, yet owned in private, that he expected to lose that part of his cause; probably because he was sensible, that if such a right had ever existed, it was taken away by a very accurate and plain statute.

It was found necessary to put this statute to the torture, in order to force it to affirm what it never meant, and to unsay what it had distinctly said, for the conduct of authors, and purchasers of manuscripts. Was this interpretation admitted, all the honour it does to the composers and enacters would be lost; and in its place would come a most distinguished *dolus malus*, being the very reverse of the stile of common honesty; the characteristic of which is plainness and simplicity.

While some of the great proprietors affirmed, that an assignment from an author, or proprietor of the trade, gave the same right to a copy that any gentleman had to his estate, they were every day doing things inconsistent with the professed principle. The law of compleat property is **{6}** not confined to subjects of the same nation towards one another, but the subjects of every nation are obliged to do mutual justice; and may be, and daily are prosecuted, for violating the perfect rights of strangers. Through the whole republic of letters, the learned and ingenious authors of one nation are reprinted by another, without being followed by any private process, or complaint of national injury.

Enlightened and generous nations rejoice to see their literary fame wafting over land and seas. Those who write for the good of mankind, rejoice to see their design prosperous; nor are the most learned and ingenious men insensible to merited fame.

It is not the reprinting of books in any other places of Great Britain that any way sensibly hurts the London trade; on the contrary, they load themselves by engrossing,[201] and diminish

[196] *Midwinter v Kincaid* (1751) 1 Pat App 488.

[197] Philip Yorke*, earl of Hardwicke (1690–1764), lord chancellor, 1737–56.

[198] Dudley Ryder†† (1691–1756), attorney-general 1737–54.

[199] Alexander Hume* (1708–60), lord clerk register, 1756–60.

[200] William Grant†* (Lord Prestongrange) (1701–64), lord advocate 1746–54, judge of the court of sessions 1754–64.

[201] For a contemporary explanation of the crime of engrossing: William Blackstone, *Commentaries on the Laws of England*, gen. ed. Wilfrid Prest (Oxford, 2016), iv, 158–9 (Prest, pp. 103–4).

their own trade by endeavouring to bind the hands of their brethren all over the kingdom, who, if free and independent, would be able to trade with them more extensively, and on more equitable terms.

A great proportion of London properties are not original compositions, but compilations: of these compilations there is no end, because the same matter may be abridged, may be enlarged, may be put in ten thousand various forms, without any real improvement, but always with great promises, in advertisements and title-pages. The good sale of one compilation of this kind gives rise to another, in hopes of turning the former from a standard book to waste paper, and this other coming in its place. This gives rise to numberless books with the word NEW before them. New Dictionaries, New Grammars, New Systems of Arithmetic, and New Systems of every other subject; not excepting even the New Practice of Piety, the New Companion to the Altar, and the New whole Duty of Man.

Independent of this cause, learning of itself hath a tendency to swell to such a degree as to render choice in reading a necessary and difficult matter, because human life is too short to read the numerous volumes that have been written on a single subject. It often happens, that a learned author, in order to introduce a few new thoughts, undertakes a whole system, and repeats whatever he thinks hath been well said before him. The reign of Henry IV. of France produced so many historians, that there are more unpublished manuscripts on the history of that **{7}** reign, in the King of France's library, than would take four hundred years to read once over, at the allowance of sixteen hours a day.

A learned advocate* for the monopoly, has laid the whole stress of the cause on the property an author has in his doctrine;[202] but it is obvious this can be of service to extremely few, since few authors contain any new doctrine; besides, novelty may be separated both from truth and goodness, and is of no value when alone. The same ingenious author defines a book a production of the mind; yet, until it be put on paper by the hand, it hath no title to any of the names given to compositions in any language in the world. The same gentleman, in order to show the inferiority of a machine to a book, defines it a production of the hand, as if any new machine had ever been invented without the inventor's thinking. If this is so, how comes it, that so many, who employ themselves in this branch, become crazed by too intense thinking?

The similarity of the faculties of the human mind necessarily produces agreement in the manner of thinking of all who are successful in the search of truth. Truth itself is the same, in all ages, and in all countries. Are the objects of inquiry the abstract relations and properties of being, of quantity, of number, of dimension? the successful enquirers, though without concert, must discover the same relations and properties, as those who add rightly the same account must agree in the same sum. How then can that be the peculiar property of one, which is common to human nature?

One philosopher, living in an earlier age of the world, may draw from the original fountain of nature, what none has communicated to the world before him; yet, many ages after, and in many different countries, the same truths will be drawn anew from the same fountain, since the love of truth is co-natural to the human mind; and, like the sublime in sentiment, the perpetual object of delightful admiration. If there is any philosopher, of so cold and

[202] William Warburton* (1698–1779), *A Letter from an Author to a Member of Parliament, Concerning Literary Property* (Knapton, 1747) (ESTC: T37853). The letter is also available in *The Works of the Right Reverend William Warburton*, ed. Richard Hurd (12 vols, 1811), xii, 405.

selfish a cast, as to have no pleasure in communicating his discoveries to society, and is influenced by money only, he discovers an evident mark of a groveling mind, rarely found united to a great genius.

As nature is one whole, so the discoveries of mankind must be linked together: because, upon this union, the progress made in the discovery **{8}** of new truths is accelerated, propositions priorly demonstrated serve as steps in the demonstration of new propositions. The Elements of Euclid[203] are a scientific arrangement of the propositions discovered by his predecessors; which, by the union he has given them, have become profitable to every age and country of science: and, without allowing that the truths, of general use to human society, may be freely employed for their benefit, the discoveries of separate men can never be made one whole. The idea of the property of the author lying in his doctrine, is, therefore, inconsistent with the advancement of science: and although he should be disposed to hoard his knowledge, as a miser his money, yet Providence hath put it out of his power to hinder others from coming after him in the discovery of the same truths.

But we hope, after the decision of the House of Peers,[204] it will be needless to detect any more sophisms on this subject; it being now evident, that all the reasonings upon which they grounded their monopoly, beyond what was granted by the statute of the eight of Queen Anne, have neither solidity of reasoning, nor truth of fact. Yet to one, who has taken only an occasional view of this subject, it may appear in a plausible point of light, as encouraging both learning and printing; but then, let such a gentleman consider, that neither authors nor printers can tell to what a degree a work will succeed, nor how long it will continue to be called for. The proofs of this uncertainty from examples are without number. And Mr. Millar owned, that if perpetual property were established by law, they could not afford to give authors any more; because, unless their money returned, with profits, by the first run, they were put to a stand, and could not go on with their trade; and a book, that did not sell quickly at first, he called a blank in the lottery of bookselling.

If perpetual property was established by law, printers and booksellers must be reduced to a smaller number: because, almost the whole books, which have been printed in Great Britain, by the accident of their having been printed in London, are claimed by the London booksellers, as their property: for the moderns are not only the successors, but the heirs of those who went before them; and a book, not reprinted since the reign of Queen Elizabeth, is still in property.

Dr. Cudworth's[205] learned book of the Intellectual System of the Universe, **{9}** was printed above a century since, and never after reprinted. A Professor of the University of Glasgow[206] desired Mr. Millar to be informed, that if he would reprint that book, a considerable number of copies would be taken at the University immediately. He wrote for answer, that the certainty of the number taken immediately was encouraging, but that he was at a loss how to proceed, because he had only the eighteenth share of the property; and that his partners might either refuse to join with him, or to sell their shares on easy terms.

[203] The first English translation was by Henry Billingsley* (*d.* 1606) in 1570.

[204] *Donaldson v Beckett* (1774) *Cobbett's Parl. Hist.*, xvii, col. 953.

[205] Ralph Cudworth* (1617–88), *Intellectual System of the Universe* (Royston, 1678) (ESTC: R27278).

[206] This was probably the quaestor at the university, who was responsible for buying books. It is unclear when this occurred so the professor in question cannot be identified.

However, the book was printed;[207] and a learned gentleman appointed to take care of the edition; but, as he was not a Greek scholar, he did not pretend to correct the numerous Greek quotations, which are left with all the errors made by the printers.

On what principles is this idea of property founded? Can any man have a private right contrary to the general good? The origin of private property is the good of society; and the lawful government of every country hath a right to limit and regulate it so far as is necessary for the greatest good of society. Thus, if the legislature were to render literary property perpetual, they would not, however, put it in the power of the bookseller to dispose of these properties as he may his books, to booksellers in any quarter of the world; because, if he was to sell the property of them, to be executed in France or Holland, then the political interests of the country would over-rule, as it would appear plainly, that by the sale, the country had lost a valuable manufacture, and become dependent for a great national benefit, besides the loss of the profit it brings as a manufacture.

Suppose a few enterprising Scotsmen had purchased the properties of Knapton, Tonson, and Millar,[208] and thereby become proprietors, by assignments of the common-law-right, to the most capital English authors, and that such a trial had ensued as was lately before the House of Peers, would not the very persons, who now complain of the decision as ruinous to them, have rejoiced in it as a national and personal benefit? and would not every impartial Briton have shared the joy? For why, would they say, should England be deprived of having the works of those great men printed in their own country, to whom it gave birth, to whom it gave education, and to whom it gave many emoluments and honours? **{10}**

The great endowments bestowed by the Author of nature, are not solely for the benefit of the persons on whom they are bestowed, they ought to be employed in the service of their parents, their children, their friends and relations, their country, and mankind. Is it in their power by any noble work to extend their service to all ages? nothing can be more enchanting to the generous mind than so extensive a hope: what nobler enthusiasm can warm the breast, and elevate the genius of an author? Why then treat every great British author as if he had been venal and mercenary? Why for a pittance, or for nothing, should he be condemned forever to be printed only by a few of a single corporation? When there is no interest to conceal the disinterestedness of authors, many will be found to have laboured for the good of mankind; the property of whose works are bought and sold, although, like the Earl of Shaftesbury,[209] they never had any concern in the commerce.

When books are out of monopoly, they can be printed forever in the place of their original publication; and all buyers in that place will be better and cheaper served when the price is kept moderate by free competition; but so long as the right of printing is transferable, the proprietor can sell his right of printing to a bookseller in the remotest part of the Isle; it is, therefore, too great a power to remain long in private hands.

Virtue and piety are the greatest happiness of an individual, and consequently, of every nation; therefore, all regulations that tend to make these more universal are to be esteemed wise, are to be esteemed just; because they produce the sum of good on the whole. Useful

[207] Ralph Cudworth, *Intellectual System of the Universe* (Walthoe, 1743) (ESTC: T140741).

[208] John Knapton* (1696–1770); Jacob Tonson* (1714–67); Andrew Millar.

[209] Anthony Ashley Cooper*, 3rd earl of Shaftesbury (1671–1713).

knowledge and worthy sentiments are the nourishment of the soul, and therefore on a level with the first necessaries of life, where a monopoly appears insufferable to all.

The wisest men of antiquity thought there could be no stable friendship but among good men. That which unites two, and makes them as it were one, if diffused over all, will unite the whole. If the same authors fit to form the mind are diffused among the whole body of the people, it will tend to give one cast to the whole, to produce mutual esteem and good will, and to implant in every mind a consciousness of the necessity of private, to the compleating of public virtue.

As virtue cannot survive with the loss of liberty, so liberty, though **{11}** never so compleat, cannot make bad men happy; nor will it long remain where justice has fled; therefore, the Legislature ought, as much as possible, to second every endeavour to promote national piety and virtue; and to let those great authors, who by the valuable writings they have left behind them continue to instruct their country, do all the good they can. The more universally they are printed, the more universally will they be read. Piety and virtue will render the common people more innocent, and crimes and punishments become more rare.

It is but just that authors should have all the honours that their works can bestow on them. It is just that they dispose of them in the most profitable manner; and to sell to a London bookseller has hitherto been found the surest road to success, because there are few authors whose works it is not in their power to suppress; and when the author retains the property, he must be highly esteemed if they cannot mar his circulation. The same interest leads them to discourage all undertakings in which they themselves are not concerned.

From such reflexions, and many others that might be made, it appears, that the profit arising from the sale of manuscripts neither is a sufficient, nor ought to be the only encouragement to learning. These works that are the effects of the most profound genius, and the greatest application, are above the capacity of the generality of mankind, and on that account called for by few, and, consequently, bring no profit to the author; nor fame, unless he can afford to lose money by printing them, or move some uncommonly discerning and generous patron.

Few are ignorant of what importance the Mathematics are to the generality of arts, on which national greatness and prosperity depend; yet, how much they have declined is but too obvious. Nor can it happen otherwise, while there are so few establishments for giving subsistence to such as are willing to devote their lives to objects of such intense application.

The Legislature gave Mr. Buckley a privilege for his splendid edition of Thuanus[210] by act of Parliament.[211] Might it not, on this occasion, be suitable to the wisdom of the Legislature, both as an enlargement of the field of British printing, and as an encouragement to the printers and booksellers of London who have been lately disappointed, to enact, That every foreign book, published after the commencement of the supposed **{12}** act, upon its being reprinted in Great Britain, and entered in stationers hall, should have the same monopoly with those composed and written in Great Britain; only, that every book, not exceeding thirty sheets, should be restricted to the privilege of five years; a book of fifty or sixty sheets, ten years; and every book of a hundred, or upwards, fourteen years; but not

[210] Jacques-Auguster de Thou, *Jac. Augusti Thuani Historiarum sui temporis Tomus primus. Lib. I.–XXIV. MDXLVI.–MDLX. Hen. II–Fran. II* (Buckley, 1733) (ESTC: T98490).

[211] Printing of Thuanus Histories Act 1733 (7 Geo. II, c. 24).

to prohibit the importation of the editions of the original publisher, which would be an useful check to prevent bad and incorrect printing, or too high a price?

As the German, Spanish, and Portuguese languages are understood by few, all books of voyages, of mines, metals, and mineralogy, in any of these languages, translated into English, might be allowed the same privilege. All books on mechanics, useful or fine arts; all books on agriculture, or any branch of the mathematics, translated into English from any language, might have the same privilege granted them. All foreign books in their original languages, if printed on British paper, might be allowed, as an encouragement to exportation, the drawback of the excise on what shall be exported. Notwithstanding, if any book, reprinted in consequence of the above act, shall be all sold off, and the proprietor delay putting a new edition to the press, it shall be lawful for any person whatsoever to reprint the same, and the person reprinting shall have the same exclusive right until the end of the term of years, granted by the statute, that the first proprietor had, whose right shall cease.

As London is the chief market for foreign editions, this act would prove a most profitable one for the printers and booksellers of London, and much more than compensate their disappointment. Nor could any foreign country think it a hardship; it is agreeable to the practice of Holland, which grants a privilege to the person who exhibits the first copy of any foreign book. It is not meant that this should extend to classics; nor that this privilege should be granted in consideration of any editions already printed, but only to encourage such editions as shall be made after the act; and on condition that they be printed on good paper, and correct.

Printing was carried on for above seventy years after its invention, without a single privilege. Froben[212] bought manuscripts at great prices for about thirty years, without ever applying for any privilege; after **{13}** that term Erasmus[213] applied in his favour for a privilege of two years, in consideration of his great merit, and the numbers who reprinted upon him; and this privilege extended only to new works, or those considerably augmented by him.

The stationers company in London itself carried on their business till the reign of Henry VIII. without any charter[214] or peculiar privilege; nor did their charter entitle them to any more than the making by-laws for regulating their own trade within the city of London, as other companies of stationers might have done, had they existed, in every burgh or village in Britain.

By long possession they imagined they had acquired property, independent of, and contrary to, the act of the eight of Queen Anne, although to that act they owe all their power in Scotland; for, previous to that, they had no more connection with Scotland than with China. The assignment of an author in England owes its legality in Scotland to a British act of parliament; this was tacitely acknowledged by the printers and booksellers in London, for they never complained of the Scots although they reprinted whatever they pleased, until the act of the eight of Queen Anne. The Tatlers and Spectators were reprinted in Edinburgh at their first publication. Nor does it appear that the trade of the stationers in London is

[212]Johann Froben (c. 1460–1527); Valentina Sebastiani, *Johann Froben, Printer of Basel: A Bibliographical Profile and Catalogue of His Edition* (Leiden, 2018).

[213]Desiderius Erasmus Roterodamus (1469–1536).

[214]The Stationers' Company obtained its charter in 1557.

diminished by the increase of printing in other places. Even with Dublin itself, their trade is probably greater than it was before they began to reprint their books; wherever printing takes place, it diffuses the taste for books wider, and the rich chuse the more expensive editions.

If the booksellers of London were convinced, that they had a right to their copies by the common-law, how comes it they never prosecuted the printers and booksellers of Ireland for violating this common-law-right, since the common-law of England and Ireland is the same? nor have they ever prosecuted an American, and this is the more extraordinary, as they had nothing to fear from the partiality of an Irish or American court, the last appeal being to the most respectable courts in Great Britain. The truth is, they knew very well they had no such right, though they languished after it; and hoped, by sham-processes, by favourable juries, by multiplied applications for injunctions, and by a learned author's publishing a pamphlet in their favour, to make the public believe, **{14}** that the encouragement of learning was inseparable from their doctrine, although the reverse may be proved.

Give any farmer more land than he can cultivate for nothing, will this induce him to rent or purchase more? it will certainly have contrary effect. When one offers him land to purchase or rent, he would say, "Sir, I have got already as much as I can cultivate, and therefore stand in need of no more. I know the fertility of my own ground from experience; what yours will produce I know not. Nevertheless, if you will give it me for a trifle, I will run all risks. A few of us farmers have got all the cultivated land into our possession, and no others now remain to whom you can either let or sell." This would be the language of a corporation, who had engrossed all, to an author.

Take away competition among buyers, and goods become cheap. Take away competition among sellers, and goods become dear. Monopoly annihilates competition among sellers, by taking away their rivals. Common interest produces combination in a corporation of sellers. A combination of book-sellers must, therefore, be a combination against book-buyers; because their ultimate intention is their own profit. The fewer undertakers there are for purchasing and publishing manuscripts, the fewer competitors there will be for that kind of property; therefore; an extension of monopoly must make the price of unpublished manuscripts sink.

As extension of monopoly would make new manuscripts cheap, so it would make the property of old saleable authors dear. By putting a restraint on all but the monopolist, the value of the property of an old book must be added to the expences of an edition, as the price given for a manuscript is at present. Every time this property shifts hands, the last purchaser is in the same state with one who has bought a new manuscript; he is, therefore, under a necessity of loading the public with this additional expence. The more stock he lays out upon old property, the less will remain to purchase new; this, consequently, must cause the price of new manuscripts to fall.

As the common interest of combined monopolists is purchasing manuscripts cheap, (for authors are no part of the corporation) so it is the common interest of all those who have acquired many copy-rights to blow up the nominal as well as the real value; because when the value **{15}** of copies swells on all hands, and all the great proprietors are both selling and buying, whatever the nominal prices may be, it is in reality only the exchange of one property for another; and when the properties transferred are equal in value, nominal price hurts neither party, whether they count by thousands or by hundreds, it only gives the appearance of great transactions to such as are in reality small. This may be illustrated by what happened to a bookseller in London. He purchased a number of unsaleable books in quires, at the price of waste paper, a catalogue of which he sent to Holland, stating each book at its full price, with an offer of exchange; and the Dutch bookseller matched him so well, that he lost by the bargain.

This swelling of the nominal value of old property is a more serious matter to young beginners, who have nothing to give for what properties they purchase but money; and are obliged to buy very small shares at high estimations, let the original price given to the author be never so small.

Nothing hinders export more than the dearness of goods. Monopolies swell the price of goods, consequently prevent export; and monopolists lean almost entirely to home consumption. The higher goods are priced in any one country, the more readily a neighbouring country will become its rival. Thus, Holland has become the rival of France in reprinting almost all their saleable books; which they had never succeeded so well in, if the Parisians had not trusted too much to their privileges.

The necessity of making the first editions of books splendid, empowers the booksellers in Dublin to sell that book for a crown[215] which costs a pound in Great Britain. If they had no such rivals in Dublin, they would spring up at the Hague. As the English language becomes more universal, English books will be more frequently reprinted on the Continent.

Printing-presses, every where, are chiefly employed in reprinting. Give all saleable books to one company, and all printing-houses not employed by them must be shut up; because, if they are not regularly employed, they cannot have workmen, nor is it possible to preserve printing materials in order for occasional employment.

Whoever has the monopoly of any book depends upon his matter, **{16}** not upon his manner of printing. He considers what price those who want the book will give, and puts it as high as is consistent with its currency. But where there is no monopoly there is a contention for cheapness, for correctness, for elegance, and legibility; and that which is most generally esteemed, will be most successful.

When great authors can be printed with classical freedom,[216] it is to be hoped they will be printed not only with elegance and correctness, but sometimes have the advantage of learned editors to explain obscure passages by their comments, correct mistakes by their notes, and supply defects by their additions taken from later discoveries. This liberty would be an ample recompence to all authors who survive the twenty-eight years, and to all the learned in general who wish to become editors, as this employment is sometimes found more profitable, and less laborious than being an author.

By the freedom of books after a determined period, many antient, respectable, and opulent families will find themselves at liberty to do honour to the memory of their ancestors, by splendid and ornamented editions of their works.

As none of us have been bred to the profession of the law, we cannot pretend to any peculiar skill of that kind; what we would wish to have the honour to do, is to lay such facts before the Legislature as tend to make it plain, that it is not the interest of authors to have the monopoly extended, that it is not the interest of honest industry among the whole body of London booksellers themselves, and is a restraint on the industry of every printer and bookseller without the capital, whether he lives in England or Scotland.

[215] Five shillings.

[216] That fits with the allowance for printing classics: Copyright Act 1709, s. 7.

The London corporation have long enjoyed advantages to which every other Briton had the same title, to the loss of the public, and to the advantage of none but a few of themselves. It is surprising that in so long a course of years, no bookseller in England appealed to the House of Peers before Alexander Donaldson.[217] We, in this part of the kingdom, had no title to concern ourselves in this appeal if the same corporation had not endeavoured to establish the same dominion here; probably from ignorance that the common-law of England does not extend to Scotland, and that the common-law of Scotland never gave any property without a privilege; but as they are just now endeavouring to **{17}** obtain a statute, which must extend an enlarged monopoly, over the whole Island, unfelt before; and for reasons of so limited a kind, as do not seem to us to justify a grant, confined within the bounds of London itself.

When judgment was given against Mr. Taylor,[218] a bookseller said, he was ten thousand pounds richer than he was in the morning. If the decision added so much to his wealth, how does it agree with his conviction that he had a common-law-right before? If he had no common-law-right before, what has the decision of the House of Peers taken from him?

If those gentlemen gave Mr. Taylor terms not to appeal to the House of Peers, are not they themselves the cause of their own misfortune? If so, why grant a new monopoly on that account? It is to be hoped that experience will prevent the repetition of what has been so often seen, that

—Though Wisdom wake, Suspicion sleeps
At Wisdom's gate, and to Simplicity
Resigns her charge, while Goodness thinks no ill
Where no ill seems: which now for once beguil'd
Uriel, though regent of the sun, and held
The sharpest sighted spirit of all in heaven.[219]

Is it a mark of conviction to shun the light? Is it not rather a mark of fear, lest an appeal might throw new light on the cause? Their methods of shunning a final decision by making up matters with different litigators, is a proof of this fear. They knew that what they alledged to be the common-law of England, was only the common use and wont of their own private corporation, which they could over-rule within themselves when they pleased: and their conduct, with respect to rights, is a series of inconsistencies; now grounding property on an assignment of an author; then claiming the property of an anonymous book; of a book published after the author's death, as Shakespear by players, who were neither heirs nor assigns; and again, calling that an assignment where the price given was restricted to the quantity sold. How often is the property of the Bible annihilated by notes? How many properties are **{18}** devoured by dictionaries of arts and sciences, trade and commence? How many lesser works are retailed in magazines and news-papers?

In the case of Milton's Paradise Lost, the second payment[220] was made only because the number necessary to make it a profitable bargain was sold. One would think the bookseller,

[217]But in Scotland there was an earlier appeal: see *Midwinter v Kincaid* (1751) 1 Pat App 488.

[218]It is presumed this is *Millar v Taylor* (1769) 4 Burr 2303 (98 ER 201).

[219]From John Milton, *Paradise Lost*, Book 3.

[220]Kerry MacLennan, 'John Milton's Contract for "Paradise Lost": A Commercial Reading', *Milton Quarterly*, xliv (2010), 221.

of consequence, had given nothing for the continuation of the property, since he made his bargain so as to make the author's second payment depend upon his success. Mr. Richard Baxter's[221] method of dealing with his booksellers seems to have some resemblance to this; he made no assignment of property, but agreed with his bookseller to receive from him eighteen pence for each ream of paper he printed.

Suppose any man undergoes an extraordinary loss by his own credulity, if any are to bear the weight of that but himself, ought it not to be such brethren as are become rich by the same peculiar privileges, not those who have undergone difficulties by their combination, and illegal monopolizing.

Would it be just to make a new law extending to Scotland, on account of an English common-law-right, which did not extend to Scotland?

Had Mr. Millar, or his executors, given warrandice, that the common-law-right was a well-grounded and lasting right, Mr. Johnson[222] might have had recourse for damage; but then, such warrandice would certainly have raised the price: and wherever any one purchases a doubtful right, he is like a man that buys a lottery-ticket, he may lose or gain; as he would have enjoyed all the profit, so nobody, in case of a blank, thinks himself concerned to share the loss.

Were the Legislature to give precedents of loading the public with private losses, not made in public service, cases may be supposed where they would find abundance of applications.

A gentleman in Scotland, of the name of Lesley, left an estate, which fell to Count Lesley, a cadet of the family, established in Germany; another gentleman claimed it, as nearer in blood; the cause came before the House of Peers, and sentence was passed in favour of Count Lesley. A process was begun afterwards on a new ground, that Count Lesley, being an alien, could not inherit; and the Count lost his estate by a decision of the House of Peers.[223] Supposing this estate not entailed, a purchaser **{19}** might have lost his money, since the Count could transfer to him no better right than he had, and had given no warrandice. Should the purchaser plead, that he trusted to the first decision of the House of Peers, would that engage the Legislature to make up his private loss by a tax on the public?

Laws are not made for single persons,[224] but for the general good of the society obliged to obey them. It is impracticable to prevent those inconveniences which are inseparable from the freedom of manufactures and commerce. To claim any right for compensation in such a case, is to set one's private interest against national prosperity.

There are sometimes inconveniences arising from manufacturing too many, or too few goods for the market; these cause events which distress manufacturers, but the remedy must be left to their own discretion. The interposal of the Legislature would destroy manufactures; and the only natural remedy is to quit manufacturing the over-done branch till increase of demand raises the price, and balances past inconveniences.

[221] Richard Baxter* (1615–91).

[222] William Johnston.

[223] This is a reference to *Antonius, Son of Count Leslie v James Leslie* (1742) 1 Paton 324 (*LJ*, xxvi, 108); and *Charles Cajetan, Count Leslie v Peter Leslie Grant* (1763) 2 Paton 68 (*LJ*, xxx, 326).

[224] This ignores private legislation which clearly is made for a single person or area.

The ingenious and worthy Mr. Glover[225] has shewn that liberty is the nurse of commerce; and certainly manufacturers supply the fund of commerce, and they are no less nourished by liberty. They furnish subsistence, on which population depends.

If freedom makes every other manufacture to prosper, should a manufacture connected with learning, be oppressed by a double monopoly? Shall compassion for a few rich, induce the Legislature to load hundreds of others, who are comparatively poor? Shall the general interest of the whole, be sacrificed to the exaggerated complaints of so small a part?

Have not the universities of Oxford and Cambridge done more honour to England abroad, by their editions of antient authors, than all the compilations brought forth by the company of stationers? Have not these universities an interest in the freedom of printing, who have daily occasion for books? They are judges both of correctness and elegance, and they are fit to give editions that may be trusted.

The clergy have certainly an interest in the freedom of printing. The rich and dignified clergy can afford expensive editions; but a book may be bulky and dear, without being magnificent or elegant. In the fetters of monopoly, there can be little competition for distinguished approbation.

{20} Do not those vicars of the clergy, improperly called curates, deserve compassion? How can they go through their duty in furnishing religious instructions to so many thousands of the people of England, without the help of books? And how can their scanty allowance afford books made dear by monopoly?

The clergy of Scotland are, indeed, generally better provided for than these last; yet, since the Union of the kingdoms, the expence of living is so greatly increased, by the diminution of the value of money, and by the change of manners, that few of them have libraries so extensive as formerly; and literature must decline among them, if their access to books is cut off by highness of price.

It is not many years since the books used in the schools, and universities of Scotland were imported from Holland. It is less time since the paper, used in printing in London, was generally Dutch or Genoa. The printers in Glasgow have ever used either English paper, or their own manufacture.

Some yet alive remember Nicholas de Champ, a French refugee, who erected the first paper-mill in Scotland;[226] since that time, by the gradual increase of printing, paper-mills have multiplied, and are still becoming more numerous, to the increase of the revenue and the national wealth; but must soon be annihilated, if we are obliged, by the oppression of monopoly, to lock up our printing-houses.

Before the late Mr. Caslon[227] began to make types, those used in Great Britain were, for the most part, imported from foreign countries, especially Holland; now none are imported. The types made in Britain are deemed superior to the foreign; and there are types

[225] Richard Glover* (1712–85); the reference would be to two of his poems: *Leonidas* (1737) which praised liberty, and *London, or the Progress of Commerce* (1739).

[226] Nicholas de Champ worked a mill in 1710 on the Stoneywood Estate near Aberdeen, owned by James Moir. However, it was not the first paper mill in Scotland, for that was established in 1590 at Dalry, Edinburgh, by Mungo and Gideon Russell: A.G. Thomson, *The Paper Industry in Scotland, 1590–1801* (Edinburgh, 1974), 18; Alastair Mann, 'The Anatomy of the Printed Book in Early Modern Scotland', *Scottish Historical Review*, lxxx (2001), 182–3.

[227] William Caslon* (1692–1766).

manufactured in this city,[228] after the models of the Stevens,[229] the Vascosans,[230] and the Elzevirs,[231] both in the Greek and Roman characters.

Thus, arts and manufactures have a mutual connection and dependence; and while one branch is discouraged, it falls heavy on others connected. By destroying one the series is broken, and the whole moulders away. After manufactures and arts have been destroyed by discouragement, it damps the spirit of a country, and renders it almost impossible to renew them.

Besides, the extending monopoly to Scotland, will be of little service to the London booksellers; if we may judge by times past, they will be **{21}** losers by it; because, while the Scots printed little they imported less. As the taste for books in Scotland hath been spread by printing, so it will contract with its decay. Some living remember when there was but one bookseller in Glasgow, who imported any books from London.

When Scotland had few manufactures they were entirely clad in their own; since their manufactures and trade increased, the demand for English manufactures hath increased; all, except the shirt, are commonly English; and all assortments of goods exported are chiefly English.

At Glasgow the art of printing, and commerce of books, are intimately connected with the other arts, manufactures, and commerce of the place. Every manufacture in Glasgow, and the country round, depends chiefly on their export-trade. Every discouragement that manufacturers meet with here, tends to diminish the materials of foreign trade.

When trade and commerce are low here, the immense quantity of English goods continually importing for consumption and export, are in proportion diminished, and the payments flower; it is, consequently, not the interest of England to discourage the lawful industry of Scotland; besides, the large stock of money employed in the trade of Glasgow, enables them to pay the greater part of English goods many months before they can possibly have any return, but the dealers with the merchants who reside here are obliged to give them much longer credit.

If these English goods, which are exported from this place, were the consequence of consignments and commissions, the same consignments and commissions might possibly be sent to London; but that is not the nature of the commerce of the place, it is bold adventure, by which goods are made to travel into every inhabited part of America, the most remote from the sea-shore; and, without such attention, the people would be under a necessity of manufacturing for themselves; and, consequently, the manufacturers in Great Britain in proportion diminished.

The printers of Glasgow have not entirely confined themselves to the printing of English, some of them have printed a few books in the French and Italian languages, and more extensively, classical books in the Greek and Roman languages, which have made their way thro' Holland, France, Germany, Italy, and, more or less, to places much more **{22}** remote. Undertakings of this nature are little envied because they are rather honourable

[228] For a discussion of the typefaces used for printing classics, Philip Gaskell, 'Printing the Classics in the Eighteenth Century', *The Book Collector*, i (1952), 98.

[229] Philemon Stephens (*d.* 1670), St Paul's Churchyard.

[230] A reference to Michel de Vascosan (*d.* 1577) a French printer known for his elegant editions: *Oxford Companion to the Book*, ed. Suarez and Woudhuysen, ii, 1238.

[231] As to the Dutch printing family, see David Davies, *The World of the Elseviers, 1580–1712* (The Hague, 1954).

than profitable; and need to be intermixed with undertakings in which there are a greater proportion of home-consumption.

The mathematical works of Dr. Simson,[232] which have been printed,[233] and are printing here, could not have been executed in the manner he chose without the art of engraving in wood; and there are others which could not have been executed without the art of engraving on copper. These two last arts are connected with the printing of linens and cottons, which are taxed so as to bring a great revenue to the crown;[234] and such manufactures are numerous in this country; it is, consequently, the interest of government to encourage arts subservient to the wealth of the country, and the increase of the revenue.

Yet the efforts made in this way, amidst great difficulties, could neither have subsisted as they have done for above twenty years, nor been undertaken, without the assistance afforded by the exercise of printing; nor would that alone have done, without the assistance of opulent and generous protectors: for the attempt was not confined to engraving in wood and copper, a drawing-school was established,[235] where many gentlemen, some of whom have been remarkably distinguished, have laid the first foundations of that part of education. This year the first prize for history-painting in Rome was adjudged to a painter[236] bred at this school. But as this would carry us too far from our main subject, we here put an end to it, with the Memorial itself, most humbly submitting the whole to the wisdom and justice of the Honourable the Commons of Great Britain.

If we err, we err unwillingly, having never offered any thing as fact which we did not know, or believe to be true; nor any reasoning which did not appear to us to be solid. We know there are many omissions of things of weight, but our Memorial is already too long. Our ignorance of the nature of the bill makes it impracticable for us to be more particular. If any act is made which gives them a right to books unnamed, they will find means of including the whole under that cover; and it will become a source of endless litigations.

Formerly, in Scotland, the distance between the sentence and the punishment of a capital crime was so short, that there was not sufficient **{23}** time to represent to the King the severity of a sentence in a particular case, that a pardon could be obtained. This was afterwards remedied by an act of parliament.[237]

In the making of laws that affect the interests or rights of the people of Great Britain, a similar inconveniency happens, when the quickness of the passing a law, makes it impossible for those who live remote from the seat of the Legislature to counter-petition, or represent the difficulty of their case.

In the present question, your Memorialists hope they have nothing to fear. It belongs to superior wisdom to distinguish between feigned lamentation, and the voice of nature in real distress.

[232]Robert Simson* (1687–1768), professor of mathematics at Glasgow University.

[233]This is probably *Euclid* (Edinburgh, 1775) (ESTC: T161020).

[234]There was a 15% import duty: Taxation Act 1711 (10 Anne, c. 18), s. 69 (extended by Continuance of Laws, etc. Act 1742 (16 Geo. II, c. 26), s. 4, and made perpetual by Duties (Logwood, etc) Act 1766 (7 Geo. III, c. 47), s. 6).

[235]This is referring to the Glasgow Academy of the Fine Arts: David Murray, *Robert and Andres Foulis and the Glasgow Press: With Some Account of the Glasgow Academy of the Fine Arts* (Glasgow, 1913), 81–2.

[236]David Allan* (1744–96) was given the gold medal in 1774 by the Academy of St Luke for 'The Origin of Portraiture' (also known as the 'The Maid of Corinth').

[237]Bail in Criminal Cases (Scotland) Act 1724 (11 Geo c 26), s 10.

May we presume to say, that it appears to us, that the honour of the Legislature is interested in the intention of this memorial; because the harmony of all the legislative powers renders a government at once awful and venerable; and what decision ever commanded more respect, or is more universally applauded than the late solemn decision of the Peers, assisted by the twelve Judges?[238] Nor does any difference of opinion that happened on that occasion in the least diminish its authority; because it gave occasion to a more full investigation of facts, than unanimity would have done; and, thereby, gave a weight to the decree, founded on a compleat knowledge of the subject.

Would not an increase of the monopoly have a similar effect with a reversal of the decision?

If this appears to be the case to the wisdom of the Honourable the Commons, they certainly will not put the House of Peers under the necessity of guaranteeing to the public the extensive advantages of their late decree.

We, the Printers and Booksellers of Glasgow, most humbly beg pardon for the length, and all the other defects of this Memorial; which we have appointed Robert Foulis,[239] Printer to the University, for us, and in our name, to subscribe.

GLASGOW,
April 25. 1774.

{24} COLBERT'S Political Testament, addressed to his master, Lewis XIV. translated into English by Bernard, Professor of Moral Philosophy in Oxford. Lond. 1695.[240]

"The booksellers trade in the country stands in much need of your Majesty to appoint it some other laws. Because it is subject to the inquisition of the booksellers of Paris; who, by means of the privileges which they obtain out of the Chancery, hold all others of the kingdom in such dependence, that they must either starve, or run the hazard of being ruined. If it please your Majesty to have compassion on their distress, you must restrict those privileges to the city of Paris, that all who live in any other place of the kingdom, may be allowed to follow freely their own methods with security. Paris, of itself alone, is worth more than all the rest of the kingdom; and it is not just that above two thousand families should perish, to increase the wealth of a few booksellers in the capital."

"The Council is full of examples of this nature, in similar cases; and it is the interest of your Majesty to pronounce in favour of the oppressed; for the books which we have from Paris are so dear, that the poor cannot reach the price: yet a priest, who hath but a hundred crowns revenue, hath no less need of instruction than he who hath two thousand; he ought, therefore, to be enabled to do his duty by being furnished with the means; which he must be deprived of so long as these people are empowered to keep their feet on his neck."

{7}*A LETTER from an Author on LITERARY PROPERTY, addressed to a Member of Parliament. Lond 1747.

[238] *Donaldson v Beckett* (1774) *Cobbett's Parl. Hist.*, xvii, col. 953.

[239] Robert Foulis* (1707–76).

[240] Jean Baptiste Colbert (1619–83), *The Political Last Testament of Monsieur John Baptist Colbert*, trans. John Bernard (Brome, 1695) (ESTC: R215457).

General Observations/Hints

General Observations on the Expediency of granting Relief in Literary Property [Copy held at: Bodleian, Oxford University/Longer Version published as 'Hints and Comments' in *Morning Chronicle*, 5, 6, 7, 9, 10, 13 May and 2 June].

[Variant 1: *Morning Chronicle* (MC)/Variant 2: General Observations (GO)]

[MC: *Hints and Grounds of Argument in the Cause of the London Booksellers.*]
[GO: GENERAL OBSERVATIONS
On the Expediency of granting Relief
In LITERARY PROPERTY.]

{MC5} The present application of such of the booksellers as are copyholders to Parliament for relief, stands distinguished by a variety of [material/striking] circumstances. [GO: and] Encouraged by the candid reception with which their petition has been honoured, [I am/they are] induced to state several facts, which may be material for the consideration of legislators, tho' they could have no weight in a court of law.

[MC: The principal ground of the application: that a number of men of character and respectable situations in life are ruined by a misconception of law, which had the sanction of the first law court in the kingdom, has been ably and amply stated. So remarkable a plea can only be successfully opposed by considerations of public and general utility. If it should appear that the public have no interest in laying open Literary Property, the interested struggles of individuals can have little weight.]

The petitioners, with [great/some] reason, think themselves much injured by the indiscriminate manner in which the term [booksellers/bookseller] is applied; it is necessary that the material distinctions in the professional character of different booksellers should be pointed out, as a general prejudice has arisen against the *whole* trade on account of the too great licentiousness of the press. Lord Camden observed with great justice, that the question of Copy-Right relates solely to the works of men of genius and learning;[241] no considerations, therefore, on the low ribaldry, personal abuse, flimsy complications, and the various species of bad books, which are daily obtruded on the public, under promising titles, relate to this case; they are published by men who are indeed booksellers, but they are not copyholders, nor do they make any efforts to procure the works of [GO: such] authors [which/as] have [any/a] chance of becoming valuable copies. It is from this source that the public are pestered with so many frivolous libellous and obscene pamphlets, such a number of paltry novels, and these are the book makers who are continually deceiving the world by retailing literary rubbish in 6d numbers. Between these men and the proprietors of bookstalls, there has ever subsisted a close connection, as the remainder of such publications must there be disposed of; they have, therefore, with great alacrity, joined their benefactors in a petition to parliament against those booksellers who print such books as they (the proprietors of the stalls) receive no kind of benefit from: and this petition [is announced in the votes to be/they modestly call] the petition of a number of the booksellers of

[241] *Donaldson v Beckett* (1774) *Cobbett's Parl. Hist.*, xvii, col. 953, at 999–1000.

London and Westminster, who apprehend that they will be injured, if copy-holders are relieved.

The proprietors of circulating libraries, the publishers of libellous papers, and of every trifling or contemptible production of the press, are all included in the same general class; and thus the friend of government, and the friend of virtue, who does not attend to the distinction, may be led to consider the cause of the copy-holders as the cause of bad men. The proprietors of good books have ever been injured in their property by booksellers of this stamp, and the claim of brotherhood appears to be peculiarly dangerous to them at this important crisis of their cause; with the same truth might the Blackwell-hall factor and the piece broker, the Virginia merchant and the retailer of snuff, be deemed brethren, but with this material difference, that in these instances, the humbler tradesmen is of use to his principal.

Pope,[242] and all the favourite authors of the last age, abound with complaints against Booksellers [GO: such as these], particularity the infamous Curl.[243] This has created a prejudice against the trade, which [GO: neither] the very honourable conduct of a Tonson, **{GO2}** a Millar, a Dodsley, a Knapton,[244] [to which/nor that of] many living names [might be added, has not been/has been] able to efface. [MC: This] Curl was a determined enemy to Copy Right, and on every occasion invaded, without scruple, the right of Authors and the property of his brethren[,/though] at the same time that he was doing them so material [an/a] injury in their professional character. A Bookseller's job is a very invidious [term, and/epithet, but it is] very indiscriminately applied, and the most severe terms of reprehension are used in arraigning the conduct of Booksellers, [as the/upon a supposition that the] practices of the whole body are [MC: said to be] equally injurious to authors and to the public. [MC: The Attorney General[245] would do well to support this opinion by some strong facts which might tend to justify the strange farrago of low abuse he has used, and the savage joy he expressed on hearing that a very worthy man, with a large family, was ruined. He must be indeed a Lawyer, who can thus exult in the effects of that glorious uncertainty of the law, by which thousands have been ruined, and by which lawyers alone are benefited.]

[GO: Nothing however can be a greater error than to confound the purchasers of Copy Right, with the freebooters in literature; the first not only pay a valuable consideration to Authors for their works, but can have no hope of reaping any advantage from their bargains, beyond the proportion which they bear in the scale of public entertainment or utility—Whereas the latter, paying no copy money whatever for their publications, injure every Author as far as they print, and instead of benefiting the world (even admitting what is *false* in *fact* to be *true* in *argument*) by selling cheaper than the Copy-holders, they in reality impose upon the Reader, because the more they multiply editions of any Writer, the more they make this Writer imperfect.—The Copyholder, like the lord of a soil, is sensible that his emolument must be estimated by the cultivation, and therefore pays a sum of money to have every edition, or fresh crop of his literary acres improved to the utmost advantage;

[242] Alexander Pope.

[243] Edmund Curll* (c. 1675–1747), bookseller, Covent Garden; *Pope v. Curl* (1741) 2 Atk. 342 (26 ER 608).

[244] Jacob Tonson* (1714–67), app. 1729–31, tr. 1732–67; John Knapton, app. 1712–19, Robert Dodsley* (1704–64); Andrew Millar.

[245] Edward Thurlow†* (1731–1806).

whereas the freebooters, like a tenant at will, considers only his temporary interest, and if that can be promoted in a single instance, cares not how he plays upon the easiness of the community.— To support this reasoning, it is barely necessary to recollect from what quarters *all* the valuable books have originated, as well as the quarters from which the *best*, nay from which the *cheapest* editions have issued, *after* the term allowed by the statute of Queen Anne.[246]— Without hesitating, the Copy-holders may venture to affirm that all the late improvements in literature, have been made either at the particular risque of their predecessors, or their own, and that besides being always interested to give *better*, they are always interested to give *cheaper* editions of their copies to the Public, than their enemies. The profits in the bookselling trade do not arise from the *particular price* of any book, but from the *number* of the books sold; the purchaser of the copy, who often assists in planning the work, knowing where additions are wanted, or where abridgments are necessary (much sooner in the nature of things than any body else can know, because his property hangs upon the general opinion) adds or retrenches with all imaginable expedition; and conscious, moreover, that he will be pirated in a degree equal to the value of his publication, studies assiduously to prevent the *possibility* of being undersold. By this means the Public have his own interest as a guarantee for the *correctness*, as well as for the *cheapness* of his work, and the very avarice imputed to the Copy-holder, must of consequence be the strongest security which can be desired both for his probity and for his moderation. Having thus considered the subject in one light, let it be now viewed in another, to shew how far the enemies to Copy Right deserve the superior attention of Parliament.]

{MC6} To patronize authors, and to promote the general progress of literature, has ever been esteemed a shining ornament in the character of Princes.—The Augustan age, that of Leo X. and Lewis XIV.[247] have given the most splendid proofs of what may be expected from patronising the arts and literary men: but [considerations of a very different kind appeared to have great weight in the later decision. We were told/it is now said,] that men of genius are born for the general benefit of their fellow creatures, and that their productions are *Publici Juris*, that no pecuniary rewards are necessary for them, [for/because] the love of fame, in this particular order of beings, is superior even to [the love of eating; and that /a solicitude necessary for the means of existence; and because] they will employ their whole time in producing works to delight and [MC: to] instruct mankind, without any wish to reap [GO: that] pecuniary benefit [from them/which is requisite to procure an establishment for themselves].

The Booksellers well know that modern authors are as tenacious of pecuniary benefit, as any men whatever; and some reasons may be given which tend to prove **{GO3}** that this has ever been the case in all ages, and in all [countries/nations]. But as facts are most certain in domestic experience, [I/they] will confine [myself to our/themselves to their] own country.

That Shakespeare did not publish his plays[248] is generally thought to proceed from an indifference for that fame, for that immortality by which authors are supposed to be solely affected. That the love of fame [GO: however,] was not his inducement to write, is very clear; and why may we not suppose, [MC: that] the consideration that the copy was of no value,

[246]Copyright Act 1709, s. 1.

[247]Leo X (1475–1521), pope from 1513; Louis XIV, king of France 1643–1715.

[248]This is not actually correct, see A.W. Pollard, *Shakespeare's Fight with the Pirates* (2nd edn, 1920), ch. 2.

deterred him from a most laborious task. The emoluments he sought, he had reaped by [their/the] representation [GO: of his works] on the stage. Every admirer of his prodigious genius is concerned that there was wanting some motive to induce him to a careful revisal of his works; what might not have been expected from his mature judgment, if he had thus employed the leisure he afterwards enjoyed. Much has been done by commentators and alterers, without lessening the regret, we [conceive that/feel for seeing] so much was left to them; yet, whatever elucidation the works of this immortal bard [has/have] received, has been principally received at the expence of Booksellers. They have paid to various commentators, whose names [found/stand] high in the republic of letters, many thousand pounds: and the last edition of Shakespeare is one of the most complete Variorum editions[249] that has ever been published of any author. All this has been done without advancing the price of Shakespeare's works to the public; [GO: for] they are now sold cheaper than by the publisher of Hemming's and Condel's edition;[250] but that a low price in books of consequence is not in the public idea essential, is evident from the much greater sale of the [MC: more] elegant editions of Shakespeare, than of those in which the convenience of the purchasers has been more consulted.

The price which Milton received for his Paradise Lost, has been [MC: triumphantly] mentioned as an irrefragable proof,[251] that it is unnecessary to give encouragement or reward to men of genius.

[MC: Milton was, during the greater part of his life, in a reputable situation, and employed by the government under which he lived. When the times were changed, he lost his employment, and by the loss of his eyes, was left without resource. He directed the whole force of his genius to the composition of that divine poem, which has indeed rendered his name immortal; but the author was greatly disappointed in his expectation of profit and of reputation; for during his life, to the disgrace of the age in which he lived, the work was unnoticed. That a man of his firm mind did not burn his poem because it was undervalued by his bookseller, or even by the public, is certainly no matter of surprise; and I am fully convinced, that no consideration would have induced Milton to have wrote an obscene poem in compliance with the depraved taste of the times. But shall this lessen our regret, that he died in obscurity and low circumstances? But are we to seek for the effects of this disappointment in Paradise Lost? Certainly not. It was written with brilliant expectation; the effects are to be found in Paradise Regained.[252] What a falling off is there! every mark of negligence and indifference glares through the whole poem.

The natural sentiment of every reader of the life of Milton, is to regret that he did not receive that reward for this noble work, which would have placed him in a state of chearful competence. And shall the very severe disappointment he suffered, be urged as a reason why the rewards of genius should be curtailed.]

[GO: —The neglect, however, of doing what ought to be performed, is no excuse for leaving it undone. If Milton deserved reward, as he undoubtedly did, for his works, the

[249] William Shakespeare, *The Plays* (Bathurst, 1773) (ESTC: T138855).

[250] William Shakespeare, *Mr William Shakespear's Comedies, Histories and Tragedies* [dedicated to John Heminge* (1566–1630) and Henry Condell* (1576–1627), and commonly called the 'First Folio'] (Jaggard and Blout, 1623) (ESTC: S111228).

[251] The contract can be seen in MacLennan, 'John Milton's Contract for "Paradise Lost"', 221.

[252] John Milton, *Paradise Regain'd* (Starkey, 1671) (ESTC: R299).

reward should have been paid him: The injury done to this great poet is no reason for offering an injury to other Authors; and when we recollect, that the solider, the divine, the physician, the lawyer, and the statesman, are all, even in the highest ranks of their profession, *paid* for their labours, who will seriously say, that Authors of distinguished merit should be the only men unentitled to a compensation for their talents? Or who does not weep at the idea of Milton's grand daughter being reduced to implore the charity of the Public? Authors, in proportion to their merits, are generally exquisite in their feelings, and have as just a relish for the rational pleasures of society as other men; why, therefore, because they are allowed to be peculiarly honourable, peculiarly serviceable to their country, they should not be allowed the common chance of getting bread with other men, is a paradox which time is left to unravel, and which fate has set apart for a determination in this kingdom. —The sciences of painting, architecture, sculpture, and music, are encouraged with the greatest avidity. The literary sciences, of course, which are universally complimented with a pre-eminence, can never be doomed to a proscription in a nation like this; nor can the unfortunate man of letters be the only individual prohibited (on account of his very merit) from procuring either a livelihood for himself, or an establishment for posterity.—But to go on with a cursory mention of Authors.]

Ben Johnson[253] [GO: from a want of encouragement,] lived a life of distress, and has left [MC: us] many specimens of his dexterity in drawing up begging petitions.[254] [MC: He does not, however, appear to have had those delicate sensations which must have rendered this talk distressing to a man of finer feelings.]

Otway[255] lived and died in the extremity of poverty and wretchedness.

Butler's[256] fate was nearly similar [MC: to the indelible disgrace of his ungenerous, unfeeling, and even ungrateful sovereign].

How pathetically does Cowley[257] exclaim,

"Is there a man, ye Gods, I ought to hate?"
"Attendance and dependence be his fate."[258]

The genius of Dryden[259] was infinitely superior to the greater part of his works: he reiterates his complaints on the disagreeable necessity he was under to comply with the vicious taste of the times, and from the narrowness of his circumstances, **{GO4}** and the low price of his labours, [MC: he was obliged] to be more attentive to the quantity, than to the excellence of his works. In the fire of original genius, in the brilliancy of his imagination, and even in the harmony of his verse, Dryden is superior to Pope,[260] but Pope lived in better times: he made an ample fortune by his works, and he was never under any necessity to publish a hasty unfinished line.

[253] Benjamin Jonson* (c. 1572–1637).

[254] Frances Teague, 'Ben Jonson's Poverty', *Biography*, ii (1979), 260.

[255] Thomas Ottaway* (1652–85).

[256] Samuel Butler* (1612–80).

[257] Abraham Cowley* (1618–67).

[258] Extract from Abraham Cowley, *The Works of Mr Abraham Cowley* (Macock, 1668) (ESTC: R9310), Martial. Lib. 2, *Vota tui breviter, etc.*

[259] John Dryden.

[260] Alexander Pope.

The [reign/reigns] of Anne, and Geo. I [was/were] indeed the golden age for good writers. Newton, Locke, Prior, Congreve, Swift, Addison, Steele, Cibber, Young,[261] and some others, were all within a few years employed or promoted by government. [MC: The greatest encouragement was given to Subscriptions, and several of the nobility appeared to be desirous of emulating the reputation of Maecenas.[262] At this distance of time we should have supposed that all this encouragement produced none but good authors, but the Dunciad[263] has happily preserved the names of many, whose works are forgotten.]

During the whole reign of George II authors were not encouraged either by the court, or by the nobility; but happily for them, the idea of copy-right prevailed, and the number of readers were so much increased, that the Booksellers have been enabled to take upon themselves the task of patronising authors; and they have performed it beyond what can be expected from the (pecuniary) bounty of princes; they have in that time paid more money to GOOD authors than the whole body [GO: of writers] had [GO: previously] received since the invention of printing.

While authors were supposed to have a Common Law-right to their own works, any man who could earn reputation from the public, might procure from the Booksellers a price for his labours, which would place him in any easy and independent situation.

{MC7} The patronage of the great has generally been confined to the poets, and to works of imagination; the natural consequence of which was, that the bulk of our writers were poets. But there are many other works necessary to form a [good/valuable] library. At the accession of the late King, we had no good history of our own country, except a translation from the French.[264] Very imperfect transcripts of the histories of foreign nations.— No Dictionary of our language, except for school boys.[265] No Dictionaries of arts, sciences, or trade; and many of the best *prose* classicks were still locked up in their original languages.

While so unfavourable an idea of Booksellers prevails, it may probably be deemed very presumptuous language, if the Booksellers should say, that the principal works which have appeared [this/these] 40 years, owe their existence to them; or rather to their mistaken idea of Copy-right. It is therefore necessary that some instances should be brought in support of this assertion.

Johnson's Dictionary,[266] a work much wanted, and which is executed on a plan so excellent, that it has been adopted in almost every language in Europe. This great effort of learning, solid judgment, and persevering industry, by which the standard of the English tongue is in some measure fixed, owes its existence to Booksellers. Hear the Author's own words. In an address to Lord Chesterfield, he says: "When first I undertook to write an English Dictionary, I had no expectation of any higher patronage than that of the propri-

[261] Issac Newton* (1642–1726), John Locke, Matthew Prior* (1664–1721), William Congreve* (1670–1729), Jonathan Swift* (1667–1745), Joseph Addison* (1672–1719), Sir Richard Steele, Colley Cibber* (1671–1757), Edward Young* (1683–1765).

[262] Gaius Cilnius Maecenas, a patron of the Roman poets in the time of Augustus.

[263] Alexander Pope, *The Dunciad* (1728) (ESTC: T5543).

[264] This is presumably a reference to (Paul) Rapin De Thoyras (1661–1725), *The History of England Written in French*, trans. N. Tindal (Knapton,1725) (ESTC: T160963).

[265] These were essentially spelling books.

[266] The first edition was Samuel Johnson, *A Dictionary of the English Language* (Strahan, 1755) (ESTC: T117231). For a history, see Allen Reddick, *The Making of Johnson's Dictionary 1746–1773* (Cambridge, 1996).

etors of the copy, nor prospect of any other advantage than the price of my labour."[267] And a little farther, "I had read indeed of times, in which princes and statesmen thought it part of their honour to promote the improvement of their native tongues; and in which Dictionaries were written under the protection of greatness. To the patrons of such undertakings I willingly paid the homage of believing that they, who were thus solicitous for the perpetuity of their language, had reason to expect that their actions would be celebrated by posterity, and that the eloquence which they promoted would be employed in their praise. But I considered such acts of beneficence as prodigies, recorded rather to raise wonder than expectation; and content with the terms that I had stipulated, had not suffered my imagination to flatter me with any other encouragement."[268]

The occasion of this address to his Lordship was this: after Mr. Johnson had made some progress in this work, the labour appeared to him to be too great for the price stipulated; he addressed himself publicly to his Lordship, with an expectation of raising a subscription to enable him to finish his task. He did not succeed; and the Booksellers agreed to give him 500l. more than the original agreement, by which he was enabled to finish the work; and the proprietors of the copy father expended **{GO5}** in paper, print, and [GO: other] necessary [expences/disbursements], upwards of 2000l. before they received one shilling from the public.[269]

When the copy was thus purchased, and published at so great a risk, can it be thought from the nature and reason of the thing, that every man had an equitable right to print it? and [I would ask/it may be asked], if this property was not protected by the laws, whether [such laws are/the laws were] not in this instance imperfect? The term of 14 years given by the Statute of Anne,[270] is a very inadequate term [GO: for a capital work]; double that time has been barely sufficient to reimburse the proprietors. How are the public interested, that it should become common; as it is now printed, [GO: be the printer whom he may,] the price cannot be reduced [, whoever prints it; and/; but] that the lower ranks of the people might not be [MC: wholly] deprived of so excellent a [work/book], the proprietors paid the author a farther sum to abridge his own [works/performance] in two vols octavo, now sold for 10s.

In this work the claim of the proprietors [is/was] not an exclusive right to ideas, nor [does/did] it arise from invention or discovery. The plan of the Dictionary was *publici juris* the moment it was published; it has been imitated by every dictionary writer since, and by the new editions of old Dictionaries. The proprietors did not think themselves injured by any imitation; they expected only that they should have the sole right to print Johnson' Dictionary, and that it should not be directly or indirectly copied, so that on a fair and candid examination it should appear to be substantially the same book.

In other words, it is not the idea of the work nor the plan on which it is executed,[271] which copy-holders wish should be protected; but the composition, which must ever be a work of great labour and assiduity, and for which they were always ready to pay large sums

[267] From Samuel Johnson, *The Plan of a Dictionary of the English Language, addressed to the Right Honourable Philip Dormer, Earl of Chesterfield, One of His Majesty's Principal Secretaries of State* (Knapton, 1747) (ESTC: T42414), 1.

[268] *The Plan of a Dictionary*, 2–3.

[269] See contradiction of this story: Cavendish, {79}.

[270] Copyright Act 1709, s. 1.

[271] *Millar v Taylor* (1769) 4 Burr 2303 (98 ER 201 at 242, 251) had not taken up this distinction.

to good authors, while they conceived that they could convey [MC: to them] an exclusive right to multiply copies.

[MC: It may here be observed that Mr. Johnson was many years employed by the Booksellers, and received very considerable sums, for which he produced his Dictionary, the Rambler, Idler &c.[272] and a great number of excellent lives and moral essays, for several periods, not works of reputation. He has now enjoyed for thirteen years a pension from government, for which he has produced *two political pamphlets*.]

Postlethwayte's Dictionary[273] is another of those books which the public have long been accustomed to treat with contempt under the term [GO: of] *Bookseller's job.* On the appearance of Savary's Dictionary,[274] the booksellers conceived that the same plan, adapted to England, would be agreeable to the public. The task was undertaken by Mr. Postlethwayte, and he performed it superior to the highest expectations of his employers; he too, when the work was nearly finished, demanded and obtained 500l. more than his original agreement, and he has since been paid a considerable sum for the additions and improvements of a new edition. Here a plan, and a great part of the contents are translated from M. Savary, undoubtedly any man may [do the same/translate the same author]; the proprietors do not [presume/pretend] to any farther right than to the labours of Mr. Postlethwayte, who was employed by them, and paid a valuable consideration, without any expectation of [GO: their] being reimbursed under a much longer term than 14 years.

Chamber's Dictionary,[275] a work which must ever be considered with astonishment as the work of one man; a work which would have done honour to a learned society, was in fact produced by the encouragement [GO: of], and at an immense expence to the Booksellers with whom Mr. Chambers lived many years: he was furnished with a number of books beyond the reach of a private fortune, and with every collateral assistance and necessary information at their [expence/charge]. It was this performance which stimulated the French to that immense work the Encyclopediae[276] [, which cost.

The proprietors of the work/The proprietors], finding themselves injured by the publications of mutilated copies of this work, published in weekly numbers, in which was inserted a great deal of crude indigested matter, under pretence of new discoveries and improvements in arts and sciences, employed the late O. Ruffhead, Esq;[277] and several of the most eminent authors in the different walks of science, to whom they have already paid 1500l. to correct the said work, and to introduce into it every thing that was really of importance in the modern discoveries and experiments. The proprietors have no expectation that they will be reimbursed this large sum for many years; they considered themselves as the proprietors

[272] *The Idler* was a series of essays (most of which were written by Johnson) published in the *Universal Chronicle* between 1758 and 1760 and printed in a book: Samuel Johnson, *The Idler* (Newberry, 1761) (ESTC: T153829); *The Rambler* was also a periodical, brought together as Samuel Johnson, *The Rambler* (Payne and Bouquet, 1752) (ESTC: N67176); Samuel Johnson, *A Dictionary of the English Language* (Strahan, 1755) (ESTC: T117231);

[273] Malachy Postlethwayt* (?1707–1767), *Universal Dictionary of Trade and Commerce* (Knapton, 1751–5) (ESTC: N35479).

[274] Jacques Savary des Brûlons (1657–1716), *Dictionnaire Universel De Commerce: Contenant Tout Ce Qui Concerne* (Waesbergl, 1724). The work was completed by his brother Philémon-Louis Savary (1654–1727).

[275] The first edition of the work was Ephraim Chambers (1680–1740), *Cyclopædia: or, An Universal Dictionary of Arts and Sciences* (Knapton, 1728) (ESTC: T114002).

[276] *Encyclopédie, ou dictionnaire raisonné des sciences, des arts et des métiers*, ed. Denis Diderot (1713–84) and Jean Le Rond d'Alembert (1717–83) (17 vols, 1754–72).

[277] Owen Ruffhead.

of the soil, and they were earnest for its improvement, whether the benefits arising should be reaped by themselves or their children.

The ancient and modern Universal History[278] is now in the same situation; though the work had great merit and [was/were] well received, [it was/they were] too difuse and ill digested. **{GO6}** The proprietors of the copy employed the first authors, who have most carefully corrected and digested the whole [MC: work], originally in 65 Vols. 8vo. [is now/and they are] prepared for the press in 12 Vols. 4to. For these corrections 1000l. has been paid to the different [authors, and/writers, but] it is now become a matter of doubt whether it is prudent to print either of these works; and if either of them [are/is] printed, it is very clear, that as the law [MC: now] stands explained, they are the last great works that will be thus carefully prepared for the press.

{MC9} [As I conceive that the facts stated in my last/As the facts stated in the foregoing remarks] are very different from the general conceptions of the world concerning Booksellers, [I have here added the following extracts in support of my assertions/it may be necessary to add the following extracts from Writers of unquestionable authority who have been intimately connected with literary Copy-holders].

The Bishop of Gloucester in his Preface to Shakespeare, says, "If, from all this, Shakespeare or good letters, have received any advantage, and the public any benefit or entertainment, the thanks are due to the *proprietors*, who have been at the expence of *procuring* this edition. And I should be unjust to several deserving men of a reputable and useful profession, if I did not, on this occasion, acknowledge the fair dealing I have always found amongst them; and profess my sense of the unjust prejudice which lies against them; whereby they have been, hitherto, unable to procure that security for their property, which they see the rest of their fellow-citizens enjoy. A prejudice in part arising from the frequent *piracies* (as they are called) committed by members of their own body. But such kind of members no body is without. And it would be hard that this should be turned to the discredit of the honest part of the profession, who suffer more from such injuries than any other men. It hath, in part too, arisen from the clamours of profligate scribblers, ever read, for a piece of money, to prostitute their bad sense for or against any cause prophane or sacred; or in any scandal, public or private; these meeting with little encouragement from men of account in the trade, (who, even in this enlightened age, are not the very worst judges or rewarders of merit) apply themselves to people of condition; and support their importunities by false complaints against *booksellers*."[279]

[MC: This very strong testimony may probably carry more weight when we consider that the language of panegyric is by no means familiar to his Lordship.]

Mr. Stevens[280] in the advertisement prefixed to the last edition of the same poet gives the character of Mr. Tonson, of which the following as an extract:

[GO: "*To the Reader*".]

"To those who have advanced the reputation of our Poet, it has been endeavored, by Dr. Johnson, in the foregoing preface, impartially to allot their dividend of fame; and it is

[278]For a history, Guido Abbattista, 'The Business of Paternoster Row: Towards a Publishing History of the Universal History (1736–65)', *Publishing History*, xvii (1985), 5.

[279]William Warburton, *The Works of Shakespeare* (Knapton, 1747) (ESTC: T138851), i, pp. xx–xxi.

[280]Samuel Johnson and George Stevens, *The Plays of William Shakespeare* (Bathurst, 1773) (ESTC: T138855), 91.

with great regret [MC: that] we now add to the catalogue, another, [MC: the consequences of] whose death will affect not only the works of Shakespeare, but of many other writers. Soon after the first appearance of this edition, a severe disease deprived the world of Mr. JACOB TONSON; a man, whose zeal for the improvement of English literature, and whose liberality to men of learning, gave him a just title to all the honours which men of learning can bestow. [MC: It may be justly said of Mr. TONSON, that he had enlarged his mind beyond solicitude about petty losses, and refined it from the desire of unreasonable profit. He was willing to admit those with whom he contracted, to the just advantage of their own labours; and had never learned to consider the author as an under agent to the bookseller. The wealth which he inherited or acquired, he enjoyed like a man conscious of the dignity of a profession subservient to learning. He was the last commercial name of a family which will be long remembered; and if Horace thought it not improper to convey the SOSII[281] to posterity; if rhetoric suffered no dishonour from Quintilian's dedication to TRYPHO,[282] let it not be, thought that we disgrace Shakespeare, by joining to his works the name of TONSON.]"

[GO: Besides the foregoing very respectable testimonies in favour of the London Booksellers, letters can be produced from other writers of distinguished reputation, such as Dr. Hurd, Dr. Robertson, Dr. Beattie, and David Hume, Esq;[283] to prove that Authors of the first character, not only entertain an advantageous idea of the Petitioners for relief in Literary Property, but even think that the Interest of Letters must be materially affected, unless this relief is benevolently granted by the Legislature.—The Scotch Booksellers complain, that the encouragement given to Men of Learning in London, almost entirely confines the original printing of every Scotch author's works to this capital; the Scotch Booksellers, nevertheless, with the same breath, call the Copy-holders of London, *oppressors* of Genius, and represent the very rewards bestowed on writers of talents, as an absolute injury to the advancement of literature.—It may, however, be safely affirmed, that the progress of learning will keep pace with the security of Copy Right; the mere love of **{GO7}** fame will not stimulate many men of genius to write, were all the men of genius even as happily affluent in their circumstances, as, generally speaking, they are known to be otherwise.—When the first men of family in every other profession deem it no less necessary than honourable, to receive a proper recompence for the dedication of their abilities, it would be hard that the literati only should be allowed a precarious portion of praise, and that those talents should be wholly useless to themselves, which are expected to be universally beneficial to society.— But it is needless to dwell upon a point so evidently clear.—The literati if rich, will not slave for the benefit of others, where the labour is certain, and the glory at best but probable; if they are poor, they cannot afford to devote that time to the pursuit of reputation which must be employed in procuring a subsistence for their families. Considering the question barely in this light, the lamp of science will be in danger of extinction, unless the Booksellers are favoured with relief; and, if we view the subject in a different point, if we take up letters as a capital manufacture, the bread of thousands, and the interest of the state, will appear essentially dependent upon the indulgence granted to Copy-holders. The good consequence upon one hand infinitely overbalance every possible inconvenience on

[281] Horace, *Epistulae*, i. 20, 2.

[282] Marcus Fabius Quintilianus (c. 35–c. 100), *Institutio Oratoria*.

[283] Richard Hurd, William Robertson, James Beattie and David Hume.

the other. Nay, the Scotch Booksellers themselves must be actually gainers by the relief, if every thing is properly considered.—For, should the London Booksellers be eventually prevented from buying new copies, the Scotch will be eventually prevented from printing or vending new books after the expiration of the statute term in the old ones; and something like the fable of the belly and the members be realized, to the general destruction of British literature.]

[From this point, it was only printed in the *Morning Chronicle*]

Of this very amiable man, Lord Camden, appeared to have conceived a different opinion, when after speaking with great severity of booksellers in general, he told us that they were the "Tonsons of the age,"[284] he might with the same propriety have used the name of Marlborough[285] as a term of reproach to a soldier.

Farther testimonies might be extracted from Dr. Morrell's[286] preface to Ainsworth's Dictionary,[287] and from several others; that odd being Geo. Psalmanazar,[288] in his own life, informs us that he had spent the greater part of it in writing for the trade. Of the characters of booksellers 50 years ago he speaks in the same severe terms as the writers of the last age, but of the modern booksellers in the warm terms of friendship and esteem, and in this posthumous work his sincerity cannot be doubted.

I know not how far the name of Hume may be with propriety added to those who have given their testimony in favour of the useful influence of Booksellers. Perhaps something may be collected from his answer to Millar and others who have repeatedly pressed him to continue his excellent history down to the present times. "I am too old, too lazy, and too RICH to write any more;"[289] undoubtably he, who from any motive, is superior to the influence of money, is out of the reach of Booksellers; titles and honours are only in the gift of Princes. But whether any of our great men wish to see their portraits drawn by so capital a master, must be left to them. Robertson,[290] and every author of reputation, have every inducement to write from those whose profession (as Goldsmith[291] expresses it) leads them to consult the wants of the public.

That the large sums given to authors raises the price of books is an argument which had been strongly urged, and appeared to have great weight; and Hawkesworth's Voyages[292] are

[284] *Donaldson v Beckett* (1774) *Cobbett's Parl. Hist.*, xvii, col. 953, at 1000.

[285] John Churchill*, duke of Marlborough (1650–1722).

[286] Thomas Morrall* (1703–84).

[287] Robert Ainsworth* (1660–1743), *Robert Ainsworth's Dictionary, English and Latin* (Rivington, 1773) (ESTC: T88659), pp. iii–iv.

[288] George Psalmanazar* (c. 1679–1763). He is described as odd as he falsely said he was from Formosa when he was French. Part of his deceit was a new language he created.

[289] The anecdote is mentioned in the *London Evening Post*, 12–14 Aug. 1773. It has not been possible to find the original source, but the origin suggested by E.C. Mossner, *The Life of David Hume* (Oxford, 1980), 556, is later (*New Evening Post*, 6 Dec. 1776) or wrong (Royal Society of Edinburgh Hume MSS, VII. 63, now National Library of Scotland, MS 23157.63).

[290] William Robertson.

[291] Oliver Goldsmith.

[292] John Hawkesworth* (?1715–73), *An Account of the Voyages undertaken by the Order of His Present Majesty for Making Discoveries in the Southern Hemisphere* (Cadell, 1773) (ESTC: T74465).

to be every way a loss to the too credulous booksellers. That an Account of three voyages round the world, which were so much the object of national attention and expence, drawn up by a man, whose literary reputation was deservedly high, should be so unimportant, so poor a work, was as much a surprise to the purchasers of the copy, as of disappointment to the public. From the affected secrecy with which the whole was conducted, the booksellers were not permitted to see what they purchased; but the severe loss they have suffered will probably teach them a useful scepticism; will include them to doubt, and to enquire closely into the subject and merit of the work, let the names or authorities which may be offered to them appear ever so recommendatory.

But to determine on a general question from so particular an instance, is certainly inaccurate and unjust.

I shall to-morrow, (with your indulgence, Mr. Woodfall)[293] attempt to examine the point, and I hope it will appear that the price of books is far from being a general grievance, and that the public have no interest whatever in laying open Literary Property, and consequently, as there does not at present appear to be any intention of altering the law, as now explained, there cannot be any important reason why the Booksellers should not be relieved; there are no circumstances in their conduct, as a body of men, that should restrain the natural, the benevolent wish to lessen a loss so severe and unexpected.

{MC10} As the litigation concerning copy-right has been so warmly pursued, the public may be naturally led to conceive, that the business of bookselling is indeed a golden one.— This, however, is far from being the case, in proportion to the property employed, and to the very great care, attention and assiduity, necessary to conduct a business in which every attempt is hazardous: there is perhaps none in which so few fortunes are made, and in which so many are tied down to the drudgery of procuring a bare subsistence. If the profits and losses of all the new productions of the press in any one year, were thrown into a general account, I believe the loss would very considerably exceed the gains.

The experience of booksellers teaches them to throw a large part of this loss on authors; for as the confidence of bad authors in generally much superior to that of good ones, they have no difficulty in standing the risk: — if they are able; but that is no means frequently the case, and the booksellers from an anxiety to procure good copies, are continually turning their fingers. If we ask them why they do this — the same answer will serve for them, as for a manager who brings forward a bad play, a father who attempts to give a blockhead a learned education, or every man who ruins himself, by endeavors to make a fortune, — they were mistaken, — to form a judgment of any new work is always difficult, as there are many books, of which every man speaks well, and yet few will purchase. These examples may caution, but they must not deter. A bookseller must venture, or be the drudge of his more spirited brethren. If amongst many bad and (what is nearly the same) tolerable new pieces, he procures some which are so well received by the public, that the right of multiplying copies becomes valuable, he considers himself as a successful adventurer in a very hazardous battery, of at least a thousand blank to a prize, and sits down contented with the rewards of a life of labour and anxiety.

But the followers of the camp are determined, that the soliders shall no longer enjoy the fruits of their warfare—they have drove the veterans off, and seized at once on all their stores,

[293]William Woodfall* (1745–1803), the editor of the *Morning Chronicle.*

and he who has till now been the dredge of a Sutler's tent,[294] may wield the truncheon of a General. The triumphs of these maroders might be borne with more patience, if they would not pretend to handle their arms better than their predecessors; if they would speak their natural language, and entertain us with the oeconomical reformation they intend to produce — if they would assert no more, than that they will reduce the price of books, and leave us to guess at the havoc they will make, in correctness and perspicuity.

The counter petitioners very modestly appeal to Baskerville[295] and to the Foulis's, as specimens of the elegance which they will produce. Are these respectable gentlemen amongst the number of those who wish to invade the equitable right of authors, or was it ever pretended that their expensive editions were calculated for general sale? Baskerville found no difficulty in procuring permission to print the most valuable copies, which he sold at very high prices, and yet he lost a considerable sum by printing.

They tell us, that they never had any doubt, but that they would gain their cause; and have therefore for some years persued that plan, by which they presume that the art of printing will be so much improved, and the cause of literature so highly benefited. This they have done by printing cheap editions of the most valuable authors. Their ideas of cheapness is entirely confined to reducing the prices. In order to do this, they disclaim all connection with authors, and chuse to print only such works as others have paid for; these they execute on a bad paper and letter, and most slovenly press-work, if with the farther aid of saving the expence of a corrector of the press, or the still more oecomomical stroke of having cut part of the author's work; by such means making a difference of sixpence in a volume, or a volume in a sett, they have atchieved work for which they claim the protection of the laws. Had Pope (who tho' very attentive to pecuniary reward, was yet sufficiently jealous of his reputation) lived to see the books called Pope's Works, and translations, published by Donaldson, they would have given him the keenest mortification.

The Counter Petitioners make a very pompous part of their case, in charging the purchasers of copies with publishing a quarto edition of every new book of consequence which appears: the fact is certainly true, and the reward to the Author must depend on the probability of its sale. A quarto is the favourite size with every gentleman who wishes to form an elegant library, and if it is not published some time before the useful octavo or duodecimo editions, experience has shewn, that the great expence of the quarto is too hazardous. But were it otherwise, how do the objections to the mode of a first publication affect the present question, the right of authors or their assigns to a term of fourteen years as uncontrovertible? what instance can be pointed out, in which an edition as cheap as is consistent with its being well and correctly printed, has not been published long before fourteen years has been expired?

The Booksellers well know that they have no interest in opposition to that of the public, for that good books, well printed, and sold at a moderate price, are in the event, more profitable than any attempts to impose on the world. At a time when the copy-holders had no doubt of the perpetuity of their right, they gave a most remarkable instance of this conviction on the great rise of leather in year 1767, the price of binding was necessarily advanced, and there was no alternative but to raise the price of books to the public, or

[294] A sutler was a civilian merchant who followed the army to sell goods.

[295] John Baskerville* (1707–75).

to reduce the profits of the copy-holders, they chose the latter, and the public still have the editions of our best authors, printed in duodecimo, at three shillings per volume, the same price at which they were sold fifty years ago, though paper is advanced near thirty per cent. and the wages and materials of binders nearly in proportion. Their conduct in those cases where authors have thought proper to publish their own works, has been equally beneficial to the public. Blackstone published his Commentaries in four vols. 4to. at four guineas,[296] and thought proper to abridge the trade of a large part of their usual profit; after he had sold three editions, Mr. Cadell[297] gave him 3500l. for the copy, and immediately published an edition at 1l 10s. Mrs Macaulay was paid a considerable sum for permission to print an octavo edition of her History.[298] From these, and many other instances that may be produced, it will appear, that booksellers do sell books cheaper than authors generally would if they were to print their own works.

The principal context lies between the English and Scotch booksellers; and it is scarcely possible to speak of the conduct of the latter with patience. If a Scotch author has written any work, he may seek in vain for a reward for his labours in his own country. The English bookseller, after having paid him an ample price for his labours, must expect a piracy from those who refused to purchase; and see a Sir John Dalrymple alternately negociate for the sale of his copy[299] and publicly plead against the existence of an author's right. The pretended comparison of the price of books as published by Donaldson,[300] is an imposition of the most glaring kind, as has been proved in many instances, and that on which the suit was instituted in Scotland is a sufficient specimen. Stackhouse's Bible printed in England in two large vols. folio,[301] with a number of good copper-plates, is sold at three guineas, which is as low as an edition, so executed, can be sold; Donaldson's edition is in six vols. octavo,[302] in a small letter and crowded page, and totally illegible to the bulk of the readers of such a work, who are principally persons in years; the prints with which he has not ornamented, but disgraced the work, are inferior to those usually given to children; the book is dear at six crowns,[303] and yet this article makes one of the most glaring differences in his catalogue; his cause would indeed be a lame one if it were to stand or fall by the comparison, and Mr. Graves,[304] though a friend to the Counter Petitioners, very candidly said these editions are unfit for any gentleman's library.[305]

[296]The first four English editions of Blackstone's *Commentaries* were printed at the Clarendon Press, Oxford University. None acknowledge Cadell's role. The 5th edition, also published by Clarendon, does mention it was published for him and others (ESTC: T57759). As this note was probably by Cadell it might simply be that the agreement with Cadell was not mentioned on the 4th edition (ESTC: T57758).

[297]Thomas Cadell, app. 1758–65, tr. 1766–93.

[298]Catherine Macaulay* (1731–91), *The History of England from the Accession of James I to that of the Brunswick Line* (Cadell, 1763–83) (ESTC: T106230).

[299]The book was Sir John Dalrymple, *Memoirs of Great Britain and Ireland. From the Dissolution of the Last Parliament of Charles II, until the Sea-battle off La Hogue* (1771) (ESTC: T145644).

[300]Printed Books, below.

[301]Thomas Stackhouse, *A History of the Holy Bible* (Hinton, 1762) (ESTC: N64746).

[302]Thomas Stackhouse, *A History of the Holy Bible* (Donaldson, 1767) (ESTC: T101785).

[303]30 shillings (£1 10*s*).

[304]William Graves† (?1724–1801), MP for West Looe.

[305]Cavendish {S18}.

There are a number of material circumstances in this case which I cannot now proceed on, and which I shall postpone for a few days; but I must just caution my worthy friend, the Counter Petitioner of yesterday, not to be so eager to get rid of difficulties; finding himself pressed by the characters of Millar[306] and Tonson,[307] he boldly tells us that the idea of a Common-Law right was unknown to them. He appears indeed through his whole performance to write on that of which he knows nothing; but it is strange that he should be ignorant that the material decision in this cause in the court of King's Bench was obtained after many years struggle in the cause of *Millar* and Taylor.[308]

As the event of the petition depends greatly on the determination of this day, I have no doubt but that it will be considered with all that attention which a cause of so much consequence to literature demands; when th wretched fate of authors in former times, and the havock which will be made by permitting every man to print the works of any author, are considered as arguments which strongly aid the petition of a body of men, who suffer a severe and unmerited distress, and whose plea for relief is opposed by no considerations of general and public utility.

T.C.[309]

Hints and Grounds of Argument in the Cause of the LONDON BOOKSELLERS

{MC13} AS the 2d reading of the Booksellers Bill was unexpectedly deferred 'till this day, I take the liberty to state some farther arguments in their case, which, from its peculiar nature cannot be generally known; and concerning which, the honourable House has received very little information at their bar.

The House of Commons are desired to believe, that the Booksellers did not mistake the Law. The Booksellers, without pretending to the learning, or to the abilities of the sages of the law, had no difficulty in perceiving that the Question was of a complicated and intricate nature, and this they heard from many lawyers, and frequently from judges and chancellors; had they even seen Lord Hardwicke's large Q,[310] they could not; from thence, have inferred that there was no doubt on their case; or were they to learn it from his Lordship's declaration, that he would not take upon him to decide the point; but if the argument was insisted on he would make a question of it for all the judges.

When they had the pleasure of hearing the ingenious and learned argument of Lord Mansfield on the determination of Millar and Taylor,[311] without attempting to fathom the depth of metaphysical subtleties, they had no difficulty in perceiving the force, the beauty and the truth of the argument; when they heard his Lordship declare, that it was agreeable to natural principles, moral justice, and fitness. that an author should enjoy the pecuniary benefit arising from the labours of his own mind, was it possible that *ignorant, uninformed*

306 Andrew Millar.

307 Jacob Tonson.

308 *Millar v Taylor* (1769) 4 Burr 2303 (98 ER 201).

309 T.C. suggests Thomas Cadell.

310 Baron Eyre judgment in *Donaldson v Beckett* (1774) *Cobbett's Parl. Hist.*, xvii, col. 953, at 973 (where he suggests a large Q in a judgment implies Lord Hardwicke was unsure of the issue).

311 *Millar v Taylor* (1769) 4 Burr 2303 (98 ER 201).

men should know that this forcible conclusion drawn from eternal and immutable truths, was of no consequence, without a case in the books?

And tho' they have penetration enough to see, that an argument said to be conceived by Warburton,[312] and adopted by Mansfield, is not a proper subject for the wit of a Mr. Murphy,[313] they cannot learn from the late decision, that theirs is a case in which there can be no excuse for a mistake or difference of opinion? To suppose that the Booksellers would have carried on a Chancery suit on the terms they did, and brought on the question immediately before the House of Lords, with an expectation of being defeated, is to suppose them madmen: I well know that not one of the present petitioners had any doubt but that they should gain their cause 'till the last day, and that many continued of that opinion 'till the question was put. And notwithstanding the high respect I bear for the most august Court of Judicature in the world, I feel myself strongly inclined to doubt whether the equity of the case was not governed by a very fallible Common Law maxim.

In the late ample and learned discussion of the question of Literary Property, the copyholders appeared to be in a very unfortunate predicament. The maxim, that nothing can be esteemed common law, unless there be some precedent in point in the books, is undoubtedly a very safe one as a general rule. But to them it was necessarily a complete bar, whatever the merits of their case may be. An exclusive right of multiplying copies had never been determined; for not being valuable, it could not be the subject of litigation. The analogy between literary composition and mechanical invention was therefore relied on, and the cases pronounced to be similar.

Why the composition of a book should be deemed an invention I cannot perceive; for here is no invention or property in ideas contented for. A man of genius, whose talents have been cultivated by a learned education, applies the whole force of his mental powers in a continual series of labour and study, and produces a book, which if be written on useful subjects, or in an agreeable manner, the right of multiplying copies, becomes valuable property. Though it was long ago very truly observed by Addison,[314] that an author cannot hope to discover new truths, or produce new ideas; all he can hope is, by improvements in language, by correctness, elegance, and perspicacity, to place them in a new or more agreeable light.

Should it, however, so happen, that any book contains a new idea, however excellent, how does the claim of literary property confine it. It may be transposed abridged, translated, any thing but copied and published as the work of the author.

The discoveries of Newton[315] are most certainly *publici juris*; every purchaser of Newton's works has free liberty to make what use he pleases of the knowledge he may obtain; he may comment and explain as much as he pleases; nothing he can publish will be complained of as an injury by the proprietors of the copy, except a new edition of the works of Newton.

It may now be necessary to enquire into the distinction which the right of invention will admit. Every invention, or improvement, of real utility, undoubtedly gives to its author a claim to a gratuity from the public, in return for the benefit received. But this must always

[312] William Warburton, *A Letter from an Author*.

[313] Arthur Murphy, junior counsel for counter-petitioners.

[314] This appears to be an interpretation of Joseph Addison's famous 'Pleasures of the Imagination', *The Spectator*, issues 411–21: *The Spectator* (Buckley and Tonson, 1712–15) (ESTC: N24116).

[315] Sir Issac Newton.

be governed by the circumstances of the case; and whenever they are opposed, the interests, and even the rights of individuals, must give way to public utility.

The industry of the bulk of mankind is daily and necessarily confined to mechanical employments. An ingenious workman is understood to be one who is continually introducing various little improvements into the mysteries of his profession, for which he is rewarded by more constant employment or better prices. Such improvements are immediately imitated by other workmen, without any idea of injury in either party. The general interests of trade require that such improvements should be mutually adopted.

In those trades which depend on the arts of design, as silk-weavers, calico-printers, &c. the nature of the case requires that they should use each other's patterns;[316] for otherwise the business of every other man must be at a stand, while the favorite of the moment triumphs, and in his turn gives way to next meteor. To be new, is here more material than to be excellent; and to get the start of a few days in the market, will always be a sufficient spur and reward to pattern drawers. If a farther claim is urged in a case of one or those discoveries by which the public receive a great and permanent benefit, as the Mariner's Compass, Optical Glasses, Printing, Worlidge's Machine,[317] the Orrery, and Harrison's Time-piece, a pecuniary sum of the public money is properly paid as the price of the invention.[318]

But this mode of rewarding authors can only be applied to very particular cases, and the singular circumstances in the printing and bookselling business, on which any other must depend, require to be pated at large.

Sir J. Dalrymple took great pains to state the number of times which the Booksellers have applied to parliament.[319] Had he perceived it, he would not have mentioned why this was done. Applications to parliament are so expensive, that he who has been twelve times refused, must have forcible reasons who comes a thirteenth.

The reason is, that the trade cannot be carried on without a mutual security, either legal or by combination, that one Bookseller shall not print an edition of any book which another has already printed. This circumstance, so peculiar to the Bookseller; has been already mentioned at the bar of the House of Lords,[320] and I shall endeavour to throw farther light upon the matter.

The price paid to an author, the setting types, corrections from the press, and various other expences, are all incurred by one, as much as by one thousand copies; and if only one was printed, the book which is now sold for five shillings, would cost 500l. or perhaps 1500l. the farther expences of paper and printing are the same per book; but if 10,000 are printed, the 1500l. must be divided by 10,000, which is three shillings per book. It is therefore evident that a large number MUST be printed: but in books of the highest reputation, with all the advantages of a clear and unrivalled market, the necessary quantity are from ten to twenty years in selling, and frequently longer. What would be the consequence, if for want of mutual intelligence, or from opposition, two or three editions were printed at

[316]Nevertheless, protection for calico printers was introduced 13 years later: Designing and Printing of Linens, etc. Act 1787 (27 Geo. III, c. 38).

[317]The Worlidge machine was a form of seed-drill.

[318]As to prizes which were awarded for inventions by parliament: see the list in Johnson, *Privatised Law Reform*, 150–1.

[319]See Cavendish {248–9}.

[320]*Donaldson v Beckett* (1774) *Cobbett's Parl. Hist.*, xvii, col. 953.

the same time, they would not be sold in 40 years, for books not being necessaries of life, a difference of 6d. or 1s. in the price, makes but a very immaterial difference in the quantity consumed; and if the holders of such books are forced by the necessities of their affairs to sell suddenly to the trade, the purchasers will make large deductions in calculating the value of a book, which will be worth 5s. thirty or forty years hence. This is the reason why honorary Copy Right is supported, which is not pretended to have any legal foundation, yet stands on the broad ground of the necessity of the case; to instance, the Delphin edition of Horace, the number necessarily printed to enable the Bookseller to sell it for six shillings, are twenty years in selling; if the honorary proprietors should be deterred by the danger of rivalship from printing the book, and it should be twenty years out of print, old ones would probably sell for five times that sum, and it would then be equally imprudent to print it.

Coke upon Littleton was last printed in 1736;[321] it has now been some years out of print: though sold by the publisher for 1l. 16s. it is now sold for seven guineas, and will probably be ten or twelve before it be reprinted; but should two printers do it at the same time, they would both of them be ruined. Many of the Law Reporters and curious books in antiquities, &c. are in the same situation.

And, whatever has been said to the contrary, I am bold to affirm, that Copy Right, or something equivalent to Copy Right, must exist in every country where printing is carried on.

In Ireland, as in Scotland, they disclaim all connection with authors; and there the Copy-Right is thus founded: they employ an agent here to procure a sheet of any new work that is printed, and on the receipt of it, paste up the title at the corner of a particular street in Dublin; those who paste up on the same day are proprietors and partners in the work; he who, from any accident, does not paste up till the next day, has lost his chance; and in this case the felonious act of a journeyman printer is frequently the foundation of a right, which perhaps cost in England several thousand pounds. This kind of Copy-Right is, from the necessity of the case, religiously observed; as may be found in the appendix to Sir Charles Grandison,[322] in the seventh volume of the first edition.

In Holland, as has been already stated,[323] the person who is in possession of the last books of a former edition is intitled to a licence to reprint. In France every thing is *Avec privilege du Roi*; and the smallness of the states in Italy, which has also been mentioned,[324] is probably the reason why literature is there at so low an ebb, and the state of printing so very bad.

It is very immaterial to reply to the low abuse which has been thrown on the Petitioners, on the supposition that they have the direction of our public News-papers;[325] it does not relate to the case, and it can be proved that they have no concern whatever in the conducting of them; but were it otherwise, the retort to the lawyers is very obvious.

[321]Sir Edward Coke, *Institutes of the Laws of England or Commentary upon Littleton* (Nutt, 1738) (ESTC: T112990).

[322]Samuel Richardson (1689–1761), *The History of Sir Charles Grandison* (Hitch and Hawes, 1754) (ESTC T58995).

[323]It is unclear to which earlier reference this relates.

[324]Cavendish {237}.

[325]Cavendish {229–32}.

If they should, for want of other matter, employ a short-hand writer to take down many of the speeches pronounced in Westminster-hall,[326] such speeches would form the most scandalous newspaper that has been published for these fifty years.

Convinced, as I sincerely am, of the justice, the equity, and the expediency of granting the Booksellers petition from the right of authors, the nature of the Booksellers business, and the peculiarly distressed situation of the petitioners, a number of farther topics occur to me. But I must particularly urge that if no regard is paid to the feelings of the Booksellers as men, by forcing them into a combination to support what they have hitherto conceived to be their right, many ill consequences will ensue, and the most obvious are, that in all combinations, the worst men naturally take the lead; the more moderate and reasonable must give way to prevent its dissolution; and that in such a combination, an author will have but one market for his copy, and it will be in vain for him to print in opposition, experience proves, that authors have always[327] been liberally paid, but when the belief[328] of a legal perpetuity in copies prevailed; and as rights of Mr. Donaldson are so warmly urged, it may be proper to observe, that he has gained too much: before the decision he only pirated on the copyholders, but now every man has a right to print, and it will probably be a loss to every man who exercises that right. I presume it was this consideration that made him so lukewarm after the decision of the Lords, that the Attorney General complained in the House of Commons, that he had lost his client.[329]

The Stall men who petition, are doubtless sincere in their complaints, and are seriously angry that they are not admitted into the Queen's Arms[330] sales, the principal cause of which is, that the sales are upon credit, and they are men whom no prudent tradesmen will trust.

[It continued again in the *Morning Chronicle*, 2 June 1774, ready for first reading in the House of Lords]

THE Booksellers, urged by the pressing necessities of their case, again approach the Bar of the House of Lords; from which they so lately retired, defeated in an expectation highly interesting to them, and of which they had entertained the warmest hope.

The opinion that authors or their assigns have a right to multiply copies, however supported by great names or ingenious arguments, can never be again urged; and the Petitioners have every consolation which their unexpected loss admit, from the reflection that they have been fully heard, and their claims determined with all that deliberation and solemn attention, which could be expected in a cause rendered so important from its connection with the interests of literature, and with that of society.

Amidst the agitations natural to men who find that the provision which they had made with so much care for the support of declining age and that of their numerous families,

[326] Where the common law courts sat.

[327] The text of the original is lost, but the context suggests 'always' is the missing word.

[328] The text of the original is lost, but the context suggests 'belief' is the missing word.

[329] The attorney-general had acted for Donaldson, but as a member he was not allowed to act before the Commons: *CJ*, viii, 646 (6 Nov. 1666).

[330] In St Paul's Churchyard ('the west end of St. Pauls'); Bryant Lillywhite, *London Coffee Houses: A Reference Book of Coffee Houses of the Seventeenth, Eighteenth and Nineteenth Centuries* (1963), 461–4, no. 1332.

—is deemed to be *common property* —together with that of the widows and orphans of several of their friends, they presume to petition the Legislature for whatever relief may be allowed them in a case so very peculiar in its nature, and where a *mistake in law* from the circumstances of the case, has been held to be an exception to the general maxim by which such mistakes are deemed inexcusable.

Their Petition has been opposed in the House of Commons with the utmost warmth and perseverance. Yet the Petitioners have had the happiness of seeing, that in all the numerous divisions in every stage of the bill, it has been carried by a very large majority.

It has been said that the ground of their petition is false in fact, for that they never did mistake the law. On a point which has been so much debated, it is unnecessary to reply farther than by observing, that those who have laid out their whole fortune in the purchase of Copy Right, and who are now ruined by the late decision, have given proofs of the sincerity of their conviction beyond the power of words; and that it was not a gambling speculation, is evident, from the price of copies which has, in many instances, been upwards of 20 years purchase.

The Petitioners are charged with an attempt to continue a monopoly; and their opponents have gone largely into the *general* argument against monopolies; which fortunately for them, is copious and unanswerable; and yet it is equally true, that the confining particular arts and trades to certain channels is sometimes necessary, and frequently useful. But these instances can only be considered as exceptions to a very proper general rule, by which they are condemned. The exemption must arise intirely from the circumstances the case, which are reserved for the consideration of the Legislature; and the peculiar nature of the case of printing was so evident to Parliament in the time of James the First, that this alone is excepted in the general statute against Monopolies.[332]

In every other business the value of numbers is a multiplication of the expences of one. In this, the expences of one is found by a division of the expences of the whole number printed.

If a cypher is given to a seal engraver, who will charge five guineas for the first; should a thousand seals be ordered, he may probably reduce the price so far, as to execute the whole for four thousands guineas. If an author's manuscript is given to a Printer, with an order to print only one copy, he must charge two, five, or perhaps fifteen hundred pounds for that one; allow him to print the proper number, and he will sell one copy for five, for ten, or for twenty shillings. It is here evidently the interest of the Public that he should enjoy that security for the sale or monopoly which may be necessary to induce a prudent man to print the necessary quantity.

From the unalterable nature of this business are large stocks now on hands; and it has been warmly urged, that, by permitting the Counter-Petitioners to print cheaper editions, those which are more elegant, correct, and expensive would be kept out of the market, and the printing of proper manufactures *thereby* promoted; and as a corollary, it was said, that the voyages to China would be more frequent if the Americans had an opportunity of destroying greater quantities of tea. But the Petitioners have no apprehension that the Parliament will adopt such a principle of commerce, as that trade is to be supported by the ruin of those who have, or who may be, engaged in it.

[332] Statute of Monopolies, s. 10.

In those articles which are not necessaries of life, the idea of dearness, is entirely arbitrary. Before the invention, Printing, the book which may now be esteemed dear at 5s. would probably have wavered in its price from 50 to 500l. and a large estate passed as an equivalent for a single volume. This extreme scarcety, and consequent enormous price of books, was doubtless a material cause why so many persons in the first ranks of society were totally illiterate.

Circumstances are now so materially changed, that it may be necessary to enquire whether there is not some danger or inconvenience in the opposite extreme. Whether it is advantageous of useful to the state that the labourer should be tempted to lay out his 3d. in the purchase of Thompson's Seasons,[332] or to *amuse* himself in the fields, in comparing the beauties of nature with the descriptions of the poet. That our streets and alleys should abound with book-stalls, of which obscenity and infidelity form the the largest part, or that country alehouses should be crouded with itinerant auctioneers, who return the same commodities to their gaping audiences.

To be content with our situation is the greatest blessing in society, and even policy demands that this blessing should be extended as much as possible. How is it consistent with the necessary subordination in ranks, that the elegance and refinement in polite life, should become familiar in idea to those who are daily and necessarily confined to low cares and severe labour. Men, in this state, who read and who study, are too apt to discover those great rights which will probably never be exerted but in speculation; as that men are born equal, that accident alone has thrown them into their humble sphere, and that they have power and inclinations to enjoy splendour and abundance. From this moment they are wretched; their humble dwellings become hateful; labour is an evil, and they spend a life of discontent.

Without attempting to render literary persuits more familiar to the lower ranks of the people, enough has been done to enable shoe-makers, rope-makers, stay-makers, and ploughmen to commence authors; but there is no very striking instance of their success, which can compensate for those who have been rendered unhappy in themselves, and useless to the community, by attempts which their situation and abilities totally disqualified them for; nor are there any works of such authors for which the proprietors wish to enlarge the term of the statute.

A Lord of session,[333] whose literary character adds great weight to his opinion, has carried his ideas of the use of cheap editions very far; he was pleased to see a threepenny number of Millar's Gardeners Dictionary,[334] printed on a dirty brown paper, in the hands of his Gardener. If this man held that rank in his Lordship's service, that a general knowledge of botany, of the classes. genera, and species of plants, the Sexual system, and the various excellencies and defects of the Linean and other systems, was necessary or useful for him; the proprietor's handsome edition of that work, with all the different plants engraved with that accuracy which is particularly necessary in botanical studies, could not be out of his reach if the services of such a man were properly rewarded, but it would probably have soon become expedient to provide him proper assistants, for his Lordship ought not to have been surprised or disappointed if the arrangement of his green-house, or the necessaries of his

[332]The subject of both *Millar v Taylor* (1769) and *Donaldson v Beckett* (1774) *Cobbett's Parl. Hist.*, xvii, col. 953.

[333]Henry Home (Lord Kames).

[334]It is not clear any such edition existed, but there were abridged editions, albeit produced by the same London Booksellers: Philip Miller (1691–1771), *Gardeners Dictionary. Abridgments* (Rivington, 1771) (ESTC: T59414).

kitchen-garden were neglected, while the botanist was ranging the neighbouring ditches for a new species of the Poliandra Triginia; and should the descriptions in the threepenny number chance to be incorrectly printed, it might lead him into a very fatal mistake, by confounding the *Antithora*[335] with the blue *Aconitum*,[336] and induce him to send to his Lordship's table a poisonous herb, which in the *simplicity of his knowledge* he might conceive to be an agreeable addition to a sallad. Would his Lordship have been equally pleased to have seen his Elements of Criticism[337] printed on a dirty brown paper, in the hands of his footman?

(*To be continued*)[338]

Further Remarks

Further Papers on the Clauses of the Booksellers Bill, with Remarks, annexed to one version of 'Petitions' (ESTC: T197622).

Further REMARKS and PAPERS
ON THE
BOOKSELLERS BILL

CLAUSES of the BILL, with REMARKS

Title of the Bill. "FOR vesting copies in the purchasers of such copies from Authors or their Assigns."

Remark. The professed intention of this Bill is to relieve Booksellers who *have* purchased. The petition on which it is founded complains of the loss that will arise from purchases that *have* been made, and prays relief from *such* loss; but the title of the bill is general, and may include future purchases, instead of confining it to vest the copies in those *who have* purchased.

Preamble. "WHEREAS, BY an act of the 8th of Queen Anne, it was enacted, That Authors, and those who had purchased from Authors, should have 21 years and no longer in such copies as were before published or purchased."

Remark. Why is this particular clause recited in the preamble, (as it was also in their petition), can an act made in 1710, vesting a property for 21 years, with an express limitation that it should exist *no longer*, be a reason that, in 1774, they should have it 21 years further? But it is supposed they mean, that, as the Booksellers, in 1710, found relief because they had bought on a supposition of having a property in them, so the Booksellers, in 1774, ought to have a similar relief on the same ground.—But the cases are very dissimilar; in 1710, it had never been ascertained and **{2}** settled by the legislature; 1774 it had.—In 1710, this property had undergone a very great alteration by the expiration of an act of the legislature,[339] and a revolution in the government;—in 1774 no such alteration can be

[335] Wholesome Wolf's Bane (closely related to the poison).

[336] Monk's Hood.

[337] The first edition was Henry Home, *Elements of Criticism* (Millar, 1762) (ESTC: T32597).

[338] It never was continued, as the Booksellers' Bill was defeated the same day it was published.

[339] This is a reference to the Licensing of the Press Act 1665 (17 Chas. II, c. 4), which was restored and continued by the Administration of Intestates' Estates Act 1685 (1 Jas. II, c. 17), s. 15.

pretended.—In 1710, they might justly say they had been induced to purchase copy-rights by the protection afforded them by an act of the legislature, and by the established form of government before the Revolution, but after 1710 they cannot pretend they purchased beyond the time given by the act, but in hope of supporting their purchases by an unjust combination.

Preamble. "AND WHEREAS it has been a prevailing opinion with Booksellers and others, that Authors and their Assigns had a common law right, and that the said act was not intended to take away or abridge that right."

Remark. In 1759, Mr. Whiston, in a letter to Mr. Merril,[340] calls the preventing the sale of Irish and Scotch books *A scheme now entered into*; which proves they before had even no scheme, much less law, for preventing the sale of them; and even then, if they had imagined they had a legal claim, they surely would have brought it to a final judgement before 1774.

Preamble. "In consequence of this opinion many Booksellers have invested the whole or great part of their fortunes in the purchase of them, and on which the support of them and their families in a great measure depend, and by the late decision many are likely to be involved in ruin"—

Remark. The truth of this they have been called on in vain to prove. No man has invested any considerable property therein but what was previously made thereby.

Mr. Wilkie has stated the sum of 49,000l.[341] to have been laid out in copy-right in the last 20 years. He could only ascertain it by casting up the sale books, and by that method he has acknowledged that he did cast up the same copy-rights divers times. This consideration must reduce very considerably that estimate. The copies by which they have been reimbursed ought to be deducted, and also those that fall under the following descriptions: 1st, All books that are under the protection of the statute, provided, if before the limitation of the statute expires, they can reimburse themselves. 2d, All copies that have not succeeded, and by which they will still be losers if this bill passes into a law. 3d, Most books that have many copperplates, for, in most of those the possession of the plates will secure them to the present possessors. 4th, Many large works which, by their connections and union they will still be able to preserve. 5th, The sum of 13,000 l. pocketed by some of the petitioners for the Bill, at Tonson's sale, in 1767; they having actually purchased his copy-rights *privately*, for Ten thousand pounds, and immediately resold these copy-rights, in Tonson's name, for 23,000l. It may also be considered the advantage they will still have over others, by means of their wealth, influence, combinations and connections, and there is no evidence of any man who has any very considerable property in copy-rights, but will still have remaining a large fortune made by their illegal pretensions to them.

{3} *1st Clause.* "BE IT ENACTED, That from every *Author*, who hath not transferred the copy-right, and his executors or assigns"—

Remark. The title of the Bill makes no mention of *Authors* or their *Assigns* who have not yet disposed of their copies; and the professed intention of the Bill is only to save harmless Booksellers who *have* made purchases. Is there any reason why an Author, who has not sold the copy-right, but already enjoyed the profits of his book for 28 years, should still enjoy it 21 years longer, when an Author who publishes his book immediately after the passing

[340] The Five Letters, below.

[341] Petition Committee Report, *CJ*, xxxiv, 590, c. ii.

of the Act will have no more than 14 or 28? This clause seems to be in favour of Authors, but it is in fact a very artful and important clause in favour of Booksellers. There are very few Authors of works whose copy-rights are of any value, that reserve to themselves their copies till the expiration of the monopoly, therefore few Authors can derive advantage from this clause.— The Booksellers can produce assignments from Authors for but few of the old copies, but they will claim and enjoy them all; for, if others begin to print an edition, this clause will give them an opening to procure for a trifle an assignment from the real or fictitious representative of the Author.

2d Clause. "Or the person or persons who hath purchased or *otherwise acquired*."

Remark. This is a very extraordinary attempt indeed! they petition to be relived from the loss they shall sustain, by being deprived of copies *they have purchased*, and now they insert a clause, that they may have copies that they have *not purchased*, but *otherwise* acquired; nay, under this clause, they perhaps will claim a prescriptive right, and claim copies because they have been in possession of them, although such possession has been by means of combinations and the mutual interests and agreements of tradesmen.—In the very title of the Bill they say *purchased*, and yet in this clause they say, purchased or *otherwise acquired*.

3d Clause. "Bodies politic or corporate, who have purchased or *otherwise acquired*."

Remark. The Stationers Company, the body here intended, do not possess their copies by purchase, but by grants from the crown, which grants were made them at a time when the prerogative ran high, and it is supposed they are illegal,[342] and some of their rights are now in litigation, and the rest are intended to be tried; therefore this is an attempt to establish their illegal claims that are even now at trial.—A Bill was ordered in, according to the prayer of the petition, and a Bill is now presented with a clause foreign to that prayer.

4th Clause. "And if any other person shall reprint or import any such books without the proprietors consent, or shall sell, or expose to sale, knowing them to be so reprinted, shall forfeit"—

Remark. By this clause, any person importing a bale of books, not knowing them to be within this act, will be subject to the forfeit: Why not *import*, **{4}** *knowing* them to be so reprinted, as well as *sell*, *knowing* them to be so reprinted?

5th Clause. "And that every such offender shall forfeit for every sheet *found* in his possession, printed or printing, or exposed to sale, to any person that sues for the same."

Remark. Why a forfeit to the proprietor and penalties to the informer? Is a person to be punished twice for the same offence? and by this clause, a person having a bale consigned to him, though ignorant of its contents, may become subject to the penalties to the informer. It also seems to arm the Booksellers with a general warrant to search houses.[343]

6th Clause. "That nothing in this act shall extend to any book, unless it is entered in Stationers Hall."

7th Clause. "If the clerk refuses to enter it he shall forfeit to the proprietor; and the proprietor shall then give notice in the Gazette, and receive the same advantage as if it had been entered in Stationers Hall."

8th Clause. "Every work, published under this act, shall give to the public Libraries copies."

[342]The Stationers' Company's patent rights in almanacks were successfully challenged a year later: *Stationers' Company v. Carnan* (1775) 2 Black W. 1004 (96 ER 590).

[343]General warrants had been unlawful for less than a decade at this point: *Wilkes v Wood* (1763) Loft 1 (98 ER 489).

Remark. Clause 6th, seems to be intended, that all books should be entered at Stationers Hall, that every person may know who claims the copy, and the protection of the statute. But by clause 7th, the whole is rendered nugatory; for, if the Bookseller does not enter the book, what is the consequence? Why, the *Bookseller* may prosecute the clerk; and that the Bookseller certainly will not do, he need only advertise it in the Gazette, and he will then receive the whole benefit of the statute; avoid entering his book; defraud the public libraries of their copies; and thus the whole is rendered nugatory and useless. And, it is remarkable, that this clause is now added, and is not in the 8th of Queen Anne, from whence clause 6th is copied; and is therefore a contrivance to effect the important point of locking up their claims in obscurity, and defraud the public libraries of their copies, as they have hitherto in a great measure done.

9th Clause. "That nothing in this act shall extend to books printed and published before the passing this act."

Remark. This clause will leave an opening to endless vexatious law-suits that may involve and perplex many innocent people. A person may import a parcel of books, bearing date 1773; perhaps they will prove it to be a false date, and that it was actually printed in 1775. And thus Booksellers may be harassed with law-suits that they cannot possibly avoid. Nay, the proprietors of books actually printed before the passing of the act may be still pestered by these monopolists on false pretexts of the books not bearing the true date.—Injunctions may be got, the sale of valuable editions stopped, till they have reprinted the same works, and altho' the defendant prevails he will find himself greatly injured.

{5} The London Booksellers, holders of copy-right, having now give in all the evidence they chuse to produce, and their counsel having finished all they chose to say, in defence of their claim to a monopoly; the petitioners, against the Bill, hope they may be permitted to make a few observations. The witness before the Committee was Mr. Johnston.[344] On his evidence this Bill was ordered in. The material facts in his evidence were: "That the sales of copy-right are open to every man who sells books; that no man of the trade is excluded." And, "That the Booksellers did make those purchases of copy-right, under a belief that they were an undoubted perpetual property which the law did acknowledge and would protect:" With respect to the first assertion, it is now proved to be false; with respect to the second, they have not offered any proof; and the only circumstance from whence they pretend to infer it, is, that the Booksellers did purchase shares of copy-rights that were not under the protection of the statute; but the fallacy of this inference appears from his own evidence, wherein he acknowledges, that they did purchase copies which could have no legal title; and to which he declares, he never imagined they had a legal claim: It is evident therefore, that they might purchase. It is evident they did purchase without depending on a legal title. Their excluding Booksellers from the sales for invasion of their pretended property, and requiring bonds, are evidence that they were sensible of having power, without law, in a great measure, to protect their pretended copy-rights; and, in fact, under that protection, they did purchase copy-rights long before they made any attempt to establish their claims on the ground of the common law. Their counsel would willingly, and perhaps wisely, have declined producing any proof in support of their unjust pretensions; but at least venture to produce one single

[344] William Johnston.

solitary witness, the only one on whom they could depend; the only one that they thought could or would answer their purpose; and indeed they made a tolerable choice; but he contradicts Mr. Johnston, that the sales are open to every man who sells books. But then he tells us, that none are excluded but those who are not of sufficient credit to be trusted: Affidavits are ready to be produced of the falsity of the assertion; it appears also to be false, by considering that all country booksellers are excluded from the sales at the Queen's Arms. Will the London Booksellers say, that no country Bookseller is of sufficient credit to be trusted, when they are giving them credit every day to a very large amount? Nay, some Booksellers are admitted to the Globe sales[345] who are not admitted to the Queen's Arms, and yet the same credit is given at both. But the obvious reason is, that at the Queen's Arms, most of the copy-rights are sold, and the country booksellers, and some of London, are to be kept out of the business transacted there; for, as to purchasing shares of copies by private contract, it is not usual; and the only person among the counter-petitioners, that has attempted to obtain them by that method, finds, that in purchasing this *honorary* property, he has purchased moonshine only; although others have made like purchases, from whence they have derived large fortunes. — He has declared, that, after having paid the money, got a receipt and the assignment under which his predecessor claimed and enjoyed it, yet he could never obtain his share of the books from these *honorary gentlemen*; yet the sagacious counsel asks if we have any copies. The John Wilkie declares, that few of the persons who have signed the petition against the Bill are shopkeepers, yet **{6}** evidence on oath is ready to be produced, that every one of them are; and even this witness has not mentioned one that is not.

These worthy petitioners have filled the news-papers (*in which, to be sure, they have no concern*) with various accounts of the petitioners against the Bill! At one time, they were quite unknown to them; at another, they were only stall keepers; and, at another, they were proprietors of all the news-papers, libels, flimsy compilations, paultry novels, and literary rubbish, published in Sixpenny numbers, with which the present age abounds. But what have they proved against the counter-petitioners? Three of the persons who signed the counter petition were candidly pointed out by the petitioners themselves, as having signed it, as some thought, improperly. They called on their adversaries to point out a fourth. Their evidence cannot find him. Their counsel, indeed, with superior sagacity, finds out one, that, as he says, sells old clothes; but the witness, when called, is as much a stranger to it as the counter-petitioners themselves. Whether this gentleman followed the instructions of his brief in this notable discovery, or whether it was only a sudden start of his own imagination I know not; if the latter, it was a pity he suppressed it so suddenly. The counter-petitioners would have avoided the invidious talk of excepting against individuals, but it is hoped they may follow the example set them. It is said, one of the counter-petitioners sells spelling-books and school-books chiefly.—On the other hand, two printers have signed the petition *for* the bill, whom we can not find to have any other copy-rights than shares in a spelling-book: there are two other printers, whom, after the strictest inquiry, we cannot find to have any copy-right whatever. Two printsellers and an engraver have signed; and the rear is brought up by the clerk of the Stationers Company.— And indeed this Wilkie acknowledges there are eight or nine of them whom he does not know to have any copy-right whatever.[346]— What! present a petition to the legislature, complaining of the loss

[345] Globe Tavern and Coffee House, Fleet Street: Bryant Lillywhite, *London Coffee Houses*, 234–7, no. 466.

[346] For his evidence, *Morning Chronicle*, 16 May 1774.

they shall sustain in having purchased copy-rights, and yet have no copy-right at all to lose or gain by.—Surely these men ought not to object to even the three of the fifty-two counter-petitioners, the only exceptions against whom are, that one sells prints as well as books; that another has a wife who sells some toys; and a third, who, after having been thirty years in the Bookselling business only, was necessitated to keep a chandlery shop, from the difficulties under which the poorer Booksellers labour, from the oppressive claims of the rich monopolists. Surely the poorest Bookseller, even if he kept only a stall, has a proper claim on the justice and humanity of Parliament, that they may not be deprived of the means of existence, in following the only trade by which they can support themselves and families, in order to enrich a few. The exclusive right now sought after will be extremely prejudicial to the poorest Booksellers in Town and Country, who, although they have not money to print with, yet want cheap editions to sell; whereas larger editions will not be marketable for them; for although the copyholders hold out for shew the voluminous works of our most esteemed authors, yet they are not the copies for which they are so anxious; those articles will not lie out of print for fear of competition, for no competition can they apprehend; the purses and influence of the rich Booksellers of London will prevent any person from interfering with them in these: Neither are they their most valuable copies; the subject of this contest is for trivial articles in universal use; the copy-right of Dyche's spelling-book[347] has been sold for more, than the copy-rights of all the **{7}** works of Newton, Locke, Tillosion, Boyle, Bacon,[348] and a dozen more of our most esteemed authors would sell for, among those patrons of learning the petitioning Booksellers. It is certainly necessary, that those common books, in general use among the lower class of people, should be sold as cheap as possible, and not be loaded with a monopoly. If a poor labouring man buys spelling books for his children at 6 d. each; instead of 1 s. it is the same to him as though he saved that money in the necessaries of life; yet the Booksellers say, a monopoly of books is not oppressive, because they are not necessaries of life. The sale of single plays, for the use of the audience at the Theatres, is another great subject of this monopoly. One of the petitioners has gained a fortune by claiming and enjoying the copy-rights of most of our old plays that are still acted: To obtain and enjoy this claim, numberless injuries and oppressions have they been guilty of. But although a monopoly of this branch of trade may raise large fortunes to a few men by selling them for 6 d. each; yet it is certainly more compassionate to allow a hundred poor men to support themselves and families by selling them for 3 d. which they can do, and yet print them as well as the pretended proprietors. As a monopoly will be so very prejudicial in the lowest class of books, so it will be to the second, which are the common books in estimation, such as Pope, Swift, Spectators, Rambler, &c. This will evidently appear from comparing the editions of books that were published from the expiration of the monopoly in 1731, till about the year 1760 (when the Booksellers began to entertain hope of a perpetual one) with the new editions of old copies printed since that time; and more particularly since the judgment of the Court of King's Bench. See the last editions of the Rambler, Grandison, Jewish Spy, &c.[349]

[347]Thomas Dyche, *A Guide to the English Tongue* (1707) (ESTC: N6605).

[348]Issac Newton, John Locke, John Tillotson, Robert Boyle, Francis Bacon.

[349]The latest editions appear to be Samuel Johnson, *The Rambler* (Millar, 1767) (ESTC: N12562); Samuel Richardson, *The History of Sir Charles Grandison* (Rivington, 1770) (ESTC: T58982); Jean-Baptiste de Boyer (marquis d'Argens) (1703–71), *The Jewish Spy* (Millar, 1766) (ESTC: T131033).

The case of Mr. Strahan's[350] lately purchasing Blackston's Commentaries at a large price has been mentioned to excite compassion, although there is little doubt but that he will soon more than reimburse himself, under the limitation of the statute. The learned Judge has not reaped all the harvests, but left some profitable ones for the Bookseller.

The influence of a monopoly on printing, is obvious, from considering the various editions of the Spectators. Before the year 1731 no good edition of them was printed. After that time they gradually improved; and, in the year 1747, when the honorary monopoly was invaded, Tonson printed a small cheap edition, but it did not take with the public. He, about the year 1750, printed the best edition in 12mo, with engraved titles and frontpieces,[351] and sold this fine edition at little more than half the sum for which he before sold the ordinary editions. And the next time their counsel looks over the list of editions given by his clients at the cheap rate of 3 s. *per* volume, let him consider that this edition of the Spectators was sold by Tonson for 10d. halfpenny *per* volume in sheets, whereas, those 3 s. volumes sold by his clients are almost all of them worse printed, and are sold by them for 1 s. 7 d. halfpenny *per* vol. And it may be necessary to observe, that the Spectator being the cheapest book that is sold by London booksellers, is owing to that competition: For they have not yet thought it expedient to raise the price, but it is certain that the two last editions are printed worse. With respect to the third class of books, viz. elegant editions, it can as little be expected that a monopoly will be advantageous. Of every new work, when first published, they give an expensive quarto edition, and the monopoly given by the statute will insure to the public such elegant editions; **{8}** but those who compare them with the products of the Paris press, will entertain no very favourable idea of their elegance. It is only by competition and emulation that improvement and perfection are to be expected. That competition has raised the Paris printers to an high rank of reputation. There are some presses, in our country, that have attained an equal, if not superior rank, but they were not raised under the influence of monopolizing London Booksellers. The Paris printers cannot print without privileges; but the sale of French books not being confined to that kingdom, they print for other countries; and therefore no privilege can answer the purpose of securing the sale to them, for they are immediately reprinted in Holland, and frequently in various towns of France; therefore the Paris printers secure their trade by preserving the first rank of reputation for printing; so that a Paris edition is always preferred, and bears an higher price than the Dutch; although the latter far surpass the London editions. Let the London Booksellers preserve their trade by the same means; they have it equally in their power; and, while the other printers are loading the kingdom with *coarse* editions, and *ruining themselves* by publishing them, let the London Booksellers flourish and increase in wealth and *reputation* (an increase in the latter there is great room for) by publishing elegant and splendid editions that will do honour to English literature, and not suffer foreigners, who adorn their libraries with specimens of British printing, to despise the capital, and seek after the products of the presses of Strawberry Hill, Birmingham, and Glasgow. We trust the rich London Bookseller will no longer be suffered to disgrace their country and themselves. And on the whole, if this Bill be rejected, and the public derive not from a free trade the advantage they have a just

[350] William Strahan, 10 New Street, Shoe Lane.

[351] The octavo edition was *The Spectator* (Tonson, 1747) (ESTC: T144210); the 12mo edition with front plates was *The Spectator* (Tonson, 1750) (ESTC: T97950).

reason to expect, it must be owing to the truth of a maxim that the petitioners console themselves with: *That after all, the London Booksellers will be able, in a great measure, to give laws to the trade.*[352]

It is said, if this bill does not pass, there will be an inundation of bad editions; if so, this act will not prevent, but promote it, as those already printed may be legally sold; and a multitude of editions may be printed in the country with false dates; but at present their fears are only pretended, to impose upon the legislature.

The money expended on new editions of old books is oftener for the advantage of the Bookseller than the public; for although the improvements are much boasted of in the titles, yet they are frequently trivial and intended to depreciate the prior editions, and to tempt the public to load themselves with divers copies of the same book. This conduct, of which they now boast, is justly noticed by the Bishop of Carlisle as a hardship on the public;[353] who observes, that they ought to sell the improvements separate to the purchasers of the former editions. But will less money be expended in improving editions if this Bill does not pass? On the contrary, much more; for, as the improvements will be protected by the old statute, it will be one of the means by which they will maintain their monopoly; they have also given a list of books of which they have been long selling the impressions, but it is only printed for shew: a monopoly of them they would not think worth accepting; and many of these copies the present proprietors did not print, but combined at Tonson's sale,[354] and bought them for considerably less than they cost printing.

Not an argument do they use that applies to the present Bill; and however they may now affect to venerate the late decision, yet every one of their assertions militates against it; or if they prove any thing, prove the necessity of a perpetuity. Are they thieves who have reprinted their copies after the expiration **{9}** of the limitations of the statute? Then surely they can be no less who reprint them after the expiration of the term now prayed. Will an open trade, in printing, disgrace literature, and introduce an inundation of incorrect editions? Will it do less 15 years hence? Will it occasion valuable books going out of print? Will it have a less fatal effect then? They say they shall lose if this Bill does not pass: They may say the same, and with equal truth, at the expiration of the 14 years, in a petition for another Bill.

The conduct of the other London Booksellers, and the country ones, has certainly been laudable. Although conscious that their opulent brethren usurped their natural right, yet, they patiently, though anxiously, waited the determination of this cause. Few and but trivial instances of any invasion of those pretended rights can be justly laid to their charge; a much greater number may be adduced of the petitioners themselves having trespassed on each other's claims.

As the conduct of those rich monopolists has been most oppressive and injurious; so, it is hoped, the patient acquiescence of the other Booksellers under it, till the question was

[352]See Cavendish {S18}.

[353]This appears to be a development of what was said in Edmund Law* (1703–87), *Observations Occasioned by the Contest about Literary Property* (Archdeacon, 1770) (ESTC: T13046), 17 n. 1.

[354]*Catalogue of Books in Quires, being the Genuine Stock of Jacob and Richard Tonson, which will be sold by Auction, to a Select Number of the Booksellers of London and Westminster, on Tuesday, May 26, 1767* (ESTC: T130034).

finally decided, will not be accounted to deserve so severe a punishment, as to be now deprived of their rights for the emolument of their oppressors.

WILLIAM CAVELL,[355] of the parish of St. Andrew, Holborn in the county of Middlesex, Bookseller, saith, That he hath been at three of the Booksellers sales at the Queen's Arms:[356] That, at one as those sales, he saw William Watts,[357] one of the petitioners against the Bill: That, in the midst of the sale, William Johnston,[358] bookseller, came in to the said room, and demanded of the proprietor or manager of the said sale what he invited such company for; immediately on which, the manager of the sale, he believes it was John Wilkie, called the said William Watts out of the said sale room; and, he believes he, the said William Watts, hath not been there since. And he, the said William Cavell saith, That the said William Watts was and is reputed to be a man of considerable substance and credit. He never did hear or understand that the said William Watts was excepted against for being deficient in his payments, or for pirating any copy-right or pretended copy-right whatever: That he, the said William Cavell, at another of the said sales, did see J. Murray[359] called on, in order, as he understood, to be turned out for being in possession of a Scotch printed book; but that the said J. Murray denied the charge: That, at one of the said sales, he, the said William Cavell, was informed by Thomas Evans,[360] one of the petitioners for the Bill, that some gentlemen had refused to buy if he continued in the room, for, that he had sold pirated books, and desired or required him to withdraw; or words to that effect: That Thomas Lowndes,[361] one of the petitioners for the bill, came to him, the said William Cavell, and informed him that, if he sold any Scotch or pirated books, they were determined to ruin him, and, that a considerable sum of money was subscribed for that purpose: That soon after, he, the said William Cavell, was served with three injunctions,[362] for selling George Barnwell, Cato, and the Beggar's Opera.[363] And, the said William Cavell saith, That, to the best of his knowledge and belief, he hath not printed or sold any books contrary to law; and saith, That all the books or plays, which he hath ever sold, which the pretended proprietors deemed to be pirated, did not amount to the sum of 10 l. And saith, That he hath seen the servant of the said Thomas Lowndes, in the shop of the said Thomas Lowndes, one of the petitioners for the Bill, take out the titles of **{10}** plays which they deemed to be pirated, and insert titles to the said plays; which titles purported that the said plays were printed at London,

[355] William Cavell tr. 1766–1804, 29 Middle-Row.

[356] Queen's Arms Tavern, St Paul's Churchyard: Bryant Lillywhite, *London Coffee Houses*, 461–4, no. 1032.

[357] William Watts* (1752–1851) sold engravings at Kemp's Row, Chelsea. However, he was not known to trade before 1779. There was a bookbinder with the same name and a similar date of death (1852) whose trade dates would cover 1774 (and it may be the same person).

[358] William Johnston.

[359] John Murray (1745–93), 32 Fleet St.

[360] Thomas Evans (1742–84), app. 1757, tr. 1769–85, bookseller, 195 Strand, London.

[361] Lowndes, 77 Fleet Street, ran a circulating library.

[362] Two injunctions can be identified from Gomez-Arostegui, *Register of Copyright Infringement Suits: Strahan & Others v Cavell & Others* (1771–4) (TNA, C 12/1327/44) (*Cato*); *Rivington & Others v Lloyd and Cavell* (1771–4) (TNA, C 12/1327/28) (*Beggar's Opera*).

[363] The editions that resulted after the litigation were Joseph Addison, *Cato* (Cavell, 1774) (ESTC: T185727) and George Lillo* (1691/3–1739), *The London Merchant: The History of George Barnwell* (Cavell, 1776) (ESTC: N55250). The infringement edition was probably John Gay* (1685–1732), *The Beggar's Opera* (1770) (ESTC: N14823).

for the said Thomas Lowndes and others. And he, the said William Cavell saith, That he, the said William Cavell, did purchase several copy-rights of John Fuller:[364] That an edition being printed of Cole's Dictionary,[365] one of the said copy-rights, he did apply to William Johnston and others, for his share of the said books, but that he never has had any part of the same, although he hath the receipt of the said John Fuller, and the assignment to the said John Fuller, under which he, the said John Fuller, did claim and enjoy the copy-right of the said book. And further saith, That all the persons who have signed the counter-petition are shopkeepers, and that 30 of the said persons sell books only, and that 15 others of the said persons sell books and stationary only, to the best of his knowledge and belief. Of all which particulars he is ready to make oath when required.

WILLIAM CAVELL.

SIMON VANDENBERGH,[366] of the parish of St. James, in the city of Westminster, Bookseller, saith, That, about the year 1760, he complained to John Rivington,[367] one of the petitioners for the Bill, that he, the said Simon Vandenbergh, was not allowed to attend the Queen's Arms sales: That he, the said John Rivington, replied, That he, the said Simon Vandenbergh, might attend the said sales, if he, the said Simon Vandenbergh, would pay 5 l. and sign the same agreement as other Booksellers did, or words to that effect: That he asked what agreement that was, and the said John Rivington replied, that it was a bond not to reprint any book claimed by them, or words to that effect: That he, the said Simon Vandenbergh, inquired of John Wilkie why he, the said Simon Vandenbergh, was not invited to the said sales: That the said John Wilkie replied, that he, the said Simon Vandenbergh was not in the list, or words to that effect; and that he did never hear, or could obtain any other reason for such refusal: That he hath frequented the sales at the Globe for and during the last 16 years, and catalogues of them have been usually sent to his house: That he, the said Simon Vandenbergh, hath given a great number of notes of hand for books bought at the said sales, which said notes he regularly paid: That he hath never imported any Scotch or Irish books; nor hath he ever printed any book claimed by the London Booksellers, except Joe Miller's Jests:[368] That, the said book having been long out of print, he, the said Simon Vandenbergh, not apprehending that any person claimed an exclusive right thereto, did, about the year 1766, reprint the same: That he did receive a letter, purporting to be a letter from the attorney of William Nicoll,[369] one of the petitioners for the Bill, and others, threatening him, the said Simon Vandenbergh, with a law-suit for reprinting the said book; and that the said William Nicoll did threaten the said Simon Vandenbergh, and assert, that himself, and three other London Booksellers, had an exclusive right to print the said book: And, That he, the said William Nicoll, did induce the said Simon Vandenbergh to promise not to reprint the same. Of all which particulars he is ready to make oath when required,

SIMON VANDENBERGH.

[364]John Fuller, app. 1713–24, tr. from 1726, Bible & Dove, 6 Ave Maria Lane.

[365]Elisha Coles* (c. 1608–1688), *An English Dictionary* (Crouch, 1676) (ESTC: R38819).

[366]Simon Vandenbergh (1728–1808), of Bow Street, Westminster, ran a circulating library.

[367]John Rivington, 62 Paternoster Row (settled in north America in 1760).

[368]The first edition of this was *Joe Miller's Jests or the Wit Vade-melum* (Reid, 1739) (ESTC: T124768).

[369]He was the partner of his brother George Nicoll on the Strand.

{11} WILLIAM FOX,[370] of the parish of St. Andrew, Holbourn, in the county of Middlesex, Bookseller, saith, That he, in or about the year 1769 received a catalogue of a sale at the Globe Tavern,[371] directed to him by name: That he did go to the said sale, in consequence thereof: That, when he had been in the room about an hour, the clerk of the said sale, did inform him that his company was objected to by some of the company; and the proprietor, Mr. Millan,[372] desired he would retire, or words to that effect: That he did go away in consequence thereof: And he was not told any other reason, nor doth he know of any other reason for such procedure: And the said William Fox further saith, That he received a catalogue of a book-sale at the Queen's Arms in St. Paul's Church-yard, in or about the year 1769, which catalogue was directed to him by name: That he did go to the said sale in consequence thereof: That after he had been in the sale-room about an hour, he did understand and believe, by the method of proceeding, that he would be turned out; and therefore, and for no other reason, did leave the sale-room for fear of insult: And saith, That he the said William Fox, was invited, by catalogue, and did attend the trade-sales of books held at the Globe Tavern, from the year 1766, to the year 1770: That, in the course of that time, he did give a great number of notes of hand for books there purchased; and which notes he did regularly discharge and pay; nor did he ever hear of any complaints being pretended of not payment thereof: That in or about the years 1769–70, he, the said William Fox, refused to join in an agreement to combine together at the public auctions of libraries, in order not to bid against each other, but to purchase the books and afterwards resel them and divide the surplus, that, in consequence thereof, he did receive, in June, 1770, from ———Noble, then servant to Mr. Thomas Payne,[373] Bookseller, at the Mews, the following letter, *viz*. "To Mr. Fox. June 12, 1770. Sir, There will be an universal joining of the trade, to-morrow, at Peel's auction; unless you prevent so very necessary a measure for the good of the trade, which, in old books, will soon come to nothing, if every broker, and auctioneer can make more of them than we can give, and which they could not do were the trade to be unanimous; therefore, it is hoped, that you will not be the only person who will not agree in the measure proposed: for otherwise people will be angury, and you, yourself, will not be asked any where. I wish your compliance; and am, Sir, your most humble servant, Thomas Payne." That he, the said William Fox, did go to the said Mr. Thomas Payne, and inform him, That he could not approve or agree to the said terms, as he thought such conduct unjustifiable or words to that effect: And saith, That he, the said William Fox, hath not been at any trade-sale, at the Globe or Queen's Arms, since the said 12th day of June 1770, and doth not know, nor ever heard, any other reason why he is not allowed to come to the said sales at the Globe, but his refusal, as aforesaid: And he, the said William Fox, hath often been told by Booksellers, that he might again attend the said sales, if he would agree to join the combination before mentioned: And the said William Fox further saith, That he did never reprint, nor was he ever concerned in reprinting, any book, the copy-right of which was claimed: And that he never did import or convey, or cause to be imported or conveyed, any

[370] William Fox tr. 1773–83, 128 Holborn Hill (opposite Fetter Lane), became a pamphleteer in the abolitionist movement: Timothy Whelan, 'William Fox, Martha Gurney, and Radical Discourse of the 1790s', *Eighteenth-Century Studies*, xlii (2009), 397.

[371] Globe Tavern and Coffee House, Fleet Street: Bryant Lillywhite, *London Coffee Houses*, 234–7, no. 466.

[372] John Millan (c. 1700–1782), tr. 1727–81, bookseller, Charing Cross.

[373] Thomas Payne.

Scotch or Irish editions of English books, and that he never did sell any pirated editions, or any editions deemed **{12}** by the Booksellers to be pirated, to the value or amount of 20 s. except in the following case. In the year 1767, he exchanged with a Dublin Bookseller for some Dublin editions of books, to the value of about 18 or 20 l.: That, when he purchased the said books, he did not know they were prohibited by law; for that he had seen such editions at the sale or sales of Mr. William Cater,[374] one of the petitioners for the bill; and had purchased of the said Mr. William Cater, Dr. Young's Works, a Dublin edition,[375] then not knowing that to sell such editions were illegal: That soon after he had purchased the said books, a person did purchase the whole of the said books, except about eight or ten books, which person was employed by some Bookseller or Booksellers to inform against him: That he did acquaint them with the above circumstances, and would have confirmed it on oath, and further offered to give security never to sell any such editions: That the said Bookseller or Booksellers did refuse the said terms; and did bring actions on the statute of the 12 Geo. 2.[376] which cost him about 80 l. And the said William Fox saith, That he was present when 50 of the London Booksellers signed the petition against the Bill: That all the said persons are shopkeepers: That 30 of the said persons sell books only: That other 15 of the said persons sell books and stationary only; and that two others of the said persons sell books and some medicines, and no other commodity, to the best of his knowledge and belief; and that one other person is a printer and bookseller. Of all which particulars he is ready to make oath when required.

WILLIAM FOX.

JOHN WADE,[377] of the parish of St. Andrew, Holbourn, in the county of Middlesex, Bookseller, saith, That he hath been invited, and has attended most of the Booksellers sales at the Globe Tavern in Fleetstreet for and during the last 14 years: That he hath, during that time, given notes of hand for books purchased at those sales, to the amount of some thousand pounds; which said notes were regularly discharged and paid the days when they respectively became due, if then brought and tendered for payment: That he, the said John Wade, was not invited to any Booksellers sale at the Queen's Arms, till September 1765: That he did attend the said sale, and did pay the purchase money when due: That the clerk, or manager, of the said sales, hath not since invited him to the said sales, or sent him any catalogues of them: That he has never been informed of the reason for such proceeding: That he, the said John Wade, was desired, by a proprietor of a Queen's Arms sale, in or about the year 1771, to attend and purchase at his sale; but he did refuse to attend the said sale, because not invited in the usual manner, by the clerk of the said sale; and was apprehensive, that he would be turned out of the room if he went: That he, the said John Wade, knoweth the Booksellers who have signed the petition against the Booksellers Bill: That they are all shopkeepers: That he was present when 47 of the said persons signed the said petition. And he saith, That 30 of the said persons, to the best of his knowledge and belief, sell books only: That 15 other of the said persons sell books and some stationary, and two other of the

[374] William Cater tr. 1759–82, 274 High Holborn.

[375] Probably Edward Young, *The Works of the Author of Night Thoughts* (Ewing, 1764) (ESTC: T78086).

[376] Importation Act 1738 (12 Geo. II, c. 36).

[377] John Wade app. 1766, tr. 1771–1801, 163 Fleet Street.

said persons sell books and some medicines. Of all which particulars he is ready to make oath when required.

JOHN WADE.

Country Booksellers' Petitions

Votes 1774, pp. 684–5; *CJ*, xxxiv, 757 (16 May).

A Petition of *George Sagg*, of *New Malton*, in the County of *York*, Bookseller, Bookbinder, and Stationer, and *William Arnell*, Bookseller: And also,

A Petition of *William Ward* and *Samuel Creswell*, Bookseller and Printers in *Nottingham*: And also,

A Petition of *John Baines*, of *Bawtry*, Bookseller, and others: And also,

A Petition of *John Binns*, *Griffith Wright*, *Daniel Smith*, and *James Bowling*, Booksellers, Stationers, and Printers of the Town of *Leeds*, in the County of *York:* And also,

A Petition of *Ely Hargrove*, Booksellers and Stationer, of the Town of *Knaresborough*, in the County of *York*;

Were severally presented to the House, and read; Setting forth, That the Petitioners observe, by the Votes, that Leave has been given to bring in a Bill, for the Relief of some Booksellers in *London* and *Westminster*, by granting them the sole and exclusive Privilege, for a further limited Time, of re-printing Books not protected by the Act of the 8th of Queen *Anne*; and that the Petitioners view this Bill as highly detrimental to the Community at large, as well as particularly injurious to them and all Country Booksellers, Printers, and others, dependent on those Branches of Business: And therefore praying, That the Statute of the 8th of Queen *Anne*, for vesting Copies in Authors, *&c.* may stand in full Force, as lately explained by the House of Lords, and be neither amended or extended; and that the Petitioners may be heard, by Counsel, against the said Bill being passing into a Law.

Burke's Notes on Copyright Bill

Edmund Burke, *Correspondence of the Right Honourable Edmund Burke* (4 vols, 1844), iv.

{459} NOTES ON COPY-RIGHT BILL AND MONOPOLIES GENERALLY

"MONOPOLY" is contrary to "Natural Right."

"Free-Trade" is the same thing as "Use of Property"

[*Definition.*— Monopoly is the power, in one man, of exclusive dealing in a commodity or commodities, which others might supply if not prevented by that power.]

No monopoly can, therefore, be prescribed in; because contrary to common right.

Its only lawful origin is in the convention of parties, which gets the better of law.

[*Note.*—The convention is valid, not merely by the will of the parties, but on account of a presumed compensation for the right that is given up.]

The State, representing all its individuals, may contract for them; and therefore may grant a monopoly.

{460} They ought not to grant this monopoly on arbitrary principles, but for the good of the whole.

What ought to be their rules in granting a monopoly?

1st. The principle of encouraging men to employ themselves in useful inventions.

2nd. The principle of encouraging them to great risks in useful undertakings.

A matter may be of great difficulty in the invention, and of great use in the imitation; a monopoly here may be equitable, in favour of the inventor.

The beginnings of many useful undertakings may be full of risk and danger of all kinds; the following of them safe. Here, therefore, is another equity for monopoly.

[*Note.*—Nothing here said of monopoly purchased from the State; nor of that monopoly which grows out of the power of dealing on a large capital, or of disadvantageous intelligence, &c. This last is not monopoly, properly so called. The former is in the nature of a tax.]

Concerning the Duration of Monopolies.

I know of no dealing, except in books of the author's own invention, wherein a perpetual monopoly can be reasonable.

{461} A book is an invention which, taken in the whole, it is not probable that any other man in the world, but the individual author, could have supplied. It is that which, of all others, is the most readily multiplied by copies; with this advantage, that all the copies are as good as the original; in which it differs from pictures and agrees with machines.

The equity of a monopoly in favour of *mechanical inventions*, is not so strong and evident, because it is not improbable that many men may hit on a contrivance, in all respects the same, without communication; and it has so happened. Monopolies ought, therefore, not to granted in perpetuity for such contrivances.

As to new *undertaking*, where, not the invention, but the risk gives a sort of title to monopoly, the duration of the monopoly ought not, in equity, to be continued longer than till the undertaker is compensated the full value of the risk.

Perhaps the best way of estimating this risk, is by the supposed loss of the capital, and the ordinary *simple* interest of the money, or the current value of insurance. This ought to be the utmost extent. If he has gained his capital with *compound* interest, this ought to be the very utmost; it seems, indeed, rather too much.

1st. Because, by suffering others to trade, he **{462}**is not excluded, but is at least on equal footing with others.

2nd. Because he has advantages from prior possession of market, which does, in many cases, operate as a monopoly.

3rd. Because the new dealer does himself run a risk, and therefore stands upon the equity of the former; and he runs a risk for a beneficial purpose, as much as the first dealer does; for to *extend* trade is beneficial as well as to *discover* it; and risks are run in extending as well as discovering.

There will be some difference where, in the original grant of the monopoly, a price has been limited.

Such monopolies may, therefore, have limits; in most cases they *ought* to have limits; else they will transgress the purposes of their establishment, which was to discover a benefit for the most beneficial, that is, the most generally beneficial purposes.

Copies of Five Letters[378]

'Petitions' {20–4}.

{20} In the following Letters, we have a very accurate account of the rise of *a scheme*, the effects of which have been severely felt by many booksellers—a scheme which they have been some years, and are even now, attempting to mature into law;—but whatever they may now pretend, it appears that they did not then pretend to a common law right, but only to a *scheme*, to prevent the sale of Irish, Scotch, or any editions that they deemed piratical. The method they pursued in the execution of this scheme is an indisputable proof that they were not ignorant of the nature of their claims, but were conscious they had no legal foundation.

About the year 1746, the London booksellers commenced a suit in the Court of Session[379] in Scotland, and grounded their complaint on the statute. So far from thinking they had a common law right, it does not appear that they had the least idea of it in commencing that suit; but during the progress of that cause, their counsel (fond, as is usual, of discovering new fields of litigation) *first found out the Common Law Right*, and when it was brought by appeal into the House of Lords, Mr. *Murray*, (now Lord *Mansfield*), their counsel, pleaded in defence that common law right: and although Lord *Hardwicke*[380] told them, that notwithstanding that point could not then be determined, yet the field was open, they might bring an action and have the opinion of the House; but they then saw so little prospect of success, that they declined the contest, we must suppose, by advice of their counsel.

They had not, for some years after, even a *scheme* for preventing this pretended invasion of their property. Scotch, Irish, and country editions of books were sold by every country bookseller in the three kingdoms. The London trade, indeed, they had principally to themselves, because it was the interest of the principal London booksellers to support each other in their pretensions. But, however, plays, and some books were printed in London by the lower class of booksellers, without any interruption, till about a year before the writing of these letters.

In the year 1756, Mr. *Murray* was created Lord *Mansfield*, and made Lord Chief Justice. In 1758, they commenced the *first action that ever was brought* in defence of a common law right to their copies; but, conscious that it was an hazardous enterprize, they attempted to establish it by a collusive action in the court of king's bench, in the case of *Millar* against *Collins*.[381] *Foster, Dennison,* and *Wilmot*,[382] were then the puisne judges in that court. The collusion was discovered, and judgment was deferred on that account. This was a situation of which they availed themselves; for, under pretence that it was a property in contest at common law, they found they could obtain injunctions from the Court of Chancery. On that *fortunate* circumstance, these worthy gentlemen project this *laudable scheme* of proceeding in Chancery with the *utmost severity* against every person that should presume to sell

[378]The Letters dated 23 and 26 Apr. and 2 Nov. 1759 are also published, with commentary, in the earlier Alexander Donaldson, *Some Thoughts on the State of Literary Property* (Donaldson, 1764) (ESTC: N023843; T049411).

[379]The year is wrong: it is *Midwinter v Hamilton* (1743) Kam Rem 154; Mor 8295.

[380]Philip Yorke, earl of Hardwicke.

[381]This is usually called *Tonson v Collins* (1762) 1 Black W 321 (96 ER 180).

[382]Sir Thomas Denison, Sir Michael Foster, Sir John Eardley Wilmot.

the books prohibited by them. Would not the faintest idea of true *honour* or *morality* have taught these men to have first ascertained their common law right before they harrassed and ruined their poor brethren, with injunctions and suits in Chancery. Their common law right had been transgressed by almost every bookseller in the three kingdoms, Why did they not bring an action against some one of them? On *what principle* did they dare to call themselves *proprietors*? On what *justifiable principle* did they presume to bring *injunctions*, and yet not ascertain their claim by a *bona fide* action on the common law right? But the event has proved, that they acted with *prudence at least*. The cause has at last come to a determination. *But not yet abashed*, they return to the charge, mutter **{21}** complaints against Lord *Mansfield* for not defending them to the last, when it was obvious that their cause was totally indefensible; and then, would fain persuade the world that their conduct deserves the *applause of mankind*, and that their *miscarriage* in their *worthy attempt*, ought to recommend them to the *compassion* of the *legislature*.

COPIES of FIVE LETTERS

To Mr. JOHN MERRILL,[383] Bookseller in Cambridge.

{11} DEAR SIR, London, April 23, 1759.

—WE have *a scheme now entered into*, for totally preventing the sale of Scotch and Irish books, which were first printed in England; and near two thousand pounds is already subscribed for carrying it into immediate execution. And *every person in England, selling such books, will be proceeded against in Chancery, with the utmost severity:* and after May 1, *agents will be sent out to all parts of England, to detect such as have them in their shops, except classics, (Greek and Latin books.)* Your father, Mr. Millar, and I, have had a meeting upon it,* and your father approves of it, and has promised to subscribe ten guineas towards it: Mr. Fletcher[384] of Oxford will do the same. But as the subscribers will do every thing equitably, they take all the Scotch books you have in sheets, off your hands, at the lowest price they are sold at in Scotland to booksellers, and will give you the same value in the same books, English editions. You may therefore send up, *this week*, all the Scotch and Irish editions you have in sheets, and direct them for your father, at the Globe Tavern, Fleetstreet.[385] I have wrote to James Fletcher of Oxford, by this post, to send his up directly. But your father will write in general to you; but desired me to be particular in my letter. The books will be mostly, I suppose, as follows: Spectators, Tatlers, Guardians,[386] Shakespeare, Prior, Gay's poems and fables,[387] Swift's

[383]John Merrill (c. 1731–1801), son of Thomas Merrill (*d.* 1781), booksellers, Regents Walk, Cambridge: David McKitterick, *A History of Cambridge University Press, Vol. II* (Cambridge, 1992), 151–2.

[384]James Fletcher (1710–95), bookseller, The Turl, Oxford.

[385]Bryant Lillywhite, *London Coffee Houses*, 234–6, no. 466.

[386]*The Spectators* (Tonson, 1757) (ESTC: T63449); *The Tatler* (Tonson, 1759) (ESTC: T63451); *The Guardian* (Tonson, 1756) (ESTC: T97930).

[387]It is not clear which edition is being referred to. The following are the most likely, comparing the date of publication, it being published in London: John Gay, *Poems on Several Occasions* (Lintot, 1752) (ESTC: T13899); *Fables. By the late Mr Gay* (Hitch and Hawes, 1757) (ESTC: N9617, N9616); Matthew Prior, *Poems on Several* 387 *(continued)* *Occasions* (Tonson, 1755) (ESTC: N472915). There were a vast number of imprints of Shakespeare, but see for instance *The Works of Shakespeare: In Eight Volumes* (Hitch and Hawes, 1757) (ESTC: N26030).

works, Temple's works,[388] Prideaux's connection, Barrow's works, Rollin's ancient history, &c.[389] Gil Blas, Whiston's Josephus, Burnet's theory, 2 vols,[390] Young's works, Thomson's seasons, &c. Milton's poetical works,[391] Parnell's poems, Hudibras, Waller's poems,[392] Fable of the bees, 2 vols, Young's night thoughts, Turkish spy, Travels of Cyrus.[393] If *I have omitted any, don't you fail to send all* you have in sheets, and an account how many you have of each bound; and sell none after the first of May, for fear you are informed against. Please to shew this letter to Mess. Thurlbourn and Woodyer,[394] and Matthews.[395] I suppose they will have a letter from Beecroft[396] on the same subject. As to *Maps*,[397] he will be detected and punished severely; so I shall give him no information about it, nor do you, for I would not have him spared. But as for your shop, Mr. Thurlbourn, and Fletcher,[398] all things shall be done in a friendly manner. I beg you would not fail sending the Scotch and Irish books this week.— I am

Yours sincerely,
JOHN WHISTON.

---

*He here attempts to draw in the son, by telling him his father (who was then in town) approved the scheme. His veracity may be seen by comparing this with the fourth letter (to the father then at Cambridge) wherein he threatens the father, and pleads the example of the son to the father, as he here does that of the father to the son.

{22} To Mr. JOHN MERRILL

DEAR SIR, April 26, 1759.

—YEsterday was a general meeting of the considerable booksellers, and indeed almost all the whole trade. The scheme was read and approved of, and an agreement was entered into,

388 Jonathan Swift, *The Works of Jonathan Swift* (Bathurst, 1755) (ESTC: T52755); Sir William Temple* (1628–99), *The Works of Sir William Temple* (Clarke, 1757) (ESTC: T136594).

389 Humphrey Prideaux* (1648–1724), *The Old and New Testament Connected* (Tonson, 1749) (ESTC: T88603); Isaac Barrow* (1630–77), *The Works of Isaac Barrow* (Millar, 1741) (ESTC: N62058); Charles Rollin, *The Roman History from the Foundation of Rome to the Battle of Actium* (Knapton, 1754) (ESTC: T121677).

390 Alain-René Lesage (1668–1747), *The Adventures of Gil Blas de Santillane* (Anderson, 1759) (ESTC: T186763); *The Genuine Works of Flavius Josephus*, trans. William Whiston* (1667–1752) (Browne, 1755) (ESTC: T106436); Thomas Burnet* (?1635–1715), *Sacred Theory of the Earth* (Hooke, 1726) (ESTC: T144579).

391 Edward Young, *The Poetical Works of Rev Edward Young* (1755) (ESTC: N41838).

392 Thomas Parnell* (1679–1718), *Poems on Several Occasions* (Lintot, 1747) (ESTC: N20766); Samuel Butler, *Hudibras* (Brown, 1750) (ESTC: N17555); Edmund Waller* (1606–87), *The Works of Edmund Waller* (Tonson, 1758) (ESTC: T116990); James Thomson* (1700–48), *The Seasons* (Millar, 1758) (ESTC: T141530); John Milton, *The Poetical Works of Mr John Milton* (Tonson, 1721) (ESTC: T491785) (it is likely there was another edition subsequent to this, but this is the closest London edition on the ESTC).

393 Bernard Mandeville* (1670–1733), *The Fable of the Bees* (Roberts, 1733) (ESTC: T77578); Edward Young, *The Complaint: Or Night Thoughts* (Millar, 1758) (ESTC: T151056); Giovanni Marana (1642–93), *The Eight Volumes of Letters Writ by a Turkish Spy* (Wilde, 1754) (ESTC: T91589); Chevalier (Andrew) Ramsay (1686–1743), *The Travels of Cyrus* (Bettenham, 1752) (ESTC: T129760).

394 William Thurlbourn (*d.* 1768), tr. 1724–68, bookseller, Cambridge. John Woodyer (*d.* 1782) ended the partnership with Thurlbourn in the 1760s.

395 Richard Matthews (*d.* 1778), Regent Walk (University Street), Cambridge.

396 John Beecroft (*d.* 1779), app. 1731–8, tr. 1740–9, 23 Paternoster Row.

397 This may be William Mapes, North Buckenham, Norfolk.

398 Probably Thomas Fletcher of Cambridge.

and signed by all present but one,* (Worral in Bellyard.)[399] Wren[400] signed, and Pottinger,[401] and both subscribed 25 pound. Only a fifth of the money will be called for. The substance of the articles agreed to, and signed by above sixty, near seventy booksellers present, are,

No one, *after the first day of May next*, shall sell any Scotch or Irish editions of books first printed in England, *classics excepted*; or shall purchase, or take in exchange, or bring in by any means whatsoever, such Scotch or Irish books. As soon as may be, after the first of May, all such books in sheets shall be sent up to London by the booksellers in the country, to the proprietors of the copies of the said books, and the proprietors shall return to the said booksellers directly, the value in English editions of the same books. An account shall be sent how many they have *bound*, of such Scotch or Irish editions. All *such editions* now in London, and all pirated editions printed in England, shall be delivered up directly to the several proprietors. Any bookseller or printer knowing of any person bringing in, or selling, such editions, or piratical edition, shall give immediate notice to one of the committee, who shall directly order a prosecution against such offender, to be paid out of the common fund. Notice of this agreement shall be sent directly to *all* the booksellers in the country. No person who refuses to sign this agreement, and to subscribe something towards it, shall be admitted to any sale of quire books,[402] or copies; *neither shall any subscriber buy any books for such person in any sale*, under the penalty of five pounds for each offence, *and himself to be excluded all future sales*, and the benefit of this agreement. The committee chosen are, Mess. Tonson, Millar, Hitch, John and James Rivingtons, John Ward, and William Johnston.[403] At the end of three months a meeting of the subscribers to be called, and the proceedings of the committee to be laid before them for their approbation. All second-hand Scotch and Irish books, *coming in parcels or libraries*, to be sent up to the committee, and they are to pay, in money, the *real value* to the person who sent them. Riders shall be appointed, the first of May, to inspect all the booksellers shops in England, and give intelligence of what they can find out. Mr. Tonson subscribed 500 pounds, Millar 300, Hitch 150. All the wholesale dealers, Dodd, Baldwin, both Rivingtons, Ward, Beecroft, Longman, Crowder and Comp. Ware, Richardson, Dodsley, Davey and Comp. Johnston, Newberry,[404] 100 pound each, T. Osborne 50,[405] Brown, Whiston, L. Davis, Sandby, Shuckburgh, Bathurst, Hawkins, Wren, Pottinger, Buckland, Field, Stuart, Caslon, &c &c. 25 pound each;[406] in all amounting to

[399]John Worrall (*d.* 1771), tr. 1758–65, Bell Yard, Temple Bar.

[400]John Wren (*d.* 1768), app. 1745, tr. 1764–8, Strand, Bible & Crown, Salisbury Court (it is suggested he finished trading in 1757; but a J. Wren was trading on the Strand between 1761 and 1768; this is likely to be the same person).

[401]Probably James Pottinger tr. 1745–70, Royal Bible, Paternoster Row.

[402]A quire book has 24 sheets.

[403]Jacob Tonson, Strand; Andrew Millar, Strand; Charles Hitch (*d.* 1786), app. 1718–25, 32 Paternoster Row; John Rivington app. 1735–42; James Rivington* (1724–1802/3), John Ward (*d.* 1760), app. 1746, tr. to 1760; and William Johnston.

[404]Benjamin Dodd (*d.* 1765), app. 1748, tr. 1752–65, Ave Maria Lane; Richard Baldwin, 47 St Paul's Churchyard; John Beecroft, 23 Paternoster Row; Thomas Longman, Ship and Black Swan; Stanley Crowder, 12 Paternoster Row; Joseph Richardson, 26 Paternoster Row; Robert Dodsley, Pall Mall; Peter Davey (*d.* 1760); Francis Newberry (*d.* 1780), 20 Ludgate Street.

[405]Thomas Osborne, Gray's Inn.

[406]Daniel Brown (*d.* 1762), app. 1732–40, tr. 1736–63, near Temple Bar; John Whiston, Boyle's Head, 64 Fleet Street; Lockyer Davis* (1719–91), app. 1732–46, tr. 1753–91, Gray's Inn Gate, 326 High Holborn; William Sandby (c. 1717–1799), app. 1734–41, tr. 1743–96, The Ship, Fleet Street; John Shuckburgh (*d.* 1761), app. 1741–21, tr.

3150 pounds. A fifth to be called for May 1. T. Payne will subscribe 25 pound,[407] but could not be there. The thing is set about in earnest, and will be conducted with spirit and discretion. Your father should by all means subscribe ten guineas, and will; so **{23}** will Fletcher and S. Baker:[408] and I hope Mr. Thurlbourn,[409] as probably never more than two guineas will be called for. The money to be deposited in Ald. Gosling's[410] hands.— I will serve you, my friend, in every thing I can; but this is a right measure, and must be steadily pursued.

Yours, sincerely,
JOHN WHISTON.

{22} *Mr. Worral had purchased copy-rights to larger amount than most of the subscribers; he certainly would not have opposed a scheme so essential to his interest, but from a conviction of the iniquity of it. Mr. Worral was well known to be a very worthy man.

To Mr. JOHN MERRILL,

With 11 Mainwaring's Sermons.

DEAR SIR, April 30, 1759.

I was out all Friday on particular business, and Mr. White not opening your letter, I had it not till near nine at night, when it was too late to send you any more Mainwaring's sermons. I send you with this, *eleven*, making in all *eighteen*. I have not any such sort of a Bible as you want. You will all soon have letters from the committee relating to the Scotch and Irish editions — when they must come up. The carriage will be paid by the committee, out of the general fund of money subscribed, and *that is another reason* why your father should subscribe. As only two guineas will be called for, I hope you will not grudge so small a sum, for the general good of the trade: besides, I know he can afford it *better* than the person you mention: And if that person *is wrong* in his acting meanly on this occasion, his example is not to be followed. You did right to inform Mr. Paris.[411] I doubt not but you received my full letter by Thursday's post, and that it was clear and satisfactory. Your father *again tells me*, he laid by two or three Grey's Hudibras,[412] 2 vols. with cuts, and some other books, for me, against I came to Cambridge.—Pray send me the Hudibras this week. I have been much

406 *(continued)* 1728–61, The Sun, near Temple Gates, Fleet Street; Charles Bathurst (1709–86), app. 1727–39, 26 Fleet St; George Hawkins (1705–80), app. 1720–30, Milton's Head, Temple Gates, Fleet St; John Wren, Bible & Crown, Salisbury Court, Fleet St; James Buckland (c. 1711–1790), tr. 1736–89, 57 Paternoster Row; Thomas Field, Paternoster Row; Zachariah Stuart (*d.* 1773), app. 1758, tr. 1759–73, Paternoster Row; Thomas Caslon, 4 Stationers Court, Ludgate St.

407 Thomas Payne.

408 Thomas Fletcher, app. 1732, tr. 1749–62, St Mary the Great, Cambridge; Samuel Baker, York Street, Covent Garden.

409 William Thurlbourn.

410 Francis Gosling (1719–68), alderman Farringdon Without, 1756–68. In 1742 he was made a partner in what became Gosling's Bank; *History of Barclays Bank Limited*, comp. P.W. Matthews, ed. A.W. Tuke (1926).

411 John Paris (*d.* 1781), app. 1743, tr. 1749–81, St Benedict's parish, Cambridge.

412 Zachary Grey* (1688–1766), *Critical, Historical, and Explanatory Notes upon Hudibras, by way of Supplement to the Two Editions Published in the Years 1744 and 1745* (Norris, 1752) (ESTC: T139122).

hurried on Friday and Saturday with Le Bas's affairs,[413] at Nine Elms.[414] Your father dined with us there both days, and spent all yesterday with me. I hope to have a little leisure this week, for I was too much hurried with variety of affairs last week. I am, with kind respects to all of you,

Your sincere friend
JOHN WHISTON.

To Mr. THOMAS and JOHN MERRILL, Booksellers at Cambridge,
By Mrs. Cooper's Parcel

SIR,

June 8, 1759

I Received both yours, and am glad to hear you are all well. I must insist upon the two which Dr. Walker[415] has promised me to put out. As for the Dean of York's,[416] we will talk of it when at Cambridge. As to the other affair, I am sorry to see you are an advocate still for pirates, who plunder people of their property, which they have paid a valuable consideration for. And had you a property in Spectators, Swift, Tillotson, Barrow, Pope's Homer, or any valuable author which you had paid a considerable sum of money for, very sure I am, you would cry out *loudly* and *justly*, upon any person who should reprint and undersel you, and render your copy of no worth, *because he paid no copy-money*. Shew the case, as here stated, to any man of common sense, and he must see where justice lies. But I shall say no more but this, *There will come a time*, when **{24}** you will heartily wish you had followed my friendly advice. *And this time*, I can assure you, *is not far off*. But you will do what you please, and not what is right; so you must take the consequence to yourself. Only, *then remember*, I would have been your friend, and you would not let me. I must speak the truth, whether it please or not. I heartily wish you and all your family well, and will serve you as long as I can. Soon it will not be in my power, I doubt. Pray shew this letter to your son John, whom I highly esteem, for his equitable sentiments. I am, if you will believe me,

Your sincere friend,
JOHN WHISTON.

Copy of a printed Letter which was circulated to all the Booksellers in England.

SIR,

St. Paul's Church-yard, London, Nov. 2, 1759.

THE authors of books, as well as the persons to whom, for valuable considerations, they have transferred their copy-right, having for some years past been greatly injured in their property, by sundry persons fraudulently and clandestinely in England, and openly in Scotland and Ireland, reprinting and vending the same, to the particular loss and injury of the said authors

[413]Jacques-Philippe Le Bas (1707–83), a leading French engraver.

[414]A town in Surrey at the time, now in Battersea, London.

[415]It is not possible to be certain which Dr Walker was being referred to here, but a likely candidate is Dr Richard Walker* (1679–1764), vice master of Trinity College, Cambridge.

[416]John Fountayne* (1714–1802), dean 1747–1802.

and proprietors, and to the detriment of the fair trader in general; the booksellers of London, in their own defence, have been forced to take proper measures to stop this growing evil: and, upon mature consideration, with the advice of persons *eminent in the law*, have come to a general agreement to prosecute, by due course of law, all such persons as shall be detected in either printing or vending piratical editions of the books which are their property. And in pursuance of this necessary agreement, several persons detected are now under prosecution for the same.

But the booksellers of London being desirous to stop these illicit practices *by the most gentle methods*, and not to harass persons by a law-suit, who may through ignorance or inadvertency be liable thereto, have directed me to give you this notice; that, if you have any Scotch, or other pirated editions of English books, they will take them off your hands, at the real price they cost you, and give you in return to the same value in the genuine editions of the said books, at the lowest market-price; *upon condition*, that you will engage not to purchase or vend any such pirated editions for the future. And they doubt not but this fair proposal will induce the country booksellers in general (as many have already done) to deliver up their piratical editions directly, and no more encourage this illicit trade.

If, after this notice, any person shall be detected in selling any pirated book, and is prosecuted for so doing, he must not blame any one but himself, as it will not be in the power of any of his correspondents to compromise the suit for him, for no favour will be shewn to one person more than to another; but it is hoped this notice will have the desired effect, that both authors and booksellers may not be under the disagreeable necessity of supporting their rights and properties, by those methods which the law has prescribed.

By order of the Committee,
JOHN WILKIE.

Printed Books

Books Printed by the Booksellers of London and Westminster, in different Sizes and Prices, of which there remains a large Stock on Hand: BL, two different versions: ESTC: T16363, T89000 (Copies available at: Bodleian: (Vet.) 2581 c.5 (2); Eighteenth Century Collection Online).

A: [ESTC: T16363]:

BOOKS,
Printed by the BOOKSELLERS of LONDON and WESTMINSTER, in different Sizes and Prices; of which there remains a large Stock on Hand: With the Number of Years an Impression of each is in selling.

B: [ESTC: T89000]:

A LIST of BOOKS
Printed by the BOOKSELLERS of LONDON and WESTMINSTER, in different Sizes; by which it will appear that *Cheap Editions* of all useful Books, that are capable of being reduced into a small Size, have been published by the said Booksellers: With the Number of Years an Impression of each is selling.

	£.	s	d	Years in selling
Addison's Works, 4 vols, 4to.	2	8	0	33
the same, Royal, 4to. by Baskerville	3	3	0	13
4 vols. large 8vo	1	0	0	8
his miscellaneous Works, 3 vols. 12mo	0	9	0	6
Ainsworth's Dictionary, 2 vols. folio	4	4	0	22
the same in 4to.	1	7	0	12
Dictionary abridged, 2 vols. 8vo.	0	12	0	16
Ditto, in one vol. 8vo. new Edition, 1774, ready for publication				
[**B**: Akenside's Works, 4 to.	1	1	0	
the same, 8vo.	0	6	0]	
Anson's Voyage, 1 vol. 4to.	1	1	0	6
Ditto, 1 vol. 8vo.	0	6	0	12
Ditto, 1 vol. 12mo.	0	3	0	13
Beveridge's private Thoughts, 2 vols. 8vo.	0	8	0	30
the same in 1 vol. 12mo.	0	2	0	6
Blackstone's Commentaries, 4 vols. 4to.	4	4	0	
Ditto, 4 vols. 8vo.	1	10	0	
Boyer's Royal Dictionary, French and English, 4to.	1	5	0	8
abridged, 1 vol. 8vo.	0	7	0	5
Telemachus, 2 vols. 12mo.	0	6	0	7
the same, 2 vols. [**A**: 18mo] [**B**: 18: vo].	0	4	0	[**B**:25]
[**B**: Burn's Justice, 2 vols. 4to	1	16	0	
4 vols. 8vo.	1	4	0	
Burn's Ecclesiastical Law, 2 vols. 4to.	2	6	0	
4 vols. 8vo.	1	4	0]	
Cave's Historia Literaria, 2 vols. fol.	2	10	0	34
Characteristics, (Lord Shaftesbury) 3 vols. 8vo.	0	18	0	30
the same, 3 vols. 18mo.	0	6	0	25
Clarke's (Dr. Samuel) Works, 4 vols. fol. fine Paper				26
the same, 4 vols. fol. on good Paper	5	0	0	26
his Sermons, 11 vols. 8vo.	2	15	0	24
the same in 8 vols. 8vo.	2	0	0	18
the same, 11 vols. [**A**: 18mo] [**B**: 18: vo]	1	0	0	25
[**A**: Clarissa, 8 vols. 12mo.	1	4	0	6
7 vols. 8vo.	1	15	0]	
[**B**: Clarissa, 7 vols. 8vo.	1	15	0	
8 vols. 12mo.	1	4	0	6]
Duncan's Cæsar, 1 vol. fol.	3	3	0	22
2 vols. 8vo.	0	12	0	19
Don Quixote by Jarvis, 2 vols. 4to.	0	12	0	18
the same, 2 vols, 8vo.	0	12	0	26
the same, 4 vols, 12mo. 1767	0	12	0	
by Motteaux, 4 vols. 12mo. 1741	0	10	0	

by ditto, 4 vols. 18mo.	0	8	0	25
by Dr. Smollet, 4 vols. 12mo.	0	12	0	5
by ditto, 4 vols. 18 mo.	0	8	0	
Dryden's Works, 4 vols. 8vo.	1	4	0	14
4 vols. Crown 8vo. printed 1767	0	12	0	
Doddridge's Rise and Progress of Religion, 8vo.	0	5	0	8
the same in 1 vol. 12mo.	0	3	0	4
[**B**: Francis's Horace, 2 vols. 4to	2	2	0	
the same, 4 vols. 8vo.	1	0	0	
the same, 4 vols. 12mo.	0	12	0]	
{**A2; B2**} Freeholder, 8vo.	0	5	0	16
the same, 12mo.	0	3	0	13
Ferguson's Astronomy, 1 vol. 4to.	0	18	0	9
the same, 1 vol. 8vo.	0	9	0	
Lectures, 1 vol. 4to.	0	18	0	9
the same, 1 vol. 8vo.	0	7	6	
Fielding's Works, 4 vols. 4to.	5	5	0	
the same, 8 vols. 8vo.	2	12	6	
the same, 12 vols. 12mo	1	16	0	8
Tom Jones, 6 vols. 12mo	0	18	0	
the same, 4 vols. 12mo	0	12	0	4
the rest of his Works, printed and sold separately				
Guardian, 2 vols. 8vo	0	10	0	14
2 vols. 12mo	0	5	0	13
2 vols. 18vo.	0	4	0	24
Gay's Works, 4to. 1727 [**B**:	1	5	0]	
2 vols. 12mo	0	6	0	
Fables, 2 vols. 8vo.	0	10	0	
the same, one vol. 8vo.	0	6	0	
the same, one vol. Crown, 8vo. with Cuts	0	3	0	3
[**A**: the same without Cuts	0	2	3	3]
[**B**: the same without Cuts	0	2	0	3]
Grandison, Sir Charles, 6 vols. 8vo	1	10	0	20
7 vols. 12mo	1	1	0	4
Gil Blas, 4 vols. 12mo	0	12	0	7
4 vols. 18mo	0	8	0	10
Gordon's Tacitus, 2 vols. fol.				
the same, 4 vols. 8vo	1	4	0	
the same, 5 vols. 12mo	0	15	0	15
[**B**: Hampton's Polybius, 2 vols. 8vo	2	8	0	
the same, 4 vols, 8vo.	1	4	0	
Hume's History of England, 6 vols. 4to.	4	10	0	
the same, 8 vols. 8vo.	2	8	0]	

Hudibras, by Dr Grey, 2 vols. 8vo	0	14	0	8
in 12mo. with Cuts	0	3	6	10
the same, one vol. 18mo	0	3	0	24
Hook's Roman History, 4 vols. 4to. printed in 1771.	4	4	0	3
Ditto, 11 vols. 8vo. 1771.	3	6	0	
Johnson's Dictionary, 2 vols. fol.	4	10	0	8
Dictionary abridged, 2 vols. 8vo	0	10	0	4
[**A**: Locke's Works, 3 vols. fol.	3	3	0	9
Ditto, 4 vols. 4to.	4	4	0	6]
[**B**: Locke's Works, 4 vols. 4to.	4	4	0	6]
Most of his Pieces printed to sell separate				
Leland (Dr.) on Christian Revelation, 2 vols. 4to.	1	10	0	10
the same, 2 vols. 8vo.	0	12	0	7
[**B**: Leland's Demosthenes one vol. 4to.	1	5	0	
the same, 3 vols. 8vo.	0	15	0	
Lowth's (Bishop) English Grammar, 8vo.	0	4	0	
the same, Crown 8vo.	0	3	0	
the same, in 12mo.	0	1	6	
Lyttelton (Lord)'s Henry II, 4 vols. 4to.	4	14	6	
the same, 6 vols. 8vo.	1	16	0	
Macaulay's History of England, 5 vols. 4to.	4	10	0	
the same, 5 vols. 8vo.	1	10	0]	
Milton's Paradise Lost and Regained, 2 vols. 8vo.	0	11	0	33
Bentley's Edition				43
Paradise Lost, 2 vols. 4to. by Dr. Newton	2	10	0	12
the same in 2 vols. 8vo.	0	12	0	6
Paradise Lost, 12mo.	0	3	6	6
the same [**A:,** 1 vol. 18mo] [**B**:, 18vo.]	0	2	0	17
Paradise Regained, 4to.	1	5	0	22
the same, 2 vols. 8vo.	0	10	0	8
{B3} [**A**: the same] [**B**: Milton's Paradise Regained], 1 vol. 12mo.	0	3	0	8
the same, 1 vol. [**A**: 18mo] [**B**: 18: vo]	0	2	0	17
Miller's Gardener's Dictionary, fol.	3	3	0	9
Ditto abridged, 4to.	1	5	0	7
Newman's Chemistry, 1 vol. 4to.	0	18	0	5
the same, 2 vols. 8vo. [**B**: 1773]	0	12	0	
Nature Displayed, 7 vols. 8vo.	2	2	0	26
the same, 7 vols. 12mo.	1	4	6	8
Plutarch's Lives, 8 vols. 8vo.	2	0	0	30
{A3} Plutarch's Lives, 6 vols. 8vo	1	10	0	16
the same, 9 vols. [**A**: 18mo] [**B**: 18: vo]	0	16	0	24

Prideaux's Connection, 2 vols. fol. printed 1717. [**B**:	2	0	5]	
the same, 4 vols. 8vo	1	0	0	24
Pope's Works, 5 vols. 4to. printed 1769.	5	5	0	
9 vols. Medium, 8vo	2	14	0	7
9 vols. Crown, 8vo	1	7	0	7
10 vols. Pott, 8vo	1	1	0	18
6 vols. 12mo.printed 1771.	0	18	0	
Pope's Homer, 11 vols. 4to				
9 vols. Medium, 8vo	3	3	0	13
9 vols. Crown, 8vo. printed 1771.	1	11	6	
9 vols. 12mo. printed 1771.	1	7	0	
7 vols. 12mo	1	1	0	7
Pamela, 4 vols. 8vo	1	4	0	
4 vols. 12mo	0	12	0	5
[**B**: Robertson's Scotland, 2 vols. 4to	1	10	0	
the same, 2 vols. 8vo.	0	12	0	
Charles V. 3 vols. 4to.	3	3	0	
the same, 4 vols. 8vo	1	4	0]	
Rowe's Friendship in Death, 8vo	0	6	0	
the same, 2 vols. 12mo	0	6	0	
the same, one vol. 18mo	0	3	0	
Rollin's Antient History, 10 vols. 8vo	2	10	0	24
the same, 7 vols. 8vo. printed 1768.	2	2	0	
the same, 10 vols. 12mo	1	10	0	28
the same, 8 vols. 12mo. a new Edition	1	2	0	
the same, 12 vols. 18mo	1	2	0	25
Rollin's Roman History, 16 vols. 8vo	4	0	0	20
the same, 10 vols. 8vo. printed 1768	3	0	0	
Rollin's Belles Lettres, 4 vols. 8vo	1	0	0	
the same, 3 vols 8vo. printed 1768	0	18	0	
the same, 4 vols. 12mo	0	12	0	4
Rollin's Arts and Sciences, 4 vols. 8vo.	1	2	0	31
the same, 3 vols. 8vo. printed 1768.	0	18	0	
[**B**: Secker's (Archbishop) Lectures on the Catechism, 2 vols. 8vo	0	10	0	
the same, 12mo.	0	3	6]	
Shakespear, by Pope, 6 vols. 4to	6	6	0	48
by Theobald, 7 vols. 8vo	1	15	0	41
by ditto, 8 vols. 12mo	1	8	0	6
by Sir Thomas Hanmer, 6 vols. 8vo	1	10	0	28
the same, 9 vols. 18mo	0	16	0	12
by Bishop Warburton, 8 vols. 8vo	2	8	0	28
by Mr. Chapel, 10 vols. 8vo. printed 1768.	2	2	0	

by Samuel Johnson, 8 vols. 8vo	2	8	0	
by Johnson and Steevens, 10 vols. 8vo	3	0	0	
Sharpe's (Archbishop) Sermons, 7 vols. 8vo	1	11	6	25
the same, 7 vols. 12mo	1	1	0	20
[**B**: Shenstone's Works, 3 vols. large 8vo	0	18	0	
the same, 3 vols. Crown 8vo	0	9	0]	
Spectator, 8 vols. 8vo	2	0	0	16
the same on a large Letter, 16 vols	2	0	0	50
{B4} [**A**: the same] [**B**: Spectator], 8 vols. 12mo	0	16	0	5
the same, 8 vols. [**A**: 18mo] [**B**: 18vo]	0	14	0	25
Spencer's Fairy Queen, by Mr. Upton [**B**:, 2 vols. 4to	1	7	0]	18
the same, 2 vols. 8vo	0	10	0	16
Spencer's Works, 6 vols. 12mo	0	18	0	26
the same, 6 vols. 18mo	0	12	0	24
Scot's Christian Life, fol.	1	1	0	35
the same, 5 vols. 8vo	1	1	0	17
Seneca's Morals, by Sir Richard L'Estrange, 8vo	0	5	0	18
the same in one Volume, 12mo	0	3	0	9
Swift's Works, 11 vols. 4to				11
the same, Medium 8vo. 23vols	6	18	0	6
the same, Crown 8vo. 24vols.	3	12	0	7
{A4} [**A**: Swift's Work] [**B**: the same], 21 vols. [**A**: 18mo] [**B**: 18vo]	2	2	0	8
Tatler, 4 vols. 8vo	1	0	0	15
4 vols. 12mo	0	10	0	9
4 vols. 18mo	0	8	0	22
Temple's Works, 2 vols. fol.	1	14	0	23
the same, 4 vols. 8vo	1	4	0	13
Tillotson's Works, 3 vols. fol.	3	3	0	21
the same, 12 vols. 8vo	3	0	0	16
the same, 12 vols. [**A**: 18mo] [**B**: 18vo]	1	1	0	25
Thesaurus Græcæ Poeseos, 1 vol. 4to	1	1	0	13
Thomson's Seasons, 12mo	0	3	0	3
the same in a small 12mo. just printed	0	2	6	20
[**B**: Waller's Works, 4to.	0	18	0	8
Ditto, 12mo	0	3	6	
West's Pindar, 4to.	0	15	0	
the same, 3 vols. Crown 8vo.	0	9	0	
World, 6 vols. 12mo	0	18	0	
the same, 4 vols. 12mo	0	12	0]	
Young's Works, 4 vols. 12mo	0	12	0	[**A**: 8]
[**A**: the same in a small 12mo] [**B**: Night Thoughts, 12mo	0	3	0]	

Expense of Printed Books

AN ACCOUNT of the EXPENCE of Correcting and Improving Sundry BOOKS (ESTC: T88997, T16364).

[Variant 1: ESTC: T88997 (A) /Variant 2: ESTC T16364 (B)]

[The BOOKSELLERS now petitioning the Legislature for Relief, most humbly beg Leave to observe,/*IN Behalf* of the BOOKSELLERS now petitioning the Honourable *House of Commons* for Relief, it may be truly said,] that there is scarce an Instance of a new Edition of any living Author's Work printed without submitting it to his Correction and Improvement: For though a Bookseller [at first generally purchases/buys] an Author's absolute Right, yet he [never fails to pay/pays] him for his Trouble in correcting every Edition; and in [such/those] Works, as most are capable of some Improvement, the Authors sometimes receive, in [Process of Time/the Course of the Sale], as much Money for Corrections and Improvements, as was at first paid for the Copy. Many are a continual Expence to the Printers of them, as every Edition [requires to be improve as well as/must be] carefully corrected; and for Dictionaries, Lexicons, &c, some Hundred Pounds are often paid for their Improvement.

The following Book are amongst others that might be quoted in support of the above the Assertion:

	l.	*s.*	*d.*	*l.*	*s.*	*d.*
Abridgment of the Law, vol. 1, 2, 3, 2d Edition	80	5	0			
3d ditto	105	0	0			
revising vol 4, 2d ditto	22	10	0			
vol 5, 2d ditto	32	12	6			
				240	7	6
Mr. *Ainsworth* for the first Edition of his Dictionary	666	17	6			
his Executors for the 2d Edition	250	0	0			
to Dr. Patrick for his Improvements, &c	101	11	9			
to Dr. Ward of Gresham College	26	5	0			
The 2d Edition cost	377	16	9			
3d Edition, to Mr. Kimber	21	0	0			
4th Edition, to Mr. Thomas	105	0	0			
5th Edition, to Dr. Morell	218	8	0			
The Folio Edition, to Mr. Young	184	10	0			
8vo. Edition, to Mr. Thomas	156	18	0			
Total paid since the 1st Edition				1063	12	9
Barretti's Italian Dictionary, 2d Edition	236	0	0			
3rd Edition, to Mr. Baretti	105	0	0			
				341	0	0
Boyer's Dictionary, French and English, 4to.						
Mr. Durand in 1752	67	14	6			
Mr Moore in 1759	56	9	3			
Ditto, in 1764	37	10	0			
Mr. Moore in 1773	40	0	0			

Mr. Prieur,	165 7 6		
		205 7 6	
			367 1 3
	Carried forward	£	2012 1 6
{2}	Brought over	£	2012 1 6
Beaumont and Fletcher's Plays, 10 vols. 8vo printed in 1750, (24 Years since it was printed, and the Impression not all sold)			
To Mr. Theobald		157 10 0	
Mr. Simpson		66 15 0	
Mr. Seward		52 10 0	
			276 15 0
Ben Johnson's Works, 7 vols. 8vo. Printed in 1756.			
Copies to the Rev. Mr. Whaley, to the Amount of			210 0 0
Burkitt on the New Testament, folio, on every Edition of 3000 Copies, to the Author's Widows and Heirs *for ever*,			112 10 0
Chamber's Dictionary and Supplement, for a new Edition now preparing for the Press,			1500 0 0
Cruden's Concordance, for improving the 2d Edition		123 8 0	
For improving 3d Edition,		88 4 0	
			211 12 0
Cunningham's Law Dictionary, 2d Edition,			147 0 0
Dictionary of Arts and Sciences, 4 vols. 8vo for correcting and improving 2d Edition			157 10 0
Dryden's Miscellanies, 4 vols. 8vo to the Editor of the last Edition 2d Edition in 1760			157 10 0
Hederici Lexicon, Greek and Lat. 4to.			
Dr. Patrick, 2d Edition		40 0 0	
Mr. Young, 3d ditto		52 10 0	
Dr. Morrell, 4th ditto		105 0 0	
Dr. Morrell, 5th ditto, now printing		105 0 0	
			302 10 0
Jacob's Law Dictionary, for improving the 8th Edition		105 0 0	
Ditto, for the 9th Edition, to Mr. Ruffhead and Mr. Morgan		315 0 0	
			420 0 0
Johnson's English Dictionary, 2 vols. folio, to the Author for Improvements in the third Edition			300 0 0
Milton's Paradise Lost and Regained			
Dr. Bentley in 1732 for Paradise Lost		105 0 0	
Dr. Newton, in Copies for his Subscribers, to the Amount of		630 0 0	

Dr. Newton for Paradise Regained	105	0	0			
Miller's Gardener's Dictionary, 1 vol, folio.				840	0	0
For a new Edition in 1752, as by original Agreement on every Impression, to him and his Heirs *for ever*	40	0	0			
For 50 sheets additional, &c	94	0	0			
	134	0	0			
For the Addition and Improvements in a new Edition in 1759, which was published in weekly Numbers, at 6*d. per* Number (including the Money to be paid as before mention on every Impression) and 30 Copies	300	0	0			
For the Edition in 1768, and 15 Copies	200	0	0			
				634	0	0
Carried forward			£	7281	8	6
{3} Brought forward			£	7281	8	6
Miller's Abridgment of the Gardner's Dictionary, in 1 vol. 4to printed in 1764, with 12 Copies	120	0	0			
The Edition printed in 1771, with 12 Copies	120	0	0			
				240	0	0
Postlewayte's Dictionary of Trade and Commerce, 2 vols. folio.						
For Improvements in the 3rd Edition				300	0	0
The Editors of SHAKESPEAR						
Mr. Rowe	36	10	0			
Mr. Hughes	28	7	0			
Mr. Pope	217	12	0			
Mr. Fenton	30	12	0			
Mr. Gay	35	19	0			
Mr. Whatley	12	0	0			
Mr. Theobald	652	10	0			
Mr. Warburton	500	0	0			
Mr. Capel	300	0	0			
Mr. Johnson, Copies to the Amount of	375	0	0			
Ditto, a new Edition in 1774	100	0	0			
				2288	10	6
Schrevelius's Lexicon, for improving the Edition just published				52	10	0
Universal History, Ancient and Modern, for revising, correcting and digesting it, for a new Edition				1575	0	0
Wood's Institutes, to the Author's Son, as by original Agreement on every impression, in 1762	29	10	0			
For Corrections,	45	3	6			
	74	13	6			
In 1772, to the Author's Son	30	0	0			
To a learned Serjeant at Law, for revising	63	0	0			
				167	13	6
Young's Dictionary, for Improvements made in the last Edition				47	12	6
Paid to Authors and Editors, over and above the original Sum given for the Copy of the above mentioned Books.			£	11952	15	0

Booksellers' Bill

An Act for Relief of Booksellers and others, by vesting the Copies of Printed Books in the Purchasers of such Copies from Authors, or their Assigns, for a limited Time: Ingrossment: Parliamentary Archives, HL/PO/JO/10/2/53; *Caledonian Mercury*, 2 May (with blanks); House Bill (Lords) (Two different copies available at British Library) (ESTC: T147200, T130708).

Note on Transcription

The official, and definitive version of the Bill is that held by the Parliamentary Archives. If the Bill had passed the Lords, it would have become the act of parliament, but it includes no punctuation, as was normal. The clause headings are only in the House Bill, that used for consideration in the Lords, as side headings (ESTC: T147200; T130708). The *Caledonian Mercury*, 2 May 1774, was based on the version presented at first reading in the house of commons, it therefore includes blanks. Accordingly, it is possible to see any amendments to the Bill made during its passage through the committee: blanks are completed with underline and in bold, other additions are underlined and deletions crossed out.[417] The recital and clause numbers are not in any original and have been added editorially. Page numbers in the House Bill are not marked.

An Act for Relief[418] of Booksellers and others, by vesting the Copies of Printed Books in the Purchasers of such Copies from Authors, or their Assigns, for a limited Time.[419]

Preamble

[(1)] Whereas by an Act made and passed in the Eighth Year of the Reign of Her late Majesty Queen Anne, intituled, "An Act for the Encouragement of Learning, by vesting the Copies of Printed Books in the Authors or Purchasers of such Copies during the Times therein mentioned," it was (amongst other Things) enacted, that from and after the Tenth Day of April, One thousand seven hundred and ten, the Authors of any Book or Books then printed, who had not transferred to any other the Copy or Copies of such Books, Share or Shares thereof, or the Bookseller or Booksellers, Printer or Printers, or other Person or Persons, who had purchased or acquired the Copy or Copies of any Book or Books in order to print or reprint the same, should have the sole Liberty of printing such Book and Books for the Term of Twenty-one Years, to commence from the Tenth Day of April, One thousand seven hundred and ten, and no longer:

[(2)]And whereas it hath been a prevailing Opinion with Booksellers and others, that Authors and their Assigns had by the Common Law, independently of the said Act of Queen Anne, the sole Right of printing and reprinting Copies of their Works; and that the

417 The additions and deletions, other than those filling in blanks, could be transcription errors in the newspaper.

418 The *Caledonian Mercury* opens with 'A Bill for Relief'.

419 The *Caledonian Mercury* for 'for a limited time' has 'for a Time therein to be limited'.

said Act was not intended to take away or abridge any such Right; and in consequence of this Opinion, many of them have from time to time invested the Whole, or the greatest Part, of their Fortunes in the Purchase of such Copy Rights, on which the Support of them and their Families at this Time doth in a great Measure depend:

[(3)] And whereas it hath lately been adjudged in the House of Lords, that no such Copy Right in Authors or their Assigns doth exist at Common Law; in consequence whereof Purchasers of such Copy Rights must be great Sufferers by their Misapprehension of the Law in respect thereof, and many of them likely to be involved in Ruin, unless they shall obtain the Aid and Assistance of Parliament:

May it therefore please Your most Excellent MAJESTY,

[Cl. 1] Property of Books vested in the Authors, their Executors, Administrators and Assigns, for 14 Years from the 4th June 1774.

That it may be Enacted, and be it Enacted by the King's most Excellent Majesty, by and with the Advice and Consent of the Lords Spiritual and Temporal, and Commons, in this present Parliament assembled, and by the Authority of the same, That from and after the **Fourth** Day of **June One thousand seven hundred and seventy-four**, every Author of any Book or Books already printed and published, who hath not transferred to any other the Copy Right of such Book or Books, or Share or Shares thereof, and his Executors, Administrators, and Assigns, or the Person or Persons, Bodies Politic or Corporate, who hath or have purchased, or otherwise acquired the Whole Interest of the Author in the Copy Right of any such Book or Books, or any Share or Shares thereof, from the Author or Authors of the same, or his, her, or their respective Executors, Administrators, or Assigns, in order to print or reprint the same, and the Executors, Administrators, and Assigns of such Purchaser or Purchasers respectively, shall have the sole and exclusive Right and Liberty of printing such Book or Books for the Term of **Fourteen Years** to commence from **the said Fourth Day of June**, and no longer; and that if any other Bookseller, Printer, or Person whatsoever, from and after the **said Fourth** Day of **June**, within the Time granted and limited by this Act as aforesaid, shall print, reprint, or import, or cause to be printed, reprinted, or imported any such Book or Books, without the Consent of the Proprietor or Proprietors thereof respectively first had and obtained in Writing, signed in the Presence of **Two** or more credible Witnesses, or, knowing the same to be so printed or reprinted without the Consent of the Proprietor or Proprietors thereof respectively, shall sell, publish, or expose to Sale, or cause to be sold, published, or exposed to Sale any such Book or Books without such Consent first had and obtained as aforesaid, then such Offender or Offenders shall forfeit **such Book or Books, and all and every Sheet and Sheets being Part of such Book or Books,** to the Proprietor or Proprietors of the Copy Right thereof respectively, who shall forthwith **damask and make Waste Paper of the same;** and further, that all and every such Offender and Offenders as aforesaid, shall forfeit **Ten Pounds** for every Book ~~Sheet~~ which shall be found in his, her, or their Custody, either printed or printing, published, or exposed to Sale contrary to the true Intent and Meaning of this Act; One **Moiety** thereof to the King's most Excellent Majesty, His Heirs and Successors, and the other **Moiety** thereof to any Person or Persons that shall sue for the same; to be recovered in any of His Majesty's Courts of Record at Westminster, by

Action of Debt, Bill, Plaint, or Information, in which no Wager of Law, Essoign, Privilege, or Protection, or more than One Imparlance shall be allowed.[420]

[Cl. 2] No Person liable to the Penalty unless the Title of the Book be entered with the Company of Stationers, before the 29th of September 1774.

And whereas many Persons may through Ignorance offend against this Act, unless some Provision be made, whereby the Property in every such Book as is intended by this Act to be secured to the Proprietor or Proprietors thereof may be ascertained and known, be it therefore further Enacted by[421] the Authority aforesaid, That nothing in this Act contained shall be construed to extend to subject any Bookseller, Printer, or other Person whatsoever to the **Forfeitures or Penalties** herein mentioned, for or by reason of the Printing or Reprinting any Book or Books without such Consent as aforesaid, unless the Title ~~of~~ to the Copy of such Book or Books shall, on or before the **Twenty-ninth Day of September, One thousand seven hundred and seventy-four**, be entered into the Register-Book of the Company of Stationers kept for that Purpose, in such Manner as hath been usual; for every of which several Entries so to be made as aforesaid, **the Sum of Two Shillings and Sixpence** shall be paid, and no more; which said Register-Book may at all reasonable and convenient Times be referred to and inspected by any Bookseller, Printer, or other Persons for the Purposes before mentioned, without any Fee or Reward; and the Clerk of the said Company of Stationers shall, when and as often as thereunto required, give a Certificate under his Hand of such Entry or Entries, and for every such Certificate may take a Fee, not exceeding **Sixpence**.

[Cl. 3] If the Clerk to the said Company refuse or neglect to make such Entry, and Notice thereof given in the London Gazette, then the Proprietors to have the like Benefit as if the Entries had been made, and the Clerk to forfeit 20l.

And be it further Enacted, That if the Clerk of the said Company of Stationers for the time being shall refuse or neglect to register or make such Entry or Entries, or to give such Certificate, being thereunto required by the Proprietor of such Copy or Copies in the Presence of **Two** or more credible Witnesses; then such Proprietor (Notice being first duly given of such Refusal by an Advertisement in the Gazette) shall have the like Benefit as if such Entry or Entries, Certificate or Certificates had been duly made and given; and the Clerk so refusing shall for every such Offence forfeit to the Proprietor or Proprietors of such Copy or Copies the Sum of **Twenty Pounds**, to be recovered in any of His Majesty's Courts of Record at Westminster, by Action of Debt, Bill, Plaint, or Information, in which

[420] These were various ways of delaying or defending a claim. An 'essoin' was an excuse for not appearing in court at the appointed time for reasons such as illness or being on the king's service; 'imparlance' was a way of extending time whereby a defendant said they were going to speak to the plaintiff about settling the matter; 'wager of law' was an offer to make oath with 11 compurgators of innocence. It became increasingly common for acts of parliament to restrict these pleas during the 17th century and this was more or less routine by the reign of Queen Anne (including in the Copyright Act 1709). They were abolished during the 19th century (starting with Process in Courts of Law at Westminster Act 1832 (2 & 3 Will. IV, c. 39) and removed from the statute book by the Statute Law Revision Act 1948 (11 &12 Geo. VI, c. 62), s. 4 (a)).

[421] The house of lords ingrossment has the word 'by' omitted.

no Wager of Law, Essoign, Privilege, Protection, or more than One Imparlance shall be allowed.

[Cl. 4] Ten Copies of every Book that after the 4th Day of June shall be published, to be delivered to Warehouse Keeper of the Company of Stationers, for the Use of certain Libraries.

Provided always, and it is hereby Enacted, That **Ten** Copies, upon the best Paper, of every Book, Volume or Volumes that, from and after the **Fourth** Day of **June, One thousand seven hundred and seventy-four**, shall be reprinted and published under this Act, and which shall not have been entered, and of which a Copy or Copies shall not have been given before, shall, by the Proprietor, Bookseller, or Printer or Printers thereof, be delivered to the Warehouse Keeper of the said Company of Stationers for the time being, at the Hall of the said Company, before such Publication made, for the Use of the Royal Library, the Libraries of the Universities of Oxford and Cambridge, the Library of the British Museum, the Libraries of the Four Universities of Scotland, the Library of Sion College in London, and the Library commonly called, The Library belonging to the Faculty of Advocates at Edinburgh, respectively; which said Warehouse Keeper is hereby required, to receive the same into the Warehouse of the said Company, and within **Seven Days** after such Delivery to give Notice in Writing of the Title, and Delivery of such Book, Volume or Volumes, to the several Agents of the Keepers of the said several Libraries respectively, in case there shall be any such Agents resident within the Bills of Mortality, whose Appointment and Place of Abode hath been notified to the said Warehouse Keeper; and also within Ten Days after Demand by the Keepers of the said respective Libraries, or any Person or Persons by them or any of them authorized to demand such Copies, to deliver the same for the Use of the aforesaid Libraries respectively; and if any Proprietor, Bookseller, or Printer, or the Warehouse Keeper of the said Company of Stationers for the time being, shall not observe the Direction of this Act therein, that then he or they so making Default in delivering the said printed Copies as aforesaid, shall forfeit the Sum of **Five Pounds** for every Copy not so delivered, and also **the Value of the said Printed Copies** not so delivered; the same to be recovered by the King's Majesty, His Heirs and Successors, and by the Chancellor, Masters, and Scholars of any of the said Universities, and by the Principal of the British Museum, and by the President and Fellows of Sion College, and the said Faculty of Advocates at Edinburgh, with their **Full** costs respectively.

[Cl. 5] The Act not to prevent Persons selling Books already printed, and which might have been lawfully sold by such Persons if the Act had not passed; nor to deprive Authors of the Right they had before passing the Act.

Provided also, and be it further Enacted, That nothing in this Act contained shall extend or be construed to extend to prevent any Person or Persons from selling such Impressions or Copies of any Book or Books as shall have been actually printed and published before the Passing of this Act, and might have been lawfully sold by such Person or Persons in case this Act had not been made; and also, that nothing herein contained shall extend or be construed to deprive any Author or Authors, who shall not before the Passing of this Act have sold, or for a valuable Consideration disposed of, or by Writing shall have given his, her, or their whole Right or Interest in or to the Copy or Copies of any Book or Books so printed and published as aforesaid, to the Printers or Publishers thereof respectively, of any Right or Interest in or to such Copy or Copies, or the sole and exclusive Power of reprinting and publishing the same, which he, she, or they had or was or were intitled to before the Passing of this Act, or might or ought to have had and enjoyed in case this Act had not been made.

[Cl. 6] Limitation of Actions.

And be it further Enacted by the Authority aforesaid, That if any Action or Suit shall be commenced or brought against any Person or Persons whatsoever for doing or causing to be done any Thing in pursuance of this Act, the Defendants in such Action may plead the General Issue, and give the Special Matter in Evidence;[422] and if upon such Action a Verdict be given for the Defendant, or the Plaintiff become Nonsuited, and discontinue his Action, then the Defendant shall have and recover his **Full** Costs, for which he shall have the same Remedy as a Defendant in any Case by Law hath.

[Cl. 7] Saving the Right of the English and Scotch Universities.

Provided always, and be it further Enacted, That nothing in this Act contained shall extend, or be construed to extend to prejudice any Right, that the Universities of Oxford and Cambridge in that Part of Great Britain called England, or the Four Universities in that Part of Great Britain called Scotland, or any of them, have or claim to have to the Printing or Reprinting of any Book or Books already printed, or hereafter to be printed.

[Cl. 8] Penalties incurred in Scotland, to be recovered there.

Provided always, and be it further Enacted, That if any Person or Persons shall incur any of the **Penalties** contained in this Act in that Part of this Kingdom called Scotland, the **Penalty or Penalties**, in any such Case, shall be recoverable by any Action before the Court of Sessions in Scotland.

[Cl. 9] Publick[423] Act.

And be it further Enacted by the Authority aforesaid, That this Act shall be adjudged, deemed, and taken to be a publick Act, and shall be judicially taken Notice of as such by all Judges, Justices, and other Persons whatsoever, without specially pleading the same.

Donaldson's House of Lords Petition

Alexander Donaldson's house of Lords Petition (never presented): Historical Society of Pennsylvania: ESTC: N65331.

[422] The general issue was a simple not guilty plea requiring proof of every element of the action.

[423] The *Caledonian Mercury* has the modern spelling 'public', the ingrossment is ambiguous as the form of spelling in the substantive provision is the older spelling.

[COPY of ALEXANDER DONALDSON'S Petition to the House of Lords, against the *London* Booksellers Bill.][424]

TO THE RIGHT HONOURABLE
The LORDS SPIRITUAL and TEMPORAL,
in PARLIAMENT assembled;
The humble PETITION of ALEXANDER DONALDSON, Bookseller in *St. Paul's Church-Yard, London*;

SHEWETH,

THAT a Bill having passed the House of Commons, for the Purpose of vesting certain *London* Booksellers with a Monopoly, for fourteen Years, of all the Literature of this Kingdom; the same, if passed into a Law, will be subversive of a solemn Decree of this Honourable House, obtained by your Petitioner,[425] after a very expensive Litigation for eleven Years past; and will, by an *ex post facto* Law, not only deprive him of the Benefit of the said Decree, but also prove highly injurious to the Community at large, especially to the Printers and Booksellers in *Scotland*; who will have the Mortification of seeing their natural and undoubted Rights, confirmed to them by the fourth and seventeenth Articles of Union,[426] abridged, or taken away, in favour of a few Booksellers of *London* and *Westminster.*

YOUR Petitioner embarked in the Trade and Business of a Bookseller in the Year 1750; and, in the Year 1759, your Petitioner found that a Combination of the *London* Booksellers was formed, and carried on with the most arbitrary Spirit, in Order to work a total Suppression, throughout *England*, of all Books whatever printed in *Scotland*, without paying any regard to the Time when first published. Threatening Letters were every where circulated, in the Name of some principal Booksellers in *London*, with Intent to terrify the Country Booksellers; who were told, in a Tone of Menace, that all Books printed in *Scotland* were an actual Piracy; and that those who dealt in such Copies would be liable to severe Prosecutions, and heavy Damages, in Consequence thereof. In the Letters so circulated, it was allowed to the Country Booksellers to expose to Sale no Editions whatever, except such as were printed in *London*. The Alarm was spread wide through the Country; and a Subscription of no less than three Thousand one Hundred and Fifty Pounds, was declared to have been actually made, for the Purpose of supporting an illegal Conspiracy of all the opulent Booksellers in *London*.

YOUR Petitioner was determined that he would not submit to Oppression: Accordingly, in 1763, he established a Shop in *London* for the Purpose of vending his own Editions; and with Intent to shew the Country Booksellers, that such Trade was well warranted by the Laws of the Land.

{2} FROM the Year 1763, to your Lordships late Determination on the 23d of *February* last, no less than thirteen Suits in Chancery were carried on against him, besides, Actions in the Court of Session; for the Exercise of a legal Right, in printing Books, at Prices the most

[424] All square brackets are in the original.

[425] *Donaldson v Beckett* (1774) *Cobbett's Parl. Hist.*, xvii, col. 953.

[426] Article IV (freedom of trade and navigation between and within United Kingdom and dominions); Article XVII (standardised weights and measures in United Kingdom). It is probable that reference was intended to be made to Article XIX, which preserved a separate Scottish legal system.

easy to the Public, which were not protected by the Statute of Queen *Anne*. In the Variety of Suits in which he has been involved, above one Hundred of the most opulent Booksellers in *London* and *Westminster* have, in their Turn, been Plaintiffs against your Petitioner; but he was resolved not to yield to a Monopoly most unjustly claimed: It was his fixed Purpose, that the Law should be finally settled in the supreme Court of the Kingdom.—That he has at length accomplished this Point, is now his Crime with the *London* Booksellers: But he humbly conceives, that his honest Efforts, against a powerful Combination, will not subject him to the Censure of your Lordships; with whom, he hopes, the Rights of the Subject will never want Protection.

YOUR Petitioner begs Leave to submit, that, in the Number of *London* Booksellers who petitioned the House of Commons for the Bill, there are not above twenty Persons who have any considerable Pretensions to call themselves Holders of Copy-Right.[427] To those Twenty a further Monopoly of fourteen Years cannot be worth less than L. 150,000; and, in Order to throw that Sum, or perhaps more, into the Hands of a Few, the Rights, so lately and so solemnly determined by your Lordships, of all the rest of his Majesty's Subjects are to be taken away; the common Law of *Scotland* is to be altered; and those who live in the remote Parts of the Kingdom are not to have a Book in their Hands, unless they buy it in *Pater-noster-Row;* the Country Booksellers throughout *England*, and a large Number of Booksellers in *London* and *Westminster*, who are all excluded from the Sales at the *Queen's-Arms* in *St. Paul's Church-Yard*, (where Books in Quires, and Copy-Rights, are sold cheaper than any where else), are to be debarred front exercising their inherent Rights, allowed to them by the common Law of the Land; and your Petitioner, who has proved that it has cost him above L.1000 in the just Defence of his Rights, is now to suffer the severest Punishment, altogether without a Precedent, and to lose, by an *ex post facto* Law, what he has long contended for, with the final Approbation of your Lordships.

YOUR Petitioner begs Leave to submit, that a Proceeding like this may throw his Majesty's Subjects into the most dangerous State of Uncertainty; inasmuch as Men may fear to apply to the Laws of the Land for the Recovery of their most valuable Franchises, lest, if the Contention be with an opulent Company, the Law which gives the Right, almost as soon as Judgment is pronounced, may be wrested from him.

YOUR Petitioner begs leave to observe, that the Recital of the Bill acknowledges, that, by your Lordships Decision, it has been found, that a perpetual Property at common Law never existed in this Country; but the same Recital states, that the Booksellers of *London* and *Westminster* always thought otherwise: Meaning, no doubt, that the Opinion of the Booksellers is a Counter-Balance to your Lordships Determination. But your Petitioner begs Leave to submit, that it is an important and universal Maxim, that Ignorance of the Law shall **{3}** excuse no Man: But now, by some new Rule of Logic, a Mistake of the common Law is not only to be an Excuse for a Combination of Booksellers, but it is even to be a Plea of Merit, and to procure for them the Reward of a further Monopoly for fourteen Years.

YOUR Petitioner begs Leave to add, that what the Booksellers call Ignorance of the Law, was a most wilful Misconstruction of the plain and obvious Meaning of the Statute of the 8th of Queen Anne, as appears by various Acts of the Booksellers, and particularly

[427] Cavendish {229}.

by their Petition in 1734–5, for a Bill to render more effectual the Act of Queen *Anne*, by granting them a further Term of seven Years only, in all Books printed before the said Act of Queen *Anne*; and, in all new Publications, a Term of twenty-one Years, and no longer.[428] A further Proof of a wilful Misconstruction of Law, may be drawn from the Endeavours of the *London* Booksellers to establish an exclusive Privilege by Oppression, by engrossing the Market, which should be free and open, and, finally, by commencing a fraudulent Action, in the Case of Tonson and Collins,[429] in Order, by Collusion, to obtain, at any Rate, a Judgment in their own Favour.

YOUR Petitioner begs Leave to add, that what the *London* Booksellers did not attempt, at the Bar of the House of Commons, to make any Proof of the Recital of their Bill; but, in a most unprecedented Manner, said, by their Counsel, that they relied upon the Examination of a Witness[430] who attended the Committee to whom their Petition had been referred. But your Petitioner submits, that such Examination was not taken in the Presence of your Petitioner's Counsel; and that, by the Rules of Law, that very Witness was inadmissible, as he owned himself deeply interested, in a Surplus to come to himself from the Sale of his Stock in Trade, after the Payment of his just Debts.

YOUR Petitioner begs Leave to submit, that the Clause in the Bill now depending, which provides, "That any Person, or Persons, may continue to sell Impressions, or Copies, of any Book, or Books, already printed and published,"[431] will not be an adequate Saving for your Petitioner, and several other Booksellers in the Country, and in *Scotland*, The Clause, on the contrary, will open a Door, for much Mischief; and the Difficulty of satisfying the *London* Booksellers, as to the Point of Time when such Books were printed, will leave your Petitioner, and Others, liable to a Variety of Suits; in which, from what has already past, he has no Reason to think the opulent Booksellers of *London* will be sparing.

YOUR Petitioner begs Leave to observe, that the Consequence of a free and open Trade in Printing and Publishing, must inevitably be an Emulation amongst the Booksellers to print in the neatest Manner, and at the most moderate Prices. Whereas, should the Bill pass into a Law, a very dangerous Monopoly will be thrown into the Hands of a few wealthy Booksellers, who have already enjoyed the Fruits of Usurpation, and will, no Doubt, make the best Use of the further Time now expected, by continuing such Prices as will best answer their Thirst of Gain; to the great Detriment of the Public, to the Injury of Letters, and the utter Ruin of the inferior Booksellers both in Town and Country.

{4} IT is also submitted, when the *London* Booksellers pretend that they shall be great Sufferers, if a further Monopoly is not granted to them in old Copies, that they ought to have proved what Sums have been paid by each of them respectively for their old Copies, how long they have been in Possession, and what Profits have been made. But a Discovery of this Kind is avoided, for the Purpose of concealing that they have already gained infinitely more than they ever paid to the Author or his Assigns.

YOUR Petitioner begs Pardon for so long an Intrusion upon your Lordships Patience, and only craves Leave to add, that he has at this very Time a large Sum invested in Books actually printed; and that he is engaged in a Variety of new Editions now actually at the Press,

[428] Copyright Act 1709, s. 1.

[429] *Tonson v Collins* (1761) 1 Black W 301 (96 ER 169).

[430] William Johnston.

[431] Booksellers' Bill 1774, cl. 5.

(the Expence of Printing the same being in some Measure already incurred), and which when finished, as he proposes, in the most correct and elegant Manner, will cost him several Thousand Pounds. Many of the Printers and Booksellers in the Country of *England*, and in *Scotland*, are in the same Situation. If, therefore, any Inconvenience must arise from the late Determination, he humbly hopes, that your Lordships will not think it just that the Loss should fall upon those who have obeyed the Law, while the opulent Booksellers, who have grown rich in Defiance of an Act of Parliament, made for the Regulation of their Trade, shall, by false Glosses and mere Colours, excite an unmerited Compassion, and be, perhaps, rewarded with an Extension of a Monopoly, which has hitherto subsisted by all the Arts of illegal Combination.

YOUR Petitioner, therefore; most humbly prays, that the Statute of Queen Anne, *which was expressly made for the Encouragement of Learning, may not now be altered or suspended, for the Encouragement of the* London *Booksellers* only; *and that your Petitioner may not lose the Right of which he may be deemed a Purchaser, at the Price of* L.1000, *laid out in a long Course of Litigations.*

ALEX. DONALDSON.

St. Paul's Church-yard,
May 31. 1774.

[The Bill was thrown out the 2nd of *June*, on a Division 22 against 11.]

SELECT BIBLIOGRAPHY

Archives

Birmingham Library

MS 3147/2/35/28: Notes on second reading of Hornblowers' Patent Bill

MS 3147/2/36/5: Calling card relating to Hornblowers' Patent Bill

Bodleian Library

(Vet.) 2581 c.5 (2): The Case of the Booksellers of London and Westminster; Remarks on the Petitions of Mr Alexander Donaldson and other, against the Petition now depending in Parliament for affording Relief to the Booksellers of London and Westminster in Literary Property; General Observations on the Expediency of granting Relief in Literary Property; Books: Printed by the Booksellers of London and Westminster, in different Sizes and Prices; of which there remains a large Stock on Hand

MS Carte 207: The Case of the Booksellers of London and Westminster

British Library

Add. MS 64869: Cavendish Parliamentary Diaries (Transcription of Shorthand by Timothy Joyce)

Burney Collection [newspapers]

Egerton MSS 215, 220, 223, 254, 255, 257, 259, 260, 263, 263*: Cavendish Parliamentary Diaries

Hampshire Archives

MS 9M73/G715: James Harris's Parliamentary Diary

Lincoln's Inn

MS 10: William Melmoth's Reports

MS 102, f. 307: The Case of the Free Workmen-Printers, Relating to the Bill of Preventing the Licentiouness of the Press

MSS 347–50: Yorke's Case Books

MS 384: Alexander Wedderburn's Case Notes

London Metropolitan Archives

CLC/253/MS03332/002: Isaac Hitchcock, *A Supplement to English Liberty* [MS Notes]

Parliamentary Archives

HL/PO/JO/5/1/121: Manuscript Journal of the House of Lords

HL/PO/JO/10/2/38: Act for the Better Encouragement of Learning (Booksellers' Bill 1735)

HL/PO/JO/10/2/39: Act for the more Effectual Encouragement of Learning (Booksellers' Bill 1737)

HL/PO/JO/10/3/263/50: Donaldson v Beckett Petition, 1772

HL/PO/JO/10/2/53: Bill for the relief of Booksellers (Booksellers' Bill 1774)

HL/ARC/VAR/319: O.C. Williams, *The Topography of the Old House of Commons* (1953) (unpublished monograph)

Sheffield City Archives

BK 1/1557: Letter from Dennis O'Bryen to Edmund Burke, Mar. 1782

Stationers' Archives

Literary Print Culture – The Stationers' Company Archive, 1554–2007 (Adam Matthew, 2017) and *The Records of the Stationers' Company 1554–1920* (Chadwick Healey, 1986)

Court Book C, TSC/1/B/01 (reel 56)

Register of Entries of Copies, 1710–46, TSC/1/E/06/08 (reel 6)

An Act to vest the Sole Right of Printing Almanacks in that Part of Great Britain called England in the Two Universities of Oxford and Cambridge and the Company of Stationers of the City of London Respectively: TSC/1/E/EnglishStock/E/10/10 (reel 99)

The National Archives

C 5/290/70: *Horne v Baker* (1710)

C 11/2249/4: *Benjamin Mott v Arthur Betteworth and George Faulkner* (1735)

C 12/61/24: *Beckett v Donaldson* (1771)

C 12/496/2: *Dodsley v Kinnersley* (1759)

C 12/1042/11: *Beckett & Others v Donaldson* (1771)

C 12/1321/9: *Beckett v Donaldson* (1771)

C 12/1321/36: *Dodsley v Donaldson* (1770–3)

C 12/1323/15: *Rivington v Donaldson* (1771)

C 12/1817/67: *Gay v Walker* (1729)

C 33/439: Chancery: Entry Books of Decrees and Orders, Book A

PROB 11/928/110: will of Jacob Tonson

PROB 11/940/163: will of Andrew Millar

The National Library of Scotland

Hume MS 23157.63

Wiltshire History Centre

MS 1946/4/2F/1/3: Parliamentary diaries and speeches of 2nd Earl Radnor

Printed Sources

Unless stated otherwise, the place of publication of books cited is London

Guido Abbattista, 'The Business of Paternoster Row: Towards a Publishing History of the Universal History (1736–65)', *Publishing History*, xvii (1985)

J.L. Abbott, 'John Hawkesworth: Friend of Samuel Johnson and Editor of Captain Cook's Voyages and of the Gentleman's Magazine', *Eighteenth-Century Studies*, iii (1970)

H.B. Abrams, 'The Historic Foundation of American Copyright Law: Exploding the Myth of Common Law Copyright', *Wayne Law Review*, xxix (1983)

H.B. Abrams, 'The Persistent Myth of Perpetual Common Law Copyright', in *What is the Point of Copyright History* (CREATe Working Paper 2016/04)

G.A. Akerlof, 'The Market for "Lemons": Quality Uncertainty and the Market Mechanism', *Quarterly Journal of Economics*, lxxxiv (1970)

John Almon, *The Debates and Proceedings of the British House of Commons* (Almon, 1775) (ESTC: N66572)

Hugh Amory, 'The New England Book Trade, 1713–1790', in *The Colonial Book in the Atlantic World*, ed. Hugh Amory and D.D. Hall (Chapel Hill, NC, 2010)

Alexander Andrews, *The History of British Journalism* (2 vols, 1859)

Anon, *Decision of the Court of Session upon the Question of Literary Property* (1774) (ESTC: T8898)

Anon, *Donaldson v Beckett: Case of the Appellants and Respondents in the Cause of Literary Property* (ESTC: T90592)

Anon, *Observations, Rules and Order Collected out of Divers Journals of the House of Commons* (1717)

Anon, *The Case of the Coffee-Men of London and Westminster. Or, An Account of the Impositions and Abuses put upon Them and the Whole Town by the Present Set of News-Writers* (Smith, 1728) (ESTC: T128525)

Anon, *The Cases of the Appellants and Respondents in the Cause of Literary Property, before the House of Lords* (Bew, 1774) (ESTC: T90592)

Anon, *The Pleadings of the Counsel before the House, in the Great Cause concerning Literary Property* (Wilkin, 1774) (ESTC: T90593)

Sir William Anson, *Autobiography and Political Correspondence of Augustus Henry, 3rd Duke of Grafton* (1898)

Edward Arber, *A Transcript of the Registers of the Company of Stationers of London, 1557–1640* (5 vols, 1875–94)

Arthur Aspinall, *Politics and the Press, 1780–1850* (1949)

Arthur Aspinall, 'Statistical Accounts of the London Newspapers in the Eighteenth Century', *EHR*, lxiii (1948)

Arthur Aspinall, 'The Reporting and Publishing of the House of Commons Debates 1771–1834', in *Essays Presented to Lewis Namier*, ed. Richard Areas and A.J.P. Taylor (1956)

Ivon Asquith, 'Advertising and the Press in the late Eighteenth and Early Nineteenth Centuries: James Perry and the *Morning Chronicle* 1790–1821', *Historical Journal*, xviii (1975)

Raymond Astbury, 'The Renewal of the Licensing Act in 1693 and its Lapse in 1695', *The Library*, xxxiii (1978)

Martyn Atkins, 'Persuading the House: The Use of the Commons Journal as a Source of Precedent', in *Essays on the History of Parliamentary Procedure: In Honour of Thomas Erskine May*, ed. Paul Evans (2017)

J.H. Baker, 'Why the History of Law has not been Finished', *Cambridge Law Journal*, lix (2000)

Sir John Baker, *An Introduction to English Legal History* (Oxford, 2019)

T.A. Baloch, 'Law Booksellers and Printers as Agents of Unchange', *Cambridge Law Journal*, lxvi (2007)

Hannah Barker, *Newspapers, Politics and English Society 1695–1855* (1999)

Sir Jonah Barrington, *Historic Memoirs of Ireland* (1833)

B.M. Benedict, 'Readers, Writers, Reviewers and the Professionalization of Literature', in *The Cambridge Companion to English Literature, 1740–1830*, ed. Thomas Keymer and John Mee (Cambridge, 2004)

Lionel Bently, 'A Few Remarks on Copyright at Common Law in 1774', in *What is the Point of Copyright History? Reflections on Copyright at Common Law in 1774* (CREATe Working Paper 2016/04)

Lionel Bently and J.C. Ginsburg, '"The Sole Right ... Small Return to the Authors": Anglo-American Authors' Reversion Rights from the Statute of Anne to Contemporary U.S. Copyright', *Berkeley Technology Law Journal*, xxv (2010)

Wendell Bird, *Press and Speech Under Assault* (Oxford, 2015)

Augustine Birrell, 'The "Battle of the Booksellers" for Perpetual Copyright', in *Seven Lectures on the Law and History of Copyright in Books* (1899)

Jeremy Black, 'Eighteenth-Century English Politics: Recent Work and Current Problems', *Albion: A Quarterly Journal Concerned with British Studies*, xxv (1993)

Jeremy Black, *English Press in the Eighteenth Century* (1987)

William Blackstone, *An Analysis of the Laws of England* (Oxford, 1771) (ESTC: N66987)

William Blackstone, *Commentaries on the Laws of England*, ed. Wilfrid Prest (Oxford, 2016)

Cyprian Blagden, 'The English Stock of the Stationers' Company: An Account of its Origins', *The Library*, 5th ser. x (1955)

Cyprian Blagden, 'The English Stock of the Stationers' Company in the Time of the Stuarts', *The Library*, 5th ser. xii (1957)

Cyprian Blagden, 'Thomas Carnan and the Almanack Monopoly', *Studies in Bibliography*, xiv (1961)

P.W.M. Blayney, *The Stationers' Company and the Printers of London, 1501–1557* (Cambridge, 2013)

E.A. Bloom, 'Johnson on Copyright', *Journal of English and Germanic Philology*, xlvii (1948)

Dan Bogart, 'Political Party Representation and Electoral Politics in England and Wales, 1690–1747', *Social Science History*, xl (2016)

Maurice Bond, *Guide to the Records of Parliament* (HMSO, 1971)

Thomas Bonnell, 'When Book History Neglects Bibliography: Trouble with the "Old Canon" in The Reading Nation', *Studies in Bibliography*, lvii (2005–6)

James Boswell, *The Decisions of the Court of Session upon the Question of Literary Property in the Cause of John Hinton of London, Bookseller, against Alexander Donaldson and John Wood, Booksellers in Edinburgh and James Meurose, Bookseller in Kilmarnock* (Edinburgh, 1774) (ESTC: T88998)

James Boswell, *The Life of Samuel Johnson*, ed. David Womersley (2008)

W.W. Boulton, *A Guide to Conduct and Etiquette at the Bar of England and Wales* (1953)

Huw Bowen, '"The Pests of Human Society": Stockbrokers, Jobbers and Speculators in Mid-Eighteenth-Century Britain', *History*, lxxviii (1993)

Kathy Bowrey, 'Who's Painting Copyright's History?', in *Dear Images: Art, Copyright and Culture*, ed. Daniel McClean and Karsten Schubert (2002)

Kathy Bowrey, 'Who's Writing Copyright History?', *European Intellectual Property Review* (1996)

J.E. Bradley, 'Parliament, Print Culture and Petitioning in Late Eighteenth-Century England', *Parliamentary History*, xxvi (2007)

Frank Brady, *James Boswell: The Later Years 1769–1795* (New York, 1984)

George Bramwell, *The Manner* of *Proceedings on Bills in the House of Commons* (1823)

Brewer, John, *Party Ideology and Popular Politics at the Accession of George III* (Cambridge, 1976)

John Brewer, *The Sinews of Power: War, Money and the English State 1688–1783* (Cambridge, MA, 1990)

Britain in the First Age of Party, 1680–1750: Essays Presented to Geoffrey Holmes, ed. Clyve Jones (1987)

A.L. Brown, 'The Authorization of Letters Under the Great Seal', *BIHR*, xxxvii (1964)

Browne's General Law List, 1777 (ESTC: T085768), 1887 (ESTC: T085770)

George Brunton and David Haig, *An Historical Account of the Senators of the College of Justice in MDXXXII* (Edinburgh, 1832)

Adriano Brunttini, 'Advertising and the Industrial Revolution', *Economic Notes*, iv (1973)

Samuel Buckley, *Reasons Humbly Offered to the Lords Spiritual and Tempers in Parliament Assembled, for granting to S Buckley such privilege for Thuanus in Latin as is already granted to every British Subject who is possessed of the Copy of any Book* (1733) (ESTC: T46461)

Adam Budd, *Circulating Enlightenment: The Career and Correspondence of Andrew Millar, 1725–68* (Oxford, 2020)

Patrick Bullard, 'Parliamentary Rhetoric, Enlightenment and the Politics of Secrecy: the Printer's Crisis of March 1771', *History of European Ideas*, xxxi (2005)

Edmund Burke, *Annual Register for the Year 1774* (Dodsley, 1775) (ESTC: T212980)

Robert Burrell and Catherine Kelly, 'Parliamentary Rewards and the Evolution of the Patent System', *Cambridge Law Journal*, lxxiv (2015)

Robert Burrell and Catherine Kelly, 'Public Rewards and Innovation Policy: Lessons from the Eighteenth and Nineteenth Centuries', *Modern Law Review*, lxxvii (2014)

Sir William Burroughs, *The Question Concerning Literary Property, Determined by the Court of King's Bench of 20th Apr 1769, in the Cause between A.M and R. Taylor. With the Separate Opinion of the Four Judges* (1773) (ESTC: T88999)

Paul Cairney, *The Politics of Evidence-Based Policy Making* (New York, 2016)

Theophilus Cibber, *Lives of the Poets of Great Britain and Ireland* (5 vols, 1753)

C.S. Clegg, *Press Censorship in Elizabethan England* (Cambridge, 1997)

Fredrick Clifford, *A History of Private Bill Legislation* (2 vols, 1968) (originally published in 1885)

Lord Coalston, *Information for Alexander Donaldson and John Wood* (Edinburgh, 1773) (ESTC: T90591)

William Cobbett, *Parliamentary History of England from the Earliest Period to the Year 1803* (1813)

Sir Edward Coke, *Institutes of the Law of England or Commentary Upon Littleton* (Nutt, 1738) (ESTC: T112990)

Sir Edward Coke, *The Third Part of the Institutes of the Laws of England* (1644)

A.S. Collins, *Authorship in the Days of Johnson* (1928)

R.C. Cole, *Irish Booksellers and English Writers 1740–1800* (1986)

R.J. Coombe, 'Challenging Paternity: Histories of Copyright', *Yale Journal of Law and the Humanities*, vi (1994)

Catriona Cooper, 'The Sound of Debate in Georgian England: Auralising the House of Commons', *Parliamentary History*, xxxviii (2019)

Anna Maria de Burgh Coppinger, *Modest Plea: Doctor Dissected (Stella). Modest Exceptions, from the Court of Parnassus to Mrs Macauly's Modest Plea* (Ben, 1774) (ESTC: T129596)

William Cornish, Patrick Polden *et al.*, *The Oxford History of the Laws of England* (Oxford, 2010)

Correspondence of Edmund Burke, ed. T.W. Copeland (10 vols, Cambridge, 1958–78)

Correspondence of King George the Third, from 1760 to December 1783, ed. Sir John Fortescue (6 vols, 1967)

W.J. Couper, 'Copyright in Scotland Before 1709', *Records of the Glasgow Bibliographical Society*, ix (1931)

Brian Cowan, *The Social Life of Coffee: The Emergence of the British Coffeehouse* (New Haven, CT, 2005)

William Coxe, *Memoirs of Horatio, Lord Walpole* (1802)

William Coxe, *Memoirs of the Life and Administration of Sir Robert Walpole* (1798) (ESTC: T133960)

T.E. Crispe, *Reminiscences of a K.C.* (1909)

A.L. Cross, 'The English Criminal Law and Benefit of Clergy During the Eighteenth and Early Nineteenth Century', *The American Historical Review*, xxii (1917)

Henry Curwen, *A History of Booksellers, the Old and New* (1873)

Thomas Dabbs, 'The Rise and Fall of Dodsley's Old Plays', *Studies in Language and Culture*, xx (1994)

Sir John Dalrymple, *Memoirs of Great Britain and Ireland. From the Dissolution of the Last Parliament of Charles II, until the Sea-battle off La Hogue* (Stachan and Caddell, 1771) (ESTC: T145644)

David Davies, *The World of the Elseviers, 1580–1712* (The Hague, 1954)

Lee Davison *et al.*, 'Introduction' to *Stilling the Grumbling Hive. The Response to Social and Economic Problems in England 1689–1750* (Stroud, 1992)

Giles Dawson, 'The Copyright of Shakespeare's Dramatic Works', in *Studies in Honor of A.H.R. Fairchild*, ed. C.T. Prouty (Columbia,1946)

Ronan Deazley, 'The Myth of Copyright at Common Law', *Cambridge Law Journal*, lxii (2003)

Ronan Deazley, *On the Origin of the Right to Copy: Charting the Movement of Copyright Law in Eighteenth Century Britain (1695–1775)* (Oxford, 2004)

Ronan Deazley, *Rethinking Copyright: History, Theory, Language* (Cheltenham, 2006)

Debates of the House of Commons, ed. Anchitell Grey (Becket and De Hondt, 1769) (ESTC: T145287)

John Debrett, *The History, Debates and Proceedings of Both Houses of Parliament* (Bew, 1792) (ESTC: T32171)

Sir Simonds D'Ewes, *The Journal of all the Parliaments During the Reign of Elizabeth* (Shannon, 1682)

Grayson Ditchfield, 'Numbered, Weighed and Divided: The Voting of the House of Commons During the Reign of George III', *Parliamentary History*, xv (1996)

Grayson Ditchfield, 'The Subscription Issue in British Parliamentary Politics 1772–9', *Parliamentary History*, vii (1988)

Grayson Ditchfield, David Hayton and Clyve Jones, *British Parliamentary Lists, 1660–1800* (1995)

Dennis Dixon, 'Godden v. Hales Revisited – James II and the Dispensing Power', *Journal of Legal History*, xxvii (2006)

Alexander Donaldson, *Pleadings of the Counsel before the House of Lords in the Great Cause Concerning Literary Property* (1774) (ESTC: T90593)

Alexander Donaldson, *Some Thoughts on the State of Literary Property* (1764) (ESTC: T049411; N023843)

Alan Dowling, 'The Doctrine of Lost Modern Grant', *Irish Jurist*, xxxviii (2003)

Graham Dutfield and Uma Suthersanen, 'Pope v Curll (1714) Revisited', in *Forgotten Intellectual Property Lore: Creativity, Entrepreneurship and Intellectual Property,* ed. Shubha Ghosh (Cheltenham, 2020)

Donald Eddy, 'Dodsley's "Collection of Poems by Several Hands" (6 vols), 1758 Index of Authors', *The Papers of the Bibliographical Society of America*, ix (1966)

J.E. Elliott, 'The Cost of Reading in Eighteenth-Century Britain: Auction Sale Catalogues and the Cheap Literature Hypothesis', *English Literary History*, lxxvii (2010)

Markman Ellis, 'Philip Yorke and Thomas Birch: Scribal News in the Mid 18th Century', *Parliamentary History*, xli (2022)

Markman Ellis, 'Coffee-House Libraries in Mid-Eighteenth Century London', *The Library*, x (2009)

Markman Ellis, *The Coffee House: A Cultural History* (2004)

Sir Henry Ellis, *Original Letters of Eminent Literary Men of the Sixteenth, Seventeenth and Eighteenth Century* (Camden Society, xxiii, 1843)

William Enfield, *Observations on Literary Property* (Johnson, 1774) (ESTC: T41748)

Erskine May's Treatise on The Law, Privileges, Proceedings and Usage of Parliament, ed. Sir David Natzler and Mark Hutton (25th edn, 2019)

Paul Evans and Andrej Ninkovic, 'From Manual to Authority: The Life and Times of the Treatise', in *Essays on the History of Parliamentary Procedure: In Honour of Thomas Erskine May*, ed. Paul Evans (2017)

Failed Legislation: Extracted from the Commons and Lords Journal, 1660–1800, ed. Julian Hoppit (1997)

John Feather, *A History of British Publishing* (2005)

John Feather, 'British Publishing in the Eighteenth Century: A Preliminary Subject Analysis', *The Library*, 6th ser., viii (1986)

John Feather, *Publishing, Piracy and Politics: An Historical Study of Copyright in Britain* (1994)

John Feather, 'The Book Trade and the Law 1695–1799', *Publishing History*, xii (1982)

John Feather, 'The Book Trade in Politics: The Making of the Copyright Act 1710', *Publishing History*, viii (1980)

John Feather, 'The Significance of Copyright History for Publishing History and Historians', in *Privilege and Property: Essays on the History of Copyright*, ed. Ronan Deazley, Martin Kretschmer and Lionel Bently (Cambridge, 2010)

John Ferris, 'Before Hansard: Records of Debates in the Seventeenth Century House of Commons', *Archives*, xx (1992)

David Fielding and Shef Rogers, 'Copyright Payments in Eighteenth-Century Britain, 1701–1800', *The Library*, 7th ser., xviii (2017)

David Fielding and Shef Rogers, 'Monopoly Power in the Eighteenth-Century Book Trade', *European Review of Economic History*, xxi (2017)

Jessé Foot, *The Life of Arthur Murphy, Esq* (1811)

John Forster, *The Life and Times of Oliver Goldsmith* (1855)

Sir John Fortescue, *The Correspondence of King George the Third, from 1760 to December 1783* (Frank Cass 1967)

Elizabeth Read Foster, *The House of Lords, 1603–1609: Structure, Procedure, and the Nature of its Business* (University of Carolina Press 1983)

J.M. Gaba, 'Copyrighting Shakespeare: Jacob Tonson, Eighteenth Century English Copyright, and the Birth of Shakespeare Scholarship', *Journal of Intellectual Property*, xix (2011)

Ian Gadd, 'The Stationers' Company in England Before 1710', in *Research Handbook on the History of Copyright Law*, ed. Isabella Alexander and H. Tomás Gómez-Arostegui (Cheltenham, 2016)

Philip Gaskell, 'Printing the Classics in the Eighteenth Century', *The Book Collector*, i (1952)

Sir Geoffrey Gilbert, *The Law of Evidence* (4th edn, 1777) (ESTC: N10446)

James Gillman, *The Life of Samuel Taylor Coleridge* (1838)

A.K. Goldstein, 'A Short History of Discovery', *Anglo-American Law Review*, x (1981)

H. Tomás Gómez-Arostegui, 'Copyright at Common Law in 1774', *Connecticut Law Review*, xlvii (2014)

H. Tomás Gómez-Arostegui, 'Equitable Infringement Remedies Before 1800', in *Research Handbook on the History of Copyright* Law, ed. Isabella Alexander and H. Tomás Gómez-Arostegui (Cheltenham, 2016)

H. Tomás Gómez-Arostegui, 'The Untold Story of the First Copyright Suit Under the Statute of Anne in 1710', *Berkeley Technology Law Journal*, xxv (2010)

H. Tomás Gómez-Arostegui, 'What History Teaches us About Copyright Injunctions and the Inadequate-Remedy-at-Law Requirement', *Southern California Law Review*, lxxxi (2008)

M.D. Gordon, 'The Collection of Ship-Money in the Reign of Charles I', *Transactions of the Royal Historical Society*, iv (1910)

W. Forbes Gray, 'Alexander Donaldson and the Fight for Cheap Books', *Juridical Review*, xxxviii (1926)

J.N. Green, 'The Middle Colonies, 1720–1790', in *The Colonial Book in the Atlantic World*, ed. Hugh Amory and D.D. Hall (Chapel Hill, NC, 2010)

Jeremy Greenwood, *Newspapers and the Post Office, 1635–1835* (Reigate, 1971)

Grenville Papers: Correspondence of Richard Grenville and the Rt Hon George Grenville, ed. W.J. Smith (4 vols, 1852–3)

Dennis Griffiths, *Fleet Street: Five Hundred Years of the Press* (2006)

Thomas Gurney, *Brachygraphy, or Swift Writing made Easy to the Meanest Capacity* (1750) (ESTC: T134667)

William Hakewill, *Modus Tenedi Parliamentum or the Manner of Holding Parliaments in England* (Benson, 1659) (ESTC: R210040)

William Hakewill, *The Manner How Statutes are Enacted in Parliament by Passing of Bills* (Belson, 1641) (ESTC: R11690)

P.A. Hamburger, 'The Development of the Law of Seditious Libel and the Control of the Press', *Stanford Law Review*, xxxvii (1985)

Lansing van der Heyden Hammond, *Laurence Sterne's Sermons of Mr. Yorick* (New Haven, CT, 1948)

Francis Hargrave, *An Argument in Defence of Literary Property* (2nd edn, 1774) (ESTC: T14300)

Bob Harris, 'Parliamentary Legislation, Lobbying and the Press in Eighteenth-Century Scotland', *Parliamentary History*, xxvi (2007)

Ian Harris, 'Publishing Parliamentary Oratory: The Case of Edmund Burke', *Parliamentary History*, xxvi (2007)

Ian Harris, 'What was Parliamentary Reporting? A Study of Aims and Results in London Daily Newspapers, 1780–1796', *Parliamentary History*, xxxix (2020)

Michael Harris, 'The Structure, Ownership and Control of the Press 1620–1780', in *Newspaper History: From the Seventeenth Century to the Present Day*, ed. George Boyce, James Curran and Pauline Wingate (1978)

Robert Harris, *A Patriot Press: National Politics and the London Press in the 1740s* (Oxford, 1993)

John Hatsell, *Precedents of Proceedings in the House of Commons* (Dodsley, 1781) (ESTC: T114572)

John Hatsell, *Precedents of Proceedings in the House of Commons* (4 vols, 1818)

Sir John Hawkins, *The Life of Dr Samuel Johnson* (Buckland, 1787) (ESTC: T113903)

John Hawkesworth, *An Account of the Voyages undertaken by the Order of His Present Majesty for Making Discoveries in the Southern Hemisphere* (Strahan and Cadell, 1773) (ESTC: N34379).

Nikki Hessell, *Literary Authors, Parliamentary Reporters: Johnson, Coleridge, Hazlitt, Dickens* (Cambridge, 2012)

Bridget Hill, *The Republican Virago: The Life and Times of Catharine Macaulay, Historian* (Oxford, 1992)

Brian Hillyard, 'The Edinburgh Society's Silver Medals for Printing', *Papers of the Bibliographical Society of America*, lxxviii (1984)

History of Barclays Bank Limited, comp. P.W. Matthews, ed. A.W. Tuke (1926).

History of Parliament. The House of Commons, 1604–1629, ed. Andrew Thrush and John Ferris (Cambridge, 2010)

History of Parliament. The House of Commons, 1754–1790, ed. Sir Lewis Namier and John Brooke (1964)

Christopher Hitchens, *God is Not Great: How Religion Poisons Everything* (2007)

Norma Hodgson and Cyprian Blagden, *The Notebook of Thomas Bennet and Henry Clements* (Oxford Bibliographic Society, new ser., vi, 1956)

Sir William Holdsworth, *A History of English Law* (1938)

Geoffrey Holmes, *British Politics in the Age of Anne* (1987)

Henry Home, Lord Kames, *Essays on the Principles of Morality and Natural Religion* (1751) (ESTC: T70373)

Henry Home, Lord Kames, *Principles of Equity* (Kincaid, 1760) (ESTC: T70419)

John Hooker, '*Sessions of Parliament in the Reign of Elizabeth*', in Lord Mountmorres, *The History of the Principal Transactions of the Irish Parliament from the Year 1634 to 1666* (Caddell, 1792) (ESTC: T70500)

B.B. Hoover, *Samuel Johnson's Parliamentary Reporting* (Berkeley, CA, 1953)

Julian Hoppit, 'Petitions, Economic Legislation and Interest Groups in Britain, 1660–1800', *Parliamentary History*, xxxvii (2018)

David Ibbetson, 'Legal Printing and Legal Doctrine', *Irish Jurist*, xxxv (2000)

David Ibbetson, 'Report and Record in Early-Modern Common Law', in *Case Law in the Making: The Techniques and Methods of Judicial Records and Law Reports: Volume 1: Essays*, ed. Alain Wijffels (Berlin, 1997)

Irish Book in English, 1500–1800, ed. Raymond Gillespie and Andrew Hadfield (Oxford, 2005)

W.A. Jackson, *Records of the Court of the Stationers' Company, 1602–1640* (Bibliographic Society, 1957)

F.G. James, 'The Irish Lobby in the Early Eighteenth Century', *EHR*, lxxxi (1966)

Phillip Johnson, *Parliament, Patents and Inventions* (2018)

Phillip Johnson, *Privatised Law Reform: A History of Patent Law Through Private Legislation, 1620–1907* (2017)

Phillip Johnson, 'The Myth of Mr Burke and Mr Watt: For Want of a Champion!', *Queen Mary Journal of Intellectual Property*, vi (2016)

Samuel Johnson, *A New Prologue Spoken by Mr Garrick* (Payne, 1750) (ESTC: T39922)

Samuel Johnson, *The False Alarm* (Cadell, 1770) (ESTC: T88127)

Clyve Jones, 'New Parliamentary Lists, 1660–1800', *Parliamentary History*, xxvi (2006)

Clyve Jones, 'Seating Problems in the House of Lords in the early Eighteenth Century: The Evidence of the Manuscript Minutes', *BIHR*, li (1978)

Judges of England, 1272–1990, a List of Judges of the Superior Courts, comp. Sir John Sainty (Seldon Society, supp. ser. x, 1993)

Peter Jupp, *The Governing of Britain, 1688–1848: The Executive, Parliament and the People* (2006)

William Kenrick, *An Address to Artists and Manufacturers of Great Britain: Respecting an Application to Parliament for the Father Encouragement of New Discoveries and Inventions in the Useful Arts; to which is added an Appendix Containing Strictures on some singular Consequences Attending the Late Decision on Literary Property* (Domville, 1774) (ESTC: T20406; N30789)

Frank Kidson, *British Musical Publishers* (1900)

Mark Knights, '"The Lowest Degree of Freedom": The Right to Petition Parliament, 1640–1800', *Parliamentary History*, xxxvii (2018)

Vicesimus Knox, *The Spirit of Despotism* (1795) (ESTC: N21542)

C.R. Kyle, 'Introduction' to *Parliament, Politics and Elections 1604–1648* (Camden Society, 5th ser., xvii, 2001)

Sheila Lambert, *Bills and Acts: Legislative Procedure in Eighteenth-Century England* (Cambridge, 1971)

John Langbein, 'Historical Foundations of the Law of Evidence: A View from the Ryder Sources', *Columbia Law Review*, xcvi (1996)

Last Journals of Horace Walpole: During the Reign of George III, ed. A.F. Steuart (2 vols, 1910)

Edmund Law, *Observations Occasioned by the Contest About Literary Property* (Archdeacon, 1770) (ESTC: T13046)

S.M. Lee, 'Parliament, Parties and Elections (1760–1815)', in H.T. Dickinson, *A Companion to Eighteenth-Century Britain* (Oxford, 2000)

Letters of David Hulme, ed. John Greig (Oxford, 1932)

Letters of Samuel Johnson, ed. Bruce Redford (3 vols, Oxford, 1992–4)

Letters of Sir William Blackstone, ed. W.R. Prest (Seldon Society, lxvi, 2006)

Libraries and the Book Trade, ed. Robin Myers, Michael Harris and Giles Mandelbrote (New Castle, DE, 2000)

Life of Lord Campbell, ed. Mary Hardcastle (2 vols, 1881)

Bryant Lillywhite, *London Coffee Houses: A Reference Book of Coffee Houses of the Seventeenth, Eighteenth and Nineteenth Centuries* (1963)

Liverpool Tractate: An Eighteenth-Century Manual on the Procedure of the House of Commons, ed. Catherine Strateman (New York, 1937)

F.P. Lock, *Edmund Burke, 1730–1784* (Oxford, 1998)

Philip Loft, 'Petitioning and Petitioners to the Westminster Parliament, 1660–1788', *Parliamentary History*, xxxviii (2019)

Charles Longman, *The House of Longman, 1724–1800* (1936).

William Lowe, 'Peers and Printers: The Beginnings of Sustained Press Coverage of the House of Lords in the 1770s', *Parliamentary History*, vii (1988)

Catharine Macaulay, *A Modest Plea for the Property of Copyright* (Cruttwell, 1774) (ESTC: T57030)

Michael MacDonagh, *The Reporters' Gallery* (1913)

Kerry MacLennan, 'John Milton's Contract for "Paradise Lost": A Commercial Reading', *Milton Quarterly*, xliv (2010)

Hector MacQueen, 'Intellectual Property and the Common Law in Scotland', in *The Common Law of Intellectual Property: Essays in Honour of Professor David Vaver*, ed. Catherine Ng, Lionel Bently and Giuseppina D'Agostino (2010)

Hector MacQueen, 'Literary Property in Scotland in the Eighteenth and Nineteenth Centuries', in *Research Handbook on the History of Copyright Law*, ed. Isabella Alexander and H. Tomás Gómez-Arostegui (Cheltenham, 2016)

Hector MacQueen, 'The War of the Booksellers: Natural Law, Equity, and Literary Property in Eighteenth-Century Scotland', *Journal of Legal History*, xxxv (2014)

F.W. Maitland, *The Forms of Action at Common Law* (Cambridge, 1936)

James Maitland, Lord Lauderdale, *An Inquiry into the Nature and Origin of Public Wealth* (1804)

A.P.W. Malcomson and D.J. Jackson, 'Sir Henry Cavendish and the Proceedings of the Irish House of Commons, 1776–1800', *Parliamentary History*, xx (2001)

Alistair Mann, 'Scottish Copyright Before the Statute of 1710', *Juridical Review*, xi (2000)

Alistair Mann, 'The Anatomy of Copyright Law in Scotland Before 1710', in *Research Handbook on the History of Copyright Law*, ed. Isabella Alexander and H. Tomás Gómez-Arostegui (Cheltenham, 2016)

Alastair Mann, 'The Anatomy of the Printed Book in Early Modern Scotland', *Scottish Historical Review*, lxxx (2001)

Paul Mantoux, 'French Reports of British Parliamentary Debates in the Eighteenth Century', *American Historical Review*, xii (1907)

W. Matthews, 'The Piracies of Macklin's *Love-à-la-Mode*', *The Review of English Studies*, x (1934)

Ian Maxted, *The British Book Trades 1710–1777: An Index of Masters and Apprentices* (Exeter Working Papers in Book History, ii, 1983)

Ian Maxted, *The British Book Trades, 1731–1806: A Checklist of Bankrupts* (Exeter Working Papers in Book History, iv, 1985)

Ian Maxted, *The London Book Trades 1775–1800: A Preliminary Checklist of Members* (Exeter Working Papers in Book History, 1977)

Ian Maxted, *The London Book Trades 1735–1775: A Checklist of Members in Trade Directories and in Musgrave's Obituary* (Exeter Working Papers in Book History, iii, 1983)

Thomas Erskine May, *A Treatise upon the Law Privileges, Proceedings and Usage of Parliament* (1844)

M.W. McCahill, *The House of Lords in the Age of George III, 1760–1811* (Oxford, 2009)

Matthew McCormack, *The Independent Man: Citizenship and Gender Politics in Georgian England* (Manchester, 2005)

Warren McDougall, 'Copyright Litigation in the Court of Session, 1738–1749, and the Rise of the Scottish Book Trade', *Edinburgh Bibliographical Society Transactions*, v (1971–87)

G.D. McEwen, '"What is a Conger?": John Dunton and Scottish Booksellers', *Studies in Scottish Literature*, i (1963)

D.F. McKenzie, 'Milton's Printers Matthew, Mary and Samuel Simmons', *Milton Quarterly*, xiv (1980)

D.F. McKenzie and Maureen Bell, *A Chronology and Calendar of Documents Relating to the London Book Trade, 1641–1700* (3 vols, Oxford, 2005)

D.F. McKenzie, *Stationers' Company Apprentices 1701–1800* (Oxford, 1978)

David McKitterick, *A History of Cambridge University Press* (Cambridge, 1992)

Memoirs of James Stephen, ed. Merle Bevington (1954)

S.F.C. Milsom, *A Natural History of the Common Law* (New York, 2003)

Sandra Mollin, 'The Hansard Hazard: Gauging the Accuracy of British Parliamentary Transcripts', *Corpora*, ii (2008)

James Moran, *Printing Presses: History and Development from the Fifteenth Century to Modern Times* (1973)

William Morgan, 'An Eighteenth-Century Election in England', *Political Science Quarterly*, xxxvii (1922)

E.C. Mossner, *The Life of David Hume* (Oxford, 1980)

Arthur Murphy, *An Essay on the Life and Genius of Samuel Johnson* (1793) (ESTC: T4523)

Arthur Murphy, *The Gray's-Inn Journal* (Faden and Vaillant, 1756) (ESTC: T112211)

David Murray, *Robert and Andrew Foulis and the Glasgow Press: With some Account of the Glasgow Academy of the Fine Arts* (Glasgow, 1913)

Sir Lewis Namier, 'Country Gentlemen in Parliament 1750–1783', *History Today* (1954)

Sir Lewis Namier, 'The Circular Letter: An Eighteenth-Century Whip to Members of Parliament', *EHR*, xliv (1929)

Sir John Neale, *The Elizabethan House of Commons* (1949)

F.B. Newman, 'Consideration of the Bibliographical Problems Connected with the First Edition of "Humphrey Clinker"', *The Papers of the Bibliographical Society of America*, xliv (1950)

John Nichols, *Literary Anecdotes of the Eighteenth Century, Comprising Biographical Memoirs of William Bowyer* (1812)

J.M. Norris, 'Samuel Garbett and the Early Development of Industrial Lobbying in Great Britain', *Economic History Review*, x (1958)

James Oldham, 'Informal Law-Making in England by the Twelve Judges in the Late Eighteenth and Early Nineteenth Century', *Law and History Review*, xxxix (2011)

A.G. Olson, 'Parliament, the London Lobbies, and Provincial Interests in England and America', *Historical Reflections*, vi (1979)

A.G. Olson, '"The London Mercantile Lobby" and the Coming of the American Revolution', *Journal of American History*, lxix (1982)

A.G. Olson, 'The Virginia Merchants of London: A Study in Eighteenth-Century Interest-Group Politics', *William and Mary Quarterly*. xl (1983)

Oxford Companion to the Book, ed. M.F. Suarez and H.R. Woudhuysen (Oxford, 2010)

Stephen Parks, *John Dunton and the English Book Trade* (1976)

L.R. Patterson, *Copyright in a Historical Perspective* (Nashville, TN, 1968)

Jason Peacey, '"Rushworth Shall Not Take Any Notes Here": Journals, Debates and the Public, 1640–60', *Parliamentary History*, xxxiii (2014)

Jason Peacey, 'The Print Culture of Parliament, 1600–1800', *Parliamentary History*, xxvi (2007)

Mark Perry, 'The Legacy of *The Seasons*: Confusion and Misdirection', in *Forgotten Intellectual Property Lore: Creativity, Entrepreneurship and Intellectual Property*, ed. Shubha Ghosh (Cheltenham, 2020)

R. Ross Perry, *Common-law Pleading: Its History and Principles* (1897)

George Petyt (Phillips), *Lex Parliamentaria: A Treatise on the Law and Customs of the Parliaments of England* (Goodwin, 1690) (ESTC: R4908)

Laurent Pfister, 'Author and Work in the French Print Privileges System: Some Milestones', in *Privilege and Property: Essays on the History of Copyright*, ed. Ronan Deazley, Martin Kretschmer and Lionel Bently (Cambridge, 2010)

John Phillips, 'The Structure of Electoral Politics in Unreformed England', *Journal of British Studies*, xix (1979)

J.H. Plumb, *Sir Robert Walpole: The King's Ministers* (2 vols, 1960)

J.H. Plumb, *The Growth of Political Stability in England, 1675–1725* (1967)

A.W. Pollard and G.R. Redgrave, *A Short-Title Catalogue of Books Printed in England, Scotland, & Ireland and of English Books Printed Abroad 1473–1640* (London Bibliographical Society, iii, 1991)

A.W. Pollard, *Shakespeare's Fight with the Pirates* (Cambridge, 1920)

A.W. Pollard, 'Some Notes on the History of Copyright in England, 1662–1774', *The Library*, iv (1922)

Graham Pollard, 'The English Market for Printed Books: The Sanders Lectures 1959', *Publishing History*, iv (1978)

Mary Pollard, *A Dictionary of Members of the Dublin Book Trade, 1550–1800* (2000)

Mary Poovey, *Genres of the Credit Economy: Mediating Value in Eighteenth- and Nineteenth-Century Britain* (Chicago, ILL, 2008)

Alexander Pope, *The Last Will and Testament of Alexander Pope, of Twickenham, Esq; to which is added an inscription wrote by himself* (Dodd, 1744) (ESTC: N19354)

Alexander Pope· *The Odyssey of Homer* (Lintot, 1725–6) (ESTC: T67134)

Wilfrid Prest, *William Blackstone: Law and Letters in the Eighteenth Century* (Oxford, 2008)

Privilege and Property: Essays on the History of Copyright, ed. Ronan Deazley, Martin Kretschmer and Lionel Bently (Cambridge, 2010)

Proceedings and Debates of the British Parliament Respecting North America, 1754–1783, ed. R.C. Simmons and P.D.G. Thomas (6 vols, New York, 1982–6)

H.H. Ransom, *The First Copyright Statute: An Essay on An Act for the Encouragement of Learning, 1710* (Austin, TX, 1956)

Mary Ransome, 'The Reliability of Contemporary Reporting of the Debates of the House of Commons, 1722–1741', *BIHR*, xix (1942)

James Raven, 'Booksellers in Court: Approaches to Legal History of Copyright in England Before 1842', *Law Library Journal*, civ (2012)

James Raven, *Publishing Business in Eighteenth-Century England* (Woodbridge, 2014)

James Raven, 'The Book Trades', in *Books and Their Readers in Eighteenth-Century England: New Essays*, ed. Isabel Rivers (Leicester, 2001)

James Raven, 'The Importation of Books in the Eighteenth Century', in *The Colonial Book in the Atlantic World*, ed. Hugh Amory and D.D. Hall (Chapel Hill, NC, 2010)

R.R. Rea, *The English Press in Politics, 1760–1774* (Lincoln, NE, 1963)

Allen Reddick, *The Making of Johnson's Dictionary 1746–1773* (Cambridge, 1996)

Josef Redlich, *The Procedure of the House of Commons: A Study of its History and Present Form*, trans. A.E. Steinthal (3 vols, 1908)

Christopher Reid, 'Whose Parliament? Political Oratory and Print Culture in the Later Eighteenth Century', *Language and Literature*, ix (2000)

Loren Reid, 'Speaking in the Eighteenth Century House of Commons', *Speech Monographs*, xvi (1949)

Mark Rose, *Authors and Owners: The Invention of Copyright* (Cambridge, MA, 1993)

Mark Rose, 'Donaldson and the Muse of History', in *What is the Point of Copyright History?* (CREATe Working Paper 2016/04)

Mark Rose, 'The Author in Court: Pope v Curll (1741)', *Cultural Critique* (1992)

Mark Rose, 'The Author as Proprietor: *Donaldson v Beckett* and the Genealogy of Modern Authorship', *Representations*, xxiii (1988)

Mark Rose, 'The Author as Proprietor: *Donaldson and Beckett* and the Genealogy of Modern Authorship', in *Of Authors and Origins: Essays on Copyright Law*, ed. Brad Sherman and Alain Strowell (Oxford, 1994)

I.S. Ross, *Lord Kames and the Scotland of His Day* (Oxford, 1972)

Trevor Ross, 'Copyright and the Invention of Tradition', *Eighteenth-Century Studies*, xxvi (1992)

Trevor Ross, 'The Emergence of Literature: Making and Reading the English Canon in the Eighteenth Century', *English Literary History*, lxiii (1996)

J.C. Sainty and David Dewar, *Divisions in the House of Lords: An Analytical List 1685–1857* (1976)

J.E. Sandys, *A History of Classical Scholarship* (3 vols, Cambridge, 1908)

David Saunders, 'Copyright, Obscenity and Literary History', *Journal of English Literary History*, lvii (1990)

G.O. Sayles, 'Contemporary Sketches of the Members of the Irish Parliament in 1782', *Proceedings of the Royal Irish Academy*, lvi (1953)

L.G. Schwoerer, 'Press and Parliament in the Revolution of 1689', *HJ*, xx (1977)

L.G. Schwoerer, 'Liberty of the Press and Public Opinion 1660–1695', in *Liberty Secured? Britain Before and After 1688*, ed. J.R. Jones (Stanford, CA, 1992)

Henry Scobel, *Memorials of the Method and Manner of Proceedings in Parliament in Passing Bills* (1670) (ESTC: R203067)

Valentina Sebastiani, *Johann Froben, Printer of Basel: A Bibliographical Profile and Catalogue of His Editions* (Leiden, 2018)

Caroline Shenton, *The Day Parliament Burned Down* (Oxford, 2012)

R.B. Sher, *The Enlightenment and the Book: Scottish Authors and Their Publishers* (Chicago, IL, 2006)

Brad Sherman and Lionel Bently, *The Making of Modern Intellectual Property Law* (Cambridge, 1999)

T.M. Sherwood, *A Treatise upon the Proceedings to be Adopted by Members in Conducting Private Bills* (1828)

Sir Henry Cavendish's Debates of the House of Commons, During the Thirteenth Parliament of Great Britain, commonly called the Unreported Parliament, ed. John Wright (1841)

Sketches of Irish Political Characters of the Present Day [by H. MacDougall] (1799)

Will Slauter, *Who Owns the News? A History of Copyright* (Stanford, CA, 2019)

Stef Slembrouck, 'The Parliamentary Hansard "Verbatim" Report: The Written Construction of Spoken Discourse', *Language and Literature*, i (1992)

John Small, 'The Development of Musical Copyright', in *The Music Trade in Georgian England*, ed. Michael Kassler (Farnham, 2011)

James Smyth, 'Lewis Namier, Herbert Butterfield and Edmund Burke', *Journal for Eighteenth-Century Studies*, xxxv (2012)

Henry Snyder, 'The Eighteenth Century Short Title Catalogue', *IFLA Journal*, xvi (1990)

Andrew Sparrow, *Obscure Scribblers: A History of Parliamentary Journalism* (2003)

Speeches or Arguments of the Judges of the Courts of King's Bench in the Cause of Millar against Taylor (Coke: Leith, 1771) (ESTC: T117122)

William St Clair, *The Reading Nation in the Romantic Period* (Cambridge, 2004)

Phillip Dormer Stanhope, *The Works of Lord Chesterfield* (1838)

State Trial of Doctor Henry Sacheverell, ed. Brian Cowan (Parliamentary History Texts & Studies, vi, 2012)

Henry Stephens, *A Treatise on the Principles of Pleadings in Civil Actions* (1824)

M.F. Suarez, 'Dodsley's "Collection of Poems" and the Ghost of Pope: The Politics of Literary Reputation', *The Papers of the Bibliographical Society of America*, lxxxviii (1994)

R.J Sullivan, 'England's "Age of Invention": The Acceleration of Patents and Patentable Invention During the Industrial Revolution', *Explorations in Economic History*, xxvi (1989)

Frances Teague, 'Ben Jonson's Poverty', *Biography*, ii (1979)

P.D.G. Thomas, 'Check List of MPs Speaking in the House of Commons, 1768 to 1774', *BIHR*, xxxv (1962)

P.D.G. Thomas, 'Division Lists, 1760–1774', in *The Parliamentary Lists of the Early Eighteenth Century: Their Complication and Use*, ed. Aubrey Newman (Leicester, 1973)

P.D.G. Thomas, 'John Robinson's "State" for the General Election of 1774', *Parliamentary History*, xxx (2011)

P.D.G. Thomas, *John Wilkes: A Friend to Liberty* (Oxford, 1996)

P.D.G. Thomas, 'John Wilkes and the Freedom of the Press (1771)', *BIHR*, xxxiii (1960)

P.D.G. Thomas, 'Party Politics in Eighteenth-Century Britain: Some Myths and a Touch of Reality', *Journal of Eighteenth-Century Studies*, x (1987)

P.D.G. Thomas, 'Sir Henry Cavendish (1732–1804), Parliamentarian in Two Countries', *Parliamentary History*, xxxvi (2017)

P.D.G. Thomas, 'Sources for the Debates of the House of Commons, 1768–1774', *BIHR*, special supp. iv (1959)

P.D.G. Thomas, 'The Beginning of Parliamentary Reporting in Newspapers 1768–1774', *EHR*, lxxiv (1959)

P.D.G. Thomas, *The House of Commons in the Eighteenth Century* (Oxford, 1971)

P.D.G. Thomas, 'The Parliamentary Diary of John Clementson, 1770–1802', *Camden Miscellany, XXV* (Camden Society, 4th ser., xiii, 1974)

A.G. Thomson, *The Paper Industry in Scotland 1590–1861* (Edinburgh, 1974)

J.L. Thorson, 'The Publication of "Hudibras"', *The Papers of the Bibliographical Society of America*, lx (1966)

James Tierney, 'The Museum, the "Super-Excellent Magazine"', *Studies in English Literature, 1500–1900*, xiii (1973)

G.M. Trevelyan, 'The Two-Party System in English Political History', in G.M. Trevelyan, *An Autobiography and Other Essays* (1949)

Josiah Tucker, *Four Tracts on Political and Commercial Subjects* (Raikes, 1774) (ESTC: T85923)

Van Vechten Veeder, 'The English Reports, 1537–1865', *Harvard Law Review*, xv (1901)

Victoria History of the County of Buckingham, ed. William Page (1925)

Voting Records of the British House of Commons, 1761–1820, ed. D.E. Ginter (6 vols, 1995)

Dror Wahrman, 'Virtual Representation: Parliamentary Reporting and Languages of Class in the 1790s', *Past and Present*, cxxxvi (1992)

James Walker, 'The Censorship of the Press During the Reign of Charles II', *History*, xxxv (1950)

J.W. Wallace, *The Reporters Arranged and Characterized … Fourth Edition Revised* (Boston, MA, 1882)

Patrick Wallis, Cliff Webb and Chris Minns, 'Leaving Home and Entering Service: The Age of Apprenticeship in Early Modern London', *Continuity and Change*, xxv (2010)

Horace Walpole, *Memoirs of the Reign of King George the Third*, ed. Sir Denis Le Marchant (1845)

Gwyn Walters, 'The Booksellers in 1759 and 1774: The Battle for Literary Property', *The Library*, 5th ser., xxix (1974)

William Warburton, *A Letter from an Author to a Member of Parliament, Concerning Literary Property* (Knapton, 1747) (ESTC: T37853)

Tessa Watt, *Cheap Print and Popular Piety* (Cambridge, 1991)

Timothy Whelan, 'William Fox, Martha Gurney, and Radical Discourse of the 1790s', *Eighteenth-Century Studies*, xlii (2009)

J.F. Whicher, 'The Ghost of Donaldson v Becket', *Bulletin of the Copyright Society of the USA*, ix (1962)

J.H. Wigmore, 'The History of the Hearsay Rule', *Harvard Law Review*, xvii (1904)

Harold Williams, *The Correspondence of Jonathan Swift* (5 vols, Oxford, 1965)

O.C. Williams, *The Clerical Organization of the House of Commons 1661–1850* (Oxford, 1954)

O.C. Williams, *The Historical Development of the Private Bill Procedure and the Standing Orders of the House of Commons* (2 vols, 1948)

W.H.D. Winder, 'The Courts of Requests', *Law Quarterly Review*, lii (1936)

William Windham, *Speeches in Parliament of the Right Honourable William Windham* (3 vols, 1812)

D.W. Wing, *A Short-Title Catalogue of Books Printed in England, Scotland, Ireland, Wales, and British America and of English Books Printed in Other Countries 1641–1700* (Modern Language Association of America, 1972–98)

Calhoun Winton, 'The Southern Book Trade in the Eighteenth Century', in *The Colonial Book in the Atlantic World*, ed. Hugh Amory and D.D. Hall (Chapel Hill, NC, 2010)

E.J. Wood, *Curiosities of Clocks and Watches: From the Earliest Times* (1866)

William Woodfall, *An Impartial Sketch of the Debate in the House of Commons of Ireland, on a Motion for leave to bring in a Bill for effectuating the intercourse and commerce between Great Britain and Ireland, on permanent and equitable Principles* (Dublin, 1785) (ESTC: N16791)

Graham Wootton, *Pressure Groups in Britain 1720–1970* (1975)

Works of the Right Reverend William Warburton, ed. Richard Hurd (12 vols, 1811)

Nathanial Wraxall, *Historical Memoirs of My Own Time* (1815)

Writings and Speeches of Edmund Burke, Vol III, ed. W.M. Elofson (Oxford, 1996)

David Zaret, *Origins of Democratic Culture, Printing, Petitions, and the Public Sphere in Early-Modern England* (Princeton, NJ, 2000)

Unpublished Theses

Vivienne Dietz, 'Before the Age of Capital: Manufacturing Interests and the British State, 1780–1800, University of Princeton PhD, 1991

Zoe Dyndor, 'The Political Culture of Elections in Northampton, 1768–1868', University of Northampton PhD, 2010

William Lowe, 'Politics in the House of Lords, 1760–1775', University of Emory PhD, 1975

Anita Rees, 'The Practice and Procedure of the House of Lords 1714–1784', University of Aberystwyth PhD, 1987

Robert Tennyson, 'Private Legislation: Function and Procedure in the Eighteenth Century', University of Berkeley PhD, 2009

Peter Thomas, 'The Debates of the House of Commons 1768–1774', University of London PhD, 1958

Acts of Parliament

1483 Importation Act (1 Ric. III, c. 12)
1533 Printers and Binders Act (25 Hen. VIII, c. 15)
1535 Signet Privy Seal (27 Hen. VIII, c. 11)
1584 Queen's Bench Act (27 Eliz. I, c. 8)
1623 Statute of Monopolies (21 Jas. I, c. 3)
1660 Attainer of the Regicides Act (12 Chas. II, c. 30)
1662 Licensing of the Press Act (13 & 14 Chas. II, c. 33)
1664 Licensing of the Press Act (16 & 17 Chas. II, c. 7)
1665 Licensing of the Press Act (17 Chas. II, c. 4).
1685 Administration of Intestates' Estates Act (1 Jas. II, c. 17)
1688 Bill of Rights Act (1 Will. & Mar., c. 2)
1694 Meeting of Parliament Act (6 & 7 Will. & Mar., c. 2)
1706 Act of Union (6 Anne, c. 11)
1708 Fortifications Act (7 Anne, c. 26)
1709 Copyright Act ('The Statute of Anne') (8 Anne, c. 19)
1711 Taxation Act (10 Anne, c. 18)
1716 Septennial Act (1 Geo. I, St. 2, c. 38)
1733 Printing of Thuanus Histories Act (7 Geo. II, c. 24).
1734 Engraving Copyright Act (8 Geo. II, c. 13)
1738 Importation Act (12 Geo. II, c. 36).
1740 Meinzie's Patent Act (24 Geo. II, c. 28)
1742 Continuance of Laws, etc. Act (16 Geo. II, c. 26)
1753 British Museum Act (26 Geo. II, c. 22)
1766 Engraving Copyright Act (7 Geo. III, c. 38)
Duties (Logwood, etc.) Act (7 Geo. III, c. 47)
Malt Duties Act (7 Geo. III, c. 6)
1770 Parliamentary Elections Act (10 Geo. III, c. 16)
1772 Royal Marriages Act (12 Geo. III, c.11)
1773 Supply Act (13 Geo. III, c. 77)
1774 Parliamentary Elections Act (14 Geo. III, c. 15)
Boston Port Act (14 Geo. III, c. 19)
Administration of Justice Act (14 Geo. III, c. 39)
Massachusetts Government Act (14 Geo. III, c. 45)
Quartering Act (14 Geo. III, c. 54)
Legal Rate of Interests Act (14 Geo. III, c. 74)
1775 Porcelain Patent Act (15 Geo. III, c. 52)
Copyright Act (15 Geo. III, c. 53)
1787 Designing and Printing of Linens etc. Act (27 Geo. III, c. 38)

1789 Designing and Printing of Linens etc. Act (29 Geo. III, c. 19)
1793 Parliament (Commencement) Act (33 Geo. III, c. 13)
1794 Linens, etc. Act (34 Geo. III, c. 23)
1814 Copyright Act (54 Geo. III, c. 156)
1832 Process in Courts of Law at Westminster Act (2 & 3 Will. IV, c. 39)
1842 Copyright Act (5 & 6 Vic., c. 45)
1843 Evidence Act (6 & 7 Vic., c. 85)
1851 Evidence Act (14 & 15 Vic., c. 99)
1858 Parliamentary Witnesses Act (21 & 22 Vic., c. 78)
1911 Copyright Act (1 & 2 Geo. V, c. 46)
1948 Statute Law Revision Act (11 & 12 Geo. VI, c. 62)
1988 Copyright, Designs and Patents Act (1988, c. 48)

Parliamentary Papers

1747 *Standing Orders and Resolutions of the House of Commons* (Steward, 1747) (ESTC: T114967)
1807 *Committee for the Reform and Improvement of the Post Office* (1807 HC Papers 1), ii, 105
1844 *Select Committee on Public Petitions Report* (1844)
1849 *Resolutions Relating to the Ingrossing and Inrolling of Bills* (1849 HC Papers 20), xlv
1894 *Report from the Select Committee on Parliamentary Debates* (1893–4 HC Papers 213), xiii
1907 *Select Committee on Parliamentary Debates* (1907 HC Papers 239), vii
1976 *Sound Broadcasting Joint Select Committee* (1975–6 HC Papers 494), xv
Sound Broadcasting Joint Select Committee Second Special Report (1975–6 HC Papers 723), xv

Reported Cases

H. Tomás Gómez-Arostegui, *Register of Copyright Infringement Suits & Actions from c. 1560 to 1800* (2009).
Proceedings of the Old Bailey, 1674–1913 (available at: www.oldbaileyonline.org)

Aldred v Ashcroft, 537 US 186 (2003)
Antonius, son of Count Leslie v James Leslie (1742) 1 Paton 324 (*LJ*, xxvi, 108)
Baskett v Cambridge University (1758) 2 Burr 661 (97 ER 499)
Bent v Baker (1789) 3 Term Reports 27 (100 ER 437)
Bridgeman v Dove (1744) 3 Atk 201 (26 ER 917)
Burnet v Chetwood (1721) 2 Mer 441 (35 ER 1008)
Carnan v Bowles (1786) 2 Brown's Chancery Cases 80 (29 ER 45)
Charles Cajetan, Count Leslie v Peter Leslie Grant (1763) 2 Pat App 68 (*LJ*, xxx, 326)
Darcy v Allin (1602) 11 Co Rep 84 (77 ER 1260)
Dodsley v Kinnersley (1761) Amb 403 (27 ER 270)
Donaldson v Beckett (1774) 2 Br PC 129 (1 ER 837); *Cobbett's Parl. Hist.*, xvii, col. 953
Douglas v Hello [2007] UKHL 21, [2008] 1 AC 1
East India Company v. Sandys (1683) Skinner 223 (90 ER 103)
Giles v Wilcocks (1740) 2 Atk 141 (26 ER 489)

Godden v Hales (1686) 11 State Trials 1165
Greswolde v Kemp (1842) Car & M 63 (174 ER 668)
Hinton v Donaldson (1773) *Boswell's Report*; Mor 8307; 5 Br Supp 508; 5 Pat 505
Irvine v Talksport [2002] EWHC 367 (Ch), [2002] 1 WLR 2355
King v Bray (1736) Cases Temp Hardwicke 358 (95 ER 232)
Macklin v Richardson (1770) Amb 694 (27 ER 451)
Midwinter v Hamilton (1743) Kam Rem 154; Mor 8295
Midwinter v Kincaid (1751) 1 Pat App 488
Millar and Osborne v Donaldson (1765) 2 Eden 327 (28 ER 924)
Millar v Taylor (1769) 4 Burr 2303 (98 ER 201)
Mitchel v Reynolds (1711) 1 Peere Williams 181 (24 ER 347)
Osborne & Others v Donaldson (1763) 2 Eden 328 (28 ER 924)
Osbourne v Donaldson (1765) 2 Eden 327 (28 ER 924)
Partridge v Strange and Croker (1553) 1 Plowd 77 (75 ER 123)
Ponder v Braydall /Braddill (1679) 1 Lilly's Modern Entries 67
Pope v Curl (1741) 2 Atk 342 (26 ER 608)
Proceedings against Lord Lovat (1746) 18 State Trials 529
Rex v Hampden (1637) 3 State Trials 825
Regeneron Pharmaceuticals Inc. v Kymab Ltd [2020] UKSC 27, [2020] RPC 22
Rundell v Murrary (1821) 1 Jacob 311 (37 ER 868)
Stationers' Company v Carnan (1775) 2 Black 1004 (96 ER 590)
Stationers' Company v Parker (1685) Skin 233 (90 ER 107)
Stationers' Company v Partridge (1712) 1 Mod 105 (88 ER 647)
Stationers' Company v Seymour (1676) 3 Keb 792 (84 ER 1015); 1 Mod 256 (86 ER 865)
Tillman v Egon Zehnder Ltd [2019] UKSC 32, [2020] AC 154
Tonson v Collins (1761) 1 Black W 301 (96 ER 169)
Tonson v Collins (1762) 1 Black W 321, 329 (96 ER 180, 184)
Tonson v Walker (1739) 1 Black W 331
Tonson v Walker (1752) 3 Swans 672 (36 ER 1017)
Tyson (Tyssen/Tissen) v Clarke (1773) 3 Will KB 419, 514, 558 (95 ER 1133, 1201, 1210); (1773/4) 2 Wm Bl 891, 941 (96 ER 524, 556); (1774) 3 Will KB 541 (95 ER 1201); (1774) Loft 496 (98 ER 766)
Walton v Shelley (1786) 1 Term Reports 296 (99 ER 1106)
Whiston & Others v Donaldson (1771), TNA, C 12/64/26
Wilkes v Wood (1763) Loft 1 (98 ER 489)
Wyatt v Barnard (1814) 3 Ves. & B. 78 (35 ER 408)

Newspapers and periodicals

Annual Register, Baldwin's Weekly Magazine, Caledonian Mercury, Craftsman or Say's Weekly Journal, Daily Advertiser, Edinburgh Advertiser, Edinburgh Evening Courant, Gazetteer and New Daily Advertiser, General Evening Post, Gentleman's Magazine, Lloyd's Evening Post, London Chronicle, London Evening Post, London Magazine, Middlesex Journal and Evening Advertiser, Monthly Review or Literary Journal, Morning Chronicle, Morning Post, New Evening Post, Public Advertiser, Public Ledger, Scots Magazine, St James's Chronicle, The Times

Index

Abel, Carl Fredrick
Petition, *see* Bach, Johann
Assignments (of copyright), 101–103, 187, 220, 291, 394–5, 425, 428, 431, 436, 437
Blackstone (William), 230, 237, 349, 350
Burney (Frances), 102
evidence of, 184, 230, 271, 357, 361, 395, 402, 465,
Harrington (James), 427
legality, 433
Milton (John), 207, 214, 237, 350
perpetual, 154, 235, 395
presumption, 396, 402, 404
reversion, 103–4
Seasons, The, 106
value, 102
Auction, books, 99–101, 208, 210, 213, 332
authors and, 24
Alexander Donaldson excluded, 101 n 65
exclusion of some, 384, 473
double counting, 101
Clerk, 30 n 106, 97,
'public' 100, 384
Tonsons, resale, 406
value of sales, 101, 280, 289, 399
also see Coffee Houses, Globe and Queens Arms
Authors
fame (write for), 102, 115, 197, 213, 242, 248, 351, 355, 356, 359, 428, 432, 444, 450
interest, 114–5, 198–9, 210–1, 221, 247–8
remuneration, 102, 104
support by booksellers, 114, 395, 443, 447
also see Assignments (of copyright)

Bach, Johann Christian,
Petition 51, 58, 272–3, 379–380
Battle of the Booksellers, 84–86
Scotland, 84–5
Beckett, Thomas, 7, 91
Bills,
bill Committee, 63–8
committee, 48–53 (*also see* Committee (on Petition)
first reading, 54–5,
Ingrossment, 69–70
judicial nature (private bills), 45
leave for a bill, 53
Petition, 45–47, 49, 57–8
presenting the petition, 47–8
private/public, 44–5
Report on Bill Committee, 68
scope, 56–7
second reading, 58–60
third reading, 70–71
witnesses, 60
Blackstone, William (Sir), 230, 333
as counsel, 7, 27, 90
as judge, 86, 245
as law reporter, 27, 29
as professor, 341
assignments of copyright, 230, 237, 349, 350
bias, 90
his *Commentaries*, 55, 89, 90, 117, 154, 188, 222, 287–8, 295, 338, 342, 344, 349, 355, 455, 369
Booksellers Bill (1735), 6, 82, 183, 202, 205, 366, 372
Booksellers Bill (1737), 6, 82–3, 183, 202, 366, 372
Booksellers Bill (1774), general
division Lists, 36, 41–2, 297, 374, 376, 377
not overturning *Donaldson v Beckett*, 147, 194–5
Petitions, 45, 272, 312–3, 378–379, 407–417, 475
public/private, 44–5
Booksellers Bill (1774), passage (main stages)
bill Committee, 153–156, 223–252, 257–8, 346–64
first Reading (Lords), 157, 371–7
first Reading, 147–8, 193–194, 303–312
Petition Committee, 141–2, 271–2, 273–280
Petition Report, 142–147, 170–193, 255–6, 280–303
Petition, 141, 267–271
Report, 156, 252–3, 364–7
second Reading, 148–153, 194–223, 256–7, 315–46
third Reading, 156, 253–254, 367–71
also see Table of Contents
Booksellers Bill (1774), the text
deposit, 122, 495
ex post facto, 120–1
exclusive right, 119, 464–5, 493-2
preamble, 119, 463–4
registration, 121–2,
savings, 122, 495–6, 304, 305, 466
Book, trade 160–2
after 1774, 160–2
Buckley's Act (Printing of Thuanus Histories Act 1733), 81–82, 231, 246, 432
Burke, Edmund, 16, 23, 54, 66, 94, 97, 114, 117, 132
friend of Goldsmith, 24
monopolies, 107, 108, 115, 147
Note of copyright, 475–476
on procedure, 62, 65, 66, 154,
speaking, 134, 136, 137, 147, 153

speeches, *see* Cavendish Diary, speeches and Newspapers (reports of speeches)
votes, 37, 296

Cases (in favour/against Bill), 15, 378–500
'facts', 22
as historical source, 21
authorship, 23–4
booklet, 23
conversation between, 16
cost, 17
Goldsmith, Oliver (authorship), 24
printing, 16
size, 16
style, 21–2
timing, 22–3
use in debate, 25–6
also see Part IV (Petitions, Cases and Reports)
Cartel/Combination, 11–12, 60, 61, 87–88, 187, 210, 277, 278, 237, 258, 328, 414, 473, 497
after failure of Booksellers Bill, 159
exclusion from sales, 101 n 65
for the rich, 285
formation (1759), 414, 497–8
legality, 88, 178, 182, 236, 240–1, 282, 283, 284, 298, 320, 326, 330, 372, 415, 417
letters setting it up, 477–482
monopoly, 391, 434
necessity for, 88
prosecutions, 295
rationale for, 88, 178, 382–3
subscription 178, 189
Cavendish Diary, general
description, 165–8
Booksellers Bill, Part II (The Diaries)
earlier publication, 166
Cavendish Diary, speeches
Ambler, Charles, 231–2
Barré, Issac, 223
Beauchamp, Lord, 219, 246–9, 252, 254
Burke, Edmund, 189–192, 216, 218, 222, 224–5, 227, 229, 232, 251
Burke, William. 223, 228, 232, 252, 253
Carnac, John, 219
Cavendish, Henry, 252
Cholmley, Nathaniel, 233
Dalrymple, *John* (Counsel), 194–204
Dempster, George, 188–9, 192, 194, 216, 217, 218, 232, 233, 250, 252, 253
Dunning, John, 181–84, 217
Fielde, Paul, 170–1, 273, 194, 221, 224, 227–8, 229, 234, 235–40, 244–6, 250–1, 251, 252, 253
Folkestone, Lord, 192, 234
Fox, Charles, 216, 217, 218, 219, 223, 224, 228, 233, 240–241, 252, 253
Fox, Stephen, 253
Fuller, Rose, 193
Graves, William, 184–5, 185
Harris James, 251, 252
Hett, John (Counsel), 215–216
Johnstone, George, 212, 216, 217, 219, 222, 229–31, 249–50, 251
Jollifee, William, 248–9
Mackworth, Herbert, 193, 233, 251
Mansfield, James (Counsel), 208–212, 212–215
Montague, Frederick, 232
Morton, John, 219
Murphy, Arthur (Counsel), 205–208, 219–221
North, Lord, 185
Norton, Fletcher (Speaker), 212, 218, 223, 228, 231, 232, 244, 253
Onslow, Col George, 186–8, 194, 232, 242–244, 250, 252
Onslow, George, 223
Popham, Alexander, 218, 233
Pulteney, William, 252
Saville, Sir George, 192–3, 232
Sawbridge, John, 173, 219, 221, 229, 231
Sutton, Sir Richard, 216, 244, 246, 252, 253
Thurlow, Edward (Attorney General), 173–180, 217, 218, 221, 223, 225–7, 229
Wedderburn, Alexander (Solicitor General), 185–186, 252
Whitworth, Richard, 233, 251
Wilkie, John (Witness), 216, 218, 219
Cavendish, Henry (Sir),
biography, 164–5
shorthand, 166, 167
speeches, *see* Cavendish Diary, speeches and Newspapers (reports of speeches)
vote, 38
Coffee Houses, 3, 10–11, 32, 34, 146, 185, 190, 285, 292, 318
The Chapter, 10–1
Devil Tavern, fp, 11, 389,
Globe Tavern, 100, 317–318, 320, 325, 329, 331, 467, 472, 473, 474
Queen Arms Tavern, 100, 317–318, 320, 325, 329, 331, 467, 473, 474
reading newspapers, 18
treating witnesses, 30
Committee (on Bill), 63–4
filling blanks, 272
notice, 65–7, 224–234
procedure, 64
proving preamble, 64
Report, 68
whole house, 67–8
Committee (on Petition),
Counterpetition, 49
list of books, 48
powers, 48
purpose of committee, 49
quorum, 48
Report drafting, 51
Report presentation, 51–2
witnesses 49–51
Common law right
'Battle of the booksellers', 84–6
belief in, 46, 73, 74–95
belief vs existence, 74

Blackstone, 89–90
history, 73–89
honorary monopoly, 86–89
origin, 89
also see Ignorance of the law, *Millar v Taylor* and *Donaldson v Beckett*
Conger, *see* Cartel/Combination
Copyright,
corrections, 106–7
protection of idea, 106
reversion, 103–4
term, 83, 120, 160
translations, 106
Universities' Copyright Act 1775, 158–9
also see Common law right, Statute of Anne

Debates,
why speak, 136–7
Divisions, 53–54
conduct of, 54
lists (for Booksellers Bill), 36, 41–2, 297, 374, 376, 377
tables of (those involved in Bill), 36–40, 41–42
Donaldson v Beckett 1, 2, 5, 7, 8, 22, 24, 25, 34, 91–2
affecting justification for copyright, 117–8
costs, 92
counsel, 16, 23, 52, 58, 78
Goldsmith, Oliver and, 24
Johnson, Samuel and, 24–5
law reports, 26
Mansfield, Lord, 92
newspaper reporting, 31
Petition following, 9
price of books, 32
public, victory for, 92
rejoicing in Scotland, 96
Scotland, 123
tracts in support, 35 n 154
vote, 40 n 183, 86, 94
Donaldson, Alexander,
cases connected with, 24, 25
in business, 5, 6, 109, 414
litigation 28,29-30, 29 n 92, 89, 89 n 205
lobbying, 16, n 87
Petition (HL), 23 n 19, 72, 496
Petition, 22, 25, 52, 58, 312–3, 413
publication of *The Seasons*, 7,
share of monopoly, 107
also see Donaldson v Beckett
Donaldson, James
ownership of Edinburgh Advertiser, 1, fn 4, 260

Employment, effect 111–2
everyone selling books, 112, 212
loss of jobs, 112, 197, 420

Folkstone, Lord (Jacob Pleydell Bouverie)
biography, 169–70
diary, 255–8

speeches, *see* Cavendish Diary, speeches and Newspapers (reports of speeches)
vote, 39

Hogarth, William
Engraving Copyright Act 1766, 121, 155, 246, 352, 356, 360, 420, 423
Honorary property, 11, 25, 74, 86–7, 187, 213, 283, 290, 298, 394, 402, 416, 459, 465, 467
combination, 403
invasion, 469
not classics, 402
not protected by law, 88
ownership, 103
also see Cartel/Combination and *Monopoly*
House of Commons,
acoustics, 55, 132
attendance, 13
divisions, *see* divisions
precedent books, 43, 54–5
procedure, 163–4
procedure for Bills, *see* Bills
quorum, 48, 68–70
secrecy of proceedings, 125–126
speaking in, 13
sitting time, 50, 66, 131
strangers (emptying gallery), 126
reporting of proceedings, *see* Reporting, Parliament

ignorance of law, 116–7, 151, 152, 191, 194, 195, 219, 234, 253, 257, 282, 292, 299, 319, 320, 436, 498
mistake to estate title, 116, 117, 145, 189, 205, 227, 234, 235, 257, 282, 298, 319, 428, 437
taking counsel's opinion, 117, 184, 185–6, 191, 234, 351, 368
interest groups, 9
economic groups, 9
Parliaments responsiveness, 10
coffee houses, 10–1
political groups (Wilkesite), 9–10
booksellers, 10–12
also see Cartel/Combination
Investment
Johnston, William, 98–9
loss, reporting, 96
only some booksellers, 97
proof, 98
single copy enough, 103, 185
valuation, 99
value of loss, 96–7

Johnson, Samuel
views on lobbying, 11
Parliamentary reporter, 127, 162
false claim of endorsement, 24, 114
claims regarding Dictionary, 32, 106, 230–1, 338, 349

against perpetual right, 25
Judicial Notice, 63, 496

Law reports, 29–30
how cited, 26–7
manuscript, 27, 29–30
printed 27–8, 29, 30
short notes, 27
use in parliamentary debate, 26, 28–30
Legal deposit (of books), 122, 252
Letters, in newspapers, 33–34
authorship, 33
large number, 34
sharing, 33
'Lobbying'
treating, 16
personal contacts, 15–6
Scottish Burghs, 15, 16 n 82,
also see interest groups
London Stallholders, 24, 32, 87, 91, 100, 110, 409–411
not actually selling books, 97 n 13
not holding copyright, 5–6
Licensing Acts, 77, 99, 176, 192, 201, 213, 249, 257, 351, 357, 382, 390, 410

Mansfield, Lord (William Murray), 93–4, 95, 172, 234, 244, 258
competency of witnesses, 62
Counsel in literary property cases, 7, 350, 477, 478
failure to give opinion, 92–93, 147, 154, 308, 311, 373, 386
injunctions, 85
reading case reports, 28
reliance on his opinion, 294, 298, 355, 404, 456,
also see Millar v Taylor
Millar, Andrew, 114 n 249, 216, 406, 452
books by 425, 426, 462
business, approach to 427, 104
combination and, 11, 52 n 106, 478, 480,
sale of copyright 395, 428, 430, 431, 384
will 98, 99 n 41, 385
Millar v Taylor, 6, 7, 25–6, 28–30, 74, 84–6, 90–91, 93, 106, 117, 178, 206, 281, 285, 289, 298, 397
judicial notice, 63
purchases since, 220
reports, 172
Monopolies, 2, 33, 82, 87, 98, 107–109, 124, 143, 147, 150, 155, 162, 163,
Burke, Edmund and, 107, 108, 115, 147
prices, 160
retrospective, 107
revenue, 112
Stationers, 76
also see honorary property

Newspapers, 19, 259–377
circulation, 17, 31
coverage of booksellers disputes, 31–2
errant behaviour, 115–6, 195–6, 207, 209–10, 242
franking privileges, 18
historic record, 157
length, 34, 135–6
letters, 33–34
links to book trade, 31
ownership, 260–1
printing, 17
public opinion, 19, 32
publication of cases, 32
readership, 18–19, 32
also see Reporting parliament, and Newspapers (reports of speeches)
Newspapers (reports of speeches)
Apsley LC, 372, 373, 374, 376
Bareé, Issac, 340
Beauchamp, Lord, 340, 352–3, 356, 360, 368, 370
Burke, Edmund, 277, 288–9, 292, 295, 297, 299, 300, 337, 338, 340, 344, 347, 348, 350, 354
Burke, William, 337, 340, 350
Burrell, Peter, 275
Camden, Lord, 372–3, 374, 375, 376
Campbell, Lord Fredrick, 305, 306, 311
Cavendish, Henry, 369
Cornwall, Charles, 340
Dalrymple, Sir John (Counsel), 315–7, 322–4, 324, 325–6, 327–8, 328–9
Dempster, George, 276, 277, 278, 287–8, 292, 295, 297, 299, 303, 305, 306, 307, 308, 310, 311, 337, 348, 354, 365, 366, 368, 369, 370
Denbigh, Earl of, 371, 373, 374, 376
Dundas, Sir Laurence, 306, 310–11
Dunning, John, 283–4, 291, 294, 296, 298, 299, 300, 301, 337, 340
Fielde, Paul, 279, 280, 289–90, 293, 296, 297–8, 299, 300, 301, 303, 304, 306, 307, 308, 309–310, 311, 325, 329, 338, 340, 342, 343, 347, 350–1, 352, 353, 354, 355, 358, 360, 365, 367, 369
Folkestone, Lord 276, 289, 292, 295, 297, 299–300, 301, 350, 354–5, 357–8, 360
Fox, Charles, 337, 339, 340, 344, 346–7, 349, 350, 351, 353, 354, 358–9, 359–60, 362, 365, 367–8, 369, 370
Fox, Stephen, 368, 369, 370
Graves, William, 268, 271, 272, 284–5, 291, 294, 296, 298, 299, 300
Harley, Thomas 267, 268, 269, 270, 272
Harris, James, 357, 361
Hett, John, 329, 334, 343, 344–5
Johnstone, George, 312, 313, 337, 339, 340, 345, 349, 354, 360, 366
Joliffee, William, 353, 356, 360
Lyttleton, Lord, 371–2, 373, 374, 376
Mackworth, Herbert, 349, 354
Mansfield, James (Counsel), 301, 317, 324, 329, 330–5, 336–7, 342, 344, 345
Morton, John, 337, 340
Murphy, Arthur, 318, 319–322, 324–5, 326–7, 328, 329, 335–6, 338, 340, 343, 345
North, Lord, 292, 297
Norton, Fletcher (Speaker), 347
Onslow, George, 276, 277, 300, 344

Onslow, George, Colonel, 278, 286–7, 292, 295, 297, 299, 303, 305–6, 307, 308, 310, 311, 339, 351–2, 355–6, 359, 360
Popham, Alexander, 349
Saville, Sir George, 289, 295, 354, 365
Sawbridge, John, 267, 268, 269, 270, 281, 290, 293, 296, 298, 338, 350
Stewart, William, 364
Sutton, Sir Richard, 337, 352, 356, 360
Thurlow, Edward (Attorney General), 271, 272, 281–3, 290, 293–4, 296, 299, 300, 301, 338, 339, 340–1, 343, 347, 354, 360
Turner, Charles, 337
Walpole, Richard, 271, 272
Walsh, John, 337
Wedderburn, Alexander (Solicitor General), 285–6, 292, 294, 299, 300, 357
Whitworth, Richard, 274–5, 277, 349, 353, 354, 360, 367
North America
'crisis', 2, 4, 51, 132, 158, 185, 199, 292, 314, 461
trade, 112–3, 150, 196, 199, 200, 211, 323, 326, 372, 375, 434, 439,

Old books (out of copyright), 5, 6, 74, 78, 82, 86, 87, 88, 110, 119, 202, 234, 329, 398, 418,, 470, 473
Ordinances (Commonwealth), 76–7, 78, 176, 201, 237, 390

Patent law, 249
book patents, 75–7, 162 n 46, 172, 200, 206, 213, 236, 316, 465 n 342,
comparison with books, 108–9, 110 n 194
petitioning, 57
saving in Booksellers Bill, 304, 305
saving in Statute of Anne, 79 n 74, 107 n 159, 215, 383
saving in Statute of Monopolies, 238
term extension, 33 n 139, 46, 391 n 61, 411 n 141,
Petitioning,
against bill, 57–8
average presented per day, 14
formal lobbying, 14
in 1730s, 82–4
indoor agents, 15
private bill, 45–46
Petition, Booksellers 267–71, 378
deadline, 46
lack of detail 45–7
presentation, 47–48
scope, 46
Plays (and literature), 34–36
Love-A-La Mode, 59, 205, 319
Macaulay, Catharine, 35
The Author, 34
Political parties,
divisions, 36
importance (or otherwise), 13, 36–37
links to vote, 13–4
role in 18C, 12–13
stance on Booksellers Bill, 36–40, 41–42
little role in bill, 42
Precedent books, 43, 54–5
Price of books, 109–10, 196–7, 385, 415, 419, 422, 444, 445, 452–3
Printing,
Caxton, William, 75–6
cost, 104–5, 186, 238, 430, 436–7, 458–9
early history in England, 74–8
reusing type, 105–6
selling an impression, 105
Proclamations, 63, 76, 128 n 45, 176, 201, 234, 269; *also see* Star Chamber
Public/Private, Bills, 44–5

Quorum, 68–70
breaking quorum, 69
Quality of book, 110–11, 185, 198, 208, 431–2, 453, 454, 457, 469
Donaldson and, 110–11, 152, 211, 418

Reporting, Parliament, 162–3
accuracy, 157 (*also see* Chapter 8)
acoustics (and noise), 132
copying, 134–5, 261–7 (*also see* Part 3)
earlier reporters, 126–7
Hansard compared, 135–6, 137, 139, 168
'improving' speeches, 135, 137–9
long shifts, 131, 139
members providing reports, 133–4
'Memory Woodfall', 133
notetaking, 133–4
press gallery (no), 131
Printers' Case, 128–130
restriction, 125–6
seating, 131–2
speeches, *see* Newspapers (reports of speeches)
standing order, 126
style, 133–4
Revenue (taxation), 112, 197, 198, 420

Seasons, The, 106, 160
Star Chamber, 63, 76, 121 n 37, 122, 172, 176, 201, 215, 234, 236–7, 257, 357; *also see* Proclamations
Statute of Anne (Copyright Act 1709), 61, 78–9, 94, 98–9, 119–20
Buckley's Act 81–2
classics, 82 n 104, 123–4
Copyright Bills before, 201 n 290
copyright term, 82, 107, 448
deposit, 122, 252
exclusive right, 80, 81, 119
Horne v Baker, 28, 30, 84–5, 155, 176–7, 200
musical compositions, 273
old books, 5, 6, 74, 78, 82, 86, 87, 88, 110, 119, 202, 234, 329, 398, 418,, 470, 473
Petition of booksellers, 45
proviso, 79, 122
registration, 121
remedies, 80, 84
whether public act, 44 n12, 63

Stationers' Company, 1, 202, 204, 220, 254, 382, 383, 428, 438, 465–6,
by-laws, 63 n 230, 76 n 29, 78, 176, 433
Charter and patents, 75, 76, 433
licences to print, 77
litigation, 162
register books, 48, 121, 268, 269, 270, 304, 305, 356, 363, 398, 432, 494–5
regulation, 77–8
subscription for bill, 12
Strahan, William (Master of the Stationers), 97, 316
Blackstone's *Commentaries*, 469
letters to (regarding bill), 24–5, 117, 243

Taverns, *see* Coffee Houses
Taxation, *see* Revenue (Taxation)
Trade-off (between different booksellers), 104, 185, 241, 254, 371
Tragedy of the commons, 33 n 134
Tonson, Jacob (II), 456, 110
combination, 11, 480
copyrights, 208, 254, 395, 406, 431, 464, 470
litigation, 321
Shakespeare, 205
testimonials, 114, 443, 450–1, 452, 456
Tonson v Collins, 26, 27, 29 44, 75, 172, 283, 384, 397, 499
wealth, 364

Wilkes, John,
Printers case, 129–30
Wilkesite lobbying groups, 9, 10
Witnesses (for private bill), 30–31, 60, 73–4
bill committee, 334–337
competence, 61-53
examination of, 31, 60–1
number required, 73, 187, 400
on Booksellers bill, 30
Petition committee, 49–51, 273–280
statements (declarations), 31, 471–5